Sports
Movies

**CineBooks Home Library Series
No. 5**

Sports Movies

**a guide
to nearly 500 films
focusing on sports**

CineBooks

CineBooks, Inc.
Evanston, Illinois, 1989

Editor in Chief: Jeffrey H. Wallenfeldt

President: Anita L. Werling; **Editorial Director:** William Leahy; **Editors:** James J. Mulay, Daniel Curran, Jenny Mueller; **Research Director:** William C. Clogston; **Associate Editors:** Jeannette Hori, Jennifer Howe, Michaela Tuohy.

Business Manager: Jack Medor; **Assistants:** Bernie Gregoryk, Lena Hicks; **Advertising Manager:** Craig Carter.

Editorial & Sales Offices
CINEBOOKS
990 Grove Street
Evanston, Illinois 60201

ISBN: 0-933997-24-8

Printed in the United States
First Edition

1   2   3   4   5   6   7   8   9   10

Table of Contents

Introduction

Sports and movies, two of America's favorite entertainments, have long been partners in the business of mythmaking, equally involved with larger-than-life heroes. The drama of athletics is well suited to filmic treatment. If sports movies are not as satisfying as real-life sporting events, the outcomes of which are less predictable than cinematic depictions, it can also be said that the drama, comedy, and insight into the human condition that sports occasionally offer are frequently more deeply felt in movies. It isn't always true that slow motion, a variety of camera angles, and evocative music heighten sporting glory, but when not overused these filmmaking techniques can create a powerful effect (something NFL Films has long known).

Regrettably, sports films gravitated to formula presentations almost from the beginning. Given the nature of athletic competition, however, it should come as little surprise that the Big Game, Match, or Race so often provides the climax of these pictures; likewise, it follows that determination and hard work, individual effort, and teamwork are frequent themes. But when the formula is done right (KNUTE ROCKNE—ALL AMERICAN; ROCKY; HOOSIERS) or when it is subverted (PERSONAL BEST), stood on its head (BULL DURHAM), altered in terms of tone (BANG THE DRUM SLOWLY; SLAP SHOT), or invested with social significance (THIS SPORTING LIFE), the sports film is among the most engaging the cinema has to offer and one of Hollywood's specialties.

It isn't easy to define the difference between a sports film and a film with *sports in it*. This book focuses on those films in which sports play a central role. For that reason, a film like THE GREAT SANTINI is not included—though the competition on the basketball court between father and son is an important facet of their relationship, it is only part of a much larger story. On the other hand, BREAKING AWAY, another film with an important father-son relationship at its core, is included because bicycling is essential to the story. Similarly, the Frankie Avalon-Annette Funicello "Beach" movies are not included, while RIDE THE WILD SURF, in which surfing is more than just a backdrop, is. For the most part, this book is concerned only with films about competitive sports; therefore, movies about hunting, fishing, and mountain climbing are not included—nor are Esther Williams or Sonja Henie starrers, in which the swimming and skating are generally noncompetitive. Films revolving around martial arts and hot rodding have also been excluded, but all other major sports and most minor ones are represented here, provided the film is feature-length and received a theatrical release.

While the films in this book have been evaluated with the general viewer in mind, special consideration has been given to their appeal to the sports fan and sports movie lover. Consequently, though a film fails dramatically, it may still contain some special element of interest for the sports fan and thus receive a higher star rating.

Whenever possible, we have tried to note when a film includes particularly well-shot sporting action, significant documentary footage, and the presence of athletes-turned-actors or sporting figures making cameo appearances. We have also tried to appraise the accuracy of biographical portrayals, the degree to which the actors have succeeded in their depiction of athletes in action, whether the filmmakers have captured the details or essence of the sport they have chosen to portray, and whether they have done so imaginatively. In addition we have, when able, included background information on the special preparation undertaken by actors for their roles as athletes, as well as noting their prior experience in sports.

What we have tried to do, then, is offer a guide that will lead you to the best Big Games, the most convincing reformations of crooked managers and floozie-distracted fighters, the most compelling strong-willed climbs from defeat to victory, the funniest lampooning of sports conventions, and the finest, most insightful biographies—films that not only tell us who won, but that really give us the score.

—Jeffrey H. Wallenfeldt

FILMS BY SPORT

All films included in this volume are listed below by the sport which is featured in the film. Films in which more than one sport is featured are listed under each sport which plays a role in the film.

Arm Wrestling
OVER THE TOP

Australian Rules Football
GREAT MACARTHY, THE

Auto Racing
BIG WHEEL, THE
BLONDE COMET
BOBBY DEERFIELD
BORN TO SPEED
BURN 'EM UP O'CONNER
BURNING UP
CHECKPOINT
CROWD ROARS, THE (1932)
DANGER ON WHEELS
DEVIL'S HAIRPIN, THE
FIREBALL 500
FIREBALL JUNGLE
GRAND PRIX (1934)
GRAND PRIX (1966)
GREASED LIGHTNING
GREEN HELMET, THE
HEART LIKE A WHEEL
HIGH GEAR
HIGH SPEED
INDIANAPOLIS SPEEDWAY
JOHNNY DARK
JUMP
LAST AMERICAN HERO, THE
LE MANS
LIVELY SET, THE
PIT STOP
RACE FOR LIFE, A
RACERS, THE
RACING STRAIN, THE
RACING YOUTH
RED HOT TIRES
RED LINE 7000
ROAD DEMON
ROADRACERS, THE
ROAR OF THE CROWD
SEPARATE WAYS
SIX PACK
SPEED
SPEED LOVERS
SPEEDWAY
SPINOUT
STOCK CAR
STRAIGHTAWAY
STROKER ACE
TEN LAPS TO GO

THUNDER ALLEY
THUNDER IN CAROLINA
THUNDER IN DIXIE
TO PLEASE A LADY
TOMBOY
TRACK OF THUNDER
WILD RACERS, THE
WINNING
YOUNG RACERS, THE

Baseball
ALIBI IKE
ANGELS IN THE OUTFIELD
BABE RUTH STORY, THE
BAD NEWS BEARS, THE
BAD NEWS BEARS GO TO JAPAN, THE
BAD NEWS BEARS IN BREAKING TRAINING, THE
BANG THE DRUM SLOWLY
BIG LEAGUER
BINGO LONG TRAVELING ALL-STARS AND MOTOR KINGS, THE
BLUE SKIES AGAIN
BULL DURHAM
COLLEGE
DAMN YANKEES
DEATH ON THE DIAMOND
EIGHT MEN OUT
ELMER THE GREAT
FAST COMPANY (1929)
FEAR STRIKES OUT
FIREMAN, SAVE MY CHILD
GREAT AMERICAN PASTIME, THE
HERE COME THE TIGERS
HOT CURVES
IT HAPPENED IN FLATBUSH
IT HAPPENS EVERY SPRING
JACKIE ROBINSON STORY, THE
KID FROM CLEVELAND, THE
KID FROM LEFT FIELD, THE
KILL THE UMPIRE
MOONLIGHT IN HAVANA
NATURAL, THE
PRIDE OF ST. LOUIS, THE
PRIDE OF THE YANKEES, THE
RHUBARB
ROOGIE'S BUMP
SAFE AT HOME
SLUGGER'S WIFE, THE
SQUEEZE PLAY
STEALING HOME

STRATTON STORY, THE
TAKE ME OUT TO THE BALL GAME
THEY LEARNED ABOUT WOMEN
TRADING HEARTS
WINNING TEAM, THE
YOUNG MAN OF MANHATTAN

Basketball
AMAZING GRACE AND CHUCK
BASKETBALL FIX, THE
BIG FIX, THE
COACH
CORNBREAD, EARL AND ME
DRIVE, HE SAID
FAST BREAK
FISH THAT SAVED PITTSBURGH, THE
GO, MAN, GO!
HALLS OF ANGER
HARLEM GLOBETROTTERS, THE
HOOSIERS
INSIDE MOVES
MAURIE
MIXED COMPANY
ONE ON ONE
SCORING
TALL STORY
THAT CHAMPIONSHIP SEASON

Bicycling
AMERICAN FLYERS
BREAKING AWAY
RAD
RIDING HIGH (1937)

Bowling
DREAMER

Boxing
ALL-AMERICAN BOY, THE
BATTLING BUTLER
BIG PUNCH, THE
BODY AND SOUL (1947)
BODY AND SOUL (1981)
BORN TO FIGHT
BOWERY BLITZKRIEG
BOXER
BUSTED UP
CAIN AND MABEL
CHAMP, THE (1931)
CHAMP, THE (1979)
CHAMPION
CITY FOR CONQUEST

CONFLICT
CONTENDER, THE
COWBOY AND THE PRIZEFIGHTER, THE
CROOKED CIRCLE, THE
CROWD ROARS, THE (1938)
DUKE OF CHICAGO
EDITH AND MARCEL
FAT CITY
FIFTY-SHILLING BOXER
FIGHTER, THE
FIGHTING CHAMP
FIGHTING FOOLS
FIGHTING GENTLEMAN, THE
FIGHTING MAD
FLESH AND FURY
FLYING FIFTY-FIVE
FLYING FISTS, THE
GENTLEMAN JIM
GIRL FROM MONTEREY, THE
GLORY ALLEY
GOLDEN BOY
GOLDEN GLOVES
GOLDEN GLOVES STORY, THE
GREAT JOHN L., THE
GREAT WHITE HOPE, THE
GREATEST, THE
HARD TIMES
HARDER THEY FALL, THE
HEART PUNCH
HERE COMES MR. JORDAN
HOLD EVERYTHING
HUMPHREY TAKES A CHANCE
IN THIS CORNER
IRON MAN, THE (1931)
IRON MAN, THE (1951)
JOE LOUIS STORY, THE
JOE PALOOKA, CHAMP
JOE PALOOKA IN THE BIG FIGHT
JOE PALOOKA IN THE
  COUNTERPUNCH
JOE PALOOKA IN THE SQUARED
  CIRCLE
JOE PALOOKA IN TRIPLE CROSS
JOE PALOOKA IN WINNER TAKE
  ALL
JOE PALOOKA MEETS HUMPHREY
KID COMES BACK, THE
KID FROM BROOKLYN, THE
KID FROM KOKOMO, THE
KID GALAHAD (1937)
KID GALAHAD (1962)
KID MONK BARONI
KID NIGHTINGALE
KILLER McCOY
KING FOR A NIGHT
KNOCKOUT
LAST FIGHT, THE
LAUGHING IRISH EYES
LEATHER-PUSHERS, THE

LEATHER SAINT, THE
LET'S DO IT AGAIN
LIFE OF JIMMY DOLAN, THE
MADISON SQUARE GARDEN
MAIN EVENT, THE (1938)
MAIN EVENT, THE (1979)
MAN FROM DOWN UNDER, THE
MAN I LOVE, THE
MANNEQUIN
MATILDA
MIGHTY MC GURK, THE
MILKY WAY, THE
MIRACLE KID
MR. HEX
MONKEY ON MY BACK
NAVY BOUND
NAVY WAY, THE
PALOOKA
PATENT LEATHER KID, THE
PERSONALITY KID, THE
PITTSBURGH KID, THE
POLICE CALL
PRISON SHADOWS
PRIZE FIGHTER, THE
PRIZEFIGHTER AND THE LADY,
  THE
RAGING BULL
REQUIEM FOR A HEAVYWEIGHT
RIGHT CROSS
RIGHT TO THE HEART
RING, THE
RINGSIDE MAISIE
RIPPED-OFF
ROCKY
ROCKY II
ROCKY III
ROCKY IV
SECRETS OF A NURSE
SET-UP, THE
SHAKEDOWN, THE
SOCIAL LION, THE
SOCIETY GIRL
SOME BLONDES ARE DANGEROUS
SOMEBODY UP THERE LIKES ME
SPEAKEASY
SPIKE OF BENSONHURST
SPIRIT OF YOUTH
SPLIT DECISIONS
SQUARE JUNGLE, THE
SQUARE RING, THE
STEADY COMPANY
STING II, THE
STREETS OF GOLD
SUNDAY PUNCH
SWELLHEAD, THE
SWING FEVER
SWINGIN' AFFAIR, A
TAKE IT FROM ME
TENNESSEE CHAMP
THERE AIN'T NO JUSTICE

THEY MADE ME A CRIMINAL
THEY NEVER COME BACK
WALKOVER
WHIPLASH
WINNER TAKE ALL (1932)
WINNER TAKE ALL (1939)
WOMAN-WISE
WORLD IN MY CORNER
YOUNG MAN OF MANHATTAN

Bullfighting
BLOOD AND SAND (1922)
BLOOD AND SAND (1941)
BULLFIGHTER AND THE LADY, THE
KID FROM SPAIN, THE
MAGNIFICENT MATADOR, THE
MANOLETE
MOMENT OF TRUTH, THE

Crew
BOY IN BLUE, THE
COLLEGE
FRESHMAN LOVE
MILLION DOLLAR LEGS

Cricket
FINAL TEST, THE
PLAYING AWAY

Figure Skating
ICE CASTLES

Football
ALL-AMERICAN, THE (1932)
ALL-AMERICAN, THE (1953)
ALL THE RIGHT MOVES
BAND PLAYS ON, THE
BEAR, THE
BEST OF TIMES, THE
BIG GAME, THE
COLLEGE COACH
COLLEGE HUMOR
COLLEGE LOVE
COLLEGE LOVERS
COLLEGE RHYTHM
COWBOY QUARTERBACK
CRAZYLEGS, ALL AMERICAN
EASY LIVING
EVERYBODY'S ALL-AMERICAN
FAN'S NOTES, A
FATHER WAS A FULLBACK
FIGHTING YOUTH
FINNEY
FORTUNE COOKIE, THE
FRESHMAN, THE
GOOD NEWS (1930)
GOOD NEWS (1947)
GRIDIRON FLASH
GUS
GUY WHO CAME BACK, THE

Skiing
DOWNHILL RACER
LOVE ON SKIS
RENO AND THE DOC
SKI PATROL
Soccer
ARSENAL STADIUM MYSTERY, THE
CUP-TIE HONEYMOON
GREAT GAME, THE
GREAT GAME, THE
HOT SHOT
LAST GAME, THE
SMALL TOWN STORY
VICTORY
YESTERDAY'S HERO
Speedboat Racing
MARK IT PAID
MOTOR MADNESS
RACING FEVER
Surfing
BIG WEDNESDAY
NORTH SHORE
PUBERTY BLUES
RIDE THE WILD SURF
Tennis
PAT AND MIKE
PLAYERS
RACQUET
SPRING FEVER
Track and Field
BILLIE
BOB MATHIAS STORY, THE
CHARIOTS OF FIRE
COLLEGE
GAMES, THE
GOLDENGIRL
JIM THORPE—ALL AMERICAN
LOCAL BOY MAKES GOOD
LONELINESS OF THE LONG
   DISTANCE RUNNER, THE
MILLION DOLLAR LEGS
MILLION TO ONE, A
ON THE EDGE
PERSONAL BEST
RUNNING
RUNNING BRAVE
SAM'S SON
SECOND WIND
WALK, DON'T RUN
WEE GEORDIE
WORLD'S GREATEST ATHLETE,
   THE
Volleyball
SPIKER
Weightlifting
STAY HUNGRY
Wrestling
. . . ALL THE MARBLES
BLOOD AND GUTS

BODYHOLD
DECEPTION
FLESH
GRUNT! THE WRESTLING MOVIE
MR. UNIVERSE
ONE AND ONLY, THE
PARADISE ALLEY
SPORT PARADE, THE
SWING YOUR LADY
TAKE DOWN
VISION QUEST
WRESTLER, THE

FILMS BY STAR RATING

All films included in this volume are listed below by their Star Ratings. The ratings indicate the following:
*****: masterpiece; ****: excellent; ***: good; **: fair; *: poor; zero: without merit

*****

BODY AND SOUL (1947)
CHAMPION
HARDER THEY FALL, THE
HUSTLER, THE
LUSTY MEN, THE
PRIDE OF THE YANKEES, THE
RAGING BULL
SET-UP, THE

****

BLACK STALLION, THE
BLOOD AND SAND (1941)
CHARIOTS OF FIRE
FAT CITY
FEAR STRIKES OUT
FORTUNE COOKIE, THE
FRESHMAN, THE
GENTLEMAN JIM
GOLDEN BOY
HERE COMES MR. JORDAN
HOOSIERS
HORSE FEATHERS
IT HAPPENS EVERY SPRING
JIM THORPE—ALL AMERICAN
KNUTE ROCKNE—ALL AMERICAN
LONELINESS OF THE LONG
    DISTANCE RUNNER, THE
M*A*S*H
NATIONAL VELVET
PAT AND MIKE
ROCKY
THIS SPORTING LIFE

***1/2

ANGELS IN THE OUTFIELD
BAD NEWS BEARS, THE
BANG THE DRUM SLOWLY
BREAKING AWAY
BROADWAY BILL
BULL DURHAM
CHAMP, THE (1931)
CITY FOR CONQUEST
COLOR OF MONEY, THE
CROWD ROARS, THE (1932)
DOWNHILL RACER
GREAT WHITE HOPE, THE
JOE LOUIS STORY, THE
KID GALAHAD (1937)
LONGEST YARD, THE
MILKY WAY, THE
NORTH DALLAS FORTY
PHAR LAP

PRIDE OF ST. LOUIS, THE
REQUIEM FOR A HEAVYWEIGHT
SARATOGA
SOMEBODY UP THERE LIKES ME
STAY HUNGRY
STRATTON STORY, THE
TAKE ME OUT TO THE BALL GAME
WINNER TAKE ALL (1932)

***

ALIBI IKE
AMAZING GRACE AND CHUCK
BABE RUTH STORY, THE
BASKETBALL FIX, THE
BATTLING BUTLER
BINGO LONG TRAVELING ALL-
    STARS AND MOTOR KINGS, THE
BLOOD AND SAND (1922)
BLUE GRASS OF KENTUCKY
BOOTS MALONE
BULLFIGHTER AND THE LADY, THE
CADDYSHACK
CASEY'S SHADOW
CHAMPIONS
COLLEGE
CROWD ROARS, THE (1938)
DAMN YANKEES
EDITH AND MARCEL
EIGHT MEN OUT
ELMER THE GREAT
FINAL TEST, THE
FLESH
GO, MAN, GO!
GOOD NEWS (1947)
GREASED LIGHTNING
GREAT JOHN L., THE
HALLS OF ANGER
HARD TIMES
HEART LIKE A WHEEL
HEAVEN CAN WAIT
HOME IN INDIANA
IRON MAJOR, THE
IRON MAN, THE (1931)
J.W. COOP
JUNIOR BONNER
KENTUCKY
KID FROM BROOKLYN, THE
KID FROM SPAIN, THE
KING OF THE TURF
LAST AMERICAN HERO, THE
LAST GAME, THE

LE MANS
LET'S DO IT AGAIN
MATILDA
MILLION DOLLAR LEGS (1932)
NATURAL, THE
ON THE EDGE
ONE AND ONLY, THE
PALOOKA
PAPER LION
PERSONAL BEST
PIGSKIN PARADE
PRIZEFIGHTER AND THE LADY,
    THE
PUBERTY BLUES
RACERS, THE
RIDING HIGH (1948)
RIGHT CROSS
ROCKY II
SALTY O'ROURKE
SATURDAY'S HERO
SLAP SHOT
SPORTING BLOOD (1931)
SQUARE RING, THE
STREETS OF GOLD
THEY MADE ME A CRIMINAL
TOUCH AND GO
TROUBLE ALONG THE WAY
UNDER MY SKIN
VISION QUEST
WALK, DON'T RUN
WALKOVER
WEE GEORDIE
WINNING
WINNING TEAM, THE
WORLD'S GREATEST ATHLETE,
    THE

**1/2

. . . ALL THE MARBLES
ALL THE RIGHT MOVES
BEAR, THE
BLOOD AND GUTS
BOB MATHIAS STORY, THE
BOBBY DEERFIELD
CHAMP, THE (1979)
CHECKPOINT
CORNBREAD, EARL AND ME
CRAZYLEGS, ALL AMERICAN
DRIVE, HE SAID
EASY LIVING
EVERYBODY'S ALL-AMERICAN
FAST COMPANIONS
FATHER WAS A FULLBACK

FIGHTER, THE
FIGHTING MAD
FIGHTING THOROUGHBREDS
FINNEY
FIREMAN, SAVE MY CHILD
FLESH AND FURY
FOLLOW THE SUN
FOLLOW THRU
FROM HELL TO HEAVEN
GREAT AMERICAN PASTIME, THE
GREAT DAN PATCH, THE
GREAT MACARTHY, THE
GUY WHO CAME BACK, THE
HARLEM GLOBETROTTERS, THE
HOLD 'EM YALE
HOLD EVERYTHING
IDOL OF THE CROWDS
INSIDE MOVES
IRON MAN, THE (1951)
IT HAPPENED IN FLATBUSH
JACKIE ROBINSON STORY, THE
JOE PALOOKA, CHAMP
JOE PALOOKA IN THE BIG FIGHT
JOE PALOOKA IN THE
   COUNTERPUNCH
JOE PALOOKA IN WINNER TAKE
   ALL
JOE PALOOKA MEETS HUMPHREY
JOHNNY DARK
KID COMES BACK, THE
KID FROM LEFT FIELD, THE
KID NIGHTINGALE
KILL THE UMPIRE
KILLER McCOY
KING FOR A NIGHT
KNOCKOUT
LIFE BEGINS IN COLLEGE
LIFE OF JIMMY DOLAN, THE
MIXED COMPANY
MONKEY ON MY BACK
ONE ON ONE
PAPERBACK HERO
PARADISE ALLEY
PEGGY
PLAYING AWAY
RACKETY RAX
RED LINE 7000
RHUBARB
RIDE THE WILD SURF
RING, THE
RISE AND SHINE
ROLLERBALL
SALUTE
SAM'S SON
SATURDAY'S MILLIONS
SEMI-TOUGH
SERGEANT MURPHY
SIX PACK
SPIKE OF BENSONHURST
SPIKER

SPLIT DECISIONS
SQUARE JUNGLE, THE
STORY OF SEABISCUIT, THE
SUNDAY PUNCH
TAKE DOWN
TENNESSEE CHAMP
THAT CHAMPIONSHIP SEASON
THOROUGHBREDS DON'T CRY
THRASHIN'
TO PLEASE A LADY
TOUCHDOWN
UNWELCOME STRANGER
WALL OF NOISE
WHIPLASH
WORLD IN MY CORNER
YOUNG MAN OF MANHATTAN
YOUNGBLOOD

**

ALL-AMERICAN, THE (1932)
ALL-AMERICAN, THE (1953)
AMERICAN FLYERS
ARENA
ARSENAL STADIUM MYSTERY, THE
BEST OF TIMES, THE
BIG FIX, THE
BIG GAME, THE
BIG PUNCH, THE
BIG WHEEL, THE
BILLIE
BLUE SKIES AGAIN
BORN TO FIGHT
BORN TO SPEED
BOXER
BURN 'EM UP O'CONNER
BURNING UP
CADDY, THE
CAIN AND MABEL
COLLEGE COACH
COLLEGE LOVE
COLLEGE RHYTHM
CONFLICT
CONTENDER, THE
COWBOY AND THE PRIZEFIGHTER,
   THE
CROOKED CIRCLE, THE
DANGER ON WHEELS
DEVIL'S HAIRPIN, THE
DUKE OF CHICAGO
FAN'S NOTES, A
FAST COMPANY (1929)
FAST COMPANY (1953)
FIFTY-SHILLING BOXER
FIGHTING FOOLS
FIGHTING YOUTH
FIREBALL, THE
FIREBALL 500
FIREBALL JUNGLE
FLYING FISTS, THE
FOUR AGAINST FATE

FRESHMAN LOVE
GAMES, THE
GIRL FROM MONTEREY, THE
GLORY
GLORY ALLEY
GOLDEN GLOVES
GOLDEN GLOVES STORY, THE
GOOD NEWS (1930)
GRAND PRIX (1934)
GRAND PRIX (1966)
GREAT GAME, THE (1930)
GREAT GAME, THE (1952)
GRIDIRON FLASH
GUS
HARMON OF MICHIGAN
HARRIGAN'S KID
HEART OF VIRGINIA
HEART PUNCH
HOLD 'EM JAIL
HOLD 'EM NAVY!
HOLD THAT CO-ED
HOLD THAT LINE
HOT CURVES
HOT SHOT
ICE CASTLES
IN THIS CORNER
INDIANAPOLIS SPEEDWAY
JOE PALOOKA IN THE SQUARED
   CIRCLE
JOE PALOOKA IN TRIPLE CROSS
JOHN GOLDFARB, PLEASE COME
   HOME
JUMP
KANSAS CITY BOMBER
KID FROM CLEVELAND, THE
KID FROM KOKOMO, THE
KID GALAHAD (1962)
KID MONK BARONI
KING OF HOCKEY
LADY'S FROM KENTUCKY, THE
LAUGHING IRISH EYES
LEATHER-PUSHERS, THE
LEATHER SAINT, THE
LIGHTNING—THE WHITE STALLION
LITTLE FAUSS AND BIG HALSY
LIVELY SET, THE
LOCAL BOY MAKES GOOD
LOVE ON SKIS
MADISON SQUARE GARDEN
MAGNIFICENT MATADOR, THE
MAIN EVENT, THE (1979)
MAN FROM DOWN UNDER, THE
MAN I LOVE, THE
MANIACS ON WHEELS
MANOLETE
MARK IT PAID
MAYBE IT'S LOVE
MIGHTY MC GURK, THE
MILLION DOLLAR LEGS (1939)
MILLION TO ONE, A

MR. CELEBRITY
MR. HEX
MR. UNIVERSE
MOMENT OF TRUTH, THE
MONEY FROM HOME
MOONLIGHT IN HAVANA
NADIA
NAVY BLUE AND GOLD
NAVY BOUND
$1,000 A TOUCHDOWN
OVER THE GOAL
PACE THAT THRILLS, THE
PATENT LEATHER KID, THE
PERSONALITY KID, THE
PRIDE OF MARYLAND
PRIDE OF THE BLUE GRASS (1954)
PRIDE OF THE BLUEGRASS (1939)
QUARTERBACK, THE
RACETRACK
RACING ROMANCE
RAINBOW JACKET, THE
RED HOT TIRES
RETURN OF OCTOBER, THE
RIDING HIGH (1937)
RIGHT TO THE HEART
RINGSIDE MAISIE
RIPPED-OFF
ROCKY III
RODEO
ROOGIE'S BUMP
ROSE BOWL
ROSE BOWL STORY, THE
SAFE AT HOME
SATURDAY'S HEROES
SECOND WIND
SEPARATE WAYS
70,000 WITNESSES
SHAKEDOWN, THE
SIDEWINDER ONE
SKI PATROL
SMALL TOWN STORY
SMITH OF MINNESOTA
SO THIS IS COLLEGE
SOCIETY GIRL
SPEED
SPEED TO BURN
SPEEDWAY
SPINOUT
SPIRIT OF NOTRE DAME, THE
SPIRIT OF WEST POINT, THE
SPORT OF KINGS
SPORT PARADE, THE
SPORTING BLOOD (1940)
SPORTING LOVE
STEADY COMPANY
SWEEPSTAKES
SWELLHEAD, THE
SWING YOUR LADY
SWINGIN' AFFAIR, A
TAKE ME TO PARIS

TALL STORY
THAT GANG OF MINE
THAT'S MY BOY (1951)
THAT'S MY MAN
THERE AIN'T NO JUSTICE
THEY LEARNED ABOUT WOMEN
THEY NEVER COME BACK
THOROUGHBREDS
THUNDER IN CAROLINA
THUNDER IN DIXIE
TOUCHDOWN, ARMY
TRACK OF THUNDER
TRADING HEARTS
TRIPLE THREAT
TWO MINUTES TO PLAY
UNHOLY ROLLERS
VICTORY
WE WENT TO COLLEGE
WHITE LIGHTNING
WINNER TAKE ALL (1939)
WINNER'S CIRCLE, THE
WINNERS TAKE ALL
WOMAN-WISE
YESTERDAY'S HEROES
YOUNG RACERS, THE

*1/2
AMERICAN ANTHEM
BAD NEWS BEARS GO TO JAPAN,
     THE
BIG LEAGUER
BIG WEDNESDAY
BLONDE COMET
BLUE BLOOD
BODYHOLD
BOY FROM INDIANA
BOY IN BLUE, THE
COLLEGE HUMOR
COLLEGE LOVERS
COWBOY QUARTERBACK
CUP-TIE HONEYMOON
DAREDEVILS OF EARTH
DEATH ON THE DIAMOND
DREAMER
FAST BREAK
FIGHTING GENTLEMAN, THE
FISH THAT SAVED PITTSBURGH,
     THE
GAME THAT KILLS, THE
GREATEST, THE
GREEN HELMET, THE
HIGH GEAR
HIGH SPEED
HOME ON THE RANGE
HUDDLE
HUMPHREY TAKES A CHANCE
KENTUCKY BLUE STREAK
KING OF THE GAMBLERS
LAST FIGHT, THE
MAURIE

MOTOR MADNESS
NAVY WAY, THE
NORTH SHORE
NUMBER ONE
OVER THE TOP
PITTSBURGH KID, THE
PRIZE FIGHTER, THE
RACE FOR LIFE, A
RACING BLOOD (1954)
RACING LADY
RACING LUCK (1935)
RACING YOUTH
RETURN TO CAMPUS
RIDE, KELLY, RIDE
ROAD DEMON
ROAR OF THE CROWD
RUN FOR THE ROSES
RUNNING
RUNNING BRAVE
SECRETS OF A NURSE
SILVER DREAM RACER
SOCIAL LION, THE
SPEAKEASY
SPEED LOVERS
SPIRIT OF STANFORD, THE
SPIRIT OF YOUTH
SPORTING CHANCE
SPRING FEVER
STOCK CAR
STROKER ACE
SWING FEVER
SWING THAT CHEER
TAKE IT FROM ME
THAT'S MY BOY (1932)
THIS SPORTING AGE
THUNDER ALLEY
WILD RACERS, THE
WILDCATS
YESTERDAY'S HERO

*

ALL-AMERICAN BOY, THE
BAD NEWS BEARS IN BREAKING
     TRAINING, THE
BAND PLAYS ON, THE
BODY AND SOUL (1981)
BOWERY BLITZKRIEG
BUSTED UP
COUNTY FAIR, THE
DECEPTION
FIGHTING CHAMP
FLYING FIFTY-FIVE
GOLDENGIRL
GRUNT! THE WRESTLING MOVIE
HERE COME THE TIGERS
HIGH SCHOOL HERO
MAIN EVENT, THE (1938)
MANNEQUIN
MIRACLE KID
PIT STOP

PLAYERS
POLICE CALL
POLO JOE
PRISON SHADOWS
RACING BLOOD (1938)
RACING FEVER
RACING LUCK (1948)
RACING STRAIN, THE
RACQUET
RAD
RENO AND THE DOC
ROADRACERS, THE
ROCKY IV
SCORING
SIDECAR RACERS
SKATEBOARD
SLUGGER'S WIFE, THE
SOME BLONDES ARE DANGEROUS
SQUEEZE PLAY
STEALING HOME
STING II, THE
STRAIGHTAWAY
SUNNY SKIES
TEN LAPS TO GO
TOMBOY
WRESTLER, THE

zero
COACH
JOHNNY BE GOOD

FILMS BY PARENTAL RECOMMENDATION

All films included in this volume are listed below by their Parental Recommendation (PR). The Parental Recommendations indicate the following: AA: Good for children; A: Acceptable for children; C: Cautionary—some scenes may be objectionable; O: Objectionable

AA
ALIBI IKE
ANGELS IN THE OUTFIELD
BABE RUTH STORY, THE
BLACK STALLION, THE
BLUE BLOOD
BLUE GRASS OF KENTUCKY
BOB MATHIAS STORY, THE
CHAMP, THE (1931)
CHAMP, THE (1979)
CHARIOTS OF FIRE
CRAZYLEGS, ALL AMERICAN
FISH THAT SAVED PITTSBURGH,
    THE
GLORY
GOOD NEWS (1947)
GREAT DAN PATCH, THE
GUS
HOLD EVERYTHING
HOME IN INDIANA
IT HAPPENS EVERY SPRING
JACKIE ROBINSON STORY, THE
JOE PALOOKA, CHAMP
JOE PALOOKA IN THE BIG FIGHT
JOE PALOOKA IN THE
    COUNTERPUNCH
JOE PALOOKA IN TRIPLE CROSS
JOE PALOOKA IN WINNER TAKE
    ALL
JOE PALOOKA MEETS HUMPHREY
KENTUCKY
KID FROM BROOKLYN, THE
KID FROM LEFT FIELD, THE
KID FROM SPAIN, THE
KILL THE UMPIRE
KING OF HOCKEY
KNUTE ROCKNE—ALL AMERICAN
LIFE BEGINS IN COLLEGE
MILKY WAY, THE
NATIONAL VELVET
PALOOKA
PRIDE OF ST. LOUIS, THE
PRIDE OF THE BLUEGRASS (1939)
PRIDE OF THE YANKEES, THE
STRATTON STORY, THE
TAKE ME OUT TO THE BALL GAME
THOROUGHBREDS
WORLD'S GREATEST ATHLETE,
    THE

A
ALL-AMERICAN, THE (1932)
ALL-AMERICAN, THE (1953)
ARENA
ARSENAL STADIUM MYSTERY, THE
BAND PLAYS ON, THE
BASKETBALL FIX, THE
BATTLING BUTLER
BIG FIX, THE
BIG GAME, THE
BIG LEAGUER
BIG PUNCH, THE
BILLIE
BLONDE COMET
BLUE SKIES AGAIN
BODYHOLD
BOOTS MALONE
BORN TO FIGHT
BORN TO SPEED
BOWERY BLITZKRIEG
BOXER
BOY FROM INDIANA
BROADWAY BILL
BULLFIGHTER AND THE LADY, THE
BURN 'EM UP O'CONNER
BURNING UP
CADDY, THE
CAIN AND MABEL
CASEY'S SHADOW
CHECKPOINT
CITY FOR CONQUEST
COLLEGE
COLLEGE COACH
COLLEGE HUMOR
COLLEGE LOVE
COLLEGE LOVERS
COLLEGE RHYTHM
CONFLICT
CONTENDER, THE
COUNTY FAIR, THE
COWBOY AND THE PRIZEFIGHTER,
    THE
COWBOY QUARTERBACK
CROWD ROARS, THE (1938)
CUP-TIE HONEYMOON
DAMN YANKEES
DANGER ON WHEELS
DAREDEVILS OF EARTH
DEATH ON THE DIAMOND
DECEPTION
DEVIL'S HAIRPIN, THE

DREAMER
DUKE OF CHICAGO
ELMER THE GREAT
FAST BREAK
FAST COMPANIONS
FAST COMPANY (1929)
FAST COMPANY (1953)
FATHER WAS A FULLBACK
FIFTY-SHILLING BOXER
FIGHTER, THE
FIGHTING CHAMP
FIGHTING FOOLS
FIGHTING GENTLEMAN, THE
FIGHTING MAD
FIGHTING THOROUGHBREDS
FIGHTING YOUTH
FINAL TEST, THE
FINNEY
FIREBALL, THE
FIREBALL 500
FIREMAN, SAVE MY CHILD
FLESH AND FURY
FLYING FIFTY-FIVE
FLYING FISTS, THE
FOLLOW THE SUN
FOLLOW THRU
FOUR AGAINST FATE
FRESHMAN LOVE
FRESHMAN, THE
GAME THAT KILLS, THE
GAMES, THE
GENTLEMAN JIM
GIRL FROM MONTEREY, THE
GO, MAN, GO!
GOLDEN BOY
GOLDEN GLOVES
GOLDEN GLOVES STORY, THE
GOOD NEWS (1930)
GRAND PRIX (1934)
GREAT AMERICAN PASTIME, THE
GREAT GAME, THE (1930)
GREAT GAME, THE (1952)
GREAT JOHN L., THE
GREEN HELMET, THE
GRIDIRON FLASH
GUY WHO CAME BACK, THE
HARLEM GLOBETROTTERS, THE
HARMON OF MICHIGAN
HARRIGAN'S KID
HEART OF VIRGINIA
HEART PUNCH
HERE COMES MR. JORDAN
HIGH GEAR
HIGH SCHOOL HERO

THEY MADE ME A CRIMINAL
THEY NEVER COME BACK
THIS SPORTING AGE
THUNDER ALLEY
THUNDER IN CAROLINA
THUNDER IN DIXIE
TO PLEASE A LADY
TOUCHDOWN
TOUCHDOWN, ARMY
TRACK OF THUNDER
TRIPLE THREAT
TWO MINUTES TO PLAY
UNDER MY SKIN
UNWELCOME STRANGER
WALK, DON'T RUN
WALL OF NOISE
WE WENT TO COLLEGE
WEE GEORDIE
WHIPLASH
WHITE LIGHTNING
WINNER TAKE ALL (1932)
WINNER TAKE ALL (1939)
WINNER'S CIRCLE, THE
WINNING TEAM, THE
WOMAN-WISE
WORLD IN MY CORNER
YESTERDAY'S HEROES
YOUNG MAN OF MANHATTAN

A-C

AMAZING GRACE AND CHUCK
BANG THE DRUM SLOWLY
BIG WEDNESDAY
BIG WHEEL, THE
BINGO LONG TRAVELING ALL-
    STARS AND MOTOR KINGS, THE
CROOKED CIRCLE, THE
CROWD ROARS, THE (1932)
EASY LIVING
EDITH AND MARCEL
FORTUNE COOKIE, THE
HARD TIMES
HOOSIERS
JOHN GOLDFARB, PLEASE COME
    HOME
JUNIOR BONNER
KID GALAHAD (1937)
LET'S DO IT AGAIN
MAIN EVENT, THE (1979)
MAN FROM DOWN UNDER, THE
PLAYING AWAY
RAD
RIGHT CROSS
ROCKY
ROCKY II
ROCKY III
SALTY O'ROURKE
SAM'S SON
THRASHIN'
TRADING HEARTS

VICTORY
WILD RACERS, THE
WINNING

C

. . . ALL THE MARBLES
ALL THE RIGHT MOVES
AMERICAN ANTHEM
AMERICAN FLYERS
BAD NEWS BEARS, THE
BAD NEWS BEARS GO TO JAPAN,
    THE
BAD NEWS BEARS IN BREAKING
    TRAINING, THE
BEAR, THE
BLOOD AND SAND (1922)
BLOOD AND SAND (1941)
BOBBY DEERFIELD
BODY AND SOUL (1947)
CHAMP, THE (1931)
CHAMPION
CHAMPIONS
CORNBREAD, EARL AND ME
DOWNHILL RACER
FAN'S NOTES, A
FAT CITY
FEAR STRIKES OUT
FIREBALL JUNGLE
FLESH
FROM HELL TO HEAVEN
GLORY ALLEY
GREASED LIGHTNING
HEAVEN CAN WAIT
HERE COME THE TIGERS
HUSTLER, THE
IRON MAN, THE (1951)
KID MONK BARONI
KING FOR A NIGHT
LAST AMERICAN HERO, THE
LAST GAME, THE
LUSTY MEN, THE
MIXED COMPANY
MONKEY ON MY BACK
NADIA
NATURAL, THE
NORTH SHORE
NUMBER ONE
ONE AND ONLY, THE
OVER THE TOP
PACE THAT THRILLS, THE
PHAR LAP
PRIZE FIGHTER, THE
RACING FEVER
RED LINE 7000
REQUIEM FOR A HEAVYWEIGHT
RETURN TO CAMPUS
ROCKY IV
RUN FOR THE ROSES
RUNNING
RUNNING BRAVE

SET-UP, THE
SIDEWINDER ONE
SILVER DREAM RACER
SIX PACK
SKATEBOARD
SOMEBODY UP THERE LIKES ME
SPIKE OF BENSONHURST
SPRING FEVER
STEALING HOME
STING II, THE
STREETS OF GOLD
STROKER ACE
TAKE DOWN
TALL STORY
WALKOVER
WINNERS TAKE ALL
WRESTLER, THE
YOUNG RACERS, THE

C-O

BODY AND SOUL (1981)
BOY IN BLUE, THE
BREAKING AWAY
CADDYSHACK
COACH
COLOR OF MONEY, THE
EIGHT MEN OUT
EVERYBODY'S ALL-AMERICAN
GRAND PRIX (1966)
GREAT MACARTHY, THE
GREAT WHITE HOPE, THE
GREATEST, THE
HALLS OF ANGER
HEART LIKE A WHEEL
INSIDE MOVES
LONELINESS OF THE LONG
    DISTANCE RUNNER, THE
M*A*S*H
NORTH DALLAS FORTY
PERSONAL BEST
RIPPED-OFF
SEMI-TOUGH
SLUGGER'S WIFE, THE
SPIKER
TOUCH AND GO
WILDCATS
YESTERDAY'S HERO

O

ALL-AMERICAN BOY, THE
BEST OF TIMES, THE
BLOOD AND GUTS
BULL DURHAM
BUSTED UP
DRIVE, HE SAID
GOLDENGIRL
GRUNT! THE WRESTLING MOVIE
HARDER THEY FALL, THE
JOHNNY BE GOOD
KANSAS CITY BOMBER

Sports
Movies

Film
Reviews

A

ALIBI IKE***

(1935) 73m WB bw

Joe E. Brown *(Frank X. Farrell)*, Olivia de Havilland *(Dolly)*, Roscoe Karns *(Cary)*, William Frawley *(Cap)*, Joseph King *(Owner)*, Ruth Donnelly *(Bess)*, Paul Harvey *(Crawford)*, Eddie Shubert *(Jack Mack)*, George Pat Collins *(Lieutenant)*, Spencer Charters *(Minister)*, Gene Morgan *(Smitty)*, Jack Norton *(Reporter)*, George Riley *(Ball Player)*, Cliff Saum *(Kelly)*.

Throughout the 1930s rubber-faced, wide-mouthed comedian Joe. E Brown starred in films with sports themes, including three baseball features: FIREMAN SAVE MY CHILD (1932), ELMER THE GREAT (1933), and this film, perhaps the best of his diamond comedies. In it he plays Frank X. Farrell, a heavy-hitting rookie pitching sensation with the Cubs who finds an excuse for every mistake he makes, earning him the nickname "Alibi Ike." When not engaging in on-field antics, Farrell falls for Dolly (Olivia de Havilland, in her film debut), the team owner's sister-in-law, and proposes to her, though she turns him down. As the Big Game approaches, Brown is kidnaped by gamblers, but manages to escape and, after a wild chase, returns to the playing field just in time to save the game and win Dolly. A one-time semiprofessional ball player who once spent a number of weeks practicing with the New York Yankees, Brown was a baseball fanatic: not only was he a part owner of the Kansas City Blues, but his contract with Warner Bros. stipulated that they provide him with his own team, the Joe E. Brown All-Stars. ALIBI IKE, like ELMER THE GREAT, was adapted from a story by baseball and short story writer Ring Lardner.

p, Edward Chodorov; d, Ray Enright; w, William Wister (based on a story by Ring Lardner); ph, Arthur Todd; ed, Thomas Pratt.

Baseball/Comedy **(PR:AA MPAA:NR)**

ALL-AMERICAN, THE**

(1932) 73m UNIV bw

Richard Arlen *(Gary King)*, Andy Devine *(Andy Moran)*, Gloria Stuart *(Ellen Steffens)*, James Gleason *(Chick Knipe)*, John Darrow *(Bob King)*, Preston Foster *(Steve Kelly)*, Merna Kennedy *(Gloria Neuchard)*, Harold Waldrige *(Willie Walsh)*, Huntley Gordon *(Harcourt)*, Walter Brennan.

When All-American football player Gary King (Richard Arlen) hangs up his cleats and his schoolbooks after his last game, forgoing a degree to get rich quick selling bonds, he loses his money and stature in short order thanks to cheap women and gambling. Before his brother (John Darrow), who also becomes a college star, falls victim to the same fate, Gary returns to the playing field—in a game that features current All-Americans and past stars—and brings

his brother's ego back to earth. This relatively well-told gridiron yarn is enlivened by the comedic presence of Andy Devine and boasts the presence of some of the 1930s' top coaches, as well as a number of authentic college football players.

d, Russell Mack; w, Frank Weed, Ferdinand Reyney (based on story by Richard Schayer, Dale Van Every); ph, George Robinson.

Football **(PR:A MPAA:NR)**

ALL-AMERICAN, THE**

(1953) 82m UNIV bw (GB: THE WINNING WAY)

Tony Curtis *(Nick Bonelli)*, Lori Nelson *(Sharon Wallace)*, Richard Long *(Howard Carter)*, Mamie Van Doren *(Susie Ward)*, Gregg Palmer *(Cameron)*, Paul Cavanagh *(Prof. Banning)*, Herman Hickman *(Jumbo)*, Barney Phillips *(Clipper Colton)*, Jimmy Hunt *(Whizzer)*, Stuart Whitman *(Zip Parker)*, Douglas Kennedy *(Tate Hardy)*, Donald Randolph *(David Carter)*, Frank Gifford *(Stan Pomeroy)*, Tom Harmon *(Tom Harmon)*, Jim Sears *(Dartmore Quarterback)*, Elmer Willhoite *(Kenton)*.

Tony Curtis stars as Nick Bonelli, an All-American quarterback who quits school after his parents are killed in a bus accident on their way to see him play. After a brief period of mourning and moping, Nick transfers to a snobby school, where he begins working magic again on the football field. Withstanding the taunts of his wealthy teammates and avoiding the temptation of the off-limits bar tended by the voluptuous Susie (Mamie Van Doren), Nick again becomes a gridiron star with the help of his understanding girl friend (Lori Nelson). Like its 1932 namesake, THE ALL-AMERICAN is pleasant enough entertainment, and features both a fine performance by Curtis and appearances by real-life one-time All-Americans Tom Harmon of Michigan and Frank Gifford of USC. Another Trojan All-American, Jesse Hibbs, was the director, and still another, D.D. Beauchamp, coscripted the film.

p, Aaron Rosenberg; d, Jesse Hibbs; w, D.D. Beauchamp, Robert Yale Libett (based on a story by Leonard Freeman); ph, Maury Gertsman; ed, Edward Curtiss.

Football **(PR:A MPAA:NR)**

ALL-AMERICAN BOY, THE*

(1973) 118m WB c

Jon Voight *(Vic Bealer)*, Carol Androsky *(Rodine)*, Anne Archer *(Drenna Valentine)*, Gene Borkan *(Rockoff)*, Ron Burns *(Larkin)*, Rosalind Cash *(Poppy)*, Jeanne Cooper *(Nola Bealer)*, Peggy Cowles *(Bett Van Daumee)*, Leigh French *(Lovette)*, Ned Glass *(Arty)*, Bob Hastings *(Ariel Van Daumee)*, Kathy Mahoney *(Shereen Bealer)*, Art Metrano *(Jay David Swooze)*, Jaye P. Morgan *(Magda)*, Harry Northup *(Parker)*.

Divided into six "rounds," THE ALL-AMERICAN BOY stars Jon Voight as a talented would-be Olympic boxer willing to step over anyone on his way to the top (which he never reaches), including his girl friend (Anne Archer of

FATAL ATTRACTION fame), whom he gets pregnant and then deserts. Writer-director Charles Eastman seems to view Voight as a tragic antihero, but as the film wears on, it and Voight's performance become increasingly irritating and manipulative. Shot in 1969, THE ALL-AMERICAN BOY sat mercifully on the producer's shelf until 1973, and perhaps it should have remained there.

p, Joseph T. Naar, Saul J. Krugman; d, Charles Eastman; ph, Philip Lathrop; ed, Christopher Holmes.

Boxing (PR:O MPAA:R)

... ALL THE MARBLES**½

(1981) 112m MGM/UA c (GB: THE CALIFORNIA DOLLS)

Peter Falk *(Harry)*, Vicki Frederick *(Iris)*, Laurence Landon *(Molly)*, Burt Young *(Eddie)*, Tracy Reed *(Diane)*, Ursaline Bryant-King *(June)*, John Hancock *(Big John)*, Claudette Nevins *(Solly)*, Richard Jaeckel *(Referee)*.

Veteran action director Robert Aldrich's last film, this curious mixture of mildly sexual comedy and sports (well, professional wrestling, anyway) is uneven, but occasionally very funny and compelling. Peter Falk gives a strong performance as Harry, the scheming, penny-pinching manager of the California Dolls (Vicki Frederick and Laurence Landon), a second-rate women's tag team. The three rumble from one industrial town to another as the Dolls try to claw their way into the pro wrestling spotlight. Harry secures a non-title match against the world champion Toledo Tigers, whom the Dolls defeat. A rematch ends up with the Tigers on top, but they give the Dolls a shot at their championship in Reno. The 20-minute wrestling finale is a wild and woolly affair, with the Dolls battling not just the Tigers but also the referee, who has been bribed by a mobster Harry crossed.

p, William Aldrich; d, Robert Aldrich; w, Mel Frohman; ph, Joseph Biroc (Metrocolor); ed, Irving C. Rosenblum, Richard Lane; m, Frank De Vol.

Wrestling **Cas.** (PR:C MPAA:R)

ALL THE RIGHT MOVES**½

(1983) 91m FOX c

Tom Cruise *(Stef)*, Craig T. Nelson *(Nickerson)*, Lea Thompson *(Lisa)*, Charles Cioffi *(Pop)*, Paul Carafotes *(Salvucci)*, Christopher Penn *(Brian)*, Sandy Faison *(Suzie)*, Paige Price *(Tracy)*, James A. Baffico *(Bosko)*, Donald A. Yanessa *(Coach)*, Walter Briggs *(Rifleman)*, Leon Robinson *(Shadow)*.

Stef (Tom Cruise), a high-school football star, dreams of escaping a stifling steel-mill existence via an athletic scholarship. While Stef is deluged with recruitment offers, his coach (nicely essayed by Craig T. Nelson) positions himself for a college job, and needs a big win against the little town's affluent suburban rival. Just as the team appears ready to wrap up the game, one of Stef's friends fumbles, handing their opponents victory. When the coach blows his cool after the game, Stef protects his friend and

is suspended; later, he is unjustly implicated in the vandalism of the coach's house and kicked off the team permanently. His hopes for a scholarship appear to be dashed and he turns to his girl friend (Lea Thompson, in a fine performance) and father for help in putting his life back together. This well-executed, competently acted but ultimately cliche-ridden film is a cut below the similarly themed SATURDAY'S HERO (1951), but head and shoulders above the abysmal JOHNNY BE GOOD (1988). Cruise is good, although he displays less charisma and charm than in THE COLOR OF MONEY (1987). The directorial debut of veteran cinematographer Michael Chapman, ALL THE RIGHT MOVES was filmed in Johnstown, Pennsylvania, where area coach Don Yanessa acted as the technical advisor and also did a turn as the opposing coach.

p, Stephen Deutsch; d, Michael Chapman; w, Michael Kane; ph, Jan DeBont; ed, David Garfield; m, David Campbell.

Football **Cas.** (PR:C MPAA:R)

AMAZING GRACE AND CHUCK***

(1987) 115m Turnstar-Rastar-ML Delphi/Tri-Star c

Jamie Lee Curtis *(Lynn Taylor)*, Alex English *(Amazing Grace Smith)*, Gregory Peck *(President)*, William L. Petersen *(Russell Murdock)*, Joshua Zuehlke *(Chuck Murdock)*, Dennis Lipscomb *(Johnny B. Goode)*, Lee Richardson *(Jeffries)*, Frances Conroy *(Pamela Murdock)*, Dean Alexander *(Sports Broadcaster)*, Red Auerbach *(Himself)*, Alan Autry *(George)*, Michael Bowen *(Hot Dog)*, James Cotterell *(Third Baseman)*, Clarence Felder *(Dick Ferguson)*, Lynne Turner Fitzgerald *(Network Anchor)*, Brian R. Hager *(First Baseman)*, Robert Harper *(Bowman)*, James Lindley Hathaway *(Jerome)*, Matt Kerns *(Shortstop)*, Cortney Kutner *(Carolyn)*, Harvey Martin *(Mad Dog)*, Johnny Most *(Himself)*, Natalie Oliver *(Boston Reporter)*, Kurt Olsson *(Tommy)*, Gwen Petersen *(Teacher)*.

AMAZING GRACE AND CHUCK is the heartwarming and uplifting tale of what happens when all American professional sports events are halted in an appeal for a nuclear disarmament agreement. And it's all due to the determination of Chuck Murdock (Joshua Zuehlke), a 12-year-old Little League pitcher from Montana who refuses to pitch again after learning about the potential horrors of nuclear war. The news media take this story and run with it, inspiring Boston Celtics star Amazing Grace Smith (Alex English) to hang up his sneakers and join Murdock's campaign. Soon other athletes follow his example, until all of pro sports comes to a standstill, putting pressure on the US president (Gregory Peck) and the Soviet premier (Vasek C. Simek) to reach an agreement. Ironically, English, who delivers a fine performance, is actually a longtime Denver Nuggets star. When legendary Boston coach Red Auerbach, who appears in the film as himself, was informed that English would be playing a Celtic, he said, "I only wish I could keep him." English, who has also published three books of poetry, was well prepared for his film role as an activist, having been instrumental in "Hands Across America" and at the forefront of the Ethiopian Relief Fund. Helmed by Mike Newell (the English director of DANCE WITH A STRANGER, not the former Houston Rocket), who might have fared better had he employed a more whimsical touch, the picture features venerable Boston Garden, as well as veteran Celtics' voice Johnny Most. The NBA arranged to have a special exhibition game between the Celtics and the 76ers for the film.

p, David Field; d, Mike Newell; w, David Field; ph, Robert Elswit (Metrocolor); ed, Peter Hollywood; m, Elmer Bernstein.

Basketball   **Cas.**   **(PR:A-C   MPAA:PG)**

AMERICAN ANTHEM*½

(1986) 100m Fields-Doug Chapin-Lorimar/COL bw-c

Mitch Gaylord *(Steve Tevere)*, Tiny Wells *(Jake)*, Janet Jones *(Julie Lloyd)*, Michael Pataki *(Coach Soranhoff)*, Patrice Donnelly *(Danielle)*, R.J. Williams *(Mikey Tevere)*, John Aprea *(Mr. Tevere)*, Michelle Phillips *(Linda Tevere)*, Katherine Gosney *(Landlady)*, Stacy Maloney *(Kirk Baker)*, Peter Tramm *(Ron Denver)*, Maria Anz *(Becky Cameron)*, Jenny Ester *(Tracey Prescott)*, Andrew M. White *(Arthur)*, Dick McGarvin *(Announcer Prelim Meet)*, Mark Oates *(Danny Squire)*, Jan Claire *(Announcer Final Meet)*, Megan Marsden *(Jo-Ellen Carter)*, Li Yuejiu *(Ling Xiang)*.

Mitch Gaylord, who won a gold, a silver, and two bronze medals in gymnastics at the 1984 Los Angeles Olympics, makes a big stretch and stars here as a one-time champion gymnast whose glory days appear to be behind him. Enter Julie (Janet Jones), a gymnast who comes to town to try to earn a spot on the national team. Predictably, Steve (Gaylord) falls for Julie and, newly inspired, begins training again for competition, setting up the highlight of the film, its nicely photographed finale in which Steve and Julie strive for spots on the team. Governed by a rock video aesthetic (which comes as little surprise, considering that it was directed by Albert Magnoli, the man responsible for Prince's PURPLE RAIN), AMERICAN ANTHEM employs some flashy and occasionally effective visuals, but its screenplay and characterization leave a lot to be desired, and the film is ultimately disappointing. Hockey fans are likely to recognize Jones as the woman who broke the heart of Edmonton Oiler fans when she married Wayne Gretzky.

p, Robert Schaffel, Doug Chapin; d, Albert Magnoli; w, Evan Archerd, Jeff Benjamin (based on a story by Evan Archerd, Jeff Benjamin, Susan Williams); ph, Donald E. Thorin (Panavision, MGM Color); ed, James Oliver; m, Alan Silvestri.

Gymnastics   **Cas.**   **(PR:C   MPAA:PG-13)**

AMERICAN FLYERS**

(1985) 114m WB c

Kevin Costner *(Marcus Sommers)*, David Grant *(David Sommers)*, Rae Dawn Chong *(Sarah)*, Alexandra Paul *(Becky)*, Janice Rule *(Mrs. Sommers)*, Luca Bercovici *(Muzzin)*, Robert Townsend *(Jerome)*, John Amos *(Dr. Conrad)*, Doi Johnson *(Randolph)*, John Garber *(Belov)*,

Jennifer Grey *(Leslie)*, James Terry, Jessica Nelson *(Hitchhikers)*, Tom Lawrence *(Timekeeper)*, Brian Drebber *(Race Announcer)*, Judy Jordan *(Woman Reporter)*, Katherine Kriss *(Vera)*, Jan Speck *(Receptionist)*, Greg Walker *(Photographer)*, Sig Frohlich *(Mail Clerk)*, Eddie Merckx *(Himself)*.

Combining instances of family turmoil and courage in the face of death, AMERICAN FLYERS focuses on the cycling Sommers brothers. Twenty-one-year-old David (David Grant) is a college dropout who thinks only about bicycle racing. His brother, Marcus (Kevin Costner), a doctor of sports medicine, is convinced that David is prone to the same physical condition that brought about their father's premature death. Along with Marcus' girl friend, Sarah (Rae Dawn Chong), the brothers travel cross-country to the Colorado Rockies to compete in the "Hell of the West Race," in which their major competitor is Sarah's ex-husband. The race produces some shocking medical results, as well as displays of great courage, en route to the film's emotional finale. Unfortunately, the script by Steve Tesich—who wrote the Oscar-winning screenplay for BREAKING AWAY (1979), an immeasurably better film about cycling and family relationships—is disjointed and underdeveloped. John Badham's direction is equally uninspired, although the climactic race, shot on location during the Coors International Bicycle Classic, is filmed with an abundance of breathtaking helicopter shots that capture the beautiful scenery.

p, Gareth Wigan, Paula Weinstein; d, John Badham; w, Steve Tesich; ph, Don Peterman (Panavision, Technicolor); ed, Frank Morriss, Dallas Puett, Jeff Jones; m, Lee Ritenour, Greg Mathieson.

Bicycling   **Cas.**   **(PR:C   MPAA:PG-13)**

ANGELS IN THE OUTFIELD***½

(1951) 99m MGM c (GB: ANGELS AND THE PIRATES)

Paul Douglas *(Guffy McGovern)*, Janet Leigh *(Jennifer Paige)*, Keenan Wynn *(Fred Bayles)*, Donna Corcoran *(Bridget White)*, Lewis Stone *(Arnold P. Hapgood)*, Spring Byington *(Sister Edwitha)*, Bruce Bennett *(Saul Hellman)*, Marvin Kaplan *(Timothy Durney)*, Ellen Corby *(Sister Veronica)*, Jeff Richards *(Dave Rothberg)*, John Gallaudet *(Reynolds)*, King Donovan *(McGee)*, Don Haggerty *(Rube Robinson)*, Paul Salata *(Tony Minelli)*.

Silly but fun, this delightful baseball comedy stars Paul Douglas as Guffy McGovern, the irascible manager of the Pittsburgh Pirates, who are firmly entrenched in the basement of the National League until the prayers of a little girl (Donna Corcoran) prompt the Angel Gabriel to intervene. When Guffy sees the divine light and turns over a new leaf, angels (baseball greats of the past) lend a helping glove, and the Bucs start winning ball games, shooting to the top of the standings. Reporter Jennifer Paige (Janet Leigh) suspects the Pirates are receiving help from above, and begins an investigation into the matter. Great performances by all make this a little gem of a film. Dwight Eisenhower, interviewed during his presidency, named this his favorite movie. Note the fleeting presence of Hall of Famers Ty Cobb and Joe DiMaggio.

p, Clarence Brown; d, Clarence Brown; w, Dorothy Kingsley, George Wells (based on a story by Richard Conlin); ph, Paul C. Vogel; ed, Robert J. Kern; m, Daniele Amfitheatrof.

Baseball/Comedy   **(PR:AA MPAA:NR)**

ARENA**

(1953) 83m MGM c

Gig Young *(Hob Danvers)*, Jean Hagen *(Meg Hutchins)*, Polly Bergen *(Ruth Danvers)*, Henry Morgan *(Lew Hutchins)*, Barbara Lawrence *(Sylvia Morgan)*, Robert Horton *(Jackie Roach)*, Lee Aaker *(Teddy Hutchins)*, Lee Van Cleef *(Smitty)*, Marilee Phelps *(Smitty's Wife)*, Jim Hayward *(Cal Jamison)*, George Wallace *(Buster Cole)*, Stuart Randall *(Eddie Elstead)*.

Hotshot rodeo star Hob Danvers (Gig Young) takes up with rodeo groupie Sylvia (Barbara Lawrence) when his loving wife, Ruth (Polly Bergen), leaves him, unable to stand his selfish irresponsibility. At a big rodeo in Tucson (the footage is from the *Fiesta de Los Vaqueros*), Hob's life is saved by his former partner (Henry [Harry] Morgan), a onetime top cowboy reduced to the status of rodeo clown, who rushes in front of a rampaging Brahma bull before it can get to Hob and is fatally injured in the act. After witnessing his pard's sad end, Hob decides to hang up his spurs and reconcile with Ruth. This melodramatic reworking of Nicholas Ray's THE LUSTY MEN (1952) was originally released in 3-D.

p, Arthur M. Loew, Jr.; d, Richard Fleischer; w, Harold Jack Bloom (based on a story by Arthur M. Loew, Jr.); ph, Paul C. Vogel (AnscoColor); ed, Cotton Warburton.

Rodeo   **(PR:A MPAA:NR)**

ARSENAL STADIUM MYSTERY, THE**

(1939, Brit.) 84m G&S/GDF bw

Leslie Banks *(Inspector Slade)*, Greta Gynt *(Gwen Lee)*, Ian Maclean *(Sgt. Clinton)*, Esmond Knight *(Raille)*, Liane Linden *(Inga)*, Brian Worth *(Philip Morring)*, Anthony Bushell *(Jack Dyce)*, Richard Norris *(Setchley)*, Wyndham Goldie *(Kindilett)*, Dennis Wyndham *(Commissionaire)*, Maire O'Neill *(Mrs. Kirwan)*.

Based on a novel by Leonard Gribble, this mildly intriguing mystery involves the poisoning of an English soccer star (Anthony Bushell) during a big match in London's historic Arsenal Stadium and the ensuing investigation of the case. Not surprisingly, the dead man's teammates are the prime suspects. The cast includes the real-life Gunner footballers who called Arsenal Stadium home in 1939.

p, Josef Somio, Richard Norton; d, Thorold Dickinson; w, Thorold Dickinson, Donald Bull (based on the novel by Leonard Gribble); ph, Desmond Dickinson.

Soccer/Mystery   **Cas.**   **(PR:A MPAA:NR)**

B

BABE RUTH STORY, THE***

(1948) 106m MON/AA bw

William Bendix *(Babe Ruth)*, Claire Trevor *(Claire Hodgson)*, Charles Bickford *(Brother Mathias)*, Sam Levene *(Phil Conrad)*, William Frawley *(Jack Dunn)*, Gertrude Niesen *(Nightclub Singer)*, Fred Lightner *(Miller Huggins)*, Stanley Clements *(Western Union Boy)*, Bobby Ellis *(Babe Ruth as a Boy)*, Lloyd Gough *(Baston)*, Matt Briggs *(Col. Ruppert)*, Paul Cavanagh *(Dr. Menzies)*, Pat Flaherty *(Bill Corrigan)*, Tony Taylor *(The Kid)*, Richard Lane *(Coach)*, Mark Koenig *(Himself)*, Harry Wismer, Mel Allen *(Sports Announcers)*, H.V. Kaltenborn *(News Announcer)*, Knox Manning *(Narrator)*.

The Sultan of Swat is ably enacted here by the wonderful lantern-jawed character actor William Bendix, who brings bravado and color to every frame of this sanitized but enjoyable biopic that glosses over the Babe's legendary excessiveness. THE BABE RUTH STORY begins in Baltimore as the young George Herman Ruth (Bobby Ellis) is taken from his father's waterfront saloon and placed in St. Mary's Industrial School for Boys, where the kindly Brother Mathias (Charles Bickford) introduces him to sandlot baseball. Bendix takes over as the Babe begins his stellar career on the diamond first as a brilliant pitcher with the Boston Red Sox, then as a New York Yankee, swinging for the fences as no one (save Hank Aaron) has done since, pounding out 60 home runs in 1927 and winning the hearts of baseball fans everywhere. Claire Trevor does a nice turn as the second Mrs. Ruth and Fred Lightner is excellent as famed manager Miller Huggins, but Bendix is unquestionably the star of the show. Having studied films of Ruth endlessly, until he was able to imitate his stance, walk, unique mannerisms, and facial expressions, Bendix became so good at being the Babe that it is difficult to tell where the Bendix action shots leave off and the newsreel clips of the real Ruth begin. Sadly, cancer claimed the Bambino shortly after the release of the film. Note the presence of real-life sportscasters Harry Wismer and Mel Allen.

p, Roy Del Ruth; d, Roy Del Ruth; w, Bob Considine, George Callahan (based on the book by Bob Considine); ph, Phillip Tannura; ed, Richard Heermance; m, Edward Ward.

Baseball/Biography   **Cas.**   **(PR:AA MPAA:NR)**

BAD NEWS BEARS, THE***½

(1976) 102m PAR c

Walter Matthau *(Coach Buttermaker)*, Tatum O'Neal *(Manda Whurlizer)*, Vic Morrow *(Roy Turner)*, Joyce Van Patten *(Cleveland)*, Ben Piazza *(Councilman Whitewood)*, Jackie Earle Haley *(Kelly Leak)*, Alfred Lutter *(Ogilvie)*, Brandon Cruz *(Joey Turner)*, Shari Summers *(Mrs. Turner)*,

Joe Brooks *(Umpire),* Maurice Marks *(Announcer),* Quinn Smith *(Lupus),* Gary Lee Cavagnaro *(Engelberg),* Erin Blunt *(Ahmad),* David Stambaugh *(Toby Whitewood).*

As amusing for adults as it is for children, this charming, funny film takes a gentle poke at Little League baseball and at the obsession with winning. Morris Buttermaker (Walter Matthau, in a comic tour de force), a one-time minor leaguer, becomes the manager of the Bears, a team of multiracial rejects in a southern California little league. With Morris' help this hapless, foul-mouthed bunch, led by its star female hurler, Manda Whurlizer (Tatum O'Neal), begins improving and winning ball games, although the priorities of the players begin to take a disappointing turn in the process. The Bears make it all the way to the championship, but director Michael Ritchie (SMILE; DOWNHILL RACER), working from a script by Burt Lancaster's son Bill, provides a nice twist on the expected outcome. Although the film could have been preachy, Ritchie handles the story and theme with such deftness that what you'll remember about THE BAD NEWS BEARS is its emotion and humor. So popular was the film that it produced two sequels—THE BAD NEWS BEARS IN BREAKING TRAINING (1977) and THE BAD NEWS BEARS GO TO JAPAN (1978)—and at least one imitation, HERE COME THE TIGERS (1978).

p, Stanley R. Jaffe; d, Michael Ritchie; w, Bill Lancaster; ph, John A. Alonzo (Movielab Color); ed, Richard A. Harris; m, Jerry Fielding.

Baseball/Comedy   Cas.   (PR:C MPAA:PG)

BAD NEWS BEARS GO TO JAPAN, THE*½

(1978) 91m PAR c

Tony Curtis *(Marvin Lazar),* Jackie Earle Haley *(Kelly Leak),* Tomisaburo Wakayama *(Coach Shimizu),* Hatsune Ishihara *(Arika),* George Wyner *(Network Director),* Lonny Chapman *(Louis the Gambler),* Matthew Douglas Anton *(E.R.W. Tillyard III),* Erin Blunt *(Ahmad Rahim),* George Gonzales *(Miguel Agilar),* Brett Marx *(Jimmy Feldman),* David Pollock *(Rudy Stein),* David Stambaugh *(Toby Whitewood),* Jeffrey Louis Starr *(Mike Engleberg),* Scoody Thornton *(Mustapha Rahim).*

Despite a script by THE BAD NEWS BEARS (see above) originator Bill Lancaster, producing chores handled by that film's director, Michael Ritchie, and the presence of several of the players from the first two films, this third entry in the "Bad News Bears" cycle never gets to first base. It's somewhat more energetic than the previous year's BREAKING TRAINING and the Japanese locations are a plus, but so much silliness has been substituted for the solid situations and characterizations of the first film that it's hard to believe the same people had anything to do with both pictures. This time around the Bears—guided by Marvin Lazar (Tony Curtis), a shifty wheeler-dealer who is reformed by his young charges—venture to the Land of the Rising Sun to take on the Japanese Little League champion. When the pressures imposed by all-too-competitive adults become too much, the Bears and their Japanese counterparts play the game on their own, fair and square.

p, Michael Ritchie; d, John Berry; w, Bill Lancaster; ph, Jean Polito, Kozo Okazaki (Movielab Color); ed, Richard A. Harris; m, Paul Chihara.

Baseball/Comedy   Cas.   (PR:C MPAA:PG)

BAD NEWS BEARS IN BREAKING TRAINING, THE*

(1977) 99m PAR c

William Devane *(Mike Leak),* Clifton James *(Sy Orlansky),* Jackie Earle Haley *(Kelly Leak),* Jimmy Baio *(Carmen Ronzonni),* Chris Barnes *(Tanner Boyle),* Erin Blunt *(Ahmad Abdul Rahim),* Jaime Escobedo, George Gonzales *(Agilar Boys),* Alfred Lutter *(Ogilvie),* Brett Marx *(Jimmy Feldman),* David Pollock *(Rudi Stein),* Quinn Smith *(Timmy Lupus),* David Stambaugh *(Toby Whitewood),* Jeffrey Louis Starr *(Mike Engleberg),* Fred Stuthman *(Caretaker),* Dolph Sweet *(Coach Manning),* Lane Smith *(Officer Mackie),* Pat Corley *(Coach Morrie Slater).*

Some of the kids return for this pale sequel to THE BAD NEWS BEARS (see above), but the adults have moved on to greener ball fields and the picture suffers from their absence. Director Michael Pressman is no Michael Ritchie, and Paul Brickman's script is weak, sending the Bears to Houston, where Kelly Leak (Jackie Earle Haley) recruits his dad (William Devane) to coach the kids in an Astrodome playoff game. Whereas a lot of the language was off-color but cute in the original, this time it's just plain smarmy. The original THE BAD NEWS BEARS was a home run, but the sequels are little more than weak trips back to the mound.

p, Leonard Goldberg; d, Michael Pressman; w, Paul Brickman (based on characters created by Bill Lancaster); ph, Fred J. Koenekamp (Movielab Color); ed, John W. Wheeler; m, Craig Safan.

Baseball/Comedy   Cas.   (PR:C MPAA:PG)

BAND PLAYS ON, THE*

(1934) 87m MGM bw

Robert Young *(Tony),* Stuart Erwin *(Stuffy),* Leo Carrillo *(Angelo),* Betty Furness *(Kitty),* Ted Healy *(Joe),* Preston Foster *(Howdy),* Russell Hardie *(Mike),* William Tannen *(Rosy),* Robert Livingston *(Bob Stone),* Norman Phillips, Jr. *(Stuffy as a Child),* David Durand *(Tony as a Child),* Sidney Miller *(Rosy as a Child),* Beaudine Anderson *(Mike as a Child),* Betty Jean Graham *(Kitty as a Child).*

In this monotonous tale, four street punks (Robert Young, Stuart Erwin, Russell Hardie, and William Tannen) are brought before a kindly judge for stealing a Ford. He assigns the boys to a special program run by a football coach (Preston Foster) who teaches them the meaning of teamwork, loyalty, and honor, and they prove themselves to be gifted athletes. In addition to its other problems, the film is marred by a poor job of matching newsreel footage of football crowds with the staged shots. Harry Stuhldreher, one of Notre Dame's famous "Four Horsemen," was the coauthor of one of the stories on which THE BAND PLAYS ON is based.

d, Russell Mack; w, Bernard Schubert, Ralph Spence, Harvey Gates (based on the stories "Blackfield" by Byron Morgan, J. Robert Bren and "The Gravy Game" by Harry Stuhldreher, W. Thorton Martin); ph, Leonard Smith; ed, William Levanway.

Football (PR:A MPAA:NR)

BANG THE DRUM SLOWLY***½

(1973) 96m PAR c

Robert De Niro *(Bruce Pearson)*, Michael Moriarty *(Henry Wiggen)*, Vincent Gardenia *(Dutch Schnell)*, Phil Foster *(Joe Jaros)*, Ann Wedgeworth *(Katie)*, Patrick McVey *(Pearson's Father)*, Heather MacRae *(Holly Wiggen)*, Selma Diamond *(Tootsie)*, Barbara Babcock, Maurice Rosenfield *(Team Owners)*, Tom Ligon *(Piney Woods)*, Andy Jarrell *(Ugly Jones)*, Marshall Efron *(Bradley Lord)*, Barton Heyman *(Red Traphagen)*, Donny Burks *(Perry)*, Hector Elias *(Diego)*, Tom Signorelli *(Goose Williams)*, Jim Donohue *(Canada Smith)*, Nicolas Surovy *(Aleck Olson)*, Danny Aiello *(Horse)*, Hector Troy *(George)*, Tony Major *(Jonah)*, Alan Manaon *(Dr. Loftus)*, Ernesto Gonzales *(Dr. Chambers)*, Jack Hollander, Lou Girolami *(Tegwar Players)*, Dorothy Nuebert *(Bruce's Mother)*, Pierrino Mascarino *(Sid Goldman)*.

A well-done but depressing film, BANG THE DRUM SLOWLY is a sort of baseball version of "Brian's Song," the TV movie that told the story of the extraordinary friendship between the Chicago Bears' Gale Sayers and Brian Piccolo, who died of cancer. In this film, Bruce Pearson (Robert De Niro) is the dying athlete, a journeyman big league catcher who has contracted Hodgkin's disease. Henry Wiggen (Michael Moriarty), the team's star pitcher, becomes dedicated to his batterymate when he learns of Pearson's fatal illness and prevents him from being sent to the minors. When Wiggen, the classic golden boy, and the thick-headed bumpkin Pearson suddenly become inseparable, their teammates begin to wonder. Once they learn the truth, however, the rest of the players finally make Pearson feel like one of the boys and, surprisingly, his play even improves. Alas, it's all a little too late. One of De Niro's earliest roles, Bruce Pearson, the quintessential bumpkin (who wears a "Smiley Face" t-shirt under his sports jacket), is poles apart from the enigmatic loners that became the actor's specialty. To prepare for the part, De Niro not only practiced with the Cincinnati Reds, but also traveled to Georgia to perfect his accent, and his hard work resulted in a wholly believable performance. Moriarty is also very effective as Henry Wiggen, the central character in a number of baseball novels by Mark Harris, who adapted one of them for this film. Harris' story had previously been presented on TV with Paul Newman and Albert Salmi in the leads, but under John Hancock's fine direction it became one of the best baseball movies ever. Vincent Gardenia received an Academy Award nomination for supporting work as the manager and Phil Foster is wonderful as a coach.

p, Maurice Rosenfield, Lois Rosenfield; d, John Hancock; w, Mark Harris (based on the novel by Mark Harris); ph,

Richard Shore (Movielab Color); ed, Richard Marks; m, Stephen Lawrence.

Baseball **Cas.** **(PR:A-C MPAA:NR)**

BASKETBALL FIX, THE***

(1951) 65m Realart bw

John Ireland *(Pete Ferreday)*, Marshall Thompson *(Johnny Long)*, Vanessa Brown *(Pat Judd)*, William Bishop *(Mike Taft)*, Hazel Brooks *(Lily Courtney)*, John Sands *(Jed Black)*, Bobby Hyatt *(Mickey Long)*, Walter Sande *(Nat Becker)*, Ted Pierson *(Lt. Garrett)*, Johnny Phillips *(Reporter)*, Lester Sharp *(Jewelry Salesman)*.

John Ireland plays Pete Ferreday, the sportswriter who narrates this compelling tale of a college basketball scandal. Up-and-coming cager Johnny Long (Marshall Thompson) finds himself up to his neck in gambling debts and tries to shave a few points off the Big Game so tough guy Mike Taft (William Bishop) will stop putting the squeeze on him. Unfortunately, but not unexpectedly, Long's cheating is detected by the powers that be. Surprisingly, the scandal in THE BASKETBALL FIX was small potatoes compared to the one that rocked the real basketball world in 1951 (see THE BIG FIX, below).

p, Edward Leven; d, Felix Feist; w, Peter R. Brooke, Charles K. Peck, Jr.; ph, Stanley Cortez; ed, Francis D. Lyon; m, Raoul Kraushaar.

Basketball **(PR:A MPAA:NR)**

BATTLING BUTLER***

(1926) 7 reels MGM bw

Buster Keaton *(Alfred Butler)*, Sally O'Neil *(The Girl)*, Snitz Edwards *(His Valet)*, Francis McDonald *(Alfred "Battling Butler")*, Mary O'Brien *(His Wife)*, Tom Wilson *(The Trainer)*, Eddie Borden *(His Manager)*, Walter James *(The Girl's Father)*, Buddy Fine *(The Girl's Brother)*.

Boxing was the subject of a number of movies in the silent era, including a pair of two-reelers that featured Charlie Chaplin: Keystone's THE KNOCKOUT (1914), a Fatty Arbuckle starrer in which Chaplin plays a referee, and Essanay's THE CHAMPION (1915), wherein Chaplin puts on the gloves himself. Probably the best-remembered boxing film of the era, however, is BATTLING BUTLER, starring that other great silent comedian, Buster Keaton. In it he plays Alfred Butler, a wealthy fop who passes himself off as a famous boxer (who happens to share his name) to impress a beautiful young woman he encounters while vacationing in the mountains. The humor comes in Alfred's pathetic attempt to train for an upcoming match. The film's climax is more on the serious side, however, as Alfred finds himself in a brutally realistic fight with the true "Battling Butler," an encounter that director Keaton dwells on before shifting to the more lighthearted finale.

d, Buster Keaton; w, Albert Boasberg, Paul Gerard Smith, Lex Neal, Charles Smith (based on the musical "Battling

Butler," by Stanley Brightman, Austin Melford); ph, Bert Haines, Dev Jennings.

Boxing (PR:A MPAA:NR)

BEAR, THE**½

(1984) 110m EM c

Gary Busey *(Paul "Bear" Bryant)*, Cynthia Leake *(Mary Harmon Bryant)*, Carmen Thomas *(Mae Martin Bryant)*, Cary Guffey *(Grandson Marc)*, Harry Dean Stanton *(Coach Thomas)*, Jon-Erik Hexum *(Pat Trammell)*, Pat Greenstein *(Joe Namath)*, Michael McGrady *(Gene Stallings)*, William Wesley Neighbors, Jr. *(Billy Neighbors)*, Brett Rice *(Don Hutson)*, Buddy Farmer *(Herman Ball)*, Owen E. Orr *(Ermal Allen)*, Charles Gabrielson *(Steve Meilinger)*, D'Urville Martin *(Billy)*, Ken Taylor *(Jimbo)*, Muriel Moore *(Miss Vernon)*, Ivan Green *(Mr. Gallagher)*, Scott Campbell *(Dennis Goehring)*, Robert Craighead *(Jack Pardee)*, Damon Sarafian *(Don Watson)*, Tod Spangler *(Bobby Keith)*, Michael Prokopuk *(Bob Lockett)*, Jeff Tyler *(Dee Powell)*, Eric Hipple *(Tony Eason)*.

Gary Busey stars as Paul "Bear" Bryant in this reverential biography of the colorful Alabama college football coach, faithfully portraying him over a 50-year span, from his playing days with the Crimson Tide to his death in 1983. The film's chief fault is that it presents the Bear's life story without drama or conflict, and the only reason to watch this if you're not a Bryant devotee (a moot question in Alabama) is Busey's outstanding performance. Busey had already proven his ability to *become* a character as the lead in THE BUDDY HOLLY STORY (1978), and he went on to play another legendary sports figure, Joe DiMaggio, in INSIGNIFICANCE (1985). Making an appearance in THE BEAR is former Detroit Lions quarterback Eric Hipple, who plays Illini quarterback Tony Eason in Alabama's thrilling 1982 Liberty Bowl victory.

p, Larry G. Spangler; d, Richard Sarafian; w, Michael Kane; ph, Laszlo George (DeLuxe Color); ed, Robert Florio; m, Bill Conti.

Football/Biography (PR:C MPAA:PG)

BEST OF TIMES, THE**

(1986) 104m Kings Road Entertainment/UNIV c

Robin Williams *(Jack Dundee)*, Kurt Russell *(Reno Hightower)*, Pamela Reed *(Gigi Hightower)*, Holly Palance *(Elly Dundee)*, Donald Moffat *(The Colonel)*, Margaret Whitton *(Darla)*, M. Emmet Walsh *(Charlie)*, Donovan Scott *(Eddie)*, R.G. Armstrong *(Schutte)*, Dub Taylor *(Mac)*, Carl Ballantine *(Arturo)*, Kathleen Freeman *(Rosie)*, Tony Plana *(Chico)*, Kirk Cameron *(Teddy)*, Robyn Lively *(Jaki)*, Eloy Casados *(Carlos)*, Jeff Doucette *(Olin)*, Anne Haney *(Marcy)*, Bill Overton *(Luther Jackson)*, William Schilling, Hugh Gillin, Jake Dengel *(Caribous)*, Peter Van Norden *(Mando)*, Patrick Brennan *(Ronny)*, Linda Hart, Marie Cain, Peggy Moyer *(Blenders)*, Jeff Severson *(Johnny "O")*, Hap Lawrence *(Dickie Larue)*, Nick Shields *(Bam Bam)*.

What if the Cleveland Browns' Ernest Byner hadn't fumbled on his way into the end zone in the 1987 AFC championship game? THE BEST OF TIMES doesn't examine that possibility, but it does give Jack Dundee (Robin Williams) a chance to make up for the pass he dropped 13 years previously, costing his high-school team a victory against its arch rival. Ever since then his life has been mired in failure, while his friend Reno Hightower (Kurt Russell), the legendary quarterback of that team, has been equally plagued by apathy, bad luck, and a shaky marriage. Struck by inspiration, Jack decides to restage the game, but no one in the town—including Reno—wants any part of the scheme until Jack goes on a rampage dressed as their rival's mascot. The game, of course, is played with a predictable uplifting result. Director Roger Spottiswoode emphasizes the slapstick elements of his material at the expense of the more intriguing elements of his story, encouraging the audience to laugh at rather than with his well-observed small-town characters. Although Russell and Williams have a good rapport, Williams' unique improvisational talents are restricted by the script (save for the hilarious training sequence) and the film suffers for it.

p, Gordon Carroll; d, Roger Spottiswoode; w, Ron Shelton; ph, Charles F. Wheeler (Panavision, Technicolor); ed, Garth Craven; m, Arthur B. Rubinstein.

Football/Comedy Cas. (PR:O MPAA:PG-13)

BIG FIX, THE**

(1947) 82m PRC bw

James Brown *(Ken Williams)*, Sheila Ryan *(Lillian)*, Noreen Nash *(Ann Taylor)*, Regis Toomey *(Lt. Brenner)*, Tom Noonan *(Andy Rawlins)*, John Shelton *(Del Cassini)*, Charles McGraw *(Armiston)*, Charles Mitchell *(Harry)*, John Morgan *(Joe)*, Nana Bryant *(Mrs. Carter)*, Howard Negley *(Coach Ambrose)*.

This confused story about the fixing of college basketball games follows cager Ken Williams (James Brown) as he is framed by Ann Taylor (Noreen Nash), who is killed, but not before admitting that she brought in the gangsters who corrupted the players. In the absurd finale, Williams' teammates come to the rescue by giving the gangsters a well-deserved thumping. Interestingly, life imitated art when the basic premise of THE BIG FIX was enacted for real from 1947 to 1951, in a college basketball scandal that involved 7 teams, 32 players, and 86 fixed games.

p, Ben Stoloff, Marvin D. Stahl; d, James Flood; w, George Bricker, Aubrey Wisberg (based on a story by Sonja Chernus and George Ross, adapted by Joe Malone); ph, Virgil Miller; ed, Al De Gaetano, Norman Colbert; m, Emil Cadkin.

Basketball (PR:A MPAA:NR)

BIG GAME, THE**

(1936) 73m RKO bw

Phillip Houston *(Clark)*, James Gleason *(George)*, June Travis *(Margaret)*, Bruce Cabot *(Calhoun)*, Andy Devine *(Pop)*, C. Henry Gordon *(Brad Anthony)*, Guinn "Big Boy" Williams *(Pete)*, John Arledge *(Spike Adams)*, Frank M. Thomas *(Coach)*, Barbara Pepper *(Lois)*, Margaret Seddon *(Mrs. Jenkins)*, Billy Gilbert *(Fisher)*, John Harrington *(Dawson)*, Murray Kinnell *(Dean)*, Jay Berwanger *(U. of Chicago)*, William Shakespeare *(Notre Dame)*, Robert Wilson *(Southern Methodist)*, Irwin Klein *(NYU)*, Gomer Jones *(Ohio State University)*.

Gamblers influence college admissions requirements when they recruit uneducated coal miners to play on *their* school's football team. When a star player is kidnaped and a riot occurs on the football field, this expertly photographed film gains momentum, but despite its top-notch technical work, it remains a flat effort. Several college gridiron stars of the day appear, including the University of Chicago's Jay Berwanger, winner of the first Heisman Trophy, which was awarded in 1935.

p, Pandro S. Berman; d, George Nicholls, Jr.; w, Irwin Shaw (based on the story by Francis Wallace); ph, Harry Wild; ed, Frederic Knudtson.

Football   **(PR:A   MPAA:NR)**

BIG LEAGUER*½

(1953) 70m MGM bw

Edward G. Robinson *(John B. "Hans" Lobert)*, Vera-Ellen *(Christy)*, Jeff Richards *(Adam Polachuk)*, Richard Jaeckel *(Bobby Bronson)*, William Campbell *(Julie Davis)*, Carl Hubbell *(Himself)*, Paul Langton *(Brian McLennan)*, Lalo Rios *(Chuy Agilar)*, Bill Crandall *(Tippy Mitchell)*, Frank Ferguson *(Wally Mitchell)*, John McKee *(Dale Alexander)*, Mario Siletti *(Mr. Polachuk)*, Al Campanis *(Himself)*.

Director Robert Aldrich's first film, BIG LEAGUER is replete with the usual baseball movie corniness and true fans may well be asleep before the end of the first inning. Edward G. Robinson plays John Lobert, an aging former player who now runs the tryout camp for the New York Giants in Florida. His job is to sort the wheat from the chaff among a bunch of would-be big leaguers, and, actually, the plot here is not unlike AN OFFICER AND A GENTLEMAN or THE D.I., with Robinson acting the role of the tough drill sergeant. Richard Jaeckel plays a "natural"; Lalo Rios is a Cuban hopeful; Bill Crandall secretly hates the game and is only trying out to please his father, a former major league star; and Jeff Richards is a sure thing. One-time Giants great-turned-scout Carl Hubbell appears as himself, as does Al Campanis, the long-time Dodger general manager whose career came to a sudden halt after his controversial comments on TV's "Nightline" concerning the absence of blacks in management positions in major league baseball.

p, Matthew Rapf; d, Robert Aldrich; w, Herbert Baker (based on a story by John McNulty and Louis Morheim); ph, William Mellor; ed, Ben Lewis; m, Alberto Colombo.

Baseball   **(PR:A   MPAA:NR)**

BIG PUNCH, THE**

(1948) 50m WB bw

Wayne Morris *(Chris Thorgenson)*, Lois Maxwell *(Karen Long)*, Gordon MacRae *(Johnny Grant)*, Mary Stuart *(Midge Parker)*, Eddie Dunn *(Ed Hardy)*, Marc Logan *(Milo Brown)*, Charles March *(Sam Bancroft)*.

Chris Thorgenson (Wayne Morris) hangs up the gloves and takes up the cloth, while Johnny Grant (Gordon MacRae) refuses to throw a fight and is framed for the murder of a policeman in this mediocre tale of two boxers. Look elsewhere for truly satisfying ring drama.

p, Saul Elkins; d, Sherry Shourds; w, Bernard Girard (based on a story by George Carleton Brown); ph, Carl Guthrie; ed, Frank Magee; m, William Lava.

Boxing   **(PR:A   MPAA:NR)**

BIG WEDNESDAY*½

(1978) 126m WB c

Jan-Michael Vincent *(Matt)*, William Katt *(Jack)*, Gary Busey *(Leroy)*, Patti D'Arbanville *(Sally)*, Lee Purcell *(Peggy Gordon)*, Sam Melville *(Bear)*, Robert Englund *(Fly)*, Barbara Hale *(Mrs. Barlow)*, Fran Ryan *(Lucy)*, Reb Brown *(Enforcer)*.

The most pretentious film of its kind, BIG WEDNESDAY may have cost more than all of the other surfing movies ever made put together. While Bruce Brown (ENDLESS SUMMER) captured the beauty and fun of his favorite sport in his "surfumentaries," John Milius, who always seems to have some weighty symbolic intent underlying his work, infuses BIG WEDNESDAY with heavy-handed philosophy and all-around stupidity. Divided into four segments—1962, 1965, 1968, 1974—the film chronicles the coming of age of three surfing buddies (Jan-Michael Vincent, William Katt, and Gary Busey) against a backdrop of great American social change. Busey and Katt are believable despite the absurd dialog that Milius and cowriter Dennis Aaberg saddle them with, but the best part of the film is Greg MacGillvray's spectacular and sympathetic photography of the surfing.

p, Buzz Feitshans; d, John Milius; w, John Milius, Dennis Aaberg; ph, Bruce Surtees (Panavision, Metrocolor); ed, Robert L. Wolfe, Tim O'Meara; m, Basil Poledouris.

Surfing   **Cas.**   **(PR:A-C MPAA:PG)**

BIG WHEEL, THE**

(1949) 92m UA bw

Mickey Rooney *(Billy Coy)*, Thomas Mitchell *(Red Stanley)*, Michael O'Shea *(Vic Sullivan)*, Mary Hatcher *(Louise Riley)*, Spring Byington *(Mrs. Mary Coy)*, Lina Romay *(Dolores Raymond)*, Steve Brodie *(Happy)*, Allen Jenkins *(George)*, Richard Lane *(Reno Riley)*.

Mickey Rooney stars as Billy Coy, the racing car driver son of the late, great auto racer Cannonball Coy, who was killed in the Indianapolis 500. While racing out West, the young Coy accidentally causes the death of another driver and, burdened with a reputation as a daredevil, he is unable to find an owner who will give him a car to race and is forced to move to the Eastern circuit, where his name isn't a liability. Louise Riley (Mary Hatcher), who sticks with him through thin and thinner, is finally rewarded when Billy comes to his senses after finishing third at Indy, his car in flames.

p, Harry M. Popkin, Samuel H. Steifel, Mort Briskin; d, Edward Ludwig; w, Robert Smith; ph, Ernest Laszlo; ed, Walter Thompson; m, Nat Finston.

Auto Racing   Cas.   (PR:A-C MPAA:NR)

BILLIE**

(1965) 86m UA c

Patty Duke *(Billie)*, Jim Backus *(Howard Carol)*, Jane Greer *(Agnes Carol)*, Warren Berlinger *(Mike Benson)*, Billy De-Wolfe *(Mayor Davis)*, Charles Lane *(Coach Jones)*, Dick Sargent *(Matt Bullitt)*, Susan Seaforth *(Jean Matthews)*, Ted Bessell *(Bob Matthews)*, Richard Deacon *(Principal Wilson)*, Bobby Diamond *(Eddie Davis)*, Michael Fox *(Ray Case)*, Clive Clerk *(Ted Chekas)*, Harlan Warde *(Dr. Hall)*, Jean MacRae *(Nurse Webb)*, Allan Grant *(Himself)*, Georgia Simmons *(Mrs. Hosenwacker)*, Arline Anderson *(Mrs. Clifton)*, Layte Bowden *(Miss Channing)*.

Patty Duke plays the title role, a tomboy high-school track star who, running and jumping to the very different beat that drums in her head, outperforms all of the men on the Harding High School team, including her macho boy friend (Warren Berlinger). All of this causes big problems for her politically ambitious father (Jim Backus), who is running for mayor on an unashamedly male chauvinist platform. BIL-LIE is a technically competent film, and Duke's portrayal of a capable athlete and independent woman is ahead of its time (although she eventually does demonstrate that she "knows her place"), but ultimately the film is undone by its predictable and all too easily resolved situations.

p, Donald Weis; d, Donald Weis; w, Ronald Alexander (based on his play "Time Out for Ginger"); ph, John Russell (Technicolor); ed, Adrienne Frazan; m, Dominic Frontiere.

Track and Field   (PR:A MPAA:NR)

BINGO LONG TRAVELING ALL-STARS AND MOTOR KINGS, THE***

(1976) 110m Motown-Pan Arts/UNIV c

Billy Dee Williams *(Bingo)*, James Earl Jones *(Leon)*, Richard Pryor *(Charlie Snow)*, Rico Dawson *(Willie Lee)*, Sam "Birmingham" Briston *(Louis)*, Jophery Brown *(Champ Chambers)*, Leon Wagner *(Fat Sam)*, Tony Burton *(Isaac)*, John McCurry *(Walter Murchman)*, Stan Shaw *(Esquire Joe Calloway)*, Dewayne Jesse *(Rainbow)*, Ted Ross *(Sallie Potter)*, Mabel King *(Bertha)*, Sam Laws *(Henry)*, Alvin Childress *(Horace)*, Ken Force *(Honey)*.

It's hard to understand why this good-natured look at the old Negro Leagues didn't do better at the box office. The script is a fine mix of humor, pathos, and honest drama; the direction is brisk; and the photography and production design are first-rate. Tired of being abused by the owners of all-black teams, Bingo Long (Billy Dee Williams) forms an independent team, and is joined by other black stars. Their former employers conspire to put the Bingo Long All-

Stars out of business, but the team succeeds in barnstorming the country, playing amateur white teams and achieving some success. In the climactic final game, Long's squad is pitted against a team of all-stars from the black league. If his team wins, it gets a spot in the league, but if it loses, the players have to return to their former teams. Williams and James Earl Jones are very good in their roles as the star pitcher and catcher, and Richard Pryor does a nice comic turn as the player who poses as a Cuban and then as an Indian in an attempt to overcome major league baseball's color barrier. Entertaining and well worth a look.

p, Rob Cohen; d, John Badham; w, Hal Barwood, Matthew Robbins; ph, Bill Butler (Panavision, Technicolor); ed, David Rawlins; m, William Goldstein.

Baseball/Comedy   Cas.   (PR:A-C MPAA:PG)

BLACK STALLION, THE****

(1979) 118m UA c

Kelly Reno *(Alec Ramsey)*, Mickey Rooney *(Henry Dailey)*, Teri Garr *(Alec's mother)*, Clarence Muse *(Snoe)*, Hoyt Axton *(Alex's Father)*, Michael Higgins *(Neville)*, Ed McNamara *(Jake)*, Doghmi Larbi *(The Arab)*, John Burton, John Buchanan *(Jockeys)*, Kristen Vigard *(Becky)*, Fausto Tozzi *(Rescue Captain)*.

This touching and beautifully photographed tale of a boy and his horse follows the escapades of young Alec Ramsey (Kelly Reno), who is traveling across the ocean with his father. The ship sinks and Alec is saved by Black, a handsome Arabian stallion the boy befriended earlier in the journey. After being shipwrecked on a deserted island, Alec and Black are rescued and returned to their small town home. Eventually, Black is cared for by former horse trainer Henry Dailey (Mickey Rooney), who later takes Kelly under his wing to be trained as a jockey. Naturally, it all leads up to the big race—a stunningly photographed sequence that brims with tension. A simple film, as pleasurable for adults as it is for children, THE BLACK STALLION is one of the finest movies about children and horses since Elizabeth Taylor was seen in NATIONAL VELVET. It's also a pleasure to see Rooney and Clarence Muse again in the horse barn—Rooney having appeared many years back in NATIONAL VELVET; THOROUGHBREDS DON'T CRY; and STABLEMATES; Muse having played a poor racehorse owner in THAT GANG OF MINE. A sequel, titled THE BLACK STALLION RETURNS and released in 1983, was more a Saharan adventure than a sports picture.

p, Tom Sternberg, Fred Roos; d, Carroll Ballard; w, Melissa Mathison, Jeanne Rosenberg, William Witliff (based on the novel by Walter Farley); ph, Caleb Deschanel; ed, Robert Dalva; m, Carmine Coppola.

Horse Racing   Cas.   (PR:AA MPAA:G)

BLONDE COMET*½

(1941) 65m PRC bw

Virginia Vale *(Beverly Blake)*, Robert Kent *(Jim Flynn)*, Barney Oldfield *(Himself)*, Vince Barnett *(Curly)*, William

Halligan (Cannonball Blake), Joey Ray (Red), Red Knight (Tex), Diana Hughes (Jennie).

This thinly plotted auto-racing drama features the legendary Barney Oldfield as a mechanic-inventor who hires Jim Flynn (Robert Kent) to drive a car that contains the new carburetor he has designed, in the hope that some racing success will make his invention famous. Beverly Blake (Virginia Vale), the fair-haired driver who gives the film its name, wheels her way around the track in order to save her father's failing tire business. As things have a way of happening in this sort of film, these two racing rivals fall in love, and both Beverly's old man and Oldfield wind up in the black. Oldfield, the first great auto racer, also appeared in several silent racing films.

p, George R. Batchellor; d, William Beaudine; w, Martin Mooney (based on a story by Philip Juergens and Robin Daniels); ph, Mervyn Freeman; ed, Holbrook N. Todd.

Auto Racing (PR:A MPAA:NR)

BLOOD AND GUTS**½

(1978, Can.) 92m Ambassador c

William Smith (Dan O'Neil), Micheline Lanctot (Lucky Brown), Henry Beckman (Red Henkel), Brian Patrick Clark (Jim Davenport), John McFadyen (Jake McCann), Ken James (Harry Brown).

There have been a number of attempts to re-create the ambience of the professional wrestling arena on-screen, and BLOOD AND GUTS may come the closest to succeeding. Directed by Paul Lynch, this fast-moving film follows a down-and-out wrestling troupe as it travels the tank-town circuit. William Smith, who was so good when he battled Clint Eastwood in ANY WHICH WAY YOU CAN (1980), plays a sympathetic, aging wrestler who becomes enmeshed in a love triangle involving a younger wrestler (Brian Patrick Clark, whom Yale football fans may remember) and the radiant Lucky Brown (Micheline Lanctot). Henry Beckman, who can frequently be seen overacting on TV, gobbles up the Canadian scenery as the wrestling troupe's boss. BLOOD AND GUTS just misses being the definitive wrestling picture because of some bumps in the script and Beckman's histrionics; otherwise, it's a worthwhile look at the spectacle of professional wrestling.

p, Peter O'Brian; d, Paul Lynch; w, Joseph McBride, William Gray, John Hunter; ph, Mark Irwin; ed, William Gray; m, Milton Barnes.

Wrestling Cas. (PR:O MPAA:R)

BLOOD AND SAND***

(1922) 8 reels FP/PAR bw

Rudolph Valentino (Juan Gallardo), Lila Lee (Carmen), Nita Naldi (Dona Sol), George Field (El Nacional), Walter Long (Plumitas), Rosa Rosanova (Senora Augustias), Leo White (Antonio), Charles Belcher (Don Joselito), Jack Winn (Potaje), Marie Marstini (El Carnacione), Gilbert Clayton (Garabato), Harry La Mont (El Pontelliro), George Periolat (Marquise de Guevara), Sidney De Grey (Dr. Ruiz),

Fred Becker (Don Jose), Dorcas Matthews (Senora Nacional), William Lawrence (Fuentes).

Eternal heartthrob Rudolph Valentino gives an impassioned performance in this silent classic as Juan Gallardo, a youthful matador who becomes the idol of bull-ring aficionados with his skill and valor. As his career courses upward, he weds Carmen (Lila Lee), the beauty who has long adored him, only to fall later for the charms of the fiery Dona Sol (Nita Naldi), while Carmen remains faithful throughout her husband's affair. One afternoon, the matador's concentration is broken by the sight of Dona Sol in the company of another man, and he is badly gored. As a new young hero accepts the plaudits of the crowd, Juan dies in his loving wife's arms. Originally a costly matte process was to have been used to artificially transport Valentino—who was reportedly greatly disappointed that the film wasn't shot on location in Spain, where he had hoped to be schooled in the art of bullfighting—into a Madrid arena, but editor Dorothy Arzner's adroit intercutting of stock shots made it possible to cut corners on the production. BLOOD AND SAND was remade in 1941 (see below).

d, Fred Niblo; w, June Matthis (based on the novel Sangre y Arena by Vicente Blasco Ibanez and the play by Tom Cushing); ph, Alvin Wyckoff; ed, Dorothy Arzner.

Bullfighting Cas. (PR:C MPAA:NR)

BLOOD AND SAND****

(1941) 123m FOX c

Tyrone Power (Juan Gallardo), Linda Darnell (Carmen Espinosa), Rita Hayworth (Dona Sol des Muire), Anthony Quinn (Manolo de Palma), Alla Nazimova (Senora Augustias), J. Carrol Naish (Garabato), John Carradine (Nacional), Laird Cregar (Natalio Curro), Lynn Bari (Encarnacion), Vicente Gomez (Guitarist), Monty Banks (Antonio Lopez), George Reeves (Capt. Pierre Lauren), Pedro De Cordoba (Don Jose Alvarez), Fortunio Bonanova (Pedro Espinosa), Victor Kilian (Priest), Michael Morris (La Pulga), Charles Stevens (Pabelo Gomez), Ann E. Todd (Carmen as a Child), Rex Downing (Juan as a Child), Cora Sue Collins (Encarnacion as a Child), Russell Hicks (Marquis), Maurice Cass (El Milquetoast), John Wallace (Francisco), Jacqueline Dalya (Gachi), Cullen Johnson (Manolo as a Child), Schuyler Standish (Nacional as a Child).

Dashing Tyrone Power took over Rudolph Valentino's cape in this magnificent Technicolor remake of the 1922 silent classic BLOOD AND SAND (see above), playing Juan Gallardo, the son of a famous matador killed in the bull ring who follows in his father's footsteps. Wealth, fame, and a beautiful wife (Linda Darnell) all come Juan's way as a result of his bullfighting prowess, but, as in so many films dealing with the smaller ring, it all goes to his head, which is also turned by a sultry vamp (Rita Hayworth). Before long Juan's wife leaves him, he is responsible for the deaths of two friends, his career goes into a tailspin, and the vamp is as taken with a rising rival (Anthony Quinn) as the crowd. Finally, supported by his loving wife, who has never really given up on him, Juan makes a triumphant but tragic comeback. Director Rouben Mamoulian reportedly said that he didn't want to just photograph BLOOD AND SAND, but that he wanted to "paint it," and from its beautiful sets and scenery to its extravagant costumes his film recalls the works of Spanish masters. The performances are first rate, and Power spent much time perfecting his capework under the watchful eye of one-time matador and soon-to-be director Budd Boetticher (who would helm his own bullfight films—THE BULL-FIGHTER AND THE LADY, 1951; THE MAGNIFICENT MATADOR, 1955), though the romantic leading man was never actually allowed anywhere near a real bull.

p, Darryl F. Zanuck; d, Rouben Mamoulian; w, Jo Swerling (based on the novel *Sangre y Arena* by Vincente Blasco Ibanez); ph, Ernest Palmer, Ray Rennahan (Technicolor); ed, Robert Bischoff; m, Alfred Newman.

Bullfighting   **Cas.**   **(PR:C   MPAA:NR)**

BLUE BLOOD*½

(1951) 72m MON c

Bill Williams *(Bill Manning)*, Jane Nigh *(Eileen)*, Arthur Shields *(Tim)*, Audrey Long *(Sue)*, Harry Shannon *(Buchanan)*, Lyle Talbot *(Teasdale)*, William Tannen *(Sparks)*, Harry Cheshire *(McArthur)*, Milton Kibbee *(Ryan)*.

Monogram Pictures tried to duplicate its success with BLUE GRASS OF KENTUCKY (see below) in this film, but fell short by several furlongs. For BLUE BLOOD, W. Scott Darling (who also wrote the earlier film's fine screenplay) adapted a story by Peter B. Kyne about the rescue of a horse from a dog food factory. Arthur Shields (who looks and sounds like Barry Fitzgerald, with good reason—he was his brother) plays an old trainer who does his best to get the reprieved horse to overcome a troubling phobia and back on the winning track. The characters played by Bill Williams and Jane Nigh, the stars of BLUE GRASS OF KENTUCKY, don't know each other at the start of BLUE BLOOD, and this might have been a more interesting film if their relationship from the earlier film had been carried over into this one.

p, Ben Schwalb; d, Lew Landers; w, W. Scott Darling (based on a story by Peter B. Kyne); ph, Gilbert Warrenton (Cinecolor); ed, Roy Livingston; m, Ozzie Caswell.

Horse Racing   **(PR:AA   MPAA:NR)**

BLUE GRASS OF KENTUCKY***

(1950) 69m MON c

Bill Williams *(Lin McIvor)*, Jane Nigh *(Pat Armistead)*, Ralph Morgan *(Maj. Randolph McIvor)*, Robert "Buzz" Henry *(Sandy McIvor)*, Russell Hicks *(Armistead)*, Ted Hecht *(Layton)*, Dick Foote *(Jim Brown)*, Jack Howard *(Armistead Jockey)*, Stephen Harrison *(Attendant)*, Pierre Watkin *(Head Steward)*.

A fast-moving racing film with romance, action, and lots of heart, BLUE GRASS OF KENTUCKY rises a cut above most stories of its ilk by virtue of its extremely intelligent

screenplay by W. Scott Darling. Lin McIvor (Bill Williams), who owns a racehorse with his father (Ralph Morgan), is in love with millionairess Pat Armistead (Jane Nigh), whom he adamantly refuses to marry because she comes from a higher station in life. The twist is that Lin doesn't know that his beloved horse was sired by a thoroughbred belonging to Pat's father. Williams is totally believable in his part, and the direction by William Beaudine, a first-rate second-feature director whose career spanned more than 40 years, is darn near perfect. Horse-racing fans will be glad to know that there's lots of track action, with many scenes shot at Louisville's famed Churchill Downs, home of the Kentucky Derby.

p, Jeffrey Bernerd; d, William Beaudine; w, W. Scott Darling; ph, Gilbert Warrenton (Cinecolor); ed, Otho Lovering, Roy Livingston.

Horse Racing   **(PR:AA   MPAA:NR)**

BLUE SKIES AGAIN**

(1983) 96m SB c

Harry Hamlin *(Sandy)*, Mimi Rogers *(Liz)*, Kenneth McMillan *(Dirk)*, Robyn Barto *(Paula)*, Dana Elcar *(Lou)*, Joey Gian *(Calvin)*, Doug Moeller *(Carroll)*, Tommy Lane *(The Boy)*, Andy Garcia *(Ken)*, Marcos Gonzales *(Brushback)*, Cilk Cozart *(Wallstreet)*.

A baseball movie in the tradition of IT HAPPENS EVERY SPRING and ANGELS IN THE OUTFIELD—which is to say you'd better be willing to suspend your disbelief from the opening pitch—BLUE SKIES AGAIN is a light comedy about a female second baseman's assault on the major league's gender barrier. Its implausibility, however, stems less from the attempt by softball player Paula Frakin (Robyn Barto) to make a big league roster than from the ludicrously contrived spring training camp and baseball environment the film presents. Harry Hamlin plays the team's bachelor owner, and his attraction to Frakin's personal manager (Mimi Rogers of SOMEONE TO WATCH OVER ME fame) causes him to think twice about his male chauvinism. All in all, this is a pleasant film, and it should bring smiles to the faces of young women who are involved in real-life struggles to bring down sporting gender barriers. Still, THE BAD NEWS BEARS this isn't.

p, Arlene Sellers, Alex Winitsky; d, Richard Michaels; w, Kevin Sellers; ph, Don McAlpine (WarnerColor); ed, Danford B. Greene; m, John Kander.

Baseball/Comedy   **Cas.**   **(PR:A   MPAA:PG)**

BOB MATHIAS STORY, THE**½

(1954) 79m AA bw

Bob Mathias *(Bob Mathias)*, Ward Bond *(Coach Jackson)*, Melba Mathias *(Melba Mathias)*, Howard Petrie *(Dr. Mathias)*, Ann Doran *(Mrs. Mathias)*, Diane Jergens *(Pat Mathias)*, Paul Bryar *(Andrews)*.

It's hard to imagine anyone who would be any more convincing in the role of Olympic great Bob Mathias than Bob Mathias, and the producers of this biopic obviously didn't feel like trying. Two years after winning his second gold medal in the decathlon (only Britain's Daley Thompson has duplicated this feat), Mathias plays himself in this low-budget effort that makes interesting use of documentary footage from the 1948 and 1952 Summer Games. Mathias' wife, Melba, also makes the big stretch and plays herself.

p, William E. Selwyn; d, Francis D. Lyon; w, Richard Collins; ph, Ellsworth Fredericks; ed, Walter Hannemann.

**Track and Field/
Biography** (PR:AA MPAA:NR)

BOBBY DEERFIELD**½

(1977) 124m COL c

Al Pacino *(Bobby Deerfield)*, Marthe Keller *(Lillian)*, Anny Duperey *(Lydia)*, Walter McGinn *(Leonard Deerfield)*, Romolo Valli *(Uncle Luigi)*, Stephan Meldegg *(Karl Holtzmann)*, Jaime Sanchez *(Delvecchio)*, Norman Neilsen *(The Magician)*, Mickey Knox, Dorothy James *(Tourists)*.

Bobby Deerfield (Al Pacino), a top-flight but seemingly emotionless Formula One driver, meets Lillian (Marthe Keller), a complex lady of leisure, at a Swiss hospital. Before long this man who has never loved anyone has fallen for Lillian. Ah, but it's too late; she's dying of leukemia. Don't be put off by this cliche premise, though; BOBBY DEERFIELD is a better picture than it starts out to be. Yes, tears are rather forcibly jerked, but plenty of sparks also fly in the relationship between Keller (whose German accent works against the credibility of her Italian jet-setter) and Pacino, and their love story is ultimately interesting, if not always affecting. Scripted by Alvin Sargent and directed by Sidney Pollack, this gorgeously shot film is a trifle long at just over two hours, and much of the racing footage could have been dispensed with, along with the sudsiest of the emotions.

p, Sidney Pollack; d, Sidney Pollack; w, Alvin Sargent (based on the novel by Erich Maria Remarque); ph, Henri Decae, Tony Maylam (Metrocolor); ed, Frederic Steinkamp; m, Dave Grusin.

Auto Racing Cas. (PR:C MPAA:PG)

BODY AND SOUL*****

(1947) 104m Enterprise/UA bw (AKA: AN AFFAIR OF THE HEART)

John Garfield *(Charlie Davis)*, Lilli Palmer *(Peg Born)*, Hazel Brooks *(Alice)*, Anne Revere *(Anna Davis)*, William Conrad *(Quinn)*, Joseph Pevney *(Shorty Polaski)*, Canada Lee *(Ben)*, Lloyd Goff *(Roberts)*, Art Smith *(David Davis)*, James Burke *(Arnold)*, Virginia Gregg *(Irma)*, Peter Virgo *(Drummer)*, Joe Devlin *(Prince)*, Mary Currier *(Miss Tedder)*, Milton Kibbee *(Dan)*.

Despite its having all the boxing cliches—gangsters, crooked managers, good girls and bad girls—BODY AND SOUL is one of the finest fight films ever. John Garfield portrays Charlie Davis, a Jewish prizefighter whose parents want him to hang up the gloves and get an education.

When his father is killed in a bomb explosion, however, the proud Charlie prevents his mother (Anne Revere) from accepting government relief, turns pro, and rises quickly to the top of the fight game, winning the championship from Ben (one-time welterweight Canada Lee), who is left with a life-threatening blood clot in his brain. As the champ, Charlie slides into a dissipated lifestyle and throws over his artist girl friend, Peg Born (Lilli Palmer), for a floozy (Hazel Brooks), falling deeper into the clutches of the gangster who owns him (Lloyd Goff) in the process. After his best friend (Joseph Pevney) is killed, Charlie returns to Peg and asks Ben to help him train for an upcoming fight, which Goff commands him to lose. When Ben, too, dies it appears as if Charlie will throw the contest, but then he learns of the bets that his Jewish neighbors have placed on him, and, in the ring, at the last moment, he decides to redeem himself. Rivaling this film's greatness are CHAMPION and THE SET-UP (both 1949); however, Garfield's riveting, Oscar-nominated performance lifts BODY AND SOUL to the masterpiece level, as do Robert Rossen's superb direction and the marvelous photography of James Wong Howe. The fight sequences, in particular, brought a kind of realism to the genre that had never before existed (Howe wore skates and rolled around the ring shooting the fight scenes with a hand-held camera). A knockout on all levels.

p, Bob Roberts; d, Robert Rossen; w, Abraham Polonsky; ph, James Wong Howe; ed, Robert Parrish; m, Hugo Friedhofer.

Boxing Cas. (PR:C MPAA:NR)

BODY AND SOUL*

(1981) 109m CANNON c

Leon Isaac Kennedy *(Leon Johnson)*, Jayne Kennedy *(Julie Winters)*, Perry Lang *(Charles Golphin)*, Nikki Swassy *(Kelly Johnson)*, Mike Grazzo *(Frankie)*, Kim Hamilton *(Mrs. Johnson)*, Muhammad Ali *(Himself)*, Peter Lawford *(Big Man)*.

Not to be confused with the 1947 BODY AND SOUL, this disastrous remake is five minutes longer than the original and has as much drama in it as a worn piece of linoleum. The best thing about the movie is Muhammad Ali, who shows, in his extremely limited screen time, just why he is without question the Greatest. Ali, with no training, is a far better player than writer-actor Leon Isaac Kennedy (PENITENTIARY), who plays a medical student-turned-prizefighter. Gorgeous Jayne Kennedy also proves herself to be a better actor than her then-husband; however, that can be said of just about everyone else in this film, with the possible exception of Peter Lawford as a mobster.

p, Menahem Golan, Yoram Globus; d, George Bowers; w, Leon Isaac Kennedy; ph, James Forrest; ed, Samm Pollard, Skip Schoolnick; m, Webster Lewis.

Boxing Cas. (PR:C-O MPAA:R)

BODYHOLD*½

(1950) 63m Col bw

Willard Parker *(Tommy Jones)*, Lola Albright *(Mary Sim-*

mons), Hillary Brooke (Flo Woodbury), Allen Jenkins (Slats Henry), Roy Roberts (Charlie Webster), Gordon Jones (Pat Simmons), Sammy Menacker (Red Roman), Frank Sully (Killer Cassidy), John Dehner (Sir Raphael Brokenridge), Billy Varga (Marvelous Milton), Henry Kulky (Mike Kalumbo), Wee Willie Davis (Azusa Assassin), Matt McHugh (Gus Stotz), George Lloyd (Chuck Hadley), Ruth Warren (Kitty Cassidy).

The corrupt world of professional wrestling provides the backdrop for this exploitation film inspired by the boom the sport underwent after it began appearing on television. Tommy Jones (Willard Parker) is a plumber who happens to be doing some repairs in the office of promoter Charlie Webster (Roy Roberts) just as the latter is looking for a new wrestler to replace the former champion (Gordon Jones), who was crippled by Webster's men after he demanded a bigger share of the take. Tommy rises up through the ranks, but when he gets some ideas of his own, he is subjected to the same treatment as the former champ. This time, however, Webster's strong-arm tactics backfire. Mercifully brief.

p, Rudolph C. Flothow; d, Seymour Friedman; w, George Bricker; ed, James Sweeney; m, Mischa Bakaleinkoff.

Wrestling (PR:A MPAA:NR)

BOOTS MALONE***

(1952) 102m COL bw

William Holden (Boots Malone), Johnny Stewart (The Kid), Stanley Clements (Stash Clements), Basil Ruysdael (Preacher Cole), Carl Benton Reid (John Williams), Ralph Dumke (Beckett), Ed Begley (Howard Whitehead), Hugh Sanders (Matson), Harry Morgan (Quarter Horse Henry), Ann Lee (Mrs. Gibson), Anthony Caruso (Joe), Bill Pearson (Eddie Koch), John W. Frye (Foxy Farrell), Harry Hines (Goofy Gordon), Toni Gerry (Jenny West), Hurley Breen (Rod), Whit Bissell (Lou Dyer), Earl Unkraut (Cabbage Head), Harry Shannon (Colonel Summers), John Call (Touting Clocker), Pat Williams (Receptionist), Ken Christy (Beanery Owner), Hank Worden (Mechanic), Harlan Warde (Private Investigator), Emory Parnell (Evans), Ralph Volkie (Soft Drink Man), Earle Hodgins (Owner).

Almost as much authentic racetrack lore is crowded into BOOTS MALONE as one finds in a Dick Francis novel. William Holden plays the title character, a down-on-his-luck jockey's agent looking for an opportunity to turn around his fortunes. Into his life comes a 15-year-old rich kid (Johnny Stewart, making his acting debut) with a passion for racing and a hankering to learn how to ride. With dollar signs flashing before his eyes, Boots takes the Kid under his wing, and before long the two have grown attached to each other. Difficulties arise when the boy's mother is determined to put an end to her son's blooming career, and another, more deadly complication enlivens the plot when gangsters instruct Boots to make sure the Kid doesn't win the Big Race or else. The melodrama is unraveled successfully and plausibly when the crooks are thwarted and the boy's faith in his mentor is restored. Much of BOOTS

MALONE was shot at actual racetracks, reenforcing this entertaining film's authenticity.

p, Milton Holmes; d, William Dieterle; w, Milton Holmes; ph, Charles Lawton Jr.; ed, Al Clark; m, Elmer Bernstein.

Horse Racing (PR:A MPAA:NR)

BORN TO FIGHT**

(1938) 64m Conn bw

Frankie Darro (Baby Face), Kane Richmond (Bomber), Jack LaRue (Smoothy), Frances Grant (Nan), Stella Manors (Ada), Monty Collins (Gloomy Gus), Eddie Phillips (Duffy), Fred "Snowflake" Toones (Snowflake), Philo McCullough (Goodall), Hal Price (Heckler), Donald Kerr (Broadcaster), Gino Corrado (Maitre de Hotel), Charles McMurphy (Cop), Bob Perry (Referee), Olin Francis (Hobo), Harry Harvey (Reporter).

This routine boxing film features Kane Richmond as a fight trainer hiding from the crooked gambler he has accidentally injured. While on the lam, he meets Baby Face (Frankie Darro), an up-and-coming contender, and manages him to a title.

d, Charles Hutchinson; w, Sascha Baranley (based on a story by Peter B. Kyne); ph, Arthur Reed; ed, Richard G. Ray.

Boxing (PR:A MPAA:NR)

BORN TO SPEED**

(1947) 61m PRC bw

John Sands (Johnny Randall), Terry Austin (Toni Bradley), Don Castle (Mike Conroy), Frank Orth (Breezy Bradley), Geraldine Wall (Mrs. Randall), Joe Haworth (Duke Hudkins).

Midget auto racing is the backdrop for this familiar tale. Johnny Randall (John Sands) is the son of a driver who died in a fiery crash. With the help of old-time mechanic Breezy Bradley (Frank Orth), Johnny rebuilds his father's car, wins out over his rival both in a big race and in the pursuit of Breezy's daughter (Terry Austin). A trite story, though the race sequences are well done.

p, Marvin D. Stahl; d, Edward L. Cahn; w, Crane Wilbur, W. Scott Darling, Robert B. Churchill (based on the story "Hell On Wheels" by Robert B. Churchill); ph, Jackson Rose; ed, W. Donn Hayes; m, Albert Levin.

Auto Racing (PR:A MPAA:NR)

BOWERY BLITZKRIEG*

(1941) 62m MON bw (GB: STAND AND DELIVER)

Leo Gorcey (Muggs McGinnis), Bobby Jordan (Danny Breslin), Huntz Hall (Limpy), Warren Hull (Tom Brady), Charlotte Henry (Mary Breslin), Keye Luke (Clancy), Bobby Stone (Monk Martin), Donald Haines (Skinny), Marsha Wentworth (Mrs. Brady), David Gorcey (Peewee), Ernest Morrison (Scruno), Jack Mulhall (Officer).

Leo Gorcey—carrying the unaccustomed moniker Muggs

McGinnis—is saved from a life of crime when he becomes a Golden Gloves champ. This is no mean feat for Muggs, in that he gives blood to a stricken pal in an emergency transfusion just before he steps into the ring! A sort-of entry in the "Bowery Boys" series, BOWERY BLITZKRIEG is as awful as it is unfunny.

p, Sam Katzman; d, Wallace Fox; w, Sam Robins; ph, Marcel Le Picard; ed, Robert Golden.

Boxing/Comedy (PR:A MPAA:NR)

BOXER**

(1971, Pol.) 96m Polski Film bw

Daniel Olbrychski (Antoni), Tadeusz Kalinowski (Manager), Leszek Drogosz (Walczak), Malgorzata Wlodarska (Girl).

This well-done Polish film features Daniel Olbrychski as a young boxer who ponders the events that have brought him to the verge of the biggest fight of his career. In flashback, he trains, gets drunk, is thrown in jail, goes to the Olympics, and, in the final bout, defeats a Russian fighter.

d, Julian Dziedzina; w, Bohdan Tomaszewski, Jerzy Suszko; ph, Miklaj Sprudin; ed, L. Romanis.

Boxing (PR:A MPAA:NR)

BOY FROM INDIANA*½

(1950) 66m Ventura/EL bw (GB: BLAZE OF GLORY)

Lon McCallister (Lon Decker), Lois Butler (Betty Richards), Billie Burke (Zelda Bagley), George Cleveland (Mac Dougall), Rol Laughner (Wilkinson), Victor Cox (Thorne), Jerry Ambler (Burke), Allen Church (Corbett), Jeanne Patterson (Pretty Girl), Texas Dandy (Dandy).

Midwestern lad Lon Decker (Lon McCallister) lands a job jockeying the racehorse owned by Mac Dougall (George Cleveland), unaware that the owner has been using drugs to push the pony along. After "Texas Dandy" is gored by a bull, its participation in the climactic race is jeopardized, but thanks to Lon's tender loving care, the horse not only runs the race, but wins it. Replete with silly dialog and poor acting, this familiar racetrack drama has enough cliches for two or three movies.

p, Frank Melford; d, John Rawlins; w, Otto Englander; ph, Jack Mackenzie; ed, Merrill White.

Horse Racing (PR:A MPAA:NR)

BOY IN BLUE, THE*½

(1986, Can.) 98m Denis Heroux-John Kemeny/FOX c

Nicolas Cage (Ned), Cynthia Dale (Margaret), Christopher Plummer (Knox), David Naughton (Bill), Sean Sullivan (Walter), Melody Anderson (Dulcie), James B. Douglas (Collins), Walter Massey (Mayor), Austin Willis (Bainbridge), Philip Craig (Kinnear), Robert McCormick (Trickett), Tim Weber (Cooney), George E. Zeeman (Cop), Geordie Johnson (Bothwell), Brian Thorne (Plaisted), Greg

Swanson (Oscar Hale), Gordon Masten (Toad), Doris Malcolm (Aunt Gert), Jeff Wincott (Riley).

In the late 19th century, rowing was a popular sport, with fierce competition and high-stakes spectator gambling, and Ned Hanlan was a Canadian rowing champion who honed his skills by running moonshine in his skiff on Lake Ontario. Hanlan (disappointingly portrayed here by Nicolas Cage, who lacks his usual energy) survived unscrupulous competitors, crooked gamblers, and alcoholism to become an international star in the sport, setting many records that have stood for more than 100 years and later achieving success in Canadian politics. Although his film biography features a beautiful production design and employs more than 1,400 costumes, it is, unfortunately, perfunctory, flat, and predictable. David Naughton (AN AMERICAN WEREWOLF IN LONDON) plays Hanlan's on-again, off-again mentor, Christopher Plumber is his unscrupulous manager, and Cynthia Dale is his love interest.

p, John Kemeny; d, Charles Jarrott; w, Douglas Bowie (based on an idea by John Trent); ph, Pierre Mignot (Panavision, Deluxe Color); ed, Rit Wallis; m, Roger Webb.

Crew/Biography **Cas.** (PR:C-O MPAA:R)

BREAKING AWAY***½

(1979) 100m FOX c

Dennis Christopher (Dave Stohler), Dennis Quaid (Mike), Daniel Stern (Cyril), Jackie Earle Haley (Moocher), Barbara Barrie (Mrs. Stohler), Paul Dooley (Mr. Stohler), Robyn Douglass (Katherine), Hart Bochner (Rod), Amy Wright (Nancy), Peter Maloney (Doctor), John Ashton (Mike's Brother), P.J. Soles (Suzy), Lisa Shure (French Girl), Jennifer K. Mickel (Girl), David K. Blace (Race Announcer), William S. Armstrong (Race Official), Howard S. Wilcox (Race Official), J.F. Briere (Mr. York), Jimmy Grant (Black Student Leader), Gail L. Horton (Fight Spectator), Woody Hueston (Owner of Car Wash), Dr. John W. Ryan (University President).

Set in Bloomington, Indiana, and nominated for an Oscar for Best Picture, BREAKING AWAY is a funny, touching story about love, growing up, bicycle racing, and class consciousness. Dave Stohler (Dennis Christopher) and three of his friends (Dennis Quaid, Daniel Stern, and Jackie Earle Haley) are recent high-school graduates, but, more important, to Indiana University students they are "cutters," declasse Bloomington townies, so named because many of the locals earn their living in limestone quarries. Stohler, an avid bicycle racer, immerses himself in an alternative identity, pretending to be Italian, and does his best to woo an IU coed. After a team of real Italian bicycle racers comes to town and treats Stohler horribly, he discards his false identity, but not his desire to prove himself the equal of the college students. He and his cutter buddies (who barely know one end of a racing bicycle from another) enter the university's "Little 500" bicycle race with not-so-surprising results at the film's uplifting finish. Steve Tesich won an Oscar for his amusing screenplay; Barbara Barrie, as Stohler's mother, was nominated for Best Supporting Actress; and director Peter Yates also received a nomination from the Academy. Christopher, Stern, and Quaid, who have all continued to make their marks in the movies, deliver excellent performances here. Cyclists of the world unite. You have nothing to lose but your chains!

p, Peter Yates; d, Peter Yates; w, Steve Tesich; ph, Matthew F. Leonetti (Deluxe Color); ed, Cynthia Sheider; m, Patrick Williams.

Bicycling/Comedy   Cas.   (PR:C-O MPAA:PG)

BROADWAY BILL***½

(1934) 90m COL bw (GB: STRICTLY CONFIDENTIAL)

Warner Baxter *(Dan Brooks)*, Myrna Loy *(Alice)*, Walter Connolly *(J.L. Higgins)*, Helen Vinson *(Margaret)*, Douglas Dumbrille *(Eddie Morgan)*, Raymond Walburn *(Colonel Pettigrew)*, Lynne Overman *(Happy McGuire)*, Clarence Muse *(Whitey)*, Margaret Hamilton *(Edna)*, Frankie Darro *(Ted Williams)*, Inez Courtney *(Mae)*.

Dan Brooks (Warner Baxter), pressured by his witch of a wife (Helen Vinson) into working in her family's business, abandons both his job and his marriage to start life anew as the owner of a racehorse, Broadway Bill. Dan runs into trouble with fees, jockeys, gamblers, the law, and an often-ill horse, but he receives emotional support from his charming sister-in-law, Alice (Myrna Loy). Broadway Bill wins the climactic race, but dies in the Winner's Circle. Having lost his championship horse, Dan finds solace in the loving arms of Alice. This enjoyable track picture is given an extra dash of excitement and humor by director Frank Capra. Baxter is a likable hunk in the lead role, but Loy steals the show with her elegant wit.

p, Harry Cohn; d, Frank Capra; w, Robert Riskin (based on a story by Mark Hellinger); ph, Joseph Walker; ed, Gene Havlick.

Horse Racing   (PR:A MPAA:NR)

BULL DURHAM***½

(1988) 108m Mount/Orion c

Kevin Costner *(Crash Davis)*, Susan Sarandon *(Annie Savoy)*, Tim Robbins *(Ebby Calvin "Nuke" LaLoosh)*, Trey Wilson *(Joe "Skip" Riggins)*, Robert Wuhl *(Larry Hockett)*, Jenny Robertson *(Millie)*, Max Patkin *(Himself)*, William O'Leary *(Jimmy)*, David Neidorf *(Bobby)*, Danny Gans *(Deke)*, Tom Silardi *(Tony)*, Lloyd T. Williams *(Mickey)*, Rick Marzan *(Jose)*, George Buck *(Nuke's Father)*, Timothy Kirk *(Ed)*, Don Davis *(Scared Batter)*, Tobi Eshelman *(Bat Boy)*, Charles K. Bibby *(Mayor)*, Henry G. Sanders *(Sandy)*, Jeff Greene, Kelly Heath, Mo Johnson, Todd Kopeznski, Tom Shultz, Sam Veraldi, El Chico Williams *(Baseball Players)*.

Featuring outstanding lead performances by Kevin Costner, Susan Sarandon, and Tim Robbins; a witty, literate script; and an insider's familiarity with life around minor league baseball, BULL DURHAM is both one of the best films ever made about the national pastime and a charming romantic comedy. As smart as she is sexy, Annie Savoy (Sarandon), the No. 1 fan of the Class A Durham Bulls,

chooses one player a year to be her student in the art of lovemaking as well as in metaphysics and literature. This summer, two players compete for her attentions: Nuke Laloosh (Robbins), a bonus baby pitcher "with a million-dollar arm and five-cent head," and Crash Davis (Costner), the power-hitting longtime minor league catcher brought to the club to prepare Nuke for the big leagues. Much inspired hilarity and no shortage of poignant moments accompany Nuke's rise to the majors and Crash and Annie's eventual coupling. Working from his own screenplay, first-time director Ron Shelton—who spent five years in the Baltimore Orioles farm system—suffuses his film with carefully realized bush league details and evokes laugh after rich laugh. Costner, a one-time high-school shortstop, is wholly convincing as a pro ball player, delivering the best performance of his career; Sarandon sizzles; and BULL DURHAM is an extremely sexy movie that uses bared souls rather than bared bodies to turn up the heat. The diamond action was shot at El Toro Field, home of the real Durham Bulls. Max Patkin, "the Clown Prince of Baseball," also appears.

p, Thom Mount, Mark Burg; d, Ron Shelton; w, Ron Shelton; ph, Bobby Byrne (DeLuxe color); ed, Robert Leighton, Adam Weiss; m, Michael Convertino.

Baseball/Comedy   Cas.   (PR:O MPAA:R)

BULLFIGHTER AND THE LADY, THE***

(1951) 87m REP bw

Robert Stack *(Chuck Regan)*, Joy Page *(Anita de la Vega)*, Gilbert Roland *(Manolo Estrada)*, Virginia Grey *(Lisbeth Flood)*, John Hubbard *(Barney Flood)*, Katy Jurado *(Chelo Estrada)*, Antonio Gomez *(Antonio Gomez)*, Ismael Perez *(Panchito)*, Rodolfo Acosta *(Juan)*, Ruben Padilla *(Dr. Sierra)*, Dario Ramirez *(Pepe Mora)*.

John Wayne produced and Budd Boetticher directed this semiautobiographical tale illustrating the art of bullfighting. While south of the border, American Chuck Regan (Robert Stack) falls in love with a lovely senorita, Anita de la Vega (Joy Page) and, to impress her, convinces renowned matador Manolo Estrada (Gilbert Roland) to make him his protege. Learning quickly, Chuck becomes too cocky and his carelessness causes Manolo's death, incurring the hatred of the locals and Anita. Chuck, however, reenters the ring and takes on a bull in Manolo's honor. Good performances, lush visuals, and a genuine appreciation of Mexican culture make THE BULLFIGHTER AND THE LADY a fine film about bullfighting. Certainly no American filmmaker was more familiar with the brutal sport than Boetticher, a former college football player and boxer who traveled to Mexico in 1930s and began a lifelong passion for bullfighting as a matador, serving as the technical advisor for Rouben Mamoulian's BLOOD AND SAND (see above) in 1941. After THE BULLFIGHTER AND THE LADY, Boetticher went on to direct another bullfighting film, THE MAGNIFICENT MATADOR, in 1955, and following great success as a director of westerns spent seven years, beginning in 1960, working on a documentary about the famous matador Carlos Arruza.

p, John Wayne; d, Budd Boetticher; w, James Edward Grant (from a story by Budd Boetticher and Ray Nazarro); ph, Jack Draper; ed, Richard L. Van Enger; m, Victor Young.

Bullfighting   **Cas.**   **(PR:A MPAA:NR)**

BURN 'EM UP O'CONNER**

(1939) 70m MGM bw

Dennis O'Keefe *(Jerry O'Conner)*, Cecilia Parker *(Jane Delano)*, Nat Pendleton *(Buddy Buttle)*, Harry Carey *(P. G. Delano)*, Addison Richards *(Ed Eberhart)*, Charley Grapewin *(Doc Heath)*, Alan Curtis *(Jose "Rocks" Rivera)*, Tom Neal *(Hank Hogan)*, Tom Collins *(Lefty Simmons)*, Frank Orth *(Tim McElvy)*, Frank M. Thomas *(Jim Nixon)*, Si Jenks *(Mr. Jenkins)*.

This weird auto-racing film features Harry Carey as a slightly manic car manufacturer set on breaking speed records even if his drivers are killed in the process. Enter bumpkin Jerry O'Conner (Dennis O'Keefe), who wins a midget car race witnessed by P.G. Delano (Carey) and his daughter, Jane (Cecilia Parker). Delano signs the driver to a contract, Jane falls for her father's new sucker, and O'Keefe, determined to succeed where other drivers have failed, stumbles across the real reason why so many have been killed driving Delano's cars. It seems that Doc Heath (Charley Grapewin), whose son was killed driving for Delano, has been drugging the drivers' drinks before they head out to the track.

p, Harry Rapf; d, Edward Sedgwick; w, Milton Berlin, Byron Morgan (based on the book by Sir Malcolm Campbell); ph, Lester White; ed, Ben Lewis.

Auto Racing   **(PR:A MPAA:NR)**

BURNING UP**

(1930) 60m PAR bw

Richard Arlen *(Lou Larrigan)*, Mary Brian *(Ruth Morgan)*, Francis McDonald *(Bullet McGhan)*, Sam Hardy *(Windy Wallace)*, Charles Sellon *(James P. Morgan)*, Tully Marshall *(Dave Gentry)*.

A short and, consequently, sweet early talkie, BURNING UP concerns the difficulties of maintaining an auto racing romance. Lou Larrigan (Richard Arlen) and Ruth Morgan (Mary Brian) are the lovers, and Bullet McGhan (Francis McDonald), Larrigan's one-time partner, is his rival both on the racetrack and in the romantic arena. Luckily, Sam Hardy, Charles Sellon, and Tully Marshall are on the premises to lighten things up with some hokey comedy.

d, Edward A. Sutherland; w, William Slavens McNutt, Grover Jones; ph, Allen Siegler; ed, Richard H. Digges, Jr..

Auto Racing   **(PR:A MPAA:NR)**

BUSTED UP*

(1986, Can.) 90m Busted Up-Rose & Ruby/Shapiro c

Paul Coufos *(Earl Bird)*, Irene Cara *(Simone)*, Stan Shaw *(Angie)*, Tony Rosato *(Irving Drayton)*, Frank Pellegrino

(Nick Sevins), Gordon Judges *(Tony Tenera)*, Nika Kaufhold *(Sara)*, Mike D'Aguilar *(Granite Foster)*, George Buza *(Capt. Hook)*, John Dee *(Daddy Ray)*, Nick Nichols *(Mr. Greene)*, John Ritchie *(Phil)*, Rick Orman *(Teddy)*, Garfield Andrews *(Bobby)*, Al Bernardo *(Al)*, Lawrence King-Phillips *(Kenny)*, David Mitchell *(Greg Bird)*, Sonja Lee *(Darlene)*, Tony Morelli *(Jackson)*, Louis Di Bianco *(Frankie)*.

More than a decade (and three sequels) after the smashing success of ROCKY, low-level producers are still pirating Sylvester Stallone's boxing film formula. In this ragged, predictable variation, pug Earl Bird (Paul Coufos) and his friend Angie (Stan Shaw) own a neighborhood gym that nasty real estate men want to close down. Irving Drayton (Tony Rosato), the chief bad guy, also plans on evicting local residents so the area can be redeveloped; however, he gives Bird a chance to save both the club and the neighborhood in the ring. The outcome of this bout is, of course, already predestined, but to give Bird just a little more incentive, the film introduces his ex-girl friend (Irene Cara), who demands custody of the daughter she had with Bird (and belts out no less than four tunes). Several blood-soaked punches later . . . well, you figure it out.

p, Damien Lee, David Mitchell; d, Conrad E. Palmisano; w, Damien Lee; ph, Ludvik Bogner; ed, Gary Zubeck; m, Charles Barnett.

Boxing   **Cas.**   **(PR:O MPAA:NR)**

C

CADDY, THE**

(1953) 95m PAR bw

Dean Martin *(Joe Anthony)*, Jerry Lewis *(Harvey)*, Donna Reed *(Kathy Taylor)*, Barbara Bates *(Lisa Anthony)*, Joseph Calleia *(Papa Anthony)*, Fred Clark *(Mr. Baxter)*, Marjorie Gateson *(Mrs. Taylor)*, Frank Puglia *(Mr. Spezzato)*, Lewis Martin *(Mr. Taylor)*, Romo Vincent *(Eddie Lear)*, Argentina Brunetti *(Mama Anthony)*, William Edmunds *(Caminello)*, Keith McConnell *(Mr. Benthall)*, Henry Brandon *(Mr. Preen)*, Maurice Marsac *(Mr. Leron)*, Donald Randolph *(Miller, Sr.)*, Stephen Chase *(George Garrison, Sr.)*, Tom Harmon *(Announcer)*, Ben Hogan *(Himself)*, Sam Snead *(Himself)*, Byron Nelson *(Himself)*, Julius Boros *(Himself)*, Jimmy Thomson *(Himself)*, Harry E. Cooper *(Himself)*.

The world of professional golf gets the Martin and Lewis treatment in this mildly funny film. Harvey Miller (Jerry Lewis) has all the tools to be a great professional golfer, but he has one rather big problem: he comes totally unglued in front of a gallery. Knowing he'll never be able to play the tour himself, Harvey teaches everything he knows to the debonair Joe Anthony (Dean Martin), acting as his protege's caddy when he enters a big tournament. However, crowds still transform Harvey into a nervous wreck, and as Joe's game improves and his head swells, he begins to see his "caddy" as a liability. At a tournament at Pebble

Beach, the two engage in an argument over club selection that degenerates into chaos, after which they decide their talents are better suited to show business. Lewis does his slapstick thing, Martin croons several tunes, and they duet on "That's Amore." Numerous real-life professional golfers also make cameo appearances, including Ben Hogan, Sam Snead, Byron Nelson, and Julius Boros.

p, Paul Jones; d, Norman Taurog; w, Edmund Hartman, Danny Arnold, Ken Englund (based on a story by Danny Arnold); ph, Daniel L. Fapp; ed, Warren Low.

Golf/Comedy　　　　　**(PR:A　MPAA:NR)**

CADDYSHACK***

(1980) 99m Orion/WB c

Chevy Chase (Ty), Rodney Dangerfield (Al), Ted Knight (Judge), Michael O'Keefe (Danny), Bill Murray (Carl), Sarah Holcomb (Maggie), Scott Colomby (Tony), Cindy Morgan (Lacey), Dan Resin (Dr. Beeper), Henry Wilcoxon (Bishop), Elaine Aiken (Mrs. Noonan), Albert Salmi (Noonan), Ann Ryerson (Grace), Brian Doyle Murray (Lou), Hamilton Mitchell (Motormouth), Peter Berkrot (Angie), John F. Barmon, Jr. (Spaulding), Lois Kibbee (Mrs. Smalls), Brian McConnachie (Scott).

A swanky golf club is the setting for this slapstick comedy in the National Lampoon vein. Rodney Dangerfield plays a newly wealthy patron whose lack of sophistication offends the sensibilities of the club's more staid members, particularly the Judge (Ted Knight), a pompous prig who considers the club his private fiefdom. In truth, there is something in CADDYSHACK to offend just about everybody's sensibilities, but the whole affair is so drenched in lowbrow satire, broad stereotypes, and mindless slapstick that it consistently garners guilty laughter. Chevy Chase plays a brilliant but dissipated golfer, Michael O'Keefe is a clean-cut caddy who tries to win a college scholarship in a tournament, and Bill Murray is hilarious as the grubby groundskeeper who spends his time fantasizing about the club's female members and devising ways to rid the course of a pesky gopher. If you want to experience the mastery and drama of golf, watch the US Open; if you want to laugh, stick with Rodney and company.

p, Douglas Kenney; d, Harold Ramis; w, Brian Doyle-Murray, Harold Ramis, Douglas Kenney; ph, Stevan Larner (Technicolor); ed, William Carruth; m, Johnny Mandel.

Golf/Comedy　　**Cas.**　　**(PR:C-O　MPAA:R)**

CAIN AND MABEL**

(1936) 89m COS/WB bw

Marion Davies (Mabel O'Dare), Clark Gable (Larry Cain), Allen Jenkins (Dodo), Roscoe Karns (Reilly), Walter Catlett (Jake Sherman), David Carlyle (Ronny Cauldwell), Hobart Cavanaugh (Milo), Ruth Donnelly (Aunt Mimi), Pert Kelton (Toddy), William Collier, Sr. (Pop Walters), Sammy White (Specialty), E.E. Clive (Charles Fendwick), Allen Pomeroy (Tom Reed), Robert Middlemass (Cafe Proprietor), Joseph Crehan (Reed's Manager), Eily Malyon (The Old Maid).

Clark Gable plays a heavyweight boxer and Marion Davies is a musical comedy star who are linked romantically after their managers decide that it will be good publicity for both. The not-so-surprising twist is that they really do fall for each other, with disastrous results for Gable's career. Along the way, there is plenty of singing, dancing, and boxing and several wonderful production numbers; however, CAIN AND MABEL proves to be something of a disaster despite the presence of Gable (sans mustache, because director Lloyd Bacon thought a fighter should be clean shaven), a raft of superior second bananas, and a handful of wonderful songs by Harry Warren and Al Dubin. Nothing could triumph over the inept performance by Davies, publisher William Randolph Hearst's lover. For a more satisfying film about the real-life romance between middleweight champion Marcel Cerdan and chanteuse Edith Piaf see EDITH AND MARCEL (1984).

p, Sam Bischoff; d, Lloyd Bacon; w, Laird Doyle (based on a story by H.C. Witwer); ph, George Barnes; ed, William Holmes.

Boxing/Musical　　　　**(PR:A　MPAA:NR)**

CASEY'S SHADOW***

(1978) 116m COL c

Walter Matthau (Lloyd Bourdelle), Alexis Smith (Sarah Blue), Robert Webber (Mike Marsh), Murray Hamilton (Tom Patterson), Andrew A. Rubin (Buddy Bourdelle), Stephen Burns (Randy Bourdelle), Susan Myers (Kelly Marsh), Michael Hershewe (Casey Bourdelle), Harry Caesar (Calvin Lebec), Joel Fluellen (Jimmy Judson), Whit Bissell (Dr. Williamson), Jimmy Halty (Donovan), William Pitt (Dr. Pitt), Dean Turpitt (Dean), Sanders Delhomme (Old Cajun), Ed Hyman (All American Network Announcer), Robert Dudich (Race Announcer).

Walter Matthau is Lloyd Bourdelle, a poor Cajun horse trainer attempting to raise his three sons (Andrew A. Rubin, Stephen Burns, and Michael Hershewe) all alone. His horse, Casey's Shadow, named after his youngest son, is set to run in the rich quarter-horse event at New Mexico's Ruidoso track, then is injured, but Lloyd nurses the thoroughbred back to health in record time. Tom Patterson (Murray Hamilton) and Sarah Blue (Alexis Smith) want to buy the animal, while Mike Marsh (Robert Webber) would like to have it destroyed. The outcome of the race isn't much of a surprise, the narrative is slow but steady, and the action flags occasionally, but in the end, CASEY'S SHADOW is a sincere, good-natured, well-performed family picture.

d, Ray Stark, Martin Ritt; w, Carol Sobieski (based on the short story "Ruidoso" by John McPhee); ph, John A. Alonzo (Panavision, Metrocolor); ed, Sidney Levin; m, Patrick Williams.

Horse Racing　　**Cas.**　　**(PR:A　MPAA:PG)**

CHAMP, THE***½

(1931) 85m MGM bw

Wallace Beery (Champ), Jackie Cooper (Dink), Irene Rich

(Linda), Roscoe Ates *(Sponge)*, Edward Brophy *(Tim)*, Hale Hamilton *(Tony)*, Jesse Scott *(Jonah)*, Marcia Mae Jones *(Mary Lou)*.

Wallace Beery won an Oscar for his role here as a down-at-the-heels ex-heavyweight boxing champion who trains for a comeback in Tijuana in between boozing and gambling. His son (Jackie Cooper) and the pipe dream of returning to the ring are what keep him going. When he wins some money, the "Champ" buys the boy a racehorse, but promptly loses it in a crap game. The boy's mother (Irene Rich) and her wealthy husband (Hale Hamilton) appear at the track where the boxer works and convince him that the boy would be better off with them. He reluctantly agrees, but the boy later sneaks back to his father's side. In the final reel, the old boxer finally battles a much younger opponent while his son, lower lip quivering, looks on. Although the Champ wins the fight it takes so much out of him that he dies in his son's arms in the locker room. Audiences sobbed at almost every performance of this tailored-to-make-you-cry picture. Writer Frances Marion won her second Oscar for the original story of THE CHAMP, and Beery tied with Fredric March for his Oscar as Best Actor; director King Vidor and the picture were also nominated. There are those cynics who belittle the emotions of THE CHAMP and call it mawkish and overly sentimental; however, they probably didn't cry when Bambi's mother died, either. Avoid those people at all costs and see this film when you can. Remade in 1979 (see below) and in a nonsporting context as THE CLOWN in 1953.

p, Harry Rapf; d, King Vidor; w, Leonard Praskins (based on an original story by Frances Marion); ph, Gordon Avil; ed, Hugh Wynn.

Boxing   **Cas.**   **(PR:AA MPAA:NR)**

CHAMP, THE**½

(1979) 121m UA/MGM c

Jon Voight *(Billy)*, Faye Dunaway *(Annie)*, Ricky Schroder *(T.J.)*, Jack Warden *(Jackie)*, Arthur Hill *(Mike)*, Strother Martin *(Riley)*, Joan Blondell *(Dolly Kenyan)*, Mary Jo Catlett *(Josie)*, Elisha Cook, Jr. *(Georgie)*, Stefan Gierasch *(Charlie Goodman)*, Allan Miller *(Whitey)*, Joe Tornatore *(Hesh)*, Shirlee Kong *(Donna Mae)*, Jeff Blum *(Jeffie)*, Dana Elcar *(Hoffmaster)*, Randall Cobb *(Bowers)*, Christoff St. John *(Sonny)*, Bill Baldwin *(Race Track Announcer)*.

The original film took 85 minutes, this one 121, but the extra length has not improved the story. This time, Jon Voight is Billy, a prizefighter-cum-racetrack hanger-on in Florida. A drunk and a gambler, he dreams about a ring comeback while his son T.J. (Ricky Schroder, who looks remarkably like Voight, adding to the believability of their relationship) keeps an eye on him. Annie (Faye Dunaway), Billy's ex-wife, now a pillar of society, wants to get T.J. back and a bitter custody battle looms. The rest of the film is an updated version of the more gritty original, given an inappropriately lush look by director Franco Zeffirelli. Voight, who makes a more likely looking boxer than beefy Wallace Beery does, had already played a fighter in THE ALL-AMERICAN BOY (1973).

p, Dyson Lovell; d, Franco Zeffirelli; w, Walter Newman (based on a screenplay by Leonard Praskins and a story by Frances Marion); ph, Fred J. Koenekamp (Metrocolor); ed, Michael J. Sheridan; m, Dave Grusin.

Boxing   **Cas.**   **(PR:AA MPAA:PG)**

CHAMPION*****

(1949) 99m Screen Plays/UA bv c

Kirk Douglas *(Midge Kelly)*, Marilyn Maxwell *(Grace Diamond)*, Arthur Kennedy *(Connie Kelly)*, Paul Stewart *(Tommy Haley)*, Ruth Roman *(Emma Bryce)*, Lola Albright *(Mrs. Harris)*, Luis Van Rooten *(Jerome Harris)*, John Day *(Johnny Dunne)*, Harry Shannon *(Lew Bryce)*.

Released two years after BODY AND SOUL and based on a Ring Lardner short story, CHAMPION is another truly great fight film. Midge Kelly (Kirk Douglas) travels to California with his crippled brother Connie (Arthur Kennedy), hoping to buy a diner but ending up working there and falling for the owner's daughter, Emma (Ruth Roman), who becomes his shotgun bride. Soon Midge decides to put his boxing skills to use as a professional, and leaves Emma. Managed by Tommy Haley (Paul Stewart), Midge rises through the middleweight ranks until he gets a title shot, which, true to boxing-film formula, he is supposed to throw but doesn't. Nonetheless he becomes the crime syndicate's boy, growing more corrupt daily, hooking up with a flashy blonde (Marilyn Maxwell), then dumping her in favor of the mob boss' wife (Lola Albright). Later, while preparing for what is to be his last fight, a seemingly reformed Midge seduces Emma, who is now in love with Connie. After tangling with Connie in the dressing room, Midge enters the ring and takes a beating from his opponent, but comes back to win, though he dies in the locker room. Douglas' riveting performance as the ruthless fighter earned him an Oscar nomination and made him an overnight sensation. Mark Robson's direction is all action, wasting no time in telling this compelling story, and Carl Foreman's script is sharply observant of the boxing milieu.

p, Stanley Kramer; d, Mark Robson; w, Carl Foreman (based on the story by Ring Lardner); ph, Franz Planer; ed, Harry Gerstad; m, Dimitri Tiomkin (song, "Never Be It Said," Tiomkin, Goldie Goldmark).

Boxing   **Cas.**   **(PR:C MPAA:NR)**

CHAMPIONS***

(1984) 115m United British Artists/EMB c

John Hurt *(Bob Champion)*, Gregory Jones *(Peter)*, Mick Dillon *(Snowy)*, Ann Bell *(Valda Embiricos)*, Jan Francis *(Jo)*, Peter Barkworth *(Nick Embiricos)*, Edward Woodward *(Josh Gifford)*, Ben Johnson *(Burly Cocks)*, Kirstie Alley *(Barbara)*, Alison Steadman *(Mary Hussey)*, Jonathan Newth *(Mr. Griffith Jones)*, Andrew Wilde *(Graham)*, Judy Parfitt *(Dr. Merrow)*, Carolyn Pickles *(Sally)*, Julie Adams *(Emma Hussey)*, Michael Byrne *(Richard Hussey)*, Anthony Carrick *(Ken)*, Frank Mills *(Charles)*, Richard Adams *(Nicky Hussey)*, Edwin Richfield *(Ashton)*, Noel Dyson *(Mrs. Champion)*, John Woodnutt *(Mr. Champion)*.

In 1979, Bob Champion (John Hurt), one of England's most successful jockeys, is diagnosed as having cancer and given only eight months to live. However, through chemotherapy and extraordinary will power, he survives the disease and makes a victorious comeback, winning the 1981 Grand National Steeplechase. Hollywood hokum, right? Wrong. True story, and an involving, well-performed film. Although overly dependent on the standard slow-motion treatment, the race footage gives a good indication of how it must feel for the horse and rider, particularly one in as much pain as Champion is. Hurt is excellent as the jockey, as is Jan Francis, the woman who appears mysteriously at his side in the hospital and remains faithful to him. The horse that Champion actually rode, Aldaniti, "plays" itself and a few of the actors are real-life track people, too. The real Bob Champion retired after the race to open his own training facilities.

p, Peter Shaw; d, John Irvin; w, Evan Jones (based on the book *Champion's Story* by Bob Champion, Jonathan Powell); ph, Ronnie Taylor (Rank Color); ed, Peter Honess; m, Carl Davis.

Horse Racing/
Biography   **Cas.**   **(PR:C MPAA:PG)**

CHARIOTS OF FIRE****

(1981, Brit.) 123m Enigma/FOX c

Ben Cross *(Harold Abrahams)*, Ian Charleson *(Eric Liddell)*, Nigel Havers *(Lord Andrew Lindsay)*, Nicholas Farrell *(Aubrey Montague)*, Ian Holm *(Sam Mussabini)*, John Gielgud *(Master of Trinity)*, Lindsay Anderson *(Master of Caius)*, Nigel Davenport *(Lord Birkenhead)*, Cheryl Campbell *(Jennie Liddell)*, Alice Krige *(Sybil Gordon)*, Dennis Christopher *(Charles Paddock)*, Brad Davis *(Jackson Scholz)*, Patrick Magee *(Lord Cadogan)*, Peter Egan *(Duke of Sutherland)*, Struan Rodger *(Sandy McGrath)*, David Yelland *(Prince of Wales)*, Yves Beneyton *(George Andre)*, Daniel Gerroll *(Henry Stallard)*, John Young *(Rev J.D. Liddell)*, Benny Young *(Rob Liddell)*, Yvonne Gilan *(Mrs. Liddell)*, Gerry Slevin *(Col. Keddie)*, Stephen Mallatratt *(Watson)*, Colin Bruce *(Taylor)*, Alan Polonsky *(Paxton)*, Edward Wiley *(Fitch)*, Philip O'Brien *(American Coach)*, Pat Doyle *(Jimmie)*.

Winner of four Academy Awards, nominated for four others, and the winner also of British awards for best picture and costume design, CHARIOTS OF FIRE is almost, but not quite, worthy of all the accolades it received. This true story, directed by Hugh Hudson from an original script by Colin Welland, is about what it means to win and what one must do to achieve it. Eric Liddell (Ian Charleson) is a serious Scottish Christian who runs for the glory of Jesus. Harold Abrahams (Ben Cross) is an English Jew who is extremely sensitive to prejudice and whose main motivation is to be accepted. The movie delineates and crosscuts the lives of both men as they meet and compete at the 1924 Olympics in Paris. The real-life Liddell became a Christian missionary, went to China, and eventually died in a Japanese prisoner of war camp, true to his faith to the end. Harold Abrahams went on to become the spokesman for English amateur athletics, was knighted, and died in 1978, a venerated and respected elder statesman. CHARIOTS OF FIRE won Oscars for Best Picture, Best Screenplay, Best Costume Design, and Best Musical Score; Oscar nominations went to Hudson, Ian Holm, and Terry Rawlings. Few who see the film can forget the gorgeously photographed scene of the runners striding through the surf in slow motion to the accompaniment of Vangelis' stirring score.

p, David Puttnam; d, Hugh Hudson; w, Colin Welland; ph, David Watkin; ed, Terry Rawlings; m, Vangelis Papathanassiou.

Track and Field/
Biography   **Cas.**   **(PR:AA MPAA:PG)**

CHECKPOINT**½

(1957, Brit.) 84m Rank c

Anthony Steel *(Bill Fraser)*, Odile Versois *(Francesca)*, Stanley Baker *(O'Donovan)*, James Robertson Justice *(Warren Ingram)*, Maurice Denham *(Ted Thornhill)*, Michael Medwin *(Ginger)*, Paul Muller *(Petersen)*, Lee Patterson *(Johnny)*, Anne Heywood *(Gabriela)*, Anthony Oliver *(Michael)*, Philip Gilbert *(Eddie)*.

This fast-paced British car-racing story features James Robertson Justice as Warren Ingram, a wealthy auto magnate who sends O'Donovan (Stanley Baker) to Italy to try to lure an auto designer away from his firm. When O'Donovan is unable to do so, he steals crucial blueprints and murders a guard. To avoid detection by the police, he joins the racing team led by Bill Fraser (Anthony Steel), and, in the pedal-to-the-floor finale, tries to make good his escape by hijacking a car from codriver Fraser. The camerawork and cutting during the intense racing scenes are particularly strong, but race fans will probably find the film more enjoyable than those looking for an involving plot.

p, Betty E. Box; d, Ralph Thomas; w, Robin Estridge; ph, Ernest Stewart; ed, Frederick Wilson; m, Bruce Montgomery.

Auto Racing   **(PR:A MPAA:NR)**

CITY FOR CONQUEST***½

(1941) 105m WB/FN bw

James Cagney *(Danny Kenny)*, Ann Sheridan *(Peggy Nash)*, Frank Craven *("Old Timer")*, Donald Crisp *(Scotty McPherson)*, Arthur Kennedy *(Eddie Kenny)*, Frank McHugh *("Mutt")*, George Tobias *(Pinky)*, Blanche Yurka *(Mrs. Nash)*, Elia Kazan *("Googi")*, Anthony Quinn *(Murray Burns)*, Bob Steele *(Callahan)*, George Lloyd *("Goldie")*, Jerome Cowan *(Dutch)*, Lee Patrick *(Gladys)*, Joyce Compton *(Lilly)*, Thurston Hall *(Max Leonard)*, Ben Welden *(Cobb)*, John Arledge *(Salesman)*, Selmer Jackson, Joseph Crehan *(Doctors)*.

James Cagney is at his dynamic best as a Gotham truck driver who puts on the gloves to finance his brother's promising career as a composer. Meanwhile, his girl friend, Peggy (Ann Sheridan), tries to gain fame as a dancer, though Danny (Cagney) suspects that she is involved with her partner (unctuously portrayed by Anthony Quinn). In the welterweight championship bout, Danny is blinded by his opponent's resin-laced gloves and ends up selling newspapers on a street corner, where Peggy, whose own career has failed, comes to rekindle their love. During their reunion, the symphony composed by Danny's brother (Arthur Kennedy, another boxer's brother in CHAMPION) comes on the radio. CITY FOR CONQUEST is an often heavy melodrama, but it has consistently good dialog, a sprightly style, and a captivating powerhouse performance by Cagney, who drew on his experience as an amateur boxer and longtime fight fan. He was 42 when he made the film, and training like a fighter, shed 30 pounds for the role. His fight scenes are realistically photographed by veteran cameramen Sol Polito and James Wong Howe, and in many cases hard blows were actually exchanged between the actor and his opponents. Director Anatole Litvak and Cagney argued over just about every scene, and most of Cagney's ideas, including much of his fight choreography, were edited out of the final version. Moreover, Cagney felt that the story had been ruined and sent a note of apology to its author, novelist Aben Kandel. Those who've seen this poignant film know Cagney was wrong.

p, Anatole Litvak; d, Anatole Litvak; w, John Wexley (based on the novel by Aben Kandel); ph, Sol Polito, James Wong Howe; ed, William Holmes; m, Max Steiner.

Boxing   **(PR:A   MPAA:NR)**

COACH zero

(1978) 100m Crown International c

Cathy Lee Crosby (Randy), Michael Biehn (Jack), Keenan Wynn (Fenton), Steve Nevil (Ralph), Channing Clarkson (Bradley), Jack David Walker (Ned), Meredith Baer (Janet), Myron McGill (Danny), Robyn Pohle (Candy), Kristine Greco (Darlene), Brent Huff (Keith), Rosanne Kayon (Sue), Lenka Novak (Marilyn), Otto Felix (Tom), Milt Oberman (Coach).

Upset with the high-school basketball team's record, Fenton (Keenan Wynn), the local bigwig, has the coach fired. Using a computer to analyze possible replacements, he decides to hire Randy Rawlings (Cathy Lee Crosby), unaware that he is a she. When Randy arrives, her physique attracts more than a few glances from her players and the hostility of local female prudes. The appropriately named Randy whips the team into shape and gives its star player (Michael Biehn) some special off-the-court attention. If you haven't already guessed, COACH is an idiotic drive-in entry, with the usual peek-a-boo nudity and "sexy" situations.

p, Mark Tenser; d, Bud Townsend; w, Stephen Bruce Rose, Nancy Larson (based on an idea by Tenser); ph, Mike Murphy (Metrocolor); ed, Robert Gordon; m, Anthony Harris.

Basketball   **Cas.**   **(PR:C-O MPAA:PG)**

COLLEGE***

(1927) 6 reels   Joseph M. Schenck/UA bw

Buster Keaton (Ronald), Ann Cornwall (Mary Haines, the Girl), Flora Bramley (Her Friend), Harold Goodwin (Jeff Brown, a Rival), Grant Withers, Buddy Mason (His Friends), Snitz Edwards (The Dean), Carl Harbaugh (Crew Coach), Sam Crawford (Baseball Coach), Florence Turner (Ronald's Mother), Paul Goldsmith, Morton Kaer, Bud Houser, Kenneth Grumbles, Charles Borah, Leighton Dye, "Shorty" Worden, Robert Boling, Erick Mack (Themselves), USC Baseball Team.

One of Buster Keaton's least successful films, but entertaining nonetheless, COLLEGE stars the great silent comedian as Ronald, a nerd whose high-school valedictory speech, "The Curse of Athletics," pushes his girl friend, Mary (Ann Cornwall), into the arms of Jeff Brown (Harold Goodwin), the school's star jock. All three matriculate to the same college, and Ronald, determined to win back Mary, tries his hand at several sports, failing miserably at baseball and track. With the support of the dean (Snitz Edwards), however, Ronald becomes the coxswain for the crew, stealing victory from the jaws of a near defeat engineered by his own ineptness. Later, when Mary, who has warmed to Ronald again, is held captive by Jeff, Ronald gets a chance to prove his athleticism once and for all, running, jumping, and vaulting to the rescue. Keaton, of course, was anything but unathletic, and only for the pole vault did he deign to use a stunt man (Olympian Lee Barnes). Despite the fact that Ronald doesn't know his chest protector from deep center field, Keaton himself was a lifelong lover of baseball. Not only was one of the two questions he asked those applying for work with his production company "Can you play baseball?" but when things got sticky on the set, Keaton would interrupt shooting and organize an impromptu game.

d, James W. Horne; w, Carl Harbaugh, Bryan Foy; ph, J. Devereux Jennings, Bert Haines; ed, J.S. Kell.

**Baseball/Crew/Track
and Field**   **Cas.**   **(PR:A   MPAA:NR)**

COLLEGE COACH**

(1933) 75m WB bw (GB: FOOTBALL COACH)

Dick Powell (Phil Sargent), Ann Dvorak (Claire Gore), Pat O'Brien (Coach Gore), Arthur Byron (Dr. Phillip Sargent), Lyle Talbot (Buck Wearer), Hugh Herbert (Barnett), Guinn "Big Boy" Williams (Matthews), Donald Meek (Spencer Trask), Harry Beresford (Professor).

A cynical and unsympathetic, but often amusing look at college football and big-headed coaches, this William Wellman-directed film features a woefully miscast Dick Powell as a singing gridiron star who lacks discipline but manages to get it all right in the big game. Pat O'Brien is a delight as the tyrannical coach who does the disciplining, but his greatest coaching role was yet to come (see KNUTE ROCKNE—ALL AMERICAN, 1940).

p, Robert Lord; d, William A. Wellman; w, Niven Busch, Manuel Seff; ph, Arthur Todd; ed, Thomas Pratt.

Football   (PR:A   MPAA:NR)

COLLEGE HUMOR*½

(1933) 68m PAR bw

Bing Crosby (Frederick Danvers), Jack Oakie (Barney Shirrel), Richard Arlen (Mondrake), Mary Carlisle (Barbara Shirrel), Mary Kornman (Amber), George Burns (Himself), Gracie Allen (Herself), Joseph Sawyer (Tex Roust), Lona Andre (Ginger).

When campus queen Barbara Shirrel (Mary Carlisle) falls for singing professor Frederick Danvers (Bing Crosby), her football star admirer, Mondrake (Richard Arlen), becomes jealous and his interest in his sport diminishes, jeopardizing the team's future. Never fear; Barbara's brother, Barney (Jack Oakie), takes Mondrake's place in the lineup and everything is hunky-dory. Sloppily made, COLLEGE HUMOR was an early vehicle for Crosby, who was on the verge of the most important stage of his career.

d, Wesley Ruggles; w, Claude Binyon Butler, Frank Butler (based on a story by Dean Fales); ph, Leo Tover.

Football   (PR:A   MPAA:NR)

COLLEGE LOVE**

(1929) 80m UNIV bw

George Lewis, Dorothy Gulliver, Eddie Phillips, Churchill Ross, Hayden Stevenson, Sumner Getchell.

When teammate Flash Thomas (Eddie Phillips) is suspected of having been drunk on the day of a game, college football star Bob Wilson (George Lewis) takes the blame for his pal's indiscretion and loses his starting position. When the going gets tough in a crucial contest, however, both Flash and Bob, who also happen to be rivals for the affections of a pretty coed (Dorothy Gulliver), are called upon to make the big plays. Hokey, part-talkie football picture that has the unmistakable Carl Laemmle, Jr., assembly-line signature on it.

p, Carl Laemmle, Jr.; d, Nat Ross; w, Leonard Fields, John B. Clymer, Pierre Couderc, Albert De Mond; ph, George Robinson.

Football   (PR:A   MPAA:NR)

COLLEGE LOVERS*½

(1930) 61m FN bw

Jack Whiting (Frank Taylor), Frank McHugh ("Speed" Haskins), Guinn "Big Boy" Williams (Al "Tiny" Courtlay), Russell Hopton (Eddie Smith), Wade Boteler (Coach Donovan), Marian Nixon (Mary Hutton), Phyllis Crane (Josephine), Richard Tucker (Gene Hutton).

College football players Eddie Smith (Russell Hopton) and Tiny Courtlay (Guinn Williams) try to outdo each other on the gridiron to win the heart of campus cutie Mary Hutton (Marion Nixon), who—unknown to them—is already in love with a bookworm (Jack Whiting). The amusing finale of this otherwise lackluster romantic comedy finds Eddie and Tiny trying to determine which of them will carry the ball the final yard into the end zone to win the big game as the final gun sounds. A number of songs are worked into the proceedings, including "Up and at 'Em" and "One Minute of Heaven."

d, John Adolfi; w, Douglas Doty (based on a story by Earl Baldwin); ph, Frank Kesson; ed, Fred Smith.

Football/Comedy   (PR:A   MPAA:NR)

COLLEGE RHYTHM**

(1934) 75m PAR bw

Joe Penner (Joe), Lanny Ross (Larry Stacey), Jack Oakie (Finnegan), Helen Mack (June Cort), Lyda Roberti (Mimi), Mary Brian (Gloria Van Dayham), George Barbier (J.P. Stacey), Franklin Pangborn (Peabody), Mary Wallace (Peggy Small), Dean Jagger (Coach), Joseph Sawyer (Spud Miller), Julian Madison (Jimmy Pool), Robert Mc-Wade (Whimple).

An odd combination of the "Hey kids, let's put on a show!" formula and the standard football drama, this musical comedy revolves around the competition between two rival department stores. Eventually, the singing and dancing college kids who populate the film decide that a football game is the best way to settle things. Joe Penner, a radio comedian best known for his association with his famous duck, makes an easy transition to the screen here, adding some much needed humor to this rather lifeless mixed bag.

d, Norman Taurog; w, Walter DeLeon, John McDermott, Frances Martin (based on a story by George Marion, Jr.); ph, Leo Tover, Teddy Tetzlaff.

Football/Musical   (PR:A   MPAA:NR)

COLOR OF MONEY, THE***½

(1986) 119m Touchstone/BV c

Paul Newman (Eddie), Tom Cruise (Vincent), Mary Elizabeth Mastrantonio (Carmen), Helen Shaver (Janelle), John Turturro (Julian), Bill Cobbs (Orvis), Robert Agins (Earl), Keith McCready (Grady Seasons), Carol Messing (Band Singer), Steve Mizerak (Duke), Bruce A. Young (Moselle), Alvin Anastasia (Kennedy), Elizabeth Bracco (Diane at Bar), Donald A. Feeney, Andy Nolfo (Referees), Grady Mathews (Dud), Lloyd Moss (Narrator—Resorts International), Michael Nash (Moselle's Opponent), Iggy Pop (Skinny Player on the Road).

Twenty-five years after being banned from ever again setting foot in a big-time pool room in THE HUSTLER, Paul Newman's "Fast Eddie" Felsen resurfaces—older, wiser, and much more cynical—in THE COLOR OF MONEY. Eddie, who no longer plays himself, now fronts money to pool hustlers for a percentage. He takes young hot shot Vincent (Tom Cruise) and his worldly-wise girl friend, Carmen (Mary Elizabeth Mastrantonio), on the road, teaching the flamboyant, "flaky" kid how to "dump": that "Sometimes if you lose, you win." Vincent has trouble learning to lose, Eddie begins to yearn to play again himself, and they part ways, meeting again in a big tournament in Atlantic City. There the pupil surprises his rehabilitated teacher with how well he's learned his lessons. Approached by Newman, who felt "Fast Eddie" was due for a new exploration, director Martin Scorsese and novelist-cum-screenwriter Richard Price (*The Wanderers*) came up with a fine film that retains only the title and Eddie Felsen character from novelist Walter Tevis' sequel to *The Hustler*. Although one of Scorsese's most commercial undertakings, THE COLOR OF MONEY relinquishes none of his unique style and vision, and he uses his camera placement for maxim impact. The film also boasts three bravura performances—most notably, Newman finally, and deservedly, won an Oscar for Best Actor; Mastrantonio was nominated as Best Supporting Actress; and Cruise contributes the best work of his career.

p, Irving Axelrad, Barbara De Fina; d, Martin Scorsese; w, Richard Price (based on the novel by Walter Tevis); ph, Michael Ballhaus (DuArt color); ed, Thelma Schoonmaker; m, Robbie Robertson.

Pool   **Cas.**   **(PR:C-O   MPAA:R)**

CONFLICT**

(1937) 60m UNIV bw

John Wayne *(Pat)*, Jean Rogers *(Maude)*, Tommy Bupp *(Tommy)*, Eddie Borden *(Spider)*, Frank Sheridan *(Sam)*, Ward Bond *(Carrigan)*, Margaret Mann *(Ma Blake)*, Harry Wood *(Kelly)*, Bryant Washburn *(City Editor)*, Frank Hagney *(Malone)*.

Set in the 1890s, CONFLICT stars John Wayne as a fighter who travels from one lumber camp to another, staging crooked fights with the help of Carrigan (Ward Bond). After some relatively convincing fight scenes, Wayne sees the light when confronted with the love of a beautiful blonde (Jean Rogers) and an orphan. Although based on Jack London's "The Abysmal Brute," this Trem Carr-produced film is also reminiscent of FAST COMPANIONS, a 1932 story that featured James Gleason and Tom Brown as a pair of racetrack schemers, Maureen O'Sullivan as the redeeming female, and Mickey Rooney as the orphan.

p, Trem Carr; d, David Howard; w, Charles A. Logue, Walter Weems (based on the story "The Abysmal Brute" by Jack London); ph, Archie Stout; ed, Jack Ogilvie.

Boxing   **(PR:A   MPAA:NR)**

CONTENDER, THE**

(1944) 63m PRC bw

Buster Crabbe *(Gary)*, Arline Judge *(Linda)*, Julie Gibson *(Rita)*, Donald Maye *(Mickey)*, Glenn Strange *(Biff)*, Milton Kibbee *(Pop)*, Roland Drew *(Kip)*, Sam Flint *(Commandant)*, Duke York *(Bomber)*, George Turner *(Sparky)*.

Buster Crabbe plays a truck driver who turns to prizefighting to keep his kid in an expensive military academy

(shades of CITY OF CONQUEST), but he ends up on the skids due to hooch and a money-grabbing blonde. Luckily, his old friends come to his rescue in the nick of time. He makes up with his old girl friend and has a happy reunion with his son, who, it turns out, didn't want to go to the swanky school anyway.

p, Bert Sternbach; d, Sam Newfield; w, George Sayre, Jay Dolen, Raymond Schrock (based on a story by Sayre); ph, Robert Cline; ed, Holbrook N. Todd.

Boxing   **(PR:A   MPAA:NR)**

CORNBREAD, EARL AND ME**½

(1975) 94m AIP c

Moses Gunn *(Blackwell)*, Rosalind Cash *(Sarah)*, Bernie Casey *(Atkins)*, Madge Sinclair *(Leona)*, Keith Wilkes *(Cornbread)*, Tierre Turner *(Earl)*, Antonio Fargas *(One Eye)*, Vincent Martorano *(Golich)*, Charles Lampkin *(Jenkins)*, Stack Pierce *(Sam)*, Logan Ramsey *(Deputy Coroner)*, Thalmus Rasulala *(Charlie)*, Bill Henderson *(Watkins)*.

A young black basketball star raised in the ghetto, the hope of his community, is mistakenly slain by a police officer. Although its script is uneven, CORNBREAD, EARL AND ME still manages to portray ghetto life in a moving way without reverting to stereotypes. Keith Wilkes (former UCLA All-American and later Golden State Warrior) plays the lead with charm and conviction, and the picture goes to great lengths to portray the sensitive situation in complex terms. Unfortunately, the courtroom scenes bog it down.

p, Joe Manduke; d, Joe Manduke; w, Leonard Lamensdorf (based on the novel *Hog Butcher* by Ronald Fair); ph, Jules Brenner (Movielab Color); ed, Aaron Stell; m, Donald Byrd.

Basketball   **Cas.**   **(PR:C   MPAA:NR)**

COUNTY FAIR, THE*

(1932) 67m MON bw

Hobart Bosworth *(Col. Ainsworth)*, Marion Shilling *(Alice Ainsworth)*, Ralph Ince *(Diamond Barnett)*, William Collier, Jr. *(Jimmie Dolan)*, Snowflake the Horse *(Curfew)*, Kit Guard *(Lefty)*, Otto Hoffman *(Matthews)*, Arthur Millet *(Bradley)*, Thomas Quinn *(Tout)*, Edward Kane *(Fisher)*, George Chesebro.

Racketeers dope a horse in this poor programmer. William Collier, Jr, plays the heroic ex-jockey, Hobart Bosworth is the Kentucky colonel, Ralph Ince the villain, and Snowflake the horse. The highlight is an utterly extraneous scene of a black revival meeting.

p, I.E. Chadwick; d, Louis King; w, Harvey Gates (based on a story by Roy Fitzroy); ph, Archie Stout.

Horse Racing   **(PR:A   MPAA:NR)**

COWBOY AND THE PRIZEFIGHTER, THE**

(1950) 60m EL/EPC c

Jim Bannon *(Red Ryder)*, Little Brown Jug *(Little Beaver)*, Emmett Lynn *(Buckskin)*, Don Haggerty *(Steve)*, Karen Randle *(Sue)*, John Hart *(Palmer)*, Marshall Reed *(Osborne)*, Forrest Taylor *(Stevenson)*, Lou Nova *(Bull)*.

A mediocre entry in the popular "Red Ryder" series, THE COWBOY AND THE PRIZEFIGHTER is a western in which the punching takes place in the ring as well as on the cattle range. Steve (Don Haggerty) saves the life of Red Ryder (Jim Bannon), and they, along with sidekick Little Beaver, put an end to the nefarious schemes of a fight-promoter (John Hart) and a big boxer (Lou Nova). Red Ryder has a vested interest in capturing the crooks, since he believes that the crooked promoter was responsible for the murder of his father.

p, Jerry Thomas; d, Lewis D. Collins; w, Jerry Thomas (based on the "Red Ryder" comic strip by Fred Harman); ph, Gilbert Warrenton (Cinecolor); m, Raoul Kraushaar.

Boxing/Western   **(PR:A MPAA:NR)**

COWBOY QUARTERBACK*½

(1939) 54m WB bw

Bert Wheeler *(Harry Lynn)*, Marie Wilson *(Mazie Williams)*, Gloria Dickson *(Evelyn Corey)*, De Wolf [William] Hopper *(Handsome Sam)*, William Demarest *(Rusty Walker)*, Eddie Foy, Jr. *(Steve Adams)*, William Gould *(Col. Moffett)*, Charles Wilson *(Hap Farrell)*, Fred Tozere *(Mr. Slater)*, John Harron *(Mr. Gray)*, John Ridgely *(Mr. Walters)*, Eddie Acuff *(Airplane Pilot)*, Clem Bevans *(Lem)*, Sol Gross *(Cozy Walsh)*.

Neither Don Meredith, Roger Staubach, nor Danny White are anywhere in sight in this bland comedy about a football scout (William Demarest) who discovers a hick (Bert Wheeler) heaving sacks of potatoes around a general store and signs him up to quarterback the Green Bay Packers. Of course, the kid falls in with some gamblers and makes the inevitable last-minute push to extricate himself from their clutches in just enough time (40 seconds to be exact) to win yet another Big Game. Switching the ball in question from horsehide to pigskin, COWBOY QUARTERBACK is based on a Ring Lardner short story that was adapted by Lardner and George M. Cohan as a play. The story first came to the screen, with a baseball setting, as FAST COMPANY (1929), and was remade as ELMER THE GREAT (1933) with Joe E. Brown in the lead.

d, Noel Smith; w, Fred Niblo, Jr. (based on a story by Ring Lardner and a play by Lardner, George M. Cohan); ph, Ted McCord; ed, Doug Gould; m, Howard Jackson.

Football   **(PR:A MPAA:NR)**

CRAZYLEGS, ALL AMERICAN**½

(1953) 87m REP bw

Elroy "Crazylegs" Hirsch *(Himself)*, Lloyd Nolan *(Win Brockmeyer)*, Joan Vohs *(Ruth)*, James Millican *(Rams' Coach)*, Bob Waterfield *(Himself)*, Bob Kelley *(Himself)*, James Brown *(Bill)*, John Brown *(Keller)*, Norman Field *(Mr. Hirsch)*, Louise Lorimer *(Mrs. Hirsch)*, Joseph Crehan *(Hank Hatch)*, The Los Angeles Rams *(Themselves)*.

Pro football Hall of Famer and one-time University of Wisconsin athletic director Elroy "Crazylegs" Hirsch plays himself in this film biography that begins with his introduction to football in high school. It follows the two-time All-American through his illustrious collegiate career at Wisconsin and Michigan and on into the pro ranks—first with the Chicago Rockets of the All-American Football Conference and then with the Los Angeles Rams. Doctors tell Crazylegs that injuries he received while with the Rockets will end his career, but he fights back and, shifting from the backfield to end, goes on to NFL glory. Lloyd Nolan narrates the film and a number of contemporary Rams appear, including quarterback Bob Waterfield (who also appeared in JUNGLE MANHUNT and TRIPLE THREAT and was once married to Jane Russell). A considerable amount of actual footage of Crazylegs in action is effectively incorporated in the film. Hirsch was rather old to be playing himself as a youngster, but he proves to be a convincing actor and would later star in THE UNCHAINED (1955), playing an inmate at an experimental prison, as well as in ZERO HOUR (1957), an aviation drama. A favorite with Hirsch admirers, CRAZYLEGS, ALL-AMERICAN will have a limited appeal for others.

p, Hall Bartlett; d, Francis D. Lyon; w, Hall Bartlett; ph, Virgil Miller; ed, Cotton Warburton; m, Leith Stevens.

Football/Biography   **(PR:AA MPAA:NR)**

CROOKED CIRCLE, THE**

(1958) 72m REP bw

John Smith *(Tommy Kelly)*, Fay Spain *(Carol Smith)*, Steve Brodie *(Ken Cooper)*, Don Kelly *(Joe Kelly)*, Robert Armstrong *(Al Taylor)*, John Doucette *(Larry Ellis)*, Philip Van Zandt *(Max Maxwell)*, Richard Karlan *(Sam Lattimer)*, Robert Swan *(Carl)*, Don Haggerty *(Adams)*, Peter Mamakos *(Nick)*.

Tommy Kelly (John Smith), the younger brother of an ex-fighter, decides to leave his Maine fishing camp and enter the ring in New York. He falls in with gangsters who force him to throw fights (big surprise), and when his brother (Don Kelly), who disappeared years before after winning a fight he was supposed to lose, sees what's happening, he comes to New York. Tommy wins the next fight he is supposed to throw, and is taken for a ride by the mobsters, but Ken Cooper (Steve Brodie), a sportswriter, learns what has happened and leads the police to Tommy in the nick of time. Structured around the usual characters and situations, THE CROOKED CIRCLE is a fair fight film.

p, Rudy Ralston; d, Joe Kane; w, Jack Townley; ph, Jack Marta (Naturama); ed, Frederic Knudtson.

Boxing   **(PR:A-C MPAA:NR)**

CROWD ROARS, THE***½

(1932) 84m WB bw

James Cagney *(Joe Greer)*, Joan Blondell *(Anne)*, Ann Dvorak *(Lee)*, Eric Linden *(Eddie Greer)*, Guy Kibbee *(Dad Greer)*, Frank McHugh *(Spud Connors)*, William Arnold *(Bill Arnold)*, Leo Nomis *(Jim)*, Charlotte Merriam *(Mrs. Connors)*, Regis Toomey *(Dick Wilbur)*, Sam Hayes *(Ascot Announcer)*, Ralph Dunn *(Official)*, John Conte *(Announcer)*, John Harron *(Red)*, Robert McWade *(Tom)*.

Is there a car racing movie worth its while that doesn't wind up at the Indy 500? Yes, a few, but most aim for that Memorial Day weekend, and THE CROWD ROARS is no exception. James Cagney is Joe Greer, an auto racer who fails to keep his kid brother, Eddie (Eric Linden), away from fast tracks and fast women. Before long, Eddie is involved with a floozy (Joan Blondell) and the brothers' animosity is played out on the track, where Joe's buddy Spud Connors (Frank McHugh) is killed while trying to keep the Greers' cars apart. Devastated, Joe quits racing, takes up drinking, and doesn't get behind the wheel again until Eddie is injured while racing in the Indy 500—whereupon Joe jumps into the car, takes over, and wins the race. Filmed at Indy, Ventura, and Ascot, THE CROWD ROARS gives a fairly realistic picture of auto racing, its script having been given the once-over by Billy Arnold, winner of the 500 in 1930. Cagney was on his way to developing his ultimate screen personality—aggressive, cocky, supercilious. Though Howard Hawks (who made some of the cinema's finest comedies) fails to allow Cagney or the film to find any real humor in the story, THE CROWD ROARS is an extremely enjoyable film anyway.

d, Howard Hawks; w, John Bright, Niven Busch, Kubec Glasmon (based on the story "The Roar of the Crowd" by Seaton I. Miller, Howard Hawks); ph, Sid Hickox; ed, Thomas Pratt.

Auto Racing   **(PR:A-C   MPAA:NR)**

CROWD ROARS, THE***

(1938) 87m MGM bw

Robert Taylor *(Tommy McCoy)*, Edward Arnold *(Jim Cain)*, Frank Morgan *(Brian McCoy)*, Maureen O'Sullivan *(Sheila Carson)*, William Gargan *(Johnny Martin)*, Lionel Stander *("Happy" Lane)*, Jane Wyman *(Vivian)*, Nat Pendleton *("Pug" Walsh)*, Charles D. Brown *(Bill Thorne)*, Gene Reynolds *(Tommy McCoy as a Boy)*, Donald Barry *(Pete Mariola)*, Donald Douglas *(Murray)*, Isabel Jewel *(Mrs. Martin)*, J. Farrell MacDonald *(Father Ryan)*.

This typical 1930s fight film is distinguished by a good script, sharp direction from Richard Thorpe, and a strong starring performance by Robert Taylor as Tommy McCoy, a young boxer who gets to the top of the fight game partly due to the efforts of his alcoholic father (Frank Morgan). Tommy's nickname, "Killer," proves to have been an omen when he inadvertently kills an opponent and is charged with manslaughter. Jim Cain (Edward Arnold), a crooked bookmaker, has Tommy just where he wants him, but his beautiful daughter (Maureen O'Sullivan), who thinks Dad is on the up and up, is in love with the fighter.

Plot complications arise, including a kidnaping, a clever escape, and the usual fight that is supposed to be thrown but isn't. Taylor made one of moviedom's most convincing boxers, due in large part to the serious training for the role he underwent with his friend boxer-actor Max Baer, Sr. According to studio publicity, Taylor, who had been working out for several years when he started at MGM, added six inches to his chest and almost three inches to his biceps. He and Baer trained so furiously for the role that Baer broke two fingers and Taylor one while using lightweight gloves. Remade in 1947 as KILLER MCCOY.

p, Sam Zimbalist; d, Richard Thorpe; w, Thomas Lennon, George Bruce, George Oppenheimer (based on a story by Bruce); ph, John Seitz; m, Edward Ward.

Boxing   **(PR:A   MPAA:NR)**

CUP-TIE HONEYMOON*½

(1948, Brit.) 93m Film Studios Manchester/Mancunian bw

Sandy Powell *(Joe Butler)*, Dan Young *(Cecil Alistair)*, Betty Jumel *(Betty)*, Pat McGrath *(Eric Chambers)*, Violet Farebrother *(Mary Chambers)*, Frank Groves *(Jimmy Owen)*, Joyanne Bracewell *(Pauline May)*, Vic Arnley *(Granddad)*, Harold Walden *(Himself)*.

Joe Butler (Sandy Powell), the soccer-playing son of the company chairman, has to decide which team he will play for in a championship match, his school's or his father's. He makes the right decision, and wins the affections of a pretty secretary in the process. A bleak comedy from Manchester.

p, John E. Blakeley; d, John E. Blakeley; w, Anthony Toner, Harry Jackson; ph, Geoffrey Faithfull.

Soccer/Comedy   **(PR:A   MPAA:NR)**

D

DAMN YANKEES***

(1958) 110m WB c (GB: WHAT LOLA WANTS)

Tab Hunter *(Joe Hardy)*, Gwen Verdon *(Lola)*, Ray Walston *(Applegate)*, Russ Brown *(Van Buren)*, Shannon Bolin *(Meg)*, Nathaniel Frey *(Smokey)*, Jimmie Komack *(Rocky)*, Rae Allen *(Gloria)*, Robert Shafer *(Joe Boyd)*, Jean Stapleton *(Sister)*, Albert Linville *(Vernon)*, Bob Fosse *(Mambo Dancer)*, Elizabeth Howell *(Doris)*.

In the middle of another disappointing baseball season, Joe Boyd (Robert Shafer), a middle-aged Washington Senators fan who knows well the axiom "First in War, First in Peace, and Last in the American League," exclaims that he would sell his soul for a long-ball hitter and chance to beat the despised New York Yankees. The devil (Ray Walston) takes Joe up on his offer and transforms him into a powerful young blond Adonis (Tab Hunter) who wins a spot on the Senators' roster and tears the cover off the ball, leading the team in a pennant run. Calling himself Joe Hardy, but revealing little of his past, the transformed man boards in his own house to be close to his wife (Shannon Bolin). When Joe balks at living up to his end of the bargain, the devil sends a sexy temptress (Gwen Verdon, repeating her stage role) to change his mind, but Joe's love for his wife triumphs, as do the Senators, despite the fact the he has to make the winning catch after having been changed back into his old self. Directed by Stanley Donen, this picture had absolutely everything—except the right male lead, for Hunter is out of his element singing and dancing with such consummate pros as Verdon and Walston. The stage version of DAMN YANKEES ran more than 1,000 performances and is still produced in theaters where baseball is loved and the Yankees hated. Among the show's memorable hits are "Heart," "Whatever Lola Wants," and "Shoeless Joe from Hannibal Mo."

p, George Abbott, Stanley Donen; d, George Abbott, Stanley Donen; w, George Abbott (based on the play by George Abbott and Douglas Wallop, from the novel *The Year The Yankees Lost The Pennant* by Douglas Wallop); ph, Harold Lipstein (Technicolor); ed, Frank Bracht.

Baseball/Musical   Cas.   (PR:A   MPAA:NR)

DANGER ON WHEELS**

(1940) 61m UNIV bw

Richard Arlen *(Larry Taylor),* Andy Devine *("Guppy" Wexel),* Peggy Moran *(Pat O'Shea),* Herbert Corthell *(Pop O'Shea),* Harry C. Bradley *(Jones),* Sandra King *(June Allen),* Landers Stevens *(Lloyd B. Allen),* John Holmes *(Danny Winkler),* Jack Arnold *(Bruce Crowley),* Jack Rice *(Parker),* Mary Treen *(Esme),* Eddy Chandler *(Police Officer),* Fred Santley *(Official),* Eddie Fetherston *(Pete),* Harry Strang *(First Mechanic),* Jimmie Lucas *(Second Mechanic),* Joseph King *(Race Commissioner),* James Morton *(Police Sergeant).*

An average auto racing thriller based on the life of driver Lucky Teeter, DANGER ON WHEELS features Richard Arlen as the testing grounds chief for Atlas Motors and Andy Devine as his sidekick mechanic. A rivalry grows between Larry Taylor (Arlen) and top driver Bruce Crowley (Jack Arnold), resulting in Crowley's dismissal just before the big race. Taylor then has to drive the car himself, gets into an accident, kills the brother of the girl he loves, and nearly destroys her father's revolutionary oil-burning engine. In the end, however, he puts things right by placing the engine in the body of his car, winning an important race and the girl.

p, Ben Pivar; d, Christy Cabanne; w, Maurice Tombragel (based on a story by Pivar); ph, Elwood Bredell.

Auto Racing   (PR:A   MPAA:NR)

DAREDEVILS OF EARTH*½

(1936, Brit.) 57m Hallmark bw

Ida Lupino, Cyril McLaglen, John Loder, Marie Ault, Moore Mariott, George Merritt, Sam Wilkinson, Ginger Lees.

This below average film about dirt track motorcycle racing stars Ida Lupino as a female rider. Big Bill Summers (Cyril McLaglen), a dirt track champ and ladies' man, becomes enraged when another racer (John Loder) endangers the female competitor and he causes Loder to crash. As a result, Big Bill is barred from racing. Lots of scratchy newsreel footage. Released in Britain in 1933 as MONEY FOR SPEED.

d, Bernard Vorhaus.

Motorcycle Racing   (PR:A   MPAA:NR)

DEATH ON THE DIAMOND*½

(1934) 69m Metro bw

Robert Young *(Larry),* Madge Evans *(Frances),* Nat Pendleton *(Hogan),* Ted Healy *(O'Toole),* C. Henry Gordon *(Karnes),* Paul Kelly *(Jimmie),* David Landau *(Pop Clark),* DeWitt Jennings *(Patterson),* Edward Brophy *(Grogan),* Willard Robertson *(Cato),* Mickey Rooney *(Mickey),* Robert Livingston *(Higgins),* Joseph Sawyer *(Spencer),* James Ellison *(Sherman),* Pat Flaherty *(Pat),* Francis X. Bushman, Jr. *(Sam Briscoe),* Jack Norton *(The Gambler),* Dennis O'Keefe, Bobby Watson *(Radio Announcers),* Walter Brennan *(Hot Dog Vendor),* Sam Flint *(Baseball Commissioner),* Fred Graham *(Cardinal Player),* The Cincinnati Reds, The Chicago Cubs, The St. Louis Cardinals.

Members of the St. Louis Cardinals baseball team are being murdered, and it takes a rookie pitcher (Robert Young), who has twice been a target himself, to figure out that the killer is the crazed groundskeeper. All in all, a strikeout. Still, actual members of the Cincinnati Reds, Chicago Cubs, and the Cardinals make appearances.

p, Lucien Hubbard; d, Edward Sedgwick; w, Harvey Thew, Joseph Sherman, Ralph Spence (based on a book by Cortland Fitzsimmons); ph, Milton Krasner; ed, Frank Sullivan.

Baseball/Mystery   (PR:A   MPAA:NR)

DECEPTION*

(1933) 65m COL bw

Leo Carrillo *(Jim Hurley),* Dickie Moore *(Dickie Allen),* Nat Pendleton *(Bucky O'Neill),* Thelma Todd *(Lola Del Mont),* Barbara Weeks *(Joan Allen),* Frank Sheridan *(Leo).*

This awful film about corruption in professional wrestling stars Nat Pendleton (a real-life Olympian) as a football player who becomes a pro grappler. Bucky (Pendleton) is manipulated by a promoter (Leo Carrillo) through a string of victories until he meets the champ and is soundly thrashed. He then realizes that he's been used and drops out of sight, only to return later to beat the gang at its own game. Pendleton, who wrestled professionally until he broke his leg, also wrote the story for this waste of celluloid. He is best remembered for his long and prolific career as a character actor.

p, Bryan Foy; d, Lewis Seiler; w, Harold Tarshis (based on

a story by Nat Pendleton); ph, Chet Lyons; ed, William Austin.

Wrestling (PR:A MPAA:NR)

DEVIL'S HAIRPIN, THE**

(1957) 83m PAR c

Cornel Wilde *(Nick),* Jean Wallace *(Kelly),* Arthur Franz *(Rhinegold),* Mary Astor *(Mrs. Jargin),* Paul Fix *(Doc),* Larry Pennell *(Johnny),* Gerald Milton *(Mike Houston),* Ross Bagdasarian *(Tani),* Jack Kosslyn *(Tony Botari),* Morgan Jones *(Chico Martinez),* Louis Wilde *(The Parrot),* Jack Latham *(Race Announcer),* Mabel Lillian Rea *(Redhead),* Dorene Porter *(Blonde),* Sue England *(Brunette).*

This competent but unexciting auto racing film was produced, directed, and cowritten by its star, Cornel Wilde, who plays Nick, a one-time champion driver who left racing after an accident caused by his recklessness permanently injured his younger brother. He comes out of retirement for one more big race, however, and many of the drivers who abhor his arrogance and "win at all costs" philosophy hunger for the opportunity to give him some of his own medicine on the track. But Nick is a changed man, and in a duel in the treacherous Devil's Hairpin (where his brother's accident occurred), he backs off for safety's sake, winning back the approval of his long-suffering mother (Mary Astor). The plot motivations and parade of characters that precede the racing footage are slow, dull, and confusing, but the racing itself is well shot. Playing Wilde's hard-drinking ex is his off-screen spouse, Jean Wallace.

p, Cornel Wilde; d, Cornel Wilde; w, Cornel Wilde, James Edmiston (based on the novel *The Fastest Man on Earth* by James Edmiston); ph, Daniel L. Fapp (VistaVision, Technicolor); ed, Floyd Knudtson.

Auto Racing (PR:A MPAA:NR)

DOWNHILL RACER***½

(1969) 101m Wildwood/PAR c

Robert Redford *(Davis Chappellet),* Gene Hackman *(Eugene Claire),* Camilla Sparv *(Carole Stahl),* Karl Michael Vogler *(Machet),* Jim McMullan *(Creech),* Christian Doermer *(Brumm),* Kathleen Crowley *(American Newspaperwoman),* Dabney Coleman *(Mayo),* Kenneth Kirk *(D.K. Bryan),* Oren Stevens *(Kipsmith),* Jerry Dexter *(Engel),* Walter Stroud *(David's Father),* Carole Carle *(Lena),* Rip McManus *(Devore),* Joe Jay Jalbert *(Tommy),* Tom Kirk *(Stiles),* Robin Hutton-Potts *(Gabriel),* Heini Schuler *(Meier),* Peter Rohr *(Boyriven),* Arnold Alpiger *(Hinsch),* Eddie Waldburger *(Haas),* Marco Walli *(Istel),* Rudi Gertsch *(Selznick).*

Documentarylike in style, DOWNHILL RACER is a strangely dispassionate but captivating look behind the glamorous facade of international ski racing. Robert Redford, who did much of his own skiing, stars as Davis Chappellet, a self-centered, success-hungry skier from Colorado who is summoned to Europe when a member of the US team is injured. Over the next two racing seasons he proves himself to be one of the sport's most promising newcomers, dueling with a famous teammate (Jim McMullan) for the spotlight and clashing with his strong-willed coach (Gene Hackman), but in the process of chasing Olympic gold in the downhill, he fails to win approval from his father and is unable to maintain a relationship with a beautiful ski manufacturer's assistant (Camilla Sparv). Redford, who was determined to make a skiing film, went to great lengths to sell the project: soliciting a screenplay from James Salter, enlisting a team of ski bums and photographers to shoot 20,000 feet of action on the sly at the 1968 Grenoble Olympics, and giving Michael Ritchie, who provides a sure directorial hand, his first feature film assignment. Many of the downhill scenes were filmed by skier Joe Jay Jalbert, who raced behind Redford with a camera, adding to the film's realism and excitement. DOWNHILL RACER is fascinating viewing, even if the closest you've gotten to a ski slope is "Wide World of Sports."

p, Richard Gregson; d, Michael Ritchie; w, James Salter (based on the novel *The Downhill Racers* by Oakley Hall); ph, Brian Probyn (Technicolor); ed, Nick Archer; m, Kenyon Hopkins.

Skiing Cas. (PR:C MPAA:M)

DREAMER*½

(1979) 79m FOX c

Tim Matheson *(Dreamer),* Susan Blakely *(Karen),* Jack Warden *(Harry),* Richard B. Shull *(Taylor),* Barbara Stuart *(Angie),* Owen Bush *(The Fan),* Marya Small *(Elaine),* Matt Clark *(Spider),* John Crawford *(Riverboat Captain),* Chris Schenkel *(Himself),* Nelson Burton, Jr. *(Color Man),* Morgan Farley *(Old Timer),* Pedro Gonzalez Gonzalez *(Too),* Speedy Zapata *(Juan),* Jobe Cerny *(Patterson),* Azizi Johari *(Lady),* Dick Weber *(Johnny Watkin),* Julian Byrd *(Red),* Rita Ascot Boyd *(Grandma),* Marie E. Brady *(Old Lady),* Pat Mullins Brown *(Nurse),* Richard Cosentino *(Official),* Beverly Dunn Davis *(Betty).*

DREAMER rips off the ROCKY formula to tell the story of a small-town bowler (Tim Matheson) who lifts himself into the professional ranks and wins the national championship. Of course, a crusty old coach (Jack Warden) is on hand, as is a girl friend (Susan Blakely) who wants as much attention from her beau as his bowling ball gets. Bill Conti, who did ROCKY's memorable score, contributes the music here too (the mind boggles). A gutter ball of a film, though it does include apperances by professional bowlers Dick Weber and Nelson Burton, Jr.

p, Michael Lobell; d, Noel Nosseck; w, James Proctor, Larry Bishoff; ph, Bruce Surtees (DeLuxe Color); ed, Fred Chulack; m, Bill Conti.

Bowling Cas. (PR:A MPAA:PG)

DRIVE, HE SAID**½

(1971) 92m BBS/COL c

William Tepper *(Hector),* Karen Black *(Olive),* Michael Margotta *(Gabriel),* Bruce Dern *(Coach Bullion),* Robert Towne *(Richard),* Henry Jaglom *(Conrad),* Michael Warren *(Easly),* June Fairchild *(Sylvie),* Don Hammer *(Director of*

Athletics), Lynn Bernay *(Dance Instructor)*, Joey Walsh, Harry Gittes *(Announcers)*, Charles Robinson *(Jollop)*, Bill Sweek *(Finnegan)*, David Stiers *(Pro Owner)*, B.J. Merholz *(Pro Lawyer)*, I.J. Jefferson *(Secretary)*, Kenneth Bayle *(President Wallop)*, Cathy Bradford *(Rosemary)*, Eric Johnson *(Pfc. Johnson)*, Bill Kenney *(Phoneman)*, Lenny Lockabaugh *(Policeman)*.

The directorial debut of the Los Angeles Lakers' most famous fan, Jack Nicholson, DRIVE, HE SAID is an ambitious but confused film about basketball, draft dodging, and sleeping with professors' wives. Hector (William Tepper), the long-haired star of an Ohio college team, can't decide if he wants to turn pro or join Gabriel (Michael Margotta), his radical roommate, in bringing about the revolution; in the meantime, he's content to carry on an affair with a faculty wife (Karen Black). Gabriel, on the other hand, works so hard at convincing the draft board that he's bonkers that he really does go off the deep end. In addition to Bruce Dern, who is outstanding as Hector's coach, the cast includes future writer-directors Robert Towne and Henry Jaglom, as well as one-time UCLA basketball star Mike Warren, who would go on to make several more films and be featured in TV's popular "Hill Street Blues."

p, Steve Blauner, Jack Nicholson; d, Jack Nicholson; w, Jack Nicholson, Jeremy Larner (based on the novel by Larner); ph, Bill Butler (Metrocolor); ed, Pat Somerset, Donn Cambern, Christopher Holmes, Robert I. Wolfe; m, David Shire.

Basketball **(PR:O MPAA:R)**

DUKE OF CHICAGO**

(1949) 59m REP bw

Tom Brown *(Jimmy Brody)*, Audrey Long *(Jane Cunningham)*, Grant Withers *(Tony Russo)*, Paul Harvey *(Chester Cunningham)*, Richard "Skeets" Gallagher *(Gus Weller)*, Lois Hall *(Helen Cunningham)*, Matt McHugh *(Terry Shea)*, Joseph Crehan *(Tex Harmon)*, George Beban *(Speedy)*, Keith Richards *(Bryce)*, DeForest Kelley *(Ace Martin)*, Frankie Van *(Referee)*, Dan Tobey *(Fight Announcer)*, Dale Van Sickel *(Kroner)*.

This dull fight drama stars Tom Brown as Jimmy Brody, a retired middleweight champ now involved in the publishing business. When his company encounters big financial trouble, Jimmy is forced out of retirement to make enough money to save the firm. A match is set up by some shady gamblers who bank on the ex-champ taking a dive, but Jimmy refuses and wins despite a broken hand, enraging the gamblers, who decide to kill him but are thwarted by the timely arrival of the cops.

p, Stephen Auer; d, George Blair; w, Albert DeMond (based on a novel by Lucian Cary); ph, John MacBurnie; ed, Cliff Bell; m, Stanley Wilson.

Boxing **(PR:A MPAA:NR)**

EASY LIVING**½

(1949) 77m RKO bw

Victor Mature *(Pete Wilson)*, Lucille Ball *(Anne)*, Lizabeth Scott *(Liza Wilson)*, Sonny Tufts *(Tim McCarr)*, Lloyd Nolan *(Lenahan)*, Paul Stewart *(Argus)*, Jack Paar *(Scoop Spooner)*, Jeff Donnell *(Penny McCarr)*, Art Baker *(Howard Vollmer)*, Gordon Jones *(Bill Holloran)*, Don Beddoe *(Jaegar)*, Dick Erdman *(Buddy Morgan)*, Bill Phillips *(Ozzie)*, Charles Lang *(Whitey)*, Kenny Washington *(Benny)*, Julia Dean *(Mrs. Belle Ryan)*, Everett Glass *(Virgil Ryan)*, Jim Backus *(Dr. Franklin)*, Robert Ellis *(Urchin)*, Steven Flagg *(Gilbert Vollmer)*, The Los Angeles Rams *(Themselves)*.

Based on Irwin Shaw's "Education of the Heart" and directed by Jacques Tourneur, EASY LIVING is the melodramatic tale of an aging star halfback for the fictitious New York Chiefs (Victor Mature) who knows retirement is imminent. His adjustment to this inevitability is complicated by the loss of the college coaching job he hoped would be his but which is won by a friend (Sonny Tufts). To make matters worse, he discovers that he has a heart condition, which should keep him off the field but doesn't, because he is afraid that his selfish wife (Lizabeth Scott) will leave him if he's no longer in the limelight. All along he is supported by the team's pretty secretary (Lucille Ball), who is in love with him but contents herself with helping him through his difficulties, finally persuading him to leave the gridiron for good. Eschewing the flashy, fast-paced game action of most football films, Tourneur focuses instead on his characters and the result is a moody, generally well-crafted film.

p, Robert Sparks; d, Jacques Tourneur; w, Charles Schnee (based on the story "Education of The Heart" by Irwin Shaw); ph, Harry Wild; ed, Frederic Knudtson; m, Roy Webb.

Football **Cas.** **(PR:A-C MPAA:NR)**

EDITH AND MARCEL***

(1984, Fr.) 140m Film 13-Parafrance/Miramax c (EDITH ET MARCEL)

Evelyne Bouix *(Edith Piaf/Margot de Villedieu)*, Marcel Cerdan, Jr. *(Marcel Cerdan)*, Charles Aznavour *(Himself)*, Jacques Villeret *(Jacques Barbier)*, Francis Huster *(Francis Roman)*, Jean-Claude Brialy *(Loulou Barrier)*, Jean Bouise *(Lucien Roupp)*, Charles Gerard *(Charlot)*, Charlotte de Turckheim *(Ginou)*, Micky Sebastian *(Marinette)*, Maurice Garrel *(Margot's Father)*, Ginette Garcin *(Guite)*, Philippe Khorsand *(Jo Longman)*, Jany Gastaldi *(Momone)*, Candice Patou *(Margot's Sister)*, Tanya Lopert *(English Teacher)*, Jean Rougerie *(Theater Director)*, Fouad Sakete, Stephan Ferrara, Dominique Benkouai, Michel Chapier *(The Boxers)*.

A sentimental tale about the real-life romance between legendary French chanteuse Edith Piaf (Evelyne Bouix) and world middleweight boxing champion Marcel Cerdan (played by his son, Marcel Cerdan, Jr.). After meeting once, the two are reintroduced in 1948 in New Jersey, where Cerdan has just defeated Tony Zale for the championship. Their passion for one another burns until the following year, when Cerdan dies in a transatlantic plane crash. Intercut with their headline-making romance is an everyday love story about two young Parisians (one of whom is also played by Bouix) who admire Piaf and Cerdan. Director Claude Lelouch (A MAN AND A WOMAN, 1966) coaxes a fine performance from Bouix and a serviceable one from Cerdan, a boxer like his father who had been acting as the film's technical advisor and who replaced Patrick Dewaere when the star took his own life. Although a little saccharine for some tastes, EDITH AND MARCEL is suffused with period detail and is worth watching just to see Lelouch's evocation of postwar Paris and to hear Piaf's delicate songs. (In French; English subtitles.)

p, Claude Lelouch; d, Claude Lelouch; w, Pierre Uytterhoeven, Gilles Durieux, Claude Lelouch; ph, Jean Boffety; ed, Hugues Darmois; m, Francis Lai.

Boxing/Biography   Cas.   (PR:A-C MPAA:NR)

EIGHT MEN OUT***

(1988) 119m Orion c

Jace Alexander (*Dickie Kerr*), John Cusack (*Buck Weaver*), Gordon Clapp (*Ray Schalk*), Don Harvey (*Swede Risberg*), Bill Irwin (*Eddie Collins*), Perry Lang (*Fred McMullin*), John Mahoney (*Kid Gleason*), James Read (*Lefty Williams*), Michael Rooker (*Chick Gandil*), Charlie Sheen (*Hap Felsch*), David Strathairn (*Eddie Cicotte*), D.B. Sweeney ("*Shoeless*" *Joe Jackson*), Jim Desmond (*Smitty*), John Sayles (*Ring Lardner*), Studs Terkel (*Hugh Fullerton*), Richard Edson (*Billy Maharg*), Michael Lerner (*Arnold Rothstein*), Christopher Lloyd (*Bill Burns*), Michael Mantell (*Abe Attell*), Kevin Tighe (*Sport Sullivan*), Eliot Asinof (*Heydler*), Clyde Bassett (*Ban Johnson*), Clifton James (*Charles Comiskey*), John D. Craig (*Rothstein's Lawyer*), Michael Laskin (*Austrian*), Randle Mell (*Ahearn*), Robert Motz (*D.A.*), Bill Raymond (*Ben Short*), Barbara Garrick (*Helen Weaver*), Wendy Makkena (*Kate Jackson*), Maggie Renzi (*Rose Cicotte*), Nancy Travis (*Lyria Williams*), Brad Garrett (*PeeWee*), Robert Walsh, Matthew Harrington, Richard Lynch, Garry Williams, Michael Harris (*Writers*), Ken Berry (*Heckler*).

In 1919, major league baseball was rocked by scandal when eight members of the Chicago White Sox, one of the sport's greatest teams, were accused of fixing the World Series. After losing to the Cincinnati Reds, the "Black Sox" were tried on charges of conspiracy, tainting the national pastime so that it took a new, livelier ball and the heroics of the great Babe Ruth to save the game. Working from one-time Philadelphia Phillies farmhand Eliot Asinof's assiduously researched *Eight Men Out*, writer-director John Sayles (MATEWAN; THE BROTHER FROM ANOTHER PLANET) has fashioned a gripping account of the scandal, underlain with an unconventional (by Hollywood standards) workers vs. owners critique. Sayles not only depicts the circumstances that led to the fix (most notably Sox owner Charles Comiskey's legendary tightfistedness and the virtual servitude guaranteed by the reserve clause) and the personal motivations of the players, but also re-creates the games in great detail, making the best possible use of an athletic cast tutored by one-time White Sox Ken Berry. In attempting to bring the whole story to the screen, Sayles fails to present in-depth portraits of all the players involved, but those that he does concentrate on are well etched: pitcher Eddie Cicotte (David Strathairn); third baseman Buck Weaver (John Cusack), who spent the rest of his life protesting his innocence; the legendary "Shoeless Joe Jackson" (D.B. Sweeney, whose own baseball career was ended by a motorcycle accident and who spent 5 weeks with the minor league Kenosha Twins learning to bat left-handed for the role). Still, there isn't a weak performance from the excellent ensemble cast that includes Chicago journalist Studs Terkel as sportswriter Hugh Fullerton and Sayles as Ring Lardner; and though Sayles' direction is occasionally a little heavy-handed, EIGHT MEN OUT is a fascinating historical document not just of the scandal but of the post-WW I American loss of innocence. Bush Stadium, home of the Indianapolis Indians, is convincingly dressed up as both Comiskey Park and Redland Stadium.

p, Sarah Pillsbury, Midge Sanford; d, John Sayles; w, John Sayles (based on the book by Eliot Asinof); ph, Robert Richardson (Duart Color); ed, John Tintori; m, Mason Daring.

Baseball   Cas.   (PR:C-O MPAA:PG)

ELMER THE GREAT***

(1933) 64m WB/FN bw

Joe E. Brown (*Elmer*), Patricia Ellis (*Nellie*), Frank McHugh (*High-Hips Healy*), Claire Dodd (*Evelyn*), Preston Foster (*Walker*), Russell Hopton (*Whitey*), Sterling Holloway (*Nick*), Emma Dunn (*Mrs. Kane*), Charles Wilson (*Bull McWade*), Jessie Ralph (*Sarah Crosby*), Douglas Dumbrille (*Stillman*), Charles Delaney (*Johnny Abbott*), Berton Churchill (*Col. Moffitt*), J. Carrol Naish (*Jerry*), Gene Morgan (*Noonan*), Lloyd Neal.

This likable baseball comedy stars Joe E. Brown as a country bumpkin home-run hitter who gets the best of both gangsters and cheating pitchers to win the World Series for the Cubs against the Yankees. Brown's acting is no great shakes, but his mugging comedy talents provide many a laugh and he certainly can handle a bat, having played semi-pro ball before going into show biz (see ALIBI IKE, 1935). One-time sportswriter Ring Lardner (portrayed by John Sayles in his EIGHT MEN OUT) and George M. Cohan adapted a Lardner short story into the play on which ELMER THE GREAT is based, though the tale first came to the screen as FAST COMPANY in 1929. The inspiration for Lardner's original story was Chicago White Sox pitcher Big Ed Walsh, but for ELMER THE GREAT the positions have been changed to protect the innocent, and in 1939 the sport was changed to football for another remake, THE COWBOY QUARTERBACK.

p, Ray Griffith; d, Mervyn LeRoy; w, Tom Geraghty (based on a play by Ring Lardner and George M. Cohan); ph, Arthur Todd; ed, Thomas Pratt.

Baseball/Comedy (PR:A MPAA:NR)

EVERYBODY'S ALL-AMERICAN**½

(1988) 122m New Visions/WB c

Dennis Quaid *(Gavin Grey)*, Jessica Lange *(Babs Rogers Grey)*, Timothy Hutton *(Donnie "Cake")*, John Goodman *(Ed Lawrence)*, Carl Lumbly *(Narvel Blue)*, Raymond Baker *(Bolling Kiely)*, Savannah Smith Boucher *(Darlene Kiely)*, Patricia Clarkson *(Leslie Stone)*.

Combining big emotions and the spectacle of college and professional football, this epic sports melodrama focuses on the rise and fall of a legendary fleet-footed halfback known as the "Grey Ghost" (Dennis Quaid). Beginning in 1956, it follows the Ghost as he leads the Louisiana University Tigers (LSU in everything but name) to a miraculous Sugar Bowl victory, then traces his illustrious pro career with the Washington Redskins, and finally, shifting to 1981, presents the ghost of the Ghost in retirement. As much about love as it is about football, the film also chronicles the three-cornered relationship between the Ghost, his Magnolia Queen-turned-shrewd businesswoman wife (Jessica Lange), and the Ghost's intellectual cousin (Timothy Hutton). Director Taylor Hackford (AN OFFICER AND A GENTLEMAN) employs excellent period detail to capture the excitement of college and pro games, but the film doesn't become compelling until after the glimmer has faded from Quaid's golden boy. Quaid, who is outstanding, put on 30 pounds for his role, but that didn't prevent him breaking his collar bone in one hard-hitting scene and he had to finish the film wearing a brace. Several key on-field action sequences were shot before 80,000 spectators during halftime at some LSU games. Frank Deford, author of the novel on which the film is based, appears in a small role. A little forced, a lot sincere, and not overly manipulative, EVERYBODY'S ALL-AMERICAN won't change your life but it may bring a tear to your eye.

p, Taylor Hackford, Laura Ziskin, Ian Sander; d, Taylor Hackford; w, Thomas Rickman (based on the novel by Frank Deford); ph, Stephen Goldblatt (Technicolor); ed, Don Zimmerman; m, James Newton Howard.

Football Cas. (PR:C-O MPAA:R)

FAN'S NOTES, A**

(1972, Can.) 90m Coquihala/WB c

Jerry Orbach *(Fred)*, Patricia Collins *(Patience)*, Burgess Meredith *(Mr. Blue)*, Rosemary Murphy *(Moms)*, Conrad Bain *(Poppy)*, Julia Robinson *(Bunny Sue)*.

Based on a novel by Frederick Exley, A FAN'S NOTES follows the fortunes of Fred (Jerry Orbach), an aspiring writer and the son of a one-time football star, as he travels the States in search of self-esteem. Eventually he accepts the fact that he will never experience gridiron glory himself—that he is simply a fan, an observer—and the unsettling implication is that Fred's sideline existence applies to every other aspect of his life as well. Though its subject matter is intriguing, this is a film in search of its tone.

d, Eric Till; w, William Kinsolving (based on a book by Frederick Earl Exley); ph, Harry Makin; m, Ron Collier.

Football (PR:C MPAA:NR)

FAST BREAK*½

(1979) 107m COL c

Gabriel Kaplan *(David Greene)*, Harold Sylvester *(D.C.)*, Michael Warren *(Preacher)*, Bernard King *(Hustler)*, Reb Brown *(Bull)*, Mavis Washington *(Swish)*, Bert Remsen *(Bo Winnegar)*, Randee Heller *(Jan)*, John Chappell *(Alton Gutkas)*, Rhonda Bates *(Enid Cadwallader-Gutkas)*, K. Callan *(Ms. Tidwell)*, Marty Zagon *(Henry)*, Connie Sawyer *(Lottie)*, Doria Cook *(Snooty Girl)*, James Jeter *(Officer Wedgewood)*, Steve Conte *(Man on Bus)*, Larry Farmer *(Beaton)*, Craig Impleman *(Hollis)*, Charles Penland *(Larry)*.

Gabriel Kaplan (TV's "Welcome Back Kotter") plays David Greene, a New York City delicatessen worker who finagles a job as the head basketball coach of Nevada's Cadwalader College. To insure his success, "Coach" Greene recruits a talented assemblage of Gotham playground players whose scholastic qualifications are highly suspect. One of them (Mavis Washington) is actually a woman who goes to great pains to keep her gender a secret, but before long she and another of the players have fallen in love. In the meantime, the Cadwalader cagers demolish their small-time opposition and land a Big Game with the state's basketball powerhouse (just another of those midseason schedule additions that happen all the time). Totally implausible (though surely not meant to be taken seriously), highly predictable, and not particularly funny, FAST BREAK may be worth the attention of basketball fans interested in watching University of Tennessee and NBA standout Bernard King *act*. Michael Warren, who starred in the backcourt at UCLA when Kareem Abdul-Jabbar (then Lew Alcindor) was a Bruin and who would go on to become a featured performer on TV's "Hill Street Blues," also has a part as one of Kaplan's players.

p, Stephen Friedman; d, Jack Smight; w, Sandor Stern (based on a story by Marc Kaplan); ph, Charles Correll (Metrocolor); ed, Frank J. Urioste; m, David Shire, James Di Pasquale.

Basketball/Comedy Cas. (PR:A MPAA:PG)

FAST COMPANIONS**½

(1932) 71m UNIV bw

Tom Brown *(Marty Black)*, James Gleason *(Silk Henley)*,

Maureen O'Sullivan *(Sally)*, Andy Devine *(Information Kid)*, Mickey Rooney *(Midge)*.

Marty Black (Tom Brown), a crooked jockey, and Silk Henley (James Gleason) conspire to swindle the punters at small-town racetracks. When Midge (Mickey Rooney), a plucky orphan, arrives on the scene, Marty mends his ways and falls for Sally (Maureen O'Sullivan), a boarding-house proprietress. Although hardly a first-rate track film, FAST COMPANIONS contains enough laughs and action to make it enjoyable.

d, Kurt Neumann; w, Earle Snell, C.J. Marks (based on a story by Gerald Beaumont and Charles Logue); ph, Arthur Edeson.

**Horse Racing/
Comedy** **(PR:A MPAA:NR)**

FAST COMPANY**

(1929) 70m FP-PAR bw

Evelyn Brent *(Evelyn Corey)*, Jack Oakie *(Elmer Kane)*, Richard "Skeets" Gallagher *(Bert Wade)*, Sam Hardy *(Dave Walker)*, Arthur Housman *(Barney Barlow)*, Gwen Lee *(Rosie La Clerq)*, Chester Conklin *(C. of C. President)*, E.H. Calvert *(Platt)*, Eugenie Besserer *(Mrs. Kane)*, Bert Rome *(Hank Gordon)*, Irish Meusel, Red Rollings, Frank Greene, Lez Smith *(Themselves)*.

The first screen version of George M. Cohan and Ring Lardner's play "Elmer the Great," FAST COMPANY stars Jack Oakie as Elmer Kane, a home run-hitting hayseed who becomes a New York Yankee and singlehandedly defeats gangsters *and* the Pittsburgh Pirates to win the World Series. This mildly entertaining early sound comedy was remade in 1933 with Joe B. Brown, and again in 1939 as COWBOY QUARTERBACK, with the sport changed to football.

d, A. Edward Sutherland; w, Florence Ryerson, Patrick Kearney, Walton Butterfield, Joseph L. Mankiewicz (based on the play "Elmer The Great" by George M. Cohan and Ring Lardner).

Baseball **(PR:A MPAA:NR)**

FAST COMPANY**

(1953) 67m MGM bw

Howard Keel *(Rick Grayton)*, Polly Bergen *(Carol Maldon)*, Marjorie Main *(Ma Parkson)*, Nina Foch *(Mercedes Bellway)*, Robert Burton *(Dave Sandring)*, Carol Nugent *("Jigger" Parkson)*, Joaquin Garay *(Manuel Morales)*, Horace MacMahon *("Two Pair" Buford)*, Sig Arno *("Hungry")*, Iron Eyes Cody *(Ben Iron Mountain)*.

Carol Maldon (Polly Bergen) inherits a racehorse, but Rick Grayton (Howard Keel), the man who has been caring for it, makes sure that the horse doesn't win any races in the hope that he will be able to buy it cheaply. Carol keeps her horse anyway, and when she gets fleeced by track sharpies, Rick steps in and romance blossoms.

p, Henry Berman; d, John Sturges; w, William Roberts, Don Mankiewicz (based on a story by Eustace Cockrell);

ph, Harold Lipstein; ed, Joseph Dervim.

**Horse Racing/
Comedy** **(PR:A MPAA:NR)**

FAT CITY****

(1972) 100m COL c

Stacy Keach *(Tully)*, Jeff Bridges *(Ernie)*, Susan Tyrrell *(Oma)*, Candy Clark *(Faye)*, Nicholas Colasanto *(Ruben)*, Art Aragon *(Babe)*, Curtis Cokes *(Earl)*, Sixto Rodriguez *(Lucero)*, Bill Walker *(Wes)*, Wayne Mahan *(Buford)*, Ruben Navarro *(Fuentes)*.

Set in Stockton, California, against a backdrop of run-down bars, cheap apartments, and half-empty fourth-rate boxing halls, FAT CITY is a story of hope and despair among life's losers. Billy Tully (Stacy Keach), a 29-year-old one-time boxing contender, contemplates a comeback after nearly two years of alcoholism brought about by the loss of both his wife and the biggest fight of his career. He meets Ernie Munger (Jeff Bridges), a talented 19-year-old, and encourages him to hook up with Billy's old manager (Nicholas Colasanto), which Ernie does, beginning his own boxing career. Billy, however, continues boozing and becomes involved with Oma (Susan Tyrrell), a despondent alcoholic whose black boy friend (former welterweight champion Curtis Cokes) is in jail, while Ernie marries the high-school girl who is pregnant with his child. Eventually, Billy climbs back into the ring, barely winning a brutal battle against a once highly regarded but now very sick Mexican fighter, as the film moves toward its downbeat ending. Adapted by Leonard Gardner from his own novel and brilliantly directed by John Huston, who was himself once a rather poor professional fighter (though an amateur champion), FAT CITY is both an extraordinarily realistic look at the bottom rungs of the fight game and a moving exploration of the human condition. Keach, Bridges, Tyrrell (who received an Oscar nomination), and all the supporting players give first-rate performances, and the film, which makes good use of Kris Kristofferson's "Help Me Make It Through the Night," is never less than captivating.

p, Ray Stark; d, John Huston; w, Leonard Gardner (based on his novel); ph, Conrad Hall (Eastmancolor); ed, Marguerite Booth; m, Marvin Hamlisch.

Boxing **Cas.** **(PR:C MPAA:PG)**

FATHER WAS A FULLBACK**½

(1949) 84m FOX bw

Fred MacMurray *(George Cooper)*, Maureen O'Hara *(Elizabeth Cooper)*, Betty Lynn *(Connie Cooper)*, Rudy Vallee *(Mr. Jessop)*, Thelma Ritter *(Geraldine)*, Natalie Wood *(Ellen Cooper)*, Jim Backus *(Prof. Sullivan)*, Richard Tyler *(Joe Burch)*, Buddy Martin *(Cheerleader)*, Mickey McCardle *(Jones)*, John McKee *(Cy)*, Charles J. Flynn *(Policeman)*, William Self *(Willie)*, Joe Haworth *(Reporter)*, Gwenn Fields *(Daphne)*, Gilbert Barnett *(Stinky Parker)*, Tommy Bernard *(Delivery Boy)*, Mike Mahoney *(Sailor)*, Tom Hanlon *(Radio Announcer)*, Pat Kane *(Bellhop)*,

Forbes Murray *(College President)*, Robert Patten *(Manager)*, Louise Lorimer *(Mrs. Jones)*.

Fred MacMurray stars in this lighthearted, surprisingly human comedy as George Cooper, the coach of a losing college football team who has as much trouble with his two daughters as he does with the alumni and administration. George needs all the help he can get from his supportive wife (Maureen O'Hara) when one his daughters scandalizes the university community with an article she has written detailing her sex life. With the help of a former football star (Richard Tyler), George turns the team around and, at the same time, manages to straighten things out on the home front.

p, Fred Kohlmar; d, John M. Stahl; w, Aleen Leslie, Casey Robinson, Mary Loos, Richard Sale (based on a play by Clifford Goldsmith); ph, Lloyd Ahern; ed, J. Watson Webb, Jr.; m, Cyril J. Mockridge.

Football/Comedy   **(PR:A   MPAA:NR)**

FEAR STRIKES OUT****

(1957) 100m PAR bw

Anthony Perkins *(Jimmy Piersall)*, Karl Malden *(John Piersall)*, Norma Moore *(Mary Teevan)*, Adam Williams *(Dr. Brown)*, Peter J. Votrian *(Jimmy Piersall as a Boy)*, Perry Wilson *(Mrs. John Piersall)*, Dennis McMullen *(Phil)*, Gail Land *(Alice)*, Brian Hutton *(Bernie Sherwill)*, Bart Burns *(Joe Cronin)*, Rand Harper *(Radio Announcer)*, Howard Price *(Bill Tracy)*, George Pembroke *(Umpire)*, Morgan Jones *(Sandy Allen)*.

Anthony Perkins portrays Jimmy Piersall in this well-done true story of one of baseball's most colorful characters, who, from boyhood, was relentlessly driven by his father (Karl Malden) to make it in the major leagues. Nothing the talented Jimmy does is good enough for his dad, and, after finally making the Boston Red Sox, he breaks down, maniacally climbing the backstop after hitting a home run—one the best remembered scenes in any sports film. Jimmy is then admitted to Westborough State Hospital, where he gradually recovers under the supervision of Dr. Brown (Adam Williams), eventually returning to his wife, his repentant father, and the Red Sox lineup. In recent years, Perkins has been held up as the prime example of an actor who *should not* have been cast as an athlete; however, despite his physical awkwardness, he delivers a powerful portrayal of a young man undergoing tremendous emotional turmoil, and in the final analysis, the psychological reality of FEAR STRIKES OUT is far more important than how Perkins looks throwing the ball back into the infield. Based on Piersall's autobiography, this feature film directorial debut for Robert Mulligan also boasts an extraordinary performance by Malden as Piersall's demanding but loving father.

p, Alan Pakula; d, Robert Mulligan; w, Ted Berkman, Raphael Blau (based on the autobiography by James A. Piersall, with Albert S. Hirshberg); ph, Haskell Boggs; ed, Aaron Stell; m, Elmer Bernstein.

Baseball/Biography   **(PR:C   MPAA:NR)**

FIFTY-SHILLING BOXER**

(1937, Brit.) 74m RKO bw

Bruce Seton *(Jack Foster)*, Nancy O'Neil *(Moira Regan)*, Moore Marriott *(Tim Regan)*, Eve Gray *(Miriam Steele)*, Charles Oliver *(Jim Pollett)*, Aubrey Mallalieu *(Charles Day)*.

A clown (Bruce Seton) dreams of leaving the circus and becoming a great prizefighter, but is sidetracked from this ambition when he is spotted in a fight and offered the role of a boxer in a film. After an imbroglio on the set, he gets fired as an actor but is given his big chance as a pugilist, and so it goes en route to a poor B film ending.

p, George Smith; d, Maclean Rogers; w, Guy Fletcher; ph, Geoffrey Faithfull.

Boxing   **(PR:A   MPAA:NR)**

FIGHTER, THE**½

(1952) 78m UA bw (AKA: THE FIRST TIME)

Richard Conte *(Filipe Rivera)*, Vanessa Brown *(Kathy)*, Lee J. Cobb *(Durango)*, Frank Silvera *(Paulino)*, Roberta Haynes *(Nevis)*, Hugh Sanders *(Roberts)*, Claire Carleton *(Stella)*, Martin Garralaga *(Luis)*, Argentina Brunetti *(Maria)*, Rudolfo Hoyos, Jr. *(Alvarado)*, Margaret Padilla *(Elba)*, Paul Fierro *(Fierro)*.

Filipe Rivera (Richard Conte) travels north of the border to El Paso to join his Mexican compatriots, who are plotting to overthrow the tyrannical Porfirio Diaz. In flashback, we see how Filipe's family and sweetheart were killed and his village destroyed by Diaz's soldiers. It is this memory that gives Filipe the last-minute strength to triumph in a winner-take-all boxing match—the purse of which he contributes to the cause, providing arms for the guerrilla forces lead by Durango (Lee J. Cobb). This intriguing boxing film with a strong political underpinning was based on Jack London's story "The Mexican," which also provided the inspiration for a 1957 Russian film of the same name.

p, Alex Gottlieb; d, Herbert Kline; w, Aben Kandel, Herbert Kline (based on the short story "The Mexican" by Jack London); ph, James Wong Howe; ed, Edward Mann; m, Vicente Gomez.

Boxing   **(PR:A   MPAA:NR)**

FIGHTING CHAMP*

(1933) 57m MON bw

Bob Steele, Arletta Duncan, George Hayes, Charles King, Lafe McKee, Kit Guard, George Chesebro, Frank Ball, Henry Rocquemore, Hank Bell.

Add a bad formula boxing film plot to a bad western and you get FIGHTING CHAMP—a bad movie. Besides doing a lot of riding and shooting, cowboy star Bob Steele steps into the boxing ring and unconvincingly takes on all comers (did we leave out bad acting?).

p, Trem Carr; d, J.P. McCarthy; w, Wellyn Totman; ph, Archie Stout.

Boxing/Western   **(PR:A   MPAA:NR)**

FIGHTING FOOLS**

(1949) 89m MON bw

Leo Gorcey *(Slip)*, Huntz Hall *(Sach)*, Gabriel Dell *(Gabe Moreno)*, Frankie Darro *(Johnny Higgins)*, Billy Benedict *(Whitey)*, David Gorcey *(Chuck)*, Bennie Bartlett *(Butch)*, Lyle Talbot *(Blinky Harris)*, Teddy Infuhr *(Boomer Higgins)*, Bernard Gorcey *(Louie)*, Dorothy Vaughan *(Mrs. Higgins)*, Ben Welden *(Lefty Conlon)*, Evelyn Eaton *(Bunny Talbot)*, Bert Conway *(Dynamite Carson)*, Paul Maxey *(Editor)*, Robert Wolcott *(Jimmy Higgins)*, Bill Cartledge *(Joey Prince)*, Anthony Warde *(Marty)*, Eddie Gribbon *(Highball)*, Sam Hayes *(Bill Radar)*, Frank Moran *(Goon)*, Tom Kennedy *(Rosemeyer)*, Bud Gorman *(Call Boy)*, Roland Dupree *(Young Man in Sweetshop)*, John Duncan *(Fighter in Gym)*, Mike Pat Donovan *(Pete)*.

Leo Gorcey and Huntz Hall lead the Bowery Boys through this so-so prizefighting comedy. After a pal is killed in the ring, Slip (Gorcey) and company are determined to see that the mobsters responsible get their due. Their dead friend's brother, Johnny Higgins (Frankie Darro), an alcoholic ex-fighter, is persuaded to return to the ring to avenge his sibling's death. The gangsters do their best to screw up the Boys' plans, but Johnny ends up winning the championship anyway.

p, Jan Grippo; d, Reginald Le Borg; w, Edmond Seward, Gerald Schnitzer, Bert Lawrence; ph, William Sickner; ed, William Austin.

Boxing/Comedy (PR:A MPAA:NR)

FIGHTING GENTLEMAN, THE*½

(1932) 69m Monarch/Freuler bw

William Collier, Jr. *(Jack Duncan)*, Josephine Dunn *(Jeanette Larkin)*, Natalie Moorhead *(Violet Reed)*, Crauford Kent *(Claude Morgan)*, Lee Moran *(Mr. Hurley)*, Pat O'Malley *(Dot Moran)*, James J. Jeffries *(Referee)*, Hughie Owen, Mildred Rogers, Peggy Graves, Paddy O'Flynn, Duke Lee.

Popular leading man William Collier, Jr., here plays a mechanic who aspires to prizefighting greatness. Although Jack (Collier) gets knocked out in the first round of a carnival fight, he dedicates himself to his training and kayos his opponent in the rematch. A great future begins to unfold for Jack; however, money and fame lead him into fast living and adultery, and in no time the fighter has fallen from his lofty perch and ended up back in the garage, down but not out. There's not much to surprise or delight anyone in this run-of-the-mill fight film.

d, Fred Newmeyer; w, Edward Sinclair, F. McGrew Willis; ph, Edward Kull; ed, Fred Bain.

Boxing (PR:A MPAA:NR)

FIGHTING MAD**½

(1948) 74m MON bw

Leon Errol *(Knobby Walsh)*, Joe Kirkwood, Jr. *(Joe Palooka)*, Elyse Knox *(Anne Howe)*, John Hubbard *(Charles Kennedy)*, Patricia Dane *(Iris March)*, Charles

Cane *(George Wendell)*, Wally Vernon *(Archie Stone)*, Frank Hyers *(Ralph)*, Jack Shea *(Jeff Lundy)*, Jack Roper *(Waldo)*, Horace McMahon *(Looie)*, Jack Overman *(Truck Driver)*, Eddie Gribbon *(Scranton)*, Sarah Padden *(Mom Palooka)*, Michael Mark *(Pop Palooka)*, Evelynne Smith *(Truck Driver's Wife)*, Geneva Gray *(Hat Check Girl)*, John Indrisano *(Referee)*, Frank Reicher *(Dr. MacKenzie)*, Jay Norris *(Stevie)*.

Ham Fisher's famous comic-strip pugilist Joe Palooka is again portrayed by Joe Kirkwood here. In this installment, Palooka is blinded during a fight, then regains his eyesight through an operation, but is told by doctors not to put on the gloves again for at least a year. In the meantime, his manager, Knobby Walsh (Leon Errol), takes over the career of a heavyweight (Charles Cane) who begins to go into the tank for gamblers. Determined to save Knobby from dishonor, Palooka decides to go back into the ring, risking his eyesight but triumphing in a well-staged fight sequence. One of the better entries in the "Joe Palooka" series.

p, Hal E. Chester; d, Reginald Le Borg; w, John Bright, Monte Collins (based on a story by Ralph S. Lewis, Bernard D. Shamberg); ph, William Sickner; ed, Roy Livingston.

Boxing (PR:A MPAA:NR)

FIGHTING THOROUGHBREDS**½

(1939) 65m REP bw

Ralph Byrd *(Ben Marshall)*, Mary Carlisle *(Marian)*, Robert Allen *(Greg)*, George Hayes *(Gramp)*, Marvin Stephens *(Hefty)*, Charles Wilson *(Bogart)*, Kenne Duncan *(Brady)*, Victor Kilian *(Wilson)*, Eddie Brian *(Colton)*.

This neat horse-racing story mixes a feud and romantic conflict with fast action on the track when a Kentucky Derby winner, acting on his own instincts and without the knowledge of his owner, Bogart (Charles Wilson), sires a colt that becomes the possession of a fallen aristocrat (George Hayes) and his granddaughter Marian (Mary Carlisle). Bogart can't stand Marian and her grandfather and does his best to bring about their ruination, but his son (Robert Allen) has very different feelings. A laundry man and handsome young physician also play big roles in the proceedings, as the colt grows up to be a fine racehorse, and when the big day comes (the Derby, naturally), it is entered along with a horse belonging to (who else?) Bogart.

p, Armand Schaefer; d, Sidney Salkow; w, Wellyn Totman, Franklin Coen (based on a story by Clarence E. Marks, Robert Wyler); ph, Jack Marta; ed, Ernest Nims; m, Cy Feuer.

Horse Racing (PR:A MPAA:NR)

FIGHTING YOUTH**

(1935) 80m UNIV bw

Charles Farrell *(Larry Davis)*, June Martel *(Betty Wilson)*, Andy Devine *(Cy Kipp)*, J. Farrell MacDonald *(Coach Parker)*, Ann Sheridan *(Carol)*, Eddie Nugent *(Tonnetti)*,

Herman Bing *(Luigi)*, Phyllis Fraser *(Dodo)*, Alden Chase *(Markoff)*, Glenn Boles *(Paul)*, Charles Wilson *(Bull Stevens)*.

Radical youths bent on undermining the American Way have decided to begin by bringing down the state college football team, taking aim at its star quarterback, Larry Davis (Charles Farrell). Carol (Ann Sheridan), a particularly lovely provocateur, seduces Larry away from his loyal girl friend (June Martel), and as the All-American begins to indulge in the wild life, his performance on the gridiron plummets. However, true to formula, the pendulum swings back, and Farrell, though out of shape as a result of his deviant behavior, rushes back in the final three minutes of the season's last game to perform the usual heroics. Meanwhile, an undercover G-man (Eddie Nugent) who has been posing as a college student ensnares the radical group.

p, Fred S. Meyer; d, Hamilton Macfadden; w, Henry Johnson, Florabel Muir, Hamilton Macfadden (based on a story by Stanley Meyer); ph, Edward Snyder.

Football   **(PR:A   MPAA:NR)**

FINAL TEST, THE***

(1953, Brit.) 91m ACT Films/GFD bw

Jack Warner *(Sam Palmer)*, Robert Morley *(Alexander Whitehead)*, Brenda Bruce *(Cora)*, Ray Jackson *(Reggie Palmer)*, George Relph *(Syd Thompson)*, Adrianne Allen *(Aunt Ethel)*, Stanley Maxted *(Senator)*, Joan Swinstead *(Miss Fanshawe)*, Richard Bebb *(Frank Weller)*, Valentine Dyall *(Man In Black)*, Len Hutton *(Frank Jarvis)*.

Cricket, incomprehensible for most Americans but almost a religion for some Englishmen, is at the center of this entertaining, wry British comedy. Sam Palmer (Jack Warner), a legendary cricketer, prepares to play the last innings of his career for the English team as it takes on the Australians. His son, Reggie (Ray Jackson), an aspiring poet, wants to see the old man's final stand at the wicket but receives a conflicting invitation to the home of renowned poet Alexander Whitehead (Robert Morley), an offer he can't refuse. Everything works out for the best, though, when Whitehead turns out to be a great lover of the game, and he and Reggie rush off to the cricket ground. THE FINAL TEST features appearances by real-life cricketers Jim Laker, Alec Bedser, Denis Compton, Len Hutton, and Godfrey Evans.

p, R.J. Minney; d, Anthony Asquith; w, Terence Rattigan (based on his TV play); ph, Bill McLeod; ed, Helga Cranston; m, Benjamin Frankel.

Cricket   **(PR:A   MPAA:NR)**

FINNEY**½

(1969) 72m Gold Coast bw-c

Robert Kilcullen *(Jim Finney)*, Bill Levinson *(Billy Freeman)*, Joan Sundstrom *(Joyce Finney)*, Anthony Mockus, Dick Stanwood, Richy Hill, Dwight Lawrence, Jerry Kaufherr.

After being forced to retire from the Chicago Bears, defensive tackle Jim Finney (Robert Kilcullen) turns down a coaching job to pursue a career as an artist; however, his football-themed paintings are not accepted by the art world, and he ends up throwing his canvases into the Chicago River. His wife, a rising singer, leaves him, and, feeling depressed and rejected, with no one to turn to, he writes her a letter, receiving a publicity photo as his only reply. Much of the film consists of color football flashback sequences, with occasional returns to the black-and-white present wherein Finney tends bar. This well-photographed and -directed, but ultimately depressing, independent effort was producer-director-writer Bill Hare's first feature film.

p, Bill Hare; d, Bill Hare; w, Bill Hare; ph, Jack Richards; ed, Bill Hare; m, Dick Reynolds, Les Hooper, Eli Wolf.

Football   **(PR:A   MPAA:NR)**

FIREBALL, THE**

(1950) 83m Thor/FOX bw

Mickey Rooney *(Johnny Casar)*, Pat O'Brien *(Father O'Hara)*, Beverly Tyler *(Mary Reeves)*, James Brown *(Allen)*, Marilyn Monroe *(Polly)*, Ralph Dumke *(Bruno)*, Bert Begley *(Shilling)*, Milburn Stone *(Jeff Davis)*, Sam Flint *(Dr. Barton)*, John Hedloe *(Ullman)*, Glenn Corbett *(Mack Miller)*.

Roller derby was just getting started in the late 1940s and Hollywood was quick to jump on the bandwagon. Johnny Casar (Mickey Rooney) escapes from an orphanage run by Father O'Hara (you guessed it, Pat O'Brien) and meets Mary Reeves (Beverly Tyler), a skater who helps him land a spot on a roller derby team. Johnny soon becomes a crowd favorite, attracting the attention of Polly (Marilyn Monroe), a sexy star chaser, but as his ego and selfishness grow, he alienates his teammates. Predictably, character-building tragedy strikes when Johnny is knocked for a loop by polio, but Mary nurses him back to health and he returns to the track a new, considerably more generous man. Roller derby was later handled better in KANSAS CITY BOMBER (1972), but Rooney is a joy to watch and carries the film, challenging us to love him despite his bad attitude.

p, Bert Friedlob; d, Tay Garnett; w, Tay Garnett, Horace McCoy; ph, Lester White; ed, Frank Sullivan; m, Victor Young.

Roller Derby   **(PR:A   MPAA:NR)**

FIREBALL 500**

(1966) 91m AIP c

Frankie Avalon *(Dave)*, Annette Funicello *(Jane)*, Fabian *(Leander)*, Chill Wills *(Big Jaw)*, Harvey Lembeck *(Charlie Bigg)*, Julie Parrish *(Martha)*, Doug Henderson *(Hastings)*, Baynes Barron *(Bronson)*, Mike Nader *(Joey)*, Ed Garner *(Herman)*, Vin Scully, Sandy Reed *(Announcers)*, Sue Hamilton *(Farmer's Daughter)*, Renie Riano *(Herman's Wife)*, Len Lesser *(Man in Gorage)*, Billy Beck *(Jobber)*, Tex Armstrong *(Herman's Friend)*.

Frankie Avalon and Fabian play stock car drivers who spend their time away from the track competing for the affections of Annette Funicello. Bootleggers trick Dave (Avalon) into carrying their contraband during a cross-country race, but he gets wise and helps the Feds nail the culprits. Director William Asher, responsible for such films as MUSCLE BEACH PARTY (1964) and BEACH BLANKET BINGO (1965), offers up above-average teen-age fare with FIREBALL 500. Not surprisingly, the stars are able to find time to sing between car crashes and checkered flags.

p, Burt Topper, James H. Nicholson, Samuel Z. Arkoff; d, William Asher; w, William Asher, Leo Townsend; ph, Floyd Crosby (Panavision, Pathecolor); ed, Fred Feitshans, Eve Newman; m, Les Baxter.

Auto Racing (PR:A MPAA:NR)

FIREBALL JUNGLE**

(1968) 96m Americana c (AKA: JUNGLE TERROR)

Alan Mixon *(Cateye Meares)*, John Russell *(Nero Sagittarius)*, Lon Chaney, Jr. *(Junkyard Owner)*, Randy Kirby *(Steve Cullen)*, Chuck Daniel *(Marty)*, Nancy Donohue *(Ann Tracey)*, Vicki Nunis *(Judy)*, Billy Blueriver, Tiny Kennedy, Babs Beatty, Joie Chitwood, Ed Wisner, Candy Stebbins, Andrew Martinez, Pat Rast, Sharon Cramer, James LaRue.

Mobster Nero Sagittarius (John Russell) and his henchman Cateye Meares (Alan Mixon) bring some muscle to bear on the Southern stock-car circuit and *nobody* is going to stop them! Steve Cullen (Randy Kirby), whose brother was killed by Meares, thinks otherwise. Lots of cars are destroyed in the process, with some stunt driving by famed stock-car driver Joie Chitwood. Shot in and around Tampa, Florida, FIREBALL JUNGLE offers an opportunity to see Lon Chaney, Jr., go up in flames (if you like that kind of thing).

p, G.B. Roberts; d, Joseph Prieto; w, Harry Whittington; ph, Clifford Poland (Eastmancolor); ed, John Dalton.

Auto Racing (PR:C MPAA:NR)

FIREMAN, SAVE MY CHILD**½

(1932) 67m WB-FN bw

Joe E. Brown *(Joe Grant)*, Evalyn Knapp *(Sally)*, Lillian Bond *(June)*, George Meeker *(Stevens)*, Guy Kibbee *(Pop)*, George Ernest *(Mascot for St. Louis Team)*, Ben Hendricks, Jr. *(Larkin)*, Virginia Sale *(Miss Gallop)*, Frank Shallenbach *(Pitcher)*, Richard Carle *(Dan Toby)*, Louis Robinson *(Trainer)*, Curtis Benton *(Radio Announcer)*.

The first of three 1930s baseball comedies starring Joe E. Brown (see ELMER THE GREAT, 1933, and ALIBI IKE, 1935), FIREMAN, SAVE MY CHILD cast the former semi-pro player as Joe Grant, a firefighter in a small Kansas town who is also a diamond sensation. He pitches so well, in fact, that he lands a spot on the St. Louis Cardinals' roster, bringing with it the added distraction of team follower June (Lillian Bond), who threatens his romance with Jawhawk sweetheart Sally (Evalyn Knapp). Joe's main motivation, however, is to make enough money to complete work on an experimental fire extinguisher he hopes to patent, and he takes his field responsibilities with less than the utmost seriousness. By the frenetic comic climax however, he manages to squelch the Cards' World Series opponents as well as a raging office fire.

d, Lloyd Bacon; w, Lloyd Bacon, Robert Lord, Ray Enright, Arthur Caesar; ph, Sol Polito; ed, George Marks.

Baseball/Comedy (PR:A MPAA:NR)

FISH THAT SAVED PITTSBURGH, THE*½

(1979) 104m UA c

Julius Erving *(Moses Guthrie)*, Jonathan Winters *(H.S./Halsey Tilson)*, Meadowlark Lemon *(Rev. Grady Jackson)*, Jack Kehoe *(Setshot)*, Kareem Abdul-Jabbar *(Himself)*, Margaret Avery *(Toby Millman)*, James Bond III *(Tyrone Millman)*, Michael V. Gazzo *("Harry the Trainer")*, Peter Isacksen *("Driftwood")*, Nicholas Pryor *(George Brockington)*, M. Emmet Walsh *(Wally Cantrell)*, Stockard Channing *(Mona Mondieu)*, Flip Wilson *(Coach "Jock" Delaney)*, Marv Albert *(Himself)*, George Von Benko *(P.A. Announcer)*, Debra Allen *(Ola)*, Damian Austin *(Man Ordering)*, Alfred Beard, Jr. *(Himself)*, The Spinners, The Sylvers.

Julius Erving stars in this thinly plotted basketball comedy as Moses Guthrie, a mulitmillion-dollar player who is the only member of a fictitious Pittsburgh NBA franchise not to walk out on the team when it proves incapable of beating anyone. The water boy (James Bond III) suggests that the team recruit players whose astrological signs are the same as that of Moses, and after an astrologer (Stockard Channing) is consulted, the ranks of the Pittsburgh team are filled with Pisces. Suddenly, they start winning games (as if you couldn't guess). Dr. J. does his best in his underdeveloped role, and Harlem Globetrotter Meadowlark Lemon and Laker great Kareem Abdul Jabbar also appear, but, long on disco music and short on humor, THE FISH THAT SAVED PITTSBURGH is about as entertaining and memorable as a sports celebrity Miller Lite commercial.

p, Gary Stromberg, David Dashev; d, Gilbert Moses; w, Jaison Starkes, Edmond Stevens (based on a story by Gary Stromberg, David Dashev); ph, Frank Stanley (Technicolor); ed, Frank Mazolla, Arthur Schmidt, Bud Friedgen, Jr.; m, Thom Bell.

Basketball Cas. (PR:AA MPAA:PG)

FLESH***

(1932) 95m MGM bw

Wallace Beery *(Polikai)*, Karen Morley *(Lora)*, Ricardo Cortez *(Nicky)*, Jean Hersholt *(Mr. Herman)*, John Miljan *(Joe Willard)*, Vince Barnett *(Waiter)*, Herman Bing *(Pepi)*, Greta Meyer *(Mrs. Herman)*, Ed Brophy *(Dolan)*, Ward Bond, Nat Pendleton.

There have been many movies made about wrestling since this effort by John Ford, but few come close to the feeling generated by the actors here, particularly Wallace

Beery, playing a sweet-natured German grappler who is taken advantage of by a pair of ex-convicts. Sexy Lora (Karen Morley) persuades Polikai (Beery) to secure the prison release of her lover, Nicky (Ricardo Cortez), who she claims is her brother. When Lora becomes pregnant, Nicky disappears, and Polikai and Lora are married and emigrate to the US, where Polikai, already the German champion, becomes the world title holder. In short order, Nicky reappears, becomes Polikai's manager, and tries to get him to throw matches. However, when Nicky makes the mistake of striking Lora, Polikai kills him and is incarcerated. The three leads are excellent in demanding roles: playing a different kind of CHAMP, Beery is totally believable, German accent and all; Morley makes us like her despite her duplicity; and Cortez lends just the right amount of charm to his despicable cad.

d, John Ford; w, Moss Hart, Leonard Praskins, Edgar Allen Woolf (based on a story by Edmund Goulding); ph, Arthur Edeson; ed, William Gray.

Wrestling (PR:C MPAA:NR)

FLESH AND FURY**½

(1952) 82m UNIV bw

Tony Curtis (Paul Callan), Jan Sterling (Sonya Bartow), Mona Freeman (Ann Hollis), Wallace Ford (Jack Richardson), Connie Gilchrist (Mrs. Richardson), Katherine Locke (Mrs. Hollis), Joe Gray (Cliff), Ron Hargrave (Al Logan), Harry Guardino (Lou Callan), Harry Shannon (Mike Callan), Harry Raven (Murph), Ted Stanhope (Whitey), Louis Jean Heydt (Andy Randolph), Nella Walker (Mrs. Hackett), Ken Patterson (Dr. Lester), Virginia Gregg (Claire), Grace Hayle (Mrs. Bien), Harry Cheshire (Dr. Gundling), Tommy Farrell (Rocky), George Eldredge (Dr. Buell).

Tony Curtis plays a deaf-mute prizefighter who is moving up quickly in the rankings when he falls hard for a singer (Jan Sterling) who sees him as nothing more than a meal ticket. A pretty journalist (Mona Freeman) recognizes that he's much more than just a potential champion and helps him get an operation that restores his hearing, which he loses again during the title match, but regains after realizing which of the two women is really right for him (you guess). Good production values, strong performances, and some wry social commentary combine to make FLESH AND FURY an entertaining fight film.

p, Leonard Goldstein; d, Joseph Pevney; w, Bernard Gordon (based on a story by William Alland); ph, Irving Glassberg; ed, Virgil Vogel; m, Hans J. Salter.

Boxing (PR:A MPAA:NR)

FLYING FIFTY-FIVE*

(1939, Brit.) 72m Admiral/RKO bw

Derrick de Marney (Bill Urquhart), Nancy Burne (Stella Barrington), Marius Goring (Charles Barrington), John Warwick (Jebson), Peter Gawthorne (Jonas Urquhart), D.A. Clarke-Smith (Jacques Gregory), Amy Veness (Aunt Eliza), Ronald Shiner (Scrubby Oaks), Billy Bray

(Cheerful), Francesca Bahrle (Clare), Victor Wark, Terence Conlin, John "Skins" Miller, Norman Pierce.

After quarreling with his horse owner father, Bill Urquhart (Derrick De Marney) takes a job in the stables owned by Stella Barrington (Nancy Burne) and enters the big race on a horse that only allows him behind the reins. Ignoring a blackmail threat to throw the race, Bill wins on a technicality and later weds Stella. Don't bet on this one to win, place, or show.

p, Victor M. Greene; d, Reginald Denham; w, Victor M. Greene, Vernon Clancey, Kenneth Horne (based on the novel by Edgar Wallace); ph, Ernest Palmer.

Boxing (PR:A MPAA:NR)

FLYING FISTS, THE**

(1938) 63m Victory bw

Herman Brix (Hal Donovan), Jeanne Martel (Kay Conrad), Fuzzy Knight (Spider), J. Farrell MacDonald (Kay's Father), Guinn "Big Boy" Williams (Slug Cassidy), Dickie Jones (Dickie), Charles Williams (Meggs).

Olympic shot-putter and one-time screen Tarzan Herman Brix (better known as Bruce Bennett) plays a boxer who falls in love with a lass who doesn't think much of the prizefight game. She whistles a different tune, however, when her father is in financial trouble and Hal (Brix) returns to the ring to bail him out, battling not only his opponent, but also the thugs who have fixed the match.

d, Bob Hill; w, Basil Dickey (based on a story by Rock Hawkey); ph, Bill Hyer.

Boxing (PR:A MPAA:NR)

FOLLOW THE SUN**½

(1951) 93m FOX bw

Glenn Ford (Ben Hogan), Anne Baxter (Valerie Hogan), Dennis O'Keefe (Chuck Williams), June Havoc (Norma), Larry Keating (Jay Dexter), Roland Winters (Dr. Graham), Nana Bryant (Sister Beatrice), Sam Snead (Himself), James Demaret (Himself), Dr. Cary Middlecoff (Himself), Harold Blake (Ben Hogan, Age 14), Ann Burr (Valerie, Age 14), Harmon Stevens (Mr. Johnson), Louise Lorimer (Mrs. Clinton), Harry Antrim (Dr. Everett), Homer Welborne (Announcer), William Janssen (Major), William Forrest (General), Gil Herman (Sportswriter), Jewel Rose (Nurse), Beverlee White (Gertrude), Emmett Vogan (Temporary Chairman), Grantland Rice (Toastmaster), James Flavin (Henry Gibbs), Myrtle Anderson (Grace), Esther Somers (Mrs. Edwards), Al Demaret (Golf Pro), Warren Stevens (Radio Announcer).

If you like golf, you'll enjoy this story of one of the game's great players, Ben Hogan (essayed here by Glenn Ford). If not, FOLLOW THE SUN is still a pleasant biography of a man who finds the inner strength to overcome a debilitating injury and courageously resume his career. After an impoverished Texas childhood, caddy champion Hogan joins the pro tour, accompanied by his always supportive wife, Valerie (Anne Baxter). Lean times give way to success, but just when Hogan's career is flying high, he is involved in a near-fatal automobile crash. The rest of the film deals with his recovery, culminating in his LA Open playoff battle with Sam Snead, who plays himself, as do golfing greats Cary Middlecoff and James Demaret. Legendary sportswriter Grantland Rice also has a role. Author Frederick Hazlitt Brennan adapted his own magazine article for the screenplay, showing great sensitivity, and Ford does a fine job in a revealing portrayal of Hogan.

p, Samuel G. Engel; d, Sidney Lanfield; w, Frederick Hazlitt Brennan (based on his article in *Reader's Digest*); ph, Leo Tover; ed, Barbara McLean; m, Cyril J. Mockridge.

Golf/Biography **(PR:A MPAA:NR)**

FOLLOW THRU**½

(1930) 93m PAR c

Charles Rogers *(Jerry Downs)*, Nancy Carroll *(Lora Moore)*, Zelma O'Neal *(Angie Howard)*, Jack Haley *(Jack Martin)*, Eugene Pallette *(J.C. Effingham)*, Thelma Todd *(Ruth Van Horn)*, Claude King *(Mac Moore)*, Kathryn Givney *(Mrs. Bascomb)*, Margaret Lee *(Babs Bascomb)*, Don Tomkins *(Dinty Moore)*, Albert Gran *(Martin Bascomb)*.

Based on an immensely popular Broadway show and photographed in vivid two-color Technicolor, this entertaining early musical is set at a golf course, where pretty Lora Moore (Nancy Carroll), smitten with Jerry Downs (Charles Rogers), allows the latter to help her refine her game. Her longtime rival, Ruth Van Horn (Thelma Todd), is also interested in Jerry and begins telling tales in an attempt to disrupt the growing romance between teacher and pupil. Enraged, Lora challenges Ruth to 18 holes, but without Jerry's support she plays terribly—until Jerry's timely appearance for the final hole, that is. Carroll swings a golf club as impressively as she sings tunes by the likes of Buddy De Sylva, Lew Brown, and Ray Henderson; and Jack Haley, in his film debut, re-creates his Broadway role as a timid millionaire.

p, Laurence Schwab, Frank Mandel; d, Laurence Schwab, Lloyd Corrigan; w, Laurence Schwab, Lloyd Corrigan (based on the play by Laurence Schwab, B.G. DeSylva, Ray Henderson, Lew Brown); ph, Charles B. Boyle, Henry Gerrard (2color Technicolor); ed, Alyson Shasser.

Golf **(PR:A MPAA:NR)**

FORTUNE COOKIE, THE****

(1966) 125m Mirisch/UA bw (GB: MEET WHIPLASH WILLIE)

Jack Lemmon *(Harry Hinkle)*, Walter Matthau *(Willie Gingrich)*, Ron Rich *(Luther "Boom Boom" Jackson)*, Cliff Osmond *(Mr. Purkey)*, Judi West *(Sandy Hinkle)*, Lurene Tuttle *(Mother Hinkle)*, Harry Holcombe *(O'Brien)*, Les Tremayne *(Thompson)*, Marge Redmond *(Charlotte Gingrich)*, Noam Pitlik *(Max)*, Harry Davis *(Dr. Krugman)*, Ann Shoemaker *(Sister Veronica)*, Maryesther Denver *(Nurse)*, Lauren Gilbert *(Kincaid)*, Ned Glass *(Doc Schindler)*, Sig Rumann *(Prof. Winterhalter)*, Archie Moore *(Mr. Jackson)*,

Dodie Heath *(Nun)*, Herbie Faye *(Maury)*, Howard McNear *(Mr. Cimoli)*, Bill Christopher *(Intern)*, Judy Pace *(Elvira)*.

One of the funniest sports films ever, this morality tale is a deft mixture of cynicism, wit, and idealism as only director Billy Wilder could do it. While working the sidelines during a Browns-Vikings game in Cleveland (where much of the picture was filmed), cameraman Harry Hinkle (Jack Lemmon) is flattened by Browns running back Luther "Boom Boom" Jackson (Ron Rich) and rushed to the hospital. Although Harry is fine, his shyster brother-in-law, "Whiplash Willie" Gingrich (Walter Matthau), convinces him to fake an injury and sue the Browns, CBS, and Municipal Stadium for $1 million. Pretending to be paralyzed from the neck down and relying on an old spinal injury for X-ray proof, Harry fools a team of doctors and, under Willie's supervision, continues to deceive private investigator Purkey (Cliff Osmond), who spies on his apartment. In the meantime, Harry's wife, Sandy (Judi West), a would-be singer who ran off with another guy, returns, anxious to get in on the gravy train. Boom Boom, on the other hand, is consumed with guilt, and nurses Harry and a bottle as his football career goes into a tailspin. Just when Harry is about to become a rich man, Purkey makes some racist remarks about Boom Boom, and Harry literally swings into action en route to the upbeat finale under the lights of Municipal Stadium. Both Lemmon and Matthau—who won a Best Actor Oscar for his "Barber of Seville"-humming ambulance chaser—are superb; so are Wilder and I.A.L. Diamond's script and Joseph LaShelle's cinematography, both of which were nominated for Academy Awards. Rich's Boom Boom is a bit too noble, but his relationship with Harry is still touching, and despite some minor flaws THE FORTUNE COOKIE is a thoroughly satisfying film.

p, Billy Wilder; d, Billy Wilder; w, Billy Wilder, I.A.L. Diamond; ph, Joseph LaShelle (Panavision); ed, Daniel Mandell; m, Andre Previn.

Football/Comedy/Drama **Cas.** **(PR:A-C MPAA:NR)**

FOUR AGAINST FATE**

(1952, Brit.) 84m BL bw (GB: DERBY DAY)

Anna Neagle *(Lady Helen Forbes)*, Michael Wilding *(David Scott)*, Googie Withers *(Betty Molloy)*, John McCallum *(Tommy Dillon)*, Peter Graves *(Gerald Berkeley)*, Suzanne Cloutier *(Michele Jolivet)*, Gordon Harker *(Joe Jenkins)*, Gladys Henson *(Gladys)*, Ralph Reader *(Bill Hammond)*, Alfie Bass *(Spider Wilkes)*, Edwin Styles *(Sir George Forbes)*, Nigel Stock *(Jim Molloy)*, Arthur Hambling *(Col. Tremaine)*, Myrette Morven *(Mrs. Tremaine)*, Toni Edgar-Bruce *(Mrs. Harbottle-Smith)*, Richard Wattis *(Editor)*, Raymond Glendenning *(Commentator)*, Josephine Fitzgerald, Ewan Roberts, Leslie Weston, H.R. Hignett, Robert Brown, Gerald Anderson, Sam Kydd, Hugh Moxey.

Tracing three separate story lines, this episodic horse racing film transpires over a few hours at the track. A maid (Suzanne Cloutier) wins a raffle and is escorted to the races by her favorite film star (Peter Graves), a man and a woman (Michael Wilding and Anna Neagle) find solace with each other after both have lost loved ones in a plane crash, and a couple (Googie Withers and John McCallum) is arrested for murder while at the window collecting their winnings.

p, Herbert Wilcox, Maurice Cowan; d, Herbert Wilcox; w, Monckton Hoffe, John Baines, Alan Melville (based on a story by Arthur Austie); ph, Max Greene; ed, Bill Lewthwaite.

Horse Racing (PR:A MPAA:NR)

FRESHMAN, THE****

(1925) 7 reels   Harold Lloyd/Pathe Exchange bw

Harold Lloyd *(Harold "Speedy" Lamb)*, Jobyna Ralston *(Peggy)*, Brooks Benedict *(College Cad)*, James Anderson *(Chester A. "Chet" Trask)*, Hazel Keener *(College Belle)*, Joseph Harrington *(College Tailor)*, Pat Harmon *(The Coach)*, Charles Stevenson *(Assistant Coach)*, Oscar Smith *(The Dean's Chauffeur)*.

Harold Lloyd stars in this uproariously funny silent classic as "Speedy" Lamb, a reedy, bespectacled freshman who arrives at Tate College determined to become a campus hero, but who takes his behavioral cues from a "bad" college movie he watched before matriculating. As a result he becomes an easy target for ridicule, and when he attempts to make the football team, the coach decides he's best suited to be a blocking dummy. The big game rolls around and Speedy is on the sidelines—as the water boy—but injuries so deplete the Tate lineup that he is allowed to enter the game. As the final seconds tick away, Speedy saunters toward the goal line, but at the last moment it looks as if fate is going to prevent him from finally becoming a hero. Fat chance. Some of THE FRESHMAN's football sequences were used at the beginning of its 1947 sequel, THE SIN OF HAROLD DIDDLEBOCK (aka MAD WEDNESDAY). Lloyd also starred as a milquetoast milkman-turned-boxer in another fine sports film, THE MILKY WAY (1936).

d, Sam Taylor, Fred Newmeyer; w, John Grey, Ted Wilde, Tim Wheelan, Sam Taylor, Clyde Bruckman, Lex Neal, Jean Havez, Brooks B. Harding; ph, Walter Lundin, Henry Kohler; ed, Allen McNeil.

Football/Comedy (PR:A MPAA:NR)

FRESHMAN LOVE**

(1936) 65m WB bw (GB: RHYTHM ON THE RIVER)

Frank McHugh *(Coach Hammond)*, Patricia Ellis *(Joan Simpkins)*, Warren Hull *(Bob Wilson)*, Joe Cawthorn *(Wilson, Sr.)*, George E. Stone *(E. Prendergast Biddle)*, Mary Treen *(Squirmy)*, Henry O'Neill *(Pres. Simpkins)*, Alma Lloyd *(Sandra)*, Anita Kerry *(Princess Oggi)*, Johnny Arthur *(Fields)*, Walter Johnson *(Tony Foster)*, Joseph Sawyer *(Coach Kendall)*, Florence Fair *(Mrs. Norton)*, Spec O'Donnell *(Eddie)*.

This silly campus comedy concerns the efforts of crew coach Hammond (Frank McHugh) to keep his job by pushing his team to the limit, even though he is constantly frustrated by Joan Simpkins (Patricia Ellis), a beautiful gal who keeps luring his husky oarsmen away from practice. Hammond manages to turn the tables, however, by including a sexy photo of Joan in the letters he sends to rowers from other schools, encouraging them to enroll in his college. Finally, E. Prendergast Biddle (George E. Stone), a bandleader, is recruited as the coxswain, and the jazz beat that he introduces to the striving oarsmen is just what they need to pull off a big win. Harmless fun with a few good jazz tunes to liven things up.

p, Bryan Foy; d, William McGann; w, Earl Felton, George Bricker (based on a story by George Ade); ph, Sid Hickox; ed, James Gibbons; m, M.K. Jerome.

Crew/Comedy (PR:A MPAA:NR)

FROM HELL TO HEAVEN**½

(1933) 67m PAR bw

Carole Lombard *(Colly Tanner)*, Jack Oakie *(Charlie Bayne)*, Adrienne Ames *(Joan Burt)*, David Manners *(Wesley Burt)*, Sidney Blackmer *(Cuff Billings)*, Verna Hillie *(Sonny Lockwood)*, James Eagles *(Tommy Tucker)*, Shirley Grey *(Winnie Lloyd)*, Bradley Page *(Jack Ruby)*, Walter Walker *(Pop Lockwood)*, Berton Churchill *(Toledo Jones)*, Donald Kerr *(Steve Wells)*, Nydia Westman *(Sue Wells)*, Cecil Cunningham *(Mrs. Chadman)*, Thomas Jackson *(Lynch)*, Allen Wood *(Pepper Murphy)*.

Derivative of GRAND HOTEL, this racetrack film relates the many stories of the gamblers, horse owners, and racing enthusiasts who gather at the Luray Springs Hotel to await the Capitol Handicap. Center stage, however, is Colly Tanner (Carole Lombard), a pretty handicapper who needs $10,000 to bet on a sure thing and gets it from an old flame, Cuff Billings (Sidney Blackmer), on the condition that if her horse loses she give herself to him. Her horse, Sir Rapid, comes in third, but Cuff proves to be an honorable man, leading to a surprising romantic finale. Even though this is not one of Lombard's best efforts, FROM HELL TO HEAVEN wouldn't have even finished in the money were it not for her ebullient talents.

d, Erle Kenton; w, Percy Heath, Sidney Buchman (based on a story by Lawrence Hazard); ph, Henry Sharp.

Horse Racing (PR:C MPAA:NR)

GAME THAT KILLS, THE*½

(1937) 55m COL bw

Charles Quigley *(Alec Ferguson)*, Rita Hayworth *(Betty Holland)*, John Gallaudet *(Sam Erskine)*, J. Farrell MacDonald *(Joe Holland)*, Arthur Loft *(Rudy Maxwell)*, John Tyrrell *(Eddie)*, Paul Fix *(Dick Adams)*, Max Hoffman, Jr. *(Bill Drake)*, Dick Wessel *(Leapfrog Soule)*, Maurice Black *(Jeff)*, Clyde Dilson *(Steve Moran)*, Harry Strang *(Walter)*,

Dick Curtis *(Whitey)*, Lee Prather *(Bronson)*, Jack Dougherty, Edmund Cobb *(Cops)*, Ralph Dunn *(Detective)*.

Alec Ferguson (Charles Quigley) joins a professional hockey team to find out who was responsible for the faked rink accident that resulted in his brother's death. Rita Hayworth, in one of her first major screen roles, plays the daughter of the team's trainer. There's no reason to stay up if this one comes on the Late Show.

d, D. Ross Lederman; w, Grace Neville, Fred Niblo Jr. (based on a story by J. Benton Cheney); ph, Benjamin Kline; ed, James Sweeney; m, Morris Stoloff.

Hockey   **(PR:A   MPAA:NR)**

GAMES, THE**

(1970) 95m FOX c

Michael Crawford *(Harry Hayes)*, Stanley Baker *(Bill Oliver)*, Ryan O'Neal *(Scott Reynolds)*, Charles Aznavour *(Pavel Vendek)*, Jeremy Kemp *(Jim Harcourt)*, Elaine Taylor *(Christine)*, Athol Compton *(Sunny Pintubi)*, Fritz Wepper *(Kovanda)*, Kent Smith *(Kaverley)*, Sam Elliott *(Richie Robinson)*, Reg Lye *(Gilmour)*, Mona Washbourne *(Mrs. Hayes)*, Don Newsome *(Cal Wood)*, Emmy Werner *(Vera Vendek)*, Harvey Hall *(Stuart Simmonds)*, June Jago *(Mae Harcourt)*, Karel Stepanek *(Kubitsek)*, Gwendolyn Watts *(Barmaid)*, John Alkin *(John)*, Rafer Johnson, Rod Pickering, Adrian Metcalfe *(Commentators)*, Bob Cunningham *(Fred Gardner)*, Paddy Webster *(Jocelyn)*, Tina Carter *(Miss Gibb)*, Stephanie Beacham *(Angela Simmonds)*.

A sort of CHARIOTS OF FIRE for distance runners, THE GAMES follows four marathoners from different countries as they prepare to compete in the Rome Olympics, chronicling the obstacles each must overcome to get there. The American hopeful, Yalie Scott Reynolds (Ryan O'Neal), is a ladies man with a delicate heart condition; British milkman Harry Hayes (Michael Crawford) is trained by a hard-driving former track star (Stanley Baker) whose intense feelings for his young charge are tinged with homoeroticism; Pavel Vendek (Charles Aznavour), a 41-year-old Czech former champion, is called upon to try to recapture his past glory; while down under, a fleet-footed Aborigine, Sunny Pintubi (Athol Compton), strives against the restraints of second-class citizenship.

p, Lester Linsk; d, Michael Winner; w, Eric Segal (based on a novel by Hugh Atkinson); ph, Robert Paynter (Panavision, DeLuxe Color); ed, Bernard Gribble; m, Francis Lai.

Track and Field   **(PR:A   MPAA:G)**

GENTLEMAN JIM****

(1942) 104m WB-FN bw

Errol Flynn *(James J. Corbett)*, Alexis Smith *(Victoria Ware)*, Jack Carson *(Walter Lowrie)*, Alan Hale, Sr. *(Pat Corbett)*, John Loder *(Clinton DeWitt)*, William Frawley *(Billy Delaney)*, Minor Watson *(Buck Ware)*, Ward Bond *(John L. Sullivan)*, Madeleine LeBeau *(Anna Held)*, Rhys Williams *(Harry Watson)*, Arthur Shields *(Father Burke)*,

Dorothy Vaughn *(Ma Corbett)*, James Flavin *(George Corbett)*, Pat Flaherty *(Harry Corbett)*, Wallis Clark *(Judge Geary)*, Marilyn Phillips *(Mary Corbett)*, Art Foster *(Jack Burke)*, Edwin Stanley *(President McInnes)*, Henry O'Hara *(Colis Huntington)*, Harry Crocker *(Charles Crocker)*, Frank Mayo *(Gov. Stanford)*, Carl Harbaugh *(Smith)*, Fred Kelsey *(Sutro)*, Sammy Stein *(Joe Choynski)*, Charles Wilson *(Gurney)*, Jean Del Val *(Renaud)*, William B. Davidson *(Donovan)*, Mike Mazurki *(Jake Kilrain)*, Frank Hagney *(Mug)*, Wee Willie Davis *(Flannagan)*.

Errol Flynn's colorful temperament, capricious moods, and daring nature were perfect for the role of James J. Corbett, the brash Irish bank clerk from San Francisco who went on to defeat John L. Sullivan (nicely essayed by Ward Bond) for the heavyweight championship of the world in New Orleans in 1892. As Gentleman Jim's reputation grows, so does his ego, but in the fine scene wherein Sullivan presents Corbett with the championship belt, Corbett displays a heretofore unseen humility that finally wins the heart of the patrician woman he loves (Alexis Smith). The bout in which Corbett matches his "scientific" boxing techniques against the toe-to-toe slugging of Sullivan is particularly winning (with Ed "Strangler" Lewis doubling for Bond and one-time light champion Freddie Steele doubling for Flynn), but director Raoul Walsh is firmly in control throughout, and GENTLEMAN JIM is one of the best sports biopics ever. Warner Bros. pulled out all the stops for the production, using their largest facilities for the crowd scenes and employing the enormous SEA HAWK ship stage and huge tank to represent the San Francisco Bay for one fight. Flynn was physically ideal for the role of Corbett—a dashing 6-foot-1-inch 178 pounder who went on to a successful stage and silent screen career—however, due to heart problems, the naturally right-handed Flynn, who trained with former welterweight Mushy Callahan to effectively simulate Corbett's famous left jab, could only work for a minute at a time during the boxing sequences, which prove amazingly realistic anyway.

p, Robert Buckner; d, Raoul Walsh; w, Vincent Lawrence, Horace McCoy (based on the autobiography *The Roar of the Crowd* by James J. Corbett); ph, Sid Hickox; ed, Jack Killifer; m, Heinz Roemheld.

Boxing/Biography   Cas.   (PR:A   MPAA:NR)

GIRL FROM MONTEREY, THE**

(1943) 69m PRC bw

Armida *(Lita)*, Edgar Kennedy *(Doc Hogan)*, Veda Ann Borg *(Flossie)*, Jack LaRue *(Johnson)*, Terry Frost *(Jerry O'Leary)*, Anthony Caruso *(Baby)*, Charles Williams *(Harry)*, Bryant Washburn *(Commissioner)*, Guy Zanette *(Perrone)*, Wheeler Oakman *(Announcer)*.

A mediocre boxing romance-musical, THE GIRL FROM MONTEREY stars Armida as the manager-sister of a boxer known as Baby (Anthony Caruso) who is scheduled to fight Jerry O'Leary (Terry Frost). The trouble is she doesn't want the match to take place because she's in love with O'Leary. To make matters worse, O'Leary's crooked manager hires a bombshell (Veda Ann Borg) to seduce Baby and keep him from training so that the fight will be a cake-walk. Luckily, all the dishonest dealings are revealed to the boxing commission at the last minute and nobody gets hurt.

p, Jack Schwarz; d, Wallace Fox; w, Arthur Hoerl (based on an original story by George Green, Robert Gordon); ph, Marcel Le Picard; ed, Robert Crandall.

Boxing/Musical (PR:A MPAA:NR)

GLORY**

(1955) 99m David Butler/RKO c

Margaret O'Brien *(Clarabel Tilbee)*, Walter Brennan *(Ned Otis)*, Charlotte Greenwood *(Miz Tilbee)*, John Lupton *(Chad Chadburn)*, Byron Palmer *(Hoppy Hollis)*, Lisa Davis *(Candy Trent)*, Gus Schilling *(Joe Page)*, Theron Jackson *(Alexander)*, Hugh Sanders *(Sobbing Sam Cooney)*, Walter Baldwin *(Doc Brock)*, Harry Tyler *(Beed Wickwire)*, Leonid Kinskey *(Vasily)*, Paul Burns *(Squeaky Bob)*, Madge Blade *(Aunt Martha)*.

Set in the Blue Grass state (where else?), this overlong and predictable racetrack film focuses on Clarabel Tilbee (grown-up child star Margaret O'Brien) and her grandmother (Charlotte Greenwood), who can't raise the money to buy feed but somehow come up with the funds to enter their horse in the Kentucky Derby. Can you guess who wins?

p, David Butler; d, David Butler; w, Peter Milne (based on a story by Gene Markey); ph, Wilfrid M. Cline (Superscope, Technicolor); ed, Irene Morra; m, Frank Perkins.

Horse Racing (PR:AA MPAA:NR)

GLORY ALLEY**

(1952) 79m MGM bw

Ralph Meeker *(Socks Barbarrosa)*, Leslie Caron *(Angela)*, Kurt Kasznar *(The Judge)*, Gilbert Roland *(Peppi Donnato)*, John McIntire *(Gabe Jordan)*, Louis Armstrong *(Shadow Johnson)*, Jack Teagarden *(Himself)*, Dan Seymour *(Sal Nichols)*, Larry Gates *(Dr. Robert Ardley)*, Pat Golding *(Jabber)*, John Indrisano *(Spider)*, Mickey Little *(Domingo)*, Dick Simmons *(Dan)*.

On the eve of his attempt to win the championship, promising middleweight Socks Barbarrosa (Ralph Meeker) panics and disappears, disappointing his neighbors on the New Orleans Latin Quarter street known as Glory Alley, particularly the blind father (Kurt Kasznar) of his dancer girl friend, Angela (Leslie Caron). Socks then fights in the Korean War, earning the Congressional Medal of Honor, but though Angela has never doubted his courage, the others in the Alley still do, and it is only after Socks reenters the ring and wins the crown that they finally believe in him again. Caron's steamy rendition of "St. Louis Blues," accompanied by Louis Armstrong, is a highlight, but in general this weak psychological film is not up to the usually high standards of director Raoul Walsh.

p, Nicholas Nayfack; d, Raoul Walsh; w, Art Cohn; ph, William Daniels; ed, Gene Ruggiero.

Boxing (PR:C MPAA:NR)

GO, MAN, GO!***

(1954) 82m UA bw

Dane Clark *(Abe Saperstein)*, Pat Breslin *(Sylvia Saperstein)*, Sidney Poitier *(Inman Jackson)*, Edmon Ryan *(Zack Leader)*, Bram Nossen *(James Willoughby)*, Anatol Winogradoff *(Papa Saperstein)*, Celia Boodkin *(Mama Saperstein)*, Carol Sinclair *(Fay Saperstein)*, Ellsworth Wright *(Sam)*, Slim Gaillard *(Slim)*, Mort Marshall *(Master of Ceremonies)*, Marty Glickman, Bill Stern *(Announcers)*, Lew Hearn *(Appraiser)*, Ruby Dee *(Ima Jackson)*, Harlem Globetrotters *(Themselves)*.

Following on the heels of THE HARLEM GLOBETROTTERS (1951), GO, MAN, GO!—the second film to feature and focus on the legendary all-black basketball team—tells the story of the Trotters' beginnings. When Abe Saperstein (Dane Clark) encounters a group of talented black players, he becomes determined to give them the opportunity to show what they can do, organizes the team, and takes it barnstorming from small town to small town. In the big finale, the Globetrotters are matched against a powerhouse white team and more than rise to the challenge. Although never explicitly stated, the struggle for civil rights is at the heart of GO, MAN, GO!, and the deep friendship that develops between Saperstein and his wife and one of his players, Inman Jackson (Sidney Poitier), and his wife (Ruby Dee) is surely intended as a lesson for segregated America. Directed by renowned cameraman James Wong Howe, this interesting film includes plenty of footage of the Trotters in action and explains the origins of their trademark trickery: forced by financial constraints to travel with few substitutes, the Trotters would periodically have one player showboat while the others rested, with the clock still running. Not surprisingly, "Sweet Georgia Brown" is prominently featured.

p, Anton M. Leader; d, James Wong Howe; w, Arnold Becker; ph, Phil Steiner; ed, Faith Elliott; m, Alex North.

Basketball (PR:A MPAA:NR)

GOLDEN BOY****

(1939) 99m COL bw

Barbara Stanwyck *(Lorna Moon)*, Adolphe Menjou *(Tom Moody)*, William Holden *(Joe Bonaparte)*, Lee J. Cobb *(Mr. Bonaparte)*, Joseph Calleia *(Eddie Fuseli)*, Sam Levene *(Siggie)*, Edward Brophy *(Roxy Lewis)*, Beatrice Blinn *(Anna)*, William H. Strauss *(Mr. Carp)*, Don Beddoe *(Borneo)*, Frank Jenks *(Boxer)*, Charles Halton *(Newspaperman)*, John Wray *(Manager-Barker)*, James "Cannonball" Green *(Chocolate Drop)*, Thomas Garland *(Fighter)*, Charles Lane *(Drake)*, Harry Tyler *(Mickey)*, Stanley Andrews *(Driscoll)*, Clinton Rosemond *(Father)*, Minerva Urecal *(Costumer)*, Eddie Fetherston *(Wilson)*.

Although not strictly faithful to Clifford Odets' powerful play, GOLDEN BOY nonetheless captures its spirit of proletarian angst, propelled by the extraordinary performances of Barbara Stanwyck and William Holden in his first major role. Joe Bonaparte (Holden), a gifted violinist, is forced by poverty to enter the ring, where he proves to be a talented boxer even though he seemingly pulls his punches, afraid of damaging his musician's hands and ending the dream for which his immigrant father (Lee J. Cobb) has sacrificed so much. Lorna Moon (Stanwyck), the girl friend of Joe's manager (Adolphe Menjou), is given the task of persuading Joe to give up his musical aspirations. After falling in love with Lorna and then feeling betrayed by her duplicity, Joe returns to the ring, with tragic results. He wins, but at what cost? Still, the film manages to reveal a silver-lined ending that is far more upbeat than Odets' suicide finale. Just the same, Rouben Mamoulian does a wonderful job of retaining the essential story and basic character, building beautifully upon both through his careful scenes, and his direction of the brutal but realistic fight scenes adds much to the film's power. Menjou and Cobb offer excellent support, but this film belongs to Stanwyck and to Holden, the 21-year-old unknown who was chosen for the part over John Garfield (who did the role in the original Group Theater production), Elia Kazan, Robert Taylor, Robert Cummings, Tyrone Power, Henry Fonda, and Richard Carlson.

p, William Perlberg; d, Rouben Mamoulian; w, Lewis Meltzer, Daniel Taradash, Sarah Y. Mason, Victor Heerman (based on the play by Clifford Odets); ph, Nicholas Musuraca, Karl Freund; ed, Otto Meyer; m, Victor Young.

Boxing   Cas.   (PR:A   MPAA:NR)

GOLDEN GLOVES**

(1940) 66m PAR bw

Richard Denning (Bill Crane), Jean Cagney (Mary Parker), J. Carrol Naish (Joe Taggerty), Robert Paige (Wally Matson), William Frawley (Emory Balzar), Edward S. Brophy (Potsy Brill), Robert Ryan (Pete Wells), George Ernest (Joey Parker), David Durand (Gumdrop Wilbur), James Seay (Jimmy), Sidney Miller (Sammy Sachs), Alec Craig (MacDonald).

When sportswriter Wally Matson (Robert Paige) sets up an unsullied boxing tournament to compete with the corrupt professional game, no-good Joe Taggerty (J. Carrol Naish) bribes Pete Wells (Robert Ryan), a professional fighter, to enter and ruin the competition. Virtue triumphs, however, when Wells' opponent, Bill Crane (Richard Denning), defeats him, inspired by the pretty Mary Parker (Jean Cagney, you know who's sister). In an attempt to cash in on the growing popularity of amateur boxing, this film was released with a short, GOLDEN GLOVES. Ryan, who makes one of his first film appearances here, boxed collegiately at Dartmouth.

d, Edward Dmytryk; w, Maxwell Shane, Lewis Foster (based on a story by Shane); ph, Henry Sharp; ed, Doanne Harrison.

Boxing   (PR:A   MPAA:NR)

GOLDEN GLOVES STORY, THE**

(1950) 76m EL bw

James Dunn (Joe Riley), Dewey Martin (Nick Martel), Gregg Sherwood (Iris Anthony), Kevin O'Morrison (Bob Gilmore), Kay Westfall (Patti Riley), Arch Ward (Himself), Johnny Behr (Himself), Dickie Conon (Jerry Burke), Fern Persons (Mrs. Burke), John "Red" Kullers (Bernie Dooling), Tony Zale (Himself), Issy Kline (Himself), Jack Brickhouse (Ring Side Announcer), Dick Mastro (Announcer in Ring), Michael McGuire (Capt. Mahoney), Art van Harvey (Father McGuire).

In one corner, Nick Martel (Dewey Martin), a not-so-nice Golden Gloves boxer; in the other, Bob Gilmore (Kevin O'Morrison), a "Clean Gene"; and looking on, the real prize, Patti Riley (Kay Westfall), the referee's daughter. Gilmore wins the fight, but Martel is left with both a new outlook on life and the love of Patti. Real Golden Gloves footage livens up the proceedings, which include appearances by former middleweight champ Tony Zale, Golden Gloves founder Arch Ward, and longtime Chicago sportscaster Jack Brickhouse, who plays a ringside announcer.

p, Carl Krueger; d, Felix Feist; w, Joe Ansen, Felix Feist (based on a story by D.D. Beauchamp, William F. Sellers); ph, John L. Russell, Jr.; ed, William F. Claxton; m, Arthur Lange.

Boxing   (PR:A   MPAA:NR)

GOLDENGIRL*

(1979) 104m AE c

Susan Anton (Goldengirl), James Coburn (Dryden), Curt Jurgens (Serafin), Leslie Caron (Dr. Lee), Robert Culp (Esselton), James A. Watson, Jr. (Winters), Harry Guardino (Valenti), Ward Costello (Cobb), Michael Lerner (Sternberg), John Newcombe (Armitage), Julianna Field (Ingrid), Sheila DeWindt (Debbie).

Super model Susan Anton stars as the title goldengirl, an immensely talented runner who couldn't be better prepared for the 1980 Olympics, thanks to the conditioning program created by the German geneticist who adopted her (Curt Jurgens) and financed by a group of businessmen looking to profit from her success. She doesn't know any better, having been brainwashed into believing that by winning three gold medals she will also garner true love. Produced in association with NBC, which planned to run it on TV during the 1980 Olympic year, GOLDENGIRL is an ineptly scripted and directed excuse to show Anton in a variety of tight outfits. Politics kept the real American team from ever going to Moscow, and Anton would have fared better if she'd stayed home too.

p, Danny O'Donovan; d, Joseph Sargent; w, John Kohn (based on the novel by Peter Lear); ph, Stevan Larner (Eastmancolor); ed, George Nicholson; m, Bill Conti.

Track and Field   Cas.   (PR:O   MPAA:PG)

GOOD NEWS**

(1930) 78m MGM bw

Mary Lawlor *(Connie)*, Stanley Smith *(Tom)*, Bessie Love *(Babe)*, Cliff Edwards *(Kearney)*, Gus Shy *(Bobbie)*, Lola Lane *(Patricia)*, Thomas Jackson *(Coach)*, Delmer Daves *(Beef)*, Billy Taft *(Freshman)*, Frank McGlynn *(Prof. Kenyon)*.

Based on a 1927 musical that starred former California senator George Murphy, GOOD NEWS is a cliched rah-rah college musical that was already old hat in 1930. A football star (Stanley Smith) in danger of losing his eligibility for the big game is placed in the hands of a shy, plain tutor (Mary Lawlor) who helps him with his studies and, at the same time, blossoms from an ugly duckling into a ravishing beauty. A superior remake was released in 1947, by which time the story had become a nostalgia piece (see below).

d, Nick Grinde, Edgar J. MacGregor; w, Frances Marion, Joe Franham (based on the stage play by Lawrence Schwab, Lew Brown, Frank Mandel, Ray Henderson, B.G. De Sylva); ph, Percy Hilburn; ed, William Levanway.

Football/Musical (PR:A MPAA:NR)

GOOD NEWS***

(1947) 92m MGM c

June Allyson *(Connie Lane)*, Peter Lawford *(Tommy Marlowe)*, Patricia Marshall *(Pat McClellan)*, Joan McCracken *(Babe Doolittle)*, Ray McDonald *(Bobby Turner)*, Mel Torme *(Danny)*, Robert Strickland *(Peter Van Dyne III)*, Donald MacBride *(Coach Johnsan)*, Tom Dugan *(Pooch)*, Clinton Sundberg *(Prof. Burton Kennyone)*, Loren Tindall *(Beef)*, Connie Gilchrist *(Cora, the Cook)*, Morris Ankrum *(Dean Griswold)*, Georgia Lee *(Flo)*.

This lavish remake of the 1930 film version of the Broadway musical of the same name stars Peter Lawford as Tait College football hero Tommy Marlowe, who's having trouble making his grades, and June Allyson as Connie Lane, the student librarian who tutors him. The campus sexpot (Patricia Marshall) has her sights set on Tommy, but he succumbs to the goodness and light of Connie, and all winds up well, including the inevitable big game. New songs and sensational choreography contributed to making this an impressive debut for director Charles Walters and a big hit for MGM in 1947.

p, Arthur Freed; d, Charles Walters; w, Betty Comden, Adolph Green (based on the musical comedy by Lawrence Schwab, Frank Mandel, B.G. De Sylva, Lew Brown, Ray Henderson); ph, Charles Schoenbaum (Technicolor); ed, Albert Akst.

Football/Musical **Cas.** (PR:AA MPAA:NR)

GRAND PRIX**

(1934, Brit.) 70m Clowes and Stock/COL bw

John Stuart *(Jack Holford)*, Gillian Sande *(Jean McIntyre)*, Milton Rosmer, Peter Gawthorne, Wilson Coleman, Lawrence Andrews.

This sappy romance centers around the unrequited love of a driver (John Stuart) for the daughter (Gillian Sande) of a man who was killed in a test run of a car he (Stuart) invented. When the driver-inventor wins a big race, it proves the worth of his car and redeems him in the eyes of his beloved.

p, L.S. Stock, St. John L. Clowes; d, w, Clowes.

Auto Racing (PR:A MPAA:NR)

GRAND PRIX**

(1966) 179m Douglas & Lewis/MGM c

James Garner *(Pete Aron)*, Eva Marie Saint *(Louise Frederickson)*, Yves Montand *(Jean-Pierre Sarti)*, Toshiro Mifune *(Izo Yamura)*, Brian Bedford *(Scott Stoddard)*, Jessica Walter *(Pat)*, Antonio Sabato *(Nino Barlini)*, Francoise Hardy *(Lisa)*, Adolfo Celi *(Agostini Manetta)*, Claude Dauphin *(Hugo Simon)*, Enzo Fiermonte *(Guido)*, Genevieve Page *(Monique Delvaux Sarti)*, Jack Watson *(Jeff Jordan)*, Donald O'Brien *(Wallace Bennett)*, Jean Michaud *(Children's Father)*, Rachel Kempson *(Mrs. Stoddard)*, Ralph Michael *(Mr. Stoddard)*, Phil Hill *(Tim Randolph)*, Graham Hill *(Bob Turner)*, Lorenzo Bandini, Bob Bondurant, Joakim Bonnier, Jack Brabham, Ken Costello, Juan Manuel Fangio, Nino Farina, Paul Frere, Dan Gurney, Dennis Hulme, Tony Lanfranchi, Andre Pillette, Teddy Pillette, Peter Revson, Jochen Rindt, Ludovico Scarfiotti, Skip Scott, Mike Spence *(Themselves)*, Bruce McLaren *(Douglas McClendon)*, Evans Evans *(Mrs. Tim Randolph)*.

The personal lives and loves of four professional auto racers—played by James Garner, Antonio Sabato, Brian Bedford, and Yves Montand—are mingled with lots of impressively photographed racing footage in this stylistically inventive but narratively tedious effort directed by John Frankenheimer. The film follows the drivers through a number of important European competitions, including Monte Carlo, England's Brand's Hatch, and Italy's Monza, while their off-the-track affairs involve Eva Marie Saint, Jessica Walter, Francoise Hardy, and Toshiro Mifune as Garner's corporate sponsor. Frankenheimer pulls out all the stops to lend excitement to the racing footage—splitting the screen into ever smaller increments, mounting cameras inches above the track on cars, using slow motion—but ultimately his obsession with technique also becomes a little wearying, and the plot is simply not interesting enough to stand on its own.

p, Edward Lewis; d, John Frankenheimer; w, Robert Alan Aurthur, Bill Hanley; ph, Lionel Lindon (Cinerama-SuperPanavision, Metrocolor); ed, Frederic Steinkamp; m, Maurice Jarre.

Auto Racing **Cas.** (PR:C-O MPAA:NR)

GREASED LIGHTNING***

(1977) 96m Third World Cinema/WB c

Richard Pryor *(Wendell Scott)*, Beau Bridges *(Hutch)*, Pam Grier *(Mary Jones)*, Cleavon Little *(Peewee)*, Vincent Gardenia *(Sheriff Cotton)*, Richie Havens *(Woodrow)*, Julian

Bond *(Russell)*, Earl Hindman *(Beau Welles)*, Minnie Gentry *(Mrs. Scott)*, Lucy Saroyan *(Hutch's Wife)*, Noble Willingham *(Billy Joe Byrnes)*, Bruce Atkins, Steve Fifield *(Deputies)*, Bill Cobbs, Georgia Allen *(Mary's Parents)*, Maynard Jackson *(Minister)*, Danny Nelson *(Wayne Carter)*, Cara Dunn *(Restaurant Owner)*, Alvin Huff *(Moonshiner)*, Willie McWhorter *(Wendell, Jr.)*, Frederick Dennis Greene *(Slack)*, Bill Connell *(Speedway Announcer)*.

Directed by gifted African-American filmmaker Michael Schultz, this well-done biography of the first black NASCAR champion, Wendell Scott (Richard Pryor), covers a 25-year period from the end of WW II to 1971. The film follows the determined Scott as he strives to overcome prejudice and closed-mindedness to break auto racing's color barrier, aided by a white driver (Beau Bridges), supported by his wife (Pam Grier), and relying on his sense of humor to help make it through the bad times. Civil Rights leader Julian Bond, former Atlanta mayor Maynard Jackson, and folk singer Richie Havens all appear.

p, Hannah Weinstein; d, Michael Schultz; w, Kenneth Vose, Lawrence DuKore, Melvin Van Peebles, Leon Capetanos; ph, George Bouillet (Movielab Color); ed, Bob Wyman, Christopher Holmes, Randy Roberts; m, Fred Karlin.

**Auto Racing/
Biography   Cas.   (PR:C   MPAA:PG)**

GREAT AMERICAN PASTIME, THE½**

(1956) 89m MGM bw

Tom Ewell *(Bruce Hallerton)*, Anne Francis *(Betty Hallerton)*, Ann Miller *(Mrs. Doris Patterson)*, Dean Jones *(Buck Rivers)*, Rudy Lee *(Dennis Hallerton)*, Judson Pratt *(Ed Ryder)*, Raymond Bailey *(George Carruthers)*, Wilfrid Knapp *(Mr. Dawson)*, Bob Jellison *(Mr. O'Keefe)*, Raymond Winston *(Herbie Patterson)*, Tod Ferrell *(Man Mountain O'Keefe)*, Paul Engle *(Foster Carruthers)*, Ann Morriss *(Mrs. George Carruthers)*, Gene O'Donnell *(Samuel J. Garway)*.

This comedic look at Little League baseball, and its effects on both youngsters and adults, predates THE BAD NEWS BEARS by nearly 20 years. Bruce Hallerton (Tom Ewell), a young attorney, agrees to manage a baseball team to get closer to his son, but soon this endeavor turns into a nightmare, as parents begin pressuring him to give their kids the top spots on the team. When a sexy young widow (Ann Miller) comes on to Bruce to make sure her boy is allowed to pitch, the coach's jealous wife (Anne Francis), who hates baseball, learns how to keep score in order to keep an eye on her husband. Ewell steals the show as the somewhat bumbling coach who tries hard to keep everybody happy.

p, Henry Berman; d, Herman Hoffman; w, Nathaniel Benchley; ph, Arthur E. Arling; ed, Gene Ruggiero; m, Jeff Alexander.

Baseball/Comedy   (PR:A   MPAA:NR)

GREAT DAN PATCH, THE½**

(1949) 92m W.R. Frank/UA bw

Dennis O'Keefe *(David Palmer)*, Gail Russell *(Cissy Lathrop)*, Ruth Warrick *(Ruth Treadwell)*, Charlotte Greenwood *(Aunt Neddy)*, Henry Hull *(Dan Palmer)*, John Hoyt *(Ben Lathrop)*, Arthur Hunnicutt *(Chet)*, Clarence Muse *(Voodoo)*, Harry Lauter *(Bud Ransome)*.

One of the most famous trotters ever, Dan Patch—a horse so fast he had only his own records to race against toward the end of his career—is the subject of this film biography. Dennis O'Keefe plays the farm-raised chemist-cum-trainer who drives Dan to his greatest victories, losing his patrician wife (Ruth Warrick) along the way, but falling in love with another woman who loves harness racing as much as he does (Gail Russell).

p, John Taintor Foote; d, Joseph Newman; w, John Taintor Foote; ph, Gilbert Warrenton; ed, Fred W. Berger.

**Horse Racing/
Biography   Cas.   (PR:AA   MPAA:NR)**

GREAT GAME, THE*

(1930, Brit.) 75m GAU bw

John Batten *(Dicky Brown)*, Renee Clama *(Peggy Jackson)*, Jack Cock *(Jim Blake)*, Randle Ayrton *(Henderson)*, Neil Kenyon *(Jackson)*, Kenneth Kove *(Bultitude)*, A.G. Poulton *(Banks)*, Billy Blyth *(Billy)*, Lew Lake *(Tubby)*, Wally Patch *(Joe Miller)*, Rex Harrison *(George)*.

Problems arise for a British soccer team when Henderson (Randle Ayrton), the club's director, wants to build it up by acquiring veterans, while Jackson (Neil Kenyon), its manager, is determined to develop the youthful players already in the organization. When Jackson adds Dicky Brown (John Batten), a young striker who happens to be his daughter's boy friend, to the lineup, Henderson gives the manager the sack. However, the situation is resolved after the fashion of so many Hollywood college football films when Jackson shows up at Wembley Stadium to give the team just the advice they need to win the FA Cup. A number of English footballers of the day appear, including Jack Cock.

p, L'Estrange Fawcett; d, Jack Raymond; w, W.P. Lipscomb, Ralph Gilbert Bettinson (based on a story by William Hunter, John Lees); ph, Basil Emmott.

Soccer   (PR:A   MPAA:NR)

GREAT GAME, THE*

(1952, Brit.) 80m Advance/Adelphi bw

James Hayter *(Joe Lawson)*, Thora Hird *(Miss Rawlings)*, Diana Dors *(Lulu Smith)*, Sheila Shand Gibbs *(Mavis Pink)*, John Laurie *(Wells)*, Glyn Houston *(Ned Rutter)*, Geoffrey Toone *(Jack Bannerman)*, Jack Lambert *(Mr. Blake)*, Meredith Edwards *(Skid Evans)*, Alexander Gauge *(Ben Woodhall)*, Frank Pettingell *(Sir Julius)*, Glenn Melvyn *(Heckler)*.

Directed by the prolific Maurice Elvey, THE GREAT GAME

is a relatively interesting portrait of the downfall of the chairman of a British soccer club who compromises his integrity in an attempt to keep his First Division team from being relegated (the equivalent of a major league baseball franchise being consigned to AAA ball because of its poor record). When his shady attempt to obtain a star player is discovered, the director (James Hayter) is forced to resign, and after returning to his publishing business, he learns that it, too, has fallen on hard times.

p, David Dent; d, Maurice Elvey; w, Wolfgang Wilhelm (based on the play "Shooting Star" by Basil Thomas); ph, Phil Grindrod.

Soccer (PR:A MPAA:NR)

GREAT JOHN L., THE***

(1945) 96m Crosby/UA bw (GB: A MAN CALLED SULLIVAN)

Greg McClure (*John L. Sullivan*), Linda Darnell (*Anne Livinstone*), Barbara Britton (*Kathy Harkness*), Lee Sullivan (*Mickey*), Otto Kruger (*Richard Martin*), Wallace Ford (*McManus*), George Mathews (*John Flood*), Robert Barrat (*Billy Muldoon*), J.M. Kerrigan (*Father O'Malley*), Simon Semenoff (*Mons. Claire*), Joel Friedkin (*Michael Sullivan*), Harry Crocker (*Arthur Brisbane*), Hope Landin (*Maura Sullivan*), Rory Calhoun (*James J. Corbett*), Fritz Feld (*Claire's Manager*), Dick Curtis (*Waldo*), Thomas Jackson (*McCullough*), Edwin Maxwell (*Exhibition Ring Announcer*).

Greg McClure stars in this boxing biopic as the brash "Boston Strong Boy," John L. Sullivan, the bare-knuckle heavyweight champion of the world from 1882 to 1892. One victory follows another, and Sullivan's head and pockets swell, but as he gets used to being the champ, Sullivan takes to drinking and carousing and abandons his training discipline. When the dapper James J. Corbett (Rory Calhoun) wins the title from the flabby champ (see GENTLEMAN JIM), the not-so-great John L. loses his girl and his self-respect, sinking into the gutter. Don't bet that he'll stay there for too long, though. A strong film on almost every level, THE GREAT JOHN L. boasts excellent period sets and costumes, a humorous Irish flavor, and fine supporting performances under the direction of Frank Tuttle. This was the first major film role for McClure, a one-time stevedore who later played Ham Fisher's comic strip pugilist in JOE PALOOKA IN THE BIG FIGHT (1949) and JOE PALOOKA IN THE SQUARED CIRCLE (1950).

p, Frank R. Mastroly, James Edward Grant; d, Frank Tuttle; w, Edward Grant; ph, James Van Trees; ed, Theodore Bellinger.

Boxing/Biography (PR:A MPAA:NR)

GREAT MACARTHY, THE**½

(1975, Aus.) 93m Stony Creek/ Seven Keys c

John Jarratt (*MacArthy*), Judy Morris (*Miss Russell*), Kate Fitzpatrick (*Andrea*), Sandra MacGregor (*Vera*), Barry Humphries (*Colonel Ball-Miller*), John Frawley (*Webster*), Colin Croft (*Tranter*), Chris Haywood (*Warburton*), Colin

Drake (*Ackerman*), Ron Fraser (*Twentyman*), Max Gillies (*Stan*), Dennis Miller (*Macguinness*).

Barry Oakley's popular novel *A Salute to the Great McCarthy* gave rise to an Australian stage hit, a well-received TV series, and this film about a country lad who is abducted and brought to Melbourne to play Australian Rules Football for a team run by Col. Ball-Miller (Barry Humphries—Edna Everage of the "Barry McKenzie" films). The Colonel also puts MacArthy (John Jarratt) to work in his insurance company, but the young football star finds more to life by undertaking amorous affairs with a secretary, a night school teacher, and the Colonel's daughter.

p, David Baker; d, David Baker; w, John Romeril (based on the novel *A Salute to the Great McCarthy* by Barry Oakley); ph, Bruce McNaughton; ed, John Scott; m, Bruce Smeaton.

Australian Rules Football/Comedy (PR:C-O MPAA:NR)

GREAT WHITE HOPE, THE***½

(1970) 102m FOX c

James Earl Jones (*Jack Jefferson*), Jane Alexander (*Eleanor*), Lou Gilbert (*Goldie*), Joel Fluellen (*Tick*), Chester Morris (*Pop Weaver*), Robert Webber (*Dixon*), Marlene Warfield (*Clara*), R.G. Armstrong (*Cap'n Dan*), Hal Holbrook (*Cameron*), Beah Richards (*Mama Tiny*), Moses Gunn (*Scipio*), Lloyd Gough (*Smitty*), George Ebeling (*Fred*), Larry Pennell (*Frank Brady*), Roy E. Glenn, Sr. (*Pastor*), Rodolfo Acosta (*El Jefe*), Virginia Capers (*Sister Pearl*), Rockne Tarkington (*Rudy*), Oscar Beregi (*Ragosy*), Manuel Padilla, Jr. (*Paco*).

Adapted by Howard Sackler from his own Broadway hit, this excellent period drama is a thinly veiled depiction of the life of Jack Johnson, the first black heavyweight champion of the world. In winning the title, Jack Jefferson (James Earl Jones) incurs the wrath of the white world, and when he takes up with Eleanor, a white divorcee (Jane Alexander), he is convicted of breaking the Mann Act and sent to prison. After Jefferson escapes, disguised in the uniform of a black baseball team, he and Eleanor begin an itinerant exile that takes them to Canada, England (where he is refused a boxing license), France, and Germany. Few are willing to take on the great champion, and he is forced to make ends meet by appearing in a Hungarian version of "Uncle Tom's Cabin." After initially refusing to throw a fight in exchange for a reduced sentence, Jefferson agrees to do so when Eleanor kills herself, and the climactic fight with "The Great White Hope" (Jess Willard in everything but name) takes place in Havana. Shot in Spain, Arizona, and on the HELLO DOLLY set at Fox Studios, THE GREAT WHITE HOPE shows the climate of the time without the preachiness to which director Martin Ritt is sometimes given, touchingly portrays the love story between Alexander and Jones (who also played the role on Broadway), and gives the audience a sense of the essence of the great Jack Johnson.

p, Lawrence Turman; d, Martin Ritt; w, Howard Sackler

(based on his play); ph, Burnett Guffey (Panavision, DeLuxe Color); ed, William Reynolds; m, Lionel Newman.

Boxing/Biography (PR:C-O MPAA:GP)

GREATEST, THE*½

(1977, US/Brit.) 101m M.V./COL c

Muhammad Ali *(Himself)*, Ernest Borgnine *(Angelo Dundee)*, Lloyd Haynes *(Herbert Muhammad)*, John Marley *(Dr. Ferdie Pacheco)*, Robert Duvall *(Bill McDonald)*, David Huddleston *(Cruikshank)*, Ben Johnson *(Hollis)*, James Earl Jones *(Malcolm X)*, Dina Merrill *(Velvet Green)*, Roger E. Mosley *(Sonny Liston)*, Paul Winfield *(Lawyer)*, Annazette Chase *(Belinda Ali)*, Mira Waters *(Ruby Sanderson)*, Phillip MacAllister *(Young Cassius Clay, Jr.)*, Arthur Adams *(Cassius Clay, Sr.)*, Dorothy Meyer *(Odessa Clay)*, Lucille Benson *(Mrs. Fairlie)*, Malachi Throne *(Payton Jory)*, Ben Medina *(Ronnie)*, Paul Mantee *(Carrara)*, George Garro *(Mr. Curtis)*, Ernie Wheelwright *(Bossman Jones)*, George Cooper *(Lawyer)*, James Gammon *("Mr. Harry")*, Don Dunphy *(Commentator)*, Drew "Bundini" Brown, Rahaman Ali, Howard Bingham, W. Youngblood Muhammad, Lloyd Wells, Harold Conrad *(Themselves)*.

Muhammad Ali portrays himself in this disappointing, turtle-paced biopic covering his life up to the George Foreman fight. It shows his beginnings as a fighter under trainer Angelo Dundee (Ernest Borgnine), his conversion to Islam under the tutelage of Malcolm X, and the stripping of his world heavyweight title after he refused induction into the Army during the Vietnam War. Unfortunately, Ali the actor, while far from awful, isn't nearly as captivating here as he was in real life. There's no mistaking the unparalleled talents of Ali the boxer, however, as the film includes actual footage of Ali's fights during his rise to the top, climaxing with his retaking of the crown from Foreman in Zaire.

p, John Marshall; d, Tom Gries; w, Ring Lardner, Jr. (based on the book *The Greatest, My Own Story*, by Muhammad Ali, Richard Durham, Herbert Muhammad); ph, Harry Stradling (Metrocolor); ed, Byron Brandt; m, Michael Masser.

Boxing/Biography **Cas.** (PR:C-O MPAA:G)

GREEN HELMET, THE*½

(1961, Brit.) 89m MGM bw

Bill Travers *(Rafferty)*, Ed Begley *(Bartell)*, Sidney James *(Richie Launder)*, Nancy Walters *(Diane)*, Ursula Jeans *(Mrs. Rafferty)*, Megs Jenkins *(Kitty Launder)*, Sean Kelly *(Taz Rafferty)*, Tutte Lemkow *(Carlo Zaraga)*, Gordon Tanner *(Hastrow)*, Ferdy Mayne *(Rossano)*, Peter Colingwood *(Charlie)*, Ronald Curram *(George)*, Jack Brabham, Roy Salvadori, Steve Ouvaroff, Mike Salmon *(Themselves)*.

Made in Britain with MGM money, this predictable auto racing film revolves around an aging driver who is losing his nerve. The driver, Greg Rafferty (Bill Travers), begins racing under the sponsorship of a tire company owned by Bartell (Ed Begley) and falls in love with the wealthy American's daughter (Nancy Walters), who begs him to quit the sport. Meanwhile, waiting in the wings is Greg's younger

brother, Taz (Sean Kelly), who's promised Mom he won't get behind a wheel until Greg retires. Hoping to prove he still has what it takes, Rafferty enters a 1,000-mile Italian event, and after his mechanic-navigator (Sidney James) is killed, Taz gets his big chance. Realistic racing scenes help enliven the dull script—but not much. Real-life pro auto racer Jack Brabham is also along for the ride (so to speak).

p, Charles Francis Vetter; d, Michael Forlong; w, Jon Cleary; ph, Geoffrey Faithfull; ed, Frank Clarke; m, Ken Jones.

Auto Racing (PR:A MPAA:NR)

GRIDIRON FLASH**

(1935) 62m Radio bw (GB: THE LUCK OF THE GAME)

Eddie Quillan, Betty Furness, Grant Mitchell, Edgar Kennedy, Grady Sutton, Joseph Sawyer, Allen Wood, Margaret Dumont, Lucien Littlefield.

Grant Mitchell plays a college football coach who spots a hot prospect (Eddie Quillan) playing for a prison team and offers him parole if he will put his gridiron talents to use for Bedford College. Ready to rejoin the outside world and anxious to pull a few jobs, the con-cum-collegian jumps at the opportunity, but the clever coach persuades his niece (Betty Furness) to make a play for his new star so he won't stray too far from the playing field. He does so anyway, but, not too surprisingly, returns to give it the old college try at a crucial moment in the big game.

d, Glenn Tryon; w, Glenn Tryon (based on a story by Nicholas Barrows, Earle Snell); ph, John W. Boyle; ed, George Crone; m, Max Steiner.

Football (PR:A MPAA:NR)

GRUNT! THE WRESTLING MOVIE*

(1985) 90m NW c

Greg "Magic" Schwarz *(Mad Dog Joe De Curso)*, Marilyn Dodds Frank *(Lola)*, Steven Cepello *(The Mask)*, Robert Glaudini *(Dr. Tweed)*, Jeff Dial *(Lesley Uggams)*, Lydie Denier *(Angel Face)*, Dick Murdoch, Dick Beyer *(Grunt Brothers)*, Exotic Adrian Street *(Himself)*, Miss Linda *(Herself)*, John Tolos *(Himself)*, Victor Rivera *(Skull Crusher Johnson)*, Wally George *(Himself)*, Ian Shoals *(Merle Kessler)*, Egil Aalvik *(Swedish Eagle Deejay)*, Bill Grant *(Capt. Carnage)*.

The world of professional wrestling is given a sort of CITIZEN KANE treatment in this pseudo-documentary about a filmmaker's (Jeff Dial) attempts to locate Mad Dog Joe De Curso (Greg "Magic" Schwarz), a famous heavyweight who accidentally decapitated an opponent, was acquitted of manslaughter, and then disappeared. When a new masked wrestler appears on the scene, the filmmaker is convinced that he is actually Mad Dog. Although a number of pro wrestlers lend credibility (sic) through their participation, GRUNT! offers little more than wrestling matches linked by weak expository footage. The matches were shot at Los Angeles' Olympic Auditorium, where the boxing sequences from the original ROCKY (1976) were also lensed.

p, Don Normann, Anthony Randel; d, Allan Holzman; w, Roger D. Manning (based on a story by Holzman, Randel, Lisa Tomei, Barry Zetlin); ph, Eddie van der Enden (Foto-Kem & Du Art Color, prints by Technicolor); ed, Allan Holzman, Barry Zetlin; m, Susan Justin.

Wrestling   Cas.   (PR:O MPAA:R)

GUS**

(1976) 96m BV c

Edward Asner *(Hank Cooper)*, Don Knotts *(Coach Venner)*, Gary Grimes *(Andy Petrovic)*, Tim Conway *(Crankcase)*, Liberty Williams *(Debbie Kovac)*, Dick Van Patten *(Cal Wilson)*, Ronnie Schell *(Joe Barnsdale)*, Bob Crane *(Pepper)*, Johnny Unitas *(Himself)*, Dick Butkus *(Rob Cargil)*, Harold Gould *(Charles Gwynn)*, Tom Bosley *(Spinner)*, Dick Enberg *(Atoms Announcer)*, George Putnam *(TV Interviewer)*, Stu Nahan *(L.A. Sportscaster)*.

This typical Disney sports film might have been called "The Mule That Saved Los Angeles," in that it's a Yugoslavian quadruped that answers the prayers of Hank Cooper (Edward Asner), owner of the California Atoms, a truly abysmal football team. When Gus the mule appears on the scene and begins kicking long-range field goals, the Atoms' fortunes turn around. Predictable but pleasant fluff, GUS offers Don Knotts as the head coach and Tom Bosley and Tim Conway as the bad guys who are trying to derail the Atoms. NFL Hall of Famers Johnny Unitas and Dick Butkus and sportscaster Dick Enberg also appear.

p, Ron Miller; d, Vincent McEveety; w, Arthur Alsberg, Don Nelson (based on a story by Ted Key); ph, Frank Phillips (Technicolor); ed, Robert Stafford; m, Robert F. Brunner.

Football/Comedy   Cas.   (PR:AA MPAA:G)

GUY WHO CAME BACK, THE**½

(1951) 91m FOX bw

Paul Douglas *(Harry Joplin)*, Joan Bennett *(Kath)*, Linda Darnell *(Dee)*, Don DeFore *(Gordon Towne)*, Billy Gray *(Willy)*, Zero Mostel *(Boots Mullins)*, Edmon Ryan *(Joe Demarcus)*, Ruth McDevitt *(Grandma)*, Walter Burke *(O'Hara)*, Henry Kulky *(Wizard)*, Dick Ryan *(Station Master)*, Robert B. Williams *(Paymaster)*, Ted Pearson *(Tom)*, Mack Williams *(Captain of Waiters)*, Grandon Rhodes *(Capt. Shallock)*, John H. Hamilton *(Admiral)*, John Close *(Tufano)*, Tom Hanlon *(Announcer)*, Harry Seymour *(Piano Player)*, Thomas B. Henry *(Doctor)*.

Disheartened because his playing days appear to be over, pro football player Harry Joplin (Paul Douglas) begins losing touch with his long-suffering wife, Kath (Joan Bennett), and has an affair with a model (Linda Darnell). After giving wrestling a try, Harry gets his comeback shot, but even though the pro ranks have been depleted by the war effort, he still doesn't have what it takes—and now he knows it. By the finale, Harry has had one more moment in the sun and taken a coaching job, while the model has realized

that Harry belongs with Kath. Although its flashback structure is a little confusing, this isn't a bad film, with strong performances from the leads, particularly Douglas, who essays the role of the overweight pipe dreamer with a mixture of melancholy and humor.

p, Julian Blaustein; d, Joseph Newman; w, Allan Scott (based on the story "The Man Who Sank the Navy" by William Fay); ph, Joseph LaShelle; ed, William B. Murphy; m, Leigh Harline.

Football   (PR:A MPAA:NR)

HALLS OF ANGER***

(1970) 100m UA c

Calvin Lockhart *(Quincy Davis)*, Janet MacLachlan *(Lorraine Nash)*, James A. Watson, Jr. *(J.T. Watson)*, Jeff Bridges *(Douglas)*, Rob Reiner *(Leaky Couloris)*, Dewayne Jesse *(Lerone Johnson)*, Patricia Stich *(Sherry Vaughn)*, Roy Jenson *(Harry Greco)*, John McLiam *(Lloyd Wilkerson)*, Edward Asner *(McKay)*, Lou Frizzell *(Stewart)*, Helen Kleeb *(Rita)*, Luther Whitsett *(Fowler)*, Florence St. Peter *(Miss Rowland)*, Maye Henderson *(Mrs. Taylor)*.

Although HALLS OF ANGER is not strictly a sports film, basketball plays a crucial role in this socially conscious drama about school desegregation. Quincy Davis (Calvin Lockhart), a black English teacher in an all-white suburban high school, is reassigned as a vice-principal to the inner-city school where many of his former students are now being bused. He does his best to stem the rising tide of racial conflict, and when Douglas (Jeff Bridges), a white student, meets with violent opposition while trying to make the basketball team, Quincy, a former basketball player, puts everything on the line in a game of one-on-one with J.T. Watson (James A. Watson, Jr.), the leader of the black kids who want to keep Douglas off the team. Paul Bogart's direction is tight, the cinematography is gritty and realistic, and the acting is uniformly strong, with Lockhart especially good as the teacher caught up in a volatile situation.

p, Herbert Hirschman; d, Paul Bogart; w, John Shaner, Al Ramrus; ph, Burnett Guffey (DeLuxe Color); ed, Bud Molin; m, Dave Grusin.

Basketball   Cas.   (PR:C-O MPAA:GP)

HARD TIMES***

(1975) 92m COL c (AKA: THE STREETFIGHTER)

Charles Bronson *(Chaney)*, James Coburn *(Spencer "Speed" Weed)*, Jill Ireland *(Luby Simpson)*, Strother Martin *(Poe)*, Maggie Blye *(Gayleen Schoonover)*, Michael McGuire *(Gandil)*, Robert Tessier *(Jim Henry)*, Nick Dimitri *(Street)*, Felice Orlandi *(Le Beau)*, Bruce Glover *(Doty)*, Edward Walsh *(Pettibon)*, Frank McRae *(Hammerman)*, Maurice Kowalewski *(Caesare)*, Naomi Stevens *(Madam)*,

Robert Castleberry *(Counterman)*, Becky Allen *(Poe's Date)*, Joan Kleven *(Carol)*, Anne Welsch *(Secretary)*, Lyla Hay Owen *(Diner Waitress)*, Jim Nickerson *(Barge Fighter)*.

One of Charles Bronson's best pictures, HARD TIMES is a different kind of boxing yarn. Chaney (Bronson), an itinerant bare-knuckle street fighter in the 1930s, makes his living beating the brains out of those foolish enough to think they can take the graying tough guy. (Clint Eastwood played a similar part in EVERY WHICH WAY BUT LOOSE and ANY WHICH WAY YOU CAN.) Spencer "Speed" Weed (James Coburn) is the New Orleans promoter who arranges illegal bouts for Chaney, and Luby Simpson (Jill Ireland, Bronson's real-life wife) is the woman who has a fling with the fighter. Bronson was 54 when he made this but in excellent condition, and his performance is low key and convincing. Unfortunately, the script leaves something to be desired—namely, dramatic impetus—yet HARD TIMES is still an enjoyable film, and the Depression-era settings are painstakingly captured.

p, Lawrence Gordon; d, Walter Hill; w, Bryan Gindorff, Bruce Henstell, Walter Hill (based on a story by Gindorff, Henstell); ph, Philip Lathrop (Panavision, Metrocolor); ed, Roger Spottiswoode; m, Barry DeVorzon.

Boxing   Cas.   (PR:A-C MPAA:PG)

HARDER THEY FALL, THE*****

(1956) 109m COL bw

Humphrey Bogart *(Eddie Willis)*, Rod Steiger *(Nick Benko)*, Jan Sterling *(Beth Willis)*, Mike Lane *(Toro Moreno)*, Max Baer *(Buddy Brannen)*, Jersey Joe Walcott *(George)*, Edward Andrews *(Jim Weyerhause)*, Harold J. Stone *(Art Leavitt)*, Carlos Montalban *(Luis Agrandi)*, Nehemiah Persoff *(Leo)*, Felice Orlandi *(Vince Fawcett)*, Herbie Faye *(Max)*, Rusty Lane *(Danny McKeogh)*, Jack Albertson *(Pop)*, Val Avery *(Frank)*, Tommy Herman *(Tommy)*, Vinnie DeCarlo *(Joey)*, Pat Comiskey *(Gus Dundee)*, Matt Murphy *(Sailor Rigazzo)*, Abel Fernandez *(Chief Firebird)*, Marion Carr *(Alice)*, J. Lewis Smith *(Brannen's Manager)*, Lilian Carver *(Mrs. Harding)*.

One of the most scathing indictments of professional boxing ever committed to film, THE HARDER THEY FALL presents Humphrey Bogart as Eddie Willis, a once-scrupulous sportswriter who goes to work for Nick Benko (Rod Steiger), publicizing the mob-connected promoter's new find, Toro Moreno (6-foot-10-inch Mike Lane), a giant Argentine boxer. Although Toro has a powder-puff punch and a glass jaw, Nick fixes one fight after another, and soon the towering heavyweight, who thinks he's doing it on his own, faces Gus Dundee (Pat Comiskey), a top contender who was so battered by the current champ, Buddy Brannen (one-time heavyweight title holder Max Baer), that even Toro's feeble punches are enough to bring about a brain hemorrhage that kills him. Eddie proves to the disconsolate Toro that he couldn't have killed Dundee by having his trainer ("Jersey" Joe Walcott, another ex-champ) take Toro's best shot and then crumple him with a punch. Driven by pride, Toro enters the ring with the un-

buyable Brannen anyway and displays tremendous courage. In the end, a morally reawakened Eddie extricates Toro from Nick's clinch and promises to expose the corrupt boxing racket with a series of articles. Scripted by producer Philip Yordan from the novel by Budd Schulberg, THE HARDER THEY FALL was similar enough to the real-life story of heavyweight Primo Carnera (who lost his title to Baer) that he sued Columbia. Nothing about it is pretty, with director Mark Robson (who'd already helmed the powerful CHAMPION) moving the story along at a frenetic pace and Burnett Guffey's stark black-and-white photography lending a grim feel to the movie. All of the performers are excellent, especially Bogart, in what would be his last film appearance, as the cancer that would take his life was already beginning to exhaust him.

p, Philip Yordan; d, Mark Robson; w, Philip Yordan (based on the novel by Budd Schulberg); ph, Burnett Guffey; ed, Jerome Thoms; m, Hugo Friedhofer.

Boxing   Cas.   (PR:O MPAA:NR)

HARLEM GLOBETROTTERS, THE**½

(1951) 75m COL bw

Thomas Gomez *(Abe Saperstein)*, Dorothy Dandridge *(Ann Carpenter)*, Bill Walker *(Prof. Turner)*, Angela Clarke *(Sylvia Saperstein)*, Peter Thompson *(Martin)*, Steve Roberts *(Eddie)*, Peter Virgo *(Rocky)*, Ray Walker *(Jack Davis)*, Al Eben *(Charlie Peters)*, Ann E. Allen *(Sara)*, William Forrest *(Prof. Lindley)*, Tom Greenway *(Dave Barrett)*, Billy Brown, Roscoe Cumberland, William "Pop" Gates, Marques Haynes, Louis "Babe" Pressley, Ermer Robinson, Ted Strong, Reese "Goose" Tatum, Frank Washington, Clarence Wilson, Inman Jackson *(The Harlem Globetrotters)*.

The first film to feature the Harlem Globetrotters (GO, MAN, GO! followed three years later), this entertaining movie follows a college student (Billy Brown) as he drops out to chase fame and fortune with the Trotters. Because he's in it a little too much for himself, the new player comes into conflict with his coach (Thomas Gomez) and teammates, but with the help of his girl friend (Dorothy Dandridge), he sets himself straight. The story is just an excuse to film the Globetrotters in action, however, and the antics of basketball wizards Marques Haynes and Goose Tatum are enough to make this worthwhile viewing.

p, Buddy Adler; d, Phil Brown (basketball sequences by Will Jason); w, Alfred Palca; ph, Phillip Tannura; ed, James Sweeney; m, Arthur Morton.

Basketball   (PR:A MPAA:NR)

HARMON OF MICHIGAN**

(1941) 65m COL bw

Tom Harmon *(Himself)*, Anita Louise *(Peggy Adams)*, Forest Evashevski *(Himself)*, Oscar O'Shea *("Pop" Branch)*, Warren Ashe *(Bill Dorgan)*, Stanley Crown *(Freddy Davis)*, Ken Christy *(Joe Scudder)*, Tim Ryan *(Flash Regan)*, William Hall *(Jimmy Wayburn)*, Lloyd Bridges *(Ozzie)*, Chester Conklin *(Gasoline Chuck)*, Larry Parks *(Harvey)*.

Tom Harmon, an All-American and Heisman Trophy winner at the University of Michigan, plays himself in this film loosely based on his life. Starting out with newsreel footage of the 1940 season, it follows Harmon as he marries sweetheart Peggy Adams (Anita Louise); gives pro football a try; works as an assistant for his old coach, Pop Branch (Oscar O'Shea); takes a job with another college, where he uses an illegal formation against his mentor's team; and, finally seeing the light, returns to Branch's coaching staff. Harmon, who is relatively comfortable in front of the camera here, went on to appear in a number of other sports-themed films, including THE SPIRIT OF WEST POINT (1948); TRIPLE THREAT (1948); THE ROSE BOWL STORY (1952); PAT AND MIKE (1952); and THE ALL-AMERICAN (1953). He also had a successful career as a sportscaster and is the father of actor Mark Harmon (STEALING HOME).

p, Wallace MacDonald; d, Charles Barton; w, Howard J. Green (based on a story by Richard Goldstone, Stanley Rauh, Fredric Frank); ph, John Stumar; ed, Arthur Seid.

Football/Biography   (PR:A MPAA:NR)

HARRIGAN'S KID**

(1943) 80m MGM bw

Bobby Readick *(Benny McNeil)*, Frank Craven *(Mr. Garnet)*, William Gargan *(Tom Harrigan)*, Jay Ward *(McNamara)*, J. Carrol Naish *(Jed Jerrett)*, Douglas Croft *("Skip")*, Bill Cartledge *(Joe)*, Irving Lee *(Dink)*, Selmer Jackson *(Mr. Ranley)*, Allen Wood *(Atley)*, Jim Toney *(Sam)*, Mickey Martin *(Jockey)*, Russell Hicks *(Col. Lowry)*.

Youngster Benny McNeil (Bobby Readick) becomes the protege of an unsportsmanlike ex-jockey (William Gargan) who teaches him the ins and outs of racing—and cheating. By the film's end, though, Tom (Gargan) is the one who's learned his lesson, and Benny decides to play it straight in the climactic big race. Gargan isn't particularly believable, Readick has a propensity for overacting, and HARRIGAN'S KID is mediocre.

p, Irving Starr; d, Charles F. Reisner; w, Alan Friedman, Martin Berkeley, Henry Blankfort (based on a story by Borden Chase); ph, Walter Lundin; ed, Ferris Webster; m, Daniele Amfitheatrof.

Horse Racing   (PR:A MPAA:NR)

HEART LIKE A WHEEL***

(1983) 113m Aurora/FOX c

Bonnie Bedelia *(Shirley Muldowney)*, Beau Bridges *(Connie Kalitta)*, Leo Rossi *(Jack Muldowney)*, Hoyt Axton *(Tex Roque)*, Bill McKinney *("Big Daddy" Don Garlits)*, Anthony Edwards *(John Muldowney, Age 15-23)*, Dean Paul Martin *(Sonny Rigotti)*, Paul Bartel *(Chef Paul)*, Missy Basile *(Angela)*, Michael Cavanaugh *(NHRA Boss)*, Ellen Geer *(Mrs. Marianne Kalitta)*, Nora Heflin *(Nurse North)*, Byron Thames *(John Age, 10-13)*, Tiny Wells *(Tiny)*,

Brandon Brent Williams *(John, Age 5-8)*, Jesse Aragon *(Carlos)*, Bruce Barloe *(Bass Player)*, Catherine Paolone *(Mrs. Good Joe)*, Michel Barrere *(NHRA Guard)*.

This insightful biography of drag racing champ Shirley "Cha-Cha" Muldowney (well played by Bonnie Bedelia) begins with the foreshadowing image of little Shirley driving her father's sedan and continues with her first race in 1966. Meeting with the usual sexism, she surprises all by breaking the track record on her qualifying run. Her career soars, but her marriage to mechanic Jack Muldowney (Leo Rossi) ends in divorce when he realizes that he can't handle his wife's success. Shirley then turns to banned driver Connie Kalitta (Beau Bridges, who also appears in the similarly themed GREASED LIGHTING, 1977, the story of black NASCAR driver Wendell Scott's triumph over racial prejudice) for support and love as she goes on to win the National Hot Rod Association World Championship three times.

p, Charles Roven; d, Jonathan Kaplan; w, Ken Friedman; ph, Tak Fujimoto (DeLuxe Color); ed, O. Nicholas Brown; m, Laurence Rosenthal.

**Auto Racing/
Biography**   Cas.   (PR:C-O MPAA:PG)

HEART OF VIRGINIA**

(1948) 60m REP bw

Janet Martin *(Virginia Galtry)*, Robert Lowery *(Dan Lockwood)*, Frankie Darro *(Jimmy Easter)*, Paul Hurst *(Whit Galtry)*, Sam McDaniel *("Sunflower" Jones)*, Tom Chatterton *(Dr. Purdy)*, Bennie Bartlett *(Breezy Brent)*, Glen Vernon *(Bud Landeen)*, Edmund Cobb *(Gas Station Attendant)*.

Jimmy Easter (Frankie Darro) is a jockey who is shaken after he is responsible for the death of a fellow rider during a race. He gets back down to business, however, when the daughter of his ex-boss shows her faith in him.

p, Sidney Picker; d, R.G. Springsteen; w, Jerry Sackheim, John K. Butler; ph, John MacBurnie; ed, Irving M. Schoenberg.

Horse Racing   (PR:A MPAA:NR)

HEART PUNCH**

(1932) 62m Mayfair bw

Lloyd Hughes, Marion Schilling, George Lewis, Wheeler Oakman, Mae Busch, Walter Miller, Gordon De Main, James Leong.

A boxer (Lloyd Hughes) kills his opponent with a punch to the heart. He then falls in love with the dead man's sister in this well-photographed though routine boxing picture.

d, Breezy Eason; w, John T. Neville (based on the story by Frank Howard Clark); ph, George Meehan; ed, Jeanne Spencer.

Boxing   (PR:A MPAA:NR)

HEAVEN CAN WAIT***

(1978) 101m PAR c

Warren Beatty *(Joe Pendleton)*, Julie Christie *(Betty Logan)*, James Mason *(Mr. Jordan)*, Dyan Cannon *(Julia Farnsworth)*, Charles Grodin *(Tony Abbott)*, Jack Warden *(Max Corkle)*, Buck Henry *(The Escort)*, Vincent Gardenia *(Lt. Krim)*, Joseph Maher *(Sisk)*, Hamilton Camp *(Bentley)*, Arthur Malet *(Everett)*, Stephanie Faracy *(Corinne)*, Jeannie Linero *(Lavinia)*, Larry Block *(Peters)*, Frank Campanella *(Conway)*, Bill Sorrells *(Tomarken)*, Dick Enberg *(TV Interviewer)*, Dolph Sweet *(Head Coach)*, R.G. Armstrong *(General Manager)*, Ed V. Peck *(Trainer)*, John Randolph *(Former Owner)*, Richard O'Brien *(Former Owner's Adviser)*, Will Hare *(Team Doctor)*, Lee Weaver *(Way Station Attendant)*, Roger Bowen *(Newspaperman)*, Keene Curtis *(Oppenheim)*, William Larsen *(Renfield)*, Morgan Farley *(Middleton)*, William Bogert *(Lawson)*, Charlie Charles *(High-Wire Performer)*, Les Josephson *(Owens)*, Jack T. Snow *(Cassidy)*, Charlie Cowan, Joe Corolla *(Football Players)*, Bryant Gumbel, Jim Healy *(TV Sportscasters)*, Curt Gowdy *(TV Commentator)*, Al DeRogatis *(TV Color Analyst)*.

Warren Beatty is very nearly the whole ball game in this satisfying remake of HERE COMES MR. JORDAN (see below), producing, codirecting, cowriting (with Elaine May) and starring as Joe Pendleton, a Los Angeles Rams quarterback who is prematurely escorted to heaven by a bumbling celestial messenger (codirector Buck Henry) after an auto accident. An archangel, Mr. Jordan (James Mason), tries to redress this error by restoring Joe's corporeity, and moments after wealthy industrialist Leo Farnsworth is murdered by his adulterous wife, Julia (Dyan Cannon), and his nitwit secretary, Tony (Charles Grodin), Joe's spirit reanimates his body. Determined to play in the Super Bowl, Leo/Joe buys the Rams and hires his old coach (Jack Warden) to help him train, convincing him of his reincarnation. He also meets and falls in love with Betty Logan, an English environmental activist (Julie Christie), but just when it looks as if everything is going to work out, Julia and Tony murder Leo again. Nothing is going to keep Joe from winning a Super Bowl ring, however, and by the finale he (or at least *someone* with the glint of his eyes) also appears destined to win Betty. Although not the equal of the original and occasionally a little too cute, HEAVEN CAN WAIT, which takes its name from the Harry Segall stage play that inspired HERE COMES MR. JORDAN, is a warm, funny, and enjoyable film. Beatty, an outstanding high-school football player, makes a relatively convincing QB and the presence of several former Rams (including Les Josephson, Jack Snow, and Deacon Jones) adds further credibility to the proceedings.

p, Warren Beatty; d, Warren Beatty, Buck Henry; w, Warren Beatty, Elaine May (based on the play by Harry Segall); ph, William A. Fraker (Panavision, Movielab Color); ed, Robert C. Jones, Don Zimmerman; m, Dave Grusin.

**Football/Comedy/
Fantasy**   Cas.   (PR:C   MPAA:PG)

HERE COME THE TIGERS*

(1978) 90m AIP c (AKA: MANNY'S ORPHANS)

Richard Lincoln *(Eddie Burke)*, James Zvanut *(Burt Honneger)*, Samantha Grey *(Bette Burke)*, Manny Lieberman *(Felix the Umpire)*, William Caldwell *(Kreeger)*, Fred Lincoln *(Aesop)*, Xavier Rodrigo *(Buster Rivers)*, Kathey Bell *(Patty O'Malley)*, Noel John Cunningham *(Noel Cady)*, Sean P. Griffin *(Art Bullfinch)*, Max McClellan *(Mike "The Bod" Karpel)*, Kevin Moore *("Eaglescout" Terwilliger)*, Lance Norwood *(Ralphy)*.

Trying to cash in on the success of THE BAD NEWS BEARS, this dull comedy about a racially mixed, foul-mouthed Little League baseball team that goes from being loser to champ is nothing more than a cheap imitation of Michael Ritchie's entertaining film. Watch any "Bad News Bears" films before you decide to saddle yourself with this one. For that matter, you'll probably be more entertained by a real-life local Little League game.

p, Sean S. Cunningham, Stephen Miner; d, Sean S. Cunningham; w, Arch McCoy; ph, Barry Abrams (Movielab Color); ed, Stephen Miner; m, Harry Manfredini.

Baseball/Comedy   (PR:C   MPAA:PG)

HERE COMES MR. JORDAN****

(1941) 93m COL bw

Robert Montgomery *(Joe Pendleton)*, Evelyn Keyes *(Bette Logan)*, Claude Rains *(Mr. Jordan)*, Rita Johnson *(Julia Farnsworth)*, Edward Everett Horton *(Messenger No. 7013)*, James Gleason *(Max Corkle)*, John Emery *(Tony Abbott)*, Donald MacBride *(Inspector Williams)*, Don Costello *(Lefty)*, Halliwell Hobbes *(Sisk)*, Benny Rubin *(Bugs)*, Bert Young *(Taxi Driver)*, Joseph Crehan *(Doctor)*, William Newell *(Handler)*, Abe Roth *(Referee)*, Tom Hanlon *(Announcer)*.

Full of hilarious plot twists and blessed with brilliant performances from a stellar cast, HERE COMES MR. JORDAN is a thoroughly beguiling fantasy with a boxing subplot. Joe Pendleton (Robert Montgomery), a saxophone-playing up-and-coming prizefighter, crashes while flying his single-engine plane, and his spirit is plucked up by an anxious heavenly messenger (Edward Everett Horton) who learns later that Joe was supposed to have lived for another 50 years and was destined to be the world heavyweight champion. It's up to the messenger's superior, Mr. Jordan (Claude Rains), to help Joe find another body in which to finish his life. The first surrogate, an unscrupulous millionaire who has been murdered by his wife and his male secretary, doesn't work out well at all—though in his form Joe is introduced to Bette Logan (Evelyn Keyes), with whom he falls in love. Joe has considerably more luck, however, when he enters the body of a boxing rival who has been given a shot at the title (and put to the canvas by a gangster's bullet). And before the credits roll, he both fulfills his destiny and convinces Bette that Joe by any other name is still Joe. Montgomery and James Gleason, as his manager, were both nominated for Academy Awards, but the rest of the cast is equally believable in this most unbelievable film, which was itself nominated for a Best Picture Oscar. A weak nonsports sequel, DOWN TO EARTH, followed in 1947, and the story was remade with a football backdrop in 1978 as HEAVEN CAN WAIT (see above).

p, Everett Riskin; d, Alexander Hall; w, Sidney Buchman, Seton I. Miller (based on the play "Heaven Can Wait" by Harry Segall); ph, Joseph Walker; ed, Viola Lawrence; m, Morris Stoloff.

Boxing/Fantasy   Cas.   (PR:A MPAA:NR)

HIGH GEAR*½

(1933) 65m Goldsmith bw

James Murray (High Gear Sherrod), Joan Marsh (Anne Merritt), Jackie Searl (Jimmy Evans), Eddie Lambert (Jake Cohen), Theodore Von Eltz (Larry Winston), Ann Brody (Mrs. Cohen), Mike Donlin (Ed Evans), Lee Moran (Howard).

Emotions run high at the old auto racing track in this melodramatic programmer starring James Murray as a race-car driver in love with a female reporter (Joan Marsh). To this already hackneyed story line add a crippled boy whose father crashed into a retaining wall at the beginning of the movie and you have the typical Hollywood surrogate family that, of course, will wind up making it all legal by the fade-out.

p, Leigh Jason; d, Leigh Jason; w, Rex Taylor, Leigh Jason, Charles Saxton; ph, Edward Kull.

Auto Racing   (PR:A MPAA:NR)

HIGH SCHOOL HERO*

(1946) 69m MON bw

Freddie Stewart (Freddie), June Preisser (Dodie), Noel Neill (Betty), Ann Rooney (Addie), Jackie Moran (Jimmy), Frankie Darro (Roy), Warren Mills (Lee), Milt Kibbee (Townley), Belle Mitchell (Miss Hinklefink), Isabelita (Chi-Chi), Douglas Fowley (Coach Carter), Edythe Elliott (Mrs. Rogers), Leonard Penn (Prof. Farrell), Pierre Watkin (Gov. Huffington), Dick Elliott (Mayor Whitehead), Freddie Slack (Himself).

This tedious musical concerns the rivalry between two high schools and their football teams. The sympathetic team (the one in the white jerseys) looks as if they'll be pounded into the turf by the bad guys (black jerseys, of course), who are much better (and bigger). Don't believe it for a minute and prepare yourself instead for the Big Show—if you bother watching this at all.

p, Sam Katzman; d, Arthur Dreifuss; w, Hal Collins, Arthur Dreifuss; ph, Ira Morgan; ed, Ace Herman, Richard Currier; m, Edward J. Kay.

Football/Musical   (PR:A MPAA:NR)

HIGH SPEED*½

(1932) 60m COL bw

Buck Jones, Loretta Sayers, Wallace MacDonald, Mickey McGuire, Ed La Saint, William Walling, Ward Bond, Dick

Dickinson, Martin Faust, Joe Bordeaux, Pat O'Malley, Eddy Chandler.

Western star Buck Jones is out of the saddle and in the driver's seat in this film about a policeman who brings a mob of crooks to justice, triumphs at the speedway, befriends the son of a dead driver, and gets the girl.

d, Ross D. Lederman; w, Adele Buffington (based on a story by Harold Shumate); ph, Teddy Tetzlaff.

Auto Racing   (PR:A MPAA:NR)

HOLD 'EM JAIL**

(1932) 65m RKO bw

Bert Wheeler (Curly Harris), Robert Woolsey (Spider Robbins), Edna May Oliver (Violet Jones), Roscoe Ates (Slippery Sam Brown), Edgar Kennedy (Warden), Betty Grable (Barbara Jones), Paul Hurst (Coach), Warren Hymer (Steel), Robert Armstrong (Sports Announcer), John Sheehan (Mike Maloney), Jed Prouty (Warden Charles Clark), Spencer Charters (Governor), Lee Phelps (Spike), Ernie Adams, Monty Collins (Referees), Ben Taggart (Doorman).

Comedians Bert Wheeler and Robert Woolsey star here as a pair of salesmen who are framed for robbery and sentenced to a prison where the warden (Edgar Kennedy) and his football coach (Paul Hurst) are desperately trying to beef up their pathetic team so that a rival jailhouse eleven doesn't drop them from their schedule. Wheeler and Woolsey indulge in their usual zaniness, climaxing in the ultimate in stop-action game footage, wherein Woolsey uses chloroform to bring both teams to their knees. Although directed at a rapid clip by Oscar winner Norman Taurog (SKIPPY), this moderately funny Wheeler and Woolsey effort was a box-office bomb in 1932.

d, Norman Taurog; w, S.J. Perelman, Walter DeLeon, Mark Sandrich, Albert Ray (based on a story by Tim Wheelan, Lou Lipton); ph, Leonard Smith; ed, Artie Roberts; m, Max Steiner.

Football/Comedy   (PR:A MPAA:NR)

HOLD 'EM NAVY!**

(1937) 62m PAR bw

Lew Ayres (Tommy Gorham), Mary Carlisle (Judy Holland), John Howard (Chuck Baldwin), Benny Baker (Stuffy Miller), Elizabeth Patterson (Grandma Holland), Archie Twitchell (Jerry Abbott), Lambert Rogers (Ritter), Les Bennett (Blake), Alston Cockrell (Carner), Tully Marshall (The "Admiral"), Billy Daniels (Steve Crenshaw), George Lollier (Doctor), Pat Flaherty (Coach Hanley), Dick French (Announcer), Harold Adams (Referee), Gwen Kenyon (Caroline), Priscilla Moran (Kitty Hollingsbee), Richard Denning (Jepson), Jack Hubbard (Fruit Vendor), Frank Nelson (Radio Announcer), Wade Boteler (O'Brien).

Tommy Gorham (Lew Ayres), a freshman football player at the Naval Academy, meets and falls for Judy Holland (Mary Carlisle), who, unbeknownst to him, is the sweetie of his upperclassman teammate Chuck Baldwin (John

Howard). Not surprisingly, there's some bitterness between the Midshipmen rivals, but all is resolved when they combine their talents on the last play of the annual Army-Navy football game.

d, Kurt Neumann; w, Erwin Gelsey, Lloyd Corrigan (based on a story by Albert Shelby LeVino); ph, Henry Sharp; ed, Edward Dmytryk.

Football (PR:A MPAA:NR)

HOLD 'EM YALE**½

(1935) 61m PAR bw

Patricia Ellis *(Clarice Van Cleve)*, Cesar Romero *(Gigolo Georgie)*, Larry "Buster" Crabbe *(Hector Wilmot)*, William Frawley *(Sunshine Joe)*, Andy Devine *(Liverlips)*, George Barbier *(Mr. Van Cleve)*, Warren Hymer *(Sam The Gonoph)*, George E. Stone *(Bennie South Street)*, Hale Hamilton *(Mr. Wilmot)*, Guy Usher *(Coach Jennings)*, Grant Withers *(Cleary)*, Garry Owen, Ethel Griffies, Leonard Carey, Kendall Evans, Theodore Lorch.

Ticket scalpers Sunshine Joe (William Frawley), Liverlips (Andy Devine), Sam the Gonoph (Warren Hymer), and Bennie South Street (George E. Stone) find themselves responsible for pretty Clarice Van Cleve (Patricia Ellis) when their playboy buddy (Cesar Romero) drops her. What's more, her wealthy father charges them with putting an end to her wild ways and finding a nice boy for her to marry. Hector Wilmot (Larry "Buster" Crabbe), who rides the bench for the Yale football team, appears to fit the bill, and the fellas convince the Eli coach to let him play against Harvard, leading to the usual last-minute heroics and plenty of romance. HOLD 'EM YALE's weak plot is more than compensated for by great dialog, adapted from a Damon Runyon story by Paul Gerard Smith and Eddie Welch.

p, Charles R. Rogers; d, Sidney Lanfield; w, Paul Gerard Smith, Eddie Welch (based on a story by Damon Runyon); ph, Milton Drasner; ed, Jack Dennis.

Football/Comedy (PR:A MPAA:NR)

HOLD EVERYTHING**½

(1930) 78m WB c

Joe E. Brown *(Gink Schiner)*, Winnie Lightner *(Toots Breen)*, Georges Carpentier *(Georges LaVerne)*, Sally O'Neill *(Sue Burke)*, Edmund Breese *(Pop O'Keefe)*, Bert Roach *(Nosey Bartlett)*, Dorothy Revier *(Norine Lloyd)*.

A little singing, a little boxing, and a lot of Joe E. Brown are the ingredients that make up this enjoyable musical comedy about a flirtatious second-rate boxer who becomes embroiled in a fight fix. While preparing for his own upcoming bout and trying to stay out of his girl friend's dog house, Gink Schiner (Brown) intervenes to make sure that heavyweight Georges LaVerne (Georges Carpentier, world light heavyweight champion from 1920 to 1922) gets to take his best shots in a title fight, unencumbered by the crooked characters who would have it otherwise. No stranger to 1930s sports films, Brown does his usual mugging and his

comic sense is on target more often than not in this tuneful comedy based on a Broadway original.

d, Roy Del Ruth; w, Robert Lord (based on the play by B.G. DeSylva, John McGowan); ph, Dev Jennings; ed, William Holmes; m, Ray Henderson, Al Dubin, Lew Brown, Joe Burke.

Boxing/Musical/
Comedy (PR:AA MPAA:NR)

HOLD THAT CO-ED**

(1938) 80m FOX bw (GB: HOLD THAT GIRL)

John Barrymore *(Governor)*, George Murphy *(Rusty)*, Marjorie Weaver *(Marjorie)*, Joan Davis *(Lizzie)*, Jack Haley *(Wilbur)*, George Barbier *(Breckenridge)*, Ruth Terry *(Edie)*, Donald Meek *(Dean Thatcher)*, Johnny Downs *(Dink)*, Paul Hurst *(Slapsy)*, Guinn "Big Boy" Williams *(Mike)*, Frank Sully *(Steve)*, Brewster Twins *(Themselves)*, Billy Benedict *(Sylvester)*, Charles Wilson *(Coach Burke)*, Glenn Morris *(Spencer)*, Charles Williams *(McFinch)*, John Elliot *(Tremont)*.

In one of the best of his later performances, John Barrymore portrays a scheming politician (not unlike Louisiana's infamous Huey Long) who hitches his electoral future to the fortunes of a college football team. Hoping to win a seat in the Senate, the governor (Barrymore) does his best to build up the university's heretofore dismal football program, while his election opponent (George Barbier) does the same for another institution. Everything hinges on the big game, and when the pro wrestlers the governor has recruited are identified as ringers, it's up to a female flash (Joan Davis) to save the day. Since the film is a musical comedy, there are also a number of songs from the likes of Mack Gordon, Harry Revel, and Jule Styne.

p, Darryl F. Zanuck; d, George Marshall; w, Karl Tunberg, Don Ettlinger, Jack Yellen (based on a story by Tunberg, Ettinger); ph, Robert Planck; ed, Louis Loeffler.

Football/Comedy/
Musical (PR:A MPAA:NR)

HOLD THAT LINE**

(1952) 67m MON bw

Leo Gorcey *(Slip)*, Huntz Hall *(Sach)*, Gil Stratton, Jr. *(Junior)*, David Gorcey *(Chuck)*, Bennie Bartlett *(Butch)*, Bernard Gorcey *(Louie)*, Taylor Holmes *(Dean Forrester)*, Francis Pierlot *(Billingsley)*, Pierre Watkin *(Stanhope)*, John Bromfield *(Biff)*, Bob Nichols *(Harold)*, Mona Knox *(Katie Wayne)*, Gloria Winters *(Penny)*, Paul Bryar *(Coach Rowland)*, Bob Peoples *(Assistant Coach)*, Veda Ann Borg *(Candy Calin)*, Byron Foulger *(Prof. Grog)*, Tom Hanlon *(Football Announcer)*, George Lewis *(Mike Donelli)*.

The Bowery Boys meet "Pygmalion" in HOLD THAT LINE, as a pair of university trustees encourage Slip (Leo Gorcey) and Sach (Huntz Hall) to enroll at an Ivy League school as a kind of sow's ear-silk purse experiment. In chemistry class, Sach concocts a vitamin that transforms him into a gridiron hero, much to the dismay of the team's reigning star (John Bromfield), who is in cahoots with gamblers. When the Big Game comes around, Sach is kidnaped, but though he reappears in the nick of time, it's up to another of the Boys to perform the last minute heroics. Director William Beaudine handles the football action better than the comedy in this one, but there is still plenty of the usual Bowery Boys mayhem.

p, Jerry Thomas; d, William Beaudine; w, Tim Ryan, Charles R. Marion, Bert Lawrence; ph, Marcel Le Picard; ed, William Austin.

Football/Comedy   **(PR:A   MPAA:NR)**

HOME IN INDIANA***

(1944) 103m FOX c

Walter Brennan (J.P. "Thunder" Bolt), Lon McCallister (Sparke Thorton), Jeanne Crain (Char), June Haver (Cri-Cri), Charlotte Greenwood (Penny), Ward Bond (Jed Bruce), Charles Dingle (Godaw Boole), Robert Condon (Gordon Bradley), Charles Saggau (Jitterbug), Willie Best (Mo' Bum), George H. Reed (Tuppy), Noble "Kid" Chissell (Fleaflit Dryer), Walter Baldwin (Ed), George Cleveland (Sam), Arthur Aylesworth (Blacksmith).

Directed by Henry Hathaway, HOME IN INDIANA is a heartfelt story about Sparke Thornton (Lon McCallister), a city kid who goes to live in the country with his aunt and uncle (Charlotte Greenwood and Walter Brennan), a pair of semi-retired horse breeders with only one trotter left on their farm. Char (Jeanne Crain) and Cri-Cri (June Haver) are the two local lovelies who introduce Sparke to another side of country living (swimming holes and jitterbugging primarily—this is the 1940s). With the help of his uncle and the handyman (Willie Best), Sparke decides to raise a filly and become a champion sulky racer himself. This cheerful, upbeat film includes some nice location work on the racetracks of Kentucky, Indiana, and Ohio.

p, Andre Daven; d, Henry Hathaway; w, Winston Miller (based on the novel The Phantom Filly, by George Agnew Chamberlain); ph, Edward Cronjager (Technicolor); ed, Harmon Jones; m, Hugo Friedhofer.

Horse Racing   **(PR:AA   MPAA:NR)**

HOME ON THE RANGE*½

(1935) 54m PAR bw

Jackie Coogan (Jack), Randolph Scott (Tom Hatfield), Evelyn Brent (Georgie), Dean Jagger (Thurman), Addison Richards (Beady), Fuzzy Knight ("Cracker"), Ann Sheridan (Girl Entertainer).

Randolph Scott and Jackie Coogan play a pair of stable-owning brothers in this combination western and racetrack story that never quite comes together. One of their horses, Midnight, is a sure winner, and bad guys covet not only it but the brothers' ranch, which, true to formula, has a mortgage they can't pay. Not to worry. Midnight and young Jack (Coogan) bring an end to all this nonsense in a climactic showdown race.

p, Harold Hurley; d, Arthur Jacobson; w, Harold Shumate,

Ethel Doherty, Grant Garrett, Charles A. Logue (based on the novel Code of the West by Zane Grey); ph, William Mellor; ed, Jack Dennis.

Horse Racing/
Western   **(PR:A   MPAA:NR)**

HOOSIERS****

(1986) 114m Hemdale/Orion c

Gene Hackman (Coach Norman Dale), Barbara Hershey (Myra Fleener), Dennis Hopper (Shooter), Sheb Wooley (Cletus), Fern Persons (Opal Fleener), Brad Boyle (Whit), Steve Hollar (Rade), Brad Long (Strap), David Neidorf (Everett), Kent Poole (Merle), Wade Schenck (Ollie), Scott Summers (Whit), Maris Valainis (Jimmy), Chelcie Ross (George), Robert Swan (Rollin), Michael O'Guinne (Rooster), Wil Dewitt (Mr. Doty), John Robert Thompson (Sheriff Finley).

It should come as little surprise that the best movie ever made about basketball, HOOSIERS, is set in Indiana, where babies are given roundballs before they get rattles. Loosely based on the true story of the team from tiny Milan High School (164 students) that won the 1954 Indiana state championship, this uplifting film, set in 1951, follows Norman Dale (Gene Hackman), a big-time college coach who has fallen from grace, as he comes to Hickory, Indiana, to lead the high school basketball team. Jimmy, the town's most gifted player, is so disturbed by the death of the previous coach that he declines to join the team, but Norman refuses to pressure him into doing so, earning the reluctant respect of Myra Fleener (Barbara Hershey), the acting principal. Norman also remains determined to run the team his way, despite the animosity of the townspeople. With the expert help of Shooter (Dennis Hopper, in an Oscar-nominated performance that is one of the finest of his career), the alcoholic father of one of the players, Norman perseveres, and when Jimmy decides to play after all, the sky—or at least the state championship—is the limit. Bursting with emotion and full of exhilarating game action, HOOSIERS magnificently captures the ambience of small-town Indiana basketball, but more than that it is a universal story of pride, courage, love, and redemption. David Anspaugh's direction is assured, Fred Murphy's cinematography is gorgeous, Jerry Goldsmith's score unforgettable, and the performances are uniformly excellent. Only one thing pleased Hoosier basketball fans more than this film did in 1987—Bobby Knight's third NCAA championship at Indiana University.

p, Carter DeHaven, Angelo Pizzo; d, David Anspaugh; w, Angelo Pizzo; ph, Fred Murphy (CFI Color); ed, C. Timothy O'Meara; m, Jerry Goldsmith.

Basketball   **Cas.**   **(PR:A-C   MPAA:PG)**

HORSE FEATHERS****

(1932) 70m PAR bw

Groucho Marx (Prof. Quincy Adams Wagstaff), Harpo Marx (Harpo), Chico Marx (Chico), Zeppo Marx (Zeppo), Thelma Todd (Connie Bailey), David Landau (Jennings),

Florine McKinney *(Peggy Carrington)*, Jim Pierce *(Mullens)*, Nat Pendleton *(McCarthy)*, Reginald Barlow *(President of College)*, Robert Grieg *(Prof. Hornsvogel)*.

The Marx Brothers bring their special brand of anarchy to the world of college football in this wonderfully madcap comedy. Prof. Quincy Adams Wagstaff (Groucho) is named president of Huxley College, which hasn't won a football game since its founding in 1888. Acting on the advice of his son (Zeppo), Wagstaff attempts to recruit a pair of pro players, but a mixup at a speakeasy leads him to mistake a dog catcher (Harpo) and bootlegging iceman (Chico) for football players. Just the same, Wagstaff sends them to kidnap arch rival Darwin College's ringers; unfortunately, they fail. Meanwhile, college widow Connie Bailey (Thelma Todd), who is in cahoots with Darwin's Jennings, tries to wheedle the Huxley *signals* out of Groucho. Although there are many funny moments preceding it, the film's big payoff comes in the Huxley-Darwin game, in which Harpo, Chico, and Groucho all contribute to a zany comeback victory brought about through the use of banana peels, an elastic band, a chariot, and a surplus of footballs. Perhaps the wildest film the Brothers Marx ever made, this fast-paced laugh fest was directed by Norman Z. McLeod and written by the great humorist S.J. Perelman with help from Bert Kalmar and Harry Ruby, who also contributed the songs "I'm Against It" and "Everyone Says I Love You."

d, Norman Z. McLeod; w, Bert Kalmar, Harry Ruby, S.J. Perelman; ph, Ray June.

Football/Comedy   **(PR:A   MPAA:NR)**

HOT CURVES**

(1930) 83m Tiffany bw

Marceline [Alice] Day, Benny Rubin, Pert Kelton, Natalie Moorhead, Rex Lease, Mary Carr, John Ince, Paul Hurst, Mike Donlin.

Looking to attract Jewish fans, a big league baseball team signs the first young Jewish ball player who comes along (Benny Rubin); however, he ends up becoming a hero both on and off the field, preventing the club's star pitcher from being dragged down by a bad woman. Reportedly, HOT CURVES was inspired by the New York Giants' acquisition of Andy Cohen.

d, Norman Taurog; w, Earle Snell, Frank Mortimer, Benny Rubin (based on a story by Mortimer, A.P. Younger); ph, Max Dupont; ed, Clarence Kolster.

Baseball   **(PR:A   MPAA:NR)**

HOT SHOT**

(1987) 101m Intl. Film Marketing-Arista c

Jim Youngs *(Jimmy Kristidis)*, Pele *(Santos)*, Billy Warlock *(Vinnie Fortino)*, Leon Russom *(Coach)*, David Groh *(Jerry Norton)*, Rutanya Alda *(Georgia Kristidis)*, Peter Henry Schroeder *(Nick Kristidis)*, Weyman Thompson, Mario Van Peebles.

Jimmy Kristidis (Jim Youngs),   a brash professional soc-

cer player for the New York Rockers, is removed from the lineup as a result of his hot-dog playing style, then suspended from the team for two months after he gives the coach (Leon Russom) a tongue lashing when his best friend, Vinnie Fortino (Billy Warlock), is left paralyzed by a game injury. Frustrated, Jimmy travels to Brazil, where he meets his hero, Santos, a retired soccer star (played by real-life retired soccer star Pele) and persuades him to help him with his game. Santos' tutelage transforms both Jimmy's play and his personality, and when the American returns to New York, he's able to help out Vinnie and prove himself on the field. Director Rick King aims for the heartstrings with nearly every frame, but ends up undermining his otherwise engaging premise with cheap sentiment. Unfortunately, the acting isn't much better, and this one will probably be best appreciated by soccer devotees. If it's the great Pele that you want to watch in action, pass up HOT SHOT and go directly to John Huston's VICTORY, a much better film that puts the brilliant Brazilian's talents to much better use.

p, Steve Pappas; d, Rick King; w, Joe Sauter, Rick King, Ray Errol Fox, Bill Guttentag; ph, Greg Andracke, Edgar Moura (Deluxe Color); ed, Stan Salfas; m, William Orbit.

Soccer   **(PR:A   MPAA:PG)**

HUDDLE*½

(1932) 103m MGM bw (GB: IMPOSSIBLE LOVER)

Ramon Novarro *(Tony)*, Madge Evans *(Rosalie)*, Una Merkel *(Thelma)*, Ralph Graves *(Coach Malcolm)*, John Arledge *(Pidge)*, Frank Albertson *(Larry)*, Kane Richmond *(Tom Stone)*, Martha Sleeper *(Barbara)*, Henry Armetta *(Mr. Amatto)*, Ferike Boros *(Mrs. Armatto)*, Rockliffe Fellows *(Mr. Stone)*, Joseph Sawyer *(Slater)*.

This slow-moving football film chronicles the college career of a tough Italian kid (Ramon Novarro) who tries to use his prowess on the gridiron to become BMOC at Yale. It doesn't work, however, as he is passed over in the fraternity elections and shunned by the girl he tries to romance (Madge Evans). After four years of tough going and a significant personality change, things begin to look up for him, and he finishes his football career with a heroic flourish against Harvard.

d, Sam Wood; w, Walton Hall Smith, C. Gardner Sullivan, Robert Lee Johnson, Arthur S. Hyman (based on a story by Francis Wallace); ph, Harold Wenstrom; ed, Hugh Wynn.

Football   **(PR:A   MPAA:NR)**

HUMPHREY TAKES A CHANCE*½

(1950) 62m MON bw

Leon Errol *(Knobby)*, Joe Kirkwood, Jr. *(Joe Palooka)*, Lois Collier *(Anne Howe)*, Robert Coogan *(Humphrey Pennyworth)*, Jack Kirkwood *(Phiffeney)*, Andrew Tombes *(Sheriff Grogan)*, Stanley Prager *(Ward)*, Tim Ryan *(Bentley)*, Almira Sessions *(Mrs. Hardwig)*, Joel Friedkin *(Hootleman)*, Tom Neal *(Gordon Rogers)*, Gil Lamb *(Martin)*, Chester Conklin *(Prentice)*, Hank Mann *(Hiram)*,

Clarence Hennecke *(Zeke),* Chester Clute *(Upperbottom),* Victoria Horne *(Miss Tucker),* Mary Happy *(Mary).*

Joe Kirkwood pummels again as Joe Palooka in one of the lesser boxing comedies based on the exploits of Ham Fisher's comic-strip hero. This time, Joe and his erstwhile manager, Knobby (Leon Errol), do battle with a shady mayor and a dishonest fight promoter who have tricked a punchy boxer, the eponymous Humphrey (Robert Coogan), into signing an unfair contract. The crooks are really interested in using Humphrey to manipulate Joe into putting his name on the dotted line, but don't bet on their scheme's working out.

p, Hal E. Chester; d, Jean Yarbrough; w, Henry Blankfort; ph, William Sickner; ed, Otho Lovering.

Boxing/Comedy (PR:A MPAA:NR)

HUSTLER, THE***

(1961) 134m FOX bw

Paul Newman *("Fast" Eddie Felson),* Jackie Gleason *(Minnesota Fats),* Piper Laurie *(Sarah Packard),* George C. Scott *(Bert Gordon),* Myron McCormick *(Charlie Bums),* Murray Hamilton *(Findlay),* Michael Constantine *(Big John),* Stefan Gierasch *(Preacher),* Jake LaMotta *(Bartender),* Gordon B. Clarke *(Cashier),* Alexander Rose *(Scorekeeper),* Carolyn Coates *(Waitress),* Carl York *(Young Hustler),* Vincent Gardenia *(Bartender),* Gloria Curtis *(Girl with Fur Coat),* Willie Mosconi.

This unqualified masterpiece based on Walter Tevis' novel boasts Paul Newman in the role that made him an overnight superstar—"Fast" Eddie Felson, a pool shark who hustles his way across the country to Ames Billiard Parlor in New York, where he nearly bests the unbeatable Minnesota Fats (Jackie Gleason) before being taken to the cleaners. Penniless and alone, Eddie falls in love with Sarah Packard (Piper Laurie), an alcoholic cripple; then, after a return to small-time hustling that leads to two thug-administered broken thumbs, Eddie teams up with gambler Bert Gordon (George C. Scott), who becomes his backer but also plays a role in Sarah's suicide. The film's climactic sequence finds Eddie back at the table with Fats, and, if you don't already know, it's a very different story this time around. With the help of Gene Shufton's Oscar-winning black-and-white cinematography, producer-writer-director Robert Rossen offers a grim world where the only bright spot is the top of the pool table, yet his characters maintain a shabby nobility and grace. The performances are all excellent: Gleason is brilliantly detached, witty, and charming as Fats; self-involved but sexy Laurie offers some of the best work of her career; Scott is evil incarnate; and Newman is simply unforgettable in his Oscar-nominated role (he would have play Fast Eddie again 25 years later in the excellent sequel, THE COLOR OF MONEY, to actually win his first Academy Award). The great pool player Willie Mosconi coached Gleason and Newman in their shots. Not to be missed.

p, Robert Rossen; d, Robert Rossen; w, Sidney Carroll, Robert Rossen (based on the novel by Walter Tevis); ph,

Gene Shufton (CinemaScope); ed, Dede Allen; m, Kenyon Hopkins.

Pool Cas. (PR:C MPAA:NR)

ICE CASTLES**

(1978) 113m COL c

Lynn Holly Johnson *(Alexis Winston),* Robby Benson *(Nick Peterson),* Colleen Dewhurst *(Beulah Smith),* Tom Skerritt *(Marcus Winston),* Jennifer Warren *(Deborah Macland),* David Huffman *(Brian Dockett),* Diane Reilly *(Sandy),* Craig T. McMullen *(Doctor),* Kelsey Ufford *(Ceciel Monchet),* Leonard Lilyholm *(Hockey Coach),* Jean-Claude Bleuze *(French Coach),* Brian Foley *(Choreographer),* Teresa Willmus *(Annette Brashlout),* Diana Holden *(X-ray Technician),* Carol Williams *(TV Producer).*

Lynn Holly Johnson is Alexis Winston, a figure skater with a bright Olympic future who is blinded in a freak accident. With the help of Nick Peterson (Robby Benson), her hockey-playing, repulsively sensitive boy friend, she wages a brave battle to make it back to the top. Colleen Dewhurst is superb as the owner of a local skating rink who tries not to live out her failed dreams through Alexis, and Bill Butler's cinematography is stunning, but Johnson and Benson are entirely *too wonderful,* and ICE CASTLES collapses under the weight of sentimental overkill.

p, John Kemeny, S. Rodger Olenicoff; d, Donald Wrye; w, Donald Wrye, Gary L. Baim (based on a story by Baim); ph, Bill Butler (Metrocolor); ed, Michael Kahn, Maury Winetrobe, Melvin Shapiro; m, Marvin Hamlisch.

Figure Skating Cas. (PR:A MPAA:PG)

IDOL OF THE CROWDS½**

(1937) 62m UNIV bw

John Wayne *(Johnny Hanson),* Sheila Bromley *(Helen Dale),* Charles Brokaw *(Jack Irwin),* Billy Burrud *(Bobby),* Jane Johns *(Peggy),* Huntley Gordon *(Harvey Castle),* Frank Otto *(Joe Garber),* Russell Hopton *(Kelly),* Virginia Brissac *(Mrs. Dale),* George Lloyd *(Spike Regan),* Hal Neiman *(Squat Bates),* Clem Bevans *(Andy Moore),* Wayne Castle *(Swifty),* Lloyd Ford *(Hank),* Lee Ford *(Elmer).*

Trading his six-shooter for a slap shot, John Wayne manages to exude toughness as Johnny Hanson, a virtuous Maine chicken farmer who takes a stab at professional hockey in order to earn enough money to keep from losing his spread. His brother Bobby (Billy Burrud) also earns a spot on the team, but their lives become complicated when crooks try to get the Hansons to purposely blow some games. What's more, pretty Helen Dale (Sheila Bromley) tries to ruin Johnny's play by turning his head, but by the finale, it's she who lets romance prevent her from doing her job.

p, Trem Carr, Paul Malvern; d, Arthur Lubin; w, George Waggner, Harold Buckley (based on the story "Hell on Ice" by George Waggner); ph, Harry Neumann; ed, Charles Craft.

Hockey (PR:A MPAA:NR)

IN THIS CORNER**

(1948) 62m EL bw

Scott Brady *(Jimmy Weston)*, Anabel Shaw *(Sally Rivers)*, Charles D. Brown *(Doc Fuller)*, James Millican *(Tug Martin)*, Mary Meade *(Birdie Bronson)*, Robert Bice *(Comdr. Harris)*, Don Forbes *(TV Announcer)*, John Doucette *(Dunkle)*, Cy Kendall *(Tiny Reads)*, John Indrisano *(Tommy Hart)*, Bill Kennedy *(Barton)*.

This variation on the boxing film formula deals with a crooked manager (James Millican) who stages the fake ring death of a sparring partner when his fighter, Jimmy Weston (Scott Brady), refuses to take a dive. Jimmy, a WW II navy veteran, killed a man while boxing in the service, and this new "death" takes a heavy toll on his performance in the ring. Ah, but lucky Jimmy has his faithful girl friend in his corner, and she goes in search of the "dead" sparring partner, returning with him in just the nick of time.

p, David L. Stephenson; d, Charles F. Riesner; w, Burk Symon, Fred Niblo, Jr.; ph, Guy Roe, Joseph LaShelle; ed, Norman Colbert, Al De Gaetano.

Boxing (PR:A MPAA:NR)

INDIANAPOLIS SPEEDWAY**

(1939) 85m WB bw (GB: DEVIL ON WHEELS)

Pat O'Brien *(Joe Greer)*, Ann Sheridan *(Frankie Merrick)*, John Payne *(Eddie Greer)*, Gale Page *(Lee Mason)*, Frank McHugh *(Spud Connors)*, Granville Bates *(Mr. Greer)*, Grace Stafford *(Martha Connors)*, John Ridgely *(Ted Horn)*, Regis Toomey *(Wilbur Shaw)*, John Harron *(Red)*, William B. Davidson *(Duncan Martin)*, Ed McWade *(Tom Dugan)*, Irving Bacon *(Fred Haskill)*, Tommy Bupp *(Haskill's Son)*, Robert Middlemass *(Edward Hart)*, Charles Halton *(Mayor)*.

This remake of THE CROWD ROARS (1932) deviates little from the original Jimmy Cagney starrer, with Pat O'Brien in the lead role as Joe Greer, an auto racer who is determined to keep his younger brother Eddie (John Payne) in school and away from the racetrack. Frustrated, Eddie takes a seat behind the wheel of someone else's car, and when he and Joe battle it out on the track, Joe's friend, Spud Connors (Frank McHugh), who enacted the same role in the original, is killed. Joe then begins a downward spiral that doesn't end until he has to take over for Eddie during the Indianapolis 500. Gale Page plays Joe's girl friend and Ann Sheridan is the woman who steals Eddie's heart. Though its racing scenes are relatively well done, this Lloyd Bacon-directed film finishes a distant second to Howard Hawks' superior original.

p, Max Siegel; d, Lloyd Bacon; w, Sig Herzig, Wally Klein

(based on the story by Howard Hawks, Seton I. Miller ph, Sid Hickox; ed, William Holmes.

Auto Racing (PR:A MPAA:NR)

INSIDE MOVES**½

(1980) 113m Goodmark/Associated c

John Savage *(Roary)*, David Morse *(Jerry)*, Diana Scarwid *(Louise)*, Amy Wright *(Ann)*, Tony Burton *(Lucius Porter)*, Bill Henderson *(Blue Lewis)*, Steve Kahan *(Burt)*, Jack O'Leary *(Max)*, Bert Remsen *(Stinky)*, Harold Russell *(Wings)*, Pepe Serna *(Herrada)*, Harold Sylvester *(Alvin Martin)*, Arnold Williams *(Benny)*.

Roary (John Savage), who attempts suicide but ends up partly paralyzed, frequents a bar where other patrons are handicapped and befriends Jerry (David Morse), a basketball player with a promising future but who lacks the funds to pay for an operation to rehabilitate his knee. Eventually, Jerry gets his operation, stars for a semipro team, and earns a shot at the big time. Along the way, he forgets about his friends at Max's Bar, who are hurt by his selfishness. In the meantime, Roary learns to accept his disability and struggles through a difficult romance with Louise (Diana Scarwid). He isn't the only one who comes to know himself better, however, and by the upbeat finale, all of the old friends are reconciled. Despite a predictable plot and an abundance of stereotypes—the product of a surprisingly clunky script by Barry Levinson (THE NATURAL; DINER) and Valerie Curtin—this is a well-meaning film with strong performances all around. Harold Russell, the double amputee who won an Oscar for his performance in THE BEST YEARS OF OUR LIVES (1946), makes his second film appearance here as a card-playing bar regular.

p, Mark M. Tanz, R.W. Goodwin; d, Richard Donner; w, Valerie Curtin, Barry Levinson (based on the novel by Todd Walton); ph, Laszlo Kovacs (Panavision/ Technicolor); ed, Frank Morriss; m, John Barry.

Basketball **Cas.** (PR:C-O MPAA:PG)

IRON MAJOR, THE***

(1943) 85m RKO bw

Pat O'Brien *(Frank Cavanaugh)*, Ruth Warrick *(Florence "Mike" Ayres Cavanaugh)*, Robert Ryan *(Father Tim Donovan)*, Leon Ames *(Robert Stewart)*, Russell Wade *(Pvt. Manning)*, Bruce Edwards *(Lt. Jones)*, Richard Martin *(Davis Cavanaugh)*, Robert Bice *(Coach)*, Virginia Brissac *(Mrs. Ayres)*, Lew Harvey *(Lieutenant)*, Walter Brooke *(Lt. Stone)*, Louis Jean Heydt *(Recruiting Sergeant)*, Pierre Watkin *(Col. White)*, Walter Fenner *(Doctor)*, Willy Roy *(Bob as a Boy)*, Robert Winkler *(Frank as a Boy)*, Joel Davis *(Davie as a Boy)*, Cyril Ring *(Ross)*, Henry Roquemore *(Evans)*, Barbara Hale *(Sarah Cavanaugh)*, Kirk Alyn *(John Cavanaugh)*, James Jordan *(Philip Cavanaugh)*, Dean Benton *(William Cavanaugh)*, Margaret L. Landry *(Sis Cavanaugh)*, Myron Healey *(Paul Cavanaugh)*.

After his extraordinary performance in KNUTE ROCKNE— ALL AMERICAN in 1940, Pat O'Brien portrayed another legendary coach—Frank Cavanaugh, of Dartmouth, Boston College, and Fordham. The father of 10, a dedicated family man, and firm believer in God and country, Cavanaugh returns from WW I with the rank of major but with his eyesight damaged. Still, with his wife, Florence (Ruth Warrick), at his side, Cavanaugh continues his illustrious coaching career, consistently leading his teams to winning seasons; and even as total blindness sets in, he directs Fordham to an important win over Oregon State in 1932. Based on a book written by Florence Cavanaugh, THE IRON MAJOR includes much newsreel footage from Cavanaugh-coached games, including the famous Fordham-Oregon State contest. O'Brien's energetic and charismatic performance truly captures the spirit of the Iron Major, and Robert Ryan does a nice turn as Father Tim Donovan, Cavanaugh's priest and former teammate.

p, Robert Fellows; d, Ray Enright; w, Aben Kandel, Warren Duff (based on a story by Florence Cavanaugh); ph, Robert de Grasse; ed, Robert Wise, Philip Martin, Jr.; m, Roy Webb.

Football/Biography   (PR:A MPAA:NR)

IRON MAN, THE***

(1931) 73m UNIV bw

Lew Ayres *(Kid Mason)*, Robert Armstrong *(George Regan)*, Jean Harlow *(Rose Mason)*, John Miljan *(Paul H. Lewis)*, Eddie Dillon *(Jeff)*, Mike Donlin *(McNeil)*, Morrie Cohan *(Rattler O'Keefe)*, Mary Doran *(The Show Girl)*, Mildred Van Dorn *(Gladys DeVere)*, Ned Sparks *(Riley)*, Sam Blum *(Mandel)*, Sammy Gervon *(Trainer)*, Tom Kennedy *(Bartender)*.

When Kid Mason (Lew Ayres), a promising lightweight, loses a big fight, Rose (Jean Harlow), his domineering, money-hungry wife, leaves him to search for fame as an actress in Hollywood, much to the delight of the Kid's manager, George Regan (Robert Armstrong), who puts his lovesick fighter on a rigorous training program to prepare for a comeback. Not surprisingly, the boxer starts winning again, and before you can count to 10, Rose is back, Regan is out of a job, Paul Lewis (John Miljan)—Rose's secret lover—is installed as Kid's manager, and Kid begins losing his edge again. With a big bout close at hand and Kid wholly unprepared for it, Regan presents the fighter with startling evidence of Rose's infidelity, but though the Kid enters the ring a wiser man, he still isn't through getting his lumps. Directed by horror master Tod Browning (FREAKS; DRACULA) and based on a W.R. Burnett novel, IRON MAN is a competent if unremarkable film. Though the featured stars were Ayres and Harlow, Armstrong grabs the picture away from them with his rapid-fire delivery and hard-boiled mannerisms. THE IRON MAN was remade in 1937 as SOME BLONDES ARE DANGEROUS and again in 1951 under its original title (see below).

p, Carl Laemmle, Jr.; d, Tod Browning; w, Francis Edward Faragoh (based on the novel by W.R. Burnett); ph, Percy Hilburn; ed, Maurice Pivar, Milton Carruth.

Boxing   (PR:A MPAA:NR)

IRON MAN, THE**½

(1951) 81m UNIV bw

Jeff Chandler *(Coke Mason)*, Evelyn Keyes *(Rose Warren)*, Stephen McNally *(George Mason)*, Joyce Holden *(Tiny)*, Rock Hudson *(Speed O'Keefe)*, Jim Backus *(Max Watkins)*, Jim Arness *(Alex)*, Paul Javor *(Pete)*, Steve Martin *(Joe Savella)*, Eddie Simms *(Jackie Bowden)*, George Baxter *(Herb Riley)*, Raymond Gray *(Jo Jo Meyers)*, Walter Ekwart *(Whitey)*, John Maxwell *(Dr. Rowan)*, Larry Blake *(Ralph Crowley)*, Ken Patterson *(Herb Daly)*.

Differing considerably from the first film version of W.R. Burnett's boxing novel, this loose, relatively satisfying remake of THE IRON MAN (see above) stars Jeff Chandler as Coke Mason, a poor coal miner who is desperate to leave the mines and marry his girl friend, Rose (Evelyn Keyes). Hoping to earn enough money to buy a small radio shop, he becomes a prizefighter, but when he enters the ring he is transformed into a savage beast, administering terrible beatings to his opponents that turns crowds against him and worries both Rose and his older brother, George (Stephen McNally), who serves as his manager. They try to persuade him to hang up his gloves, but it is only when Coke is forced to fight his best friend (Rock Hudson) that he quells his killer instinct, winning the respect of the crowd and his loved ones. Director Joseph Pevney moves the story along at a rapid clip and is greatly aided by a strong cast of supporting players, including Jim Backus as a sportswriter.

p, Aaron Rosenberg; d, Joseph Pevney; w, George Zuckerman, Borden Chase (based on the story by W.R. Burnett); ph, Carl Guthrie; ed, Russell Schoengarth.

Boxing   (PR:C MPAA:NR)

IT HAPPENED IN FLATBUSH**½

(1942) 80m FOX bw

Lloyd Nolan *(Frank Maguire)*, Carole Landis *(Kathryn Baker)*, Sara Allgood *(Mrs. McAvoy)*, William Frawley *(Sam Sloan)*, Robert Armstrong *(Danny Mitchell)*, Jane Darwell *(Mrs. Maguire)*, George Holmes *(Roy Anderson)*, Scotty Beckett *(Squint)*, Joseph Allen, Jr. *(Walter Rogers)*, James Burke *(Shaunnessy)*, Roger Imhof *(Maguire)*, Matt McHugh *(O'Doul)*, LeRoy Mason *(Scott)*, Pat Flaherty *(O'Hara)*, Dale Van Sickel *(Stevenson)*.

In this better than average baseball film, Frank Maguire (Lloyd Nolan), a former player haunted by the memory of an error he made in an important game, is given a second chance in the big leagues, this time as a manager. Taking the helm of the Brooklyn Dodgers, he has to overcome both clubhouse dissension and the apathy of new owners when the team's longtime matriarch (Sara Allgood) dies. Even after the players petition to have him removed as the skipper, Frank rises to the challenge and leads them in an exciting pennant drive, falling in love with one of the new owners (Carole Landis) in the process.

p, Walter Morosco; d, Ray McCarey, Richard Day, Lewis

Creber; w, Lee Loeb, Harold Buchman; ph, Charles Clarke; ed, J. Watson Webb.

Baseball **(PR:A MPAA:NR)**

IT HAPPENS EVERY SPRING****

(1949) 87m FOX bw

Ray Milland *(Vernon Simpson)*, Jean Peters *(Deborah Greenleaf)*, Paul Douglas *(Monk Lanigan)*, Ed Begley *(Stone)*, Ted de Corsia *(Dolan)*, Ray Collins *(Prof. Greenleaf)*, Jessie Royce Landis *(Mrs. Greenleaf)*, Alan Hale, Jr. *(Schmidt)*, Bill Murphy *(Isbell)*, William E. Green *(Prof. Forsythe)*, Edward Keane *(Bell)*, Gene Evans *(Mueller)*, Al Eben *(Parker)*, Ruth Lee *(Miss Collins)*, John Butler *(Fan)*, Jane Van Duser *(Miss Mengalstein)*, Ray Teal *(Mac)*, Don Hicks *(Assistant to Announcer)*, Mickey Simpson *(Policeman)*, Johnny Calkins *(Boy)*, Harry Cheshire *(Doctor)*.

Superb actor Ray Milland shines as Vernon Simpson, a chemistry professor who stumbles onto a formula that repels any kind of wood that gets near it. Needing some extra cash so that he can marry his sweetheart (Jean Peters), Vernon, a big baseball fan, gets a tryout with the St. Louis Cardinals and, applying his special solution to the baseballs, transforms himself into an unhittable pitcher. Not only does he make the team, but he wins 38 games and almost single-handedly wraps up the World Series as his doctored *screw*balls hop, bounce, jerk, and flit around mightily swung bats. One of the funniest moments in this sidesplitting comedy comes when Vernon's catcher roommate (Paul Douglas) mistakes the solution for hair tonic and tries to take a brush to his head. Featuring a marvelous script by Valentine Davies and ably directed by Lloyd Bacon, IT HAPPENS EVERY SPRING is one of the most entertaining films ever made about the national pastime.

p, William Perlberg; d, Lloyd Bacon; w, Valentine Davies (based on a story by Davies, Shirley W. Smith); ph, Joe MacDonald; ed, Bruce Pierce; m, Leigh Harline.

Baseball/Comedy **(PR:AA MPAA:NR)**

J.W. COOP***

(1971) 112m COL c

Cliff Robertson *(J.W. Coop)*, Geraldine Page *(Mama)*, Christina Ferrare *(Bean)*, R.G. Armstrong *(Jim Sawyer)*, R.L. Armstrong *(Tooter Watson)*, John Crawford *(Rancher)*, Wade Crosby *(Billy Sol Gibbs)*, Marjorie Durant Dye *(Big Marge)*, Paul Harper *(Warden Morgan)*, Son Hooker *(Motorcycle Cop)*, Richard Kennedy *(Sheriff)*, Mary Robin Redd *(Bonnie May)*, Claude Stroud *(Rodeo Manager)*, Augie Vallejo *(Hector)*, Dennis Reiners *(Billy Hawkins)*, Myrtis Dightman *(Myrtis)*, Frank Hobbs *(Deacon)*, Billy Hogue *(Hogue)*, Billy Martinelli *(Eddie)*, Clyde W. Maye *(Cisco)*, Larry Clayman *(Finals Clown)*,

Larry Mahan *(Himself)*, John Ashby *(Johnny)*, Robert Christensen *(Bobby)*, Velma Cooper *(Maylene)*, Jim Madland *(Himself)*, Beverly Powers *(Dora Mae)*, Sharron Rae *(Herself)*.

Cliff Robertson produced, directed, cowrote, and starred in the title role of this involving film about a rodeo rider's attempt to adjust to a life on the outside after spending 10 years in prison. Both society and the rodeo have changed dramatically during Coop's incarceration, and he struggles to adapt as he undertakes a relationship with Bean (Christina Ferrare) while going after the national championship. The cast features members of the Rodeo Cowboys Association, and much of the action footage was shot during actual rodeo events.

p, Cliff Robertson; d, Cliff Robertson; w, Cliff Robertson, Gary Cartwright, Bud Shrake; ph, Frank Stanley, Adam Hollander, Ross Lowell, Fred Waugh (Eastmancolor); ed, Alex Beaton; m, Louie Shelton, Don Randi.

Rodeo **(PR:A MPAA:PG)**

JACKIE ROBINSON STORY, THE**½

(1950) 76m EL bw

Jackie Robinson *(Jackie Robinson)*, Ruby Dee *(Rae Robinson)*, Minor Watson *(Branch Rickey)*, Louise Beavers *(Jackie's Mother)*, Richard Lane *(Hopper)*, Harry Shannon *(Charlie)*, Ben Lessy *(Shorty)*, Bill Spaulding *(Bill Spaulding)*, Billy Wayne *(Clyde Sukeforth)*, Joel Fluellen *(Mack Robinson)*, Bernie Hamilton *(Ernie)*, Kenny Washington *(Tigers' Manager)*, Pat Flaherty *(Karpen)*, Howard Louis MacNeely *(Jackie as a Boy)*.

Jackie Robinson took time out after leading the Dodgers to their 1949 pennant to make the story of his life, and though he was a better infielder than he was an actor, anyone who loves baseball will be intrigued by the story of the determined man who broke the color barrier in the major leagues. Some license has been taken by the screenwriters, but for the most part this is a straightforward account of Robinson's lifelong battle against racism, following him from his impoverished childhood through his glory years at UCLA and on to his army experience and his playing days with the Kansas City Monarchs of the Negro Leagues, and finally depicting the tremendous challenge he faced while integrating first the Dodgers' Montreal farm club and then the Brooklyn team itself. The victim of more abuse than any athlete who ever stepped onto a playing field, Robinson holds his normally hot temper in check as a promise to Dodger boss Branch Rickey (nicely played by Minor Watson), courageously enduring a relentless onslaught of dehumanizing taunts from fans and players alike, constantly turning the other cheek, and forever changing the game.

p, Mort Briskin; d, Alfred E. Green; w, Lawrence Taylor, Arthur Mann (based on a story by Louis Pollock); ph, Ernest Laszlo; ed, Maurie M. Suess, Arthur H. Nadel; m, David Chudnow.

Baseball/Biography **Cas.** **(PR:AA MPAA:NR)**

JIM THORPE—ALL AMERICAN****

(1951) 107m WB bw (GB: MAN OF BRONZE)

Burt Lancaster *(Jim Thorpe)*, Charles Bickford *(Glenn S. "Pop" Warner)*, Steve Cochran *(Peter Allendine)*, Phyllis Thaxter *(Margaret Miller)*, Dick Wesson *(Ed Guyac)*, Jack Big Head *(Little Boy)*, Suni Warcloud *(Wally Denny)*, Alan Mejia *(Louis Tewanema)*, Hubie Kerns *(Tom Ashenbrunner)*, Nestor Paiva *(Hiram Thorpe)*, Jimmy Moss *(Jim Thorpe, Jr.)*, Billy Gray *(Young Jim Thorpe)*, Edwin Max *(Football Manager)*.

Burt Lancaster is terrific as America's greatest athlete, the wondrous Jim Thorpe, a native American who captured gold medals in the pentathlon and decathlon at the 1912 Stockholm Olympics, only to be stripped of them because he had played semi-professional baseball, violating his amateur status. This excellent film biography begins with Billy Gray portraying Thorpe as a youth on an Oklahoma reservation. Lancaster takes over as Thorpe matriculates to the all-Indian college at Carlisle, Pennsylvania, where he begins playing football to impress Margaret Miller (Phyllis Thaxter) as he falls in love with his future wife. Coached by the legendary Glenn "Pop" Warner (Charles Bickford), he captures All-American honors, then goes on to glory and disappointment in Stockholm, followed by an illustrious career in professional baseball and football. When his young son dies, Thorpe's spirit is broken and he turns to the bottle, losing Margaret, but by the film's close, he has regained his self-respect and is given some of the recognition due him. (In actuality, Thorpe is enshrined in the Pro Football Hall of Fame and his Olympic medals have been posthumously restored.) Directed with great zest by Michael Curtiz, JIM THORPE—ALL AMERICAN benefits from an intelligent script, a stirring score, an outstanding supporting cast, and a great portrayal by Lancaster—who performed most of his own athletic feats.

p, Everett Freeman; d, Michael Curtiz; w, Douglas Morrow, Frank Davis, Everett Freeman (based on the story "Bright Path" by Morrow, Vincent X. Flaherty, based on the biography by Russell J. Birdwell and James Thorpe); ph, Ernest Haller; ed, Folmar Blangsted; m, Max Steiner.

Football/Track and Field/Biography   **(PR:A MPAA:NR)**

JOE LOUIS STORY, THE***½

(1953) 88m UA bw

Coley Wallace *(Joe Louis)*, Paul Stewart *(Tad McGeehan)*, Hilda Simms *(Marva Louis)*, James Edwards *(Chappie Blackburn)*, John Marley *(Mannie Seamon)*, Dotts Johnson *(Julian Black)*, Evelyn Ellis *(Mrs. Barrow)*, Carl Rocky Latimer *(Arthur Pine)*, John Marriott *(Sam Langford)*, P. Jay Sidney *(Handler)*, Isaac Jones *(Johnny Kingston)*, Royal Beal *(Mike Jacobs)*, Buddy Thorpe *(Max Schmeling)*, Ruby Goldstein *(Himself)*.

Told in flashback, THE JOE LOUIS STORY is an honest, humanistic film biography that shows "the Brown Bomber" as a man, not a god, and is all the better for it. Coley Wallace, a one-time amateur boxer of some renown, plays the title role, and is an uncanny lookalike for the champ.

The story begins in Detroit as Louis slowly works his way to the top, and includes the famous bouts with the German fighter Max Schmeling (Buddy Thorpe), as well as Louis' disastrous comeback in 1951, resulting in a pummeling by Rocky Marciano. It also deals sensitively with Louis' failed marriage, and Wallace does a nice job of handling the champ's confusion regarding his celebrity status. Moreover, his work in the ring looks authentic, but for those who aren't convinced there is real-life fight footage edited in. Well directed by Robert Gordon, THE JOE LOUIS STORY was one of the first films with a nearly all-black cast to show black people in an honest, unpatronizing manner.

p, Stirling Silliphant; d, Robert Gordon; w, Robert Sylvester; ph, Joseph Brun; ed, David Kummins; m, George Bassman.

Boxing/Biography   **(PR:A MPAA:NR)**

JOE PALOOKA, CHAMP**½

(1946) 70m MON bw

Leon Errol *(Knobby Walsh)*, Elyse Knox *(Anne)*, Joe Kirkwood, Jr. *(Joe Palooka)*, Eduardo Ciannelli *(Florini)*, Joseph Sawyer *(Lefty)*, Elisha Cook, Jr. *(Eugene)*, Sam McDaniel *(Smoky)*, Robert Kent *(Brewster)*, Sarah Padden *(Mom Palooka)*, Michael Mark *(Pop Palooka)*, Lou Nova *(Al Costa)*, Russ Vincent *(Curly)*, Alexander Laszlo *(Aladar)*, Joe Louis, Manuel Ortiz, Ceferino Garcia, Henry Armstrong, Jack Roper *(Themselves)*.

The first film in Monogram's series based on Ham Fisher's comic strip, JOE PALOOKA, CHAMP rehashes the old boxing story of a talented youngster who is discovered by an astute manager and trained for a big fight. It should comes as no surprise, then, that gangsters want to see the fighter put on the canvas or that a society girl falls for him despite differences in their social classes. Although rife with cliches, the film has several strong fight sequences; Joe Kirkwood, Jr., does a nice job as Joe Palooka; and Leon Errol gives a competent performance as his manager, Knobby Walsh—roles they would repeat as the series continued. Real-life fighters Lou Nova and Jimmy McLarnin offer cameos as the champ and a referee, respectively, and boxing greats Joe Louis (see above), Manuel Ortiz, Ceferino Garcia, and Henry Armstrong also appear briefly.

p, Hal E. Chester; d, Reginald Le Borg; w, Cyril Endfield, Albert DePina (based on a story by Chester from the comic strip by Ham Fisher); ph, Benjamin Kline; ed, Bernard W. Burton.

Boxing   **(PR:AA MPAA:NR)**

JOE PALOOKA IN THE BIG FIGHT**½

(1949) 66m MON bw

Leon Errol *(Knobby Walsh)*, Joe Kirkwood, Jr. *(Joe Palooka)*, Lina Romay *(Maxine)*, David Bruce *(Tom Conway)*, George O'Hanlon *(Louie)*, Virginia Welles *(Anne Howe)*, Greg McClure *(Grady)*, Taylor Holmes *(Dr. Benson)*, Ian MacDonald *(Mike)*, Lou Lubin *(Talmadge)*, Bert Conway *(Pee Wee)*, Lyle Talbot *(Lt. Muldoon)*, Benny Baker *(Flight Secretary)*, Eddie Gribbon *(Canvas)*, Jack Roper *(Scranton)*, Frances Osborne *(Wardrobe Woman)*, Harry Hayden *(Commissioner Harris)*.

This better-than-average "Joe Palooka" film finds our hero (again played by Joe Kirkwood, Jr.) tangled up with gangsters who frame him on a drunk charge and then a murder rap, forcing Joe to undertake his own investigation to prove his innocence. Making the most of realistic dialog, director Cyril Endfield moves the film along at a nice pace while holding together a number of plot lines. Surprisingly, there isn't much boxing footage in this one.

p, Hal E. Chester; d, Cyril Endfield; w, Stanley Prager, Cyril Endfield (based on the comic strip by Ham Fisher); ph, Mack Stengler; ed, Fred Maguire.

Boxing   **(PR:AA MPAA:NR)**

JOE PALOOKA IN THE COUNTERPUNCH**½

(1949) 74m MON bw

Leon Errol *(Knobby Walsh)*, Joe Kirkwood, Jr. *(Joe Palooka)*, Elyse Knox *(Anne Howe)*, Marcel Journet *(Anton Kindel)*, Sheila Ryan *(Myra)*, Harry Lewis *(Chick Bennett)*, Frank Sully *(Looie)*, Ian Wolfe *(Prof. Lilliquist)*, Sam Hayes *(Fight Announcer)*, Walter Sande *(Austin)*, Douglas Dumbrille *(Capt. Lance)*, Douglas Fowley *(Thurston)*, Eddie Gribbon *(Canvasback)*, Suni Chorre *(Cardona)*, Ralph Graves *(Dr. Colman)*, Martin Garralaga *(Announcer)*, Roland Dupree *(Bell Boy)*, Gertrude Messinger *(Nurse)*, John Hart *(Pedro)*.

While traveling by boat to South America for a big bout against a Latin American champion, Joe Palooka (Joe Kirkwood, Jr.) and his manager, Knobby Walsh (Leon Errol), get mixed up with some counterfeiters. Joe joins forces with an on-board Fed to put an end to the criminals' scheming and injures his hand in the process, but still has plenty of punching power when he steps through the ropes. Despite a typical fight film plot and the stereotyping of Joe's ring opponent as a Latin hothead, slapstick comedy and a good dose of suspense combine to make this one of the more enjoyable films in the "Joe Palooka" series.

p, Hal E. Chester; d, Reginald Le Borg; w, Henry Blankfort, Cyril Endfield (based on the comic strip by Ham Fisher); ph, William Sickner; ed, Warren Adams; m, Edward J. Kay.

Boxing   **(PR:AA MPAA:NR)**

JOE PALOOKA IN THE SQUARED CIRCLE**

(1950) 63m MON bw

Joe Kirkwood, Jr. *(Joe Palooka)*, James Gleason *(Knobby Walsh)*, Lois Hall *(Anne Howe)*, Edgar Barrier *(Brogden)*, Myrna Dell *(Sandra)*, Robert Coogan *(Humphrey Pennyworth)*, Dan Seymour *(Crawford)*, Charles Halton *(Merkle)*, Frank Jenks *(Looie)*, Greg McClure *(Pete)*, Eddie Gribbon *(Canvas)*, Robert Griffin *(Kebo)*, John Harmon *(Phillips)*, Jack Roper *(Gunsel)*, Sue Carlton *(Felice)*, William Haade *(Bubbles)*, Stanley Prager *(TV Announcer)*.

Joe Palooka (Joe   Kirkwood. Jr.) witnesses a mob killing and vows to bring the killers to justice, but since the body

is missing, the cops can't help him. The boxer names names for the papers, however, and two of the murderers he fingers come looking for him, but are caught and sent to jail. The suspenseful fight sequence features a doped-up Joe valiantly trying to hold his crown, while manager Knobby Walsh (James Gleason, replacing series vet Leon Errol) is held by gangsters.

p, Hal E. Chester; d, Reginald Le Borg; w, Jan Jeffrey (based on the story by B.F. Melzer from the comic strip by Ham Fisher); ph, Marcel Le Picard.

Boxing   **(PR:A MPAA:NR)**

JOE PALOOKA IN TRIPLE CROSS**

(1951) 60m MON bw

Joe Kirkwood, Jr. *(Joe Palooka)*, James Gleason *(Knobby Walsh)*, Cathy Downs *(Anne)*, John Emery *(The Professor)*, Steve Brodie *(Dutch)*, Don Harvey *(Chuck)*, Rufe Davis *(Kenny Smith)*, Jimmy Wallington *(Himself)*, Mary Young *(Mrs. Reed)*, Eddie Gribbon *(Canvas)*, Sid Tomack *(Looie)*, Dickie Leroy *(Bub)*.

While on a fishing trip, Joe Palooka (Joe Kirkwood, Jr.), his wife, Anne (Cathy Downs), and his manager (James Gleason) are kidnaped by escaped convicts who use the trio as a cover to dodge the cops. One of the baddies, known only as the Professor (John Emery), decides to do away with his partners in crime and to make Joe throw a fight. The Professor comes to the arena disguised as Anne's aunt, and everything goes according to his plan until Joe allows himself to be knocked out of the ring long enough to put an end to the Professor's plotting—but not too long to beat the referee's count. This picture was the last in Monogram's "Joe Palooka" series.

p, Hal E. Chester; d, Reginald Le Borg; w, Jan Jeffrey (based on the story by Harold Bancroft from the comic strip by Ham Fisher); ph, William Sickner; m, Darrell Calker.

Boxing   **(PR:AA MPAA:NR)**

JOE PALOOKA IN WINNER TAKE ALL**½

(1948) 64m MON bw

Joe Kirkwood, Jr. *(Joe Palooka)*, Elyse Knox *(Anne Howe)*, William Frawley *(Knobby Walsh)*, Stanley Clements *(Tommy)*, John Shelton *(Greg Tanner)*, Mary Beth Hughes *(Millie)*, Sheldon Leonard *(Herman)*, Frank Jenks *(Louie)*, Lyle Talbot *(Henderson)*, Jack Roper *(Waldo)*, Eddie Gribbon *(Canvas)*, Wally Vernon *(Taxi Driver)*, Ralph Sanford *(Lt. Steve Mulford)*, Bill Martin *(Sportscaster)*, "Big" Ben Moroz *(Bobo Walker)*, Hal Fieberling *(Sammy Talbot)*, William Ruhl *(Talbot's Manager)*, Chester Clute *(Doniger)*.

William Frawley takes over the role of Joe Palooka's trusted manager Knobby Walsh in this Monogram series entry, which differs from most of the other "Joe Palooka" films in that it offers less talk and more boxing. Joe Kirkwood, Jr., is back as Ham Fisher's famous battler; Reginald Le Borg, the series' most frequently used director (JOE PALOOKA IN THE COUNTERPUNCH; JOE PALOOKA IN

THE SQUARED CIRCLE; JOE PALOOKA IN TRIPLE CROSS), is in charge; and, if you haven't already guessed, the story involves the usual Big Fight and fix-hungry gamblers.

p, Hal E. Chester; d, Reginald Le Borg; w, Stanley Rubin, Monte Collins (based on the comic strip by Ham Fisher); ph, William Sickner; ed, Otho Lovering; m, Edward J. Kay.

Boxing (PR:AA MPAA:NR)

JOE PALOOKA MEETS HUMPHREY**½

(1950) 65m MON bw

Leon Errol (Knobby/Lord Cecil Poole), Joe Kirkwood, Jr. (Joe Palooka), Robert Coogan (Humphrey), Jerome Cowan (Belden), Joe Besser (Carlton), Don McGuire (Mitchell), Pamela Blake (Anne Howe), Donald MacBride (Mayor), Curt Bois (Pierre), Clem Bevans (Mr. Edwards), Frank Sully (Looie), Eddie Gribbon (Canvas), Meyer Grace (Referee), Lillian Bronson (Prunella), Sam Balter (Announcer).

While Joe Palooka (Joe Kirkwood, Jr.) and his bride (Pamela Blake) are off on their honeymoon, Joe's manager, Knobby Walsh (Leon Errol, who also plays an English manager), books his charge for a charity fight against Humphrey (Robert Coogan), a nice-guy pug long on brawn but short on smarts. Coogan, who performs well here, repeated his role in another entry in the "Joe Palooka" series, HUMPHREY TAKES A CHANCE. Frequently amusing, though never sidesplitting, JOE PALOOKA MEETS HUMPHREY is no better or worse than most of the series' films.

p, Hal E. Chester; d, Jean Yarbrough, Dave Milton; w, Henry Blankfort (based on the comic strip by Ham Fisher); ph, William Sickner; ed, Otho Lovering; m, Edward J. Kay.

Boxing (PR:AA MPAA:NR)

JOHN GOLDFARB, PLEASE COME HOME**

(1964) 95m Parker-Orchard/FOX c

Shirley MacLaine (Jenny Ericson), Peter Ustinov (King Fawz), Richard Crenna (John Goldfarb), Jim Backus (Miles Whitepaper), Scott Brady (Sakalakis), Fred Clark (Heinous Overreach), Wilfrid Hyde-White (Mustafa Guz), Harry Morgan (Deems Sarajevo), Patrick Adiarte (Prince Ammud), Richard Deacon (Maginot), Jerome Cowan (Brinkley), Leon Askin (Samir), David Lewis (Cronkite), Milton Frome (Air Force General), Charles Lane (Editor), Jerry Orbach (Pinkerton), Jackie Coogan (Father Ryan), Telly Savalas (Harem Recruiter), Angela Douglas (Mandy), Richard Wilson (Frobish), Barbara Bouchet (Astrid Porche).

This mostly silly, sometimes amusing, but, in general, flat football comedy would have lost a fortune had not the University of Notre Dame (which objected to a scene in which Irish players were entertained by harem girls) sued the studio, drawing the curious to the theaters. "Wrong Way" John Goldfarb (Richard Crenna), an infamous football player-turned-U2 pilot, crash-lands in the fictional Middle Eastern nation of Fawzia, whose ruler (hammily portrayed by Peter Ustinov) presents the American with an ultimatum: either coach the football team the king is assembling for his son—who was cut by Notre Dame—or prepare for a trip to the USSR. The king then informs the US State Department that if it still wants to have a military base in his country, the Fighting Irish will have to take on his team in Fawzia. A international crisis brews when the Notre Dame players refuse to lie down in the climactic game, but Jenny Ericson (Shirley McLaine), a reporter who has become a member of the king's harem to do a story and who has fallen for Goldfarb, comes up with an unexpected resolution to the problem.

p, Steve Parker; d, J. Lee Thompson; w, William Peter Blatty; ph, Leon Shamroy (CinemaScope, DeLuxe Color); ed, William B. Murphy; m, Johnny Williams.

Football/Comedy (PR:A-C MPAA:NR)

JOHNNY BE GOOD zero

(1988) 98m Orion c

Anthony Michael Hall (Johnny Walker), Robert Downey, Jr. (Leo Wiggins), Paul Gleason (Wayne Hisler), Uma Thurman (Georgia Elkans), Steve James (Coach Sanders), Seymour Cassel (Wallace Gibson), Michael Greene (Tex Wade), Marshall Bell (Chief Elkans), Deborah May (Mrs. Walker), Michael Alldredge (Vinny Kroll), Jennifer Tilly (Connie Hisler), Jon Stafford (Bad Breath), Pete Koch (Pete Andropolous), Howard Cosell (Himself), Jim McMahon (Himself), George Hall (Grandpa Walker), Lucianne Buchanan (Lawanda Wade), Tony Frank (Joe Bob), Tim Rossovich (Gas Attendant), Robert Downey, Sr. (NCAA Investigator), David Denny (Benny Figg), Chris Dunn (Flick Weaver), John DeLuna (Jose Popupu), Ted Dawson.

Anthony Michael Hall, the likable teen star of the John Hughes comedy SIXTEEN CANDLES, appears here with a new image, as squeaky clean All-American quarterback Johnny Walker. Hall tries unceasingly to be a "dude" in this film, but comes off as nothing more than a phony, pesty geek. We are supposed to believe, however, that Johnny is the hottest high-school quarterback in the entire nation. The script, which might have provided a biting satire of college recruiting, instead plays on male fantasies, sexual double entendres, toilet humor, and an unhealthy portrait of women and minorities. Johnny is being courted by all the top college football programs, some more persuasive than others. Johnny, however, has a steady girl friend (Uma Thurman) with whom he has promised to attend the generic State University, which has a very good football program, but expects its students to (gasp!) attend class, pass exams, and play for the love of the game instead of recruitment promises. JOHNNY BE GOOD will probably be best remembered for the commercial that appears halfway through the film, in which Chicago Bears star QB Jim McMahon is visited by Johnny on the set of his latest promotional spot. Also on-screen are Howard Cosell, Los Angeles sportscaster Ted Dawson, KC Chiefs' linebacker Pete Koch, and the ubiquitous former footballer Tim Rossovich.

p, Adam Fields; d, Bud Smith; w, Steve Zacharias, Jeff Buhai, David Obst; ph, Robert D. Yeoman (Foto-Kem Color); ed, Scott Smith; m, Dick Rudolph.

Football   Cas.   (PR:O   MPAA:PG-13)

JOHNNY DARK**½

(1954) 85m UNIV c

Tony Curtis *(Johnny Dark)*, Piper Laurie *(Liz Fielding)*, Don Taylor *(Duke Benson)*, Paul Kelly *(Jim "Scotty" Scott)*, Ilka Chase *(Abbie Binns)*, Sidney Blackmer *(James Fielding)*, Ruth Hampton *(Miss Border-to-Border)*, Russell Johnson *(Emory)*, Joseph Sawyer *(Svenson)*, Robert Nichols *(Smitty)*, Pierre Watkin *(E.J. Winston)*, Ralph Montgomery *(Morgan)*, William Leslie *(Phil Clark)*, Scatman Crothers *(Himself)*, Vernon Rich *(Ross)*, Robert Bice *(Guard)*.

Johnny Dark (Tony Curtis) designs a race car for an independent automobile manufacturer, but discovers that he is being used by the company's owner (Sidney Blackmer) as a pawn in a battle against a stockholder (Pierre Watkin). Angered, Johnny steals the car and enters a Canada-to-Mexico cross-country race in which his main competition is an ex-buddy (Don Taylor). Everyone knows who's going to win the big race, but director George Sherman keeps things interesting along the way with some exciting action footage, and, for those who like romance mixed with their racing, there's a subplot involving Curtis and Piper Laurie. If supporting actor Russell Johnson looks familiar, think "Gilligan's Island." JOHNNY DARK was remade as THE LIVELY SET in 1964.

p, William Alland; d, George Sherman; w, Franklin Coen; ph, Carl Guthrie (Technicolor); ed, Edward Curtiss; m, Joseph Gershenson.

Auto Racing   (PR:A   MPAA:NR)

JUMP**

(1971) 97m Cannon c

Tom Ligon *(Chester Jump)*, Logan Ramsey *(Babe Duggers)*, Collin Wilcox-Horne *(April May)*, Sudie Bond *(Ernestine)*, Conrad Bain *(Lester)*, Norman Rose *(Dutchman)*, Lada Edmund, Jr. *(Enid)*, Bette Craig *(Beulah)*, Vicky Lynn *(Mercy)*, Jack Nance *(Ace)*.

Burdened by an awful (but insightfully depicted) family background, Chester Jump (Tom Ligon) tries his damnedest to make it as an auto racer, participating in everything from drag races to demolition derbies. Meeting with plenty of complications along the way, including a self-serving racing promoter, he is taken on an emotional roller-coaster ride that still isn't over as the credits begin to crawl. Despite its thin plot, JUMP profits from a fine performance by Ligon, some good support from the ensemble, and periodically incisive writing and direction, yet it never becomes the interesting picture it could have been.

p, Christopher C. Dewey; d, Joe Manduke; w, Richard Wheelwright; ph, Greg Sandor (DeLuxe Color); ed, George T. Norris.

Auto Racing   (PR:A   MPAA:GP)

JUNIOR BONNER***

(1972) 100m ABC/CINERAMA c

Steve McQueen *(Junior Bonner)*, Robert Preston *(Ace Bonner)*, Ida Lupino *(Elvira Bonner)*, Ben Johnson *(Buck Roan)*, Joe Don Baker *(Curly Bonner)*, Barbara Leigh *(Charmagne)*, Mary Murphy *(Ruth Bonner)*, Bill McKinney *(Red Terwiliger)*, Sandra Deel *(Nurse Arlis)*, Donald Barry *(Homer Rutledge)*, Dub Taylor *(Del, Bartender)*, Charles Gray *(Burt)*, Matthew Peckinpah *(Tim Bonner)*, Sundown Spencer *(Nick Bonner)*.

Steve McQueen stars in this fine Sam Peckinpah-directed film as the title character, an aging rodeo cowboy who returns to his small hometown, Prescott, Arizona, and learns that nothing stays the same. Saddened to discover that his parents (Ida Lupino and Robert Preston) have split and that his brother (Joe Don Baker) is getting rich selling off parcels of his father's land, Junior tries to regain his self-esteem by staying on a previously unrideable bull at the town's annual Fourth of July rodeo. There's much to recommend here, including some fine rodeo footage, winning characterizations from Ben Johnson as the man who supplies the livestock for the rodeo and Dub Taylor as the owner of the bar, and an especially strong performance by McQueen as the cowboy who realizes that he can't go home on the range again.

p, Joe Wizan; d, Sam Peckinpah; w, Jeb Rosebrook; ph, Lucien Ballard (Todd-AO, Movielab Color); ed, Robert Wolf; m, Jerry Fielding.

Rodeo   Cas.   (PR:A-C   MPAA:PG)

K

KANSAS CITY BOMBER**

(1972) 99m Artists Entertainment Complex/MGM c

Raquel Welch *(Diane "K.C." Carr)*, Kevin McCarthy *(Burt Henry)*, Helena Kallianiotes *(Jackie Burdette)*, Norman Alden *(Horrible Hank Hopkins)*, Jeanne Cooper *(Vivien)*, Mary Kay Pass *(Lovey)*, Martine Bartlett *(Mrs. Carr)*, Cornelia Sharpe *(Tammy O'Brien)*, William Gray Espie *(Randy)*, Dick Lane *(Len)*, Russ Marin *(Dick Wicks)*, Stephen Manley *(Walt)*, Jodie Foster *(Rita)*, Patti "Moo-Moo" Calvin *(Big Bertha Bogliani)*.

UCLA film school graduate student Barry Sandler tailored the screenplay for KANSAS CITY BOMBER (his master's thesis) for Raquel Welch, who plays K.C. Carr, a divorced mother of two who becomes one of the stars of a roller derby team when she has an affair with its owner, Burt Henry (Kevin McCarthy). The other skaters, particularly fiery Jackie Burdette (Helena Kallianiotes), are jealous of K. C.'s privileged position and make life difficult for her, but Horrible Hank (Norman Alden), a backwoods behemoth enamored of K.C., becomes her protector. Left to fend for herself when Hank is traded, K.C. asserts her independence by refusing to be a part of Henry's program.   Like roller derby, KANSAS CITY BOMBER is loud, violent, and occasionally interesting, with characterizations that range from well drawn (Kallianiotes) to obnoxious. Welch, who gives an adequate performance, did her own skating and the production was delayed for six weeks when she broke her wrist in a fall.

p, Marty Elfand; d, Jerrold Freedman; w, Thomas Rickman, Calvin Clements (based on a story by Barry Sandler); ph, Fred J. Koenekamp (Panavision, Metrocolor); ed, David Berlatsky; m, Don Ellis.

Roller Derby   **(PR:O   MPAA:PG)**

KENTUCKY***

(1938) 95m FOX c

Loretta Young (Sally Goodwin), Richard Greene (Jack Dillon), Walter Brennan (Peter Goodwin), Douglas Dumbrille (John Dillon, 1861), Karen Morley (Mrs. Goodwin, 1861), Moroni Olsen (John Dillon II 1937), Russell Hicks (Thad Goodwin, Sr., 1861), Willard Robertson (Bob Slocum), Charles Waldron (Thad Goodwin, 1937), George Reed (Ben), Bobs Watson (Peter Goodwin, 1861), Delmar Watson (Thad Goodwin, Jr., 1861), Leona Roberts (Grace Goodwin), Charles Middleton (Southerner), Billy McClain (Zeke), Madame Sul-Te-Wan (Lily), Cliff Clark (Melish), Meredith Howard (Susie May), Charles Trowbridge (Doctor), Stanley Andrews (Presiding Judge), Fred Burton (Presiding Officer), John Nesbitt (Commentator), Joan Valerie (Lucy Pemberton).

This bright, entertaining showcase for the Blue Grass State could justifiably be called "Romeo and Juliet at the Derby." Richard Greene is Jack, and Loretta Young plays Sally, lovers from families that have been feuding since the Civil War, when Jack's clan took over the stable run by Sally's grandfather. Keeping his lineage a secret, Jack begins training Sally's horse. But just before the Kentucky Derby, as their love affair is heating up, Sally discovers his identity and orders him out of the stable. When race day arrives, it's basically a contest between the rival families' horses. Walter Brennan won his second Best Supporting Oscar in as many years for his strong performance as Sally's uncle, Peter Goodwin, who was there when the feud began and does his best to keep it going.

p, Darryl F. Zanuck, Gene Markey; d, David Butler; w, Lamar Trotti, John Taintor Foote (based on the book The Look of Eagles by Foote); ph, Ernest Palmer, Ray Rennahan (Technicolor); ed, Irene Morra.

Horse Racing   **(PR:AA   MPAA:NR)**

KENTUCKY BLUE STREAK*½

(1935) 60m Puritan bw

Eddie Nugent, Patricia Scott, Junior Coghlan, Margaret Mann, Cornelius Keefe, Roy D'Arcy, Roy Watson, Joseph Girard.

A jockey imprisoned for a crime he did not commit breaks out to ride the title horse in the big race. Not only does he win, but his innocence is also proven. This 1930s program-

mer has been all but forgotten today, and with good reason.

p, C.C. Burr; d, Raymond K. Johnson; w, Homer King Gordon (based on a story by C.B. Carrington); ph, I.W. Akers.

Horse Racing   **Cas.**   **(PR:A   MPAA:NR)**

KID COMES BACK, THE**½

(1937) 61m WB bw

Wayne Morris (Rush Conway), Barton MacLane (Gunner Malone), June Travis (Mary), Dickie Jones (Bobby Doyle), Maxie Rosenbloom (Stan Wilson), James Robbins (Ken Rockwell), Joseph Crehan (Danny Lockridge), Frank Otto (Joey Meade), David Carlyle (Radio Announcer), Herbert Rawlinson (Redmann).

Prizefighter Gunner Malone (Barton MacLane) spots Rush Conway (Wayne Morris) in a street brawl and begins training the talented youngster to be a champ. Rush's sister (June Travis) soon becomes romantically involved with Gunner, but things get complicated when the rapidly rising young fighter is slated to battle his mentor. He can't bring himself to go up against his would-be brother-in-law, but Gunner, with the help of a sportswriter, tricks the kid into the ring. Although every cliche is intact, this standard fight story is well packaged nonetheless, and MacLane gives a fine performance that transcends the material. Look for an appearance by ex-fighter-turned-movie actor Maxie Rosenbloom.

p, Bryan Foy; d, B. Reeves Eason; w, George Bricker (based on the story "Trial Horse" by E. J. Flanagan); ph, Arthur Edeson; ed, Warren Low.

Boxing   **(PR:A   MPAA:NR)**

KID FROM BROOKLYN, THE***

(1946) 114m Goldwyn/RKO c

Danny Kaye (Burleigh Sullivan), Virginia Mayo (Polly Pringle), Vera-Ellen (Susie Sullivan), Walter Abel (Gabby Sloan), Eve Arden (Ann Westley), Steve Cochran (Speed MacFarlane), Lionel Stander (Spider Schultz), Fay Bainter (Mrs. E. Winthrop LeMoyne), Clarence Kolb (Wilbur Austin), Victor Cutler (Photographer), Charles Cane (Willard), Jerome Cowan (Fight Ring Announcer), Don Wilson, Knox Manning (Radio Announcers), Kay Thompson (Matron), Johnny Downs (M.C.), Pierre Watkin (Mr. LeMoyne), Frank Riggi (Killer Kelly), Frank Moran (Fight Manager), John Indrisano (Boxing Instructor), Almeda Fowler (Bystander), Snub Pollard (Man Who Reacts to Lion).

Based on the 1936 Harold Lloyd film THE MILKY WAY, THE KID FROM BROOKLYN overcomes its hokey plot with great songs and plenty of style, and the result is a happy amalgam of nonsense and laughter. Danny Kaye plays Burleigh Sullivan, a wimpy milkman who inadvertently becomes a champion prizefighter. Although the premise is patently absurd, Kaye's intricate performance pulls it off with good humor and verve. The songs were performed by everyone but Kaye, save for "Pavlova," a ballet satire written especially for him by Max Liebman and Sylvia Fine, Kaye's wife.

p, Samuel Goldwyn; d, Norman Z. McLeod; w, Don Hartman, Melville Shavelson (based on the screenplay by Grover Jones, Frank Butler, Richard Connell from the play "The Milky Way" by Lynn Root, Harry Clork); ph, Gregg Toland (Technicolor); ed, Daniel Mandell; m, Carmen Dragon.

Boxing/Comedy/
Musical   Cas.   (PR:AA MPAA:NR)

KID FROM CLEVELAND, THE**

(1949) 89m REP bw

George Brent *(Mike Jackson)*, Lynn Bari *(Katherine Jackson)*, Rusty Tamblyn *(Johnny Barrows)*, Tommy Cook *(Dan Hudson)*, Louis Jean Heydt *(Carl Novak)*, Ann Doran *(Emily Novak)*, K. Elmo Lowe *(Dave Joyce)*, Johnny Berardino *(Mac)*, Bill Veeck, Lou Boudreau, Tris Speaker, Hank Greenberg, Bob Feller, Gene Bearden, Satchel Paige, Bob Lemon, Steve Gromek, Joe Gordon, Mickey Vernon, Ken Keltner, Ray Boone, Dale Mitchell, Larry Doby, Bob Kennedy, Jim Hegan *(Cleveland Indians)*, Franklin Lewis, Gordon Cobbledock, Ed MacAuley *(Sportswriters)*, Bill Summers, Bill Grieve *(Umpires)*.

Sports announcer Mike Jackson (George Brent) takes Johnny Barrows (15-year-old Rusty Tamblyn), a juvenile delinquent abandoned by his stepfather, under his wing and introduces him to the Cleveland Indians, who do their best to straighten the kid out, pulling together to win the World Series in the process. The real treat here is a chance to see one of baseball's great championship teams in action, with actual footage of the 1948 Series included in the film. The Indians' then owner, Bill Veeck, gives a terrific performance, and Hall of Famers Lou Boudreau and Bob Feller also play prominent roles—not just on the diamond. Although it may be of only marginal interest to most, Indians fans should find THE KID FROM CLEVELAND heartening as they continue their long wait for another World Series championship team.

p, Walter Colmes; d, Herbert Kline; w, John Bright (based on a story by Kline, Bright); ph, Jack Marta; ed, Jason Bernie; m, Nathan Scott.

Baseball   (PR:A MPAA:NR)

KID FROM KOKOMO, THE**

(1939) 92m WB bw (GB: ORPHAN OF THE RING)

Pat O'Brien *(Bill Murphy)*, Wayne Morris *(Homer Baston)*, Joan Blondell *(Doris Harvey)*, Jane Wyman *(Marian Bronson)*, May Robson *(Ma "Maggie" Martin)*, Maxie Rosenbloom *(Curly Bender)*, Ed Brophy *(Eddie Black)*, Stanley Fields *(Muscles)*, Sidney Toler *(Judge Bronson)*, Winifred Harris *(Mrs. Bronson)*, Morgan Conway *(Louie)*, John Ridgely *(Sam)*, Frank Mayo *(Durb)*, Al Hill *(Lippy)*, Clem Bevans *(Jim)*, Ward Bond *(Klewicke)*, Olin Howland *(Stan)*, Reid Kilpatrick, John Harron *(Radio Announcers)*.

This unexceptional boxing comedy stars Pat O'Brien as the manager of Homer Baston (Wayne Morris), a witless fighter who believes his mother and the woman in James McNeill Whistler's famous portrait are one and the same. In order to get the reluctant Homer to put the gloves on again, a drunken kleptomaniac (May Robson) is brought in to pose as his mother, and she brings along a Hell's Kitchen buddy (Stanley Fields) to act the role of Dad. A boxing film without a big fight is like a Thanksgiving without a turkey, and former light heavyweight champion "Slapsie" Maxie Rosenbloom plays Homer's opponent in this one. Lewis Seiler's direction is competent and the film is well paced, but ultimately it's KO'd by its insipid plot, based on a story by the usually reliable Dalton Trumbo.

p, Sam Bischoff; d, Lewis Seiler; w, Jerry Wald, Richard Macauley (based on the story "Broadway Cavalier" by Dalton Trumbo); ph, Sid Hickox; ed, Jack Killifer.

Boxing/Comedy   (PR:A MPAA:NR)

KID FROM LEFT FIELD, THE**½

(1953) 80m FOX bw

Dan Dailey *(Larry "Pop" Cooper)*, Anne Bancroft *(Marian)*, Billy Chapin *(Christy)*, Lloyd Bridges *(Pete Haines)*, Ray Collins *(Whacker)*, Richard Egan *(Billy Lorant)*, Bob Hopkins *(Bobo Noonan)*, Alex Gerry *(J.R. Johnson)*, Walter Sande *(Barnes)*, Fess Parker *(McDougal)*, George Phelps *(Tony)*, John Gallaudet *(Hyams)*, Paul Salata *(Larson)*, John Berardino *(Hank Dreiser)*, Gene Thompson *(Jim Cary)*, Malcolm Cassell *(Jimmy)*, Ike Jones *(John Grant)*, Ron Hargrave *(Craig)*, John Goddard *(Riordan)*, John McKee *(Hunchy Harrison)*, Claude Olin Wurman *(Bermudez)*, Sammy Ogg *(Herman)*, George Garner, Rush Williams *(Yankee Players)*, Leo Cleary *(Yankee Manager)*, John "Beans" Reardon *(Umpire)*, James Griffith *(Proprietor)*, James F. Stone *(Mack)*.

This cute baseball story features Dan Dailey as Larry "Pop" Cooper, an ex-big leaguer reduced to hawking peanuts in the stands while his nine-year-old son, Christy (Billy Chapin), acts as the team's bat boy. With the club mired in a slump, Pop gives Christy some tips to pass on to the manager (Lloyd Bridges), and when the team starts winning, Whacker (Ray Collins), the owner, promotes the kid to the manager's position, not knowing Pop is really behind the resurgence. Although its premise is a little hard to swallow, warm, believable performances make THE KID FROM LEFT FIELD pleasant fare indeed. The story was remade in 1979 as a far less charming made-for-television movie with Gary Coleman. Note Fess Parker in a small role, one year before he donned a coonskin cap and made it big as Walt Disney's Davy Crockett.

p, Leonard Goldstein; d, Harmon Jones; w, Jack Sher; ph, Harry Jackson; ed, William Reynolds; m, Lionel Newman.

Baseball/Comedy   Cas.   (PR:AA MPAA:NR)

KID FROM SPAIN, THE***

(1932) 118m Goldwyn/UA bw

Eddie Cantor *(Eddie Williams)*, Lyda Roberti *(Rosalie)*, Robert Young *(Ricardo)*, Ruth Hall *(Anita Gomez)*, John

Miljan *(Pancho)*, Noah Beery *(Alonzo Gomez)*, J. Carrol Naish *(Pedro)*, Robert Emmett O'Connor *(Det. Crawford)*, Stanley Fields *(Jose)*, Paul Porcasi *(Gonzales, Border Guard)*, Sidney Franklin *(American Matador)*, Julian Rivero *(Dalmores)*, Theresa Maxwell Conover *(Martha Oliver)*, Walter Walker *(The Dean)*, Ben Hendricks, Jr. *(Red)*.

After being tossed out of school, Ricardo (Robert Young) invites his college roommate, Eddie (Eddie Cantor), to his home in Mexico. Their trip becomes a necessity when bank robbers mistake Eddie for their getaway driver, the only person who can identify them. Once they are south of the border, mistaken identity strikes again. This time Eddie is thought to be the offspring of a legendary matador and is forced into the bull ring, though Ricardo has arranged for him to face a tame animal that will stop its charge upon command. However, a rough character involved in one of the story's many subplots substitutes a considerably less docile bull and hilarity results as Eddie does his best not to get gored. Not strictly a sports film, THE KID FROM SPAIN is chock-full of laughs and boasts some fine songs, written mostly by Bert Kalmar and Harry Ruby (who cowrote the screenplay).

p, Samuel Goldwyn; d, Leo McCarey; w, William Anthony McGuire, Bert Kalmar, Harry Ruby; ph, Gregg Toland; ed, Stuart Heisler.

Bullfighting   (PR:AA MPAA:NR)

KID GALAHAD***½

(1937) 101m WB bw (AKA: THE BATTLING BELLHOP)

Edward G. Robinson *(Nick Donati)*, Bette Davis *(Louise "Fluff" Phillips)*, Humphrey Bogart *(Turkey Morgan)*, Wayne Morris *(Kid Galahad/Ward Guisenberry)*, Jane Bryan *(Marie Donati)*, Harry Carey *(Silver Jackson)*, William Haade *(Chuck McGraw)*, Soledad Jiminez *(Mrs. Donati)*, Joe Cunningham *(Joe Taylor)*, Ben Welden *(Buzz Stevens)*, Joseph Crehan *(Editor Brady)*, Veda Ann Borg *(Redhead at Party)*, Frank Faylen *(Barney)*, Harland Tucker *(Gunman)*, Bob Evans *(Sam McGraw)*, Hank Hankinson *(Jim Burke)*, Bob Nestell *(Tim O'Brien)*, Jack Kranz *(Denbaugh)*, George Blake *(Referee)*, Charles Sullivan *(Second)*, Joyce Compton *(Drunken Girl on Phone)*, Eddie Foster *(Louie, Pianist)*, George Humbert *(Barber)*, Emmett Vogan *(Ring Announcer)*, I. Stanford Jolley *(Ringsider)*, Mary Sunde *(Blonde)*, Billy Wayne *(Bell Captain)*, John Ridgely *(Photographer)*, Curtis Benton *(Announcer)*, Eddy Chandler *(Title Fight Announcer)*.

Edward G. Robinson and Humphrey Bogart play rival fight managers in this strong boxing film with Wayne Morris in the title role, the first of his three turns as a pugilist (THE KID COMES BACK, 1937, and THE KID FROM KOKOMO, 1939, followed). When a bellhop (Morris) knocks out highly touted heavyweight Chuck McGraw (William Haade) defending the honor of "Fluff" Phillips (Bette Davis), she dubs him Kid Galahad, and her boy friend, Nick Donati (Robinson), decides to make the young man into a prizefighter. Jealous because both Fluff and her sister appear interested in Kid, Nick arranges a bout with McGraw that he is certain his fighter will lose and assures rival manager

Turkey Morgan (Bogart) of the same. Following his manager's advice, Kid tries to slug it out with McGraw and is battered for several rounds before Nick has a change of heart and tells him to start *boxing*—which Kid does, turning around the fight and leading to a gun-wielding finale in the locker room. A solid story with good characterizations and sensational prizefight footage, KID GALAHAD was remade as THE WAGONS ROLL AT NIGHT, with the story switched to a circus, then made again as a fight film with Elvis Presley (see below). To avoid confusion with the Presley movie, the title has been changed to THE BATTLING BELLHOP for TV.

p, Hal B. Wallis; d, Michael Curtiz; w, Seton I. Miller (based on the novel by Francis Wallace); ph, Tony Gaudio; ed, George Amy; m, Heinz Roemheld, Max Steiner.

Boxing   (PR:A-C MPAA:NR)

KID GALAHAD**

(1962) 95m Mirisch/UA c

Elvis Presley *(Walter Gulick)*, Gig Young *(Willy Grogan)*, Lola Albright *(Dolly Fletcher)*, Joan Blackman *(Rose Grogan)*, Charles Bronson *(Lew Nyack)*, Ned Glass *(Lieberman)*, Robert Emhardt *(Maynard)*, David Lewis *(Otto Danzig)*, Michael Dante *(Joie Shakes)*, Judson Pratt *(Zimmerman)*, George Mitchell *(Sperling)*, Richard Devon *(Marvin)*, Jeffrey Morris *(Ralphie)*, Liam Redmond *(Father Higgins)*.

Elvis Presley puts on the gloves and gives his vocal cords a few rounds, too, in this inferior remake of the fine 1937 boxing film KID GALAHAD (see above). Taking over the Wayne Morris role, Elvis plays a sparring partner who saves Dolly Fletcher (Lola Albright), the girl friend of fight manager Willy Grogan (Gig Young), from the clutches of gangsters, earning the nickname Kid Galahad and a shot at a prizefighting career. After falling for Willy's sister (Joan Blackman), Kid decides to end his successful ring career, but when Grogan can't make good on a debt to a hoodlum, he arranges for Kid to fight an opponent certain to beat him. Wrong. Elvis plays his fighter as the nice, soft-spoken kid that he was at the time, and Charles Bronson is excellent as his trainer.

p, David Weisbart; d, Phil Karlson; w, William Fay (based on the novel by Francis Wallace); ph, Burnett Guffey (DeLuxe Color); ed, Stuart Gilmore; m, Jeff Alexander.

Boxing   Cas.   (PR:A MPAA:NR)

KID MONK BARONI**

(1952) 80m REA bw

Richard Rober *(Father Callahan)*, Bruce Cabot *(Mr. Hellman)*, Allene Roberts *(Emily Brooks)*, Mona Knox *(June Travers)*, Leonard Nimoy *(Paul "Monk" Baroni)*, Jack Larson *(Angelo)*, Budd Jaxon *(Knuckles)*, Archer MacDonald *(Pete)*, Kathleen Freeman *(Maria Baroni)*, Joseph Mell *(Gino Baroni)*, Paul Maxey *(Mr. Petry)*, Stuart Randall *(Mr. Moore)*, Chad Mallory *(Joey)*, Maurice Cass *(Pawnbroker)*, Bill Cabanne *(Seattle Wildcat)*.

A parish priest (Richard Rober) tries to reform street punk Paul "Monk" Baroni (Leonard Nimoy), whose nickname comes from his disfigured face (the weird *ears* would come later), by teaching him how to box and involving him in church activities. His plan appears to be working, until Monk hits the priest during a gang fight and flees town, becoming a successful professional fighter under the direction of Hellman (Bruce Cabot) and eventually undergoing plastic surgery. As usually happens in these films, Monk's ego swells and he becomes involved with a gold digger who cuts out when he stops winning the big purses because he spends too much ring time trying to protect his new face. Still, a happy ending is in store, and Monk wins on brownie points when he returns to his old neighborhood to become the church's athletic director.

p, Jack Broder; d, Harold Schuster; w, Aben Kandel; ph, Charles Van Enger; ed, Jason Bernie; m, Herschel Burke Gilbert.

Boxing   (PR:C   MPAA:NR)

KID NIGHTINGALE**½

(1939) 57m WB bw

John Payne (*Steve Nelson*), Jane Wyman (*Judy Craig*), Walter Catlett (*Skip Davis*), Ed Brophy (*Mike Jordan*), Charles D. Brown (*Charles Paxton*), Max Hoffman, Jr. (*Fitts*), John Ridgely (*Whitey*), Harry Burns (*Strangler Colombo/Rudolfo Terrassi*), William Haade (*Rocky*), Helen Troy (*Marge*), Winifred Harris (*Mrs. Reynolds*), Lee Phelps (*Announcer*), Frankie Van (*Trainer*), Steve Mason (*Fighter*), Claude Wisberg (*Messenger*), Creighton Hale (*Boxing Commission Official*), Constantine Romanoff, Mike Tellegen (*Wrestlers*).

Throw a few punches, sing a few songs, and next thing you know you're the world heavyweight champion, or at least that's what shady fight promoters have in mind when they send opera-singing waiter Steve Nelson (John Payne) into one fixed fight after another, confident that his post-knockout warbling will attract female fans. It's up to Steve's girl friend (Jane Wyman) to discover that the vocal coach the fighter has demanded is actually a wrestler (Harry Burns, who also plays a real voice teacher) and to get Steve back on the right track musically. For those willing to accept its goofy premise, there should be plenty of laughs in KID NIGHTINGALE, and the direction, script, and Payne's singing are all more than passable.

p, Bryan Foy; d, George Amy; w, Charles Belden, Raymond Schrock (based on the story "Singing Swinger" by Lee Katz); ph, Arthur Edeson; ed, Frederick Richards.

**Boxing/Comedy/
Musical**   (PR:A   MPAA:NR)

KILL THE UMPIRE**½

(1950) 77m COL bw

William Bendix (*Bill Johnson*), Una Merkel (*Betty Johnson*), Ray Collins (*Jonah Evans*), Gloria Henry (*Lucy*), Richard Taylor (*Bob Landon*), Connie Marshall (*Susan*), William Frawley (*Jimmy O'Brien*), Tom D'Andrea (*Roscoe Snooker*), Luther Crockett (*Sam Austin*), Jeff York (*Panhandle Jones*), Glenn Thompson (*Lanky*), Bob Wilke (*Cactus*), Jim Bannon (*Dusty*), Alan Hale, Jr. (*Harry Shay*).

William Bendix stars in this fun little film as a baseball fan so obsessed with the game he can't even hold on to a job when the national pastime is in season. He finally agrees to go to umpire school so his wife (Una Merkel) won't walk out on him, and is hired by the Texas Interstate League, where he makes a controversial call at the plate in an important game that sends the home team fans wildly chasing after him. KILL THE UMPIRE is nice light fare, deftly played by Bendix and the supporting cast.

p, John Beck; d, Lloyd Bacon; w, Frank Tashlin; ph, Charles Lawton, Jr.; ed, Charles Nelson.

Baseball/Comedy   (PR:AA   MPAA:NR)

KILLER McCOY**½

(1947) 104m MGM bw

Mickey Rooney (*Tommy McCoy*), Brian Donlevy (*Jim Caighn*), Ann Blyth (*Sheila Carrson*), James Dunn (*Brian McCoy*), Tom Tully (*Cecil Y. Walsh*), Sam Levene (*Happy*), Walter Sande (*Bill Thorne*), Mickey Knox (*Johnny Martin*), James Bell (*Father Ryan*), Gloria Holden (*Mrs. McCoy*), Eve March (*Mrs. Martin*), June Storey (*Waitress*), Douglas Croft (*Danny Burns*), Bob Steele (*Sailor Graves*), David Clarke (*Pete Mariola*).

In his first adult role, Mickey Rooney switches from singing and dancing to bobbing and weaving as Tommy McCoy, a hoofer-turned-prizefighter. Lightweight champion Johnny Martin (Mickey Knox), who headlines the show Tommy performs in with his alcoholic father (James Dunn), suggests that the kid give his fancy footwork a try in the ring, and in no time Tommy faces Martin for the championship, a brutal battle that results in the champ's death and confirms Tommy's all-too-appropriate nickname, "Killer." Distraught, Tommy falls under the influence of Jim Caighn (Brian Donlevy), a reprehensible gambler, but his daughter (Ann Blyth) falls for the confused fighter and rescues him from the tangled web of boxing. Though a bit overly melodramatic, this loose remake of the 1938 Robert Taylor film THE CROWD ROARS contains some fine performances from Rooney, Donlevy, and Dunn.

p, Sam Zimbalist; d, Roy Rowland; w, Frederick Hazlitt Brennan (based on story and screenplay by Thomas Lennon, George Bruce, George Oppenheimer); ph, Joseph Ruttenberg; ed, Ralph E. Winters; m, David Snell.

Boxing   (PR:A   MPAA:NR)

KING FOR A NIGHT**½

(1933) 78m UNIV bw

Chester Morris (*Bud Williams*), Helen Twelvetrees (*Lillian Williams*), Alice White (*Evelyn*), John Miljan (*Walter Douglas*), Grant Mitchell (*Rev. John Williams*), George E. Stone (*Hymie*), George Meeker (*John Williams*), Frank Albertson (*Dick*), Warren Hymer (*Goofy*), John Sheehan (*Manny*), Maxie Rosenblum (*Heavyweight*).

Part fight film, part murder movie, KING FOR A NIGHT traces the rise of small-town boxer Bud Williams (Chester Morris, in a sterling performance) as he punches his way toward the middleweight title over the pacifist objections of his father (Grant Mitchell), a paralyzed minister. Moving to New York City, Bud finds fame, fortune, and floozies galore, little knowing that his sister, Lillian (Helen Twelvetrees), who has been sleeping with promoter Walter Douglas (John Miljan), is responsible for his success. When he finds out, Bud plans to murder Douglas, but Lillian beats him to the punch, prompting the boxer to make the ultimate sacrifice by tampering with the evidence to implicate himself.

d, Kurt Neumann; w, William Anthony McGuire, Jack O'Donnell, Scott Pembroke (based on a story by McGuire); ph, Charles Stumar; ed, Phil Cahn.

Boxing   (PR:C   MPAA:NR)

KING OF HOCKEY**

(1936) 57m WB bw (GB: KING OF THE ICE RINK)

Dick Purcell (Gabby Dugan), Anne Nagel (Kathleen O'Rourke), Marie Wilson (Elsie), Wayne Morris (Jumbo Mullins), George E. Stone (Nick Torga), Joseph Crehan (Mike Trotter), Gordon Hart (Dr. Noble), Ann Gillis (Peggy O'Rourke), Dora Clement (Mrs. O'Rourke), Guy Usher (Mr. O'Rourke), Garry Owen (Jitters McCarthy), Max Hoffman, Jr. (Torchy Myers), Andre Beranger (Evans), Frank Faylen (Swede), Frank Bruno (Loogan), Harry Davenport (Tom McKenna).

Gabby Dugan (Dick Purcell), hockey star and jerk, is forced to retire prematurely when he is blinded in one eye after being belted by Jumbo Mullins (Wayne Morris), who believes his teammate is throwing games. Gabby's girl friend (Anne Nagel) and her terminally cute sister (Ann Gillis) scrape together the money for an operation, and Gabby returns to the ice a better man, leading his team to the championship. Stage actor Purcell, making his film debut, does well in a most unsympathetic role; the hockey action is fair; and as is often the case with films of the period, the snappy dialog outshines the plot.

p, Bryan Foy; d, Noel Smith; w, George Bricker (based on his story "The Shrinking Violet"); ph, L.W. O'Connell; ed, Harold McLernon.

Hockey   (PR:AA   MPAA:NR)

KING OF THE GAMBLERS*½

(1948) 60m REP bw

Janet Martin (Jean Lacey), William Wright (Dave Fowler), Thurston Hall ("Pop" Morton), Stephanie Bachelor (Elsie Pringle), George Meeker (Bernie Dupal), Wally Vernon (Mike Burns), William Henry (Jerry Muller), James Cardwell ("Speed" Lacey), Jonathan Hale (Sam Hyland), Selmer Jackson (Judge), Howard J. Negley (Jordon), John Holland (Symonds), George Anderson (O'Brien), Ralph Dunn (Cassidy), John Albright (Bartender).

When a football player threatens to expose a game-fixing

operation run by a gambler and sports magazine publisher, he is killed and another player is framed for the murder. A crusading district attorney, who also happens to be the publisher's stepson, defends the accused and exposes the crooked scheme. Although the acting is fair, several implausible plot twists are introduced into KING OF THE GAMBLERS' standard story, and George Blair's direction is uneven.

p, Stephen Auer; d, George Blair; w, Albert DeMond, Bradbury Foote; ph, John MacBurnie; ed, Robert Leeds.

Football   (PR:A   MPAA:NR)

KING OF THE TURF***

(1939) 88m UA bw

Adolphe Menjou (Jim Mason), Roger Daniel (Goldie), Dolores Costello (Mrs. Barnes), Walter Abel (Mr. Barnes), Alan Dinehart (Grimes), William Demarest (Arnold), Harold Huber (Santelli), George McKay (Murphy), Lee M. Moore (Carr), Oscar O'Shea (Bartender), Cliff Nazarro, George Chandler (Touts), Milburn Stone (Taylor).

Thrown together by fate, Jim Mason (Adolphe Menjou), a down-and-out one-time racehorse owner, and Goldie (Roger Daniel), a young runaway who has become a stable boy, buy a horse for $2 at an auction. After giving up the bottle, Jim becomes the horse's trainer and Goldie its jockey, but just when the two become a successful team and inseparable friends, the boy's mother (Dolores Costello) appears and Jim discovers that Goldie is the son he abandoned many years before. Hoping the boy will go back to his mother and the good life, Jim tells Goldie to throw a big race; Goldie, however, has another outcome in mind, and the situation is happily resolved by the film's end. Despite some hard to swallow plot points, this is a delightful film and Menjou and Daniel are terrific together.

p, Edward Small; d, Alfred E. Green; w, George Bruce; ph, Robert Planck; ed, Grant Whytock.

Horse Racing   (PR:A   MPAA:NR)

KNOCKOUT**½

(1941) 71m FN-WB bw

Arthur Kennedy (Johnny Rocket), Olympe Bradna (Angela Grinnelli), Virginia Field (Gloria Van Ness), Anthony Quinn (Trego), Cliff Edwards (Pinky), Cornel Wilde (Tom Rossi), William Edmunds (Louis Grinnelli), Richard Ainley (Allison), John Ridgely (Pat Martin), Frank Wilcox (Denning), Ben Welden (Pelky), Vera Lewis (Mrs. Turner), Charles Wilson (Monigan), Edwin Stanley (Doctor), Grace Hayle (Mrs. Smithers), Frank Faylen, Paul Phillips, Jack Merrick (Fighters), Frank Riggi (Hanson), Pat O'Malley (Announcer), Al Seymour (Referee), Gaylord Pendleton (Stanley), Noble "Kid" Chissell (Hawkins).

Arthur Kennedy, who played the brother of boxers in CHAMPION (1949) and CITY FOR CONQUEST (1941), throws the punches himself this time as Johnny Rocket, a promising young fighter who gives up the ring to please his new bride (Olympe Bradna). Unwilling to let the promise of a big payoff slip away, Trego (Anthony Quinn), Johnny's manager, sees to it that his fighter is unable to find any other work, and before long Johnny is winning fights again, falling for the charms of a socialite sportswriter (Virginia Field), and ruining his marriage. Trying to make a quick killing, Trego drugs Johnny before a big fight and bets against him. True to formula, Johnny loses both the fight and his fair-weather female admirer, but though things look bleak for him, he is both loved and redeemed by the finale. A strong script, consistent direction, realistic fight footage, and adequate performances combine to make this a very watchable boxing film.

p, Edmund Grainger; d, William Clemens; w, M. Coates Webster (based on a story by Michael Fessier); ph, Ted McCord; ed, Doug Gould; m, Heinz Roemheld.

Boxing (PR:A MPAA:NR)

KNUTE ROCKNE—ALL AMERICAN****

(1940) 98m WB bw (GB: A MODERN HERO)

Pat O'Brien (Knute Rockne), Gale Page (Bonnie Skilles Rockne), Ronald Reagan (George Gipp), Donald Crisp (Father Callahan), Albert Basserman (Father Julius Nieuwland), John Litel (Chairman), Henry O'Neill (Doctor), Owen Davis, Jr. (Gus Dorais), John Qualen (Lars Knutson Rockne), Dorothy Tree (Martha Rockne), John Sheffield (Knute Rockne as a boy), Nick Lukats (Harry Stuhldreher), Kane Richmond (Elmer Laydon), William Marshall (Don Miller), William Byrne (James Crowley), John Ridgely (Reporter), Dutch Hendrian (Hunk Anderson), Howard Jones, Glenn "Pop" Warner, Alonzo Stagg, William Spaulding (Themselves), Creighton Hale (Secretary), Lee Phelps (Army Coach).

Pat O'Brien gives a brilliant performance as the great Notre Dame football coach Knute Rockne in this fond biography that features Ronald Reagan as Rockne's most famous player, George Gipp. The film follows Rockne from his Norwegian immigrant beginnings through his playing days at Notre Dame (when he helped invent the forward pass) and on to his glorious tenure as head coach at his alma mater. With the support of Father Callahan (Donald Crisp), Rockne rises from assistant coach and chemistry teacher to the top spot and revolutionizes the game as he turns out winning team after winning team, blessed with great players like the "Four Horseman" and Gipp, who dies young of pneumonia and provides the inspiration for Rockne's famed "win one for the Gipper" pep talk. Along the way Rockne even finds time to romance and marry Bonnie Skilles (Gale Page). Four of Rockne's contemporaries play themselves—the grandfather of all coaches, Amos Alonzo Stagg, Howard Jones of USC, William Spaulding, and "Pop" Warner—and much of the football action is culled from newsreel footage.

p, Jack Warner, Hal B. Wallis; d, Lloyd Bacon; w, Robert Buckner (based on the private papers of Mrs. Knute Rockne); ph, Tony Gaudio; ed, Ralph Dawson; m, Ray Heindorf.

Football/Biography Cas. (PR:AA MPAA:NR)

L

LADY'S FROM KENTUCKY, THE**

(1939) 67m PAR bw

George Raft (Marty Black), Ellen Drew (Penelope "Penny" Hollis), Hugh Herbert (Mousey Johnson), ZaSu Pitts (Dulcey Lee), Louise Beavers (Aunt Tina), Lew Payton (Sixty), Forrester Harvey (Nonny Watkins), Harry Tyler (Carter), Edward Pawley (Spike Cronin), Gilbert Emery (Pinckney Rodell), Jimmy Bristow (Brewster), Mickey O'Boyle (Roman Boy), Mike Arnold (Cantankerous), Kentucky Lady (Foal), Eugene Jackson (Winfield), George Anderson (Joe Lane), Stanley Andrews (Doctor), Hooper Atchley (Surgeon), Fern Emmett (Attending Nurse), Robert Milasch (Big Longshoreman), Harry Tenbrook, George Turner (Longshoremen), Frankie Van (Taxi Driver), William Cartledge (Jones), Charles Trowbridge (Charles Butler).

Marty Black (George Raft), a bookie fallen on hard times, has nothing left but part ownership of a thoroughbred, and though the horse appears to be weakening from too much racing, Marty insists that it be prepared for a run in the Kentucky Derby—against the advice of his partner (Ellen Drew). The horse runs and wins, but is ruined as a result. Although unevenly paced, this standard track film offers competent performances.

p, Jeff Lazarus; d, Alexander Hall; w, Malcolm Stuart Boylan (based on the story by Rowland Brown); ph, Theodor Sparkuhl; ed, Harvey Johnson.

Horse Racing (PR:A MPAA:NR)

LAST AMERICAN HERO, THE***

(1973) 95m Fox c (AKA: HARD DRIVER)

Jeff Bridges (Elroy Jackson, Jr.), Valerie Perrine (Marge), Geraldine Fitzgerald (Mrs. Jackson), Ned Beatty (Hackel), Gary Busey (Wayne Jackson), Art Lund (Elroy Jackson, Sr.), Ed Lauter (Burton Colt), William Smith, II (Kyle Kingman), Gregory Walcott (Morley), Tom Ligon (Lamar), Ernie Orsatti (Davie Baer), Erica Hagen (Trina), James Murphy (Spud), Lane Smith (Rick Penny).

Based on an *Esquire* article by Tom Wolfe, this well-crafted film tells the story of real-life stock car driver Junior Johnson, who served as THE LAST AMERICAN HERO's technical advisor. As a North Carolina youth, Junior (Jeff Bridges) is a hot-rodding, small-time hoodlum until his father is busted for moonshining and hauled off to prison; then he decides to put his ability behind the wheel to good use, becoming a professional stock car racer to raise money for his father's defense. Starting at a local track, Junior begins a rise to the stock car big time, where his stubborn independence runs up against the realities of corporate sponsorship. Well-written and subtly directed, THE LAST AMERICAN HERO concentrates on the human elements of the story without becoming overly sentimental.

Its performances—including Ned Beatty as the local promoter and Valerie Perrine a trackside hanger-on—are also excellent.

p, William Roberts, John Cutts; d, Lamont Johnson; w, William Roberts (based on articles by Tom Wolfe); ph, George Silano (Panavision, DeLuxe Color); ed, Tom Rolf, Robbe Roberts; m, Charles Fox.

**Auto Racing/
Biography   Cas.   (PR:C MPAA:PG)**

LAST FIGHT, THE*½

(1983) 86m Movie and Pictures International/Best Film and Video c

Willie Colon *(Joaquin Vargas)*, Ruben Blades *(Andy "Kid" Clave)*, Fred Williamson *(Jesse Crowder)*, Joe Spinell *(Boss)*, Darlanne Fluegel *(Sally)*, Nereida Mercado *(Nancy)*, Anthony Sirico *(Frankie)*, Vinny Argiro *(Detective Pantane)*, Jose "Chegui" Torres *(Ex-Champ)*, Nick Corello *(Pedro)*, Sal Corolio *(Papa)*, Izzy Sanabria *(Slim)*.

This slow-moving boxing drama stars Panamanian actor-salsa singer Ruben Blades as Andy "Kid" Clave, a crooner who takes to the ring when his gambling debts accumulate, battling his way to a title bout with Salvador Sanchez, the then real-life featherweight champion of the world who was killed in an auto accident shortly after this film was shot. Former Oakland Raider and Kansas City Chief defensive back and one-time blaxploitation star Fred "the Hammer" Williamson wrote, directed, and appears in THE LAST FIGHT.

p, Jerry Masucci; d, Fred Williamson; w, Fred Williamson (based on a story by Masucci); ph, James Lemmo; ed, Daniel Loewenthal; m, Jay Chattaway.

Boxing   Cas.   (PR:O MPAA:R)

LAST GAME, THE***

(1963, USSR) 88m Mosfilm/Artkino bw (TRETIY TAYM)

Yu. Volkov, V. Kashpur, Mazarov Kuravlyov, Yuriy Nazarov, V. Nevinny, Gleb Strizhenov, Gennadiy Yukhtin, A. Eybozhenko, A. Metyolkin, Ye. Paptsov *(Soviet Team)*, B. Kvin, L. Ilyukhin, A. Zinovyev *(German Team)*.

Similar to John Huston's VICTORY (1981) and based on fact, this powerful film depicts a soccer match between a sterling German team and Soviet POWs during WW II. The game, intended as a propaganda coup for the Germans, takes place in occupied Kiev. The Soviets are given an ultimatum: lose or die. After realizing how much the game means to their countrymen, the Soviets defeat the Germans, only to be finally led before a firing squad.

d, Y. Karelov; w, A. Borshchagovskiy (based on the novel by Borshchagovskiy); ph, Sergey Zaytsev; ed, K. Aleyeva; m, Andrey Petrov.

Soccer   (PR:C MPAA:NR)

LAUGHING IRISH EYES**

(1936) 70m REP bw

Phil Regan *(Danno O'Keefe)*, Walter C. Kelly *(Pat Kelly)*, Evalyn Knapp *(Peggy Kelly)*, Ray Walker *(Eddie Bell)*, Mary Gordon *(Mrs. O'Keefe)*, Warren Hymer *(Tiger O'Keefe)*, Betty Compson *(Molly)*, J.M. Kerrigan *(Tim)*, Herman Bing *(Weisbecher)*, Raymond Hatton *(Gallagher)*, Clarence Muse *(Deacon)*, Russell Hicks *(Silk)*, Maurice Black *(Tony)*.

American fight promoter Pat Kelly (Walter C. Kelly) travels to Ireland to find a topnotch boxer. He returns to the States with Danno O'Keefe (Phil Regan), a singing blacksmith who wins the middleweight title, as well as the heart of Kelly's daughter (Evalyn Knapp). There isn't much here that hasn't been seen elsewhere, but the performances are believable, the fight scenes engaging, and Regan demonstrates a fine set of pipes on four songs, including the title tune.

p, Colbert Clark; d, Joseph Santley; w, Olive Cooper, Ben Ryan, Stanley Rauh (based on a story by Sidney Sutherland, Wallace Sullivan); ph, Milton Krasner, Reggie Lanning; ed, Joseph H. Lewis, Murray Seldeen.

Boxing/Musical   (PR:A MPAA:NR)

LE MANS***

(1971) 108m Solar/NG c

Steve McQueen *(Michael Delaney)*, Siegfried Rauch *(Erich Stahler)*, Elga Andersen *(Lisa Belgetti)*, Ronald Leigh-Hunt *(David Townsend)*, Fred Haltiner *(Johann Ritter)*, Luc Merenda *(Claude Aurac)*, Christopher Waite *(Larry Wilson)*, Louise Edlind *(Anna Ritter)*, Angelo Infanti *(Lugo Abratte)*, Jean-Claude Bercq *(Paul Jacques Dion)*, Michele Scalera *(Vito Scalise)*, Gino Cassani *(Loretto Fuselli)*, Alfred Bell *(Tommy Hopkins)*, Carlo Cecchi *(Paolo Scandenza)*, Richard Rudiger *(Bruno Frohm)*, Hal Hamilton *(Chris Barnett)*, Jonathan Williams *(Jonathan Burton)*, Peter Parten *(Peter Wiese)*.

Steve McQueen, an accomplished auto and motorcycle racer offscreen, brought his passion for speed (and his driving experience) to this brilliantly shot film in the role of Michael Delaney, an aging Formula One driver for the Porsche team who battles Ferrari rival Erich Stahler (Siegfried Rauch) at the famed 24-hour French race. Sidelined after a crash, Delaney falls for Lisa Belgetti (Elga Andersen), the widow of a driver killed in an accident in which Delaney was also involved a year previously. With the Porsche fortunes beginning to dim, Delaney returns behind the wheel, dueling Stahler to a surprising finish. Racing fans should love LE MANS' dazzling documentary-like photography, including actual footage from the 1969 and 1970 race, but those who are more interested in an involving story may be disappointed.

p, Jack N. Reddish; d, Lee H. Katzin; w, Harry Kleiner; ph, Robert B. Hauser, Rene Guissart, Jr. (Panavision, DeLuxe Color); ed, Donald W. Ernst, John Woodcock, Ghislaine Des Jonqueres; m, Michel Legrand.

Auto Racing   (PR:A MPAA:G)

LEATHER-PUSHERS, THE**

(1940) 64m UNIV bw

Richard Arlen (Dick), Andy Devine (Andy Grogan), Astrid Allwyn (Pat), Douglas Fowley (Slick), Charles D. Brown (Stevens), Shemp Howard (Sailor), Horace MacMahon (Slugger), Charles Lane (Mitchell), Wade Boteler (Commissioner), George Lloyd (Joe), Eddie Gribbon (Pete), Frank Mitchell (Grogan's Manager), Reid Kilpatrick (Commentator), Ben Alexander (Announcer).

When a brawl breaks out at the local gym, Dick (Richard Arlen), the trainer of wrestler Andy Grogan (Andy Devine), demonstrates some real punching power, and Slick (Douglas Fowley), a boxing promoter, persuades him to give prizefighting a try, paving his way to success with a series of fixed fights. Pat (Astrid Allwyn), a female sportswriter whose readers think she's a man, knows something is fishy, and Slick decides to sock it to her by sticking her with Dick's contract, which she wins in a raffle. She and Dick have the last laugh, though, when he starts landing punches for real.

p, Ben Pivar; d, John Rawlins; w, Larry Rhine, Ben Chapman, Maxwell Shane; ph, Stanley Cortez; ed, Arthur Hilton.

Boxing (PR:A MPAA:NR)

LEATHER SAINT, THE**

(1956) 86m PAR bw

Paul Douglas (Gus MacAuliffe), John Derek (Father Gil Allen), Jody Lawrence (Pearl Gorman), Cesar Romero (Tony Lorenzo), Richard Shannon (Tom Kelly), Ernest Truex (Father Ritchie), Ricky Vera (Pepito), Thomas B. Henry (Bishop Hardtke), Lou Nova (Tiger), Robert Cornthwaite (Dr. Lomas), Edith Evanson (Stella), Baynes Barron (Henchman), Mary Benoit (Nurse), Bill Baldwin (Flight Announcer).

This moving story about a clergyman whose belief takes him beyond the church and into the world of suffering presents John Derek as a minister who goes into the ring to raise money for polio-stricken children in his parish. Paul Douglas portrays the manager who has no idea of his fighter's true calling, and Jody Lawrence is an alcoholic torch singer redeemed by the preacher pugilist.

p, Norman Retchin; d, Alvin Ganzer; w, Norman Retchin, Alvin Ganzer; ph, Haskell Boggs (VistaVision); ed, Floyd Knudtson; m, Irvin Talbot.

Boxing (PR:A MPAA:NR)

LET'S DO IT AGAIN***

(1975) 112m First Artists/WB c

Sidney Poitier (Clyde Williams), Bill Cosby (Billy Foster), Calvin Lockhart (Biggie Smalls), John Amos (Kansas City Mack), Denise Nicholas (Beth Foster), Lee Chamberlin (Dee Dee Williams), Mel Stewart (Ellison), Julius Harris (Bubbletop Woodson), Paul E. Harris (Jody Tipps), Val Avery (Lt. Bottomley), Jimmie Walker (Bootney Farnsworth), Ossie Davis (Elder Johnson), Talya Ferro, Doug Johnson,

Richard Young, Cedric Scott (Biggie's Gang), Morgan Roberts (Fish 'n' Chips Freddie), Billy Eckstine (Zack), George Foreman (Factory Worker).

The sequel to UPTOWN SATURDAY NIGHT, this solid comedy reteams Sidney Poitier (who also directed) and Bill Cosby as Clyde Williams and Billy Foster, and again they're trying to raise money for their club, The Sons and Daughters of Shaka Lodge. The pair finds a potential bonanza in Bootney Farnsworth (Jimmie Walker), and Clyde uses hypnosis to transform the bony boxer into a champion. Former heavyweight champ George Foreman appears briefly as a factory worker.

p, Melville Tucker; d, Sidney Poitier; w, Richard Wesley (based on a story by Timothy March); ph, Donald M. Morgan (Technicolor); ed, Pembroke J. Herring; m, Curtis Mayfield.

Boxing/Comedy **Cas.** **(PR:A-C MPAA:PG)**

LIFE BEGINS IN COLLEGE**½

(1937) 90m FOX bw (GB: THE JOY PARADE)

Ritz Brothers (Themselves), Joan Davis (Inez), Tony Martin (Band Leader), Gloria Stuart (Janet O'Hara), Fred Stone (Coach O'Hara), Nat Pendleton (George Black), Dick Baldwin (Bob Hayner), Joan Marsh (Cuddles), Dixie Dunbar (Polly), Edward Thorgersen (Radio Announcer), Jed Prouty (Oliver Stearns, Sr.), Maurice Cass (Dean Moss), Marjorie Weaver (Miss Murphy), J.C. Nugent (T. Edwin Cabot), Robert Lowery (Sling), Elisha Cook, Jr. (Ollie Stearns), Lon Chaney, Jr. (Gilks), Fred Kohler, Jr. (Bret), Brewster Twins (Emmy and Mary Lou), Charles Wilson (Coach Burke), Frank Sully (Acting Captain), Robert Murphy (Rooter), Norman Willis (Referee).

One of several 1930s football comedies, LIFE BEGINS IN COLLEGE features the zany Ritz Brothers as seventh-year undergraduates working their way through school as tailors and longing for gridiron stardom. A number of subplots involving a wealthy native American player (Nat Pendleton), the coach (Fred Stone), his daughter (Gloria Stuart), and her boy friend (Dick Baldwin) lead up to an injury in the big game that finally gives the Ritzes a chance to strut their stuff on the field, culminating in a predictably wacky finish. Although not in the same class as the Marx Brothers' HORSE FEATHERS (1932), this well-paced song- and dance-filled film is fun in its own way, and contains "Spirit of '76," the Ritzes' minor classic comedy routine. Edward Thorgersen, who was the regular sports announcer for Movietone newsreels, makes a cameo appearance as the football radio announcer.

p, Harold Wilson; d, William A. Seiter; w, Karl Tunberg, Don Ettlinger, Sidney Kuller, Ray Golden, Samuel Pokrass (based on stories by Darrell Ware); ph, Robert Planck; ed, Louis Loeffler.

Football/Comedy/
Musical **(PR:AA MPAA:NR)**

LIFE OF JIMMY DOLAN, THE**½

(1933) 85m WB bw (GB: THE KID'S LAST FIGHT)

Douglas Fairbanks, Jr. *(Jimmy Dolan)*, Loretta Young *(Peggy)*, Aline MacMahon *(The Aunt)*, Guy Kibbee *(Phlaxer)*, Lyle Talbot *(Doc Woods)*, Fifi D'Orsay *(Budgie)*, Shirley Grey *(Goldie)*, George Meeker *(Magee)*, Harold Huber *(Reggie Newman)*, Farina *(Sam)*, Dawn O'Day *(Mary Lou)*, David Durand *(George)*, Mickey Rooney *(Freckles)*, Arthur Hohl *(Malvin)*, Arthur Dekuh *(Louie Primaro)*, John Wayne *(Smith)*.

Douglas Fairbanks, Jr., essays the lead role in this better than average fight film about a newly crowned champion who accidentally kills a newspaperman. When his double-crossing manager is burned beyond recognition in an automobile accident, the fighter takes his identity and goes underground, ending up at a home for crippled children. Ah, but the mortgage payment is due, so Jimmy reenters the ring to raise the cash. Note the presence of future stars Mickey Rooney, as one of the crippled kids, and John Wayne, as a fighter. THE LIFE OF JIMMY DOLAN was remade with John Garfield in 1939 as THEY MADE ME A CRIMINAL.

d, Archie Mayo; w, David Boehm, Erwin Gelsey (based on the play "The Sucker" by Bertram Milhauser and Beulah Marie Dix); ph, Arthur Edeson; ed, Bert Levy.

Boxing   **(PR:A   MPAA:NR)**

LIGHTNING—THE WHITE STALLION**

(1986) 95m Cannon c

Mickey Rooney *(Barney Ingram)*, Isabel Lorca *(Stephanie Ward)*, Susan George *(Mme. Rene)*, Billy Wesley *(Lucas Mitchell)*, Martin Charles Warner *(Emmett Fallon)*, Francoise Pascal *(Marie Ward Leeman)*, Read Morgan *(Harry Leeman)*, Stanley Siegel *(Jim Piper)*, Jay Rasumny *(Johnny)*, Debra Berger *(Lili Castle)*, Murray Langston *(Gorman)*, Rick Lundin *(Max)*, Justin Lundin *(Wiley)*, Charles Pitt *(Judge)*, Sheila Colligan *(Registrar)*, Karen Davis *(Melinda)*, Claudia Stenke *(Danielle)*, Rob Gage *(Himself)*.

Mickey Rooney stars here in yet another horse racing tale, this one the titular opposite of his 1979 film THE BLACK STALLION. Disgruntled over not having been paid for two months, a horse trainer steal his boss' favorite animal. Barney Ingram (Rooney) is the boss, a breeder whose penchant for gambling has reduced him to penury. He is heartbroken over the loss of his stallion and spends his days pouting about it and avoiding his creditors. When the horse escapes, schoolgirl Stephanie Ward (Isabel Lorca) finds it and takes it home, but her mean stepfather won't let her keep it, so she takes "Lightning" to a nearby farm owned by Mme. Rene (Susan George), arranging to work in the stables in return for the horse's board. She begins to ride and jump under Mme. Rene's instruction, eventually winning a local show-jumping contest; meanwhile, she learns that she is suffering from a degenerative eye disease and will, unless she has an expensive operation, become blind within a year. She goes on to win the state championship, finally gaining some measure of approval

from her stepfather, then, when Barney's creditors steal the horse back, Stephanie manages to rescue Lightning and ride him in the national championship, which, of course, she wins. While not as good as THE BLACK STALLION, this is not a bad film, for the performances help keep the cliches from seeming too familiar. Heavy on sweet, family-style scenes and light on actual race footage.

p, Harry Alan Towers; d, William A. Levey; w, Peter Welbeck; ph, Steven Shaw (TVC Color); ed, Ken Bornstein; m, Maurizio Abeni, Annakarin Klockar.

Horse Racing   **Cas.**   **(PR:A   MPAA:PG)**

LITTLE FAUSS AND BIG HALSY**

(1970) 98m PAR c

Robert Redford *(Big Halsy)*, Michael J. Pollard *(Little Fauss)*, Lauren Hutton *(Rita Nebraska)*, Noah Beery, Jr. *(Seally Fauss)*, Lucille Benson *(Mom Fauss)*, Ray Ballard *(Photographer)*, Linda Gaye Scott *(Mometh)*, Erin O'Reilly *(Sylvene McFall)*, Ben Archibek *(Rick Nifty)*, Shara St. John *(Marcy)*.

Little Fauss (Michael J. Pollard) is a slow-witted neophyte motorcycle racer; Big Halsy (Robert Redford) is the selfish suspended pro racer who takes Little on as a mechanic, provided that he can use his name and bike. As the pair experiences a series of on-the-road misadventures— including their mutual interest in Rita Nebraska (Lauren Hutton)—Halsy continually abuses the ever-admiring Little, and eventually they face each other in a race. Life imitated art in the making of this film, as Redford and Pollard reportedly fought constantly. Furthermore, director Sidney J. Furie is said to have wanted no part of the project (which was to have been directed by its screenwriter, Charles Eastman), and, as a result, LITTLE FAUSS AND BIG HALSY is a mixed bag, with a helter skelter plot but nicely coordinated motorcycle action and some good background music by Johnny Cash, Carl Perkins, and Bob Dylan.

p, Albert S. Ruddy; d, Sidney J. Furie; w, Charles Eastman; ph, Ralph Woolsey (Panavision, Movielab); ed, Argyle Nelson, Jr..

Motorcycle Racing   **(PR:O   MPAA:R)**

LIVELY SET, THE**

(1964) 95m UNIV c

James Darren *(Casey Owens)*, Pamela Tiffin *(Eadie Manning)*, Doug McClure *(Chuck Manning)*, Joanie Sommers *(Doreen Grey)*, Marilyn Maxwell *(Marge Owens)*, Charles Drake *(Paul Manning)*, Peter Mann *(Stanford Rogers)*, Russ Conway *(Moody)*, Carole Wells *(Mona)*, Frances Robinson *(Celeste)*.

This remake of JOHNNY DARK (1954) replaces Tony Curtis of that film with Gidget's true love, James Darren. Darren plays Casey Owens, an ex-GI and college dropout who cares more for cars than girls and works in his father's garage on a new gas turbine engine. When he meets hot-rodding buddy Chuck's (Doug McClure) sister, Eadie (Pamela Tiffin), Casey's interests broaden, and they get engaged and head for San Francisco, where Casey works on building a prototype car for millionaire Stanford Rogers (Peter Mann). Rogers fires him after he wrecks a model as a result of disregarding others' advice, but Casey scrounges up the cash to buy his engine back from Rogers and enters the Tri-State Endurance Race. He leaves the winner's circle a soberer young man, ready to wed Eadie and return to school. In addition to a five songs by Bobby Darin (sung by Darren, The Surfaris, Joanie Summers, and Wink "The Joker's Wild" Martindale), the film features cameo appearances by racers Max Schumacher, Dick Whittinghill, Mickey Thompson, James Nelson, Duane Carter, Billy Krause, and Ron Miller.

p, William Alland; d, Jack Arnold; w, Mel Goldberg, William Wood (based on a story by Goldberg, Alland); ph, Carl Guthrie (Eastmancolor); ed, Archie Marshek; m, Bobby Darin.

Auto Racing (PR:A MPAA:NR)

LOCAL BOY MAKES GOOD**

(1931) 67m FN-WB bw

Joe E. Brown *(John Miller)*, Dorothy Lee *(Julia Winters)*, Ruth Hall *(Marjorie Blake)*, Eddie Woods *(Spike Hoyt)*, Eddie Nugent *(Wally Pierce)*, John Harrington *(Coach Jackson)*, Wade Boteler, William Burress, Robert Bennett.

This silly but tolerable comedy gave Joe E. Brown a chance to do his thing as a sheepish florist who writes a letter to the girl of his dreams (Dorothy Lee) without any intention of mailing it. When one of his pals actually posts the note, the florist has to find a way to become the collegiate track star he claimed to be in his missive, and tries to make the team as javelin thrower—nearly impaling the coach, who chases him around the track in record time.

p, Robert Lord; d, Mervyn LeRoy; w, Robert Lord (based on the play "The Poor Nut" by J.C. Nugent and Elliott Nugent); ph, Sol Polito; ed, Jack Killifer.

**Track and Field/
Comedy** (PR:A MPAA:NR)

LONELINESS OF THE LONG DISTANCE RUNNER, THE****

(1962, Brit.) 104m Woodfall-Bryanston-Seven Arts/CD bw (AKA: REBEL WITH A CAUSE)

Tom Courtenay *(Colin Smith)*, Sir Michael Redgrave *(The Governor)*, Avis Bunnage *(Mrs. Smith)*, Peter Madden *(Mr. Smith)*, James Bolam *(Mike)*, Julia Foster *(Gladys)*, Topsy Jane *(Audrey)*, Dervis Ward *(Detective)*, Raymond Dyer *(Gordon)*, Alec McCowen *(Brown)*, Joe Robinson *(Roach)*, Philip Martin *(Stacey)*, Ray Austin *(Craig)*, Anthony Sayger *(Fenton)*, John Thaw *(Bosworth)*, Peter Kriss *(Scott)*, James Cairncross *(Jones)*, John Bull *(Ronalds)*, William Ash *(Gunthorpe)*, Dallas Cavell *(Lord Jaspers)*, Anita Oliver *(Alice Smith)*, Brian Hammond *(Johnny Smith)*.

One of the best of the British "Angry Young Man" films, THE LONELINESS OF THE LONG DISTANCE RUNNER follows Colin Smith (Tom Courtenay) as the ill-educated youth is sentenced to a reformatory after robbing a bakery. The borstal's governor (Michael Redgrave), a great believer in the rehabilitative powers of sports, is delighted to learn that Colin is a natural distance runner and encourages him to train for a big meet with a local public school, promising him special privileges in exchange for a victory. Most of the film is taken up with Colin's training, during which he flashes back to the events and relationships that have brought him to this point in his life. When the big race finally arrives, Colin easily outclasses his competitors, but at the finish line he shocks the governor with an unexpected act of rebellion. Adapted by Alan Sillitoe from his own short story and masterfully directed by Tony Richardson, this poignant film was also the auspicious film debut of Courtenay, whose excellent performance earned him the British Academy's Most Promising Newcomer award.

p, Tony Richardson; d, Tony Richardson; w, Alan Sillitoe (based on a story by Sillitoe); ph, Walter Lassally; ed, Anthony Gibbs; m, John Addison.

Track and Field (PR:C-O MPAA:NR)

LONGEST YARD, THE***½

(1974) 121m PAR c

Burt Reynolds *(Paul Crewe)*, Eddie Albert *(Warden Hazen)*, Ed Lauter *(Capt. Knauer)*, Michael Conrad *(Nate Scarboro)*, Jim Hampton *(Caretaker)*, Harry Caesar *(Granville)*, John Steadman *(Pop)*, Charles Tyner *(Unger)*, Mike Henry *(Rassmeusen)*, Bernadette Peters *(Warden's Secretary)*, Pervis Atkins *(Mawabe)*, Tony Cacciotti *(Rotka)*, Anitra Ford *(Melissa)*, Michael Ford *(Announcer)*, Joe Kapp *(Walking Boss)*, Richard Kiel *(Samson)*, Mort Marshall *(Assistant Warden)*, Ray Nitschke *(Bogdanski)*, Sonny Sixkiller *(Indian)*, Dino Washington *(Mason)*, Ernie Wheelwright *(Spooner)*, Joseph Dorsey *(Bartender)*, Dr. Gus Carlucci *(Team Doctor)*, Jack Rockwell *(Trainer)*, Sonny Shroyer *(Tannen)*, Roy Ogden *(Schmidt)*, Don Ferguson *(Referee)*, Robert Tessier *(Shokner)*, Tony Reese *(Levitt)*, Steve Wilder *(J.J.)*, George Jones *(Big George)*, Wilbur Gillan *(Big Wilbur)*, Wilson Warren *(Buttercup)*, Joe Jackson *(Little Joe)*.

Part prison film, part football film, this violent but outstanding comedy-drama by gifted action director Robert Aldrich (BIG LEAGUER, 1953; ALL THE MARBLES, 1981) explores the brutality inherent in both the American penal system and football. Burt Reynolds gives one of his best performances as Paul Crewe, a former pro who tires of being a kept man, steals his lover's car, and ends up in the prison ruled by Warden Hazen (Eddie Albert). Hazen compels Crewe to put together a team of prisoners to face the crack guard 11, offering him parole in exchange for a lopsided loss. Crewe assembles the "Mean Machine," then does his best to throw the game (which takes up 47 minutes of screen time), leaving it early with an "injury," but returning later to lead the Machine's comeback when the guards' savageness continues unabated. Deftly employing split screen and slow motion, Aldrich makes the most of Tracy Keenan Wynn's incisive script, aided by fine cinematography and tight editing. Both sides of the line of scrimmage feature former gridiron stars: the guards boast one-time Viking quarterback Joe Kapp and Packer Hall of Famer Ray Nitschke, while among the prisoners are Ernie Wheelwright, Pervis Atkins, and the University of Washington's legendary QB Sonny Sixkiller. No stranger to football himself, Reynolds, an All-Southern Conference halfback at Florida State, also played a pigskin hero in SEMI-TOUGH (1977).

p, Albert S. Ruddy; d, Robert Aldrich; w, Tracy Keenan Wynn (based on a story by Ruddy); ph, Joseph Biroc (Technicolor); ed, Michael Luciano, Frank Capacchione, Allan Jacobs, George Hively; m, Frank De Vol.

Football/Comedy   Cas.   (PR:O   MPAA:R)

LOVE ON SKIS**

(1933, Brit.) 65m Sokal/BL bw

Bull and Buster, Joan Austin, Ralph Rogan, Jack Lester.

Filmed in and around St. Moritz, LOVE ON SKIS is a conventional romance about two tramps from Canada who are really professional skiers and skaters. Winter sports enthusiasts will thrill to the daredevil expertise of these two comedians and the excellent skating, skiing, and ski-jumping on display; others may be happier reading the newspaper.

d, L. Vadja.

Skiing   (PR:A   MPAA:NR)

LUSTY MEN, THE*****

(1952) 113m RKO bw

Susan Hayward *(Louise Merritt)*, Robert Mitchum *(Jeff McCloud)*, Arthur Kennedy *(Wes Merritt)*, Arthur Hunnicutt *(Booker Davis)*, Frank Faylen *(Al Dawson)*, Walter Coy *(Buster Burgess)*, Carol Nugent *(Rusty Davis)*, Maria Hart *(Rosemary Maddox)*, Lorna Thayer *(Grace Burgess)*, Burt Mustin *(Jeremiah)*, Karen King *(Ginny Logan)*, Jimmy Dodd *(Red Logan)*, Eleanor Todd *(Babs)*, Riley Hill *(Hoag the Ranch Hand)*, Bob Bray *(Fritz)*, Sheb Wooley *(Slim)*, Marshall Reed *(Jim-Bob)*, Paul Burns *(Waite)*.

Director Nicholas Ray was a master of the offbeat film, and this brilliant contemporary western—easily the best movie ever made about rodeo (see also JUNIOR BONNER, 1972; J.W. COOP, 1971; RODEO, 1952)—is no exception. Washed-up rodeo champion Jeff McCloud (Robert Mitchum) takes a job on the ranch of Wes and Louise Merritt (Arthur Kennedy and Susan Hayward), and under his guidance Wes becomes a rodeo star. Meanwhile, Louise leads on the infatuated Jeff to insure his continued training of her husband, but when Wes gets too big for his britches, Jeff goes head to swelled head with him in rodeo competition, with tragic results. THE LUSTY MEN is full of action and dangerous stunts, photographed beautifully by master cinematographer Lee Garmes; Ray's direction is superb; and all three leads give bravura performances. Based on a *Life* magazine story by Claude Stanush and scripted by cowboy David Dortort, its screenplay presents classical situations, full of poetry and destiny. In his search for realism, Ray took his cameras on location, filming rodeos in

Tucson, Arizona; Spokane, Washington; Pendleton, Oregon; and Livermore, California, using a host of real rodeo stars such as Gerald Roberts, Jerry Ambler, and Les Sanborn.

p, Jerry Wald, Norman Krasna; d, Nicholas Ray; w, Horace McCoy, David Dortort (based on a story by Claude Stanush); ph, Lee Garmes; ed, Ralph Dawson; m, Roy Webb.

Rodeo   Cas.   (PR:C   MPAA:NR)

M

MADISON SQUARE GARDEN**

(1932) 70m PAR bw

Jack Oakie *(Eddie Burke)*, Marian Nixon *(Bee)*, Thomas Meighan *(Bill Carley)*, William Boyd *(Sloane)*, ZaSu Pitts *(Florrie)*, Lew Cody *(Roarke)*, William Collier, Sr. *(Doc Williams)*, Robert Elliott *(Miller)*, Lou Magnolia *(Referee)*, Jack Johnson *(Tom Sharkey)*, Damon Runyon, Jack Lait, Grantland Rice, Ed W. Smith, Westbrook Pegler, Paul Gallico.

The original Madison Square Garden is the setting for this run-of-the-mill boxing picture replete with the usual gangsters and fixed fights. Doc Williams (William Collier, Sr.), the manager of boxer Eddie Burke (Jack Oakie) and wrestler Brassy Randall (Warren Hymer), becomes the matchmaker for the venerable Gotham arena when his charges quit him, realizing it's the only way to get him to accept his dream job. In no time, Eddie falls victim to fight-fixing crooks who use the contests as a cover for their bootlegging activities, but in the film's wild finale the heavies get theirs from Garden employees, portrayed by such former sports greats as one-time heavyweight champ Jack Johnson. Alert viewers will also note the presence of writers Damon Runyon, Paul Gallico, Westbrook Pegler, and Grantland Rice.

p, Charles R. Rogers; d, Harry Joe Brown; w, P.J. Wolfson, Allen Rivkin (based on a story by Thomas Burtis); ph, Henry Sharp.

Boxing   (PR:A   MPAA:NR)

MAGNIFICENT MATADOR, THE**

(1955) 94m FOX c (GB: THE BRAVE AND THE BEAUTIFUL)

Maureen O'Hara *(Karen Harrison)*, Anthony Quinn *(Luis Santos)*, Richard Denning *(Mark Russell)*, Thomas Gomez *(Don David)*, Lola Albright *(Mona Wilton)*, William Ching *(Jody Wilton)*, Eduardo Noriega *(Miguel)*, Lorraine Chanel *(Sarita Sebastian)*, Manuel Rojas

Although best known as a director of westerns, Budd Boetticher, a one-time matador, also made two features about bullfighting, THE BULLFIGHTER AND THE LADY (1951) and this film. Anthony Quinn (who also appeared in Rouben Mamoulian's BLOOD AND SAND, on which Boetticher served as technical adviser) plays Luis Santos, a famed matador whose reputation is ruined when he flees the ring after formally introducing his young rival, Rafael (Manuel Rojas), to the bullfighting public. He finds solace in an affair with a rich American admirer (Maureen O'Hara), but her boy friend (Richard Denning) seeks revenge by denouncing Luis as a coward. Eventually, the matador returns to the ring to fight alongside Rafael, who is, we learn, much more than just a fellow bullfighter to Luis. Boetticher makes the most of Mexican locations, but the censors prevented him from showing any details of actual bullfighting that might have saved the otherwise trite plot. As a result, THE MAGNIFICENT MATADOR is a lackluster outing for both its star and director.

p, Edward L. Alperson; d, Budd Boetticher; w, Charles Lang (based on a story by Boetticher); ph, Lucien Ballard (CinemaScope, Eastmancolor); ed, Richard Cahoon; m, Raoul Kraushaar, Edward L. Alperson, Jr..

Bullfighting   **(PR:A   MPAA:NR)**

MAIN EVENT, THE*

(1938) 55m COL bw

Robert Paige (Mac Richards), Julie Bishop (Helen Phillips), Arthur Loft (Jack Benson), John Gallaudet (Joe Carter), Thurston Hall (Capt. Phillips), Gene Morgan (Lefty), Dick Curtis (Sawyer), Oscar O'Shea (Capt. Rorty), Pat Flaherty (Moran), John Tyrrell (Steve), Nick Copeland (Jake), Lester Dorr (Buck).

Essentially a crime film with a boxing backdrop, this tedious, badly mounted low-budget programmer follows a detective (Robert Paige) as he tracks a prizefighter kidnaped just before a long-awaited match.

p, Ralph Cohn; d, Danny Dare; w, Lee Loeb (based on a story by Harold Shumate); ph, Allen Siegler; ed, Al Clark.

Boxing   **(PR:A   MPAA:NR)**

MAIN EVENT, THE**

(1979) 112m Barwood/WB c

Barbra Streisand (Hillary Kramer), Ryan O'Neal (Eddie "Kid Natural" Scanlon), Paul Sand (David), Whitman Mayo (Percy), Patti D'Arbanville (Donna), Chu Chu Malave (Luis), Richard Lawson (Hector Mantilla), James Gregory (Gough), Richard Altman (Tour Guide), Joe Amsler (Stunt Double Kid), Seth Banks (Newsman), Lindsay Bloom (Girl in Bed), Earl Boen (NoseKline), Roger Bowen (Owner Sinthia Cosmetics), Badja Medu Djola (Heavyweight in Gym), Rory Calhoun (Fighter in Kid's Camp), Sue Casey (Brenda), Kristine DeBell (Lucy), Tim Rossovich.

Barbra Streisand and Ryan O'Neal are teamed in this boxing-based screwball comedy in the same vein as their earlier, more successful collaboration, WHAT'S UP, DOC? She is Hillary Kramer, a bankrupt perfume magnate; he is Kid Natural, a less-than-talented prizefighter-turned-driving instructor whose contract she took over as a tax write-off in more prosperous times. Now Hillary is deter-

mined to make some money on her investment. Becoming Kid's manager and immersing herself in the very male world of prizefighting, she forces him back into the ring. The problem is he's still a lousy fighter. Needless to say, plenty of romantic sparks fly en route to the clinch that ends this infrequently amusing battle of the sexes. THE MAIN EVENT was the film debut of Tim Rossovich, the glass-chewing former USC and Philadelphia Eagle star who plays one of O'Neal's opponents here and went on to appear in several other films, including THE LONG RIDERS (1980); CHEECH & CHONG'S NICE DREAMS (1981); and NIGHT SHIFT (1982).

p, Jon Peters, Barbra Streisand; d, Howard Zieff; w, Gail Parent, Andrew Smith; ph, Mario Tosi (Technicolor); ed, Edward Warschilka.

Boxing/Comedy   Cas.   (PR:A-C MPAA:PG)

MAN FROM DOWN UNDER, THE**

(1943) 103m MGM bw

Charles Laughton (Jocko Wilson), Binnie Barnes (Aggie Dawlins), Richard Carlson ("Nipper" Wilson), Donna Reed (Mary Wilson), Christopher Severn ("Nipper" as a Child), Clyde Cook (Ginger Gaffney), Horace [Stephen] McNally ("Dusty" Rhodes), Arthur Shields (Father Polycarp), Evelyn Falke (Mary as a Child), Hobart Cavanaugh ("Boots"), Andre Charlot (Father Antoine).

At the close of WW I, Sgt. Jocko Wilson (Charles Laughton), a former prizefighter, leaves singer Aggie Dawlins (Binnie Barnes) at an English dock and returns to Australia with two Belgian orphans in tow, raising them as his own. The girl (played as an adult by Donna Reed) is sent to private school, while the boy (Richard Carlson) becomes the Australian lightweight boxing champion. Using his winnings, they buy an estate and convert it into a hotel. Years later, Aggie—now rich, but still bitter over having been dumped—appears and wins possession of the struggling hotel in a card game. But as WW II begins she and Jocko rekindle their romance, and his "kids," who have long been afraid of their attraction to each other, learn that they aren't related.

p, Robert Z. Leonard, Orville O. Dull; d, Robert Z. Leonard; w, Wells Root, Thomas Seller (based on a story by Bogart Rogers, Mark Kelly); ph, Sidney Wagner; ed, George White; m, David Snell.

Boxing   **(PR:A-C MPAA:NR)**

MAN I LOVE, THE**

(1929) 70m PAR bw

Richard Arlen (Dum-Dum Brooks), Mary Brian (Celia Fields), Olga Baclanova (Sonia Barondoff), Harry Green (Curly Bloom), Jack Oakie (Lew Layton), Pat O'Malley (D.J. McCarthy), Leslie Fenton (Carlo Vesper), Charles Sullivan (Champ Mahoney), Sailor Vincent (K.O. O'Hearn), Robert Perry (Gateman).

Richard Arlen takes to the ring as Dum-Dum Brooks, a small-town boxer who, accompanied by his wife (Mary Brian), heads to Manhattan, where he batters the champ in an exhibition bout. Before the film is over, he gets a real shot at the title, and don't bet that he blows it.

p, David O. Selznick; d, William A. Wellman; w, Herman J. Mankiewicz, Percy Heath; ph, Harry Gerard; ed, Allyson Shaffer.

Boxing   **(PR:A MPAA:NR)**

MANIACS ON WHEELS**

(1948, Brit.) 76m Rank-Wessex/International Releasing bw (GB: ONCE A JOLLY SWAGMAN)

Dirk Bogarde (Bill Fox), Bonar Colleano (Tommy Possey), Renee Asherson (Pat Gibbon), Bill Owen (Lag Gibbon), Cyril Cusack (Duggie Lewis), Thora Hird (Ma Fox), James Hayter (Pa Fox), Pauline Jameson (Mrs. Lewis), Stuart Lindsell (Mr. Yates), Moira Lister (Dotty Liz), Sandra Dorne (Kay Fox), Sidney James (Rowton), Anthony Oliver (Derek), Dudley Jones (Taffy), Russell Waters (Mr. Possey), Frederick Knight (Chick), Michael Kent (Solicitor), June Bardsley (WAAF Sergeant).

Bill Fox (Dirk Bogarde), a young factory worker in 1930s Britain, quits his job to become a motorbike racer and, wonder of wonders, is a great success, but, like so many celluloid jocks before and after him, falls victim to his own burgeoning ego. Bill hangs up his goggles for good, however, after his wife decides to leave him. Although the performances are lifeless and the plot predictable, MANIACS ON WHEELS' racing sequences are well handled.

p, Ian Dalrymple; d, Jack Lee, R.Q. McNaughton; w, Jack Lee, William Rose, Cliff Gordon (based on the novel by Montagu Slater); ph, H.E. Fowle, L. Cave-Chinn; ed, Jack Harris; m, Bernard Stevens.

Motorcycle Racing   **(PR:A MPAA:NR)**

MANNEQUIN*

(1933, Brit.) 54m REA/RKO bw

Harold French (Peter Tattersall), Judy Kelly (Heather Trent), Diana Beaumont (Lady Diana Savage), Whitmore Humphries (Billy Armstrong), Richard Cooper (Lord Bunny Carstairs), Ben Welden (Chris Dempson), Faith Bennett (Queenie), Vera Boggetti (Nancy), Ann Lee (Babette), William Pardue, Carol Lees, Tonie Edgar Bruce.

Take one boxer, one boxer's girl friend, and one female fight fan who's only interested in winners, and you've got a standard fight film setup—and MANNEQUIN, a formula British entry that brings absolutely nothing new to the genre. Whitmore Humphries plays the boxer who tosses over his sweetheart (Judy Kelly) for a wealthy society dame (Diana Beaumont) who regards him as a plaything and even bets against him. It should come as little surprise that the fighter not only wins the big bout but also regains the affections of his ex. The boxing sequences are as phony as the plot, but MANNEQUIN does promise more than a few unintentional laughs.

p, Julius Hagen; d, George A. Cooper; w, Charles Bennett.

Boxing   **(PR:A MPAA:NR)**

MANOLETE**

(1950, Sp.) 80m Hercules bw

Jose Greco (Rafael), Paquito Rico (Dolores), Pedro Ortega (Manolete), Juanita Manso (Soledad), Manolo Moran (Favier), Ava Adamaz.

Combining actual newsreel footage with staged action, this film biography of Spanish bullfighter Manolete (played here by Pedro Ortega) has some interesting moments, despite its overplayed performances and shaky direction. Jose Greco, in particular, contributes some accomplished flamenco dancing, and that's what we're all looking for in a good sports film, aren't we?

d, Florian Rey; w, Llovety Manzano; ph, Enrique Guerner; ed, Ropence.

**Bullfighting/
Biography**   **(PR:A MPAA:NR)**

MARK IT PAID**

(1933) 69m COL bw

William Collier, Jr., Joan Marsh.

Well-done racing scenes are the best thing going for this film in which William Collier, Jr., headlines as an honest speedboat driver who refuses to throw a race and finds himself in hot water as a result.

d, D. Ross Lederman; w, Charles Condon.

Speedboat Racing   **(PR:A MPAA:NR)**

M*A*S*H****

(1970) 116m Aspen/FOX c

Donald Sutherland (Hawkeye Pierce), Elliott Gould (Trapper John McIntyre), Tom Skerritt (Duke Forrest), Sally Kellerman (Maj. Hot Lips Houlihan), Robert Duvall (Maj. Frank Burns), Jo Ann Pflug (Lt. Dish), Rene Auberjonois (Dago Red), Roger Bowen (Col. Henry Blake), Gary Burghoff (Radar O'Reilly), David Arkin (Sgt. Major Vollmer), Fred Williamson (Spearchucker), Michael Murphy (Me Lay), Kim Atwood (Ho-Jon), Tim Brown (Cpl. Judson), John Schuck (Painless Pole), Ken Prymus (Pfc. Seidman), Dwayne Damon (Capt. Scorch), Carl Gottlieb (Ugly John), Tamara Horrocks (Capt. Knocko), G. Wood (Gen. Hammond), Bobby Troup (Sgt. Gorman), Bud Cort (Pvt. Boone), Corey Fisher (Capt. Bandini), J.B. Douglas (Col. Douglas), Ben Davidson, Fran Tarkenton, Howard Williams, Jack Concannon, John Myers, Tom Woodeschick, Tommy Brown, Buck Buchanan, Nolan Smith (Football Players).

Although Robert Altman's hilarious antiwar comedy-drama M*A*S*H is primarily involved with the goofy goings-on at a Mobile Army Surgical Hospital—the Korean War-time home for the military medicos who became even more familiar to viewers of the film's beloved TV spin-off—it also includes an extended football sequence that is one of the most amusing Hollywood has to offer. When Hawkeye (Donald Sutherland) boasts about his unit's football skills, a visiting general arranges a game and a $5,000 bet.

SPORTS MOVIES   **73**

Through liberal use of a sedative and the talents of a ringer, pro football player Spearchucker Jones (former Chief and Raider defensive back Fred Williamson), the MASH unit triumphs. Both Williamson and another football player-turned-actor, Tim Brown (outstanding running back and kick returner for the Philadelphia Eagles), made their film debuts in M*A*S*H, and pro players Fran Tarkenton, Jack Concannon, Tom Woodeschick, and Buck Buchanan also appear.

p, Ingo Preminger; d, Robert Altman; w, Ring Lardner, Jr. (based on the novel by Richard Hooker); ph, Harold E. Stine (Panavision, DeLuxe Color); ed, Danford B. Greene; m, Johnny Mandel.

Football/Comedy   Cas.   (PR:C-O MPAA:R)

MATILDA*

(1978) 105m AIP c

Elliott Gould *(Bernie Bonnelli)*, Robert Mitchum *(Duke Parkhurst)*, Harry Guardino *(Uncle Nono)*, Clive Revill *(Billy Baker)*, Karen Carlson *(Kathleen Smith)*, Roy Clark *(Wild Bill Wildman)*, Lionel Stander *(Pinky Schwab)*, Art Metrano *(Gordon Baum)*, Larry Pennell *(Lee Dockerty)*, Roberta Collins *(Tanya Six)*, Lenny Montana *(Mercanti)*, Frank Avianca *(Renato)*, James Lennon *(Ring Announcer)*, Don Dunphy *(Ringside Announcer)*, George Latka *(Referee)*, Mike Willesee *(Australian Announcer)*.

Far from a routine fight film, MATILDA is a charming family picture that bounces along as happily as the kangaroo (actually a man in a kangaroo suit) that fights for the world championship in it. Despite the objections of animal lover Kathleen Smith (Karen Carlson) the title marsupial earns a shot at the heavyweight championship, and by the end of the big bout in Lake Tahoe everyone is smiling except gangland chief Uncle Nono (Harry Guardino). The excellent cast includes Robert Mitchum as a sportswriter, Elliott Gould as a two-bit promoter, Lionel Stander as the champ's nominal manager, and several real-life ring announcers, most notably Don Dunphy.

p, Albert S. Ruddy; d, Daniel Mann; w, Albert S. Ruddy, Timothy Galfas (based on the book by Paul Gallico); ph, Jack Woolf (Movielab Color); ed, Allan Jacobs.

Boxing/Comedy   Cas.   (PR:A MPAA:G)

MAURIE*½

(1973) 113m Ausable/NG c (AKA: BIG MO)

Bernie Casey *(Maurice Stokes)*, Bo Swenson *(Jack Twyman)*, Janet MacLachlan *(Dorothy)*, Stephanie Edwards *(Carol)*, Pauline Myers *(Rosie)*, Bill Walker *(Stokes)*, Maidie Norman *(Mrs. Stokes)*, Curt Conway *(Dr. Stewart)*, Jitu Cumbuka *(Oscar)*, Lori Busk *(Lida)*, Tol Avery *(Milton)*, Chris Schenkel.

Part "Brian's Song," part THE STRATTON STORY (also scripted by the writer of this film, Douglas Morrow), MAURIE is based on the ordeal of Cincinnati Royals star Maurice Stokes, who was struck with a paralysis that ended his promising career and left him hospitalized. One-time San Francisco 49er and Los Angeles Ram wide receiver Bernie Casey gives a fine performance as Maurie; Bo Swenson plays Jack Twyman, his white Royals teammate who dedicates a decade to Maurie's rehabilitation, raising money through an annual charity game and making it possible for Maurie to talk again before death ended his 10-year struggle. Unfortunately, despite the leads' fine characterizations, Morrow and director Daniel Mann lay on the sentiment so thick that the touching humanity of the remarkable real-life relationship between Twyman and Stokes is smothered.

p, Frank Ross, Douglas Morrow; d, Daniel Mann; w, Douglas Morrow; ph, John Hora (Technicolor); ed, Walter Hannemann.

Basketball/Biography

(PR:A MPAA:G)

MAYBE IT'S LOVE*

(1930) 74m WB bw

Joan Bennett *(Nan Sheffield)*, Joe E. Brown *(Speed Hanson)*, James Hall *(Tommy Nelson)*, Laura Lee *(Betty)*, Anders Randolf *(Mr. Nelson)*, Sumner Getchell *(Whiskers)*, George Irving *(President Sheffield)*, George Bickel *(Professor)*, Howard Jones *(Coach Bob Brown)*, Bill Banker *(Bill)*, Russell Saunders *(Racehorse Russell)*, Tim Moynihan *(Tim)*, W.K. Schoonover *(Schoony)*, E.N. Sleight *(Elmer)*, George Gibson *(George)*, Ray Montgomery *(Ray)*, Otto Pommerening *(Otto)*, Stuart Erwin *(Brown of Harvard)*.

Similar to many early 1930s college football programmers, this dumb but cute comedy directed by William Wellman focuses on the attempts of a college president's daughter (Joan Bennett) to improve the fortunes of Upton College's pathetic football team through a bit of inspired recruiting, doffing her glasses and batting her pretty eyelashes at All-Americans in an attempt to lure them from their alma maters. James Hall essays the role of her real love interest—a bad boy turned good—and Joe E. Brown uses his famous "big mouth" to protest his ouster from the lineup. Also included in the cast are members of the 1929 All-American team.

d, William A. Wellman; w, Joseph Jackson (based on a story by Darryl F. Zanuck); ph, Robert Kurrle; ed, Edward McDermott.

Football/Comedy   (PR:A MPAA:NR)

MIGHTY MC GURK, THE*

(1946) 83m MGM bw

Wallace Beery *(Roy "Slag" McGurk)*, Dean Stockwell *(Nipper)*, Edward Arnold *(Mike Glenson)*, Aline MacMahon *(Mamie Steeple)*, Cameron Mitchell *(Johnny Burden)*, Dorothy Patrick *(Caroline Glenson)*, Aubrey Mather *(Milbane)*, Morris Ankrum *(Fowles)*, Clinton Sundberg *(Flexter)*, Charles Judels, Torben Meyer *(Brewers)*, Stuart Holmes *(Sightseer)*, Edward Earle *(Martin)*, Tom Kennedy *(Man at Punching Machine)*, Trevor Tremaine *(Cockney)*.

Fifteen years after starring in THE CHAMP, Wallace Beery took on the role of another down-and-out boxer, here playing Roy "Slag" McGurk, an ex-champion employed by a despicable tavern owner (Edward Arnold) bent on evicting the Salvation Army from its Bowery home so that he can expand his operation. McGurk takes in a young English lad (Dean Stockwell), hoping that the boy's rich uncle will reward him, but—swayed by the boy and a Salvation Army leader (Cameron Mitchell)—the former champ sets aside his selfish ambitions and uses his once-famous fists to keep the wolves from the Army's door. More than a little sappy, this melodrama set in the 1890s presents Beery in his usual role as the lovable slob, but unless you're completely burned out on THE CHAMP, you'll find that 1931 classic a much more satisfying experience.

p, Nat Perrin; d, John Waters; w, William R. Lipman, Grant Garrett, Harry Clark; ph, Charles Schoenbaum; ed, Ben Lewis; m, David Snell.

Boxing   **(PR:A   MPAA:NR)**

MILKY WAY, THE***½

(1936) 83m PAR bw

Harold Lloyd (Burleigh "Tiger" Sullivan), Adolphe Menjou (Gabby Sloan), Verree Teasdale (Ann Westley), Helen Mack (Mae Sullivan), William Gargan (Elwood "Speed" MacFarland), George Barbier (Wilbur Austin), Dorothy Wilson (Polly Pringle), Lionel Stander (Spider Schultz), Charles Lane (Willard, Reporter), Marjorie Gateson (Mrs. E. Winthrop LeMoyne), Bull Anderson (Oblitsky), Jim Marples (O'Rourke), Larry McGrath (Referee), Henry Roquemore (Doctor), Arthur Byron (Cop), Eddie Dunn (Barber), Larry McGrath (Referee), Jack Clifford (Announcer), Jack Perry ("Tornado" Todd), Phil Tead (Radio Announcer), Jack Murphy (Newsboy), Bob Callahan (Onion), Eddie Fetherston (Cameraman), Leonard Carey (Butler), Melville Ruick (Austin's Secretary), Harry Bowen (Bartender), James Farley (Fight Promoter).

This very funny film shows the great Harold Lloyd making the transition from silent to sound films with no problems. Lloyd plays milquetoast milkman Burleigh Sullivan, who happens to be in the right place at the right time. When the middleweight champion (William Gargan) throws a punch his way, Sullivan ducks, and the punch is returned by bruiser Spider Schultz (Lionel Stander). The champ is knocked senseless and "Tiger" Sullivan gets the credit. The champ's manager (Adolphe Menjou) then decides to take the milkman on as a boxer-client, with predictable comic results. Lloyd (who almost always did his own spectacular stunts) stepped aside from producing chores on THE MILKY WAY, and was thus able to concentrate on his comedy without worrying about finances and other woes. He gives a superb performance in his patented role of the bespectacled, naive everyman who triumphs over ironic perils every time. Remade as THE KID FROM BROOKLYN (1946), starring Danny Kaye.

p, E. Lloyd Sheldon; d, Leo McCarey; w, Grover Jones,

Frank Butler, Richard Connell (based on the play by Lynn Root, Harry Clork); ph, Alfred Gilks; ed, LeRoy Stone.

Boxing/Comedy   Cas.   (PR:AA   MPAA:NR)

MILLION DOLLAR LEGS***

(1932) 64m PAR bw

Jack Oakie (Migg Tweeny), W.C. Fields (The President of Klopstokia), Andy Clyde (The Major-Domo), Lyda Roberti (Mata Machree), Susan Fleming (Angela), Ben Turpin (Mysterious Man), Hugh Herbert (Secretary of Treasury), George Barbier (Mr. Baldwin), Dickie Moore (Willie), Billy Gilbert (Secretary of the Interior), Vernon Dent (Secretary of Agriculture), Teddy Hart (Secretary of War), John Sinclair (Secretary of Labor), Sam Adams (Secretary of State), Irving Bacon (Secretary of the Navy), Ben Taggart (Ship's Captain), Hank Mann (Customs Inspector), Chick Collins (Jumper), Syd Saylor (Starter at the Games), Ernie Adams (Contestant).

Silly and surrealistic, MILLION DOLLAR LEGS is a satire of the 1932 Los Angeles Olympics made before the fact and released to coincide with the Summer Games. The coffers of the mythical nation of Klopstokia need replenishment, and, accepting the advice of an American brush salesman (Jack Oakie), the president (W.C. Fields) who holds office by virtue of his superior physical prowess, decides to send a delegation to the Olympics, hoping to put his little land on the map. This is a less ambitious notion than it first appears, because virtually every Klopstokian is a superior athlete. The rest of the film is a melange of intrigue (including an espionage parody), slapstick, chases, and very nearly a laugh every minute. Director Edward Cline called in several of the best silent-film gagsters (Ben Turpin and Hank Mann among them) to work with the inimitable Fields, and the result is a wonderful mix of physical comedy and sharp dialog that is unfortunately hampered somewhat by a script and direction that never quite tie all of the great gags together.

p, Herman J. Mankiewicz; d, Edward Cline; w, Henry Myers, Nick Barrows (based on a story by Joseph L. Mankiewcz); ph, Arthur Todd.

Track and Field/
Comedy   (PR:A   MPAA:NR)

MILLION DOLLAR LEGS**

(1939) 59m PAR bw

Betty Grable (Carol Parker), John Hartley (Greg Melton), Donald O'Connor (Sticky Boone), Jackie Coogan (Russ Simpson), Larry "Buster" Crabbe (Coach Baxter), Peter Lind Hayes (Freddie Fry), Dorothea Kent (Susie Quinn), Richard Denning (Hunk Jordan), Philip Warren (Buck Hogan), Edward Arnold (Blimp Garrett), Thurston Hall (Gregory Melton, Sr.), Roy Gordon (Dean Wixby), Matty Kemp (Ed Riggs), William Tracy (Egghead Jackson), Joyce Mathews (Bunny), Russ Clark (Referee), Wallace Rairden (Crandall), John Hart (Haldeman), Bill Boggess (Wells), Ken Nolan (Thurston), Billy Wilkerson (Rich), Jim Kelso (Carpenter).

Combining crew and horse racing, this mildly amusing B comedy is notable for the presence of several talents who went on to bigger things, including Betty Grable (whose famous legs were eventually insured for $1 million, though this has nothing to do with the film's title), a youthful Donald O'Connor, and William Holden in a bit part. Rich kid Greg Melton (John Hartley) tries to escape from his father's shadow by supplying his college's rowing team with badly needed new shells without tapping into the family funds. Taking up a collection from his teammates, he bets on a racehorse called Million Dollar Legs, and though it's a long shot, his gamble pays off, the team gets its new equipment, and the stage is set for a climactic race.

d, Nick Grinde, Edward Dmytryk; w, Lewis Foster, Richard English (based on a story by Foster); ph, Harry Fischbeck; ed, Stuart Gilmore.

Crew/Horse Racing　　　　**(PR:A　MPAA:NR)**

MILLION TO ONE, A**

(1938) 59m Puritan bw

Herman Brix [Bruce Bennett] *(Johnny Kent)*, Joan Fontaine *(Joan Stevens)*, Monte Blue *(John Kent, Sr.)*, Kenneth Harlan *(William Stevens)*, Suzanne Kaaren *(Pat Stanley)*, Reed Howes *(Duke Hale)*, Ed Piel *(Mac, the Editor)*, Ben Hall *(Joe, a Reporter)*, Dick Simmons *(A Friend)*.

Some remember Bruce Bennett as Cody in THE TREASURE OF SIERRA MADRE (1948), others recall him as one of the fraternity of screen Tarzans, and fewer know him as Herman Brix, silver medalist in the shot put at the 1928 Amsterdam Olympics. Still acting under his given name, Brix makes a big stretch and appears here as an Olympic decathlete battling for gold. Joan Fontaine is the wealthy miss who wants to marry him, Monte Blue is his father and trainer, and Reed Howes is his main competitor.

p, Fanchon Royer; d, Lynn Shores; w, John T. Neville; ph, James Diamond; ed, Edward Schroeder.

Track and Field　　　　**(PR:A　MPAA:NR)**

MIRACLE KID*

(1942) 66m PRC bw

Tom Neal *(Jimmy)*, Carol Hughes *(Pat)*, Vicki Lester *(Helen)*, Betty Blythe *(Gloria)*, Ben Taggart *(Gibbs)*, Alex Callam *(Bolger)*, Thornton Edwards *(Pedro)*, Minta Durfee *(Pheney)*, Gertrude Messinger *(Marge)*, Adele Smith *(Lorraine)*, Frank Otto *(Shady)*, Paul Bryar *(Rocco)*, Pat Gleasch *(Reporter)*, Billy McGown *(Tiger)*, Joe Gray *(Kayo Kane)*, Gene O'Donnell *(Usher)*, Warren Jackson *(Headwaiter)*.

Directed by the prolific William Beaudine, MIRACLE KID is another go-round—and a weak one at that—for the old story of the young man forced into boxing against his better inclinations. Here Tom Neal is the fighter whose ring ambitions drive away his fiancee (Carol Hughes), but who is reunited with her after the usual bouts with bright lights and bruised egos.

p, John T. Coyle; d, William Beaudine; w, Gerald Drayson

Adams, Henry Sucher, John T. Coyle; ph, Arthur Martinelli; ed, Guy V. Thayer, Jr.

Boxing　　　　**(PR:A　MPAA:NR)**

MR. CELEBRITY**

(1942) 68m PRC bw

Buzzy Henry *(Danny Mason)*, James Seay *(Jim Kane)*, Doris Day *(Carol Carter)*, William Halligan *(Mr. Mason)*, Gavin Gordon *(Travers)*, Johnny Berkes *(Johnny Martin)*, Jack Baxley *(Judge Culpepper)*, Larry Grey *(Cardo the Great)*, John Ince *(Joe Farrell)*, Frank Hagney *(Dugan)*, Jack Richardson *(Geraghty)*, Alfred Hall *(Scanlon)*, Smokey Saunders *(Smokey)*, Francis X. Bushman, James J. Jeffries.

This routine racetrack tale centers around Jim Kane (James Seay), a young veterinarian; his nephew, Danny (Buzzy Henry); and their love for horse racing. When the boy's rich grandfather demands custody of him, Danny and Jim run off to a farm that serves as a getaway for former celebrities. On the premises is Mr. Celebrity, an old horse that Jim trains for a big race, which it wins, permitting Jim and Danny to stay together. What else did you expect?

p, Martin Mooney; d, William Beaudine; w, Martin Mooney (based on the story by Charles Samuels, Mooney); ph, Arthur Martinelli; ed, Robert Crandall.

Horse Racing　　　　**(PR:A　MPAA:NR)**

MR. HEX**

(1946) 63m MON bw (GB: THE PRIDE OF THE BOWERY)

Leo Gorcey *(Slip)*, Huntz Hall *(Sach)*, Bobby Jordan *(Bobby)*, Gabriel Dell *(Gabe Moreno)*, Billy Benedict *(Whitey)*, David Gorcey *(Chuck)*, Gale Robbins *(Gloria Williams)*, Ben Welden *(Bull Laguna)*, Ian Keith *(Raymond The Hypnotist)*, Sammy Cohen *(Evil Eyes Fagin)*, Bernard Gorcey *(Louie)*, William Ruhl *(Mob Leader)*, Danny Beck *(Danny the Dip)*, Rita Lynn *(Margie)*, Eddie Gribbon *(Blackie)*, John Indrisano *(Referee Joe McGowan)*.

The Bowery Boys get involved in the fight game while trying to help a pretty singer (Gale Robbins) and her sick mother. Learning that Sach (Huntz Hall) acquires Herculean strength under hypnosis, Slip (Leo Gorcey) steers him to victory in a number of prizefights; then the dazed dynamo is set to battle a fighter who, unknown to the Boys, is a former champ whose face has been altered by plastic surgery. What's more, the ringer is hypnotized for the bout and his crooked manager sees to it that the coin Slip uses to put Satch under is stolen. Not to worry: Slip finds a replacement coin and justice is not served.

p, Jan Grippo; d, William Beaudine; w, Cyril Endfield (based on a story by Grippo); ph, James Brown; ed, Richard Currier, Seth Larson.

Boxing/Comedy　　　　**(PR:A　MPAA:NR)**

MR. UNIVERSE**

(1951) 79m Laurel/EL bw

Jack Carson (Jeff Clayton), Janis Paige (Lorraine), Vincent Edwards (Tommy Tomkins), Bert Lahr (Joe Pulaski), Robert Alda (Fingers Maroni), Dennis James, Maxie Rosenbloom, Joyce Matthews, Harry Landers, Donald Novis, Murray Rothenberg.

Long before he began making the rounds as Ben Casey, Vince Edwards checked in as a body builder-cum-professional wrestler in this low-budget comedy. Failing to realize that pro wrestling is as much theater as it is sport, honest, hard-working Tommy (Edwards) thinks his meteoric rise is due to his own ability. Meanwhile, his handlers (Jack Carson and Bert Lahr) incur the wrath of gangsters who think Tommy has been a little too successful. By the final bell, however, Tommy's very real wrestling skills reverse what otherwise promises to be a bleak outcome. Outside the ring MR. UNIVERSE falters, but the wrestling action offers some nice comic moments, and some of its caricatures of grapplers and other hangers-on are amusing.

p, Joseph Lerner; d, Joseph Lerner; w, Searle Kramer; ph, Gerald Hirschfield; ed, Geraldine Lerner; m, Dimitri Tiomkin.

Wrestling (PR:A MPAA:NR)

MIXED COMPANY**½

(1974) 109m Llenroc/UA c

Barbara Harris (Kathy), Joseph Bologna (Pete), Lisa Gerritsen (Liz), Arianne Heller (Mary), Stephen Honanie (Joe), Haywood Nelson (Freddie), Eric Olson (Rob), Jina Tan (Quan), Tom Bosley (Al), Dorothy Shay (Marge), Ruth McDevitt (Miss Bergguist), Bob G. Anthony (Krause), Ron McIlwain (Walt Johnson), Roger Price (The Doctor), Keith Hamilton (Milton), Jason Clark (Police Sergeant), Charles J. Samsill (Police Officer), Jophery Brown (Basketball Player), Rodney Hundley (Announcer), Darell L. Garretson (Referee), Calvin Brown (Santa Claus), The Phoenix Suns.

Director Melville Shavelson (YOURS, MINE AND OURS) once again explores the problems of an oversized family in this film focusing on the household headed by the struggling coach of the Phoenix Suns (Joseph Bologna), who is at odds with his star player (Ron McIlwain). On the home front, the coach's wife is determined to add to their brood of three, even though her husband has been left sterile by a middle-aged bout with the mumps. The solution: adoption. Soon the three newest members of the family—one black, one Vietnamese, one native American—are confronted with their neighbors' bigotry; meanwhile, dad's basketball team keeps losing and he is fired. Confusion and calamity reign as the film moves towards its sentimental climax. The real-life Phoenix Suns play themselves.

p, Melville Shavelson; d, Melville Shavelson; w, Melville Shavelson, Mort Lachman; ph, Stan Lazan; ed, Walter Thompson, Ralph James Hall; m, Fred Karlin.

Basketball (PR:C MPAA:PG)

MOMENT OF TRUTH, THE**

(1965, It./Sp.) 105m Federiz-A.S/Rizzoli c (VIVIR DESVIVIENDOSE; EL MOMENTO DE LA VERDAD: IL MOMENTO DELLA VERITA)

Miguel Mateo (Miguel), Pedro Basauri (Maestro Pedrucho), Jose Gomez Sevillano (Impresario), Linda Christian (American Woman).

Directed by Francesco Rosi, THE MOMENT OF TRUTH tells the story of a farm boy (Miguel Mateo) who heads for the bullrings of Barcelona and quickly becomes a top-rated toreador and press darling. His downfall is just as abrupt, however, as he dies in the ring while facing a killer bull. (In Italian, English subtitles.)

p, Antonio Cervi, Francesco Rosi; d, Francesco Rosi; w, Francesco Rosi, Pedro Portabella, Ricardo Munoz Suay, Pedro Beltran, Raffaele La Capria (based on a story by Rosi); ph, Gianni Di Venanzo, Aiace Parolin, Pasquale De Santis (Techniscope, Technicolor); ed, Mario Serandrei; m, Piero Piccioni.

Bullfighting (PR:A MPAA:NR)

MONEY FROM HOME**

(1953) 100m PAR c

Dean Martin (Honey Talk Nelson), Jerry Lewis (Virgil Yokum), Marjie Millar (Phyllis Leigh), Pat Crowley (Autumn Claypool), Richard Haydn (Bertie Searles), Robert Strauss (Seldom Seen Kid), Gerald Mohr (Marshall Preston), Sheldon Leonard (Jumbo Schneider), Romo Vincent (The Poojah), Jack Kruschen (Short Boy), Lou Lubin (Sam), Joe McTurk (Hard Top Harry), Frank Mitchell (Lead Pipe Louie), Sam Hogan (Society Kid), Phil Arnold (Crossfire), Louis Nicoletti (Hot Horse Herbie), Charles Frank Horvath.

Originally filmed in 3-D but offering few 3-D thrills, this disappointing Dean Martin-Jerry Lewis comedy-musical casts Martin as a gambler given the option of paying up his debts or fixing an upcoming horse race. He hides out from his tough-guy creditor (Sheldon Leonard) and the latter's thugs with his cousin (Lewis), who gets mixed up with an Arab sheik, pretends to be one of his harem, and ends up impersonating a famous British jockey and riding in a big race.

p, Hal B. Wallis; d, George Marshall; w, Hal Kanter, James Allardice (based on a story by Damon Runyon); ph, Daniel L. Fapp (Technicolor); ed, Warren Low; m, Leigh Harline.

Horse Racing/
Musical/Comedy (PR:A MPAA:NR)

MONKEY ON MY BACK**½

(1957) 93m UA bw

Cameron Mitchell (Barney Ross), Dianne Foster (Cathy), Paul Richards (Rico), Jack Albertson (Sam Pian), Kathy Garver (Noreen), Lisa Golm (Barney's Mother), Barry Kelley (Big Ralph), Dayton Lummis (McAvoy), Lewis Charles (Lew Surati), Raymond Greenleaf (Latham), Richard Benedict (Art Winch), Brad Harris (Spike), Robert Holton (Dr. Sullivan).

The monkey of the title is morphine addiction, and the back it's riding on is Cameron Mitchell's in a portrayal of former welter- and lightweight boxing champ Barney Ross. A flamboyant, high-living character, Ross takes off as a Marine for WW II and is awarded a medal for heroism at Guadalcanal. He soon contracts malaria, however, and is given morphine to ease the pain. Upon his return home and to the ring, Ross' need for morphine increases, nearly ruining his career and family life. The fighting sequences are especially well staged, as is Ross' four-and-a-half-month struggle in the US Federal Hospital in Lexington, Kentucky, to shake the monkey.

p, Edward Small; d, Andre de Toth; w, Crane Wilbur, Anthony Veiller, Paul Dudley; ph, Maury Gertsman; ed, Grant Whytock; m, Paul Sawtell, Bert Shefter.

Boxing/Biography   (PR:C MPAA:NR)

MOONLIGHT IN HAVANA**

(1942) 63m UNIV bw

Allan Jones *(Johnny Norton)*, Jane Frazee *(Gloria Jackson)*, Marjorie Lord *(Patsy Clark)*, William Frawley *(Barney Crane)*, Don Terry *(Eddie Daniels)*, Sergio Orta *(Martinez)*, Wade Boteler *(Joe Clark)*, Hugh O'Connell *(Charlie)*, Jack Norton *(George)*, Dorothy Babb, Marilyn Kay *(Jivin' Jills)*, Roland Dupree, Joe "Corky" Geil, Dick Humphreys *(Jivin' Jacks)*, Tom Dugan *(Doc)*, Helen Lynd *(Daisy)*, Robert E. Homans *(Mac)*, Pat McVey *(Chuck)*, Phil Warren *(Regan)*.

Gifted western director Anthony Mann's second feature is a trite tale about a singing baseball player who can only sing when he has a cold. While his team is in spring training in Havana, the catcher-crooner (Allan Jones) gets a job singing nights at a club, alternating between sickness and health as he switches from the stage to the diamond.

p, Bernard W. Burton; d, Anthony Mann; w, Oscar Brodney; ph, Charles Van Enger; ed, Russell Schoengarth.

Baseball   (PR:A MPAA:NR)

MOTOR MADNESS*½

(1937) 61m COL bw

Rosalind Keith *(Peggy McNeil)*, Allen Brook *(Joe Dunn)*, Marc Lawrence *(Slater)*, Richard Terry *(Givens)*, J.M. Kerrigan *(Cap McNeil)*, Arthur Loft *(Lucky Raymond)*, Joseph Sawyer *(Steve Dolan)*, George Ernest *(Pancho)*, Al Hill *(Jeff)*, John Tyrrell *(Pete Bailey)*, Ralph Byrd *(Mike Burns)*.

Joe Dunn (Allen Brook), a mechanic for a small boat manufacturer, falls in with some crooked off-shore gamblers, realizes his mistake, and withdraws from the gang, but feels the only way to redeem himself is by winning a big international boat race.

d, D. Ross Lederman; w, Fred Niblo, Jr., Grace Neville; ph, Allen Siegler; ed, Byrd Robinson.

Speedboat Racing   (PR:A MPAA:NR)

N

NADIA**

(1984, US/Yugo.) 100m Dave Bell-Tribune-Jadran/Tribune-Cori c

Talia Balsam, Jonathan Banks, Joe Bennett, Simone Blue, Johann Carlo, Conchata Ferrell, Carrie Snodgress, Carl Strano, Karrie Ullman, Leslie Weiner, Sonja Kereskenji, Pat Starr, Gregory Cooke, Geza Poszar, Vjenceslav Kapural, Tom Vukusic, Bozo Smiljanic, Gheorghe Berechet.

In 1976, teenage Rumanian gymnast Nadia Comaneci astounded the world with her perfect Olympic scores of 10 points, but her life after the Games was anything but perfect and this film tells that story. In the wake of her international fame, Nadia's parents divorce, the Communist Party assigns her a new coach, she begins overeating, and, in a moment of desperation, tries to take her own life. Eventually, however, Nadia makes a dramatic comeback and retires happily. Despite some fine performances—including that of Carrie Snodgress as Nadia's mother—this real-life drama is reduced to formula filmmaking, complete with a pat upbeat ending.

p, James E. Thompson; d, Alan Cooke; w, Jim McGinn (based on his story); ph, Frank Beascoechea (Foto-Kem Color); ed, Raymond Bridgers; m, Christopher L. Stone.

Gymnastics/Biography   Cas.   (PR:C MPAA:NR)

NATIONAL VELVET****

(1944) 125m MGM c

Mickey Rooney *(Mi Taylor)*, Donald Crisp *(Mr. Brown)*, Elizabeth Taylor *(Velvet Brown)*, Anne Revere *(Mrs. Brown)*, Angela Lansbury *(Edwina Brown)*, Juanita Quigley *(Malvolia Brown)*, Jackie "Butch" Jenkins *(Donald Brown)*, Reginald Owen *(Farmer Ede)*, Terry Kilburn *(Ted)*, Alec Craig *(Tim)*, Eugene Loring *(Mr. Taski)*, Norma Varden *(Miss Sims)*, Arthur Shields *(Mr. Hallam)*, Dennis Hoey *(Mr. Greenford the Farmer)*, Aubrey Mather *(Entry Official)*, Frederic Worlock *(Stewart)*, Arthur Treacher *(Man with Umbrella)*, Harry Allen *(Van Driver)*, Billy Bevan *(Constable)*, Barry Macollum *(Townsman)*.

NATIONAL VELVET is the picture that made a matinee idol of Elizabeth Taylor. The place is Sussex, England, where radiant Velvet Brown (Taylor) wins a horse, which she names Pie and plans to enter in the famous Grand National. She and Mi Taylor (Mickey Rooney) train the animal, despite the fact that the entrance fee is more than her family can afford. Although Velvet's mother (Anne Revere, who won a Best Supporting Actress Oscar for this performance) pays the fee with money she'd won years earlier for swimming the English Channel, that's not an end to their problems, for Velvet must overcome more obstacles in her quest to win the Grand National. The movie features one of the best horse-racing sequences ever filmed, as well as a host of winning performances. Although the 11-year-old Taylor had already appeared in four films, this is the one that made her a shining star. Australian jockey Snowy Baker was hired to train Taylor to ride especially for the movie, adding a certain realism to the proceedings. The story came to the screen again in 1977 as the less successful INTERNATIONAL VELVET, starring Tatum O'Neal.

p, Pandro S. Berman; d, Clarence Brown; w, Theodore Reeves, Helen Deutsch (based on the novel by Enid Bagnold); ph, Leonard Smith (Technicolor); ed, Robert J. Kern; m, Herbert Stothart.

Horse Racing   Cas.   (PR:AA   MPAA:NR)

NATURAL, THE***

(1984) 134m Natural/Tri-Star c

Robert Redford *(Roy Hobbs)*, Robert Duvall *(Max Mercy)*, Glenn Close *(Iris)*, Kim Basinger *(Memo Paris)*, Wilford Brimley *(Pop Fisher)*, Barbara Hershey *(Harriet Bird)*, Robert Prosky *(The Judge)*, Darren McGavin *(Unbilled Role)*, Richard Farnsworth *(Red Blow)*, Joe Don Baker *(The Whammer)*, John Finnegan *(Sam Simpson)*, Alan Fudge *(Ed Hobbs)*, Paul Sullivan *(Young Roy)*, Rachel Hall *(Young Iris)*, Robert Rich III *(Teb Hobbs)*, Michael Madsen *(Bump Bailey)*, Jon Van Ness *(John Olsen)*, Mickey Treanor *(Doc Dizzy)*, George Wilkosz *(Bobby Savoy)*, Anthony J. Ferrera *(Coach Wilson)*, Philip Mankowski *(Hank Benz)*, Danny Aiello III *(Emil LaJong)*, James Meyer *(Dutch Schultz)*, Michael Starr *(Boone)*, Sam Green *(Murphy)*, Kevin Lester, Joseph Charboneau, Robert Rudnick, Ken Kamholz *(Knights)*.

Transforming Bernard Malamud's fabulist first novel into a mythical morality play, THE NATURAL follows the fortunes of Roy Hobbs (Robert Redford) as the 19-year-old farm boy makes his way to try out with the Cubs. En route, he wins a bet by striking out the Whammer (Joe Don Baker), a slugger of Ruthian proportions, proving greatness is in his future. But in Chicago a mysterious women (Barbara Hershey) lures Roy to her hotel room and shoots him with a silver bullet. Fifteen years later, in 1939, Roy joins the hapless New York Knights and literally knocks the cover off the ball, leading the team back into contention. Sent by the Knights' owner (Robert Prosky), who is betting against his own team, a beautiful temptress (Kim Basinger) causes Roy to fall into a terrible slump, but the appearance of his virtuous former girl friend (Glenn Close) revives his hitting. Poisoned for the big game, without the use of his familiar "Wonderboy" bat, Roy still blasts an awe-inspiring home run into the lights, setting off a magical shower of fireworks to the strains of Randy Newman's evocative score. Somewhat overly sentimental, lacking the novel's subtlety, and less interesting when the action leaves the ball park, Barry Levinson's beautifully shot film is nonetheless a charming fairy tale. Redford, who played baseball at the University of Colorado, gives an appropriately iconic performance as Roy Hobbs—part Shoeless Joe Jackson (EIGHT MEN OUT), part Joe Hardy (DAMN YANKEES)—and the supporting roles are also well handled, especially Wilford Brimley as the manager. Filmed partly in Buffalo's

War Memorial Stadium, a minor league park built in the 1930s, THE NATURAL also offers an appearance by "Super" Joe Charboneau, who had his own miracle season with the Cleveland Indians before disappearing from the big leagues.

p, Mark Johnson; d, Barry Levinson; w, Roger Towne, Phil Dusenberry (based on the novel by Bernard Malamud); ph, Caleb Deschanel (Technicolor); ed, Stu Linder; m, Randy Newman.

Baseball   Cas.   (PR:C   MPAA:PG)

NAVY BLUE AND GOLD**

(1937) 94m MGM bw

Robert Young *(Roger Ash)*, James Stewart *(John "Truck" Cross)*, Lionel Barrymore *(Capt. "Skinny" Dawes)*, Florence Rice *(Patricia Gates)*, Billie Burke *(Mrs. Alyce Gates)*, Tom Brown *(Richard Arnold Gates, Jr.)*, Samuel S. Hinds *(Richard A. Gates, Sr.)*, Paul Kelly *(Tommy Milton)*, Frank Albertson *(Weeks)*, Barnett Parker *(Albert Graves)*, Minor Watson *(Lt. Milburn)*, Robert Middlemass *(Academy Superintendent)*, Phillip Terry *(Kelly)*, Charles Waldron *(Comdr. Carter)*, Pat Flaherty *(Coach of Southern Institute)*.

Roger Ash (Robert Young), Truck Cross (James Stewart), and Richard Gates (Tom Brown) all wear the blue and gold of the Naval Academy football squad, but when Truck admits that he's lied about his true identity because his father was cashiered out of the Navy, the center is suspended from the team just before the Midshipmen's traditional gridiron battle with Army. As in so many other football films of the era, the game goes badly until Truck is reinstated mid-contest and leads Roger into the end zone and Navy to victory. The stars were all a little long in the tooth to be playing collegians—Young was 30, Stewart 27, and Brown 24—but contemporary moviegoers didn't care much about this or that they'd already seen the story many times before. Viewers today are likely to be a little more discriminating.

p, Sam Zimbalist; d, Sam Wood; w, George Bruce (based on his novel); ph, John Seitz; ed, Robert J. Kern; m, Edward Ward.

Football   (PR:A   MPAA:NR)

NAVY BOUND**

(1951) 61m MON bw

Tom Neal *(Joe Morelli)*, Wendy Waldron *(Lisa)*, Regis Toomey *(Capt. Danning)*, John Abbott *(Pappa Cerrano)*, Murray Alper *(Chris "Warthog" Novak)*, Paul Bryar *(Robert Garrells)*, Harvey Parry *(Sweeney)*, Ric Roman *(Tony)*, John Compton *(Vincent)*, Stephen Harrison *(Pietro)*, Billy Bletcher *(Schott)*.

When his family's fishing business experiences money troubles, Navy boxing champ Joe Morelli (Tom Neal) has to hang up the gloves and return home to help out. He yearns to get back in the ring, however, and a fight is set up with a rising professional. If Joe wins, there will be enough money to get the family business going again and he'll be able to return to the Navy.

p, William F. Broidy; d, Paul Landres; w, Sam Roeca (based on the story by Talbert Joslyn); ph, Harry Neumann; ed, Otho Lovering.

Boxing (PR:A MPAA:NR)

NAVY WAY, THE*½

(1944) 74m PAR bw

Robert Lowery *(Johnny Jersey)*, Jean Parker *(Ellen Sayre)*, Bill Henry *(Mal Randall)*, Roscoe Karns *(Frankie Gimball)*, Sharon Douglas *(Trudy)*, Robert Armstrong *(Harper)*, Richard Powers *(Steve Appleby)*, Larry Nunn *(Billy Jamison)*, Mary Treen *(Agnes)*, Joseph Crehan.

This quickly made wartime propaganda film depicts the gradual conversion to the Navy Way of a prizefighter inducted into the service just before he is about to be given a title shot. Robert Lowery plays the bitter boxer and Jean Parker is his love interest.

p, William Pine, William Thomas; d, William Berke; w, Maxwell Shane; ph, Fred Jackman, Jr.; ed, Howard Smith; m, Willy Stahl.

Boxing (PR:A MPAA:NR)

NORTH DALLAS FORTY***½

(1979) 119m PAR c

Nick Nolte *(Phillip Elliott)*, Mac Davis *(Maxwell)*, Charles Durning *(Coach Johnson)*, Dayle Haddon *(Charlotte)*, Bo Svenson *(Jo Bob Priddy)*, Steve Forrest *(Conrad Hunter)*, G.D. Spradlin *(B.A. Strothers)*, Dabney Coleman *(Emmett)*, Savannah Smith *(Joanne)*, Marshall Colt *(Art Hartman)*, Guich Koock *(Eddie Rand)*, Deborah Benson *(Mrs. Hartman)*, James F. Boeke *(Stallings)*, John Bottoms *(VIP)*, Walter Brooke *(Doctor)*, Carlos Brown *(Balford)*, Danny J. Bunz *(Tony Douglas)*, Jane Daly *(Ruth)*, Rad Daly *(Conrad, Jr.)*, Cliff Frazier *(Monroe)*, Stanley Grover *(March)*, John Matuszak *(O.W. Shaddock)*.

Pro football fans may be disillusioned by this excellent, honest, and often brutal expose of the play-for-pay game. Phillip Elliott (Nick Nolte) is a veteran pass-catcher for the North Dallas Bulls, who bear a strong resemblance to the Dallas Cowboys—not surprising given that the film is based on a novel by former Cowboy wide receiver Pete Gent. The coaches (G.D. Spradlin and Charles Durning) and team owner (Steve Forrest) feel the fiercely independent Elliott has an attitude problem because of his blatant cynicism and his awareness of how he and his teammates are constantly being manipulated by management. Cast aside after being callously used to motivate a fellow player, the receiver comes to realize there is more to life than football, but that he loves the game just the same. Country singer Mac Davis, making his film debut, is quite good as the quarterback who is Elliott's best friend and knows how to play the game both on and off the field and Bo Svenson is effective as a big, dumb defensive lineman. The National Football League refused to help with the production of this film in any way, so the action is kept to a minimum (though that which is shown is brutal), but the locker room atmosphere and the off-the-field drama smack of authenticity in NORTH DALLAS FORTY, as telling a depiction of pro football as any to be found. Note the presence of one-time Oakland Raider behemoth John Matuszak, who also appears in CAVEMAN (1981) and THE ICE PIRATES (1984).

p, Frank Yablans; d, Ted Kotcheff; w, Frank Yablans, Ted Kotcheff, Peter Gent (based on his novel); ph, Paul Lohmann (Panavision, Metrocolor); ed, Jay Kamen; m, John Scott.

Football Cas. (PR:C-O MPAA:R)

NORTH SHORE*½

(1987) 96m UNIV c

Matt Adler *(Rick)*, Gregory Harrison *(Chandler)*, Nia Peeples *(Kiani)*, John Philbin *(Turtle)*, Gerry Lopez *(Vince)*, Laird Hamilton *(Lance Burkhart)*, Robert Page *(Alex Rogers)*, Mark Occhilupo *(Occy)*, John Parragon *(Professor)*, Cristina Raines *(Rick's Mother)*, Lord James Blears *(Contest Director)*.

Rick (Matt Adler), a design student from Arizona, uses his winnings from a wave-tank surfing contest to travel to Hawaii and test himself against the legendary waves of Oahu's North Shore. He experiences a series of mishaps, but, in time, is taught the ropes by Chandler (Gregory Harrison), a veteran surfer who brings a religious devotion to the sport, and en route to greater understanding and the inevitable big competition, Rick falls for a Hawaiian girl (Nia Peeples). Adler's and Harrison's performances are adequate, but the story line here is strictly for the surfin' b-b-b-birds, though the wave-riding is captured in splendid action photography. Former "Trapper John, MD" star Harrison, a real-life surfer, is credited with supervising the shooting of much of the surfing footage. Less pretentious than John Milius' BIG WEDNESDAY, NORTH SHORE is pleasant enough but not very engaging.

p, William Finnegan; d, William Phelps; w, Tim McCanlies, William Phelps (based on a story by William Phelps, Randal Kleiser); ph, Peter Smokler (Duart color); ed, Robert Gordon; m, Richard Stone.

Surfing Cas. (PR:C MPAA:PG)

NUMBER ONE*½

(1969) 105m UA c (GB: THE PRO)

Charlton Heston *(Ron "Cat" Catlan)*, Jessica Walter *(Julie Catlan)*, Bruce Dern *(Richie Fowler)*, John Randolph *(Coach Jim Southerd)*, Diana Muldaur *(Ann Marley)*, G.D. Spradlin *(Dr. Tristler)*, Richard Elkins *(Kelly Williams)*, Mike Henry *(Walt Chaffee)*, Ernie Barnes *(Deke Coleman)*, Steve Franken *(Robin)*, George Sperdakos *(Dr. Overstreet)*, Bob Bennett *(Penny Forber)*, Billy Holiday *(Trainer)*, Bobby Troup *(Harvey Hess)*, Al Hirt *(Himself)*, The New Orleans Saints *(Themselves)*.

If you find it difficult to imagine Moses in a football helmet remember that after winning an Academy Award for BEN

HUR Charlton Heston was no stranger to brutal sporting contests and screaming crowds. In NUMBER ONE he portrays Ron "Cat" Catlan, an aging quarterback for the New Orleans Saints whose already sagging career is further jeopardized when he suffers a knee injury in the final game of the preseason. While Catlin battles a talented rookie (Richard Elkins) for the starting spot, his wife (Jessica Walter) withdraws from him, becoming immersed in her design career. Doped up and wearing a knee brace, Catlin turns boos to cheers in the season opener when he leads the offense to a TD, but on the Saints' next possession he is smothered by the pass rush—and doesn't get up.

p, Walter Seltzer; d, Tom Gries; w, David Moessinger; ph, Michel Hugo, Kirk Wooster (DeLuxe Color); ed, Richard Brockway; m, Dominic Frontiere.

Football **Cas.** **(PR:C MPAA:M)**

ON THE EDGE***

(1985) 92m Alliance c

Bruce Dern *(Wes Holman)*, Pam Grier *(Cora)*, Bill Bailey *(Flash Holman)*, Jim Haynie *(Owen Riley)*, John Marley *(Elmo)*.

Masterfully photographed, tightly edited, and well acted, this ROCKY for democratic socialists details the impassioned comeback of 44-year-old distance runner Wes Holman (Bruce Dern), banned from racing 20 years previously for financial indiscretion as an amateur, but determined now to win the grueling Cielo-Sea race over Mill Valley's Mount Tamalpais to the ocean. Training under his old coach (John Marley), Wes pushes himself to the limit, while trying to come to an understanding with his unreconstructed radical Leftist father (wonderfully essayed by Bill Bailey, lifelong union organizer and Spanish Civil War veteran), who has never understood Wes' compulsion to run. (A gratuitous sexual relationship between Wes and a character played by Pam Grier is also included in one version of the film available on videocassette.) Prohibited from legally entering the race (which features a staggered start that takes into account age and sex), Wes runs as an "outlaw," and his dramatic dash for the finish is brilliantly captured by a combination of TV coverage—featuring Olympian Marty Liquori as the analyst—and inventive camera placement and movement. Suffice to say the surprising upbeat finale has as much to do with the triumph of community as with rugged individualism. Director Rob Nilsson and Dern (a dedicated runner who competed for the University of Pennsylvania) have both run in the Dipsea, the second oldest footrace in US, on which the film is based and whose treacherous northern California trails are traced by Stefan Czapsky's cameras. The inspiration for Nilsson's screenplay came from three legendary distance runners: Gerry Lindgren, the teenage phenom who disappeared in the 1970s and whose return at the Dipsea has long been rumored; Wes Hildreth, a classmate of Nilsson's who charted his strategy for the Dipsea's "point-to-point" course "like a composer"; and Norman Bright, the race's longtime record holder who returned at age 60 to win again.

p, Jeffrey Hayes, Bob Nilsson; d, Rob Nilsson; w, Rob Nilsson; ph, Stefan Czapsky (Eastmancolor); ed, Richard Harkness; m, Herb Philhofer.

Track and Field **Cas.** **(PR:O MPAA:NR)**

ONE AND ONLY, THE***

(1978) 98m First Artists/PAR c

Henry Winkler *(Andy Schmidt)*, Kim Darby *(Mary Crawford)*, Gene Saks *(Sidney Seltzer)*, William Daniels *(Mr. Crawford)*, Harold Gould *(Hector Moses)*, Polly Holliday *(Mrs. Crawford)*, Herve Villechaize *(Milton Miller)*, Bill Baldwin *(Announcer in Des Moines)*, Anthony Battaglia *(Little Andy)*, Ed Begley, Jr. *(Arnold the King)*, Peter Vrocco *(Autograph Hound)*, Brandon Cruz *(Sherman)*, Lucy Lee Flippin *(Agatha Franklen)*, Charles Frank *(Paul Harris)*, Chavo Guerrero *(Indian Joe)*, H.B. Haggerty *(Capt. Nemo)*, Dennis James *(Himself)*, Richard Karron *(The Elephant)*, Mary Woronov *(Arlene)*.

Set in the 1950s, THE ONE AND ONLY is the entertaining story of a would-be Broadway star who ends up doing his acting in the wrestling ring. Andy Schmidt (Henry Winkler), an obnoxious young cad who wants to make it big in show business, woos and wins Mary Crawford (Kim Darby) despite the lack of respect he shows her parents. After marrying, the two are off to New York, where Andy's attempts to make it in the biz lead only to a gig as a carnival wrestler. Then promoter Sidney Seltzer (Gene Saks) gets behind him, and, after trying out a number of ring personas, Andy finally dons a blond wig and becomes a professional wrestling star as The Lover. Director Carl Reiner gives his subject the human touch, and Winkler does a nice job of finding the humor in his mostly loathesome character.

p, Steve Gordon, David V. Picker; d, Carl Reiner; w, Steve Gordon; ph, Victor J. Kemper (Panavision, Movielab Color); ed, Bud Molin; m, Patrick Williams.

Wrestling **Cas.** **(PR:C MPAA:PG)**

ONE ON ONE**½

(1977) 98m WB c

Robby Benson *(Henry Steele)*, Annette O'Toole *(Janet Hays)*, G.D. Spradlin *(Coach Moreland Smith)*, Gail Strickland *(B.J. Rudolph)*, Melanie Griffith *(Hitchhiker)*, James G. Richardson *(Malcolm)*, Hector Morales *(Gonzales)*, Cory Faucher *(Tom)*, Doug Sullivan *(Young Henry)*, Lamont Johnson *(Barry Brunz)*.

In perhaps his least grating performance, Robby Benson—who has also played a distance runner (RUNNING BRAVE) and a hockey player (ICE CASTLES)—takes to the basketball court as Henry Steele, a talented but pint-sized high school cager who earns a scholarship to Western University, where he has trouble adjusting to the playing style of the sadistic coach (G.D. Spradlin). While fighting to keep his spot on the team, Henry also battles the books, aided by an attractive tutor (Annette O'Toole). Things get worse before they get better, but by the uplifting end Henry not only gets a chance to show what he can do in a crucial game situation, but also proves he's more than just a dumb jock, winning his tutor's heart in the process. Cowritten by Benson and his father, Jerry Segal, ONE ON ONE is an earnest, mostly believable study of the psychological struggle that can occur between player and coach. Handling the ball as well as he does his lines, Benson is convincing both as a basketball player and as a young man undergoing emotional turmoil.

p, Martin Hornstein; d, Lamont Johnson; w, Robby Benson, Jerry Segal; ph, Donald M. Morgan (Panavision, Technicolor); ed, Robbe Roberts; m, Charles Fox.

Basketball   **Cas.**   **(PR:A MPAA:PG)**

$1,000 A TOUCHDOWN**

(1939) 71m PAR bw

Joe E. Brown *(Marlowe Mansfield Booth)*, Martha Raye *(Martha Madison)*, Eric Blore *(Henry)*, Susan Hayward *(Betty McGlen)*, George McKay *(Mr. Fishbeck)*, John Hartley *(Bill Anders)*, Syd Saylor *(Bangs)*, Joyce Mathews *(Lorelei)*, Tom Dugan *(Popcorn Vendor)*, Matt McHugh *(Brick Benson)*, Hugh Sothern *(King Richard)*, Josef Swickard *(Hamilton McGlen, Sr.)*, Adrian Morris *(Two Ton Terry)*, Dewey Robinson *(Cab Driver)*, William Haade *(Guard)*, Jack Perrin *(McGlen's 1st Son)*, Phil Dunham *(McGlen's 2nd Son)*, Constantine Romanoff *(Duke)*, Charles Middleton *(Stage Manager)*, Dot Farley *(Hysterical Woman)*, Emmett Vogan *(Coach)*, Fritzie Brunette, Gertrude Astor *(McGlen's Sons' Wives)*, John Hart *(Buck)*, Wanda McKay *(Babe)*, Cheryl Walker *(Blondie)*.

Failed actress Martha Madison (Martha Raye) and audience-shy actor Marlowe Mansfield Booth (Joe E. Brown) transform the college she has inherited into a drama school. Having trouble coming up with students, they try to put the school on the map by developing a winning football team, using the romance course taught by knockout Betty McGlen (Susan Hayward) to attract players from other institutions. When they can't find an opponent, Martha engages a professional team to play them, betting the school's creditor (George McKay) $1,000 that her heroes will score a touchdown—then making *sure* they will by bribing the pros, who allow the college players only so many TDs before they begin running up the score themselves. Then it's up to Marlowe, who has been acting as the coach, to perform the final on-field heroics.

p, William Thomas; d, James Hogan; w, Delmer Daves; ph, William Mellor; ed, Chandler House.

Football   **(PR:A MPAA:NR)**

OVER THE GOAL**

(1937) 63m FN-WB bw

June Travis *(Lucille Martin)*, William Hopper *(Ken Thomas)*, Johnnie Davis *(Tiny Waldron)*, Mabel Todd *(Bee)*, Gordon Oliver *(Benton)*, William Harrigan *(Jim Shelly)*, Willard Parker *(Duke Davis)*, Eric Stanley *(Dr. Martin)*, Raymond Hatton *(Abner)*, Herbert Rawlinson *(Stanley Short)*, Douglas Wood *(Dr. Marshall)*, Eddie Anderson *(William)*, Hattie McDaniel *(Hannah)*, Fred McKaye *(Clay)*, Eddy Chandler *(Peters)*, George Offerman, Jr. *(Teddy)*, The USC Football Squad.

College football star Ken Thomas (William Hopper) promises his girl friend (June Travis) he'll hang up his cleats rather than risk further injury; however, his alma mater stands to get a Big Donation if it can win the Big Game. Ken's to-play-or-not-to-play dilemma is further complicated by the fact that his family has money riding on the other team. What's a gridiron hero to do? Play, of course, but not if the scheming lawyer who has Ken tossed in jail has anything to say about it. Based on William Jacobs' story "Block That Kick," this formula football film boasts the presence of members of the USC team.

p, Bryan Foy; d, Noel Smith; w, William Jacobs, Anthony Coldeway (based on the story "Block That Kick" by Jacobs); ph, Warren Lynch; ed, Everett Dodd.

Football   **(PR:A MPAA:NR)**

OVER THE TOP*½

(1987) 93m Cannon Group-Golan-Globus/WB c

Sylvester Stallone *(Lincoln Hawk)*, Robert Loggia *(Jason Cutler)*, Susan Blakely *(Christina Hawk)*, Rick Zumwalt *(Bob "Bull" Hurley)*, David Mendenhall *(Michael Cutler)*, Chris McCarty *(Tim Salanger)*, Terry Funk *(Ruker)*, Bob Beattie *(Announcer)*, Alan Graf *(Collins)*, Greg "Magic" Schwarz *(Smasher)*, Bruce Way *(Grizzly)*, Jimmy Keegan *("Big Boy"/Richie)*, John Braden *(Col. Davis)*, Tony Munafo *(Tony)*, Randy Raney *(Mad Dog Madison)*, Paul Sullivan *(Carl Adams)*, Jack Wright *(Big Bill Larson)*, Sam Scarber *(Bosco)*, Richie Giachetti *(Landis)*, Michael Fox *(Jim Olson)*, Ross St. Phillip *(McBroom)*, Flo Gerrish *(Martha the Waitress)*, Reggie Bennett *(Female Arm Wrestler)*, Joshua Lee Patton *(Arm Wrestler)*, James Mendenhall *(Minister)*.

Arm wrestling, truck driving, weird weight lifting, and tear jerking are the stuff of this predictable Sylvester Stallone starrer in which he plays Lincoln Hawk, a trucker-cum-wrist twister whose son, Michael (David Mendenhall), has been kept from him by his devious, wealthy father-in-law (Robert Loggia). With his estranged wife (Susan Blakely) on her death bed, Hawk travels the highways with his son, doing everything in his power to keep the father-in-law and his goons from taking Michael from him. After several violent, action-packed confrontations, Michael is on hand when Hawk, sweating and grunting, goes for the gusto at the arm wrestling championship in Las Vegas, where he must best a bald-headed behemoth (Rick Zumwalt) to make his fortune.

p, Menahem Golan, Yoram Globus; d, Menahem Golan; w, Stirling Silliphant, Sylvester Stallone (based on a story by Gary Conway, David C. Engelbach); ph, David Gurfinkel (Panavision, Metrocolor); ed, Don Zimmerman, James Symons; m, Giorgio Moroder.

Arm Wrestling   **Cas.**   **(PR:C MPAA:PG)**

PQ

PACE THAT THRILLS, THE**

(1952) 63m RKO bw

Bill Williams (Dusty), Carla Balenda (Eve Drake), Robert Armstrong (Barton), Frank McHugh (Rocket), Steven Flagg (Chris), Cleo Moore (Ruby), John Mallory (Blackie), Diane Garrett (Opal), John Hamilton (Sour Puss), Claudia Drake (Pearl).

Dusty (Bill Williams) is a pro racer and test rider for a motorcycle factory. His buddy, Chris (Steve Flagg), is a designer working on a new transmission that will revolutionize the machine. Unfortunately, motorcycles aren't their only common pursuit, as the charms of writer Eve Drake (Carla Balenda) throw a monkey wrench into the friendship. Issues are resolved through the plot mechanics of the Big Race, in which Dusty rides Chris' experimental bike to victory, with Eve's heart in the balance. Lots of stock motorcycle footage raises the level of excitement, but not much. Dedicated bikers may enjoy the racing sequences.

p, Lewis J. Rachmil; d, Leon Barsha; w, DeVallon Scott, Robert Lee Johnson (based on a story by Scott and Johnson); ph, Frank Redman; ed, Samuel E. Beetley.

Motorcycle Racing   **(PR:C   MPAA:NR)**

PALOOKA***

(1934) 86m Reliance/UA bw (AKA: JOE PALOOKA; GB: THE GREAT SCHNOZZLE)

Jimmy Durante (Knobby Walsh), Lupe Velez (Nina Madero), Stuart Erwin (Joe Palooka), Marjorie Rambeau (Mayme Palooka), Robert Armstrong (Pete Palooka), Mary Carlisle (Anne), William Cagney (Al McSwatt), Thelma Todd (Trixie), Franklyn Ardell (Doc Wise), Tom Dugan (Whitey), Guinn "Big Boy" Williams (Slats), Stanley Fields (Blacky), Louise Beavers (Crystal), Fred "Snowflake" Toones (Smokey), Al Hill (Dynamite Wilson).

Although not part of the Monogram "Joe Palooka" series that followed in the 1940s, this amusing comedy introduced Ham Fisher's famed comic-strip pugilist to filmgoers. Here manager Knobby Walsh (wonderfully played by Jimmy Durante in his first big role) is center stage as he discovers Joe (Stuart Erwin) knocking around a gym and trains him for the inevitable big fight with the drunken champ (William Cagney, brother of Jimmy). The dialog is clever, the direction of both the comedy and the fight scenes is assured, and "Schnozzola" even gets a chance to sing his trademark "Ink-a-Dinka-Do!"

d, Benjamin Stoloff; w, Ben Ryan, Murray Roth, Gertrude Purcell, Jack Jevne, Arthur Kober (based on the comic strip by Ham Fisher); ph, Arthur Edeson; ed, Grant Whytock.

Boxing   **Cas.**   **(PR:AA   MPAA:NR)**

PAPER LION***

(1968) 105m UA c

Alan Alda (George Plimpton), Lauren Hutton (Kate), David Doyle (Oscar), Ann Turkel (Susan), Sugar Ray Robinson, Frank Gifford, Vince Lombardi, Joe Schmidt (Themselves), Alex Karras, John Gordy, Mike Lucci, Pat Studstill, Roger Brown (Themselves—Members of the Detroit Lions).

In 1966, George Plimpton wrote a series of articles for Sports Illustrated based on his firsthand experiences in the world of professional sports, including pitching in baseball's All-Star Game and fighting a few rounds with one-time middleweight champ Sugar Ray Robinson. Adapted from Plimpton's best-selling book of the same name, PAPER LION is the amusing, occasionally insightful depiction of another of the writer's forays into pro sports, his summer spent in the training camp of the Detroit Lions. Although Plimpton (well played by Alan Alda, in his film debut), tries at first to pass himself off as a real free-agent quarterback, it becomes obvious almost immediately what he's up to, and some of the Lions resent it. But by toughing out the grueling practice regimen and remaining a good sport in the face of hostility and harassment (some of which is very funny), he eventually earns the team's grudging respect, and is taken under the wing of All-Pro tackle Alex Karras (playing himself). When the final minutes of an exhibition game with the St. Louis Cardinals roll around, No. 0 even gets an opportunity to lead the Lion offense for three plays, losing 32 yards, fumbling, knocking himself out against the goal post. Although PAPER LION presents a slightly sanitized version of pro football training camp, several real-life Lions appear in the film, including John Gordy, Mike Lucci, Pat Studstill, and Roger Brown. Karras displays an engaging film presence and went on to become an actor, appearing in several films (BLAZING SADDLES; VICTOR, VICTORIA; AGAINST ALL ODDS) and TV series. Vince Lombardi (who tells Plimpton the Packers want no part of his stunt), Sugar Ray Robinson, and Frank Gifford also appear as themselves.

p, Stuart Millar; d, Alex March; w, Lawrence Roman (based on Paper Lion by George Plimpton); ph, Morris Hartzbrand, Peter Garbarini, Steve Sabol, Fred Hoffman, Al Taffet, Jack Schatz, Joseph Wheeler, Eugene Friedman, David Marx, Richard Pollister, Fred Porrett, Morris Kellman (Techniscope, Technicolor); ed, Sidney Katz, John Carter, Louis San Andres; m, Roger Kellaway.

Football   **Cas.**   **(PR:A   MPAA:G)**

PAPERBACK HERO**½

(1973, Can.) 93m Agincourt International/Rumson

Keir Dullea (Rick), Elizabeth Ashley (Loretta), John Beck (Pov), Dayle Haddon (Joanna), Franz Russell (Big Ed), George R. Robertson (Burdock), Margot Lamarre (Julie), Ted Follows (Cagey), Linda Sorenson (Mona), Les Ruby (Jock), Jacquie Presly (Marlene), Chet Robertson (Father), Winnie Rowles (Mother), Gerry Cooke (Noogie), John Ottenberg (Heavy), Linda Findlay (Friend), Mike Shabaga (Referee), Pat Scott (Hippie).

Keir Dullea stars in this uneven Canadian effort as Rick, the best player on a not particularly talented hockey team in a tiny western Canadian town. When the businessmen who fund the team decide to pull the plug on it, threatening Rick's privileged status with the local ladies, his mental health deteriorates rapidly. Already given to wearing cowboy duds and romanticizing the Old West, he ends up involved in a robbery and shootout.

p, James Margellos, John F. Bassett; d, Peter Pearson; w, Les Rose, Barry Pearson; ph, Donald Wilder (Eastmancolor); ed, Kirk Jones; m, Ron Collier.

Hockey   **Cas.**   **(PR:O MPAA:R)**

PARADISE ALLEY**½

(1978) 107m Force Ten/UNIV c

Sylvester Stallone *(Cosmo Carboni)*, Lee Canalito *(Victor)*, Armand Assante *(Lenny)*, Frank McRae *(Big Glory)*, Anne Archer *(Annie)*, Kevin Conway *(Stich)*, Terry Funk *(Franky the Thumper)*, Joyce Ingalls *(Bunchie)*, Joe Spinell *(Burp)*, Aimee Eccles *(Susan Chow)*, Tom Waits *(Mumbles)*, Chick Casey *(Doorman)*, James Casino *(Paradise Bartender)*, Max Leavitt *(Mr. Giambelli)*, Paul Mace *(Rat)*, Polli Magaro *(Fat Lady)*, Pamela Miller *(Vonny)*, John Monks, Jr. *(Mickey the Bartender)*, Leo Nanas *(Store Owner)*, Frank Stallone, Jr. *(Singer)*, Frank Pesce *(Skinny the Hand)*.

Sylvester Stallone made his directorial debut (and, doing his usual universal thing, wrote, starred, penned the promotional novel, and even *sang the theme song* by Bill Conti) with this film set in New York's Hell's Kitchen in the 1940s. Stallone is Cosmo Carboni, one of three brothers trying to hustle their way out of the slums. Brother Lenny (Armand Assante) is an embalmer and veteran lamed in WW II who feels bitter toward all, including his girl friend, dance hall hostess Annie (Anne Archer, later of FATAL ATTRACTION). Cosmo also likes Annie, but she's loyal to Lenny, so he consoles himself with Bunchie (Joyce Ingalls), a whore-with-a-heart-of-gold, looks for quick ways to enrich himself, and hangs out at Paradise Alley, a dive that stages illegal wrestling matches. Cosmo takes a look at the aging resident champ, Big Glory (well played by Frank McRae), and correctly figures that his younger brother, Victor (boxer Lee Canalito, in his film debut), can easily beat him. Victor, a huge, gentle iceman (shades of you know who) who is patiently trying to improve his mind under the tutelage of his Chinese-American girl friend (Aimee Eccles), reluctantly agrees to go along with Cosmo's scheme and, as "Kid Salami," becomes his siblings' meal ticket. At first, Lenny and Cosmo ruthlessly exploit their "baby" brother, but they rediscover their better natures by the end, when a local hood (Kevin Conway) matches his vicious protege, Franky the Thumper (Terry Funk), up against Victor, and the Paradise Alley champ manages to beat him in a Homeric 22-round, big-money battle. Like the "Rocky" films, PARADISE ALLEY banks on audience loyalty to old-movie cliches (mistakenly this time—the film was a box-office bomb), and those who stuck with the Italian Stallion's story will be rewarded by this funny-sad up-from-the-slums tale, which benefits from some strong performances and colorful characters, evocative period detail, and superb cinematography by Laszlo Kovacs.

p, John F. Roach, Ronald A. Suppa; d, Sylvester Stallone; w, Sylvester Stallone; ph, Laszlo Kovacs (Panavision, Technicolor); ed, Eve Newman; m, Bill Conti.

Wrestling/Comedy   **Cas.**   **(PR:O MPAA:PG)**

PAT AND MIKE****

(1952) 95m MGM bw

Spencer Tracy *(Mike Conovan)*, Katharine Hepburn *(Pat Pemberton)*, Aldo Ray *(Davie Hucko)*, William Ching *(Collier Weld)*, Sammy White *(Barney Grau)*, George Mathews *(Spec Cauley)*, Loring Smith *(Mr. Beminger)*, Phyllis Povah *(Mrs. Beminger)*, Charles Bronson *(Hank Tasling)*, Frank Richards *(Sam Garsell)*, Jim Backus *(Charles Barry)*, Chuck Connors *(Police Captain)*, Owen McGiveney *(Harry MacWade)*, Joseph E. Bernard *(Gibby)*, Tom Harmon *(Sportscaster)*, Don Budge, Helen Dettweiler, Betty Hicks, Beverly Hanson, Babe Didrikson Zaharias, Gussie Moran, Alice Marble, Frank Parker *(Themselves)*.

After playing a sports-hating character 10 years earlier in WOMAN OF THE YEAR, Kathryn Hepburn essays the role of an all-around athlete not unlike the great Babe Didrikson Zaharias (who plays herself here) in this marvelous romantic comedy, which paired her again with real-life companion Spencer Tracy. Pat (Hepburn), a perky PE instructor at a southern California college and gifted athlete, falls apart whenever her professor fiance, Collier (William Ching), comes to watch her compete. Mike (Tracy), a somewhat shady sports promoter, recognizes her talent and persuades her to turn pro. Despite his unsuccessful attempt to get her to throw a match, she begins winning golf and tennis tournaments under his guidance, and gradually they fall for each other. What did you expect? Still, the point isn't what happens, but how it happens, and under the direction of George Cukor—working from an Oscar-nominated script by Garson Kanin and Ruth Gordon—Tracy and Hepburn turn in unforgettable performances. Shot mostly at the Riviera Country Club in Pacific Palisades, PAT AND MIKE gave Hepburn an opportunity to display her authentic athletic ability amidst a cast that included pro golfers Helen Dettweiler and Betty Hicks, as well tennis professionals Don Budge and Pancho Gonzales. Chuck Connors, on loan from his job as the Triple A Los Angeles Angels' first sacker, makes his film debut as a police captain.

p, Lawrence Weingarten; d, George Cukor; w, Ruth Gordon, Garson Kanin; ph, William Daniels; ed, George Boemler; m, David Raksin.

Golf/Tennis   **(PR:A MPAA:NR)**

PATENT LEATHER KID, THE**

(1927) 110m Alfred Santell/First National

Richard Barthelmess *(Patent Leather Kid)*, Molly O'Day *(The Golden Dancer)*, Arthur Stone *(Puffy)*, Lawford Davidson *(Capt. Breen)*, Matthew Betz *(Jake Stuke)*, Henry Murdock, Charles Sullivan, John Kolb, Al Alborn *(The Tank*

Crew), Raymond Turner (Mobile Molasses), Hank Mann (Sergeant), Lucien Prival (German Officer), Nigel de Bruller (French Doctor).

Taking its hero from New York's Lower East Side to the trenches of France in WW I, THE PATENT LEATHER KID stars Richard Barthelmess as the title character. While mighty cocky in the ring, the Kid ignominiously shirks his patriotic duty, preferring gloves and shorts to army fatigues. His girl friend (Molly O'Day) would prefer that he become more soldierly, and she gets her wish when the Kid is drafted (though not before he suffers defeat in the ring, as a result of turning his head in mid-fight to listen to the music of a passing military band and, of course, getting clobbered). Once in the Army, the doughboy (who, coincidentally, winds up in camp with his romantic rival *and* is assigned to the same company as his boxing trainer) is initially a wimp, but eventually acquits himself nobly in honor of a fallen comrade. He winds up wounded, but after a grisly operation scene, conquers paralysis in time for the big patriotic finale, attended by his girl friend—who has left nightclub performing for nursing. This silent film has something for everyone, from boxing to war to romance to comedy (intentional and otherwise) to flag-waving.

d, Alfred Santell; w, Winifred Dunn, Adela Rogers St. John (based on a story by Rupert Hughes); ph, Arthur Edeson, Ralph Hammerus, Alvin Knechtel; ed, Hugh Bennett.

Boxing   (PR:A   MPAA:NR)

PEGGY**½

(1950) 77m UNIV c

Diana Lynn (Peggy Brookfield), Charles Coburn (Prof. Brookfield), Charlotte Greenwood (Mrs. Emelia Fielding), Barbara Lawrence (Susan Brookfield), Charles Drake (Tom Fielding), Rock Hudson (Johnny Higgins), Connie Gilchrist (Miss Zim Nurse), Griff Barnett (Dr. Wilcox), Charles Trowbridge (Dean Stockwell), James Todd (Mr. Gardiner), Jerome Cowan (Mr. Collins), Ellen Corby (Mrs. Privet Librarian), Peter Brocco (Mr. Winters), Donna Martell (Contestant), Jack Gargan (Chauffeur), Olan Soule (Simmons), Marjorie Bennett (Flossie), Jack Kelley (Lex), Wheaton Chambers (Gateman), John Wald (Announcer), Floyd Taylor (Newsboy), Ann Pearce (Pretty Girl), James Best (Frank Addison), Tim Graham (Dr. Stanton).

Charles Coburn plays a widower who retires from his post as professor at Ohio State and moves with his daughters—Peggy (Diana Lynn) and Susan (Barbara Lawrence)—to Pasadena, California. Peggy isn't very happy about the move, however, and with good reason: she's secretly married to Buckeye football player Johnny Higgins (Rock Hudson), but can't reveal the union because her father despises the fullback. To make sure Dad stays in the dark, Peggy enters the contest to determine the Rose Queen, who, according to the rules, must be single. As you might well imagine, complications multiply—not only is Peggy crowned queen, but the Big Ten champion Buckeyes come to town to play in the Rose Bowl. Silly but entertaining, PEGGY also features plenty of footage from the 1950 Tournament of Roses parade and OSU's 17-14 victory over California.

p, Ralph Dietrich; d, Frederick de Cordova; w, George W. George, George F. Slavin (based on a story by Leon Ware); ph, Russell Metty (Technicolor); ed, Ralph Dawson.

Football   (PR:A   MPAA:NR)

PERSONAL BEST***

(1982) 124m Geffen/WB c

Mariel Hemingway (Chris Cahill), Scott Glenn (Terry Tingloff), Patrice Donnelly (Tory Skinner), Kenny Moore (Denny Stites), Jim Moody (Roscoe Travis), Kari Gosswiller (Penny Brill), Jodi Anderson (Nadia "Pooch" Anderson), Maren Seidler (Tanya), Martha Watson (Sheila), Emily Dole (Maureen), Pam Spencer (Jan), Deby LaPlante (Trish), Mitzi McMillin (Laura), Jan Glotzer (Karen), Jan Van Reenen (Yelovitch), Allan Feuerbach (Zenk), Jane Frederick (Fern Wadkins), Cindy Gilbert (Charlene Benveniste), Charlie Jones, Frank Shorter, Len Dawson (Announcers).

Oscar-winning screenwriter Robert Towne (CHINATOWN; SHAMPOO) made his directorial debut with this uneven but affecting study of romantic and athletic commitment set against the background of women's track and field. At the 1976 Olympic trials, pentathlete Tory Skinner (onetime track star Patrice Donnelly in her film debut) and hurdler Chris Cahill (Mariel Hemingway) meet after the former qualifies for the US team, while the latter runs badly. The two become lovers, and Tory persuades her reluctant coach, Terry Tingloff (Scott Glenn), to allow Chris to train with her under his guidance. Eventually, Tingloff convinces Chris to train for the pentathlon, creating a rivalry between Chris and Tory that leads to the breakup of their relationship. Later, Chris falls for Denny (Kenny Moore), a onetime Olympic medalist in swimming; then, against Tingloff's wishes, Chris renews her friendship with Tory during the 1980 Olympic trials, and in the final event of the pentathlon, the 800-meter run, sets a pace that allows Tory to win a spot on the team Chris has already made but which won't compete in the 1980 Moscow Games because of the US boycott. Although Towne's script is a little talky and heavy-handed, he nonetheless captures the essence of the competitive impulse, exploring both the "killer instinct" and the inner drive to compete only with oneself. The lesbian love story at the film's center is less well developed, but still engaging, its poignancy heightened by the well-cast Hemingway's understated performance. Visually, PERSONAL BEST is frequently interesting, if occasionally studied. Towne's over-reliance on slow motion ultimately undercuts the poetry of motion he seeks to convey, but his camera placement during the track and field action is almost always inventive, as is the film's editing. Moreover, PERSONAL BEST offers a detailed, believable insider's portrait of the world of track and field. This very different sports film isn't for everyone, but patient viewers should find many small pleasures in it. Olympic marathoner Frank Shorter and veteran sportscaster Charlie Jones provide the commentary during the Olympic trials.

p, Robert Towne; d, Robert Towne; w, Robert Towne; ph, Michael Chapman, Allan Gornick, Jr. (Technicolor); ed, Ned Humphreys, Jere Huggins, Jacqueline Cambas, Walt Mulconery, Bud Smith; m, Jack Nitzsche, Jill Fraser.

Track and Field   **Cas.**   **(PR:C-O MPAA:R)**

PERSONALITY KID, THE**

(1934) 67m WB bw

Pat O'Brien (*Ritzy McCarthy*), Glenda Farrell (*Joan McCarthy*), Claire Dodd (*Patricia Merrill*), Henry O'Neill (*Jay Stephens*), Robert Gleckler (*Gavin*), Thomas Jackson (*Bill Rankin*), Arthur Vinton (*McPhail*), Clarence Muse (*Shamrock*), Clay Clement (*Duncan King*), George Cooper (*Tiny*), George Pat Collins (*Ed*), Pudgie White (*Louie*), Jack Perry (*Sailor White*), Harry Seymour (*Referee*), Mary Russell (*Waitress*), Mushy Callahan (*Biff Sullivan*), Paul Power (*Freddie*), Marvin Shechter (*Kearney*), Phil Regan (*Murray*), Billy Arnold (*Sam Sullivan's Manager*).

Slugger Ritzy McCarthy (Pat O'Brien) lets his name go to his head and quits the ring—the wedding ring, that is, skipping out on his wife, Joan (Glenda Farrell), to paint the town red with a flashy artist (Claire Dodd). When he discovers that Joan has engineered his success by contracting for him to box only weak opponents, McCarthy decides to dump her for good. Apparently the champ hasn't neglected his wife *too* much, however, since her announcement of pregnancy inspires him to redeem himself in the ring and at home. Although O'Brien was himself a top college fighter and former champs Mushy Callahan and Marvin Schechter appear as his opponents here, the film's many boxing scenes are poorly staged, with some obvious pulling of punches.

d, Alan Crosland; w, F. Hugh Herbert, David Boehm, Erwin Gelsey (based on the story "One Man Woman" by Gene Towne, C. Graham Baker); ph, William Rees; ed, Terry Morse.

Boxing   **(PR:A MPAA:NR)**

PHAR LAP***½

(1983, Aus.) 108m FOX c (AKA: PHAR LAP—HEART OF A NATION)

Tom Burlinson (*Tommy Woodcock*), Ron Leibman (*Dave Davis*), Martin Vaughan (*Harry Telford*), Judy Morris (*Bea Davis*), Celia De Burgh (*Vi Telford*), Richard Morgan ("*Cashy" Martin*), Robert Grubb (*William Neilsen*), Georgia Carr (*Emma*), James Steele (*Jim Pike*), Vincent Ball (*Lachlan McKinnon*), Peter Whitford (*Bert Wolfe*), John Stanton (*Eric Connolly*), Roger Newcombe (*James Crofton*), Len Kaserman (*Baron Long*), Tom Woodcock (*Trainer*), Steven Bannister, Richard Terrill, Warwick Moss.

One of the most expensive and successful films in the history of Australian cinema, PHAR LAP opens in April 1932 as the title horse lies dying in a Mexican stable after winning the biggest race of his career, the Agua Caliente. The cause of death is unknown, as it is to this day, though suspicion falls on the Australian gamblers who consistently lost money as the unpedigreed Phar Lap won race after race. The film flashes back to trace the horse's career from his purchase in New Zealand by the savvy trainer Harry Telford (Martin Vaughan) and American Dave Davis (Ron Leibman); through his initially disappointing performance at the track; to the establishment of a bond of kindness between the horse and a stable boy, Tommy Woodcock (Tom Burlinson), after which Phar Lap becomes unbeatable and bookies are all but wiped out by heavy betting on the horse. Finally Phar Lap is taken to Mexico for his final triumph and mysterious death. Phar Lap is remembered in Australia much as Man O' War is in the US, as the greatest horse of its day (the Depression) and a symbol of national pride. The film plays too heavily on this patriotic theme, but is affecting on the simple boy-and-his-horse level (the real Tom Woodcock, at age 78, appears in PHAR LAP as a trainer and acted as a technical advisor). Impressively done, at times reminiscent of CHARIOTS OF FIRE, the film boasts uniformly good performances, especially that of Leibman as the American owner plagued by anti-Semitism.

p, John Sexton; d, Simon Wincer; w, David Williamson (based on the book *The Phar Lap Story* by Michael Wilkinson); ph, Russell Boyd (Panavision); ed, Tony Paterson; m, Bruce Rowland.

Horse Racing   **Cas.**   **(PR:C MPAA:PG)**

PIGSKIN PARADE***

(1936) 95m FOX bw (GB: HARMONY PARADE)

Stuart Erwin (*Amos Dodd*), Patsy Kelly (*Bessie Winters*), Jack Haley ("*Slug" Winston Winters*), Johnny Downs (*Chip Carson*), Betty Grable (*Laura Watson*), Arline Judge (*Sally Saxon*), Dixie Dunbar (*Ginger Jones*), Judy Garland (*Sairy Dodd*), Tony Martin (*Tommy Barker*), Fred Kohler, Jr. (*Biff Bentley*), Elisha Cook, Jr. (*Herbert Terwilliger Van Dyck*), Eddie Nugent (*Sparks*), Grady Sutton (*Mortimer Higgins*), Julius Tannen (*Dr. Burke*), Sam Hayes (*Radio Announcer*), Pat Flaherty (*Referee*), John Dilson (*Doctor*), Charles Wilson (*Yale Coach*), George Offerman, Jr. (*Freddy Yale Reporter*), Maurice Cass (*Prof. Tutweiler*), Jack Best (*Prof. McCormick*), Douglas Wood (*Prof. Dutton*), Charles King (*Prof. Pillsbury*), Alan Ladd (*Student*), Jed Prouty (*Mr. Van Dyke*), Emma Dunn (*Mrs. Van Dyke*).

Fifteen-year-old Judy Garland made her feature debut in this sprightly mix of music, romance, high jinks, and gridiron heroics. The Texas State University football team is coached by Slug Winters (Jack Haley) and led on the field by Amos Dodd (Stuart Erwin), a country boy who can lob watermelons further than most folks can hit a golf ball and who kicks barefooted. A scheduling mixup pits the team against Yale in New Haven, with fortune smiling on our heroes, who receive plenty of coaching help from Slug's snappy wife, Bessie (Patsy Kelly). In addition to Garland (who plays Amos' sister and sings "It's Love I'm After"), PIGSKIN PARADE features future stars Alan Ladd, Betty Grable, and Tony Martin, and the otherwise formulaic film is also notable as one of the first attempts to integrate music with plot in an original screen musical. Erwin was so good he received an Oscar nomination.

p, Bogart Rogers; d, David Butler; w, Harry Tugend, Jack Yellen, William Conselman (based on a story by Arthur Sheekman, Nat Perrin, Mark Kelly); ph, Arthur Miller; ed, Irene Morra.

Football/Musical   **(PR:A MPAA:NR)**

PIT STOP*

(1969) 92m Goldstone-Crown International bw

Brian Donlevy *(Grant Willard)*, Dick Davalos *(Rick Bowman)*, Ellen McRae [Burstyn] *(Ellen McLeod)*, Sid Haig *(Hawk Sidney)*, Beverly Washburn *(Jolene)*, George Washburn *(Ed McLeod)*.

Ambitious young stock car racer Rick Bowman (Dick Davalos) is a Class A rat: not only does he make local great Hawk Sidney (Sid Haig) crash, he also wins Sidney's old girl friend. For his next race, Bowman is assigned to work closely with his sponsor's (Brian Donlevy, in his last film) favorite, Ed McLeod (George Washburn), but works even more closely with McLeod's wife (Ellen McRae, later Burstyn). During the race, Bowman decides he wants it all and forces McLeod into a deadly crash. Shot on a low budget in and around Los Angeles, the film is padded with borrowed footage from the Phoenix International stock car race.

p, Lee Stonsnider; d, Jack Hill; w, Jack Hill; ph, Austin McKinney; ed, Jack Hill.

Auto Racing   **(PR:O MPAA:R)**

PITTSBURGH KID, THE*½

(1941) 76m REP bw

Billy Conn *(Himself)*, Jean Parker *(Patricia Mallory)*, Dick Purcell *(Cliff Halliday)*, Alan Baxter *(Joe Barton)*, Veda Ann Borg *(Barbara Ellison)*, Jonathan Hale *(Max Ellison)*, Ernest Whitman *(Feets Johnson)*, John Kelly *(Knockout Riley)*, Etta McDaniel *(Magenta)*, Dick Elliott *(Garvey)*, John Harmon *(Morrie)*, Robert Barron *(Devlin)*.

Onetime light-heavyweight champion and longtime heavyweight boxing contender Billy Conn more or less plays himself in this ring saga about a fighter whose troubles begin when his manager dies. A considerably less scrupulous boxing handler (Jonathan Hale) uses his sexy daughter, Barbara (Veda Ann Borg), to try to entice "The Pittsburgh Kid" into signing with him, but Patricia (Jean Parker), the daughter of Billy's old manager, takes over the handling of his career and the two fall for each other in the process. Before the picture's final bell, however, Billy gets a championship shot and Barbara's jealous boy friend is killed, with Billy up on murder charges you can be pretty damn sure he'll beat. Republic thought it had a coup when it signed Conn to star in this picture, inasmuch as the boxer had an upcoming championship fight with Joe Louis. What the studio didn't count on, though, was Conn's lack of acting ability and the KO punch Louis delivered in the 13th round of the fight, which the small challenger had been winning. "The Brown Bomber" and Conn fought again in 1946, and again Louis sent Conn to the canvas.

p, Armand Schaefer; d, Jack Townley; w, Earl Felton, Houston Branch (based on the story "Kid Tinsel" by Octavus Roy Cohen); ph, Reggie Lanning; ed, Ernest Nims.

Boxing   **(PR:A MPAA:NR)**

PLAYERS*

(1979) 120m PAR c

Ali McGraw *(Nicole)*, Dean Paul Martin *(Chris)*, Maximilian Schell *(Marco)*, Pancho Gonzalez *(Pancho)*, Steven Guttenberg *(Rusty)*, Melissa Prophet *(Ann)*, Drew Denny *(Chris at 10)*, Ian Altman *(Rusty at 10)*, Guillermo Vilas, John McEnroe, Ilie Nastase, Tom Gullikson, Denis Ralston, Vijay Amritraj, Jim McManus, John Alexander, David Pate, Jorge Mendoza *(Themselves)*.

Dean Paul Martin (son of Dean) and Ali McGraw star in this disappointing tennis-centered film that might have been called "40-Love Story." McGraw plays Nicole, a wealthy, 40ish sculptor; Martin is Chris, a stud some 14 years her junior who does his hustling both in bed and on the tennis court. Beginning with a Wimbledon final that pits Chris against real-life tennis star Guillermo Vilas, the story flashes back to reveal Chris' rise through the ranks of professional tennis and the deterioration of his relationship with Nicole. Although its drama is never very engaging, PLAYERS offers lots of authentic, top-flight tennis action, including appearances by such familiar faces as Pancho Gonzales (who plays Chris' coach), John McEnroe, John Lloyd, Denis Ralston, John Alexander, Jimmy Connors, and Vijay Amritraj (who would later appear in OCTOPUSSY).

p, Robert Evans; d, Anthony Harvey; w, Arnold Schulman; ph, James Crabe (Panavision, Metrocolor); ed, Randy Roberts; m, Jerry Goldsmith.

Tennis   **Cas.**   **(PR:O MPAA:PG)**

PLAYING AWAY**½

(1986, Brit.) 100m Insight/Film Four c

Norman Beaton *(Willie Boy)*, Robert Urquhart *(Godfrey)*, Helen Lindsay *(Marjorie)*, Nicholas Farrell *(Derek)*, Brian Bovell *(Stuart)*.

A comedy with a point, PLAYING AWAY uses a cricket match to explore the cultural conflicts that have arisen in increasingly multiracial Britain. Snedington, a provincial English village, hopes to top off its "Third World Week" with a *friendly* cricket match against a West Indian team from south London, the Brixton Conquerors. Derek (Nicholas Farrel), the snobby captain of the Snedington side, makes the arrangements with the Conquerors' captain, Willie-Boy (poignantly played by Norman Beaton), whose wife has returned to Jamaica and who has grown distant from his Anglicized daughter. The first third of the film cuts back and forth between both communities as they prepare for the contest, mutually afflicted by the sticky wicket of prejudice and ignorance and beset with internal dissension (class conflict in Snedington, generational confrontations in Brixton, romantic complications in both locales).

The middle section of the film depicts the weekend festivities that lead up to the match and the cross-cultural encounters that both allay racist fears and exacerbate them, and the final portion concentrates on the match. American viewers unfamiliar with cricket may find the game footage a little confusing, but an understanding of the nuances of the sport isn't necessary to appreciate the sociocultural and psychological gamesmanship that is at work here. Moreover, PLAYING AWAY is more than just a slice-of-society document; it presents its conflicts on a personal level, though occasionally individual characterizations gravitate toward stereotype. This, however, is not the case in the complex, sympathetic relationship that develops between Willie-Boy and Godfrey (Robert Urquhart), an Englishman who was more at home in Africa than in his homeland. Funny, insightful, and often poignant, PLAYING AWAY is a must-see for cricket fans and won't disappoint those who don't know the difference between a short leg and gully either.

p, Vijay Amarnani; d, Horace Ove; w, Caryl Phillips; ph, Nic Knowland; ed, Graham Whitlock; m, Simon Webb.

Cricket   **Cas.**   **(PR:A-C   MPAA:NR)**

POLICE CALL*

(1933) 63m Showmen's Pictures bw (GB: WANTED)

Nick Stuart, Merna Kennedy, Roberta Gale, Mary Carr, Warner Richmond, Walter McGrail, Robert Ellis, Eddie Phillips, Harry Myers, Ralph Freud, Charles Stevens.

This amateurish production stars athletic Nick Stuart as a young fighter trying to make it to the top honestly. Fat chance. When hoods send a henchman to talk some sense into the youth, he knocks the thug cold with a swift punch and flees, leaving his victim for dead. Not only does he get away, he gets the girl (Merna Kennedy) in the film's morally dubious finale.

d, Philip H. Whitman; w, Norman Keene, Jean Hartley (based on a story by Keene); ph, Abe Scholtz; ed, Rose Smith.

Boxing   **(PR:A   MPAA:NR)**

POLO JOE*

(1936) 65m WB bw

Joe E. Brown (Joe Bolton), Carol Hughes (Mary Hilton), Richard "Skeets" Gallagher (Haywood), Joseph King (Col. Hilton), Gordon "Bill" Elliott (Don Trumbeau), Fay Holden (Aunt Minnie), George E. Stone (1st Loafer), Olive Tell (Mrs. Hilton), David Newell (Jack Hilton), Milton Kibbee (Marker), Frank Orth (Bert), John Kelly (Rusty), Charles Foy (2nd Loafer), Sam McDaniel (Harvey the Waiter), Dudley Dickerson (Porter), Stuart Holmes (Conductor).

Joe E. Brown stars as the wealthy Joe Bolton, who has a strong aversion to horses. That's too bad, because he's a lot less repulsed by Mary Hilton (Carol Hughes), who, for some reason, will only date polo players. Naturally, Joe decides to hop in the saddle to win Mary, pretending to be

a star of the sport, with predictable—if not particularly funny—slapstick results.

d, William McGann; w, Peter Milne, Hugh Cummings; ph, L.W. O'Connell; ed, Clarence Kolster.

Polo/Comedy   **(PR:A   MPAA:NR)**

PRIDE OF MARYLAND**

(1951) 60m REP bw

Stanley Clements (Frankie), Peggy Stewart (Christine), Frankie Darro (Steve), Joseph Sawyer (Knuckles), Robert Barrat (Col. Harding), Harry Shannon (Walter Shannon), Duncan Richardson (Stevie), Stanley Logan (Sir Thomas Asbury), Joseph Crehan (Mr. Herndon), Emmett Vogan (Dr. Paley), Clyde Cook (Fred Leach), Donald Kerr (Referee), Guy Bellis (Lord Blanford).

Frankie (Stanley Clements), a young jockey with a new style of riding that brings him acclaim, is barred from the track when he starts betting on himself. Since he's been donating his winnings to an old flame and her father to help them raise a colt, the forced retirement is quite a blow. By the finale, however, his winnings add up to more than just the big race. The racing scenes employ stock footage and process photography.

p, William Lackey; d, Philip Ford; w, John K. Butler; ph, John MacBurnie; ed, Harold Minter; m, Stanley Wilson.

Horse Racing   **(PR:A   MPAA:NR)**

PRIDE OF ST. LOUIS, THE***½

(1952) 93m FOX bw

Dan Dailey (Dizzy Dean), Joanne Dru (Patricia Nash Dean), Richard Hylton (Johnny Kendall), Richard Crenna (Paul Dean), Hugh Sanders (Horst), James Brown (Moose), Leo Cleary (Manager Ed Monroe), Kenny Williams (Castleman), John McKee (Delaney), Stuart Randall (Frankie Frisch), William Frambes (Herbie), Damian O'Flynn (Johnnie Bishop), Cliff Clark (Pittsburgh Coach), Fred Graham (Alexander), Billy Nelson (Chicago Manager), Pattee Chapman (Ella), Richard Reeves (Connelly), Bob Nichols (Eddie), Al Green (Joe), Philip Van Zandt (Louis), Victor Sutherland (Kendall, Sr.), Kathryn Card (Mrs. Martin), George MacDonald (Roscoe), Joan Sudlow (Miss Johnson), Frank Scannell (Chicago 3rd Base Coach), Chet Huntley (Tom Weaver).

Thanks to a fine performance by Dan Dailey, this film biography captures the spirit of one of the most colorful figures in baseball history. Legendary St. Louis Cardinal hurler Jerome Herman "Dizzy" Dean, who is remembered almost as much for his mangling of the English language as he is for his brilliant pitching. Beginning with Dean's days as an Ozark hillbilly, the story follows him as he struggles up from poverty, into semipro ball and the minor leagues, and onto the mound for the Cardinals. He and his brother, Paul (well played by Richard Crenna), pitch their hearts out for the Cards and lead the team to a World Series championship. A sore arm and a self-pitying bout with drinking follow, but by the end of the film,

Dizzy has cleaned up his act. A warm and humorous sub-plot depicting Dizzy's courtship of his wife, Patricia (played expertly by Joanne Dru), adds depth and feeling to this good-natured story. Director Harmon Jones, who does a commendable job of mixing fact with a little fiction, doesn't fail to include the wonderful Dizzy Dean pranks, like the time he had his teammates sit down on the playing field while he struck out all three opposing hitters, much to his manager's consternation.

p, Jules Schermer; d, Harmon Jones; w, Herman J. Mankiewicz (based on a story by Guy Trosper); ph, Leo Tover; ed, Robert Simpson; m, Arthur Lange.

Baseball/Biography   **(PR:AA MPAA:NR)**

PRIDE OF THE BLUE GRASS**

(1954) 71m AA c (GB: PRINCE OF THE BLUE GRASS)

Lloyd Bridges (Jim), Vera Miles (Linda), Margaret Sheridan (Helen), Arthur Shields (Wilson), Michael Chapin (Danny), Harry Cheshire (Hunter), Cecil Weston (Mrs. Graves), Emory Parnell (Mr. Casey), Joan Shawlee (Mrs. Casey), Ray Walker (Vet).

After Linda (Vera Miles) talks trainer Jim (Lloyd Bridges) into taking care of her horse, Gypsy Prince, Jim decides to enter it in a race, but the horse falls and breaks a leg during the contest. All looks lost, but Linda won't let the horse be destroyed, insisting on caring for and retraining him. Her loyalty is rewarded when she finishes first at the track and at romance.

p, Hayes Goetz; d, William Beaudine; w, Harold Shumate (based on a story by Shumate); ph, Harry Neumann (Color Corp. of America); ed, John Fuller; m, Marlin Skiles.

Horse Racing   **(PR:A MPAA:NR)**

PRIDE OF THE BLUEGRASS**

(1939) 65m WB bw

Edith Fellows (Midge Griner), James McCallion (Danny Lowman), Granville Bates (Col. Bob Griner), Aldrich Bowker (Judge), Arthur Loft (Dave Miller), De Wolf [William] Hopper (Joe), Frankie Burke (Willie Hobson), Fred Tozere (1st Stranger), Edgar Edwards (2nd Stranger), John Butler (Mack Lowman), Sam McDaniel (Domino Jones), Bernice Pilot (Beverly), Walter Fenner (Secretary to Stewards), Raymond Brown (Sheriff Adams), Lawrence Grant (Lord Shropshire), Sam Butler (Gantry the Great).

Young Midge (Edith Fellows) persuades her father, Col. Griner (Granville Bates), to enter their colt in the Kentucky Derby. Surprisingly, it loses the race and jockey Danny Lowman (James McCallion) is suspended. The mystery is cleared up when it's discovered the racehorse is blind, but notwithstanding this handicap, the dogged Griners, and the spirited steed team up to win the Grand National and reinstate Danny. A pleasant offering.

p, Bryan Foy; d, William McGann; w, Vincent Sherman (based on the story "Gantry the Great" by Sherman); ph, Ted McCord; ed, Frank Dewar.

Horse Racing   **(PR:AA MPAA:NR)**

PRIDE OF THE YANKEES, THE*****

(1942) 127m RKO bw

Gary Cooper (Lou Gehrig), Teresa Wright (Eleanor Gehrig), Walter Brennan (Sam Blake), Dan Duryea (Hank Hanneman), Babe Ruth (Himself), Elsa Janssen (Mom Gehrig), Ludwig Stossel (Pop Gehrig), Virginia Gilmore (Myra), Bill Dickey (Himself), Ernie Adams (Miller Huggins), Pierre Watkin (Mr. Twitchell), Harry Harvey (Joe McCarthy), Addison Richards (Coach), Robert W. Meusel, Mark Koenig, Bill Stern (Themselves), Hardie Albright (Van Tuyl), Edward Fielding (Clinic Doctor), George Lessey (Mayor of New Rochelle), Vaughan Glaser (Doctor in Gehrig Home), Douglas Croft (Lou Gehrig as a Boy), Rip Russell (Laddie), Frank Faylen (Third Base Coach), Jack Shea (Hammond), George MacDonald (Wally Pip), Gene Collins (Billy), David Holt (Billy at 17), David Manley (Mayor Fiorello La Guardia), Max Willenz (Colletti), Jimmy Valentine (Sasha), Anita Bolster (Sasha's Mother), Robert Winkler (Murphy), Janet Chapman (Tessie), Eva Dennison (Mrs. Worthington), Montague Shaw (Mr. Worthington), Fay Thomas (Christy Mathewson).

Eloquently written (by Herman J. Mankiewicz and Jo Swerling from a story by Paul Gallico), stunningly photographed, and directed with great sensitivity, THE PRIDE OF THE YANKEES is the sweet, sentimental, and utterly American story of Lou Gehrig, the "Iron Man" first baseman of the indefatigable New York Yankees of the 1920s and 30s. Gary Cooper is exceptional as Gehrig and Teresa Wright marvelous as his sweetheart (and later wife) Eleanor—earning two of the film's ten Oscar nominations. Gehrig is first shown as a Columbia student, playing baseball whenever possible but dedicated to his studies. Determined to become an engineer to please his mother (Elsa Janssen), who has slaved to pay his tuition, he turns down a contract offer from the Yankees. When she requires surgery, however, Gehrig signs with the team to pay for her medical expenses, beginning his spectacular career in June 1925 and meeting his future wife during his first game, as he stumbles on a pile of bats, much to her amusement. Soon Gehrig has helped lead the Yankees to the World Series, becoming one of the best to ever play the game, until, in 1939, he learns that he has a lethal neurological disease (amyotrophic lateral sclerosis, since known as Lou Gehrig's disease) and has only a short time to live. He retires from baseball and makes a dramatic farewell at Yankee Stadium (perhaps the most famous scene in any sports film), standing at home plate and stating, "Some people say I've had a bad break, but I consider myself to be the luckiest man on the face of the earth." As the crowd gives him a deafening ovation, Gehrig walks from the field, into the dugout, and up a passageway, exiting into legend. THE PRIDE OF THE YANKEES is the story of a simple man with extraordinary talent and a soaring spirit that made him the idol of every American schoolboy. Although the film keeps the on-field action to a minimum, Cooper, a right-hander, spent many weeks under the tutelage of Lefty O'Doul learning to bunt and throw left-handed like Gehrig. To complete the illusion, Cooper wore a uniform with the numbers reversed and ran to third base instead of first so that when the film was processed, in reverse, he would appear to be swinging from the left side of the plate. Among the real-life Bronx Bomber teammates who appear in THE PRIDE OF THE YANKEES are Babe Ruth, Bill Dickey, Mark Koenig, and Bob Meusel. In 1938, Gehrig made his own acting debut, playing himself in RAWHIDE, wherein he trades in his bat for life on a ranch and ends up combating racketeers who are making life miserable for local ranchers.

p, Samuel Goldwyn; d, Sam Wood; w, Jo Swerling, Herman J. Mankiewicz (based on a story by Paul Gallico); ph, Rudolph Mate; ed, Daniel Mandell; m, Leigh Harline.

Baseball/Biography   Cas.   (PR:AA MPAA:NR)

PRISON SHADOWS*

(1936) 67m Mercury/Puritan bw

Eddie Nugent *(Gene Harris)*, Lucille Lund *(Claire Thomas)*, Joan Barclay *(Mary Grant)*, Forrest Taylor *(George Miller)*, Syd Saylor *(Dave Moran)*, Monte Blue *(Bert McNamee)*, John Elliott *(Police Captain)*, Jack Cowell *(Mr. Graham)*.

This contrived programmer takes place in the boxing ring, despite its title. Gene Harris (Eddie Nugent) is sent up for five years after killing another fighter in the ring. After serving three, he gets out to make his comeback, but deals another fighter a mortal blow. In actuality, a group of gamblers has been murdering the fighters by applying a drug to their backs via their towels—as Gene discovers when his pet dog starts chewing on a towel. When the gamblers try the towel tactic on him, he plays dead and puts the police on their trail, finally clearing his good name.

d, Robert Hill; w, Al Martin; ph, William Hyer; ed, Daniel Milner.

Boxing   (PR:A MPAA:NR)

PRIZE FIGHTER, THE*½

(1979) 99m Tri-Star/New World c

Tim Conway *(Bags)*, Don Knotts *(Shake)*, David Wayne *(Pop Morgan)*, Robin Clark *(Mike)*, Cisse Cameron *(Polly)*, Mary Ellen O'Neill *(Mama)*, Michael LaGuardia *(Butcher)*, George Nutting *(Timmy)*, Irwin Keyes *(Flower)*, John Myhers *(Doyle)*, Alfred E. Covington *(Announcer)*, Dan Fitzgerald *(Big John)*.

Set in the 1930s, THE PRIZE FIGHTER follows Shake (Don Knotts) and Bags (Tim Conway) in their efforts to promote Bags' prizefighting career, which burgeons when the villainous Mike (Robin Clark) conspires with them to fix a bunch of matches. Mike's plan is to get kindly old Pop Morgan (David Wayne) to bet his entire gym on Bags in a bout with the champ, then have Bags throw the fight. With Conway as one of the combatants, don't expect the Thriller in Manilla, but don't bet that Pop gets taken, either. Conway and Knotts' comedic potential, already not for all tastes, is further stifled by the hoary slapstick bits in this, their third picture together.

p, Lang Elliott, Wanda Dell; d, Michael Preece; w, Tim

Conway, John Myhers; ph, Jacques Haitkin (Panavision, DeLuxe Color); ed, Fabien Tordjmann; m, Peter Matz.

Boxing/Comedy   Cas.   (PR:C MPAA:PG)

PRIZEFIGHTER AND THE LADY, THE***

(1933) 102m MGM bw (GB: EVERY WOMAN'S MAN)

Myrna Loy *(Belle Morgan)*, Max Baer *(Steve Morgan)*, Primo Carnera *(Himself)*, Jack Dempsey *(Himself)*, Walter Huston *("Professor" Bennett)*, Otto Kruger *(Willie Ryan)*, Vince Barnett *(Bugsie)*, Muriel Evans *(Linda)*, Robert McWade *(Adopted Son)*, Jean Howard *(Cabaret Girl)*, Jess Willard *(Himself)*, James J. Jeffries *(Himself)*, Strangler Lewis *(Himself)*.

One-time heavyweight boxing champion Max Baer made the first of many film appearances in THE PRIZEFIGHTER AND THE LADY, in which he stars as Steve Morgan, a fighter who falls for Belle, a nightclub thrush played by Myrna Loy. The catch is, she's already the girl friend of gangster Willie Ryan (Otto Kruger); however, he's willing to let her go on the condition that Steve marry her, which the fighter does, though he is unable to keep from chasing other women. After giving Steve chance after chance to redeem himself, Belle finally goes back to Willie, but when the fighter seems about to hit the canvas for good during his battle with then-current heavyweight champion of the world Primo Carnera (playing himself), Belle is ringside and gives her husband just the encouraging look he needs to pull himself up by his bootstraps and . . . draw with the champ. The script originally called for Morgan to win the fight, but Carnera (who was the inspiration for the Budd Schulberg novel on which THE HARDER THEY FALL is based) refused to take a cinematic dive and agreed to appear only after the outcome of the fight was altered *and* he was promised extra money. Life's imitation of art wasn't so kind to Carnera, however, as Baer knocked him out in the 11th round of their very real heavyweight title bout on June 14, 1934. Baer's acting career, on the other hand, lasted much longer then his tenure as the champ, which ended with his title defense against James J. Braddock one year later. His fine performance in this film (including some song-and-dance work) brought him many subsequent roles in such films as THE NAVY COMES THROUGH (1943); Abbott and Costello's AFRICA SCREAMS (1949); THE HARDER THEY FALL (1956); and UTAH BLAINE (1957). Not only does THE PRIZEFIGHTER AND THE LADY include some extraordinarily convincing ring action, it also offers the presence of some other legendary heavyweights, including "The Manassa Mauler," Jack Dempsey, and former world champs Jim Jeffries and Jess Willard. The screenplay earned an Oscar nomination for Frances Marion.

p, Hunt Stromberg; d, W.S. Van Dyke; w, John Lee Mahin, Jr., John Meehan (based on a story by Frances Marion); ph, Lester White; ed, Robert J. Kern.

Boxing   (PR:A MPAA:NR)

PUBERTY BLUES***

(1982, Aus.) 81m Limelight/Universal Classics c

Nell Schofield *(Debbie)*, Jad Capelja *(Sue)*, Geoff Rhoe *(Garry)*, Tony Hughes *(Danny)*, Sandy Paul *(Tracy)*, Leander Brett *(Cheryl)*, Jay Hackett *(Bruce)*, Ned Lander *(Strach)*, Joanne Olsen *(Vicki)*, Julie Medana *(Kim)*, Michael Shearman *(Glenn)*, Dean Dunstone *(Seagull)*, Tina Robinson *(Freda)*, Nerida Clark *(Carol)*, Alan Cassell *(Vickers)*, Kirrily Nolan *(Mrs. Vickers)*, Rowena Wallace *(Mrs. Knight)*.

Debbie (Nell Schofield) and Sue (Jad Capelja) are a pair of Australian teenagers who want to join a group of male surfers, not because they are obsessed with guys but just because they want to surf. Slowly, they become disillusioned and embittered at the sexism that prevents them from participating fully in the sport they love. Bruce Beresford (BREAKER MORANT; TENDER MERCIES) directs this small film with a great deal of sensitivity, carefully detailing the surfing milieu from a feminine point of view, allowing Debbie and Sue's aspirations and frustrations to become both humorously and poignantly real. BEACH BLANKET BINGO this ain't. PUBERTY BLUES was based on an Australian best-seller by two erstwhile surfing groupies.

p, Joan Long, Margaret Kelly; d, Bruce Beresford; w, Margaret Kelly (based on the novel by Kathy Lette, Gabrielle Carey); ph, Don McAlpine (Panavision, Eastmancolor); ed, Jeanine Chialvo, William Anderson; m, Les Gock.

Surfing   **Cas.**   **(PR:O   MPAA:R)**

QUARTERBACK, THE**

(1940) 74m PAR bw

Wayne Morris *(Jimmy Jones/Bill Jones)*, Virginia Dale *(Kay Merrill)*, Lillian Cornell *(Sheila)*, Edgar Kennedy *("Pops")*, Alan Mowbray *(Prof. Hobbs)*, Jerome Cowan *(Townley)*, Rod Cameron *(Tex)*, William Frawley *(Coach)*, Walter Catlett *(Tom)*, Frank Burke *("Slats" Finney)*.

This minor football comedy features Wayne Morris in a dual role as a pair of twins: one smart, one dumb. The dumb one is a great football player, while his studious sibling dreams of becoming a college professor. The latter gets a football scholarship in the guise of his twin, but problems arise when both brothers woo Kay Merrill (Virginia Dale). A subplot involves the inevitable gamblers, who try to keep the gridiron hero from getting to the Big Game and "subbing" for the brainiac. As the frustrated fellow who must keep from mixing up the pair, Edgar Kennedy provides the comic high points.

p, Anthony Veiller; d, H. Bruce Humberstone; w, Robert Pirosh; ph, Leo Tover; ed, Alma Macrorie; m, Jack

Lawrence, Paul Mann, Stephen Weiss, Frank Loesser, Matty Malneck.

Football/Comedy   **(PR:A   MPAA:NR)**

RACE FOR LIFE, A*½

(1954, Brit.) 68m Hammer/Lippert bw (GB: MASK OF DUST)

Richard Conte *(Peter Wells)*, Mari Aldon *(Pat Wells)*, George Coulouris *(Dallapiccola)*, Peter Illing *(Bellario)*, Alex Mango *(Guido Rizetti)*, Meredith Edwards *(Lawrence)*, Jimmy Copeland *(Johnny)*, Jeremy Hawk *(Martin)*, Richard Marner *(Brecht)*, Edwin Richfield *(Gibson)*, Tim Turner *(Alverez)*, Stirling Moss.

Richard Conte stars as Peter Wells, a former world-class car racer who goes to Europe to make a comeback after the war, despite the objections of his wife, Pat (Mari Aldon), that the sport's too dangerous. After Peter joins an Italian team, Pat leaves him. When the Grand Prix rolls around, however, Pat can't stay away and returns to see Peter win the race. He retires thereafter, but he's proved his point.

p, Michael Carreras, Mickey Delamar; d, Terence Fisher; w, Richard Landau, Paul Tabori (based on a novel by Jon Manchip White); ph, Jimmy Harvey; ed, Bill Lenny; m, Leonard Salzedo.

Auto Racing   **(PR:A   MPAA:NR)**

RACERS, THE***

(1955) 112m FOX c (GB: SUCH MEN ARE DANGEROUS)

Kirk Douglas *(Gino)*, Bella Darvi *(Nicole)*, Gilbert Roland *(Dell'Oro)*, Cesar Romero *(Carlos)*, Lee J. Cobb *(Maglio)*, Katy Jurado *(Maria)*, Charles Goldner *(Piero)*, John Hudson *(Michel Caron)*, George Dolenz *(Count Salem)*, Agnes Laury *(Toni)*, John Wengraf *(Dr. Tabor)*, Richard Allan *(Pilar)*, Francesco de Scaffa *(Chata)*, Norbert Schiller *(Dehlgreen)*, Mel Welles *(Fiori)*, Gene D'Arcy *(Rousillon)*, Mike Dengate *(Dell'Oro's Mechanic)*, Peter Brocco *(Gatti)*.

Fans of European-style road racing will appreciate this look at the lives of those daredevils who make their way around the tracks of France, Italy, and Germany. Helmed by veteran action director Henry Hathaway, THE RACERS was the first big-budget Hollywood treatment of motor racing, and its very exciting racing footage almost compensates for the slim plot. Kirk Douglas stars as the Italian Gino, whose ambition to become a champion racer overrides all scruples. He becomes involved with Nicole (Bella Darvi), and with her money is able to get a car and win a big race. He is soon one of the top dogs on the tour, but is hurt in a crash. The next year finds him on crutches but still following the tour, and when his colleague Dell'Oro

(Gilbert Roland) needs a codriver for Le Mans, Gino signs on, taking over the wheel and winning the race when Dell'Oro is unable to continue. Now Gino steadily moves up in rank, but his ruthlessness soon loses him his fellow drivers' respect along with Nicole. In the climax, Gino gives up his chance to win a big race in order to save the injured Dell'Oro. Although the actors never left California, the film is filled with European locations that add to its appeal.

p, Julian Blaustein; d, Henry Hathaway; w, Charles Kaufman (based on the novel by Hans Ruesch); ph, Joe MacDonald (CinemaScope, DeLuxe Color); ed, James B. Clark; m, Alex North.

Auto Racing   **(PR:A MPAA:NR)**

RACETRACK**

(1933) 79m World Wide bw

Leo Carrillo *(Joe Tomasso)*, Junior Coghlan *(Jackie)*, Kay Hammond *(Myra Curtis)*, Lee Moran *("Horseface")*, Huntley Gordon *(Attorney)*, Wilfred Lucas *(Mr. Ryan)*, Joseph Girard *(Judge)*, Dick Pritchard.

In RACETRACK's familiar twist of fate, moderately crooked gambler Joe Tomasso (Leo Carrillo) finds himself turning to the straight-and-narrow after "adopting" little Jackie (Junior Coghlan), who was caught hanging around the racing stables. Thinking that the boy is an orphan, Joe takes up the kid's interest in horses and trains him to be a jockey. When Jackie's real mom (Kay Hammond) shows up, she both falls for Joe and begs him to stop the boy from racing. Recognizing that the kid needs his mom more than the corrupting influence of the turf, Joe pulls a few strings before the big race, reuniting mother and son, with a chance that he may become the boy's dad for real.

p, James Cruze; d, James Cruze; w, Walter Lang, Douglas Doty, Gaston Glass, Claire Carvalho, Ernest Pagano (based on a story by J. Walter Ruben, Wells Root); ph, Charles Schoenbaum; ed, Rose E. Loewinger.

Horse Racing   **(PR:A MPAA:NR)**

RACING BLOOD*

(1938) 61m Conn bw

Frankie Darro *(Frankie Reynolds)*, Kane Richmond *(Clay Harrison)*, Gladys Blake *(Phyllis Reynolds)*, Arthur Housman *(Legs)*, James Eagles *(Smokey Reynolds)*, Matthew Betz *(Tex O'Donnell)*, Si Wills *(Dopey)*, Fred "Snowflake" Toones *(Sad Sam)*, Bob Tansill *(Magnus)*.

When budding young jockey Frankie Reynolds (Frankie Darro) rescues a lame horse from the glue factory and nurses it back to health, he does such a good job that the horse is soon fit enough to compete in a major thoroughbred race. Before the race Frankie is kidnaped, but manages to escape by beating up his abductors, then, with a gunshot wound in his chest, he continues his string of amazing feats by stealing the ambulance that was taking him to the hospital and speeding off to the track for the big race. He gets to the gate in the nick of time (despite the fact that he has not weighed in, paraded his pony, or re-

ceived a slot in the starting gate), and nothing can stop the intrepid jockey now. The story is ridiculous, and the film's technical quality isn't much better.

p, Maurice A. Conn; d, Rex Hale; w, Stephen Norris (based on a story by Peter B. Kyne); ph, Robert Doran, William Hyer, Jack Greenhalgh; ed, Martin G. Cohn.

Horse Racing   **(PR:A MPAA:NR)**

RACING BLOOD*½

(1954) 75m FOX c

Bill Williams *(Tex)*, Jean Porter *(Lucille)*, Jimmy Boyd *(David)*, George Cleveland *(Gramps)*, John Eldredge *(Mitch)*, Sam Flint *(Doc Nelson)*, Fred Kohler, Jr. *(Emerson)*, George Steele *(Wee Willie)*, Bobby Johnson *(Mullins)*, Frankie Darro *(Jockey Ben)*.

In this equine Cinderella story, David, a stable boy (Jimmy Boyd), adopts a colt born with a split hoof that was about to be destroyed by its owners. While the trainers are busy with the colt's perfect twin, David's grandfather (George Cleveland), the stable handyman, pretends to shoot the misshapen pony and turns it over to the kid, who nurses the mutant colt, then trains it to compete against his healthier brother, on whom the stable pins hopes of big winnings. In between groomings, Boyd finds time to croon four songs.

p, Wesley Barry; d, Wesley Barry; w, Sam Roeca (based on a story by Roeca, Barry); ph, John Martin (Super Cinecolor); ed, Ace Herman; m, Edward J. Kay.

Horse Racing   **(PR:A MPAA:NR)**

RACING FEVER*

(1964) 90m AA c

Joe Morrison *(Lee Gunner)*, Charles G. Martin *(Gregg Stevenson)*, Barbara G. Biggart *(Connie Stevenson)*, Maxine Carroll *(Linda Gunner)*, Dave Blanchard *(Pop Gunner)*, Ruth Nadel *(Martha Stevenson)*, John Vella *(Johnny)*, Martha Coastworth *(Dancer)*, Rose Stone *(TV Announcer)*, Ben Hawkins *(Mechanic)*, Perry Mavrelis *(Richard Thompson)*.

The thrills and spills of hydroplane racing are detailed in this exploitation piece shot in Florida and starring Joe Morrison as Lee Gunner, who witnesses his father's death when millionaire playboy and reckless boater (aren't they all?) Gregg Stevenson (Charles G. Martin) runs the man down during Miami's International Gran Prix. Lee storms off to the scum's stately home for a confrontation—he knows where it is because his sister, Linda (Maxine Carroll), is Stevenson's mistress—but falls in love with his enemy's daughter (Barbara G. Biggart) instead. Linda, meanwhile, catches her playboy lover in the act with an exotic dancer, then announces that she is pregnant and wants to get married. Stevenson demurs, not surprisingly, since he's already married. Linda gets her revenge—but not before Lee and the millionaire meet in another hydroplane race. Awful, but amusing.

p, William Grefe; d, William Grefe; w, William Grefe; ph, Julio C. Chavez (Eastmancolor); ed, Oscar Barber.

Speedboat Racing (PR:C MPAA:NR)
.

RACING LADY*½

(1937) 59m RKO bw

Ann Dvorak (Ruth Martin), Smith Ballew (Steven Wendel), Harry Carey (Tom Martin), Berton Churchill (Judge), Frank M. Thomas (Bradford), Ray Mayer (Warbler), Willie Best (Brass), Hattie McDaniel (Abby), Harry Jans (Lewis), Lew Payton (Joe), Harlan Tucker (Gilbert).

When cynical millionaire Steven Wendel (Smith Ballew) buys a new colt, he hires the animal's former owner, Ruth Martin (Ann Dvorak), to train it. The trainer and new owner nearly strike sparks until Ruth realizes that the millionaire really cares little about the horse and is simply hoping it will gain publicity for his auto manufacturing business. Dvorak struggles painfully against the histrionic performance of Ballew, who made his film debut here after a career in radio. Harry Carey, no stranger around horses, plays down-on-his-luck-but-savvy trainer Tom Martin, father of the principled Ruth. Partially based on a Damon Runyon story.

p, William Sistrom; d, Wallace Fox; w, Dorothy Yost, Thomas Lennon, Cortland Fitzsimmons (based on the stories "All Scarlet" by Damon Runyon and "Odds Are Even" by J. Robert Bren, Norman Houston); ph, Harry Wild; ed, James Morley.

Horse Racing (PR:A MPAA:NR)

RACING LUCK*½

(1935) 59m REP bw

Bill Boyd (Dan), Barbara Worth (June), George Ernest (Jimmy), Esther Muir (Elaine), Ernest Hilliard (Walter), Onest Conley (Mose), Ben Hall (Knapsack), Henry Roquemore (Tuttle), Dick Curtis (Dynamite), Ted Caskey (Secretary).

Bill Boyd is Dan, a trainer whose prize horse takes first place in a big race, only to be disqualified when drugs are discovered in its system. Though innocent, the trainer is suspended for a year, allowing him time to discover the identity of the real culprit, and the film ends up with an even bigger race, with vindicating results for the defamed Dan.

p, George Herliman; d, Sam Newfield; w, Jack O'Donnell, George Sayre; ph, Edgar Lyons; ed, Charles Hunt.

Horse Racing (PR:A MPAA:NR)

RACING LUCK*

(1948) 66m COL bw

Gloria Henry (Phyllis Warren), Stanley Clements (Boots Warren), David Bruce (Jeff Stuart), Paula Raymond (Natalie Gunther), Harry Cheshire (Radcliffe Malone), Dooley Wilson (Abe), Jack Ingram (George), Nelson Leigh (Hendricks), Bill Cartledge (Joe), Syd Saylor (Pete).

This wretchedly produced film is basically a tedious series of horse races with a bit of human interest thrown in. The cast struggles mightily with the slim material, but the odds were against them the moment they came out of the starting gate.

p, Sam Katzman; d, William Berke; w, Joseph Carole, Al Martin, Harvey Gates; ph, Ira Morgan; ed, Henry Batista.

Horse Racing (PR:A MPAA:NR)

RACING ROMANCE**

(1937, Brit.) 63m Greenspan and Seligman/RKO bw

Bruce Seton (Harry Stone), Marjorie Taylor (Peggy Lanstone), Eliot Makeham (George Hanway), Sybil Grove (Mrs. Hanway), Elizabeth Kent (Muriel Hanway), Ian Fleming (Martin Royce), Robert Hobbs (James Archer), Charles Sewell (Mr. Lanstone).

Garage owner Harry Stone (Bruce Seton) buys a racehorse, Brownie, from Peggy Lanstone (Marjorie Taylor) and, according to formula, hires Peggy as the steed's trainer. When the filly finishes a mere second in the Oaks, Harry's snooty fiancee, Muriel (Elizabeth Kent), who never liked the setup anyway, disgustedly heads for greener pastures. Harry promptly marries Peggy, and, after an official investigation of the Oaks' results, Brownie gets revenge on the fickle Muriel.

p, A. George Smith; d, Maclean Rogers; w, John Hunter; ph, Geoffrey Faithfull.

**Horse Racing/
Comedy** (PR:A MPAA:NR)

RACING STRAIN, THE*

(1933) 64m Irving/Maxim bw

Wally Reid, Jr., Dickie Moore, Paul Fix, Eddie Phillips, Otto Yama, J. Frank Glendon, Phyllis Barrington, J. Farrell MacDonald, Ethel Wales, Mae Busch, Lorin Raker.

Having witnessed his father's death in an auto racing crash, a teenager (Wally Reid, Jr.) is terrified of cars. The kid has no problem with airplanes, however, and proves himself a crackerjack stunt pilot. In the end he overcomes his fear of auto racing and enters the big race in memory of his father. A romantic subplot pads out the mix of wings and wheels heroics.

p, Willis Kent; d, Jerome Storm; w, Betty Burbridge, Willis Kent (based on a story by Mrs. Wallace Reid); ph, William Nobles; ed, Ethel Davey.

Auto Racing (PR:A MPAA:NR)

RACING YOUTH*½

(1932) 62m UNIV bw

Frank Albertson (Teddy Blue), June Clyde (Amelia Cruikshank), Louise Fazenda (Daisy Joy), Slim Summerville (Slim), Arthur S. Hull (Brown), Forrest Stanley (Sanford), Eddie Phillips (Van), Otis Harlan (Dave).

Teddy Blue (Frank Albertson) is the spunky auto designer

of a firm inherited by Amelia Cruikshank (June Clyde). The company is in trouble if it doesn't win the upcoming race, and an unscrupulous manager tries to ruin the firm by disparaging the race car's design. Teddy jumps into action, redesigns the car in time to enter the race, and saves the day, with some mistaken-identity plot mechanics to add interest to the outcome.

d, Vin Moore; w, Earle Snell; ph, George Robinson.

Auto Racing (PR:A MPAA:NR)

RACKETY RAX**½

(1932) 70m FOX bw

Victor McLaglen ("Knucks" McGloin), Greta Nissen (Voine), Nell O'Day (Doris), Arthur Pierson (Speed Bennett), Alan Dinehart (Counsellor Sultsfeldt), Allen Jenkins (Mike Dumphy), Vince Barnett (Dutch), Esther Howard (Sister Carrie), Stanley Fields (Gilotti), Marjorie Beebe (Mrs. McGloin), Ivan Linow (Tossilitis), Ward Bond (Brick Gilligan), Eric Mayne (Dr. Vanderveer), Joe E. Brown (McGloin's Bodyguard).

This satire of college football begins as big-time racketeer "Knucks" McGloin (Victor McLaglen) decides he can make a lot of money exploiting the popularity of collegiate home games. Knucks purchases Canarsie College, in which he "enrolls" some hoods and professional wrestlers, and, when football season arrives, the boys stomp the legitimate opposition and run up ridiculously lopsided scores. With the stands full, the money comes pouring in, until a rival gang steals the idea and sets up its own bogus college. Eventually the two teams meet in a championship match, in which lead, rather than the pigskin, flies. Pretty silly stuff, but good fun.

d, Alfred Werker; w, Ben Markson, Lou Breslow (based on a story by Joel Sayre); ph, L.W. O'Connell; ed, Robert Bischoff.

Football/Comedy (PR:A MPAA:NR)

RACQUET*

(1979) 89m Harlequin/Cal-Am c

Bert Convy (Tommy), Lynda Day George (Monica), Phil Silvers (Arthur), Edie Adams (Leslie), Susan Tyrrell (Miss Baxter), Bjorn Borg (Himself), Bobby Riggs (Bernie), Dorothy Konrad (Mrs. Kaufman), Monti Rock III (Scotty), Tanya Roberts (Bambi), Bruce Kimmel (Arnold), Kitty Ruth (Melissa).

Taking a break from TV game and talk shows, Bert Convy (SEMI-TOUGH) stars here as a tennis pro who turns gigolo to raise start-up money from Beverly Hills matrons for his own tennis club. The plot rips off SHAMPOO to vastly inferior effect, mainly because Convy is no Warren Beatty. Cameos by Bjorn Borg (briefly) and Bobby Riggs (in a more substantial role) prove to be an acting double fault.

p, David Winters, Alan Roberts; d, David Winters; w, Steve Michaels, Earle Doud.

Tennis/Comedy Cas. (PR:O MPAA:R)

RAD*

(1986) 91m Taliafilm II/Tri-Star c

Bill Allen (Cru), Lori Laughlin (Christian), Talia Shire (Mrs. Jones), Ray Walston (Burton Timmer), Alfie Wise (Eliott Dole), Jack Weston (Duke Best), Bart Conner (Bart Taylor), Marta Kober (Becky), Jamie Clarke (Luke), H.B. Haggerty (Sgt. Smith), Chad Hayes (Rex Reynolds), Carey Hayes (Rod Reynolds), Kellie McQuiggin (Foxy), Beverly Hendry (Tiger).

In an acting stretch, Olympic gymnast Bart Conner made his screen debut here as a BMX bike champion; what's more, the former national hero assumes the role of movie bad guy. The plot concerns a small town's effort to gain publicity and funds through the building of a BMX racing course and promotional race. Not realizing the bigwigs behind the competition are corrupt to the gills, a local BMX nut, young Cru (Bill Allen), enters tryouts for the race, convinced he has a chance to beat the BMX factory-sponsored champ, Bart Taylor (Conner). The whole town rallies behind Cru, giving him the financial sponsorship to compete in the big race, and when the big day arrives, both Cru and the unethical Bart learn a few things about themselves. Conner's screen debut is inauspicious—to put it kindly—in the quality of both his acting and the material chosen, and someone else is obviously doing his riding. The commercial endorsement-studded RAD was directed by Hal Needham, the brains behind such triumphs as CANNONBALL RUN, and as might be expected the film's most entertaining aspects are the many good-looking stunts.

p, Robert L. Levy, Sam Bernard; d, Hal Needham; w, Sam Bernard, Geoffrey Edwards; ph, Richard Leiterman (Technicolor); ed, Carl Kress; m, James Di Pasquale.

Bicycling Cas. (PR:A-C MPAA:PG)

RAGING BULL*****

(1980) 129m UA bw-c

Robert De Niro (Jake LaMotta), Cathy Moriarty (Vickie LaMotta), Joe Pesci (Joey), Frank Vincent (Salvy), Nicholas Colasanto (Tommy Como), Theresa Saldana (Lenore), Frank Adonis (Patsy), Mario Gallo (Mario), Frank Topham (Toppy/Handler), Lori Anne Flax (Irma), James V. Christy (Dr. Pinto), Bernie Allen (Comedian), Bill Hanrahan (Eddie Eagan), Rita Bennett (Emma), Mike Miles (Sparring Partner), Floyd Anderson (Jimmy Reeves), Johnny Barnes (Sugar Ray Robinson), Louis Raftis (Marcel Cerdan), Martin Scorsese (Barbizon Stagehand).

RAGING BULL is an uncompromisingly brutal and emotionally devastating movie based on the life of middleweight boxing champion Jake LaMotta. The film chronicles the life of the fighter from 1941 until the mid-1960s, and is chiefly concerned with the irrational and violent LaMotta's struggle to find peace within himself. Loosely based on LaMotta's autobiography and filmed in gorgeous black and white, the story begins in 1941 and follows LaMotta (Robert De Niro), who is managed by his brother, Joey (Joe Pesci), as he pursues the middleweight championship. During his rise to the crown, the hostile LaMotta is distracted by both the local mafia's efforts to control his career and his romance with 15-year-old Vickie (Cathy Moriarty). Eventually, LaMotta divorces his first wife to marry Vickie, but the extremely paranoid and insanely jealous boxer abuses both his wife and his brother when he unjustly suspects them of wrongdoing. LaMotta eventually wins the championship (in a bout with Frenchman Marcel Cerdan), but quickly relinquishes it to his nemesis, Sugar Ray Robinson (Johnny Barnes), who defeated LaMotta five out of the six times they met. The collapse of his boxing career coincides with the destruction of his personal life, and, estranged from both his brother and his wife, the now-bloated boxer begins the long road back to personal salvation. The film ends on a hopeful note, with LaMotta finally attaining some sort of self-awareness. Fueled by Martin Scorsese's brilliant direction and a magnificent Oscar-winning performance by De Niro—who gained nearly 50 pounds to play the older, fatter LaMotta—RAGING BULL is one of the most powerful boxing films ever made. Often unpleasant and painful to watch, the film is a no-holds-barred look at a violent man in a brutal sport, in which, amazingly, the wholly unsympathetic LaMotta attains a state of grace at the end that is inspiring and very moving.

p, Irwin Winkler, Robert Chartoff; d, Martin Scorsese; w, Paul Schrader, Mardik Martin (based on the book by Jake LaMotta with Joseph Carter, Peter Savage); ph, Michael Chapman (Technicolor); ed, Thelma Schoonmaker.

Boxing/Biography   Cas.   (PR:O MPAA:R)

RAINBOW JACKET, THE**

(1954, Brit.) 99m EAL/GFD c

Robert Morley (Lord Logan), Kay Walsh (Barbara Crain), Edward Underdown (Geoffrey Tyler), Fella Edmonds (Georgie Crain), Bill Owen (Sam Lilley), Charles Victor (Mr. Ross), Honor Blackman (Monica Tyler), Wilfrid Hyde-White (Lord Stoneleigh), Ronald Ward (Bernie Rudd), Howard Marion Crawford (Travers), Sidney James (Harry), Michael Trubshawe (Gresham), Colin Kemball (Archie Stevens), Sam Kydd (Bruce), Herbert C. Walton (Adams).

This British horse racing saga stars Bill Owen as Sam Lilley an ex-champion jockey banned from the track for an indiscretion. Trying to relive his former glory vicariously through the exploits of young protege, Georgie Crain (Fella Edmonds), Sam vows that the kid will never let his morals slip. When Georgie's mother hits hard times, however, both Sam and the kid capitulate and throw a race for crooks offering a big price, posing more difficult ethical dilemmas down the line. A trite outcome mars this fairly entertaining film, which features real-life British racing figures Raymond Glendenning and Gordon Richards.

p, Michael Relph; d, Basil Dearden; w, T.E.B. Clarke; ph, Otto Heller (Technicolor); ed, Jack Harris; m, William Alwyn.

Horse Racing   (PR:A MPAA:NR)

RED HOT TIRES**

(1935) 61m WB bw (GB: RACING LUCK)

Lyle Talbot (Wallace Storm), Mary Astor (Patricia Sanford), Roscoe Karns (Bud Keene), Frankie Darro (Johnny), Gavin Gordon (Robert Griffin), Mary Treen (Maggie), Henry Kolker (Martin Sanford), Bradley Page (Curley Taylor), John Elliott (Governor), Eddie Sturgis (Old Convict).

Stock auto-racing footage fills out this predictable yarn, in which Lyle Talbot plays race car driver Wallace Storm, who is wrongly accused of killing his partner and rival for the affections of Patricia (Mary Astor) in an accident during a race, found guilty of murder, and sent to prison. While Wallace is behind bars, Patricia and Wallace's pal Johnny (Frankie Darro) dig up evidence that will clear his name. Before they can prove his innocence, however, Wallace escapes jail and takes off for South America, where he achieves great driving success under an alias before returning Stateside when Patricia's father needs a driver for his new car. The climax finds the judge that sent Wallace up a handy trackside witness to the wronged man's big-race heroics.

p, Sam Bischoff; d, D. Ross Lederman; w, Tristram Tupper, Dore Schary (based on a story by Tupper); ph, Arthur Todd, Warren Lynch; ed, Frank McGee.

Auto Racing   (PR:A MPAA:NR)

RED LINE 7000**½

(1965) 110m PAR c

James Caan (Mike Marsh), Laura Devon (Julie Kazarian), Gail Hire (Holly MacGregor), Charlene Holt (Lindy), John Robert Crawford (Ned Arp),   Marianna Hill (Gabrielle Queneau), James Ward (Dan McCall), Norman Alden (Pat Kazarian), George Takei (Kato), Carol Connors (Singer), Idell James (Server), Robert Donner (LeRoy).

Not one of the great director Howard Hawks' better pictures, RED LINE 7000 begins as one of the drivers in a car-racing team is killed in an accident at Daytona. His fiancee, Holly MacGregor (Gail Hire), arrives the next day and remains to team up with Lindy (Charlene Holt), who has also lost a loved one in a track accident, to manage Lindy's restaurant. Tapped to replace the dead man is new driver Ned Arp (John Robert Crawford), whom team leader Pat Kazarian's (Norman Alden) younger sister, Julie (Laura Devon), falls in love with, despite Pat's objections. A sensational driver, Ned wins his race, and decides to strike out on his own. He is replaced by Dan McCall (James Ward), who comes in from France with Gabrielle (Marianna Hill). It's not long, however, before Dan dumps Gabrielle in favor of Holly. Simultaneously, Mike Marsh (James Caan), another of Pat's drivers, begins showing an interest in Gabrielle. When Mike, seething with jealousy, attempts to run Dan off the track and cause a fatal accident, Dan survives the crash, and, once he understands Mike's motives, the two men patch things up. Mike continues with Gabrielle, Holly accepts Dan's proposal of marriage, and Julie winds up with Ned. With a plot that's strictly from sudsville and interchangeable characters, RED LINE 7000 wouldn't be worth watching if it weren't for the superb racing footage (shot by Bruce Kessler) at Daytona; Riverside, California; Charlotte, North Carolina; Darlington, Texas; and Ascot in England.

p, Howard Hawks; d, Howard Hawks; w, George Kirgo (based on a story by Hawks); ph, Milton Krasner, Haskell Boggs (Technicolor); ed, Stuart Gilmore, Bill Brame; m, Nelson Riddle.

Auto Racing   **(PR:C MPAA:NR)**

RENO AND THE DOC*

(1984, Can.) 88m Rose & Ruby/NW c

Ken Welsh *(Reginald "Reno" Coltchinsky)*, Henry Ramer *(Hugo "Doc" Billings)*, Linda Griffiths *(Savannah Gates)*, Cliff Welsh *(Cliff)*, Laura Dickson *(Agnes)*, Sean Ryerson *(Long Jack)*, Damien Lee *(Gunther Schloss)*, Rick Lewson *(Brian)*, Charles Denning *(Delgado)*, Al Safrata *(Starter)*, Paddy Macafee *(Reporter)*, Tony Avola *(Bodyguard)*, Simone Stevenson *(Orchid)*, John Prince *(Bartender)*, Woody Sidarous *(Orderly)*.

When "Reno" Coltchinsky (Ken Welsh), a 40ish mountain man and loner, meets "Doc" Billings (Henry Ramer), a former con man a few years his senior, the two quickly grow close—not surprisingly, since they're telepathic. The friendship is tested, however, when Doc convinces Reno to hit the professional ski circuit, where Reno must contend not only with obnoxious champ Gunther (Damien Lee), but with his own aging body. By the "exciting" finale, of course, Reno saves the honor of middle-aged men, wins a fortune for the gambling Doc, and impresses a pretty sports writer to boot. Dubiously advertised as "a heartwarming adventure about two irascible "old men" who refuse to grow up," RENO AND THE DOC is filled with extraneous scenes, bad acting, inane dialog, and silly plot devices (namely the telepathy, which in one embarrassing scene includes Doc experiencing Reno's orgasm). To top it all off, the ski footage is unspectacular to say the least.

p, David Mitchell, Sean Ryerson; d, Charles Dennis; w, Charles Dennis (based on a story by Damien Lee); ph, Ludvik Bogner; ed, Jim Lahti, Mairin Wilkison; m, Betty Lazebnik, Brian Bell.

Skiing   **Cas.**   **(PR:O MPAA:NR)**

REQUIEM FOR A HEAVYWEIGHT***½

(1962) 85m COL bw

Anthony Quinn *(Mountain Rivera)*, Jackie Gleason *(Maish Rennick)*, Mickey Rooney *(Army)*, Julie Harris *(Grace Miller)*, Stanley Adams *(Perelli)*, Mme. Spivey *(Ma Greeny)*, Herbie Faye *(Bartender)*, Jack Dempsey *(Himself)*, Cassius Clay [Muhammad Ali] *(Ring Opponent)*, Steve Belloise *(Hotel Desk Clerk)*, Lou Gilbert *(Ring Doctor)*, Arthur Mercante *(Referee)*, Rory Calhoun, Barney Ross, Willie Pep.

Six years after Jack Palance brilliantly essayed the character of Mountain Rivera on TV's "Playhouse 90," Anthony Quinn took on the role of the battered boxer for this big screen adaptation of Rod Serling's Emmy-winning tele-

play. As the film begins, Mountain, a veteran of 17 years in the ring, is beaten senseless by a younger, faster opponent (played by Cassius Clay, soon to be Muhammad Ali), going down for the count in the seventh round. His longtime manager, Maish (Jackie Gleason), who assured mobster Ma Greeny (Madame Spivey) that his fighter wouldn't last past the first few rounds, is given three weeks to compensate her for her betting losses—or else. Mountain, who has been told that he may go blind if he fights again, tries to get a job to come up with the money, aided by Grace (Julie Harris), a caring employment counselor, but Maish sabotages his interview for a position at a summer camp. Disappointed with Maish, but ever loyal, Mountain compromises his dignity by donning an Indian war bonnet and entering the professional wrestling ring to save his manager's life. Quinn, Gleason, and Mickey Rooney, as Mountain's erstwhile trainer, turn in magnificent performances in this unforgettable drama of abiding friendship and the abuse of trust. However, director Ralph Nelson, who also helmed the original 1956 TV production, asked that his name be removed from the credits when nonessential scenes that had been cut from the original release print were reinstated to make the feature long enough to be shown on television. Although those scenes, which slow down the narrative drive, certainly work against the film, REQUIEM FOR A HEAVYWEIGHT remains a thoroughly engaging movie.

p, David Susskind; d, Ralph Nelson; w, Rod Serling (based on his TV play); ph, Arthur J. Ornitz; ed, Carl Lerner; m, Laurence Rosenthal.

Boxing   **Cas.**   **(PR:C MPAA:NR)**

RETURN OF OCTOBER, THE**

(1948) 89m COL c

Glenn Ford *(Prof. Bassett)*, Terry Moore *(Terry Ramsey)*, Albert Sharpe *(Vince the Tout)*, James Gleason *(Uncle Willie)*, Dame May Whitty *(Aunt Martha)*, Henry O'Neill *(President Hotchkiss)*, Fred Tozere *(Mitchell)*, Samuel S. Hinds *(Judge Northridge)*, Nana Bryant *(Therese)*, Lloyd Corrigan *(Dutton)*, Roland Winters *(Col. Wood)*, Stephen Dunne *(Prof. Stewart)*, Gus Schilling *(Benny)*, Murray Alper *(Little Max)*, Horace MacMahon *(Big Louie)*, Victoria Horne *(Margaret)*.

Whimsy is the predominant note in this girl-and-her-reincarnated-horse story. Before Terry Ramsey's (Terry Moore) uncle (James Gleason) died, he remarked that if he ever returned to this world, it would be as a horse, so he could win the Kentucky Derby. When Terry spots October, she therefore decides the horse is Uncle Willie returned, ready to make a run for the roses. Terry's beliefs cause some greedy relatives who want to gain control of her estate to try to have the girl declared incompetent, but when October comes through at Churchill Downs it's cause for second thoughts, especially for the psychology professor (Glenn Ford) interested in Terry's case.

p, Rudolph Mate; d, Joseph H. Lewis; w, Melvin Frank, Norman Panama (based on a story by Connie Lee, Karen DeWolf); ph, William Snyder (Technicolor); ed, Gene

Havlick; m, George Duning.

**Horse Racing/
Comedy**   (PR:A MPAA:NR)

RETURN TO CAMPUS*½

(1975) 100m Cinepix c

Earl Keyes (Hal Norman), Ray Troha (Bruce Norman), Al Raymond (Rupp Brubaker), Robert Gutin (Pighead Smith), Paul Jacobs (Esco Schmidt), Helen Killinger (Joyce Kutner), Norma Joseph (Barbara Lewis), Arnold Palmer (Spike Belfry), John Barner (Dean of Men), Connie O'Connell (Night Club Singer), Tom Harmon, Jesse White (Sports Announcers).

Filmed in suburban Cleveland, this autobiographical fantasy produced, written, and directed by Harold Cornsweet, a onetime Ohio State football player, focuses on Hal Norman (Earl Keyes), an ex-Buckeye whose varsity career was cut short by military service. When the local high school coach (Al Raymond, real-life Shaker Heights High School football coach) asks the middle-aged former kicker to work with some of his players, visions of a return to glory dance in Hal's head. Before long, he's is back in Columbus, playing out his last year of eligibility, outfitted with a special kicking shoe that he uses to perform plenty of game-winning heroics.

p, Harold Cornsweet; d, Harold Cornsweet; w, Harold Cornsweet; ph, Steve Shuttack, Pierre Janet (DeLuxe Color); m, Gordon Zahler, Harry Fields.

Football   (PR:C MPAA:PG)

RHUBARB**½

(1951) 95m PAR bw

Ray Milland (Eric Yeager), Jan Sterling (Polly Sickles), Gene Lockhart (Thaddeus J. Banner), William Frawley (Len Sickles), Elsie Holmes (Myra Banner), Taylor Holmes (P. Duncan Munk), Willard Waterman (Orlando Dill), Henry Slate (Dud Logan), James Griffith (Oggie Meadows), Jim Hayward (Doom), Donald MacBride (Phenny), Hal K. Dawson (Mr. Fisher), Strother Martin (Shortly McGirk), Edwin Max (Fish Eye), Leonard Nimoy, Lee Miller (Ball Players).

In this adaptation of H. Allen Smith's best-selling novel, an eccentric millionaire (Gene Lockhart) becomes so taken with the golf ball-stealing antics of Rhubarb, a tough alley cat, that he takes the stray home with him. His admiration for the cat grows until Rhubarb becomes the principal heir to his vast fortune, including a lousy major league ball club, the Brooklyn Loons. With Rhubarb as its owner, mascot, and good luck charm, the team begins winning, although the cat's guardian and team press agent, Eric Yeager (Ray Milland), experiences some difficulty because his girl friend (Jan Sterling) is allergic to felines. This affliction turns out to be a godsend, however, when Rhubarb is kidnaped by gamblers who want the ball club to lose, culminating in some last-minute zaniness at the big game.

p, William Perlberg, George Seaton; d, Arthur Lubin; w, Dorothy Reid, Francis Cockrell, David Stern (based on the

novel by H. Allen Smith); ph, Lionel Lindon; ed, Alma Macrorie; m, Van Cleave.

Baseball/Comedy   (PR:A MPAA:NR)

RIDE, KELLY, RIDE*½

(1941) 59m FOX bw

Eugene Pallette (Duke Martin), Marvin Stephens (Corn Cob Kelly), Rita Quigley (Ellen Martin), Mary Healy (Entertainer), Richard Lane (Dan Thomas), Charles D. Brown (Bob Martin), Chick Chandler (Knuckles), Dorothy Peterson (Mrs. Martin), Frankie Burke (Skeeziks O'Day), Cy Kendall (Louis Becker), Spec O'Donnell (Kalinski), Ernie Adams (Sandy).

When eager young jockey Corn Cob Kelly (Marvin Stephens) accidentally falls in with some gamblers, his refusal to throw a race causes them to replace him with an older rider. However, thanks to Duke Martin (Eugene Pallette), the trainer who took Corn Cob off the ranch and onto the track, the ambitious lad enters the "fixed" race anyway, much to the gamblers' chagrin, and wins more than the heart of Duke's daughter (Rita Quigley).

p, Sol M. Wurtzel; d, Norman Foster; w, William Conselman, Jr., Irving Cummings, Jr. (based on a story by Peter B. Kyne); ph, Virgil Miller; ed, Louis Loeffler.

Horse Racing   (PR:A MPAA:NR)

RIDE THE WILD SURF**½

(1964) 101m Jana/COL c

Fabian (Jody Wallis), Shelley Fabares (Brie Matthews), Tab Hunter (Steamer Lane), Barbara Eden (Augie Poole), Peter Brown (Chase Colton), Susan Hart (Lily Kilua), James Mitchum (Eskimo), Anthony Hayes (Frank Decker), Roger Davis (Charlie), Catherine McLeod (Mrs. Kilua), Murray Rose (Swag), Robert Kenneally (Russ), David Cadiente (Ally).

Three young Californians—Jody Wallis (Fabian), Steamer Lane (Tab Hunter), and Chase Colton (Peter Brown)—pack their boards and surfari to Hawaii to take on the monster waves at Oahu's North Shore. In no time, each is involved with his own beach bunny: Lily Kilua (Susan Hart) has the hots for Steamer, though her mother despises surfers; Augie (Barbara Eden) gets the all-too-intense Chase to lighten up; and Brie (Shelley Fabares) persuades Jody that there is more to life than hanging ten. Still, when the big contest that has brought the boys to Hawaii rolls around, the surfers are all business. Steamer is forced to drop out when his board breaks, Chase nearly drowns, and when the waves swell to 40-foot peaks, only Jody is left to challenge last year's champion (Jim Mitchum). Although RIDE THE WILD SURF is hardly compelling drama, its performances are more engaging than one would expect and there's lots of outstanding surfing footage, not to mention the super-catchy title song by Jan and Dean.

p, Jo Napoleon, Art Napoleon; d, Don Taylor; w, Jo

Napoleon, Art Napoleon; ph, Joseph Biroc (PatheColor); ed, Eda Warren, Howard Smith; m, Stu Phillips.

Surfing (PR:A MPAA:NR)

RIDING HIGH**

(1937, Brit.) 68m EM/BL bw (AKA: REMEMBER WHEN)

Claude Dampier *(Septimus Earwicker)*, John Garrick *(Tom Blake)*, Kathleen Gibson *(Grace Meadows)*, Helen Haye *(Miss Broadbent)*, John Warwick *(George Davenport)*, Billy Merson *(Popping)*, Mai Bacon *(Mrs. Winterbottom)*, Peter Gawthorne *(Sir Joseph Wilmot)*, Billy Holland *(Jack Adamson)*, Billy Bray *(Ted Rance)*.

The early days of cycling (1879) are the backdrop for this British comedy, in which village blacksmith Tom Blake (John Garrick) invents a newfangled bicycle in his spare time. With the help of eccentric solicitor Septimus Earwicker (Claude Dampier), the inventor enters the bike in a race and surprises the skeptics by taking first place.

p, George King; d, David Macdonald; w, H. Fowler Mear; ph, Hone Glendinning.

Bicycling (PR:A MPAA:NR)

RIDING HIGH***

(1950) 112m PAR bw

Bing Crosby *(Dan Brooks)*, Coleen Gray *(Alice Higgins)*, Charles Bickford *(J. L. Higgins)*, William Demarest *(Happy McGuire)*, Frances Gifford *(Margaret Higgins)*, Raymond Walburn *(Prof. Pettigrew)*, James Gleason *(Racing Secretary)*, Ward Bond *(Lee)*, Clarence Muse *(Whitey)*, Percy Kilbride *(Pop Jones)*, Harry Davenport *(Johnson)*, Irving Bacon *(Hamburger Man)*, Margaret Hamilton *(Edna)*, Douglas Dumbrille *(Eddie Morgan)*, Gene Lockhart *(J.P. Chase)*, Charles Lane *(Erickson)*, Frankie Darro *(Jockey Williams)*, Paul Harvey *(Whitehall)*, Marjorie Lord *(Mathilda Winslow)*.

Frank Capra directed both BROADWAY BILL (1934) and its remake, RIDING HIGH, and the 1950 film is one of the rare instances in which the remake is as good as the original. BROADWAY BILL stars Myrna Loy and Warner Baxter are replaced here by Coleen Gray and Bing Crosby, who, not surprisingly, contributes a few tunes to the proceedings. Dan Brooks (Crosby) is devoted to both a racehorse and to wealthy meal ticket Alice Higgins (Gray), whose jealousy of the quadruped forces Dan to choose between them. Naturally, he chooses the horse, who repays his love by winning the big race and making Dan rich, then dies. One-time heavyweight champion Max Baer makes a cameo appearance as the man with whom Alice seeks solace; Oliver Hardy, in a rare Laurel-less appearance, also does a brief bit.

p, Frank Capra; d, Frank Capra; w, Robert Riskin, Melville Shavelson, Jack Rose (based on the story "Broadway Bill" by Mark Hellinger); ph, George Barnes, Ernest Laszlo; ed, William Hornbeck.

**Horse Racing/
Musical** (PR:A MPAA:NR)

RIGHT CROSS***

(1950) 90m MGM bw

June Allyson *(Pat O'Malley)*, Dick Powell *(Rick Gavery)*, Ricardo Montalban *(Johnny Monterez)*, Lionel Barrymore *(Sean O'Malley)*, Teresa Celli *(Marian Monterez)*, Barry Kelley *(Allan Goff)*, Tom Powers *(Robert Balford)*, Mimi Aguglia *(Mom Monterez)*, Marianne Stewart *(Audrey)*, John Gallaudet *(Phil Tripp)*, David Fresco *(Gump)*, Smoki Whitfield *(Nassau)*, Harry Shannon *(Haggerty)*, Frank Ferguson *(Dr. George Lamond)*, David Wolfe *(Totem)*, Marilyn Monroe *(Blonde)*, Dewey Robinson *(Hanger-On)*, Jim Pierce *(Moe)*.

RIGHT CROSS stars Ricardo Montalban as Mexican champ Johnny Monterez, who constantly worries that he's being victimized by prejudice. His manager, wheelchair-bound Sean O'Malley (Lionel Barrymore), a former top dog in the ring, now handles only Johnny—who is in love with the Irishman's daughter, Pat (June Allyson). A loner, Johnny has few friends except the O'Malleys and sportswriter Rick Gavery (Dick Powell). Although his fears of racism are shown to be largely unfounded, Johnny's paranoia causes him to believe that he will lose Pat if he doesn't keep winning, so, when his signature right cross starts to lose its sting, he signs with a top promoter, hoping to quickly make enough money to marry Pat and support her father. However, this apparent defection gives Sean a heart attack, and alienates Pat. Johnny loses his crown in one last match, but still collects a huge purse, then gets in a fight with Rick and breaks his right hand. The film ends on an upbeat note, though, when the fighter, his career ended, reconciles with Pat and Rick. RIGHT CROSS stands out among fight films, not only for the elements *missing* (there are no underworld characters, no fixed fights, and, in a refreshing turn of events, the hero loses the big fight), but also for its strong cast (including an unbilled, prestardom Marilyn Monroe in a bit part) and good fight scenes directed by John Sturges. Most notable, however, is its sensitive and relatively daring depiction of the concerns of a minority athlete.

p, Armand Deutsch; d, John Sturges; w, Charles Schnee; ph, Norbert Brodine; ed, James E. Newcom; m, David Raksin.

Boxing (PR:A-C MPAA:NR)

RIGHT TO THE HEART**

(1942) 74m FOX bw

Brenda Joyce *(Jenny Killian)*, Joseph Allen, Jr. *(John T. Bromley III)*, Cobina Wright, Jr. *(Barbara Paxton)*, Stanley Clements *(Stash)*, Don DeFore *(Tommy Sands)*, Hugh Beaumont *(Willie Donovan)*, Charles D. Brown *(Jim Killian)*, Ethel Griffies *(Minerva Bromley)*, Frank Orth *(Pete)*, Phil Tead *(McAllister)*, William Haade *(Morgan)*, Spencer Charters *(Jonah)*.

When wastrel rich kid John T. Bromley III (Joseph Allen, Jr.) is disinherited by his wealthy aunt, then disowned by his social-climbing girl friend to boot, he goes to a bar to drown his sorrows and gets knocked flat in a brawl with a former boxer. Hungry for a rematch, the humiliated blue-blood enrolls at a training camp for would-be fighters, where he falls head over heels for the trainer's daughter (Brenda Joyce). Her foster brother (Stanley Clements) doesn't care for the rich kid and gives him a hard time; gradually, however, John learns a few things about humility, gets the girl, and redeems himself all round.

p, Sol M. Wurtzel; d, Eugene Forde; w, Walter Bullock (based on a story "You Can't Always Tell" by Harold McGrath); ph, Virgil Miller; ed, Louis Loeffler.

Boxing (PR:A MPAA:NR)

RING, THE**½

(1952) 79m UA bw

Gerald Mohr (Pete), Rita Moreno (Lucy), Lalo Rios (Tommy), Robert Arthur (Billy Smith), Robert Osterloh (Freddy), Martin Garralaga (Vidal), Jack Elam (Harry Jackson), Peter Brosco (Barney Williams), Julia Montoya (Rosa), Lillian Molieri (Helen), Pepe Hern (Rick), Victor Millan (Pablo), Tony Martinez (Go-Go), Ernie Chavez (Joe).

John Sturges' RIGHT CROSS (see above) paved the way for this boxing tale exploring prejudice against Mexican Americans in southern California. Tommy (Lalo Rios) has trouble finding a decent job because of discrimination against "lazy Mexicans," prompting him to try his luck in the ring, under the management of Pete (Gerald Mohr) and over the objections of his family. At first he's successful, but the young man's need to prove himself leads to self-defeat when he begins fighting in matches for which he is undertrained. He quits the ring, only to return after a humiliating scene in a restaurant, where a waitress refuses to serve him because he is Mexican American. Tommy now believes that boxing is the only way to overcome prejudice and achieve a better life for himself and his girl friend, Lucy (Rita Moreno), but he is severely beaten in a shot at the championship, leading to deep feelings of failure. Finally, Lucy convinces him to carry on his fight outside the ring. The film takes a realist approach both to its story and the fight scenes.

p, Maurice King, Frank King, Herman King; d, Kurt Neumann; w, Irving Shulman (based on the novel by Shulman); ph, Russell Harlan; ed, Bruce Pierce; m, Herschel Burke Gilbert.

Boxing Cas. (PR:A MPAA:NR)

RINGSIDE MAISIE**

(1941) 96m MGM bw

Ann Sothern (Maisie Ravier), George Murphy (Skeets Maguire), Robert Sterling (Terry Dolan), Natalie Thompson (Cecelia Reardon), Maxie Rosenbloom (Chotsie), Margaret Moffat (Mrs. Dolan), John Indrisano (Peaches), Virginia O'Brien (Virginia O'Brien), Eddie Simms (Billy-Boy Duffy), Jack LaRue (Ricky DuPrez), Purnell Pratt (Dr. Taylor).

The fifth entry in the "Maisie" series, which starred Ann Sothern as the title spunky gal-on-her-own, places the Brooklyn blonde in the training camp of up-and-coming boxer Terry Dolan (Robert Sterling), whose manager, Skeets Maguire (George Murphy), is overly anxious to push his fledgling fighter into the big-money big time. Along the way, Skeets and Maisie strike a few romantic sparks. Among the players backing up Sothern's comedy are Rags Ragland and Maxie Rosenbloom, the latter playing the young boxer's trainer.

p, J. Walter Ruben; d, Edwin L. Marin; w, Mary C. McCall, Jr.; ph, Charles Lawton; ed, Frederick Y. Smith; m, David Snell.

Boxing/Comedy (PR:A MPAA:NR)

RIPPED-OFF**

(1971, It.) 83m White Mountain/Cinema Shares c (UN UOMO DALLA PELLE DURA; AKA: BOXER, THE)

Robert Blake, Ernest Borgnine, Catherine Spaak, Gabriel Ferzetti, Tomas Milian.

Robert Blake is as good as this second-rate Italian import (filmed in Chicago) will let him be, starring as a boxer framed for the murder of his manager. He convinces the murdered man's daughter (Catherine Spaak) of his innocence and sets out to nab the real killer with her help, all the while trying to stay one step ahead of the detective on his trail (Ernest Borgnine).

d, Franco Prosperi.

Boxing Cas. (PR:C-O MPAA:R)

RISE AND SHINE**½

(1941) 93m FOX bw

Jack Oakie (Boley Bolenciewcz), George Murphy (Jimmy M'Gonigle), Linda Darnell (Louise Murray), Walter Brennan (Grandpa), Milton Berle (Seabiscuit), Sheldon Leonard (Menace), Donald Meek (Prof. Murray), Ruth Donnelly (Mame), Raymond Walburn (Col. Bacon), Donald MacBride (Coach Graham), Emma Dunn (Mrs. Murray), Charles Waldron (President), Mildred Gover (Mrs. Robertson), William Haade (Butch), Dick Rich (Gogo), John Hiestand (Announcer), Claire Dubrey (Miss Pinkham), Francis Pierlot (Prof. Schnauzer).

Jack Oakie headlines this musical comedy as Boley Bolenciecwcz, the unbelievably dense star of the Clayton College football team. His pigskin prowess has attracted the attention of Menace (Sheldon Leonard), a gambling gangster who sends song-and-dance man Jimmy M'Gonigle (George Murphy) to see that nothing happens to Boley. In the meantime, Jimmy falls for a professor's daughter (Linda Darnell) and chooses to call the college town home. When Menace decides to bet against Clayton and has Boley kidnaped, Jimmy switches sides and comes to his rescue, permitting the gridiron flash to perform the standard last-minute heroics in the big game.

p, Mark Hellinger; d, Allan Dwan; w, Herman J. Mankiewicz (based on the book My Life and Hard Times by James Thurber); ph, Edward Cronjager; ed, Allen McNeil.

Football/Comedy/ Musical (PR:A MPAA:NR)

ROAD DEMON*½

(1938) 65m FOX bw

Henry Arthur (Blake), Joan Valerie (Joan), Henry Armetta (Gambini), Thomas Beck (Rogers), Bill Robinson (Zephyr), Jonathan Hale (Connors), Thomas MacMahon (Speed), Murray Alper, Edward Marr, Lon Chaney, Jr.

Rogers (Thomas Beck), a young Indianapolis 500 racer, is trying to follow in the footsteps of his father and save the old man's reputation in the bargain, since he was killed in a previous racing accident by racketeers who made his death appear to be the result of drunk driving. Truck driver and racing nut Blake (Henry Arthur) lends a hand, doing some fancy driving of his own to foil the hoods after they try to knock off Rogers fils as well. Mixed incongruously among old footage of Indy smashups is an appearance by Bill "Bojangles" Robinson, who does a tap dance routine in his role as a junk yard proprietor.

p, Jerry Hoffman; d, Otto Brower; w, Robert Ellis, Helen Logan; ph, Edward Snyder; ed, Jack Murray.

Auto Racing   **(PR:A MPAA:NR)**

ROADRACERS, THE*

(1959) 73m AIP bw

Joel Lawrence (Rob), Marian Collier (Liz), Skip Ward (Greg), Sally Fraser (Joanie), Mason Alan Dinehart, Jr. (Kit), Irene Windust (Alice), John Shay (Harry), Michael Gibson (Bartender), Richard G. Pharo (Wilkins).

A young driver (Joel Lawrence) is prevented from competing on the auto-racing circuit after his recklessness causes a crash in which another driver is killed. He spends some time in Europe proving his worth and piling up the trophies, then makes his comeback in the States, where he must race his arch-rival in love and on wheels (Skip Ward) in the US Grand Prix. Filled to the brim with stock footage.

p, Stanley Kallis; d, Arthur Swerdloff; w, Stanley Kallis, Ed Lasko (based on the story by Kallis); m, Richard Markowitz.

Auto Racing   **(PR:A MPAA:NR)**

ROAR OF THE CROWD*½

(1953) 71m AA c

Howard Duff (Johnny Tracy), Helene Stanley (Marcy Parker), Dave Willock (Ruster), Louise Arthur (Rose Adams), Harry Shannon (Pop Tracy), Minor Watson (Mackey), Don Haggerty (Chuck Baylor), Edna Holland (Mrs. Atkinson), Ray Walker (Tuffy Adams), Paul Bryar (Max Bromski).

Johnny (Howard Duff) wants to follow in his father's racing wake, but his fiancee, Marcy (Helene Stanley), wishes he wouldn't. A compromise is reached when Marcy marries Johnny on the condition that he stop racing after a one-time shot at the Indianapolis 500. Unfortunately, before Johnny gets to Indy, he's sidelined by a wreck. With Marcy's help, however, he's able to make it back behind the wheel for the race of races . . . finishing a disappointing ninth. Luckily, the ever-supportive Marcy decides to back

her husband's dream another year after all. The film has at least two dubious distinctions: its "realistic" ending and direction by the ubiquitous William Beaudine. Real-life racers Johnnie Parsons, Duke Nalon, Henry Banks, and Manuel Ayulo are among those appearing.

p, Richard Heermance; d, William Beaudine; w, Charles R. Marion (based on the the story by Marion, Robert Abel); ph, Harry Neumann (Cinecolor); ed, William Austin; m, Marlin Skiles.

Auto Racing   **(PR:A MPAA:NR)**

ROCKY****

(1976) 119m UA c

Sylvester Stallone (Rocky Balboa), Talia Shire (Adrian), Burt Young (Paulie), Carl Weathers (Apollo Creed), Burgess Meredith (Mickey), Thayer David (Miles Jergens), Joe Spinell (Tom Gazzo), Bill Baldwin (Fight Announcer), Al Silvani (Cut Man), George Memmoli (Ice Rink Attendant), Jodi Letizia (Marie), Diana Lewis, George O'Hanlon (TV Commentators), Larry Carroll (TV Interviewer), Stan Shaw (Dipper), Billy Sands (Club Fight Announcer), Pedro Lovell (Spider Ricco), DeForest Covan (Apollo's Corner), Simmy Bow (Club Cornerman), Jane Marla Robbins (Gloria Pet Shop Owner), Jack Hollander (Fats), Lou Filippo (Championship Fight Announcer), Joe Frazier, Butkus the Dog.

Better films have been made about the world of sports, but for many ROCKY is the sports movie. As drenched in sentiment as it is in sweat, as much love story as fight film, this classic tale of a tireless "bum" who makes good is one of the most uplifting films ever made. Set primarily in working-class Philadelphia, it follows the fortunes of Rocky Balboa (Sylvester Stallone), a 30-year-old club fighter who earns his living as a collections man for a loan shark. His boxing career has hit bottom, but Rocky's love life is looking up. He clumsily but endearingly woos Adrian (Talia Shire), the shy, repressed sister of Paulie (Burt Young), Rocky's friend who engineers their strange first date, and in no time, Rocky and Adrian are deeply in love. When a challenger's injury leaves the Ali-like world heavyweight champion Apollo Creed (ex-Oakland Raider linebacker Carl Weathers) without an opponent for his upcoming title defense, the boisterous champ decides to give a nobody a chance and chooses Rocky, "the Italian Stallion." Urged on by Mickey (Burgess Meredith), his crotchety old manager, and to the accompaniment of Bill Conti's rousing theme "Gonna Fly Now," Rocky undergoes grueling training for his title long shot: doing one-armed push-ups, pounding slabs of meat in a slaughterhouse freezer, making his now-famous run through the Philadelphia streets and up the steps of its art museum. Come fight time, Rocky wants only to go the distance with Creed, to prove he isn't "just another bum from the neighborhood." Surprising everyone, he gives Creed the fight of his life, narrowly losing a split decision. Amid the post-fight hubbub, Rocky and Adrian meet in a loving mid-ring clinch. Establishing a formula that would be duplicated over and over (especially in its own sequels—see below), the film slowly draws the audience into Rocky's struggle, until his triumph becomes that of every "little guy" who's dreamed of making it big. Reminiscent of Marlon Brando's Terry Malloy (ON THE WATERFRONT) and Paul Newman's Rocky Graziano (SOMEBODY UP THERE LIKES ME), Stallone's Rocky is magnificent, mirroring the actor's own battle for Hollywood success. As a struggling actor and screenwriter known mainly for THE LORDS OF FLATBUSH, Stallone, inspired by New Jersey club boxer Chuck Wepner's courageous loss to Muhammad Ali (a 15th-round TKO), wrote ROCKY's screenplay in three days. Determined to star in it himself, he turned down a quarter-million-dollar offer for his script, won the part, and, under John Avildsen's Oscar-winning direction, gave the screen one of its most memorable characters. What's more, both his performance and screenplay were nominated for Academy Awards, and the film won for Best Picture and Best Editing. Shire, who is wonderful as the gradually blooming Adrian, and Meredith also earned nominations. The fairy-tale championship match is generally well choreographed (by Stallone), and the training montage, in its originality, remains more gripping than the many glossier imitations it inspired. Expertly paced, benefiting from well-drawn characters and an evocative, often funny script, ROCKY simply pushes all the right buttons. Former heavyweight champ and Philly homeboy Joe Frazier appears as himself.

p, Irwin Winkler, Robert Chartoff; d, John G. Avildsen; w, Sylvester Stallone; ph, James Crabe (Technicolor); ed, Richard Halsey, Scott Conrad; m, Bill Conti.

Boxing　　　　　**Cas.**　　　**(PR:A-C　MPAA:PG)**

ROCKY II***

(1979) 119m UA c

Sylvester Stallone *(Rocky Balboa)*, Talia Shire *(Adrian)*, Burt Young *(Paulie)*, Carl Weathers *(Apollo Creed)*, Burgess Meredith *(Mickey)*, Tony Burton *(Apollo's Trainer)*, Joe Spinell *(Gazzo)*, Leonard Gaines *(Agent)*, Sylvia Meals *(Mary Anne Creed)*, Frank McRae *(Meat Foreman)*, Al Silvani *(Cutman)*, John Pleshette *(Director)*, Stu Nahan *(Announcer)*, Bill Baldwin *(Commentator)*, Jerry Ziesmer *(Salesman)*, Paul J. Micale *(Father Carmine)*.

Considerably less satisfying than the original ROCKY, but head and shoulders above the later installments, ROCKY II picks up the saga of "the Italian Stallion" during the last two rounds of his gutsy loss to world champ Apollo Creed (Carl Weathers). After the bout, Rocky (Sylvester Stallone) and Adrian (Talia Shire), his no-longer-mousy sweetheart, marry and use his fight purse to buy a car and condo. Soon Rocky learns that if he enters the ring again he runs the risk of being blinded in the eye he injured against Apollo. He does his best to provide for Adrian, but is laid off by the slaughterhouse where he works with his brother-in-law, Paulie (Burt Young). Worried about the future—which is about to include a new baby—Rocky accepts a rematch with Apollo, who is anxious to prove Rocky's showing in their first bout was a fluke. Adrian doesn't want her husband to fight, and without her support Rocky is unable to immerse himself in training, much to the chagrin of his manager, Mickey (Burgess Meredith). When Adrian falls into a coma after giving birth to their son, a despondent

Rocky stops training completely. However, after his revived wife tells Rocky to *win*, he trains again in earnest (followed up the steps to the museum by a legion of running kids) and does just that, surprising Apollo by boxing right-handed for most of the fight and switching back to his natural southpaw style only for the decisive final round. All the endearing characters from the original are back, as is Bill Conti's familiar music. This time Stallone both wrote and directed the film, and though his handling of the actors and camera is less assured than John Avildsen's in ROCKY, he keeps things moving at a good pace and delivers another charming performance himself. Again the characters and relationships are engaging—Rocky and Adrian's center-stage love still touching—and though the main plot differs little from the first film, audiences will have a hard time not becoming involved in Rocky's quixotic quest all over again. Unfortunately, the big fight is a letdown, ending preposterously as both exhausted fighters fall to the canvas, with Rocky clambering back to his feet to take the title.

p, Irwin Winkler, Robert Chartoff; d, Sylvester Stallone; w, Sylvester Stallone; ph, Bill Butler (Panavision, Technicolor); ed, Danford B. Greene, Stanford C. Allen, Janice Hampton, James Symons; m, Bill Conti.

Boxing　　　　　**Cas.**　　　**(PR:A-C　MPAA:PG)**

ROCKY III**

(1982) 99m MGM-UA c

Sylvester Stallone *(Rocky Balboa)*, Carl Weathers *(Apollo Creed)*, Mr. T. *(Clubber Lang)*, Talia Shire *(Adrian Balboa)*, Burt Young *(Paulie)*, Burgess Meredith *(Mickey)*, Ian Fried *(Rocky, Jr.)*, Hulk Hogan *(Thunderlips)*, Al Silvani *(Al)*, Wally Taylor *(Clubber's Manager)*, Tony Burton *(Duke)*.

Six years, multimillions of dollars, and thousands of Nautilus repetitions after the first ROCKY, Sylvester Stallone was back again with this third installment in his popular boxing saga. Bigger but not better—much like Stallone and his ego—ROCKY III begins with the final minutes of the last film, as Rocky (Stallone) gallantly takes the championship from Apollo Creed (Carl Weathers). The action then shifts three years and 10 successful title defenses ahead, as a wealthy Rocky considers retiring after taking on pro wrestling champion Thunderlips (real-life glam grappler Hulk Hogan) in a charity match. Interfering in his attempt to bow out gracefully, however, is Clubber Lang (well essayed by the menacing Mr. T), the loud, brutal, and *hungry* No. 1 contender. Against the wishes of his beloved manager, Mickey (Burgess Meredith), Rocky gives Lang a title shot and, having trained poorly, is knocked out by the challenger. Afterwards, in the dressing room, Mickey dies. Rocky's former nemesis, Apollo, then becomes his manager, turning the brawler into a skilled *boxer* who, after confronting his fear, fights Lang again and wins back his title. Despite the usual training montage and a big new theme song (Survivor's "Eye of the Tiger"—describing the edge Apollo tells Rocky he's lost), ROCKY III crawls along without dramatic impetus, failing to convey the big emotions and missing the humor of the first two films. Shire's Adrian is relegated to the background, Meredith's Mickey and Burt Young's Paulie have grown redundant and annoying, and Stallone's script and performance (he also directed) lack his earlier efforts' charm. Perhaps the most interesting aspect of ROCKY III is its only partly successful attempt to redress some of the inherent racism of the first two entries. The obstreperous Apollo Creed has become something less of a caricature in coming around to Rocky's side; however, Clubber Lang takes his place as an intimidating symbol of ascendant black rage.

p, Irwin Winkler, Robert Chartoff; d, Sylvester Stallone; w, Sylvester Stallone; ph, Bill Butler (Technicolor); ed, Don Zimmerman, Mark Warner; m, Bill Conti.

Boxing   **Cas.**   **(PR:A-C MPAA:PG)**

ROCKY IV*

(1985) 91m UA/MGM-UA c

Sylvester Stallone *(Rocky Balboa)*, Talia Shire *(Adrian Balboa)*, Burt Young *(Paulie)*, Carl Weathers *(Apollo Creed)*, Brigitte Nielsen *(Ludmilla)*, Tony Burton *(Duke)*, Michael Pataki *(Nicoli Koloff)*, Dolph Lundgren *(Drago)*, R.J. Adams *(Sports Announcer)*, Al Bandiero, Barry Tompkins *(American Commentators)*, Dominic Barto *(Russian Government Official)*, Daniel Brown *(Rocky Jr.'s Friend)*, James Brown *(The Godfather of Soul)*, Mark Delessandro *(Russian Cornerman)*, Marty Denkin *(Russian Referee)*, Lou Filippo *(Las Vegas Referee)*, James "Cannonball" Green *(Manual Vega)*, Dean Hammond *(Interviewer)*, Rocky Krakoff *(Rocky, Jr.)*, Sergei Levin *(Russian Ring Announcer)*, Sylvia Meals *(Mrs. Creed)*, Leroy Neiman *(Ring Announcer)*, Warner Wolf *(Commentator in Las Vegas)*.

In ROCKY IV, writer-director Sylvester Stallone follows the formula that filled box-office coffers the first three times out, taking the underdog "Italian Stallion" (or transforming him into an underdog, as is the case here and in ROCKY III) and giving him a seemingly unbeatable opponent. The main difference here is that, by 1985, the lines had begun to blur between Rocky, Stallone's blue-collar American Dreamer, and Rambo, his reactionary, jingoist mercenary. This time the good vs. evil confrontation isn't black and white; it's red vs. red, white, and blue. When Drago (Dolph Lundgren), a gargantuan, scientifically trained Soviet boxer, not only defeats but kills Rocky's now good friend Apollo Creed (Carl Weathers) in an "exhibition match," its up to Rock to avenge his friend's death and defend the country's honor, and Rocky—against Adrian's (Talia Shire) wishes—is off to the USSR to take on the Russian automaton. While Drago enhances his amazing punching power using high-tech equipment, Rocky toughens up under the guidance of Apollo's former manager in a spartan compound in the frozen Soviet countryside, using the most primitive of methods. After the appearance of Adrian and the all-important training montage, Rocky takes on the huge Soviet in front of a partisan Moscow crowd, but by the final bell he has won both the fight and the spectators' hearts. Burdened by lackluster performances, making little effort to develop its characters, wholly lacking in imagination, and philosophically repugnant, ROCKY IV is a far cry from the delights (both large and small) of its illustrious original.

p, Irwin Winkler, Robert Chartoff; d, Sylvester Stallone; w, Sylvester Stallone; ph, Bill Butler (Panavision, Metrocolor); ed, Don Zimmerman, John W. Wheeler; m, Vince DiCola, Bill Conti.

Boxing   **Cas.**   **(PR:C MPAA:PG)**

RODEO**

(1952) 71m MON c

Jane Nigh *(Nancy Cartwright)*, John Archer *(Slim Martin)*, Wallace Ford *(Barbecue Jones)*, Gary Gray *(Joey Cartwright)*, Frances Rafferty *(Dixie Benson)*, Sara Haden *(Agatha Cartwright)*, Frank Ferguson *(Harry Cartwright)*, Myron Healey *(Richard Durston)*, Fuzzy Knight *(Jazbo Davis)*, Robert Karner *(Charles Olenick)*, Jim Bannon *(Bat Gorman)*, I. Stanford Jolley *(Pete Adkins)*.

Nancy Cartwright (Jane Nigh) takes over the reins of a mismanaged rodeo and turns it into a success, but big problems arise when Barbecue Jones (Wallace Ford), an aging former bronc rider, overhears the new boss making fun of him. Determined to prove that he's still got what it takes, Barbecue hops on a dangerous mount and is seriously injured, prompting a walkout by the rest of the rodeo company. Ah, but guess who's been paying the old rider's hospital bills?

p, Walter Mirisch; d, William Beaudine; w, Charles R. Marion; ph, Harry Neumann (Cinecolor); ed, William Austin; m, Marlin Skiles.

Rodeo   **(PR:A MPAA:NR)**

ROLLERBALL**½

(1975) 129m UA c

James Caan *(Jonathan E.)*, John Houseman *(Bartholomew)*, Maud Adams *(Ella)*, John Beck *(Moonpie)*, Moses Gunn *(Cletus)*, Pamela Hensley *(Mackie)*, Barbara Trentham *(Daphne)*, Ralph Richardson *(Librarian)*, Shane Rimmer *(Team Executive)*, Alfred Thomas *(Team Trainer)*, Burnell Tucker *(Jonathan's Captain of Guard)*, Angus MacInnes *(Jonathan's Guard No. 1)*, Rick Le Parmentier *(Bartholomew's Aide)*, Burt Kwouk *(Oriental Doctor)*, Robert Ito *(Oriental Instructor)*, Nancy Blair *(Girl In Library)*.

It is the year 2018 and society is rid of war, poverty, and violence—except for the political corporation-controlled rollerball teams, who fight to the bloody finish with spikes and motorcycles in a sport combining roller derby, football, and hockey. When champion rollerball player Jonathan E. (James Caan) is asked to retire because the corporate executives who rule the world are fearful that he has become too popular with the masses, he fights the move, and to get rid of him, the corporate executives decide to change the rollerball rules and make it a fight to the death. Produced and directed by Norman Jewison, this science-fiction film envisions a time when major corporations will control the populace by offering them a brutal and compelling entertainment to distract from the real social issues at hand and act as a funnel for their frustrations, hatred, and resentment. While the questions raised about the relationship between corporate power and sporting events are valid and intriguing, ROLLERBALL is, unfortunately, hopelessly heavy-handed and ponderous. From its gloomy and solemn air to the overbearing use of baroque music, the film is far too self-important for its own good. Luckily, the performances of Caan and Ralph Richardson are excellent, and the rollerball sequences are fast-paced and interesting. The film attempts to raise some uncomfortable questions about the role of sport in society, but fails to pose them properly.

p, Norman Jewison; d, Norman Jewison; w, William Harrison (based on his story "Rollerball Murders"); ph, Douglas Slocombe (Technicolor); ed, Anthony Gibbs; m, Andre Previn, Johann Sebastian Bach, Petr Ilich Tchaikovsky, Dmitri Shostakovich, Tomaso Giovanni Albioni.

Science Fiction   Cas.   (PR:O   MPAA:R)

ROOGIE'S BUMP**

(1954) 71m REP bw (GB: THE KID COLOSSUS)

Robert Marriot *("Roogie" Rigsby)*, Ruth Warrick *(Mrs. Rigsby)*, Olive Blakeney *(Mrs. Andrews)*, Robert Simon *(Boxi)*, William Harrigan *(Red O'Malley)*, David Winters *(Andy)*, Michael Mann *(Benji)*, Tedd Lawrence *(Sports Announcer)*, Michael Keene *(Barney Davis)*, Roy Campanella, Billy Loes, Carl Erskine, Russ Meyer, Robbie the Dog.

New kid on the block "Roogie" Rigsby (Robert Marriot) is ostracized by the neighborhood kids, who won't let him play baseball with them. One day, however, the ghost of a one-time Brooklyn Dodger great (William Harrigan) who was once in love with Roogie's grandmother takes pity on the boy and gives him a magical bump, endowing Roogie with a major-league arm. Now outclassing the local kids entirely, Roogie lands a position with the Dodgers—giving the film's producers a reason to put Roy Campanella, Billy Loes, Carl Erskine, Russ Meyer, et al., on the screen—although his mother (Ruth Warrick) and manager (Robert Simon) must be ever-vigilant to keep the boy from being exploited by the team. Unfortunately, the considerable amount of Dodger footage is reportedly disappointing and sloppy; one scene, for example, appears to show Duke Snider grounding out, then coming right back to the plate to hit again.

p, John Bash, Elizabeth Dickenson; d, Harold Young; w, Jack Hanley, Dan Totheroh (based on a story by Frank Warren, Joyce Selznick); ph, Durgi J. Contner; m, Lehman Engels.

Baseball   (PR:A   MPAA:NR)

ROSE BOWL**

(1936) 75m PAR bw (GB: O'RILEY'S LUCK)

Eleanor Whitney *(Cheers Reynolds)*, Tom Brown *(Paddy O'Riley)*, Larry "Buster" Crabbe *(Ossie Merrill)*, William Frawley *(Coach Soapy Moreland)*, Benny Baker *(Dutch Schultz)*, Nydia Westman *(Susie Reynolds)*, Priscilla Lawson *(Florence Taylor)*, Adrian Morris *(Doc)*, James Conlin *(Browning Hills)*, Nick Lukats *(Donavan)*, Ellen Drew *(Mary*

Arnold), Bud Flanagan [Dennis O'Keefe] *(Jones)*, William Moore *(Peter Potter/Holt)*, Lon Chaney, Jr., Leavitt Thurlow, Jr., Miles Norton, Edward Shuey, David Horsley *(Football Players)*, Louis Mason *(Thornton)*, John Sheehan *(Orville Jensen)*, Hugh McArthur *(Russell)*, Charles Judels *(Mr. Schultz)*, Bodil Ann Rosing *(Mrs. Schultz)*.

Paddy (Tom Brown) and Dutch (Benny Baker) are school chums who become big names on the college football roster, but they still can't seem to get the girls, especially with charmer Ossie (Buster Crabbe) getting all the attention. Paddy and Dutch get their way at the end by showing up Ossie in the title gridiron game. The story begins with Paddy and Dutch in high school, though both seen a bit old for the part.

p, A.M. Botsford; d, Charles Barton; w, Marguerite Roberts (based on the novel *O'Reilly of Notre Dame* by Francis Wallace); ph, Henry Sharp; ed, William Shea.

Football   (PR:A   MPAA:NR)

ROSE BOWL STORY, THE**

(1952) 73m MON c

Marshall Thompson *(Steve Davis)*, Vera Miles *(Denny Burke)*, Richard Rober *(Coach Hadley)*, Natalie Wood *(Sally Burke)*, Keith Larsen *(Bronc Buttram)*, Tom Harmon *(Himself)*, Ann Doran *(Mrs. Burke)*, James Dobson *(Allie Bassler)*, Jim Backus *(Mike Burke)*, Clarence Kolb *(Gramps)*, Barbara Woodell *(Mrs. Hadley)*, Bill Welsh *(Himself)*.

Few trick plays are used in this standard football tale of a star quarterback, Steve Davis (Marshall Thompson), who falls in love with the pelt-draped Denny Burke (Vera Miles). He tries extra hard to impress her, believing that she is an heiress, although she's just putting on airs in a borrowed fur coat. After the coach's wife takes ill and Steve has a falling out with Denny, the QB begins to straighten up. Instead of putting his star image before team spirit, he concentrates on impressing his coach and his girl friend with sportsmanship. Natalie Wood is cast as Sally, Denny's laugh-getting little sister. In the previous year, Thompson appeared in THE BASKETBALL FIX as a star cager. Naturally, THE ROSE BOWL STORY includes an abundance of Rose Bowl stock footage and a cameo of the 1952 Rose Queen, Nancy Thorne.

p, Richard Heermance; d, William Beaudine; w, Charles R. Marion; ph, Harry Neumann (Cinecolor); ed, Walter Hannemann; m, Marlin Skiles.

Football   (PR:A   MPAA:NR)

RUN FOR THE ROSES*½

(1978) 93m Pan-American/Kodiak c (AKA: THOROUGHBRED)

Vera Miles *(Clarissa)*, Stuart Whitman *(Charlie)*, Sam Groom *(Jim)*, Panchito Gomez *(Juanito)*, Theodore Wilson *(Flash)*, Lisa Eilbacher *(Carol)*.

Young Juanito (Panchito Gomez) is the stepson of the manager of a Kentucky horse farm (Stuart Whitman) who, more than anything, wants a horse of his own. His wish comes true when one of the thoroughbreds gives birth to a colt with a deformed knee and the disgusted owner (Vera Miles) gives it to the boy. Through love and surgery, Juanito trains the horse to become a racer and, to the surprise of everyone but the audience, wins the Kentucky Derby.

p, Mario Crespo, Jr., Wolf Schmidt; d, Henry Levin; w, Joseph G. Prieto, Mimi Avins; ph, Raul Dominguez (Metrocolor); ed, Alfredo Rosas Priego; m, Raul Lavista.

Horse Racing   **Cas.**   **(PR:C MPAA:PG)**

RUNNING*½

(1979, Can.) 102m UNIV c

Michael Douglas *(Michael Andropolis)*, Susan Anspach *(Janet Andropolis)*, Lawrence Dane *(Coach Walker)*, Eugene Levy *(Richard Rosenberg)*, Charles Shamata *(Howard Grant)*, Philip Akin *(Chuck)*, Trudy Young *(Pregnant Woman)*, Murray Westgate *(Mr. Finlay)*, Jennifer McKinney *(Susan Andropolis)*, Lesleh Donaldson *(Andrea Andropolis)*, Jim McKay *(Himself)*, Lutz Brode *(Boston Race Winner)*, Deborah Templeton Burgess *(Debbie Rosenberg)*.

This lifeless rip-off of ROCKY made at the height of the Jim Fixx-inspired running craze stars Michael Douglas as Michael Andropolis, who is training to run in the Montreal Olympic marathon while trying to patch things up with his wife (Susan Anspach) and family. The 34-year-old Michael, who is attempting to redeem himself for not showing up for the Pan-American games 10 years before—among other failures—makes it to the marathon, to everyone's surprise, but is injured in the race. Determined to finish, Michael finally staggers into the stadium long after the crowd has gone home, cheered by his fellow athletes. In an cameo, Jim McKay provides commentary as the hero strives to reach his goal.

p, Robert Cooper, Ronald Cohen; d, Steven Hilliard Stern; w, Steven Hilliard Stern; ph, Laszlo George; ed, Kurt Hirschler; m, Andre Gagnon.

Track and Field   **(PR:C MPAA:PG)**

RUNNING BRAVE*½

(1983, Can.) 105m Englander/BV c

Robby Benson *(Billy Mills)*, Pat Hingle *(Coach Easton)*, Claudia Cron *(Pat Mills)*, Jeff McCraken *(Denis)*, August Schellenberg *(Billy's Father)*, Denis Lacroix *(Frank)*, Graham Greene *(Eddie)*, Margo Kane *(Catherin)*, Kendall Smith, Maurice Wolfe, Albert Angus, Barbara Blackhorse, Carmen Wolfe, Gail Omeasoo, Billy Runsabove, Seymour Eaglespeaker.

Billy Mills, the 10,000-meter-run gold medalist at the 1964 Tokyo Olympics, both ran bravely and was a "running brave" (South Dakota Sioux), hence the exceedingly appropriate title of this unexceptional biopic. The film follows Mills (Robby Benson, whom Mills himself reportedly chose for the role) from the reservation to the University of Kansas, where he distinguishes himself as a distance runner

under the watchful eye of Coach Easton (Pat Hingle), but finds adjustment to his new surroundings difficult. After marrying and joining the Marines, Mills continues training and eventually triumphs at the Tokyo Games. Benson, whose versatility as a screen athlete often transcends his acting ability, fails to bring real depth to his portrayal of Mills, though his performance here is far superior to his cloying hockey player in ICE CASTLES (1978). Those interested in seeing the actor at his cinematic sporting best, however, should pass up RUNNING BRAVE and witness instead Benson's credible portrayal of a college basketball player in ONE ON ONE (1977).

p, Ira Englander; d, D.S. Everett; w, Henry Bean, Shirl Hendryx; ph, Francois Protat (Medallion Color); ed, Tony Lower, Earl Herdan; m, Mike Post.

Track and Field/ Biography   **Cas.**   **(PR:C MPAA:PG)**

S

SAFE AT HOME**

(1962) 84m COL bw

Mickey Mantle, Roger Maris *(Themselves)*, William Frawley *(Bill Turner)*, Patricia Barry *(Johanna Price)*, Don Collier *(Ken Lawton)*, Bryan Russell *(Hutch Lawton)*, Eugene Iglesias *(Mr. Torres)*, Flip Mark *(Henry)*, Scott Lane *(Mike Torres)*, Charles G. Martin *(Henry's Father)*, Ralph Houk, Whitey Ford *(Themselves)*, Desiree Sumarra *(Mrs. Torres)*, Joe Hickman *(Joe)*.

Having recently moved to Florida from New York, Little Leaguer Hutch Lawton (Bryan Russell) tries to impress his new teammates by claiming that his widower father is a chum of Yankee superstars Mickey Mantle and Roger Maris. Backed into a corner by his lie, Hutch is then called upon to produce the Yankee sluggers or face humiliation. Unwilling to resign himself to his fate, the plucky youngster not only makes his way to the Yankees' spring training camp, but actually meets Mantle and Maris; however, when he explains his predicament to the home-run-hitting duo (Maris had broken Babe Ruth's single season round-trip record the previous year), the honesty-is-the-best-policy advocates refuse to help him. Or do they? Guess who invites the whole group to spring training? Mantle and Maris are no Redford and Newman, but then Redford and Newman couldn't hit a baseball like Mantle and Maris. Okay, in THE NATURAL, yes, but that's only the movies.

p, Tom Naud; d, Walter Doniger; w, Robert Dillon (based on a story by Naud, Steve Ritch); ph, Irving Lippman; ed, Frank P. Keller; m, Van Alexander.

Baseball   **(PR:A MPAA:NR)**

SALTY O'ROURKE***

(1945) 97m PAR bw

Alan Ladd *(Salty O'Rourke)*, Gail Russell *(Barbara Brooks)*, William Demarest *(Smitty)*, Stanley Clements *(Johnny Cates)*, Bruce Cabot *(Doc Baxter)*, Spring Byington *(Mrs. Brooks)*, Rex Williams *(Babe)*, Darryl Hickman *(Sneezer)*, Marjorie Woodworth *(Lola)*, Don Zelaya *(Hotel Proprietor)*, Lester Matthews *(Dignified Salesman)*, William Forrest *(Racing Secretary)*, William Murphy *(Bennie)*.

Alan Ladd is at his best here as the title character, a bad apple who hangs around the racetrack. He and his pal Smitty (William Demarest) have one month to pay the money they owe a tough fellow gambler, or else. Needing to get rich quick, they buy a fast horse that's sold to them cheap because it's considered unridable by all but Johnny Cates (Stanley Clements), who has been banned from riding in the US, then convince the 22-year-old Cates to use his teenage brother's birth certificate and masquerade as the younger boy in order to qualify to race. Cates is appalled when he learns that he must also go to the school run by the track for under-18 jockeys, but warms up the assignment somewhat under the tutelage of pretty schoolteacher Barbara Brooks (Gail Russell). Unfortunately, Salty also falls for Barbara, who reciprocates the gambler's feelings, and the jockey decides to exact revenge by throwing the race in Salty's debtor's favor. Cates later has a change of heart, which proves too little, too late for him, but not for the hard-boiled Salty. A tough movie with sharp dialog, well-directed by Raoul Walsh, SALTY O'ROURKE was made at the height of Ladd's popularity and is dominated by the actor's charisma. Clements (THE BABE RUTH STORY), who was actually 18 at the time the film was made, is also fine.

p, E.D. Leshin; d, Raoul Walsh; w, Milton Holmes; ph, Theodor Sparkuhl; ed, William Shea; m, Robert Emmett Dolan.

Horse Racing   **(PR:A-C   MPAA:NR)**

SALUTE**½

(1929) 83m FOX bw

George O'Brien *(Cadet John Randall)*, William Janney *(Midshipman Paul Randall)*, Frank Albertson *(Midshipman Albert Edward Price)*, Helen Chandler *(Nancy Wayne)*, Joyce Compton *(Marion Wilson)*, Clifford Dempsey *(Maj. Gen. Somers)*, Lumsden Hare *(Rear Adm. Randall)*, Stepin Fetchit *(Smoke Screen)*, David Butler *(Navy Coach)*, Rex Bell *(Cadet)*, Ward Bond, John Wayne *(Football Players)*, Lee Tracy *(Announcer)*.

It's the old story of the Army versus the Navy on a gridiron battlefield. John Randall (George O'Brien) is the Army freshman player who's a whiz on both the football field and the dance floor. Paul (William Janney) is his younger brother, the Navy's dream boy. When they meet at the final climactic game it's a 6-6 tie, with both brothers scoring the only touchdown for their respective teams. This was only the second talkie to be directed by John Ford, who makes good use of locations at Annapolis. The director also shot isolated footage of the "reel" game and intercut it with newsreel footage of a real game, probably an Army-Princeton contest from the fall of 1928. Look for a minor appearance by John Wayne and Ward Bond as football players who haze Janney's character. Bond and Wayne, at the time, were both on the football team at the University of Southern California. Ford brought the entire USC football team with him to Annapolis; when a pair of speaking parts were called for, he gave the small roles to Bond and Wayne (the latter had worked for Ford during school vacations as a laborer and prop man, and was well liked by the director, the crew, and O'Brien, the star). Ford had the advantage of generous cooperation from the superintendent of the Naval Academy, who had been a great friend of his father's (they were both from Peak's Island, Maine). Ford was to say, "The admirals' daughters were all in the picture—you know, 10 bucks a day—and we had a lot of fun."

d, John Ford, David Butler; w, John Stone, James Kevin McGuinness (based on a story by Tristram Tupper); ph, Joseph August; ed, Alex Troffey.

Football   **(PR:A   MPAA:NR)**

SAM'S SON**½

(1984) 104m Worldvision/Invictus c

Eli Wallach *(Sam Orowitz)*, Anne Jackson *(Harriet Orowitz)*, Timothy Patrick Murphy *(Gene Orowitz)*, Hallie Todd *(Cathy Stanton)*, Alan Hayes *(Robert Woods)*, Jonna Lee *(Bonnie Barnes)*, Michael Landon *(Gene Orman)*, Howard Witt *(Cy Martin)*, William Boyett *(Coach Sutter)*, John Walcutt *(Ronnie Morgan)*, David Lloyd Nelson *(Lonnie Morgan)*, William Bassett *(Mr. Turner)*, Harvey Gold *(Jake Bellow)*, James Karen *(Mr. Collins)*, David Wakefield *(Buddy)*, Martin Rudy *(Dr. Warren)*, Montana Smoyer *(Maxine Wagner)*, Gavin H. Mooney *(Police Officer)*.

This autobiographical tale written and directed by Michael Landon (TV's "Little House on the Prairie," "Bonanza," etc.) stars Timothy Patrick Murphy as Gene Orowitz (Landon's real surname) a talented but frail teenaged javelin thrower. When Gene sees SAMSON AND DELILAH (1949) at the movie theater managed by his father, Sam (Eli Wallach), he begins to emulate the Biblical strongman. He is, after all, "Sam's son," and he decides to grow long hair like his namesake. Since this is the 1950s, Gene's locks become a symbol in his struggle for individuality and a bone of contention with his school principal. Sam, meanwhile, is a frustrated writer who works on his manuscript at night and at the theater by day. Just before Gene is about to compete in a big meet, the overworked Sam has a heart attack and hands his son his completed manuscript on his deathbed. Inspired, Gene goes to the meet and throws the javelin with Samson-like strength for his dad, winning a scholarship to a college Sam could never have afforded. SAM'S SON is made-for-TV style fare from Landon, who reportedly *did* win that inspirational scholarship to USC and who makes a cameo appearance in the film.

p, Kent McCray; d, Michael Landon; w, Michael Landon; ph, Ted Voigtlander; ed, John Loeffler; m, David Rose.

Track and Field   Cas.   (PR:A-C MPAA:PG)

SARATOGA***½

(1937) 94m MGM bw

Jean Harlow *(Carol Clayton)*, Clark Gable *(Duke Bradley)*, Lionel Barrymore *(Grandpa Clayton)*, Walter Pidgeon *(Hartley Madison)*, Frank Morgan *(Jesse Kiffmeyer)*, Una Merkel *(Fritzi O'Malley)*, Cliff Edwards *(Tip O'Brien)*, George Zucco *(Dr. Beard)*, Jonathan Hale *(Frank Clayton)*, Hattie McDaniel *(Rosetta)*, Frankie Darro *(Dixie Gordon)*, Carl Stockdale *(Boswell)*, Henry Stone *(Hard Riding Hurley)*, Ruth Gillette *(Mrs. Hurley)*, Charley Foy *(Valet)*, Robert Emmett Keane *(Auctioneer)*, Edgar Dearing *(Medbury the Trainer)*, Sam Flint *(Judge)*, Harrison Greene *(Clipper)*, Si Jenks *(Gardener)*.

Jean Harlow gave her last screen performance—one of her best—in this sharp-witted and charming trackside comedy that pairs the actress with Clark Gable. Harlow, who died before the film's completion, stars as Carol Clayton, the daughter of a horse breeder (Jonathan Hale) who through gambling loses his Saratoga farm to his bookmaker friend Duke Bradley (Clark Gable). After her father dies of a heart attack, Carol forbids her stockbroker fiance, Hartley Madison (Walter Pidgeon), to make any more trackside wagers—much to the chagrin of Duke, who had planned to win back the money he lost to Hartley at Belmont. While Carol and Duke carry on a love-hate flirtation, the bookmaker schemes with his old friend Fritzi (Una Merkel) to recoup his losses, persuading top jockey Dixie Gordon (Frankie Darro) to ride Fritzi's horse in an upcoming race against Hartley's steed. By now Carol has fallen for Duke and broken off her engagement, but Duke nobly ends their budding romance, respecting her late father's wishes that she be sheltered from the wicked ways of the track. Heartbroken, Carol purchases Frankie's contract from Fritzi, and the stage is set for Duke's ruin until kindhearted Fritzi saves the day. After Harlow died in June 1937, it was decided to use a stand-in for her remaining scenes, in which Mary Dees and Geraldine Dvorak are photographed from behind while wearing a large floppy hat, with Paula Winslow speaking for the character (whom screenwriters Anita Loos and Robert Hopkins gave a cold and cough).

p, Bernard H. Hyman; d, Jack Conway; w, Anita Loos, Robert Hopkins; ph, Ray June; ed, Elmo Veron; m, Edward Ward.

**Horse Racing/
Comedy   (PR:A MPAA:NR)**

SATURDAY'S HERO***

(1951) 109m Sidney Buchman/COL bw (GB: IDOLS IN THE DUST)

John Derek *(Steve Novak)*, Donna Reed *(Melissa)*, Sidney Blackmer *(T.C. McCabe)*, Alexander Knox *(Megroth)*, Elliott Lewis *(Eddie Abrams)*, Otto Hulett *(Coach Tennant)*,

Howard St. John *(Belfrage)*, Aldo Ray *(Gene Hausler)*, Alvin Baldock *(Francis Clayborne)*, Wilbur Robertson *(Bob Whittier)*, Charles Mercer Barnes *(Moose Wagner)*, Bill Martin *(Joe Mestrovic)*, Mickey Knox *(Joey Novak)*, Sandro Giglio *(Poppa)*.

A probing of the lack of ethical standards in college recruiting just as potent today as it was in 1951, SATURDAY'S HERO is the story of Steve Novak (John Derek), a high-school football star and the son of Polish immigrants, who has hopes of rising above his New Jersey surroundings and receiving a college scholarship. As academic standards are of prime importance to Steve, he chooses a respected southern school instead of a traditional gridiron powerhouse, and becomes not only the leader of his football squad, but a promising All-American. After a serious shoulder injury in his junior year, Steve realizes that he has been victimized by the political game-playing of T.C. McCabe (Sidney Blackmer), a wealthy and powerful alumnus who callously used Steve as a means of turning the school into a football power. The determined Steve doesn't give up so easily; he settles down in his New Jersey mill town with girl friend Melissa (Donna Reed), McCabe's niece, and continues his education by attending night school while working during the day.

p, Buddy Adler; d, David Miller; w, Millard Lampell, Sidney Buchman (based on the novel *The Hero* by Lampell); ph, Lee Garmes; ed, William Lyon; m, Elmer Bernstein.

Football   (PR:A MPAA:NR)

SATURDAY'S HEROES**

(1937) 58m RKO bw

Van Heflin *(Val)*, Marian Marsh *(Frances)*, Richard Lane *(Red Watson)*, Alan Bruce *(Burgeson)*, Minor Watson *(Doc Thomas)*, Frank Jenks *(Dubrowsky)*, Willie Best *(Sam)*, Walter Miller *(Coach Banks)*, Crawford Weaver *(Baker)*, George Irving *(President Hammond)*, John Arledge *(Calkins)*, Al St. John *(Andy Jones)*, Charles Trowbridge *(President Mitchell)*, Jack Mulhall *(Desk Clerk)*, Frank Coghlan, Jr. *(Student)*.

This college football tale predates the cynicism found in 1951's SATURDAY'S HERO. College gridiron star Val (Van Heflin) refuses to put up with the patronage he receives because of his athletic ability. He wants to get through his classes through hard work and development of his mental faculties, just like everyone else. To make ends meet, Val scalps some tickets to a big game, is caught, and expelled—a glaring example of the school administration's hypocrisy. He transfers to a rival, apparently more virtuous, school, and revels in on-field heroics and the victory of his alma mater.

p, Robert Sisk; d, Edward Killy; w, Paul Yawitz, David Silverstein, Charles Kaufman (based on the story by George Templeton); ph, Nicholas Musuraca; ed, Frederic Knudtson.

Football   (PR:A MPAA:NR)

SATURDAY'S MILLIONS**½

(1933) 76m UNIV bw

Robert Young *(Jim Fowler)*, Leila Hyams *(Joan Chandler)*, Johnny Mack Brown *(Alan Barry)*, Andy Devine *(Andy Jones)*, Grant Mitchell *(Ezra "Scoot" Fowler)*, Mary Carlisle *(Thelma Springer)*, Joe Sawyer *(Coach)*, Mary Doran *(Marie)*, Paul Porcasi *(Felix)*, Lucille Lund *(Myra Blaine)*, Richard Tucker *(Mr. Chandler)*, Paul Hurst *(Doc Maloney)*, Herbert Corthell *(Baldy)*, William Kent *(Sam)*, Sidney Bracey *(Butler)*, Al Richmond, Charles K. French, Phil Dunham *(Old Grads)*, Alan Ladd *(Student)*.

In a change of pace from earlier college football films, the hero of SATURDAY'S MILLIONS, Jim Fowler (Robert Young), is a college gridiron star who despises his fans and their tendency to make fools of themselves over the game. To support himself, Jim takes numerous jobs, including delivering laundry, all the while romancing a rich man's daughter (Leila Hyams). The film's ending is surprisingly ambiguous; although Jim finally does show the proper team spirit in the climactic contest, it's suggested he might've done better to leave his heroics at home. Young's performance lends realism to his cynical character, though the plot never drifts too far from stereotype. Andy Devine is around to provide some needed laughs, Johnny Mack Brown (one-time star in the Alabama backfield and later in B westerns) and several other All-Americans lend support, and sharp-eyed viewers will spot Alan Ladd in a bit part early in his career.

p, Carl Laemmle, Jr.; d, Edward Sedgwick; w, Dale Van Every (based on the story by Lucian Cary); ph, Charles Stumar; ed, Dave Berg, Robert Carlisle.

Football (PR:A MPAA:NR)

SCORING*

(1979) 91m Intermedia Artists c

Myra Taylor, Charles Fantone, Gregg Perrie, Freya Crane, Pete Maravich, Nina Scotti, Paunita Nichols, Joseph Hardin, Gary Moss, Dick Hardiman.

Having lost what little community support they once had, the Des Moines Vixens, an abysmally bad and extraordinarily unlucky women's professional basketball team, appear headed for extinction. Their prospects brighten, however, when the Vixens' new leadership, a florist and his dope-smoking son, use the profits from their new cash crop (marijuana) to develop the team. Still, if they want to remain in town, the female cagers must prove themselves against a military men's squad. Floppy-socked LSU and NBA great "Pistol Pete" Maravich appears as a member of the Army team.

p, Michael de Gaetano, Nicholas Nizich; d, Michael de Gaetano; w, Michael de Gaetano; ph, William E. Hines; ed, Oliver B. Katz.

Basketball Cas. (PR:O MPAA:NR)

SECOND WIND**

(1976, Can.) 92m Olympic/Ambassador c

James Naughton *(Roger)*, Lindsay Wagner *(Linda)*, Kenneth Pogue *(Pete)*, Tedde Moore *(Paula)*, Tom Harvey *(Frank)*, Louis Del Grende *(Howie)*, Gerard Parkes *(Packard)*, Jonathan Welsh *(Simon)*, Cec Linder *(Graham)*, Alan Levson *(Kevin)*.

SECOND WIND is the innocuous saga of a stockbroker (James Naughton) who enhances his meaningless existence by taking up long-distance running. He decides to compete in the mile and runs every day, but for some reason never quite made clear he refuses to explain the character of his obsession to his wife (Lindsay Wagner). She gets fed up and walks, but all works out well when the proto-yuppie wins both the race and his bride's return.

p, James Margellos; d, Donald Shebib; w, Hal Ackerman; ph, Reginald Morris; ed, Donald Shebib; m, Hagood Hardy.

Track and Field Cas. (PR:A MPAA:NR)

SECRETS OF A NURSE*½

(1938) 69m UNIV bw

Edmund Lowe *(John Dodge)*, Helen Mack *(Katherine MacDonald)*, Dick Foran *(Lee Burke)*, Samuel S. Hinds *(Judge Corrigan)*, Paul Hurst *(Slice Cavanaugh)*, Leon Ames *(Joe Largo)*, David Oliver *(Spud Williams)*, Frances Robinson *(Nurse)*, Clarence Muse *(Tiger)*, Stanley Hughes *(Intern)*, Horace MacMahon *(Larry Carson)*, Dorothy Arnold *(Secretary)*, George Chandler *(Dopey)*, Clyde Dilson *(Churchill)*, Virginia Brissac *(Farlinger)*.

Helen Mack plays the title intriguer, who lovingly tends boxer Lee Burke (Dick Foran) after he is nearly beaten to death in the ring at the behest of a big-shot gambler (Horace McMahon). Burke incites the jealousy of another of her patients, dashing criminal attorney John Dodge (Edmund Lowe), but the rivalry is ended when, after Burke is framed for the murder of his former manager and sent to death row, Dodge comes to the ex-fighter's aid, extracting a crucial confession at the eleventh hour.

p, Burt Kelly; d, Arthur Lubin; w, Thomas Lennon, Lester Cole (based on the story "West Side Miracle" by Quentin Reynolds); ph, Elwood Bredell; ed, Edward Curtiss.

Boxing (PR:A MPAA:NR)

SEMI-TOUGH**½

(1977) 108m UA c

Burt Reynolds *(Billy Clyde Puckett)*, Kris Kristofferson *(Shake Tiller)*, Jill Clayburgh *(Barbara Jane Bookman)*, Robert Preston *(Big Ed Bookman)*, Bert Convy *(Friedrich Bismark)*, Roger E. Mosley *(Puddin)*, Lotte Lenya *(Clara Pelf)*, Richard Masur *(Phillip Hooper)*, Carl Weathers *(Dreamer Tatum)*, Brian Dennehy *(T.J. Lambert)*, Mary Jo Catlett *(Earlene)*, Joe Kapp *(Hose Manning)*, Ron Silver *(Vlada)*, Jim McKrell *(McNair)*, Peter Bromilow *(Interpreter)*, Norm Alden *(Coach Parks)*, Fred Stuthman *(Minister)*, Janet Brandt *(Dressmaker)*, William Wolf *(Fitter)*, Jenifer Shaw *(Stewardess)*, Kevin Furry *(Puddin)*,

Ava Roberts *(Puddin's Wife)*, Melonie Magruder *(Linda)*, Mark Franklin *(Attendant Tom)*, Dick Schaap, Lindsay Nelson, Paul Hornung *(Themselves)*.

Set against the backdrop of professional football, SEMI-TOUGH is both a three-cornered romantic comedy and a scathing satire of self-help movements. Billy Clyde Puckett (Burt Reynolds) and Shake Tiller (Kris Kristofferson) are teammates on a fictitious Super Bowl-bound Miami football team owned by Big Ed Bookman (Robert Preston), a recent convert to BEAT, the est-like way to a better life "gurued" by Friedrich Bismark (Bert Convy). Recently returned from Africa, Big Ed's twice-divorced daughter, Barbara Jane (Jill Clayburgh), reappraises her longtime friends Billy Clyde and Shake, and finds the latter, whom Bismark has led to "IT," not only a changed man but a suitable fiance. The trouble is Billy Clyde is in love with Barbara Jane; however, being a resourceful guy, he manages to poke a hole in Bismark's BEAT bubble, pull off some Super Bowl magic, and make sure that the right guy ends up with Big Ed's daughter. Based on a book by Dan Jenkins, SEMI-TOUGH is periodically funny and frequently on target in its satire, and boasts a strong performance from Reynolds (who also starred in the football-themed THE LONGEST YARD). Jenkins' novel did not include the self-help lampooning, which was introduced into the story by screenwriter Walter Bernstein at the insistence of director Michael Ritchie (THE BAD NEWS BEARS; DOWNHILL RACER). Several sportscasters and former football players appear in the film in character or as themselves, including Joe Kapp, Carl Weathers (ROCKY), Paul Hornung, and Lindsay Nelson.

p, David Merrick; d, Michael Ritchie; w, Walter Bernstein (based on the novel by Dan Jenkins); ph, Charles Rosher, Jr. (Panavision, DeLuxe Color); ed, Richard A. Harris; m, Jerry Fielding.

Football/Comedy   Cas.   (PR:C-O MPAA:R)

SEPARATE WAYS**

(1981) 92m 13 Valentine Associates/Crown International c

Karen Black *(Valentine Colby)*, Tony LoBianco *(Ken Colby)*, Arlene Golonka *(Annie)*, David Naughton *(Jerry)*, Jack Carter *(Barney)*, Sharon Farrell *(Karen)*, William Windom *(Huey)*, Robert Fuller *(Woody)*, Walter Brooke *(Lawrence)*, Jordan Charney *(Harry)*, Sybil Danning *(Mary)*, Angus Duncan *(Allen)*, Bob Hastings *(Jack)*, Noah Hathaway *(Jason)*, Katherine Justice *(Sheila)*, Josh Taylor *(Jim)*, Cissy Wellman *(Darlene)*.

This love story stars Karen Black as unhappy housewife Valentine Colby, whose former auto racer husband (Tony Lo Bianco) is allowing the family car dealership to slide downhill and carrying on an affair. Valentine accordingly begins a dalliance of her own with a fellow art student (David Naughton), then moves out and takes a waitress job in a sleazy club. The ending combines Valentine's return with her husband's triumphant comeback on the track.

p, Howard Avedis; d, Howard Avedis; w, Leah Appet (based on the story by Appet, Avedis and Marlene

Schmidt); ph, Dean Cundy (DeLuxe); ed, John Wright; m, John Cacavas.

Auto Racing   Cas.   (PR:O MPAA:R)

SERGEANT MURPHY**½

(1938) 57m WB bw

Ronald Reagan *(Dennis Murphy)*, Mary Maguire *(Mary Lou Carruthers)*, Donald Crisp *(Col. Carruthers)*, Ben Hendricks, Jr. *(Corp. Kane)*, William B. Davidson *(Maj. Gruff)*, Max Hoffman, Jr. *(Sgt. Connors)*, David Newell *(Lt. Duncan)*, Emmett Vogan *(Maj. Smythe)*, Tracey Lane *(Texas)*, Edmund Cobb *(Adjutant)*, Ellen Clancy *(Joan)*, Rosella Towne *(Alice)*, Helen Valkis *(Bess)*, Sam McDaniel *(Henry)*, Art Mix, Kansas Moehring, Lloyd Lane, James Green *(Cavalrymen)*, Edward Keane *(Maj. Biddle)*, Douglas Wood *(Maj. Gen. Truson)*, Fred Miller *(Quartermaster)*, Walter Miller *(Superintendent Dairy)*, Raymond Brown *(Turner)*, Lee Prather *(Slaughterhouse Foreman)*, William Worthington *(Judge at Horse Show)*.

It's tough to part a man and his horse, even during wartime. Ronald Reagan is Dennis Murphy, a young cavalry private whose horse, the title "sergeant," is skittish and mustered out of duty. Dennis acquires the disgraced steed and trains him into a prize-winner, incontestably proving his worth when he is smuggled into England and wins the Grand National. Along the way, the two Murphys win over the post colonel's daughter (Mary Maguire). Reportedly based on a true story, SERGEANT MURPHY is a good example of the kind of competent second feature Hollywood turned out in the 1930s and 1940s, while former cavalry reservist Reagan gets to display the equestrian form that was later to impress the British royals. Filmed on the Monterey Peninsula, SERGEANT MURPHY is an unusual B film in its extensive location shooting, with Santa Anita standing in for the Grand National.

p, Bryan Foy; d, B. Reeves Eason; w, William Jacobs (based on the story "Golden Girl" by Sy Bartlett); ph, Ted McCord; ed, James Gibbons.

Horse Racing   (PR:A MPAA:NR)

SET-UP, THE*****

(1949) 72m RKO bw

Robert Ryan *(Bill "Stoker" Thompson)*, Audrey Totter *(Julie)*, George Tobias *(Tiny)*, Alan Baxter *(Little Boy)*, Wallace Ford *(Gus)*, Percy Helton *(Red)*, Hal Fieberling *(Tiger Nelson)*, Darryl Hickman *(Shanley)*, Kenny O'Morrison *(Moore)*, James Edwards *(Luther Hawkins)*, David Clarke *(Gunboat Johnson)*, Phillip Pine *(Souza)*, Edwin Max *(Danny)*, David Fresco *(Mickey)*, William E. Green *(Doctor)*, Abe Dinovitch *(Ring Caller)*, Jack Chase *(Hawkin's Second)*, Walter Ridge *(Manager)*, Jess Kirkpatrick, Paul Dobov *(Gamblers)*, Frank Richards *(Bat)*, Jack Stoney *(Nelson's Second)*, Archie Leonard *(Blind Man)*, Lynn Millan *(Bunny)*, Bernard Gorcey *(Tobacco Man)*, Charles Wagenheim *(Hamburger Man)*, Billy Snyder *(Barker)*, W.J. O'Brien *(Pitchman)*, Frank Mills *(Photographer)*, Bobby Henshaw *(Announcer)*, Dwight

Martin *(Glutton)*, Noble "Kid" Chissell *(Handler)*, Ben Moselle *(Referee)*, Arthur Weegee Fellig *(Timekeeper)*.

One of the most realistic and gripping boxing films ever made, THE SET-UP is a tautly constructed, emotionally charged examination of one night in the life of an aging boxer, Stoker Thompson (Robert Ryan). Played out in real time as 72 uninterrupted minutes of Stoker's life, the movie begins as a crowd gathers in front of the arena in anticipation of the evening's bouts. Although almost washed up, Stoker is convinced that if he can win that night's bout he'll be back on the road to the top, "just one punch away" from being able to collect a big purse, open his own tavern, and retire. Meanwhile, his seedy manager (George Tobias) has taken $50 from a hood in return for Stoker's throwing the fight. Since, as of late, Stoker has been getting knocked out regularly after the second round, the manager simply doesn't tell the fighter about the setup. Back in the locker room, Stoker watches as the fighters—ranging from fresh-out-of-high-school talent to punchy veterans—prepare for their bouts, while he awaits the fight of his life. THE SET-UP is an amazingly powerful film. Within a very simple format (the screenplay was based on a poem), director Robert Wise and his performers present a myriad of hopes, fears, criticisms, and emotions, making for one of the most brutal condemnations of boxing ever filmed. The fighting is shown as dehumanizing and cruel, the audience as a mass of animalistic maniacs who live vicariously through the boxers. Everyone, from trainers to promoters to gangsters, is a seedy, uneducated opportunist; only the fighters themselves are shown to have any self-respect. Ryan gives the best performance of his career as the quiet, inarticulate fighter who is determined to stick with the game because he feels that he's "just one punch away" from success. Ryan, who actually boxed for four years undefeated while at Dartmouth College, handles his role with great subtlety: always soft-spoken and sincere, Stoker clings to his simple beliefs and will take whatever punishment is necessary to retain his self-respect and dignity. The fight scenes in THE SET-UP are among the best ever filmed, surpassed only by those in Martin Scorsese's incredible RAGING BULL (1980).

p, Richard Goldstone; d, Robert Wise; w, Art Cohn (based on the poem by Joseph Moncure March); ph, Milton Krasner; ed, Roland Gross.

Boxing **Cas.** **(PR:C MPAA:NR)**

70,000 WITNESSES**

(1932) 71m PAR bw

Phillips Holmes *(Buck Buchanan)*, Dorothy Jordan *(Dorothy Clark)*, Charlie Ruggles *(Johnny Moran)*, Johnny Mack Brown *(Wally Clark)*, J. Farrell MacDonald *(State Coach)*, Lew Cody *(Slip Buchanan)*, David Landau *(Dan McKenna)*, Kenneth Thomson *(Dr. Collins)*, Guinn "Big Boy" Williams *(Connors)*, George Rosener *(Ortello)*, Walter Hiers *(Old Grad)*.

A murder occurs in the middle of a football game, yielding the title 70,000 witnesses. Gridiron star Buck Buchanan (Phillips Holmes), whose brother is a noted point shaver, is framed for the killing, but when the quarter in which the death occurred is played over again at the request of the police, he is exonerated of the crime. Sharp dialog drops hints about his innocence and who is guilty along the way. Johnny Mack Brown plays the murdered player.

p, Charles R. Rogers; d, Ralph Murphy; w, Garret Fort, Robert N. Lee, P.J. Wolfson, Allen Rivkin (based on a novel by Cortland Fitzsimmons); ph, Henry Sharp.

Football/Mystery **(PR:A MPAA:NR)**

SHAKEDOWN, THE**

(1929) 70m UNIV bw

James Murray *(Dave Hall)*, Barbara Kent *(Marjorie)*, George Kotsonaros *(Battling Roff)*, Wheeler Oakman *(Manager)*, Jack Hanlon *(Clem)*, Harry Gribbon *(Bouncer)*.

This early talkie produced and directed by William Wyler (WUTHERING HEIGHTS; MRS. MINIVER) was not one of his more notable efforts, and moves at a slow pace, mixing sound and silent episodes. Dave Hall (James Murray) travels the country with his manager (Wheeler Oakman) and "rival" boxer Battling Roff (George Kotsonaros), staging fights in which Dave is the planted "local talent" who loses to Roff. The crooked scheme goes smoothly until Dave falls in with urchin Clem (Jack Hanlon) and pretty waitress Marjorie (Barbara Kent) and decides to redeem himself in the climactic final bout.

p, William Wyler; d, William Wyler; w, Charles A. Logue, Albert De Mond, Clarence Marks (based on a story by Logue); ph, Charles Stumar, Jerome Ash; ed, Lloyd Nosler, Richard Cahoon.

Boxing **(PR:A MPAA:NR)**

SIDECAR RACERS*

(1975, Aus.) 100m UNIV c

Ben Murphy *(Jeff Rayburn)*, Wendy Hughes *(Lynn Carson)*, John Clayton *(Dave Ferguson)*, John Derum *(Pete McAllister)*, Peter Graves *(Carson)*, John Meillon *(Ocker Harvey)*, Peter Gwynne *(Rick Horton)*, Serge Lazareff *(Bluey Wilson)*, Paul Bertram *(Bob Horton)*, Patrick Ward *(Tex Wilson)*, Arna Maria Winchester *(Marlene)*, Vicki Raymond *(Virginia)*, Kevin Healy *(Store Manager)*, Brian Anderson *(Store Detective)*, Brenda Senders *(Mrs. Horton)*.

Former American Olympic swimmer Jeff Rayburn (Ben Murphy) drifts around Australia, eventually taking up sidecar racing with Aussie motorcyclist Dave Ferguson (John Clayton). The two vie for the attentions of rich girl Lynn Carson (Wendy Hughes) amid the plentiful racing footage, with Dave's reputation for endangering his partners adding to the tension. Made as part of a contemporary push to bring film production to Australia, SIDECAR RACERS is an example of the type of filmmaking that was soon to be far outclassed with the rise of independent Australian cinema.

p, Richard Irving; d, Earl Bellamy; w, Jon Cleary; ph, Paul Onorato (Eastmancolor); ed, Robert L. Kimble; m, Tom Scott.

Motorcycle Racing **(PR:A MPAA:PG)**

SIDEWINDER ONE**

(1977) 96m Ibex/AE c

Marjoe Gortner *(Digger)*, Michael Parks *(J.W. Wyatt)*, Susan Howard *(Chris Gentry)*, Alex Cord *(Packard Gentry)*, Charlotte Rae *(Mrs. Holt)*, Barry Livingston *(Willie Holt)*, Bill Vint *(Jerry Fleming)*, Byron Morrow *(Gentry Executive)*.

While tearing up the terrain and working on the new "Sidewinder One" motorcycle, top motocross racer J.W. Wyatt (Michael Parks) also gets romantically involved with rich, snooty motorcycle heiress Chris Gentry (Susan Howard). His partner, Digger (Marjoe Gortner), helps smooth out the bumpy course of their love. The plot is really just an excuse to show lots of racing action, somewhat repetitively filmed, but stressing spills and chills.

p, Elmo Williams; d, Earl Bellamy; w, Nancy Voyles Crawford, Thomas A. McMahon; ph, Dennis Dalzell (DeLuxe Color); ed, Frank Bracht; m, Mundell Lowe.

Motorcycle Racing   Cas.   (PR:C MPAA:PG)

SILVER DREAM RACER*½

(1980, Brit.) 111m Wickes-RANK/Almi c

David Essex *(Nick Freeman)*, Beau Bridges *(Bruce Mc-Bride)*, Cristina Raines *(Julie Prince)*, Clarke Peters *(Cider Jones)*, Harry H. Corbett *(Wiggins)*, Diane Keen *(Tina)*, Lee Montague *(Jack Freeman)*, Sheila White *(Carol)*, David Baxt *(Ben Mendoza)*, Ed Bishop *(Al Peters)*, Nick Brimble *(Jack Davis)*, Stephen Hoye *(Clarke Nichols)*, T.P. McKenna *(Bank Manager)*, Richard Parmentier *(Journalist)*, Patrick Ryecart *(Benson)*.

Minor British pop idol ("Rock On") turned minor British film actor (STARDUST, 1974) David Essex stars as Nick Freeman, a garage mechanic with an attitude. He's also got the hot prototype motorcycle (a model actually built for Britain's Barry Hart) of his late elder brother, and fully intends to enter it in a race against American punk Bruce McBride (Beau Bridges). McBride is known as one of the dirtiest racers since Professor Fate went up against The Great Leslie in THE GREAT RACE (1965), but you'd never guess that from the racing sequences here, which are fairly unexciting. Cristina Raines is the contested love interest; Essex wrote and performed the score.

p, Rene Dupont; d, David Wickes; w, David Wickes; ph, Paul Beeson (Panavision, Eastmancolor); ed, Peter Hollywood; m, David Essex.

Motorcycle Racing   Cas.   (PR:C MPAA:PG)

SIX PACK**½

(1982) 110m Lion Share/FOX c

Kenny Rogers *(Brewster Baker)*, Diane Lane *(Breezy)*, Erin Gray *(Lilah)*, Barry Corbin *(Sheriff)*, Terry Kiser *(Terk)*, Bob Hannah *(Diddler)*, Tom Abernathy *(Louis)*, Robbie Fleming *(Little Harry)*, Anthony Michael Hall *(Doc)*, Robby Still *(Swifty)*, Benji Wilhoite *(Steven)*, Buddy Baker *(Himself)*, Gary McGurrin *(Hank)*, Charles Kahlenberg *(Stan)*, Roy Tatum *(Harley)*, Terry Beaver *(Pensky)*, Ernest Dixon *(Clarence)*, Jay McMillian, Tim Bays *(Hippies)*, Jo Ahl

(Deanna), Allison Bigger *(Ludi)*, Chuck Woolery, Chris Economaki *(TV Commentators)*.

Country-western singer and human teddy bear Kenny Rogers made his film debut in this story about a stock car racer and six orphans. Brewster Baker (Rogers), a loner who's been away from racing for a few years, one day discovers six kids trying to strip his car. No Brady Bunch, this brood has taken to stealing car parts for money, but Brewster still takes a liking to them, putting their mechanical expertise to work in his big comeback bid and teaching them to behave in the bargain. For all its cute contrivances, SIX PACK isn't a bad film and is guaranteed to warm the hearts of Rogers' fans. Among the kids, future stars Diane Lane (THE COTTON CLUB) and Anthony Michael Hall (SIXTEEN CANDLES) show their promise.

p, Michael Trikilis; d, Daniel Petrie; w, Mike Marvin, Alex Matter; ph, Mario Tosi (DeLuxe Color); ed, Rita Roland; m, Charles Fox.

Auto Racing   Cas.   (PR:C MPAA:PG)

SKATEBOARD*

(1978) 97m Blum Group/UNIV c

Allen Garfield *(Manny Bloom)*, Kathleen Lloyd *(Millicent Broderick)*, Leif Garrett *(Brad Harris)*, Richard Van Der Wyk *(Jason Maddox)*, Tony Alva *(Tony Bluetile)*, Steve Monahan *(Peter Steffens)*, David Hyde *(Dennis)*, Ellen Oneal *(Jenny Bradshaw)*, Pam Kenneally *(Randi)*, Anthony Carbone *(Sol)*, Sylvester Words *(Sol's Henchman)*, Gordon Jump *(Harris)*, Pat Hitchcock *(Mrs. Harris)*, Orson Bean *(Himself)*, Joe Bratcher *(Vito)*, Harvey Levine *(U.E.O. Clerk)*, Thelma Pelish *(Woman in Motel)*, John Fox *(Charlie)*, Damon Douglas *(Scott)*, Marilyn Roberts *(Waitress)*, David Carlile *(Palmdale Announcer)*, Chuck Niles *(Race Announcer)*.

Manny (Allen Garfield), a down-on-his-luck agent with a bookie hot on his tail, needs big money . . . fast. Luckily, he knows a group of skateboarding kids ripe for professional status, whom he organizes into a team and enters in a downhill race with a $20,000 prize. The size of the purse seems more than farfetched, as is the presence of a gangster (Anthony Carbone) who tries to get Manny to throw the big event. Flash-in-the-pan teen idol Leif Garrett plays the heroic skater who saves the day in this independent quickie made during a 70s skateboarding craze.

p, Harry N. Blum, Richard A. Wolf; d, George Gage; w, Richard A. Wolf, George Gage (based on a story by Richard A. Wolf); ph, Ross Kelsay (Technicolor); ed, Robert Angus; m, Mark Snow.

Skateboarding   Cas.   (PR:C MPAA:PG)

SKI PATROL**

(1940) 64m UNIV bw

Philip Dorn *(Viktor Ryder)*, Luli Deste *(Julia Engle)*, Stanley Fields *(Birger Simberg)*, Samuel S. Hinds *(Per Vallgren)*, Edward Norris *(Paave Luuki)*, John Qualen *(Gustaf Nerkuu)*, Hardie Albright *(Tyko Galien)*, John Arledge *(Dick*

Reynolds), John Ellis *(Knut Vallgren)*, Reed Hadley *(Ivan Dubroski)*.

At the 1936 Winter Olympics, a Russian, a Finn, and an American win the Gold, Silver, and Bronze medals in a skiing competition. The skiers are friends, and at the medal ceremony officials proudly proclaim that war is a thing of the past, but the audience knows better. The story then moves ahead to the Russo-Finnish War, during which troops on skis, including the 1936 Finnish team, must defend the mountainous border from the enemy. While the heroics and footage are stock, the film does boast photography by gifted cinematographer Milton Krasner.

p, Warren Douglas; d, Lew Landers; w, Paul Huston; ph, Milton Krasner; ed, Edward Curtiss.

Skiing (PR:A MPAA:NR)

SLAP SHOT***

(1977) 123m UNIV c

Paul Newman *(Reggie Dunlop)*, Strother Martin *(Joe McGrath)*, Michael Ontkean *(Ned Braden)*, Jennifer Warren *(Francine Dunlop)*, Lindsay Crouse *(Lily Braden)*, Jerry Houser *("Killer" Carlson)*, Andrew Duncan *(Jimm Carr)*, Jeff Carlson *(Jeff Hanson)*, Steve Carlson *(Steve Hanson)*, David Hanson *(Jack Hanson)*, Yvon Barrette *(Denis Le Mieux)*, Allan Nicholls *(Upton)*, Brad Sullivan *(Wanchuk)*, Stephen Mendillo *(Jim Ahern)*, Yvan Ponton *(Drouin)*, Matthew Cowles *(Charlie)*, Kathryn Walker *(Anita McCambridge)*, Melinda Dillon *(Suzanne Hanrahan)*, M. Emmet Walsh *(Dickie Dunn)*, Swoosie Kurtz *(Shirley)*, Paul D'Amato *(Tim McCracken)*, Ronald L. Docken *(Lebrun)*, Guido Tenesi *(Billy Charlebois)*.

Funny, frank, and violent, George Roy Hill's absorbing film about minor league hockey offers a wonderful comic performance from Paul Newman as Reggie Dunlop, the aging player-coach of the Charleston Chiefs. Mired in a long losing streak and deserted by their fans, the Chiefs learn that the franchise is to fold at the end of the season because the steel mill that employs most of their Pennsylvania town's populace is closing. Refusing to give up, Reggie encourages his team in no-holds-barred play, and, surprisingly, the recently acquired, bespectacled Hanson brothers (Jeff Carlson, Steve Carlson, and David Hanson) prove to be the ultimate monsters of high-sticking mayhem, leading the Chiefs to victory after violent victory and filling the stands. This doesn't sit well with Ned Braden (Michael Ontkean), the team's leading scorer, a Princeton grad committed to "old-fashioned" hockey. Meanwhile, Reggie plants stories that the Chiefs' unknown owner is negotiating to sell the club and tries to reconcile with his beautician wife, Francine (Jennifer Warren). The team is destined to become a tax write-off, but with pride on the line, they take on a club composed of the league's roughest players for the championship—a game with a bizarre finish unlike that of any other sports film. Upon its release, SLAP SHOT gained instant notoriety for its "locker-room" language, which may offend some, but is perfect for its milieu—in fact, screenwriter Nancy Dowd based the diction on tape recordings her brother, a minor league hockey player,

made in the locker room and on the team bus. In addition to Newman's masterful work, the film includes excellent supporting performances by Strother Martin as the Chiefs' general manager, Andrew Duncan as a sportscaster, and Lindsay Crouse as Braden's most unhappy wife. The on-ice violence is hyper-real, the emotions believable, and the laughs plentiful in this slightly off-the-wall comedy.

p, Robert J. Wunsch, Stephen Friedman; d, George Roy Hill; w, Nancy Dowd; ph, Victor J. Kemper (Panavision, Technicolor); ed, Dede Allen; m, Elmer Bernstein.

Hockey **Cas.** **(PR:O MPAA:R)**

SLUGGER'S WIFE, THE*

(1985) 105m COL c (AKA: NEIL SIMON'S THE SLUGGER'S WIFE)

Michael O'Keefe *(Darryl Palmer)*, Rebecca De Mornay *(Debby Palmer)*, Martin Ritt *(Burley De Vito)*, Randy Quaid *(Goose Granger)*, Cleavant Derricks *(Manny Alvarado)*, Lisa Langlois *(Aline Cooper)*, Loudon Wainwright III *(Gary)*, Georgann Johnson *(Marie De Vito)*, Danny Tucker *(Coach O'Brien)*, Lynn Whitfield *(Tina Alvarado)*, Al Garrison *(Guard)*, Nicandra Hood *(Nurse)*, Ginger Taylor *(Sherry)*, Kay Mclelland *(Peggy)*, Julie Kemp *(Paloma)*, Dennis Burkley *(Chuck)*, Alisha Das *(Lola)*, Dan Biggers *(Preacher)*, Justine Thielemann *(Iris Granger)*, Marc Clement *(Mr. Davis)*, Alex Hawkins *(Hawkins)*, John B. Sterling *(Himself)*, John W. Bradley *(Himself)*, Steve Daniels, Jr., Henry J. Rountree, George Jack Klarman, Collin Fagan, David M. Pallone *(Umpires)*, John Lawhorn *(Coach Reckon)*, Douglas Garland Nave, Bill G. Fite *(Catchers)*, Al Hrabosky, Mark Fidrych *(Baseball Players)*, Pete Van Wieren, Ernie Johnson *(Baseball Narrators)*, Skip Caray, Nick Charles *(Sportscasters)*.

Given the track records of its writer, Neil Simon, and director, Hal Ashby, THE SLUGGER'S WIFE should at least have been entertaining. It isn't. Instead, it is one of the most disappointing, least credible films about baseball in recent memory. Neither good-natured fantasy (ANGELS IN THE OUTFIELD; DAMN YANKEES) nor realistic drama (EIGHT MEN OUT; BANG THE DRUM SLOWLY), THE SLUGGER'S WIFE most nearly approaches the romantic comedy of BULL DURHAM, except that it's neither funny nor romantic, and it certainly isn't believable. Not only are we asked to swallow Michael O'Keefe, who plays Atlanta Brave Darryl Palmer, as a power hitter, but we are also supposed to accept that he is closing in on Roger Maris' single-season home run record. In the same way that Anthony Perkins' impassioned performance made his throwing ability irrelevant in FEAR STRIKES OUT, it might not have mattered that O'Keefe looks like anything but a long-ball hitter . . . if he or the film had anything else to offer. Neither does. The crux of the tale is the relationship that develops between Darryl and aspiring rock star Debby (Rebecca De Mornay), who eventually becomes his wife. Darryl can't hit unless Debby's there to support him, but she feels trapped in their marriage and longs to put on her rock'n'roll shoes again. Problems mount, but, as you might guess, everything is hunky-dory at the finale. Those who do decide to watch the film should be on the lookout for appearances by former major league hurlers Mark "The Bird" Fidrych and Al Hrobosky and former pro football players Alex Hawkins and Harmon Wages. Sports fans will also want to note the presence of folkie Loudon Wainwright III as Debby's lead guitar player.

p, Ray Stark; d, Hal Ashby; w, Neil Simon; ph, Caleb Deschanel (Metrocolor); ed, George Villasenor, Don Brochu; m, Patrick Williams.

Baseball/Comedy   Cas. (PR:C-O   MPAA:PG-13)

SMALL TOWN STORY**

(1953, Brit.) 69m Almanack/GFD bw

Donald Houston (Tony Warren), Susan Shaw (Patricia Lane), Alan Wheatley (Nick Hammond), Kent Walton (Bob Regan), George Merritt (Michael Collins), Margaret Harrison (Jackie Collins), Norman Williams (Elton), Arthur Rigby (Alf Benson).

A windfall of cash awaits a lowly British soccer team if it wins enough to be promoted to the third division, and Bob Regan (Kent Walton), a former Canadian soldier, appears to be just the spark they need to pull it off. His talents don't go unnoticed by other clubs, though, and one of them pays Regan's old girl friend (Susan Shaw) to try to lure him to their side. Fat chance.

p, Otto Kreisler, Ken Bennett; d, Montgomery Tully; w, George Fisher (based on a story by Franz Marischka and Maurice Weissberger); ph, Jo Jago, Peter Hamilton.

Soccer   (PR:A   MPAA:NR)

SMITH OF MINNESOTA**

(1942) 66m COL c

Bruce Smith, Arline Judge, Warren Ashe, Don Beddoe, Kay Harris, Robert Stevens, Roberta Smith, Rosemary De Camp, Maurice Murphy, Dick Hogan, Douglas Leavitt.

In the tradition of HARMON OF MICHIGAN (1941), SMITH OF MINNESOTA stars Minnesota All-American Bruce Smith in his own life story. The film's self-reflexive angle involves a screenwriter (Warren Ashe) who is assigned to write a screenplay on the star halfback, which sends him to live with Smith for some "up close and personal" research. The writer's admiration for the unassuming gridiron hero grows as Smith fills him in on some background motivation, including the story of his father's losing efforts in a 1910 Minnesota-Michigan game, which is reconstructed in the film.

p, Jack Fier; d, Lew Landers; w, Robert D. Andrews; ph, Phillip Tannura; ed, Mel Thorsen.

Football/Comedy   (PR:A   MPAA:NR)

SO THIS IS COLLEGE**

(1929) 97m MGM bw

Elliot Nugent (Eddie), Robert Armstrong (Biff), Cliff Edwards (Windy), Sally Starr (Babs), Phyllis Crane (Betty),

Polly Moran (Polly), Lee Shumway (Coach), Dorothy Dehn (Jane), Max Davidson (Moe), Ann Brody (Momma).

Academics again provide the excuse to sing a few songs and show footage from a football game: this time it's USC against Stanford in 1928 (the game was, in reality, won by USC 10-0, but through the magic of cinema the results are somewhat altered here). USC teammates Eddie and Biff (Elliott Nugent and Robert Armstrong) share the same room and the same girl, Babs (Sally Starr), but don't find out about the latter until the big game. Their coach avoids disaster with a timely speech, persuading them that winning is more important than women.

d, Sam Wood; w, Al Boasberg, Delmer Daves, Joe Farnham; ph, Leonard Smith; ed, Frank Sullivan, Leslie F. Wilder; m, Martin Broones.

Football   (PR:A   MPAA:NR)

SOCIAL LION, THE*½

(1930) 72m PAR-Publix bw

Jack Oakie (Marco Perkins), Mary Brian (Cynthia Brown), Richard "Skeets" Gallagher ("Chick" Hathaway), Olive Borden (Gloria Staunton), Charles Sellon (Jim Perkins), Cyril Ring (Ralph Williams), E.H. Calvert (Henderson), James Gibson (Howard), Henry Roquemore (Smith), William Bechtel (Schultz), Richard Cummings (McGinnis), Jack Byron ("Knockout" Johnson).

Jack Oakie stars in this satire of everything from prize fighting to polo. After suffering a humiliating defeat in the ring, boxer Marco Perkins (Oakie) successfully takes up polo, chiefly because he wants to impress society princess Gloria (Olive Borden), who, however, is merely leading him on for her own amusement. Once the would-be "social lion" realizes this, he returns to the unrefined ring and to the girl he left behind (Mary Brian). An Oakie formula story, THE SOCIAL LION combines that special touch of pathos within the comedy that was the actor's trademark.

d, A. Edward Sutherland; w, Joseph L. Mankiewicz, Agnes Brand Leahy (based on the story "Marco Himself" by Octavus Roy Cohen); ph, Allen Siegler; ed, Otho Lovering.

Boxing/Polo/
Comedy   (PR:A   MPAA:NR)

SOCIETY GIRL**

(1932) 67m FOX bw

James Dunn (Johnny Malone), Peggy Shannon (Judy Gelett), Spencer Tracy (Briscoe), Walter Byron (Warburton), Bert Hanlon (Curly), Marjorie Gateson (Alice Converse), Eula Guy Todd (Miss Halloway).

While preparing for a championship match, boxer Johnny Malone (James Dunn) meets and falls hard for socialite Judy Gelett (Peggy Shannon), much to the dismay of his trainer, Briscoe (Spencer Tracy). Instead of training for the fight, Johnny devotes all his energies to Judy, who, naturally, packs her bags and leaves him to take the 10 count, while the disgusted Briscoe also takes off. True love wins out in the end, however, and Johnny has every hope of making a comeback. The 32-year-old Tracy steals every scene he's in, making one wonder why he isn't cast in the lead, especially since he looks more like a prizefighter than Dunn.

d, Sidney Lanfield; w, Elmer Harris (based on the play by John Larkin, Jr.); ph, George Barnes; ed, Margaret Clancy.

Boxing (PR:A MPAA:NR)

SOME BLONDES ARE DANGEROUS*

(1937) 65m UNIV bw

Noah Beery, Jr. *(Bud Mason),* William Gargan *(George Regan),* Dorothea Kent *(Rose Whitney),* Nan Grey *(Judy Williams),* Roland Drew *(Paul Lewis),* Polly Rowles *(Mrs. Lewis),* John Butler *(McNeil),* Lew Kelly *(Jeff),* Eddie Roberts *(Battle O'Keefe),* Joe Smallwood *(Spike),* Edward Stanley *(Reilly),* Walter Friedman *(Dink Pappas).*

Boxer Bud Mason (Noah Beery, Jr.) dumps his manager (William Gargan) and devoted girl friend Judy (Nan Grey) when he becomes the champ, knowing he can do better by himself. He marries glamorous-but-worthless chorus girl Rose (Dorothea Kent) and sets up a match with an up-and-comer hungry for his title. On the night of the big fight, however, he learns of Rose's infidelity, which, compounded by sloppy training, bodes ill for continued mastery in the ring. Judy returns to console the big lug. The film, a remake of IRON MAN (1931), was remade again with that title in 1951.

p, E.M. Asher; d, Milton Carruth; w, Lester Cole (based on the novel and screenplay *Iron Man* by W.R. Burnett); ph, George Robinson; ed, Frank Gross.

Boxing (PR:A MPAA:NR)

SOMEBODY UP THERE LIKES ME***½

(1956) 113m MGM bw

Paul Newman *(Rocky Graziano),* Pier Angeli *(Norma),* Everett Sloane *(Irving Cohen),* Eileen Heckart *(Ma Barbella),* Sal Mineo *(Romolo),* Harold J. Stone *(Nick Barbella),* Joseph Buloff *(Benny),* Sammy White *(Whitey Bimstein),* Arch Johnson *(Heldon),* Robert Lieb *(Questioner),* Theodore Newton *(Eddie Eagan),* Steve McQueen *(Fidel),* Robert Easton *(Cpl. Quinburg),* Ray Walker *(Ring Announcer),* Billy Nelson *(Commissioner),* Robert Loggia *(Frankie Peppo),* Matt Crowley *(Lou Stillman),* Judson Pratt *(Johnny Hyland),* Donna Jo Gribble *(Yolanda Barbella),* James Todd *(Colonel),* Jack Kelk *(George),* Russ Conway *(Capt. Grifton),* Harry Wismer *(Himself).*

After pulling no punches in his brilliant study of the downside of professional boxing, THE SET-UP (1949), director Robert Wise presents a much more upbeat picture of the fight game in this entertaining biography of one-time middleweight champion Rocky Graziano. Paul Newman plays the New York slum-bred fighter, the son of a boxer whose career was stifled by the bottle. In and out of trouble for most of his young life, Rocky drifts from petty crime to re-

form school, from a dishonorable discharge from the Army to Leavenworth Prison. In the joint, however, Rocky is encouraged to develop his boxing talents, and when he is released he is taken under the wing of small-time manager Irving Cohen (Everett Sloane). Under Cohen's guidance, Rocky begins winning fights, but it isn't until he meets and marries Norma (Pier Angeli) that Rocky becomes a big winner. In time, he battles Tony Zale (brilliantly boxed by Courtland Shepard) for the championship, losing their first fight, but taking the title in the second. Newman, who spent time with Graziano and observed his speech patterns, mannerisms, movements, and boxing style, worked himself into peak condition for the role, lifting weights and sparring with top professionals, and his portrayal of the scrappy, often tongue-tied, but wholly likable boxer is superb. Although the role was originally intended for James Dean, Newman makes it his own, delivering such memorable lines as "I'll drink from the bottle like the rest of the boys" when asked if he needs a cup to complete his boxing garb.

p, Charles Schnee; d, Robert Wise; w, Ernest Lehman (based on the autobiography of Rocky Graziano written with Rowland Barber); ph, Joseph Ruttenberg; ed, Albert Akst; m, Bronislau Kaper.

Boxing/Biography Cas. (PR:C MPAA:NR)

SPEAKEASY*½

(1929) 62m FOX bw

Paul Page *(Paul Martin),* Lola Lane *(Alice Woods),* Henry B. Walthall *(Fuzzy),* Helen Ware *(Min),* Warren Hymer *(Cannon Delmont),* Stuart Erwin *(Cy Williams),* Sharon Lynn *(Mazie),* Erville Alderson *(City Editor),* James Guilfoyle *(Davey),* Joe Cawthorn *(Yokel),* Ivan Linow *(Wrestler).*

This early talkie intercuts newsreel footage with the story of Paul Martin (Paul Page), a down-and-out college fighter-turned-pro who's being ripped off by his manager (Warren Hymer). Reporter Alice Woods (Lola Lane) falls in love with the gullible slugger and helps him get back in the ring on his own. The familiar climax shows Paul getting the worst of it in the battle for the middleweight championship, his attention riveted to the empty seat where a tardy Alice should be sitting. The fight footage from Madison Square Garden and other New York City views are culled from the vaults of Movietone news.

d, Benjamin Stoloff; w, Frederick Hazlitt Brennan, Edwin Burke (based on the play by Edward Knoblock, George Rosener); ph, Joseph A. Valentine; ed, J. Edwin Robbins.

Boxing (PR:A MPAA:NR)

SPEED**

(1936) 65m MGM bw

James Stewart *(Terry Martin),* Wendy Barrie *(Jane Mitchell),* Ted Healy *(Gadget),* Una Merkel *(Josephine Sanderson),* Weldon Heyburn *(Frank Lawson),* Patricia Wilder *(Fanny Lane),* Ralph Morgan *(Mr. Dean),* Robert Livingston *(George Saunders),* Charles Trowbridge, William

Tannen *(Doctors)*, Walter Kingsford *(Uncle)*, Claudelle Kaye *(Nurse)*.

James Stewart stars as Terry Martin, a test driver for a large auto plant trying to perfect the new high-speed carburetor he and his crew have invented in time for the big race at the Indianapolis Speedway. While trying to work out some bugs in the system, Terry is encouraged by his boss' niece, Jane (Wendy Barrie), to let her engineer friend Frank (Weldon Heyburn) take a look. Frank helps out, but since both men are sweet on Jane, tension soon develops between them. The day on which the new device is tested nearly ends in disaster when the car crashes, injuring the driver. Later, when Terry is nearly asphyxiated during an attempt to break a speed record, Frank saves the day and vindicates the invention, which wins Terry more than a promotion. In addition to the starring presence of Stewart in one of his first films, SPEED contains much stock footage of races, some point-of-view shots from behind the wheel, and a tour of a Plymouth assembly line.

p, Lucien Hubbard; d, Edwin L. Marin; w, Michael Fessier (based on a story by Milton Krims, Larry Bachman); ph, Lester White; ed, Harry Poppe.

Auto Racing   (PR:A   MPAA:NR)

SPEED LOVERS*½

(1968) 102m Associates and Wilmac/Jemco c

Fred Lorenzen *(Himself)*, William McGaha, Peggy O'Hara, David Marcus, Carol Street, Glenda Brunson.

Stock car racer Fred Lorenzen appears here as himself, the role model emulated by a track mechanic's young son. If the plot sounds less than baroque, that may be because SPEED LOVERS includes *lots* of racing footage, shot at Atlanta, Riverside, Daytona Beach, Darlington, Charlotte, and other speedways.

p, William McGaha; d, William McGaha; w, Elaine Wilkerson, William McGaha, Fred Tuch; ph, Joe Shelton (Eastmancolor); ed, John Fitzstephens, David Moscovitz, William Freda; m, Carleton Palmer.

Auto Racing   (PR:A   MPAA:NR)

SPEED TO BURN**

(1938) 60m FOX bw

Michael Whalen *(Matt Kerry)*, Lynn Bari *(Marion Clark)*, Marvin Stephens *(Tim Turner)*, Henry Armetta *(Papa Gambini)*, Chick Chandler *(Sport Fields)*, Sidney Blackmer *(Hastings)*, Johnnie Pirrone *(Tony Gambini)*, Charles D. Brown *(Pop Williams)*, Inez Palange *(Mrs. Gambini)*.

Racetrack waif Tim (Marvin Stephens) raises a pony that looks like a winner, but is shocked when the trainer he works for sells the horse to the police department. Michael Whalen plays Matt, the friendly cop who helps Tim find out why his horse was not allowed to race. When it turns out the horse was nudged out of competition by gamblers, Matt and Tim conspire to get it back and enter it in a race, with all Matt's fellow men in blue betting on the speedy steed. The gamblers have yet another dirty trick up their

sleeve, but in the final analysis crime doesn't pay. Henry Armetta provides comic relief as an Italian restaurateur.

p, Jerry Hoffman; d, Otto Brower; w, Robert Ellis, Helen Logan (based on a story by Edwin Dial Torgerson); ph, Edward Snyder; ed, Fred Allen.

Horse Racing   (PR:A   MPAA:NR)

SPEEDWAY**

(1968) 92m MGM c

Elvis Presley *(Steve Grayson)*, Nancy Sinatra *(Susan Jacks)*, Bill Bixby *(Kenny Donford)*, Gale Gordon *(R.W. Hepworth)*, William Schallert *(Abel Esterlake)*, Victoria Meyerink *(Ellie Esterlake)*, Ross Hagen *(Paul Dado)*, Carl Ballantine *(Birdie Kebner)*, Poncie Ponce *(Juan Medala)*, Harry Hickox *(The Cook)*, Christopher West *(Billie Jo)*, Beverly Hills *(Mary Ann)*, Harper Carter *(Ted Simmons)*, Bob Harris *(Lloyd Meadows)*, Michele Newman *(Debbie Esterlake)*, Courtney Brown *(Carrie Esterlake)*, Dana Brown *(Billie Esterlake)*, Patti Jean Keith *(Annie Esterlake)*, Carl Reindel *(Mike)*, Gari Hardy *(Dumb Blonde)*.

Elvis Presley again plays a successful racer (see SPIN-OUT, below) in this, his 27th film. Steve Grayson (Elvis) is a nice guy who gives most of his stock car winnings away while still managing to sustain an opulent rock'n'roll lifestyle. Unfortunately, Steve's manager, Kenny Donford (Bill Bixby), has mismanaged the racer's funds (apparently he lost a lot of it betting on horses), leaving Steve flat broke. If that weren't enough, Donford has also bungled Steve's taxes, which sends the boots of Nancy Sinatra, as miniskirted IRS agent Susan Jacks, walkin' to the King's door. Track scenes were filmed at the Charlotte Speedway in North Carolina. Includes such Presley non-hits as "He's Your Uncle, Not Your Dad"; Sinatra sings "Your Groovy Self." Presley appendages The Jordanaires (as backup singers) and Col. Tom Parker (as "technical advisor") again lend their dubious support here.

p, Douglas Laurence; d, Norman Taurog; w, Phillip Shuken; ph, Joseph Ruttenberg (Panavision, Metrocolor); ed, Richard Farrell; m, Jeff Alexander.

Auto Racing/Musical   Cas.   (PR:A   MPAA:G)

SPIKE OF BENSONHURST**½

(1988) 101m Film Dallas c

Sasha Mitchell *(Spike Fumo)*, Ernest Borgnine *(Baldo Cacetti)*, Anne DeSalvo *(Sylvia Cacetti)*, Sylvia Miles *(Congresswoman)*, Geraldine Smith *(Helen Fumo)*, Antonio Rey *(Bandana's Mother)*, Rick Aviles *(Bandana)*, Maria Pitillo *(Angel)*, Talisa Soto *(India)*, Christopher Anthony Young.

A mixture of Sylvester Stallone's Rocky Balboa and Matt Dillon's tough kid from RUMBLE FISH, male model Sasha Mitchell is the eponymous Spike, a tough Italian street fighter from Brooklyn whose old man is a mafia fall guy doing time in Sing Sing and whose old lady is a spiteful lesbian. Since his father took a fall to cover for mob boss Baldo Cacetti (played with great energy and guts by Ernest Borgnine), the mobster has vowed to take care of Spike. Spike thinks his future is in the ring, so Baldo gets him a few fights, although he complains that he himself left the boxing game because "it's too old . . . too ethnic." Nevertheless, most of the fights Spike wins have been fixed by Baldo. During one bout, Spike spots pretty blonde Angel (Maria Pitillo), who turns out to be Baldo's precious daughter—a mafia princess who studies at a respected Catholic college and is planning, at her father's behest, to marry the clean-cut son of a congresswoman (Sylvia Miles). Angel wants Spike, however, and, although the boxer doesn't balk at the idea, he's something of a Neanderthal and is more concerned with his fists and his future. Combining the milieus of mobsters and fighters, SPIKE OF BENSONHURST is a likable story revolving around a boxer who, like Rocky, achieves right through might. The film deals with predictable conflicts, but manages to present them in an entertaining way.

p, David Weisman, Nelson Lyon, Mark Silverman; d, Paul Morrissey; w, Alan Bowne, Paul Morrissey; ph, Steven Fierberg; ed, Stan Salfas; m, Coati Mundi.

Boxing   **Cas.**   **(PR:C MPAA:R)**

SPIKER**½

(1986) 104m Seymour Borde c

Michael Parks *(Coach Doames)*, Patrick Houser *(Catch)*, Stephen Burns *(Sonny)*, Kristi Ferrell *(Pam Howard)*, Jo McDonnell *(Marcia Steinbeck)*, Natasha Schneider *(Wanda)*, Christopher Allport *(Newt Steinbeck)*, Ken Michelman *(Steve Landow)*, Jan-Ivan Dorin *(Polish Security Officer)*, Doug Beal.

NORTH DALLAS FORTY looked at the tainted world of professional football, then came THE NATURAL, with its story of a baseball player who struggles against external corruption and his own demons to emerge victorious. Following in their wake was SPIKER, an unflinching look at the world of men's volleyball, and it'll be hard for anyone who isn't interested in the sport to maintain an interest in this movie—which contains some great volleyball footage, but a rather predictable plotline. Michael Parks plays the tough-as-nails coach who turns a group of green kids into a lean, mean Olympic volleyball playin' machine. Along the way a few personal crises arise among the teammates, as well as some important matches against foreign opponents, but SPIKER never amounts to anything particularly memorable. Unlike other sports films, the emphasis isn't on a climactic Big Game, but on how tough it is to make the team and compete. The cast includes members of the US National Volleyball Team.

p, Roger Tilton; d, Roger Tilton; w, Marlene Matthews (based on a story by Roger Tilton, Marlene Matthews); ph, Robert A. Sherry; ed, Richard S. Brummer; m, Jeff Barry.

Volleyball   **(PR:C-O MPAA:R)**

SPINOUT**

(1966) 93m Euterpe/MGM c (GB: CALIFORNIA HOLIDAY)

Elvis Presley *(Mike McCoy)*, Shelley Fabares *(Cynthia Foxhugh)*, Diane McBain *(Diana St. Clair)*, Deborah Walley *(Les)*, Dodie Marshall *(Susan)*, Jack Mullaney *(Curly)*, Will Hutchins *(Lt. Tracy Richards)*, Warren Berlinger *(Philip Short)*, Jimmy Hawkins *(Larry)*, Carl Betz *(Howard Foxhugh)*, Cecil Kellaway *(Bernard Ranley)*, Una Merkel *(Violet Ranley)*, Frederic Worlock *(Blodgett)*, Dave Barry *(Harry)*.

Mike McCoy (Elvis Presley) is that common animal, a successful auto racer *and* rock singer. Naturally, he has more women than he can handle, including a spoiled millionairess (Shelley Fabares), a Helen Gurley Brown-ish author (Diane McBain), and the drummer in his band (Deborah Walley). Between songs, Mike manages to outrun the gals in his cool custom race cars, and eventually he hits upon a way to rid himself of their pesky attentions by marrying them off to various members of the supporting cast—although a last love interest turns up in the person of his new female drummer (Dodie Marshall). This one's okay if you like Elvis movies, but they all tend to blend together to the untrained eye. The big race was filmed at Dodger Stadium.

p, Joe Pasternak; d, Norman Taurog; w, Theodore J. Flicker, George Kirgo; ph, Daniel L. Fapp (Panavision, Metrocolor); ed, Rita Roland; m, George Stoll.

Auto Racing/Musical   **(PR:A MPAA:NR)**

SPIRIT OF NOTRE DAME, THE**

(1931) 80m UNIV bw (GB: VIGOUR OF YOUTH)

Lew Ayres *(Bucky O'Brien)*, William Bakewell *(Jim Stewart)*, Andy Devine *(Truck McCall)*, Harry Barris *(Wasp)*, Sally Blane *(Peggy)*, J. Farrell MacDonald *(Coach)*, Frank Carideo, Elmer Layden, Jim Crowley, Harry Stuhldreher, Adam Walsh, Paul "Bucky" O'Connor, Moon Mullins, Art McManmon, John O'Brien *(Themselves)*.

J. Farrell MacDonald plays legendary Notre Dame coach Knute Rockne in everything but name in this standard college football film, released only months after Rockne's tragic death and dedicated to his memory. The slim plot hinges on the conflict that arises between the inspiring coach and Bucky O'Brien (Lew Ayres), a freshman running back who becomes disenchanted when his game role shifts from carrying the ball to blocking for talented teammate Jim Stewart (William Bakewell). After refusing to do his job, Bucky finds himself in the stands when Notre Dame battles Army, but it should come as little surprise that when the chips are down and the Irish are down, Bucky is back in uniform, a team player at last. Re-creating more Rockne lore, Andy Devine plays the George Gipp-like Truck McCall, a player who is struggling against death in a hospital. A number of real-life former Irish players and coaches also appear as themselves, including Adam Walsh, Bucky O'Connor, Frank Carideo, John Law, and the Four Horsemen—Don Miller, Elmer Layden, Jim Crowley, and Harry Stuhldreher.

SPIRIT OF NOTRE DAME, THE—

p, Carl Laemmle, Jr.; d, Russell Mack; w, Christy Walsh, Walter DeLeon (based on the story by Richard Schayer, Dale Van Every); ph, George Robinson; ed, Robert Carlisle.

Football/Biography (PR:A MPAA:NR)

SPIRIT OF STANFORD, THE*½

(1942) 74m COL bw

Frankie Albert *(Himself)*, Marguerite Chapman *(Fay Edwards)*, Matt Willis *(Link Wyman)*, Shirley Patterson *(June Rogers)*, Kay Harris *(Edna)*, Robert Stevens *(Cliff Bonnard)*, Lloyd Bridges *(Don Farrell)*, Forrest Tucker *(Buzz Costello)*, Billy Lechner *(Butch)*, Harold Landon *(Skeats)*, Volta Boyer *(Mrs. Bixby)*, Ernie Nevers *(Himself)*, Dale Van Sickel *(Frosh Backfield Coach)*, John Gallaudet *(Frosh Coach)*, Arthur Loft *(Varsity Coach)*, Jim Westerfield *(Man)*, Stanley Brown *(Kenny)*, Ed Laughton *(Assistant Coach)*, Ray Walker *(Duke Connors)*.

In the grand Hollywood tradition of gridiron heroes cast as themselves (Elroy Hirsch—CRAZYLEGS, ALL AMERICAN; Doc Blanchard and Glenn Davis—THE SPIRIT OF WEST POINT; Tom Harmon—HARMON OF MICHIGAN), one-time San Francisco Forty-Niner quarterback and Stanford All-American Frankie Albert stars in this reportedly autobiographical account of the turning point in his football career. Full of himself, Albert decides to quit school and turn pro just before the Cardinals' big game, but when his roommate takes ill, the southpaw slinger reconsiders and returns to the Stanford lineup. The film's title is equally appropriate for another Stanford great who makes a brief appearance here, Hall of Famer Ernie Nevers.

p, Sam White; d, Charles Barton; w, Howard J. Green, William Brent, Nick Lucats (based on a story by Brent, Lucats); ph, Franz Planer, Charles Stumar; ed, James Sweeney.

Football/Biography (PR:A MPAA:NR)

SPIRIT OF WEST POINT, THE**

(1947) 77m FC bw

Felix "Doc" Blanchard *(Himself)*, Glenn Davis *(Himself)*, Robert Shayne *(Col. Red Blaik)*, Anne Nagel *(Mrs. Blaik)*, Alan Hale, Jr. *(Oklahoma Cutter)*, George O'Hanlon *(Joe Wilson)*, Michael Browne *(Mileaway McCarty)*, Tanis Chandler *(Mildred)*, Mary Newton *(Mrs. Blanchard)*, William Forrest *(Dr. Blanchard)*, Lee Bennett *(Cabot)*, Mickey McCardle *(Quarterback)*, John Gallaudet *(Ferriss)*, Rudy Wissler *(Young Dr. Blanchard)*, Tom Harmon *(Himself)*, Bill Stern, Harry Wismer *(Sportscasters)*, Margaret Wells *(Mrs. Davis)*, Frank Parker *(Ralph Davis)*.

Army football greats Felix "Doc" Blanchard ("Mr. Inside") and Glenn Davis ("Mr. Outside") play themselves in this re-creation of their West Point glory years. The minimal plot is primarily an excuse to recap the highlights of the backfield duo's great career, and THE SPIRIT OF WEST POINT features plenty of actual game footage that captures the brilliant running that won Blanchard the 1945 Heisman Trophy and Davis the same award a year later.

The film was made while the recently graduated Cadets were on a 60-day leave before beginning active duty.

p, John W. Rogers, Harry Joe Brown; d, Ralph Murphy; w, Tom Reed (based on a story by Mary Howard); ph, Lester White; ed, Harvey Manger.

Football/Biography Cas. (PR:A MPAA:NR)

SPIRIT OF YOUTH*½

(1937) 65m GN bw

Joe Louis, Clarence Muse, Edna Harris, Mae Turner, Mantan Moreland, Cleo Desmond.

Shortly after beginning his reign as world heavyweight champion, Joe Louis starred with a predominantly black cast in this weak film about a young fighter's rise from the streets to Golden Gloves competition and eventually on to the big time. Along the way the fighter (Louis) becomes smitten with a nightclub singer, falls prey to the temptations of life in the fast lane, allows his training regimen to suffer, and loses his first fight as a result. After repenting, he makes a comeback and earns a title shot, though he takes a terrible beating from the champ until he spots his old girl friend (read: true love) in the stands and musters the stuff champions are made of. Though Louis hardly distinguishes himself as an actor here, he went on to appear in a number of other films, including JOE PALOOKA, CHAMP and THE SQUARE JUNGLE. The Brown Bomber's own story came to the screen in 1953 in the well-done JOE LOUIS STORY, in which look-alike Coley Wallace gives a fine portrayal of the champ.

p, Lew Golder; d, Harry Fraser; w, Arthur Hoerl.

Boxing Cas. (PR:A MPAA:NR)

SPLIT DECISIONS**½

(1988) 95m Wizan/New Century-Vista c

Craig Sheffer *(Eddie McGuinn)*, Jeff Fahey *(Ray McGuinn)*, Gene Hackman *(Dan McGuinn)*, John McLiam *(Pop McGuinn)*, Jennifer Beals *(Barbara Uribe)*, Eddie Velez *(Julian "Snake" Pedroza)*, Carmine Caridi *(Lou Rubia)*, James Tolkan *(Benny Platone)*.

SPLIT DECISIONS is a tedious low-budget boxing film that contains yet another sensitive performance by Gene Hackman, but that is crippled by its predictable script and phony, ROCKY-style ending. In the mean streets of New York City, young Eddie McGuinn (Craig Sheffer) is a Golden Gloves champ who has just been accepted into a prestigious university where he hopes to train and qualify for the 1988 Olympics. His trainer-father, Dan (Hackman), couldn't be prouder, for Eddie's success helps soothe the disappointment anger he feels toward his older boy, Ray (Jeff Fahey). Ray, who is also a boxer, rejected Dan's advice and went pro, signing with a sleazy manager. Now he fights several small-time bouts a month, with little to show for it but an increasingly scarred face. Dan has disinherited Ray, but Eddie still keeps tabs on his brother, and when Ray returns to town to promote a match with a dangerous Hispanic boxer nicknamed "Snake" (Eddie Velez), Eddie quickly becomes embroiled in his brother's dangerous world. With a plot straight out of an old Warner Bros. movie, SPLIT DECISIONS isn't terribly original and one wonders why it was made at all. Director David Drury (DEFENSE OF THE REALM), a onetime amateur boxer in England, brings nothing new to the material except the gritty realism that most low-budget movies rely on (because they have to shoot on actual locations), and, with the exception of Hackman's performance, most of the acting is unremarkable. An interesting family relationship begins to build among Dan and sons, but soon the film's melodramatic machinations take over and overwhelm the scant emotional nuance that had been established, while the plot requires that logic be thrown to the wind, with the last half of the film filled with so many implausibilities and plot holes that any credibility is lost.

p, Joe Wizan, Michael Borofsky, Todd Black; d, David Drury; w, David Fallon; ph, Timothy Suhrstedt (CFI color); ed, John W. Wheeler, Jeff Freeman, Thomas Stanford; m, Basil Poledouris.

Boxing (PR:O MPAA:R)

SPORT OF KINGS**

(1947) 68m COL bw

Paul Campbell (Tom Cloud), Gloria Henry (Doc Richardson), Harry Davenport (Maj. Denning), Mark Dennis (Biff Cloud), Harry Cheshire (Theodore McKeogh), Clinton Rosemond (Josiah), Louis Mason (Bertie), Oscar O'Shea (Judge Sellers), Ernest Anderson (Alf).

Yankee brothers Tom and Biff Cloud (Paul Campbell and Mark Dennis) find themselves in possession of a Kentucky plantation that their late father won in a bet with the previous owner, noted racehorse fancier Maj. Denning (Harry Davenport). Life isn't easy for the northerners, however, since the locals treat them badly. To smooth things over, the brothers bring the major back on the premises, pretending their father left him a trust fund. Eventually, the old man soon sees through this falsehood and makes plans to leave, until the brothers decide to enter the southern gentleman's horse in a big race, putting everyone on an equal footing. Southern California locations stand in for the Bluegrass state.

p, William Bloom; d, Robert Gordon; w, Edward Huebsch (based on a story by Gordon Grand); ph, Henry Freulich; ed, Aaron Stell.

Horse Racing (PR:A MPAA:NR)

SPORT PARADE, THE**

(1932) 67m RKO bw

Joel McCrea (Sandy Baker), William Gargan (Johnny Brown), Marian Marsh (Irene Stewart), Walter Catlett (Promoter Morrison), Richard "Skeets" Gallagher (Dizzy), Robert Benchley, Clarence Wilson, Ivan Linow.

Joel McCrea and William Gargan play former college football teammates and rivals in love, one of whom ends up becoming a sportswriter, giving the filmmakers an excuse to employ a "sport parade" of stock footage of various sporting events. The climax involves a wrestling championship.

d, Dudley Murphy; w, Corey Ford, Robert Benchley, Tom Wenning, Francis Cockrell (based on a story by Jerry Horwin); ph, J. Roy Hunt.

Football/Wrestling (PR:A MPAA:NR)

SPORTING BLOOD***

(1931) 82m MGM bw

Clark Gable (Tim Scanlon), Ernest Torrence (Jim Rellence), Madge Evans (Ruby), Lew Cody (Warren), Marie Prevost (Angela), Harry Holman (Phil Ludeking), J. Farrell MacDonald (Jerry Hardwick).

Horse breeder Jim Rellence (Ernest Torrence) sells his beloved Tommy Boy to Jerry Hardwick (J. Farrell MacDonald), who, after making a lot of money with the racehorse, sells him to Angela and Phil Ludeking (Marie Prevost and Harry Holman). The greedy pair work Tommy Boy hard, eventually entering the abused horse in a race he cannot win. Phil places a bet with Tip Scanlon (Clark Gable), hoping to win back the money he has lost, but instead loses Tommy Boy to Tip, who starts running the horse himself. At first he is honest, then he deliberately has Tommy Boy lose, and finally he plans to drug the horse. Two of his employees, Ruby (Madge Evans)—who is romantically linked with Tip—and Warren (Lew Cody), deplore this treatment of Tommy Boy, and when he loses a big race, putting Tip in trouble with some gangsters, Tip transfers ownership to Madge, who returns the horse to his loving original owner, Jim. The breeder then restores Tommy Boy to condition for the Churchill Downs finale, in which all the horse's abusers get their comeuppance. Gable, sans mustache, moved from supporting to featured player with this film. Trivia buffs will note the cameo appearance of then-Vice President Charles Curtis (under Herbert Hoover) at the track, dutifully pointed out for filmgoers by the announcer.

d, Charles Brabin; w, Willard Mack, Wanda Tuchock (based on the novel Horseflesh by Frederick Hazlitt Brennan); ph, Harold Rosson; ed, William Gray.

Horse Racing (PR:A MPAA:NR)

SPORTING BLOOD**

(1940) 82m MGM bw

Robert Young (Myles Vanders), Maureen O'Sullivan (Linda Lockwood), Lewis Stone (Davis Lockwood), William Gargan (Duffy), Lynne Carver (Joan Lockwood), Clarence Muse (Jeff), Lloyd Corrigan (Otis Winfield), George Reed (Stonewall), Tom Kennedy (Grantly), Russell Hicks ("Sneak" O'Brien), George Lessey (Banker Cobb), William Tannen (Ted Milner), Helene Millard (Martha Winfield), Allen Wood (Jockey), Eugene Jackson (Sam).

Robert Young plays Myles Vanders, a none-too-honest stable owner who returns to his run-down Virginia family home and rekindles a long-standing family feud with racing rival Davis Lockwood (Lewis Stone). Despite this enmity,

Myles begins romancing one of Lockwood's daughters (Lynne Carver). He is dumped by daughter no. 1, then marries daughter no. 2, Linda (Maureen O'Sullivan), primarily to get the old man's goat. When Myles' prize pony is injured in a stable fire, he enters Linda's horse in the big race, in which it goes against her daddy's best steed. Luckily, Myles has become a nicer guy by this time, ready to reconcile with the Lockwood patriarch after the climactic final contest.

p, Albert E. Levoy; d, S. Sylvan Simon; w, Lawrence Hazard, Albert Mannheimer, Dorothy Yost (based on a story by Grace Norton); ph, Sidney Wagner; ed, Frank Sullivan; m, Franz Waxman.

Horse Racing   (PR:A   MPAA:NR)

SPORTING CHANCE*½

(1931) 63m Peerless bw

Buster Collier, Jr. *(Terry Nolan)*, Claudia Dell *(Mary Bascom)*, James Hall *(Phillip Lawrence)*, Eugene Jackson *(Horseshoes)*, Joseph Levering *(Phillip Lawrence)*, Henry Roquemore *(Mullins)*, Hedwiga Reicher *(Aunt Hetty)*, Mahlon Hamilton *(Buddy)*.

Romance blossoms at the stable between Terry and Mary (Buster Collier, Jr., and Claudia Dell), with James Hall lending support as a young rich ne'er-do-well and Eugene Jackson providing dubious comic relief as "Horseshoes," a black stableboy. The film's makers claimed to have lensed the first steeplechase ever staged for the talking screen in SPORTING CHANCE, but fast-motion photography mars this minor landmark.

p, Albert Herman; d, Albert Herman; w, King Baggott.

Horse Racing   (PR:A   MPAA:NR)

SPORTING LOVE**

(1936, Brit.) 70m Hammer/BL bw

Stanley Lupino *(Percy Brace)*, Laddie Cliff *(Peter Brace)*, Henry Carlisle *(Lord Dimsdale)*, Eda Peel *(Maud Dane)*, Bobbie Comber *(Gerald Dane)*, Clarissa Selwyne *(Aunty Fanny)*, Lu Ann Meredith *(Nellie Gray)*, Wyn Weaver *(Wilfred Wimple)*.

Percy and Peter Brace (Stanley Lupino and Laddie Cliff) are young stable owners swamped with debts. Their bid to win the English Derby only sinks them further, so they seek help from their rich aunt, but must pretend they've gotten married in order to loosen her purse strings. This adaptation of a British stage hit by star Lupino complements its racetrack milieu with singing, dancing, and large doses of farce.

p, H. Fraser Passmore; d, J. Elder Wills; w, Fenn Sherie, Ingram D'Abbes (based on the play by Stanley Lupino); ph, Eric Cross.

Horse Racing/
Comedy/Musical   (PR:A   MPAA:NR)

SPRING FEVER*½

(1983, Can.) 100m Amulet/Comworld c

Susan Anton *(Stevie Castle)*, Frank Converse *(Louis Corman)*, Jessica Walter *(Celia Berryman)*, Stephen Young *(Neil Berryman)*, Carling Bassett *(Karen Castle)*, David Mall *(Beechman)*, Lisa Brady *(Rhoda)*, Barbara Cook *(Chris)*, Maria Hontzas *(Bunny)*, Alan Fawcett *(Roger)*, Derrick Jones *(Scotty)*, Lisa Foster *(Lena)*, Brian Crabb *(Ralph)*, Martin Schecter *(Umpire)*, Stephen Shellin *(Andy)*, Shawn Foltz *(Melissa Berryman)*.

This behind-the-scenes look at a group of young competitors in a girls' junior tennis championship and their parents focuses on 13-year-old Karen Castle (Carling Bassett), an unseeded contestant who is snubbed because of her Las Vegas showgirl mom (Susan Anton). She eventually establishes a friendship with Missy (Shawn Foltz), the top-seeded daughter of rich bitch Celia Berryman (Jessica Walter), although the girls' affections are tested when they are pitted against each other in the tournament finals.

p, John F. Bassett; d, Joseph L. Scanlan; w, Fred Stefan, Stuart Gillard; ph, Donald Wilder (Film House Color); ed, Kirk Jones, Tony Lower; m, Fred Mollin.

Tennis   Cas.   (PR:C   MPAA:PG)

SQUARE JUNGLE, THE**½

(1955) 86m UNIV bw

Tony Curtis *(Eddie Quaid/Packy Glennon)*, Pat Crowley *(Julie Walsh)*, Ernest Borgnine *(Bernie Browne)*, Paul Kelly *(Jim McBride)*, Jim Backus *(Pat Quaid)*, Leigh Snowden *(Lorraine Evans)*, John Day *(Al Gorski)*, David Janssen *(Jack Lindsay)*, John Marley *(Tommy Dillon)*, Barney Phillips *(Dan Selby)*, Joseph Vitale *(Tony Anderson)*, Wendell Niles *(Chicago Ring Announcer)*, Kay Stewart *(Mrs. Gorski)*, Frank Marlowe *(Rip Kane)*, Frankie Van, Walter Ekwart *(Seconds)*, Joe Louis *(Himself)*.

Tony Curtis plays Eddie Quaid, a young man who turns to the ring to raise enough money to post bail for his father (Jim Backus) so that he can get out of jail. Though he originally wanted the money to help his dad, he ends up winning the middleweight crown. Ernest Borgnine plays the gentle and reserved trainer who guides Eddie's fighting career. In the final title bout, Eddie badly beats his opponent and then is overcome with guilt. While the main story is the stuff of standard boxing melodramas, THE SQUARE JUNGLE does highlight the dilemma of the referee, who is booed, jeered, and otherwise pressured into letting fights continue despite the risk to the boxers' lives. Good performances, especially by Borgnine as the surprisingly intellectual trainer and John Marley as the referee, help to provide freshness. Heavyweight champ Joe Louis also makes a guest appearance.

p, Albert Zugsmith; d, Jerry Hopper; w, George Zuckerman (based on a story by Zuckerman); ph, George Robinson; ed, Paul Weatherwax; m, Heinz Roemheld.

Boxing   (PR:A   MPAA:NR)

SQUARE RING, THE***

(1953, Brit.) 73m EAL/REP bw

Jack Warner *(Danny Felton)*, Robert Beatty *(Kid Curtis)*, Bill Owen *(Happy Burns)*, Maxwell Reed *(Rick Martell)*, George Rose *(Whitey Johnson)*, Bill Travers *(Rowdie Rawlings)*, Alfie Bass *(Frank Forbes)*, Ronald Lewis *(Eddie Lloyd)*, Sidney James *(Adams)*, Joan Collins *(Frankie)*, Kay Kendall *(Eve Lewis)*, Bernadette O'Farrell *(Peg Curtis)*, Eddie Byrne *(Lou Lewis)*, Vic Wise *(Joe)*, Michael Golden *(Warren)*, Joan Sims *(Bunty)*.

This boxing saga involves five different stories that take place mainly in the dressing room prior to and after various bouts. The film concentrates on the characters who have taken to the ring for one reason or another, and what the night's fights mean to them. One boxer, Kid Curtis (Robert Beatty), is estranged from his wife, and dies after taking a savage beating. Based on a stage play, the film is somewhat similar to THE SET-UP in that much of the action revolves around the locker room, where the audience is allowed a glimpse at the lives and dreams of several different fighters. Director Basil Dearden keeps the film moving at a tight pace and the boxing scenes are appropriately gritty. Look for a young Joan Collins as the girl friend of one of the boxers.

p, Michael Relph, Basil Dearden; d, Michael Relph, Basil Dearden; w, Robert Westerby, Peter Myers, Alec Grahame (based on the play by Ralph W. Peterson); ph, Otto Heller, Gordon Dines; ed, Peter Bezencenet; m, Dock Mathieson.

Boxing (PR:A MPAA:NR)

SQUEEZE PLAY*

(1978) 92m Troma c

Jim Harris *(Wes)*, Jenni Hetrick *(Samantha)*, Rick Gitlin *(Fred)*, Helen Campitelli *(Jamie)*, Rick Kahn *(Tom)*, Diana Valentien *(Maureen)*, Alford Corley *(Buddy)*, Melissa Michaels *(Mary Lou)*, Michael P. Morgan *(Bozo)*, Sonya Jennings *(Max)*, Sharon Kyle Bramblett *(Midge)*, Zachary *(Pop)*, Tony Hoty *(Koch)*, Lisa Beth Wolf *(Rose)*, Brenda Kaplan·*(Brenda)*.

This offensive film uses softball as an excuse to display body parts and tell dirty jokes. The thin plot concerns a group of girls, abandoned by their sports-loving boy friends, who form their own team, the Beaverettes, to get even. All the problems between the sexes are worked out on the playing field. It's supposed to be a comedy.

p, Lloyd Kaufman, Michael Herz; d, Samuel Weil; w, Haim Pekelis, Charles Kaufman; ph, Lloyd Kaufman; ed, George T. Norris.

Baseball/Comedy Cas. (PR:O MPAA:R)

STAY HUNGRY***½

(1976) 102m UA c

Jeff Bridges *(Craig Blake)*, Sally Field *(Mary Tate Farnsworth)*, Arnold Schwarzenegger *(Joe Santo)*, R.G. Armstrong *(Thor Erickson)*, Robert Englund *(Franklin)*, Helena Kallianiotes *(Anita)*, Robert E. Mosley *(Newton)*, Woodrow Parfrey *(Craig's Uncle)*, Scatman Crothers *(Butler)*, Kathleen Miller *(Dorothy Stephens)*, Fannie Flagg *(Amy Walterson)*, Joanna Cassidy *(Joe Mason)*, Richard Gilliland *(Hal Foss)*, Ed Begley, Jr. *(Lester)*, Dennis Fimple *(Bubba)*, Mayf Nutter *(Packman)*, Joe Spinell .

Bodybuilding and class consciousness are at the center of this moody, insightful, and frequently funny film based on a novel by Charles Gaines and directed by Bob Rafelson (FIVE EASY PIECES). Set in Birmingham, Alabama, it features Jeff Bridges as Craig Blake, the scion of a wealthy Mountain Brook family who becomes involved in a real estate deal masterminded by Jabo (Joe Spinell). One of the properties blocking the development project is a health club, which Craig visits in the hope of finding a way to persuade its owner, Thor Erickson (wonderfully played by R.G. Armstrong), to sell. In the process, however, Craig immerses himself in the world of bodybuilding, becoming friends with Joe Santo (Arnold Schwarzenegger, in his first film role), who is training for the Mr. Universe contest, and failing in love with Mary Tate Farnsworth (Sally Field), a working-class miss who questions the slumming rich kid's sincerity. Craig tries to walk a tightrope between his two worlds, but when matters become too complex, he is forced to choose. As he did in FIVE EASY PIECES, Rafelson explores the issue of class in the US, contrasting Craig's privileged, pretentious friends with the more down-to-earth denizens of The Olympic Spa, but at the same time saving his most telling censure for Craig's condescending attitude toward his new friends. Filled with interesting characters and strong performances, STAY HUNGRY not only makes its point about class prejudice, but presents a detailed portrait of southern country club culture and the bodybuilding milieu that would be so deftly captured in Schwarzenegger's next film, the fine documentary PUMPING IRON (1977).

p, Harold Schneider, Bob Rafelson; d, Bob Rafelson; w, Bob Rafelson, Charles Gaines (based on the novel by Gaines); ph, Victor J. Kemper (DeLuxe Color); ed, John F. Link II; m, Bruce Langehorne, Byron Berline.

Weightlifting Cas. (PR:O MPAA:R)

STEADY COMPANY**

(1932) 65m UNIV bw

Norman Foster, June Clyde, ZaSu Pitts, Henry Armetta, Maurice Black, J. Farrell MacDonald, Morgan Wallace, Jack Perry, Morrie Cohan, Willard Robertson.

Love and boxing mix in this minor programmer from Universal Studios. After getting badly beaten in a match, an up-and-coming pugster takes the advice of a promoter and accepts safer bouts. This pleases everyone involved, including the girl who holds the key to the fighter's heart. Typically sappy nonsense, done over and over again throughout film history.

d, Edward Ludwig; w, Earle Snell (based on a story by Edward I. Luddy); ph, Charles Stumar.

Boxing (PR:A MPAA:NR)

STEALING HOME*

(1988) 98m Mount/WB c

Mark Harmon (Billy Wyatt as an Adult), Blair Brown (Ginny Wyatt), Jodie Foster (Katie Chandler), Jonathan Silverman (Alan Appleby as a Teen), Harold Ramis (Alan Appleby as an Adult), John Shea (Sam Wyatt), William McNamara (Billy Wyatt as a Teen), Thatcher Goodwin (Billy Wyatt as a Child), Judith Kahan (Laura Appleby), Miriam Flynn (Mrs. Parks), Christine Jones (Grace Chandler), Richard Jenkins (Hank Chandler).

Structured in a series of confusing flashbacks, STEALING HOME focuses on Billy Wyatt (Mark Harmon), a thirtysomething failure who could have been somebody—namely a star with the Philadelphia Phillies. In a bush league game, Billy steals home in the bottom of the ninth to give his team a victory, and is spotted by a Phillies scout, who promises him a big future. Mom and Dad (Blair Brown and John Shea) have been hoping for a college education for their boy, but the prospect of having a major leaguer in the family changes their minds. When Dad is killed in a car wreck, Billy puts away his bat and glove. The film opens some 15 years later, as the sleepy-eyed, unshaven Billy gets a call from Mom informing him that his closest childhood friend, Katie Chandler (Jodie Foster), six years his senior, has just killed herself. "Come home," says Mom, and since "stealing home" was once his specialty, Billy agrees. Along the way he smokes cigarettes, looks longingly out the train window at those delicate memories of his past, and remembers Katie. He also does much reminiscing with former pal Alan Appleby (Harold Ramis), who now runs a sporting goods store in town. A onetime star quarterback at UCLA, Mark Harmon isn't bad here, it's just that he isn't given a darned thing to do. Not even Thom Mount and Bobby Byrne, producer and cinematographer, respectively, of the far superior BULL DURHAM, could save this mess.

p, Thom Mount, Hank Moonjean; d, Steven Kampmann, Will Aldis; w, Steven Kampmann, Will Aldis; ph, Bobby Byrne (Technicolor); ed, Anthony Gibbs; m, David Foster.

Baseball   Cas.   (PR:C   MPAA:PG-13)

STING II, THE*

(1983) 102m UNIV c

Jackie Gleason (Condorff), Mac Davis (Hooker), Teri Garr (Veronica), Karl Malden (Macalinski), Oliver Reed (Lonnegan), Bert Remsen (Kid Colors), Kathalina Veniero (Blonde with Kid Colors), Jose Perez (Carlos), Larry Bishop (Gallecher), Ron Rifkin (Eddie), Harry James (Bandleader), Frances Bergen (Lady Dorsett), Monica Lewis (Band Singer), Danie-Wade Dalton (Messenger), Val Avery (O'Malley), Cassandra Peterson (O'Malley's Girl), Jill Jaress (Gertie), Al Robertson (Redcap), Bob O'Connell (Clancy), John Hancock (Doc Brown), Larry Hankin (Handicap), Jerry Whitney (Page Boy), Michael Alldredge (Big Ohio), Danny Dayton (Ring Announcer), Tim Rossovich (Typhoon Taylor), Marty Denkin (Referee), Rex Pierson (Healy).

This repulsive sequel to George Roy Hill's THE STING is

harmed irreparably by the performances of Jackie Gleason and Mac Davis, neither of whom come anywhere near acquitting himself well in the inevitable Newman and Redford comparisons, as a couple of cons. The pair scheme to strike it rich with a boxing scam involving a nightclub owner (Karl Malden) and a likeable young woman (Teri Garr, delivering the only bright piece of acting in sight). The usual twists and turns follow, without wit or humor. It was scripted by David S. Ward, who also wrote the original, but added nothing new or special to this sequel. Former footballer Tim Rossovich plays a boxer named Typhoon Taylor, and Cassandra Peterson, best known for her television character "Elvira," has a small part.

p, Jennings Lang; d, Jeremy Paul Kagan; w, David S. Ward; ph, Bill Butler (Technicolor); ed, David Garfield; m, Lalo Schifrin.

Boxing/Comedy   Cas.   (PR:C   MPAA:PG)

STOCK CAR*½

(1955, Brit.) 68m Balblair/BUT bw

Paul Carpenter (Larry Duke), Rona Anderson (Katie Glebe), Susan Shaw (Gina), Harry Fowler (Monty Albright), Robert Rietty (Roberto), Paul Whitsun-Jones (Turk McNeil), Sabrina (Trixie), Alma Taylor (Nurse Sprott), Lorrae Desmond (Singer), Eve Raymond, Frank Thornton.

This stock-car movie runs in low gear and out of gas before the opening credits finish rolling. The British racing tale follows Katie Glebe (Rona Anderson) as she battles to keep her father's garage open after he is killed in a race. She gets some help from American racer Larry Duke (Paul Carpenter), but runs into a roadblock in Turk McNeil (Paul Whitsun-Jones), an unsympathetic creditor who wants to foreclose on the garage. Turk gets even angrier when his girl, Gina (Susan Shaw), takes a liking to Larry. While attempting to get rid of the competition Larry gets beaten up and nearly dies in a rigged race. As movie heroes are known to do, Larry makes a comeback to win the big race and walks off with the girl.

p, A.R. Rawlinson; d, Wolf Rilla; w, A.R. Rawlinson, Victor Lyndon; ph, Geoffrey Faithfull.

Auto Racing   (PR:A   MPAA:NR)

STORY OF SEABISCUIT, THE**½

(1949) 93m WB c (GB: PRIDE OF KENTUCKY)

Shirley Temple (Margaret O'Hara), Barry Fitzgerald (Shawn O'Hara), Lon McCallister (Ted Knowles), Rosemary De Camp (Mrs. Howard), Donald MacBride (George Carson), Pierre Watkin (Charles S. Howard), William Forrest (Thomas Millford), "Sugarfoot" Anderson (Murphy), William Cartledge (Jockey George Woolf), Gertrude Astor (Wife), Creighton Hale (Husband), Ral Erlenborn (Cameraman), Gil Warren (Radio Announcer).

A pleasant, harmless film, THE STORY OF SEABISCUIT brings to the screen the legendary horse in a fictionalized account. Shirley Temple plays Margaret O'Hara, the Irish niece of trainer Shawn O'Hara (Barry Fitzgerald), who roots her uncle's champion horse to victory and finds spare time to romance jockey Ted Knowles (Lon McCallister). William J. Cartledge is cast as jockey George Woolf, who rode Seabiscuit to a number of victories. The film includes three documentary segments of Seabiscuit in action—one on the track at Pimlico against War Admiral, and another in 1940's Santa Anna Handicap.

p, William Jacobs; d, David Butler; w, John Taintor Foote (based on the story by Foote); ph, Wilfrid M. Cline (Technicolor); ed, Irene Morra; m, David Buttolph.

Horse Racing (PR:A MPAA:NR)

STRAIGHTAWAY*

(1934) 60m COL bw

Tim McCoy, Sue Carol, William Bakewell, Ward Bond, Lafe McKee, Francis McDonald, Samuel S. Hinds, Arthur Rankin, Charles Sullivan.

Tim McCoy finds himself in a bind when he is threatened with a murder rap if his younger brother takes the checkered flag at an upcoming auto race. Filled with stock footage of endless cars lapping each other and crashing off walls, ineptly edited with shots of the principals, STRAIGHTAWAY is only worthwhile for its glimpses of the raceways at Indianapolis, Altoona, Providence, Elgin, and Utica.

d, Otto Brower; w, Lambert Hillyer (based on a story by Hillyer); ph, Dan Clark; ed, Otto Mayer.

Auto Racing (PR:A MPAA:NR)

STRATTON STORY, THE***½

(1949) 106m MGM bw

James Stewart (Monty Stratton), June Allyson (Ethel Stratton), Frank Morgan (Barney Wile), Agnes Moorehead (Ma Stratton), Bill Williams (Gene Watson), Bruce Cowling (Ted Lyons), Eugene Bearden (Western All-Stars Pitcher), Bill Dickey, Jimmy Dykes (Themselves), Cliff Clark (Higgins), Mary Lawrence (Dot), Dean White (Luke Appling), Robert Gist (Larnie), Mervyn Shea (White Sox Catcher), Mitchell Lewis (Conductor), Michael Ross (Pitcher), Florence Lake (Mrs. Appling), Anne Nagel (Mrs. Piet), Barbara Woodell (Mrs. Shea), Holmes Herbert (Doctor), Roy Partee (Western Pitcher), Kenneth Tobey (Detroit Player), Pat Flaherty (Western Manager), Capt. F.G. Somers (Giants Manager), Fred Millican (All-Star Catcher), John Kerr (Yankee Coach), Dwight Adams, George Vico, Lou Novikoff (Detroit Ball Players).

Directed by Sam Wood (PRIDE OF THE YANKEES), this is the true story of pitcher Monty Stratton's heroic return to professional baseball after his leg had been amputated as the result of a hunting accident. Although some liberties are taken with the story to make it play on-screen, the film doesn't stray too far from the facts. Stratton (James Stewart) is pitching in a semipro game in Texas when Barney Wile (Frank Morgan), a one-time baseball player but now a jobless hobo, recognizes his raw talent. Stratton likes the idea of hurling in the majors, and Barney offers to instruct him in the fine points that separate sandlotters from stars. The pair hitchhikes to California, where the White Sox are holding their training camp. White Sox manager Jimmy Dykes (playing himself) lets Stratton try out and the lanky right-hander is so impressive that he's given a contract. After a couple of superb years, it looks as though a great future is in store for the pitcher, until he accidentally shoots himself in the leg. With a prosthesis, Stratton learns to walk again, and then gets back into form on the pitching mound. This inspiring picture about a man who wouldn't give up (and who acted as the film's technical advisor) also features appearances by the Yankee great Bill Dickey and pitcher Gene Bearden as themselves.

p, Jack Cummings; d, Sam Wood; w, Douglas Morrow, Guy Trosper (based on a story by Morrow); ph, Harold Rosson; ed, Ben Lewis.

Baseball/Biography (PR:AA MPAA:NR)

STREETS OF GOLD***

(1986) 95m Roundhouse FOX c

Klaus Maria Brandauer (Alek Neuman), Adrian Pasdar (Timmy Boyle), Wesley Snipes (Roland Jenkins), Angela Molina (Elena Gitman), Elya Baskin (Klebanov), Rainbow Harvest (Brenda), Adam Nathan (Grisha), John Mahoney (Linehan), Jaroslav Stremien (Malinovsky), Dan O'Shea (Vinnie), Mike Beach (Sonny), John McCurry (Bobby Rainey), Jim Nickerson (Suvorov), Jeff Ward (Preston), Pete Antico (Balsamo), Dan Nutu (Semyon), Liya Glaz (Polina), Elizbieta Czyzewska (Mrs. Peshkov), Yacov Levitan (Mr. Peshkov).

Without Klaus Maria Brandauer's brilliantly nuanced performance, STREETS OF GOLD might easily have been just another predictable boxing film; with it, this story of a Russian immigrant who trains two young New Yorkers to fight against the Soviet national team is something considerably more. Alek Neuman (Brandauer), a onetime national champion who was prohibited from fighting for the Soviet Union in the Olympics because he is Jewish, emigrates to Brooklyn's Brighton Beach. After "living in Russia like an American," he now lives in "America like a Russian," working as a dish washer, and, disillusioned, he begins drinking heavily. Eventually, however, Alek begins coaching Timmy Boyle (Adrian Pasdar), a tough Irish kid, and Roland Jenkins (Wesley Snipes), an immensely gifted black fighter. Initially, Alek's charges can't stand each other, but while training together they grow close, and when Roland is hurt in a nightclub fracas and unable to fight in the US-Soviet match, his and Alek's hopes ride on Timmy's fists. Although the plot of STREETS OF GOLD offers few surprises and its rock-scored montage training sequences might have been lifted from any number of similar films, director Joe Roth does a nice job of capturing the feel of Brighton Beach's Russian community, and the relationship between the two fighters (capably portrayed by Pasdar and Snipes) and Alek is interesting if not always compelling. Brandauer, however, takes what probably would have been an interesting character and makes it a fascinating one, bringing complexity, depth, and an understated sense of humor to Alek, adding just the right spin to otherwise un-memorable lines.

p, Joe Roth, Harry Ufland; d, Joe Roth; w, Heywood Gould, Richard Price, Tom Cole (based on a story by Dezso Magyar); ph, Arthur Albert (Panavision, Deluxe Color); ed, Richard Chew; m, Jack Nitzsche.

Boxing   **Cas.**   **(PR:C   MPAA:R)**

STROKER ACE*½

(1983) 96m UNIV/WB c

Burt Reynolds (Stroker Ace), Ned Beatty (Clyde Torkle), Jim Nabors (Lugs), Parker Stevenson (Aubrey James), Loni Anderson (Pembrook Feeney), John Byner (Doc Seegle), Frank O. Hill (Dad Seegle), Cassandra Peterson (Girl with Lugs), Bubba Smith (Arnold), Warren Stevens (Jim Catty), Alfie Wise (Charlie), Jim Lewis (Crew Chief), Jonathan Williams (Man), Donna Fowler (Reporter), Hunter Bruce (Little Ace), Cary Guffey (Little Doc), Linda Vaughn (Miss Hurst Shifter), Kyle Petty, Tim Richmond, Ricky Rudd, Cale Yarborough (Nascar Drivers), Chris Economaki, Ken Squier (Announcers).

Burt Reynolds hits new lows as he mugs his way through this film, playing Stroker Ace, a race-car driver who's under the control of chicken-franchise owner Clyde Torkle (Ned Beatty). His love interest is Pembrook Feeney (Loni Anderson, the future Mrs. Reynolds), a squeaky-clean virgin. Reynolds also teams up with old pal director Hal Needham, in a script filled with "good ol' boy" humor and car crackups. Most of the fun comes from trying to spot real-life racing luminaries, including drivers Dale Earnhardt, Benny Parsons, Kyle Petty, Cale Yarborough and television announcers Chris Economaki, David Hobbs, and Ken Squier.

p, Hank Moonjean; d, Hal Needham; w, Hal Needham, Hugh Wilson (based on the novel *Stand On It* by William Neely, Robert K. Ottum); ph, Nick McLean (Technicolor); ed, Carl Kress, William Gordean; m, Al Capps.

Auto Racing   **Cas.**   **(PR:C   MPAA:PG)**

SUNDAY PUNCH**½

(1942) 76m MGM bw

William Lundigan (Ken Burke), Jean Rogers (Judy Galestrum), Dan Dailey (Olaf Jensen), Guy Kibbee (Pops Muller), J Carrol Naish (Matt Basler), Connie Gilchrist (Ma Galesu.) Sam Levene (Roscoe), Leo Gorcey (Biff), Rags Ragland (Killer), Douglass Newland (Baby Fitzroy), Anthony Caruso (Nat Cucci), Tito Renaldo (Jose), Michael Browne (Al), Dane Clark (Bill), Dick Wessel (Moxie), Dave Willock (Milkman), Lester Matthews (Smith), Ava Gardner (Ringsider).

Living in a boardinghouse full of boxers can have its un-usual moments, as chorine Judy Galestrum (Jean Rogers) discovers. Ken Burke (William Lundigan) is one of the fighters, and ends up getting knocked out by Olaf Jensen (Dan Dailey), a Swedish janitor-turned-pug. However, it's the man on the mat who wins the girl's heart, rather than

the champ, in this entertaining minor boxing comedy. Watch for a young Ava Gardner in a ringside seat.

p, Irving Starr; d, David Miller; w, Fay Kanin, Michael Kanin, Allen Rivkin (based on a story by the Kanins); ph, Paul C. Vogel; ed, Albert Akst.

Boxing/Comedy   **(PR:A   MPAA:NR)**

SUNNY SKIES*

(1930) 75m TIF bw

Benny Rubin (Benny Krantz), Marceline Day (Mary Norris), Rex Lease (Jim Grant), Marjorie "Babe" Kane (Doris), Greta Granstedt (College Widow), Wesley Barry (Sturrle), Robert Randall (Dave), James Wilcox (Smith).

It's the usual hokum about college kids and the big game: Jim Grant (Rex Lease) is a student who donates some blood to save the life of his Jewish roommate, Benny Krantz (Benny Rubin). The next day, Jim is out on the foot-ball field, winning the big game despite his weakened con-dition. Oddly enough, this sappy nonsense is a musical comedy. Suffering from a low budget and some unfortu-nate humor derived from ethnic stereotyping, SUNNY SKIES has developed a reputation as being among the worst of the spate of collegiate musicals that hit the screens in the early 1930s.

d, Norman Taurog; w, Earle Snell, George Cleveland (based on a story by A.P. Younger); ph, Paul Meyers, Arthur Reeves; ed, Clarence Kolster.

Football   **(PR:A   MPAA:NR)**

SWEEPSTAKES**

(1931) 75m RKO-Pathe bw

Eddie Quillan (Bud Doyle), James Gleason (Sleepy Jones), Marian Nixon (Babe Ellis), Lew Cody (Wally Weber), Paul Hurst (Bartender), Fred Burton (Pop Blake), King Baggott (Weber's Trainer), Billy Sullivan (Speed Martin), Lillian Leighton (Ma Clancy), Mike Donlin (The Dude).

Bud Doyle (Eddie Quillan) is a jockey unfairly barred from racing and left with no other choice but to become a sing-ing waiter in Tijuana. He manages to get himself back in the saddle again, however, winning the climactic race. His horse always gives an extra burst of speed when he hol-lers, "Whoop-tee-do," so Bud does this often and loudly. This is a silly little programmer, though Quillan handles his comedy role in a good fashion. As horse-race pictures go, SWEEPSTAKES has some relatively realistic race foot-age.

p, Charles E. Rogers; d, Albert Rogell; w, Lew Lipton, Ralph F. Murray (based on a story by Lipton); ph, Edward Snyder; ed, Joe Kane.

Horse Racing/
Comedy   **(PR:A   MPAA:NR)**

SWELLHEAD, THE**

(1930) 70m TIF bw

James Gleason *(Johnny Trump)*, Johnny Walker *(Bill "Cyclone" Hickey)*, Marion Shilling *(Mamie Judd)*, Natalie Kingston *(Barbara Larkin)*, Paul Hurst *(Mugsy)*, Freeman Wood *(Clive Warren)*, Lillian Elliott *(Mrs. Callahan)*.

THE SWELLHEAD is a simple story about a factory girl, Mamie Judd (Marion Shilling), who falls in love with Bill "Cyclone" Hickey (Johnny Walker), an overconfident, underimpressive prizefighter. Mamie engages sportswriter Johnny Trump (James Gleason) to manage the boxer, but Cyclone's attitude causes his new manager to walk out and the boxer's career takes a nosedive. Trump is finally persuaded to return and Cyclone begins to win again, paving the way for the romantic clinch between the boxer and his girl.

d, James Flood; w, Richard Cahoon, Adele Buffington, James Gleason (based on the story "Cyclone Hickey" by A.P. Younger); ph, Jackson Rose, Arthur Reeves; ed, Richard Cahoon.

Boxing   (PR:A   MPAA:NR)

SWING FEVER*½

(1943) 80m MGM bw

Kay Kyser *(Lowell Blackford)*, Marilyn Maxwell *(Ginger Gray)*, William Gargan *(Waltzy Malone)*, Nat Pendleton *(Killer Kennedy)*, Maxie Rosenbloom *(Rags)*, Curt Bois *(Nick)*, Morris Ankrum *(Dan Conlon)*, Andrew Tombes *(Clyde L. Star)*, Lou Nova *(Kid Mandell)*, Clyde Fillmore *(Mr. Nagen)*, Ish Kabibble *(Ish)*, Pamela Blake *(Lois)*, Lena Horne, The Kay Kyser Orchestra, Sully Mason, Julie Conway, Trudy Irwin *(Themselves)*.

Lowell Blackford (Kay Kyser), a young composer with a talent for hypnotizing people, is tricked by former singer Ginger Gray (Marilyn Maxwell) into using this skill on a boxer in order to fix a fight. The eclectic cast includes former pro wrestler Mike Mazurki, former boxer Maxie Rosembloom, comics Ish Kabibble and Mantan Moreland, Ava Gardner, Lena Horne, and Merriel Abbott and Her Abbott Dancers. Definitely not one of the finer MGM musicals.

p, Irving Starr; d, Tim Whelan; w, Nat Perrin, Warren Wilson (based on a story by Matt Brooks, Joseph Hoffman); ph, Charles Rosher; ed, Ferris Webster.

Boxing/Comedy/
Musical   (PR:A   MPAA:NR)

SWING THAT CHEER*½

(1938) 63m UNIV bw

Tom Brown *(Bob Potter)*, Robert Wilcox *(Larry Royal)*, Andy Devine *(Doc Saunders)*, Constance Moore *(Marian Stuart)*, Ernest Truex *(Prof. Peabody)*, Margaret Early *(Betty Wilson)*, Raymond Parker *(Jay Hill)*, Samuel S. Hinds *(Coach McGann)*, Stanley Hughes *(Winston)*, Doodles Weaver *(Bennett)*, David Oliver *(Intern)*.

Gridiron teammates and off-field best pals Bob (Tom Brown) and Larry (Robert Wilcox) suffer a rift in this comedy when the fullback gets all cheers, while his blocking buddy remains in his shadow. The latter decides to fake an injury to show the world the team can't do without him, then leaves the bench just in time to snatch big-game victory from the jaws of defeat.

p, Max H. Golden; d, Harold Schuster; w, Charles Grayson, Lee Loeb (based on a story by Thomas Ahearn, F. Maury Grossman); ph, Elwood Bredell; ed, Edward Curtiss.

Football/Comedy   (PR:A   MPAA:NR)

SWING YOUR LADY**

(1938) 72m WB bw

Humphrey Bogart *(Ed Hatch)*, Penny Singleton *(Cookie Shannon)*, Frank McHugh *(Popeye Bronson)*, Louise Fazenda *(Sadie Horn)*, Nat Pendleton *(Joe "Hercules" Skopapoulos)*, Allen Jenkins *(Shiner Ward)*, Leon Weaver *(Waldo Davis)*, Frank Weaver *(Ollie Davis)*, Loretta "Elviry" Weaver *(Mrs. Davis)*, Ronald Reagan *(Jack Miller)*, Daniel Boone Savage *(Noah Wulliver)*, Hugh O'Connell *(Smith the Referee)*, Tommy Bupp *(Rufe Horn)*, Sonny Bupp *(Len Horn)*, Joan Howard *(Mattie Horn)*, Sue Moore *(Mabel)*, Olin Howland *(Hotel Proprietor)*.

Humphrey Bogart approached his role in this silly musical comedy with all the enthusiasm as a mass murderer being dragged down the hall to the gas chamber. The straight Broadway play had been a fair success in New York, but the movie fared far less well. Bogart plays Ed Hatch, a wrestling promoter traveling in Kentucky with his one asset, numbskull wrestler Joe "The Wrestling Hercules" Skopapoulous (Nat Pendleton), an obvious parody of "The Weeping Greek from Cripple Creek," George Zaharias. Also in the entourage is Joe's trainer, Popeye Bronson (Frank McHugh); Ed's assistant, Shiner (Allen Jenkins); and Ed's girl friend, Cookie (Penny Singleton). They are just about out of money and have no ideas for making more, as this hinterlands tour has been a bust, and when their car is stuck in a morass of mud and slime, they figure this is the end of the line. Enter Sadie Horn (Louise Fazenda), a muscular Amazon who lifts the car with ease, and a light bulb flashes over Ed's head: What about a match between Sadie and "The Wrestling Hercules"? In a bit part as a sports reporter is Ronald Reagan, a former announcer in real life for the Chicago Cubs.

p, Hal B. Wallis; d, Ray Enright; w, Joseph Schrank, Maurice Leo (based on the story "Toehold on Artemus" by H.R. Marsh and the play by Kenyon Nicholson, Charles Robinson); ph, Arthur Edeson; ed, Jack Killifer; m, Adolph Deutsch.

Wrestling/Comedy/
Musical   (PR:A   MPAA:NR)

SWINGIN' AFFAIR, A**

(1963) 85m Bengal International/Emerson Film Enterprises bw (AKA: A SWINGING AFFAIR)

William Wellman, Jr., Arline Judge, Dick Dale and the Del Tones, Sandra Gale Bettin.

Johnny Kwalski (William Wellman, Jr.) is a muscular young college student who is planning on taking over his father's steamship company. His secret, which he keeps from the college so as not to be viewed as a Neanderthal, is that he is "Kid Gallant," a professional boxer. Johnny's true identity is revealed, however, when he uses his fists to help his school raise money. Filled with the surf music of Dick Dale and the Del Tones.

p, Gunther Collins; d, Jay O. Lawrence; w, Gunther Collins.

Boxing (PR:A MPAA:NR)

T

TAKE DOWN**½

(1979) 107m American Film Consortium/BV c

Edward Herrmann *(Ed Branish)*, Kathleen Lloyd *(Jill Branish)*, Lorenzo Lamas *(Nick Kilvitus)*, Maureen McCormick *(Brooke Cooper)*, Nick Beauvy *(Jimmy Kier)*, Stephen Furst *(Randy Jensen)*, Kevin Hooks *(Jasper Macgruder)*, Vincent Roberts *(Bobby Cooper)*, Darryl Peterson *(Ted Yacabovich)*, "T" Oney Smith *(Chauncey Washington)*, Salvador Feliciano *(Tom Palumbo)*, Boyd Silversmith *(Jack Gross)*, Scott Burgi *(Robert Stankovich)*, Lynn Baird *(Doc Talada)*, Ron Bartholomew *(Warren Overpeck)*, Kip Otanez *(Zeno Chicarelli)*, Larry Miller *(LeRoy Barron)*.

While waiting to hear from Harvard about a teaching post, high-school English teacher Ed Branish (Edward Herrmann) is given the chore of coaching the school wrestling team, which has been anything but successful for a long time. First Ed has to learn something about the sport (accomplished through some crash reading), then he has to find someone to wrestle at 185 pounds. Adonis Nick Kilvitus (Lorenzo Lamas) seems to fit the bill, but he couldn't be less interested in getting down on all fours on a sweaty mat. Ed, however, proves persuasive, and Nick rises to the challenge. Lighthearted and unassuming, TAKE DOWN offers a nicely modulated performance from Herrmann and a team full of interesting characters.

p, Keith Merrill; d, Keith Merrill; w, Keith Merrill, Eric Hendershot (based on an idea by Hendershot); ph, Reed Smoot (Deluxe Color); ed, Richard Fetterman; m, Merrill B. Jenson.

Wrestling Cas. (PR:C MPAA:PG)

TAKE IT FROM ME*½

(1937, Brit.) 78m WB-FN bw (GB: TRANSATLANTIC TROUBLE)

Max Miller *(Albert Hall)*, Betty Lynne *(Lilli Maguet)*, Buddy Baer *(Kid Brody)*, Clem Lawrence *(Timber Wood)*, Zillah Bateman *(Lady Foxham)*, James Stephenson *(Lewis)*, Charlotte Parry *(Mrs. Murphy)*, Joan Miller *(Secretary)*.

This light comedy features Buddy Baer as Kid Brody, a fighter who becomes the protege of the flirtatious Lady Foxham (Zillah Bateman) after he knocks out her previous favorite in a fight. They sail to England on an ocean liner, and en route the Kid's manager (Max Miller) is mistaken by gold digger Lilli Maguet (Betty Lynne) for a millionaire. Lilli learns the truth, dumps the manager, and pursues the Kid instead. This was the first film appearance of Buddy Baer, a heavyweight fighter in the 1930s and 40s who faced Joe Louis once in 1941 and again in 1942 for the championship (he lost both fights). Baer would go on to make many B pictures, including the Abbott and Costello comedy AFRICA SCREAMS (1949) with his brother, fighter Max Baer, who was the world heavyweight champ in the early 1930s. Max's son, Max, Jr., played Jethro on television's "The Beverly Hillbillys." TAKE IT FROM ME was directed by notorious Hollywood hack William Beaudine, who would later direct such classics as BILLY THE KID VS. DRACULA (1966) and JESSE JAMES MEETS FRANKENSTEIN'S DAUGHTER (1966).

p, Irving Asher; d, William Beaudine; w, John Meehan, Jr., J.O.C. Orton; ph, Basil Emmott.

Boxing (PR:A MPAA:NR)

TAKE ME OUT TO THE BALL GAME***½

(1949) 93m MGM c (GB: EVERYBODY'S CHEERING)

Frank Sinatra *(Dennis Ryan)*, Esther Williams *(K.C. Higgins)*, Gene Kelly *(Eddie O'Brien)*, Betty Garrett *(Shirley Delwyn)*, Edward Arnold *(Joe Lorgan)*, Jules Munshin *(Nat Goldberg)*, Richard Lane *(Michael Gilhuly)*, Tom Dugan *(Slappy Burke)*, Murray Alper *(Zalinka)*, Wilton Graff *(Nick Donford)*, Saul Gorss *(Steve)*, Douglas Fowley *(Karl)*, Eddie Parkes *(Dr. Winston)*, James Burke *(Cop in Park)*, Gordon Jones *(Sen. Catcher)*, Henry Kulky *(Burly Acrobat)*, Dorothy Abbott *(Girl Dancer)*, Jackie Jackson *(Kid)*, Si Jenks *(Sam)*, Jack Rice *(Room Clerk)*, Ed Cassidy *(Teddy Roosevelt)*, Dick Wessel *(Umpire)*.

Dennis Ryan (Frank Sinatra) and Eddie O'Brien (Gene Kelly) are a popular song-and-dance team on the vaudeville circuit who spend their summers playing baseball in a semiprofessional league. Ready to begin a new season, the pair are surprised and delighted to find a woman, K.C. Higgins (Esther Williams) is the new team owner as well as their manager. Both find her attractive, but K.C. is only interested in fielding a good team. When Eddie is benched for moonlighting as a dance director for a nightclub chorus line, he falls under the spell of Joe Lorgan (Edward Arnold), a seemingly benevolent man who in reality is a bigtime gambler, and trouble brews for Eddie and his team. While there's not much baseball played here, this is an amiable film, marked by the enjoyable cast and some lively, if not memorable, music. TAKE ME OUT TO THE BALL GAME was Sinatra and Kelly's follow-up to ANCHORS AWEIGH (1945), and the two are again well-matched partners. The film was based on an original idea of Kelly and Stanley Donen's that closely resembled a minor 1930 film, THEY LEARNED ABOUT WOMEN. After concocting the story, Kelly and Donen asked for the chance to direct, but it was decided to bring in the legendary Busby Berkeley—who had fallen on hard times—and the film turned out to be his last directorial effort. Kelly and Donen, however, were allowed to direct TAKE ME OUT TO THE BALL GAME's musical sequences and the producer was impressed enough to allow them to direct the next Kelly-Sinatra film, ON THE TOWN, later that year. The songs include "Take Me Out to the Ball Game" and "O'Brien to Ryan to Goldberg."

p, Arthur Freed; d, Busby Berkeley; w, Harry Tugend, George Wells, Harry Crane (based on a story by Gene Kelly and Stanley Donen); ph, George Folsey (Technicolor); ed, Blanche Sewell; m, Robert Edens.

Baseball/Musical   Cas.   (PR:AA MPAA:NR)

TAKE ME TO PARIS**

(1950, Brit.) 72m Byron/ABF-Pathe bw

Albert Modley (Albert), Roberta Huby (Linda Vane), Bruce Seton (Gerald Vane), Claire Guilbert (Annette), Richard Molinas (Pojo), George Bishop (Mr. Armstrong), Leonard Sharp (Walter), Jim Gerald (Butcher).

Some shady stable boys from Britain and France team up in a scheme to smuggle counterfeit cash across the English Channel under a horse blanket in this comedy. Their plan goes awry when the horse they had picked out is injured and withdrawn from a race. Seeking a replacement, the crooks are forced to rely on the laughingstock of the stables, Dunderhead. Dunderhead's much-maligned jockey (Albert Modley) overhears the criminals' plan and succeeds in ruining their scheme while winning the big race astride the not-so-slow steed.

p, Henry Halstead; d, Jack Raymond; w, Max Catto; ph, James Wilson.

Horse Racing   (PR:A MPAA:NR)

TALL STORY**

(1960) 91m WB bw

Anthony Perkins (Ray Blent), Jane Fonda (June Ryder), Ray Walston (Leo Sullivan), Marc Connelly (Charles Osman), Anne Jackson (Myra Sullivan), Murray Hamilton (Coach Hardy), Bob Wright (President Nagel), Bart Burns (D.A. Davis), Elizabeth Patterson (Connie), Tom Laughlin (Fred Jensen), Barbara Darrow (Frieda Jensen).

Looking much more at home on a basketball court than he did on the diamond (FEAR STRIKES OUT), Anthony Perkins costars with Jane Fonda (making her film debut) in this mostly unfunny romantic comedy based on a play by Howard Lindsay and Russel Crouse, which was in turn adapted from Howard Nemerov's novel The Homecoming Game. June (Fonda), a tall girl, matriculates to Custer College, home of one of the nation's finest men's basketball teams, hoping to land a husband from among the school's talented cagers. Setting her sights on Ray (Perkins), an All-American who also has a brain, she enrolls in the same classes as Ray and lands a cheerleading gig. In short order, Ray is proposing marriage but, worried about coming up with the funds to start their life together, he becomes susceptible to a gambler's bribe to throw an upcoming contest with the Russian national team. Letting his moral

quandary get in the way of his studies, Ray fails an exam and becomes ineligible; however, the class' instructor (Ray Walston) allows the star player to retake the exam orally, and Ray makes a last-minute appearance on the court, saving the day.

p, Joshua Logan; d, Joshua Logan; w, Julius J. Epstein (based on the play by Howard Lindsay, Russel Crouse and the novel The Homecoming Game by Howard Nemerov); ph, Ellsworth Fredericks; ed, Philip W. Anderson; m, Cyril J. Mockridge.

Basketball/Comedy   (PR:C MPAA:NR)

TEN LAPS TO GO*

(1938) 67m States Rights bw

Rex Lease (Larry Evans), Muriel Evans (Norma), Duncan Renaldo (DeSylva), Tom Moore (Corbett), Charles Delaney (Steve), Marie Prevost (Elsie), Yakima Canutt (Barney), Edward Davis (Adams).

Rex Lease plays Larry Evans, a cocky driver who gets in an accident with bad guy DeSylva (Duncan Renaldo) and loses his nerve. Strange things start occurring around the track and Larry is blamed for them, causing his girl, Norma (Muriel Evans), who is seemingly attracted to DeSylva, to doubt Larry. On the day of the big race, however, Larry heroically finds out who's causing all the trouble and takes over driving for Norma's father with 10 laps to go. Clips from newsreels are badly integrated with close-ups of the actors in this low-budget racing film.

p, Fanchon Royer; d, Elmer Clifton; w, Charles Condon (based on a story by William F. Bleecher); ph, Arthur Martinelli; ed, Edward Schroeder.

Auto Racing   (PR:A MPAA:NR)

TENNESSEE CHAMP**½

(1954) 72m MGM c

Shelley Winters (Sarah Wurble), Keenan Wynn (Willy Wurble), Dewey Martin (Daniel Norson), Earl Holliman (Happy Jackfield), Dave O'Brien (Luke MacWade), Charles Bronson (Sixty Jubel), Yvette Dugay (Blossom), Frank Richards (J.B. Backett), Jack Kruschen (Andrews), John Indrisano (Referee), Alvin J. Gordon (Sam).

Daniel Norson (Dewey Martin) is a young and very religious prizefighter from the South who is given his chance by manager Willy Wurble (Keenan Wynn). The future looks good for Daniel, until he discovers that Willy is fixing an upcoming match. He voices his disapproval and along with it his religious and moral principles, which finally get through to Willy, causing him to rethink his malicious ways. Willy promotes a fair fight between Daniel and another boxer, played by a fellow named Charles Buchinsky—who would later change his name to Bronson—for the film's finale, which implies that Daniel will find his future in God's corner rather than Willy's. The story upon which the film is based, "The Lord in His Corner," had as its main character a black fighter.

p, Sol Baer Fielding; d, Fred M. Wilcox; w, Art Cohn (based

on "The Lord in His Corner" and other stories by Eustace Cockrell); ph, George Folsey (Ansco Color); ed, Ben Lewis; m, Conrad Salinger.

Boxing (PR:A MPAA:NR)

THAT CHAMPIONSHIP SEASON**½

(1982) 110m Cannon c

Bruce Dern *(George Sitkowski)*, Stacy Keach *(James Daley)*, Robert Mitchum *(Coach Delaney)*, Martin Sheen *(Tom Daley)*, Paul Sorvino *(Phil Romano)*, Arthur Franz *(Macken)*, Michael Bernosky *(Jacks)*, James M. Langan *(Cooney)*, Joseph Kelly *(Malley)*, Tony Santaniello *(Marelli)*, William G. McAndrew *(Harrison)*, Barry Weiner *(Sharmen)*.

Playwright Jason Miller made his motion picture directorial debut with this adaptation of his own Pulitzer Prize-winning play. Though he makes little effort to treat his material cinematically, Miller nonetheless invests his production with insight and high emotion. Twenty-five years after winning the state high-school basketball championship, four ex-teammates gather for a reunion with their coach (Robert Mitchum). George Sitkowski (Bruce Dern) is now the town mayor, embroiled in a reelection bid; James Daley (Stacy Keach) is his campaign manager; Phil Romano (Paul Sorvino) is a successful but unscrupulous businessman; and Tom Daley (Martin Sheen) is a writer returning home after an absence of several years. As the booze flows, the good humor begins to fade, old wounds and jealousies mixing with more current bitterness and admissions of personal and professional disappointment. Tempers flare, and though the coach tries to keep things under control, all he has to offer are courtside homilies. Though some have found THAT CHAMPIONSHIP SEASON long and talky, patient viewers will find moments of profound insight into the masculine psyche, or at least into the macho code that governed life on the basketball court for these four characters 25 years ago and that still influences their actions. Although the performances are uneven, the cast is so excellent that even when the actors aren't at the top of their games, they are never boring.

p, Menahem Golan, Yoram Globus; d, Jason Miller; w, Jason Miller (based on his play); ph, John Bailey (Metrocolor); ed, Richard Halsey; m, Bill Conti.

Basketball **Cas.** (PR:O MPAA:R)

THAT GANG OF MINE**

(1940) 62m MON bw

Bobby Jordan *(Danny Dolan)*, Leo Gorcey *(Mugs Maloney)*, Clarence Muse *(Ben)*, Dave O'Brien *(Knuckles Dolan)*, Joyce Bryant *(Louise)*, Donald Haines *(Skinny)*, David Gorcey *(Peewee)*, Sunshine Sammy Morrison *(Scruno)*, Eugene Francis *(Algernon "Algy" Wilkes)*, Milton Kibbee *(Conrad Wilkes)*, Hazel Keener *(Mrs. Wilkes)*.

In this weak Bowery Boys effort, gang member Mugs (Leo Gorcey) aspires to be a jockey, despite the teasing he gets from his pals. When they meet Ben (Clarence Muse), a poor black man who owns a racehorse, they per-

suade him to let Mugs ride the steed in a big race. Ben agrees, but the boys must raise the money for the entry fees themselves. The gang gets the dough from Conrad Wilkes (Milton Kibbee), but he insists that a different jockey ride the horse, Muggs having proven himself talentless.

p, Sam Katzman; d, Joseph H. Lewis; w, William Lively (based on a story by Alan Whitman); ph, Robert Cline, Harvey Gould; ed, Carl Pierson.

Horse Racing (PR:A MPAA:NR)

THAT'S MY BOY*½

(1932) 71m COL bw

Richard Cromwell *(Tommy)*, Dorothy Jordan *(Dorothy)*, Mae Marsh *(Mom)*, Arthur Stone *(Pop)*, Douglas Dumbrille *(Adams)*, Lucien Littlefield *(Uncle Louie)*, Leon Waycoff *(Al Williams)*, Russell Saunders *(Pinkie)*, Sumner Getchell *(Carl)*, Otis Harlan *(Mayor)*.

This typical college football yarn concerns studious, honest Tommy (Richard Cromwell), who works his way through school while becoming the star player. He proves his pigskin prowess by hot-footing it all over the field, but foolishly becomes involved in a stock swindle that threatens to destroy his career. Luckily, the kid wises up and pays back every dime he inadvertently bilked out of hapless investors before going on to win the big game. The cast includes members of USC's national championship team of 1931.

d, Roy William Neill; w, Norman Krasna (based on the novel by Francis Wallace); ph, Joseph August; ed, Jack Dennis.

Football (PR:A MPAA:NR)

THAT'S MY BOY**

(1951) 98m PAR bw

Dean Martin *(Bill Baker)*, Jerry Lewis *("Junior" Jackson)*, Ruth Hussey *(Ann Jackson)*, Eddie Mayehoff *("Jarring Jack" Jackson)*, Marion Marshall *(Terry Howard)*, Polly Bergen *(Betty Hunter)*, Hugh Sanders *(Coach Wheeler)*, John McIntire *(Benjamin Green)*, Tom Harmon *(Sports Announcer)*.

The genuine laughs are few and far between in this ho-hum Dean Martin and Jerry Lewis comedy, in which the boys are involved in college football antics. Lewis plays Junior Jackson, the nebbish son of wealthy college alumnus and former All-American Jarring Jack Jackson (Eddie Mayehoff), who pushes his talentless son into playing football for his alma mater, Ridgeville. Realizing that Junior needs some special training to avoid being slaughtered, the domineering Jarring Jack hires Ridgeville player Bill Baker (Dean Martin) to do the tutoring. Junior, of course, goes through the spastic struggles that afflict nearly all Jerry Lewis' characters, until finally, during the obligatory final minutes of the season's big game, he is confident enough to go out and win the battle for Ridgeville. Heisman Trophy winner from Michigan and real-life sports announcer Tom Harmon has a cameo as . . . a sports announcer.

p, Hal B. Wallis; d, Hal Walker; w, Cy Howard (based on his story); ph, Lee Garmes; ed, Warren Low; m, Leigh Harline.

Football/Comedy (PR:A MPAA:NR)

THAT'S MY MAN**

(1947) 104m REP bw

Don Ameche *(Joe Grange)*, Catherine McLeod *(Ronnie)*, Roscoe Karns *(Toby Gleeton)*, John Ridgely *(Ramsey)*, Kitty Irish *(Kitty)*, Joe Frisco *(Willie Wagonstatter)*, Gregory Marshall *(Richard)*, Dorothy Adams *(Millie)*, Frankie Darro *(Jockey)*, Hampton J. Scott *(Sam)*, John Miljan *(Secretary)*, Gallant Man the Horse.

A professional gambler, Joe Grange (Don Ameche), lets his obsession nearly ruin his life. Seeing a chance to make some big dough, Joe buys a sickly colt, nurses it back to health, and then trains it until it promises to win big at the track. Placing a small fortune on the horse's head, Joe wins a bundle, but the money doesn't please his wife, Ronnie (Catherine McLeod), who feels Joe has ignored his duties as a husband (he was playing cards while she was giving birth) and father (he skipped a Christmas party to gamble). She leaves him, and his luck ends. In the end he is left with nothing but his horse. Seeking to win just one more big bet, Joe takes the nag out of retirement and runs him. Heavy on the melodramatics, but the race footage is more realistic than usual.

p, Frank Borzage; d, Frank Borzage; w, Steve Fisher, Bradley King (based on their story); ph, Tony Gaudio; ed, Richard L. Van Enger; m, Hans J. Salter.

Horse Racing (PR:A MPAA:NR)

THERE AIN'T NO JUSTICE**

(1939, Brit.) 83m Ealing-CAPAD/ABF bw

Jimmy Hanley *(Tommy Mutch)*, Edward Rigby *(Pa Mutch)*, Mary Clare *(Ma Mutch)*, Phyllis Stanley *(Elsie Mutch)*, Edward Chapman *(Sammy Sanders)*, Jill Furse *(Connie Fletcher)*, Richard Ainley *(Billy Frost)*, Gus McNaughton *(Alfie Norton)*, Nan Hopkins *(Dot Ducrow)*, Sue Gawthorne *(Mrs. Frost)*, Michael Hogarth *(Frank Fox)*, Michael Wilding *(Len Charteris)*, Richard Norris *(Stan)*.

Auto mechanic Tommy Mutch (Jimmy Hanley) discovers he has a talent for boxing and, hoping to earn quick money so he can marry his sweetheart, steps into the ring. Unfortunately he hooks up with a crooked promoter who tries to force him to take a dive. Knowing that the odds will be lopsided if it's rumored that the fight is fixed, Tommy has his father bet big on him and knocks the intended victor onto the canvas.

d, Penrose Tennyson; w, Penrose Tennyson, Sergei Nolbandov, James Curtis (based on the novel by Curtis); ph, Max Greene; ed, Ray Pitt; m, Ernest Irving.

Boxing (PR:A MPAA:NR)

THEY LEARNED ABOUT WOMEN**

(1930) 72m MGM bw

Joseph T. Schenck *(Jack)*, Gus Van *(Jerry)*, Bessie Love *(Mary)*, Mary Doran *(Daisy)*, J.C. Nugent *(Stafford)*, Benny Rubin *(Sam)*, Tom Dugan *(Tim)*, Eddie Gribbon *(Brennan)*, Francis X. Bushman, Jr. *(Haskins)*.

It's that age-old dilemma for World Series champs—the diamond or the vaudeville stage. Jack (Joseph T. Schenck) and Jerry (Gus Van) are professional baseball players who give up the bat for the footlights, becoming vaudeville singers. Mary (Bessie Love) is the dancer who offers herself to one, although she really loves the other. Another woman enters the scene and almost breaks up the singing duo, but they both end up leaving the stage and returning to baseball in time to play in the World Series.

d, Jack Conway, Sam Wood; w, Sarah Y. Mason, Arthur "Bugs" Baer (based on a story by A.P. Younger); ph, Leonard Smith; ed, James McKay, Tom Held.

Baseball/Musical (PR:A MPAA:NR)

THEY MADE ME A CRIMINAL***

(1939) 92m WB bw

John Garfield *(Johnny Bradfield/"Jack Dorney")*, Gloria Dickson *(Peggy)*, Claude Rains *(Det. Monty Phelan)*, Ann Sheridan *(Goldie)*, May Robson *(Gramma)*, Billy Halop *(Tommy)*, Bobby Jordan *(Angel)*, Leo Gorcey *(Spit)*, Huntz Hall *(Dippy)*, Gabriel Dell *(T.B.)*, Bernard Punsley *(Milty)*, Robert Gleckler *(Doc Ward)*, John Ridgely *(Charlie Magee)*, Barbara Pepper *(Budgie)*, William B. Davidson *(Inspector Ennis)*, Ward Bond *(Lenihan)*, Robert Strange *(Malvin)*, Louis Jean Heydt *(Smith)*, Ronald Sinclair *(J. Douglas Williamson)*, Frank Riggi *(Gaspar Rutchek)*, Cliff Clark *(Rutchek's Manager)*, Dick Wessel *(Collucci)*, Raymond Brown *(Sheriff)*, Sam Hayes *(Fight Announcer)*, Irving Bacon *(Speed)*, Sam McDaniel *(Splash)*.

Seeking to capitalize on the sensation made by their new young actor John Garfield in FOUR DAUGHTERS (1938), Warner Bros. immediately cast him in this remake of the 1933 boxing-crime drama THE LIFE OF JIMMY DOLAN. Garfield plays Johnnie Bradfield, a recently crowned world champion boxer whose public image is that of a kind, gentle, clean-cut kid who is devoted to his mother. In reality, Johnnie is a cynical, heavy-drinking womanizer who hasn't given so much as a thought to his mother in years. One morning, he awakens from a drunken stupor to read in the newspaper that he has murdered a reporter and then gotten killed in a fiery car crash. The boxer's seedy lawyer advises him to stay "dead" and beat it out of town, while Monty Phelan (Claude Rains), the detective assigned to the case, suspects that Johnnie is alive and becomes obsessed with finding him. THEY MADE ME A CRIMINAL begins with Garfield once again playing the fatalistic, cynical, tough guy from the slums, but his personality undergoes a change during the film and by the conclusion he has attained a minor state of grace. Seeing himself in the faces of a group of troubled youngsters (the Dead End Kids, later the Bowery Boys), Johnnie is able to identify his problems and work to eradicate them for the boys and himself. Surprisingly, the film was helmed by Busby Berkeley (best known for his brilliantly choreographed musicals), who here directed in the trademark Warners style: gritty, fast-paced, and sometimes brutally realistic, transferring his choreographic talents from the stage to the boxing ring. Berkeley and cameraman James Wong Howe created some vivid fight scenes that wouldn't be outdone until Garfield's magnum opus, BODY AND SOUL, in 1947, which was also photographed by Howe.

p, Jack Warner, Hal B. Wallis; d, Busby Berkeley; w, Sig Herzig (based on the book by Bertram Millhauser, Beulah Marie Dix); ph, James Wong Howe; ed, Jack Killifer; m, Max Steiner.

Boxing   **Cas.**   **(PR:A MPAA:NR)**

THEY NEVER COME BACK**

(1932) 67m Weiss Bros./Artclass bw

Regis Toomey *(Nolan)*, Dorothy Sebastian *(Adele)*, Gertrude Astor *(Kate)*, Earle Foxe *(Filmore)*, Greta Granstedt *(Mary Nolan)*, Eddie Woods *(Ralph)*, George Byron *(Donovan)*, James J. Jeffries *(Referee)*, Little Billy *(M.C.)*.

A boxer, Nolan (Regis Toomey), meets with an early retirement when he breaks his arm in the ring. He becomes a bouncer in a nightclub where innocent hoochie-koochie dancer Adele (Dorothy Sebastian) is the star, only to become the victim of an envious rival for her affections. Nolan, needing money to get Adele out of a jam, reenters the ring despite his crippled south paw. James J. Jeffries, world heavyweight champion from 1899 through his initial retirement in 1905, plays a referee.

d, Fred Newmeyer; w, Arthur Hoerl, Sherman Lowe (based on the story by Hoerl); ph, James Diamond.

Boxing   **(PR:A MPAA:NR)**

THIS SPORTING AGE*½

(1932) 67m COL bw

Jack Holt *(Capt. John Steele)*, Evalyn Knapp *(Mickey Steele)*, Hardie Albright *(Johnny Raeburn)*, Walter Byron *(Charles Morrell)*, J. Farrell MacDonald *(Jerry O'Day)*, Ruth Weston *(Mrs. Rita Duncan)*, Nora Lane *(Mrs. Wainleigh)*, Shirley Palmer *(Ann Erskine)*, Hal Price *(Surgeon)*.

Jack Holt is US Army captain John Steele, whose fanatical devotion to polo gets him into trouble when he takes out a personal grudge on another polo player, Charles Morrell (Walter Byron), who has compromised Steele's daughter, Mickey (Evalyn Knapp). Steele is so enraged at the news that he causes Charles to suffer a fatal accident on the playing field. The act is deemed manslaughter, and must be weighed on the scales of justice.

d, Andrew W. Bennison, A.F. Erickson; w, Dudley Nichols (based on a story by J.K. McGuinness); ph, Teddy Tetzlaff; ed, Maurice Wright.

Polo   **(PR:A MPAA:NR)**

THIS SPORTING LIFE****

(1963, Brit.) 129m Independent Artists/CD bw

Richard Harris *(Frank Machin)*, Rachel Roberts *(Mrs. Hammond)*, Alan Badel *(Weaver)*, William Hartnell *(Johnson)*, Colin Blakely *(Maurice Braithwaite)*, Vanda Godsell *(Mrs. Weaver)*, Arthur Lowe *(Slomer)*, Anne Cunningham *(Judith)*, Jack Watson *(Len Miller)*, Harry Markham *(Wade)*, George Sewell *(Jeff)*, Leonard Rossiter *(Phillips)*, Frank Windsor *(Dentist)*, Peter Duguid *(Doctor)*, Wallas Eaton *(Waiter)*, Anthony Woodruff *(Head Waiter)*, Katherine Parr *(Mrs. Farrer)*, Bernadette Benson *(Lynda)*.

From its virtuoso opening shot of a rugby scrum—from the bottom, looking up—to its final emotionally draining moments, THIS SPORTING LIFE is a captivating, visceral film experience. Not only is Lindsay Anderson's (IF; OH LUCKY MAN) first feature film one of the most poignant sports-centered movies ever made, it is also a landmark in the history of British cinema, an "Angry Young Man" classic. Adapted by David Storey (who played professional rugby at one time) from his own novel, the film follows the fortunes of Frank Machin (Richard Harris), a loutish former Yorkshire coal miner who bashes his way to local celebrity as a professional rugby player. Although pursued by a number of women, Frank starves for the love of his landlady, Mrs. Hammond (Rachel Roberts), a bitter, passionless widow, who eventually has a physical relationship with her boarder but refuses to give herself to him emotionally. Meanwhile, Frank remains the darling of the rugby club's management and supporters, and as long as he performs on the field, his sullen rebelliousness is tolerated. In time, Mrs. Hammond grows tired of Frank's callousness, they row terribly, and he moves out. Realizing how much he needs her love, Frank tries to patch things up, but tragedy awaits his attempt at reconciliation. Finally, Frank is left only with the violent world of rugby, in which he is only as good as his last game. THIS SPORTING LIFE is both a biting indictment of class-based exploitation (the club owners treat the players as mindless beasts) and a tragic story of love that founders on suppressed feelings and unconscious macho insensitivity. Nominated for an Oscar, Harris gives an extraordinary, gut-wrenching performance reminiscent of young Marlon Brando, and Roberts, who was also nominated for an Academy Award, brings considerable complexity to her exceptional portrayal of a woman whose emotional life is as dormant as Frank's is frustrated. The game action is hard-hitting and well captured, and cinematographer Denys Coop's gritty, detailed black and white is in the best tradition of British Kitchen Sink realism. Not to be missed.

p, Karel Reisz; d, Lindsay Anderson; w, David Storey (based on the novel *This Sporting Life* by Storey); ph, Denys Coop; ed, Peter Taylor; m, Roberto Gerhard.

Rugby   **Cas.**   **(PR:O MPAA:NR)**

THOROUGHBREDS**

(1945) 56m REP bw

Tom Neal *(Rusty Curtis)*, Adele Mara *(Sally Crandall)*, Roger Pryor *(Harold Matthews)*, Paul Harvey *(John Cran-*

dall), Gene Garrick *(Jack Martin)*, Doodles Weaver *(Pvt. Mulrooney)*, Eddie Hall *(Dapper)*, Tom London *(Pop)*, Charles Sullivan *(Nails)*, Alan Edwards *(Maj. Lane)*, Sam Bernard *(Pete)*, Bud Gorman *(Roberts)*, John Crawford, Jack Gardner, Robert Strange.

Cavalry sergeant Rusty Curtis (Tom Neal) is released from the Army at the same time that his beloved horse is sold to society woman Sally Crandall (Adele Mara) to run in steeplechases. Rusty is initially hired to train the horse, but is able to stop some gamblers who want the steed kept out of an important race. When the regular jockey can't ride, Rusty takes over, winning both the race and Sally's affections.

p, Lester Sharpe; d, George Blair; w, Wellyn Totman; ph, William Bradford; ed, Ralph Dixon.

Horse Racing   (PR:AA   MPAA:NR)

THOROUGHBREDS DON'T CRY**½

(1937) 80m MGM bw

Judy Garland *(Cricket West)*, Mickey Rooney *(Tim Donahue)*, Sophie Tucker *(Mother Ralph)*, C. Aubrey Smith *(Sir Peter Calverton)*, Ronald Sinclair *(Roger Calverton)*, Forrester Harvey *(Wilkins)*, Helen Troy *(Hilda)*, Charles D. Brown *(Click Donahue)*, Henry Kolker *(Doc Godfrey)*.

Judy Garland's first starring role and her first of many movies with Mickey Rooney is a predictable racehorse story with a couple of tunes tossed in to liven up the hokum plot. Young Roger Calverton (Ronald Sinclair, a 14-year-old being groomed then as the new Freddie Bartholomew) arrives in the US with his crusty grandpa Sir Peter (C. Aubrey Smith). The Calvertons own a racehorse named "The Pookah" and want to put it on American tracks and make a killing. They offer young jockey Tim Donahue (17-year-old Rooney) the chance to ride and Tim accepts, feeling that this is a winning horse he can take to the finish line ahead of the pack. Unfortunately, Tim unwisely falls victim to the scheming of his no-good father and pulls back on The Pookah's reins during the big race. The horse loses, Tim's dad makes a fortune, and Sir Peter dies of shock. Tim is overwhelmed with guilt, but his friendship with Cricket West (Garland) helps him mend his ways. Given Rooney's stature, it was only natural that he play a jockey or an ex-jockey and in years to come he did it many times, most notably in NATIONAL VELVET; STABLEMATES; and THE BLACK STALLION.

p, Harry Rapf; d, Alfred E. Green; w, Lawrence Hazard (based on a story by Eleanore Griffin, J. Walter Ruben); ph, Leonard Smith; ed, Elmo Veron.

Horse Racing   (PR:AA   MPAA:NR)

THRASHIN'**½

(1986) 92m Fries Entertainment c

Josh Brolin *(Corey Webster)*, Robert Rusler *(Tommy Hook)*, Pamela Gidley *(Chrissy)*, Brooke McCarter, Jr. *(Tyler)*, Josh Richman *(Radley)*, Brett Marx *(Bozo)*, David Wagner *(Little Stevie)*, Chuck McCann *(Sam Flood)*, Tony

Alva *(T.A.)*, Mark Munski *(Monk)*, Sherilyn Fenn *(Velvet)*, Zachary *(Skate Club Announcer)*, Rocky Giordani *(Skate Club Bouncer)*, Steve Whittaker *(Bus Driver)*, Per Welinder *(Per, Venice Freestyler)*.

WEST SIDE STORY on skateboards, THRASHIN' is a tale of rivalry between two gangs in which one gang leader's sister falls in love with the opposing gang leader. The gangs this time are "The Ramp Locals," some affluent Valley kids headed by clean-cut Corey Webster (Josh Brolin, son of James), and "The Daggers," a gang of hardcore punk rockers in leather led by Tommy Hook (Robert Rusler). Hook's kid sister, the virginal, blonde Chrissy (Pamela Gidley), is visiting from Indiana and ends up falling for Corey, but Hook doesn't want his kid sister anywhere near someone from the Valley. It all builds up to a final competition—the "LA Massacre," a dangerous 20-mile downhill race through a mountain road in which skateboarders can reach speeds of 60 mph, the winner of which gets a corporate sponsorship. While not very original or even very skillful, THRASHIN' (a skateboarding term for aggressive, gutsy skating) isn't nearly as bad as it sounds. The film takes a look—albeit a superficial one—at a strange subculture that began in Los Angeles and has since spread through the entire country in which groups of youths identify themselves as skateboarders, much like the bikers and surfers of previous generations. Unfortunately, it doesn't get any deeper than that. There is some phenomenal camerawork, however, much of it shot from a camera attached to the front of a skateboard. While the actors perform their gymnastics in a cement "pool," on a ramp, or racing down Hollywood Boulevard's sidewalks (at speeds up to 40 mph), the camera zooms along with them. Directed by David Winters, who has a fairly large part in WEST SIDE STORY as A-Rab.

p, Alan Sacks; d, David Winters; w, Alan Sacks, Paul Brown; ph, Chuck Colwell; ed, Lorenzo DeStefano, Nicholas Smith; m, Barry Goldberg.

Skateboarding   Cas. (PR:A-C   MPAA:PG-13)

THUNDER ALLEY*½

(1967) 90m AIP c

Annette Funicello *(Francie Madsen)*, Fabian *(Tommy Callahan)*, Diane McBain *(Annie Blaine)*, Warren Berlinger *(Eddie Sands)*, Jan Murray *(Pete Madsen)*, Stanley Adams *(Mac Lunsford)*, Maureen Arthur *(Babe)*, Michael T. Mikler *(Harry Wise)*.

Stock-car driver Tommy Callahan (Fabian) must retire after suffering a blackout while driving, causing the death of another racer. He therefore takes the demeaning job of staging phony crashes and spinouts at a "Thrill Circus" run by cheap promoter Pete Madsen (Jan Murray). Among those racing cars on Madsen's track are his own daughter, Francie (Annette Funicello), and her beau, Eddie (Warren Berlinger). The bored Tommy trains Eddie to race professionally and the kid actually wins his first race. Discovering a new sugar daddy, Tommy's former girl friend, Annie (Diane McBain), zeros in on Eddie, much to Francie's dismay. This leads to some tension between Tommy and his protege, but as luck would have it, the pair are entered as partners in an important 500-mile race. While zooming along at top speeds, Fabian begins to have another blackout and realizes that his fainting spells are caused by his guilt over the childhood accident in which he ran his brother over with a go-cart! Pretty funny (albeit unintentionally) stuff, directed by Richard Rush, whose next picture, HELLS ANGELS ON WHEELS, became a biker classic, and who eventually would win some respect by directing THE STUNT MAN.

p, Burt Topper; d, Richard Rush; w, Sy Salkowitz; ph, Monroe Askins (Panavision, Pathe Color); ed, Ronald Sinclair, Kenneth Crane.

Auto Racing   **(PR:A MPAA:NR)**

THUNDER IN CAROLINA**

(1960) 92m Darlington/Howco c

Rory Calhoun, John Gentry, Connie Hines .

Yet another stock-car racing film set in the South, THUNDER IN CAROLINA follows Mitch Cooper (Rory Calhoun), a former racer forced into retirement after a nasty crash that left his leg permanently injured. With nothing much else to do, Mitch takes young garage owner Les York (John Gentry) under his wing and teaches the eager mechanic how to race. Les soon becomes obsessed with racing and practically forces his beautiful wife, Rene (Connie Hines), into Mitch's arms after he (Les) is smitten with a racetrack groupie. The film includes loads of footage of the Southern 500, including scenes of crews prepping cars, a street festival, some risky practice driving through the Carolina mountains, and even some exciting race footage shot from a car-mounted camera.

p, J. Francis White; d, Paul Helmick; w, Alexander Richards; ph, Joseph Brun (Eastmancolor); ed, Rex Lipton; m, Walter Green.

Auto Racing   **(PR:A MPAA:NR)**

THUNDER IN DIXIE**

(1965) 76m Willpat/MPI bw

Harry Millard (Mickey Arnold), Judy Lewis (Lili Arnold), Nancy Berg (Karen Hallet), Mike Bradford (Ticker Welsh), Ted Erwin (Ben Forrest), Richard Kuss (Link Duggan), Pat McAndrew (Rachel), Herb Rodgers (Motel Manager), Barry Darval (Himself), Sheri Benet (Herself), Bob Wills (Track Announcer), Johnny Carlson (Spotter), George Brenholtz (Bartender), Richard Petty.

Shifting the "thunder" from the aforementioned Southern 500 in South Carolina, THUNDER IN DIXIE is a stock-car racing movie set during Atlanta's Dixie 400. Ticker Welsh (Mike Bradford) is a racer obsessed with avenging the death of his fiancee, who, he believes, was killed because of the irresponsibility of fellow racer Mickey Arnold (Harry Millard). Ticker plans to get Mickey during the big race, despite the protests of his new girl friend (Nancy Berg) and Arnold's wife (Judy Lewis). During the race, Ticker's recklessness causes an accident that lands him in the hospital,

leaving the way clear for Mickey to win. The stay in intensive care seems to sap the vengeful blood from Ticker's veins and he makes his peace with his rival. The racing scenes were filmed at the Atlanta International Raceway, with a cameo appearance by NASCAR champion Richard Petty.

p, William T. Naud; d, William T. Naud; w, George Baxt; ph, Thomas E. Spalding; m, Elliot Lawrence.

Auto Racing   **(PR:A MPAA:NR)**

TO PLEASE A LADY**½

(1950) 91m MGM bw (AKA: RED HOT WHEELS)

Clark Gable (Mike Brannan), Barbara Stanwyck (Regina Forbes), Adolphe Menjou (Gregg), Will Geer (Jack Mackay), Roland Winters (Dwight Barrington), William C. McGaw (Joie Chitwood), Lela Bliss (Regina's Secretary), Emory Parnell (Mr. Wendall), Frank Jenks (Newark Press Agent), Helen Spring (Janie), Ted Husing (Indianapolis Announcer), Richard W. Joy (TV Voice), William Welsh (Sports Announcer), John McGuire (Newark Referee), Lee Phelps (Steward), Al Hill (Steward), Raymond Brown (Newark Announcer), Joe Garson (Joe Youghal).

Fast cars and romance mix in this yarn, which stars Clark Gable as a notorious midget race car driver. On the track, Mike Brannan (Gable) draws more boos than cheers from the crowds, who won't forgive him for a crash he once caused that resulted in another driver's death. Hard-edged columnist Regina Forbes (Barbara Stanwyck) decides to give Mike a fair shake and interview him. Mike, however, wants nothing to do with her. Regina witnesses another fatal crash caused by Mike and, convinced that he is a callous individual with no respect for life, condemns him in her column. She wields enough power to get him barred from the race circuit, thereby forcing him to take up stunt-car performing in a sideshow until he manages to save enough cash to buy a full-sized racer. Before the next big race, Mike and Regina meet, but instead of despising each other, they fall in love. Although the title is TO PLEASE A LADY, the most memorable moments of the film occur on the race track. Photographed at the Indianapolis Speedway, the 12-minute finale brims with excitement that is absent from the dialog. Gable and Stanwyck do their best, but most of their interchanges fall flat, the most electric moment between them occurring when Gable, by now attracted to Stanwyck, slaps her face. Instead of running off, Stanwyck stays, proving both her love for Gable and her ability to take what he dishes out. MGM re-released TO PLEASE A LADY under the more graphic title RED HOT WHEELS.

p, Clarence Brown; d, Clarence Brown; w, Barre Lyndon, Marge Decker; ph, Harold Rosson; ed, Robert J. Kern; m, Bronislau Kaper.

Auto Racing   **(PR:A MPAA:NR)**

TOMBOY*

(1985) 91m Marimark/Crown c

Betsy Russell (Tommy Boyd), Jerry Dinome (Randy Starr),

Kristi Somers *(Seville Ritz)*, Richard Erdman *(Chester)*, Philip Sterling *(Earl Delarue)*, Eric Douglas *(Ernie Leeds, Jr.)*, Paul Gunning *(Frankie)*, Toby Iland *(Harold)*, E. Danny Murphy *(Pimples)*, Rory Barish *(Jennifer)*, Cynthia Ann Thompson *(Amanda)*, Cory Hawkins *(Carlos)*, Shane McCabe *(Goodley)*, Aaron Butler *(Tod)*, Dennis Hayden *(Bartender)*.

A few hot cars and some bared breasts are the so-called attractions of this dismal teen-oriented story of an independent woman. Tommy Boyd (Betsy Russell) is a tough-minded young lady and a top-notch garage mechanic working in East Los Angeles, where she indulges in such unfeminine activities as motorcycle riding and playing basketball with local street kids. This being an exploitation film, Tommy needs a reason to show off her body, and she does so in her love scenes with Randy Starr (Jerry Dinome), a pretty-boy race-car driver. Eventually, Randy tires of Tommy's tomboy exterior and faces off with her in a racing challenge. Of course, she wins handily, and gets a sponsor for the Daytona 500. Yeah, right. The plot and characterizations, as expected, are as ludicrous as the main character's name—Tom(my) Boy(d). Russell is likable considering the inane nature of the film, but Dinome, a former model making his feature debut, is all teeth and moussed hair.

p, Marilyn J. Tenser, Michael D. Castle; d, Herb Freed; w, Ben Zelig (based on an idea by Mark Tenser); ph, Daniel Yarussi (DeLuxe Color); ed, Richard E. Westover.

Auto Racing   Cas.   (PR:O   MPAA:R)

TOUCH AND GO***

(1986) 101m Tri-Star c

Michael Keaton *(Bobby Barbato)*, Maria Conchita Alonso *(Denise DeLeon)*, Ajay Naidu *(Louis DeLeon)*, Maria Tucci *(Dee Dee)*, Max Wright *(Lester)*, Lara Jill Miller *(Courtney)*, D.V. de Vincentis *(Lupo)*, Michael Zelniker *(McDonald)*, Jere Burns *(Levesolie)*, Dens Duffy *(Lynch)*, Steve Pint *(Green)*, Clair Dolan, Carri Lyn Levinson, Charlotte Ross *(Courtney's Girl Friends)*, Jean Bates *(Lady at Mortuary)*, Earl Boby *(Writer)*, Ed Meekat *(Diner Waiter)*, Nick De Mauro *(Maintenance Man)*, Ron Stokes *(Sportscaster)*.

Though not entirely successful, this charming comedy works thanks to the strong performances of its three leads and a conscious effort to avoid standard plot twists. Bobby Barbato (Michael Keaton), star player for a fictitious Chicago pro hockey team, becomes involved with Denise DeLeon (Maria Conchita Alonso), a pretty unwed mother, and her 11-year-old son, Louis (Ajay Naidu), after the boy is party to an attempted mugging of the hockey player. Bobby has never been one for commitment, but he finds himself grudgingly falling in love with Denise, who is menaced by Lupo (D.V. de Vincentis), a brutal teenage gang leader in the rough neighborhood she is determined to leave behind. Although Bobby does his darnedest to hang onto his independence, his path continues to cross those of Denise and Louis, and by the film's tension-filled end, you can bet one-night stands are a thing of the past for the hockey star. Although its plot is undeniably slight and its concept of re-

ality a little far-fetched (how many home games does Bobby's team have and are they played only at times that are convenient for him?), TOUCH AND GO benefits so fully from the wonderful rapport among Naidu, Alonso, and Keaton that it becomes a warm, winning film. Keaton, in particular, delivers a fine performance, mixing his usual glib wisecracking with a quieter, more straightforward dramatic approach and acquitting himself well on the ice.

p, Stephen Friedman; d, Robert Mandel; w, Alan Ormsby, Bob Sand, Harry Colomby; ph, Richard H. Kline (AstroLabs, Movielab); ed, Walt Mulconery; m, Sylvester Levay.

Hockey/Comedy/
Romance   Cas.   (PR:C-O   MPAA:R)

TOUCHDOWN**½

(1931) 79m PAR bw (GB: PLAYING THE GAME)

Richard Arlen *(Dan Curtis)*, Peggy Shannon *(Mary Gehring)*, Jack Oakie *(Babe Barton)*, Regis Toomey *(Tom Hussey)*, George Barbier *(Jerome Gehring)*, J. Farrell MacDonald *(Pop Stewart)*, George Irving *(President Baker)*, Charles D. Brown *(Harrigan)*, Charles Starrett *(Paul Gehring)*, Jim Thorpe, Howard Jones, Russell Saunders, Morley Drury, Jesse Hibbs, Nate Barrager, Tom Lieb, Roy Riegels.

Richard Arlen is Dan Curtis, a college football coach and former All-American who'll stop at nothing to bring his team victory. He loses everyone's respect after he sends an injured player into the fray—winning the game, but putting the young man in the hospital as a result. Dastardly Dan is later shown to have reformed, however, when he resists the temptation to make a lad with a *brain concussion* play in a crucial game. He forfeits victory on the field, but comes out on top in the "how to make friends and influence people" department. Comedic relief is provided by the ubiquitous Jack Oakie; J. Farrell MacDonald once again (THE SPIRIT OF NOTRE DAME) plays an old coach; the football clips include glimpses of the legendary Jim Thorpe, "Wrong Way" Roy Riegels, future "Tarzan" Herman Brix, Howard Jones, Russ Saunders, and other gridiron stars and coaches; and the source material was a novel by former Knute Rockne staff member Francis Wallace.

d, Norman Z. McLeod; w, William Slavens McNutt, Grover Jones (based on the novel *Stadium* by Francis Wallace); ph, Arthur Todd.

Football   (PR:A   MPAA:NR)

TOUCHDOWN, ARMY**

(1938) 60m PAR bw (GB: GENERALS OF TOMORROW)

John Howard *(Brandon Culpepper)*, Robert Cummings *(Jimmy Howell)*, Mary Carlisle *(Toni Denby)*, Owen Davis, Jr. *(Kirk Reynolds)*, William Frawley *(Jack Heffernan)*, Benny Baker *(Dick Mycroft)*, Minor Watson *(Col. Denby)*, Raymond Hatton *(Bob Haskins)*.

The 1938 football season was greeted with this West Point sports picture starring Robert Cummings as Jimmy Howell, a new cadet whose talent on the field far outweighs his talent in the classroom. Not extremely well-liked due to his sure-fire antidisciplinary, anti-upperclassmen attitude, Jimmy saves the game when he prevents his teammate, Brandon Culpepper (John Howard), from running the wrong way with the ball and scoring points for the opponent.

p, Edward T. Lowe; d, Kurt Neumann; w, Lloyd Corrigan, Erwin Gelsey; ph, Victor Milner; ed, Arthur Schmidt.

Football   (PR:A   MPAA:NR)

TRACK OF THUNDER**

(1967) 83m Ambassador/UA c

Tom Kirk (Bobby Goodwin), Ray Stricklyn (Gary Regal), H.M. Wynant (Maxwell Carstairs), Brenda Benet (Shelley Newman), Faith Domergue (Mrs. Goodwin), Majel Barrett (Georgia Clark), Chet Stratton (Mr. Regal), James Dobson (Bowser Smith), Paul Crabtree (Mr. Bigelow), Sam Tarpley (Col. Lee).

Big with the Southern drive-in circuit of stock car racing fans, this independently made film tells the tale of a couple of hotshot driving "good ol' boys," Bobby Goodwin (Tom Kirk) and Gary Regal (Ray Stricklyn), who battle it out on the track night after night for the checkered flag. While the track publicity people claim the pair hate each other, they're actually friends—until they set eyes on the same girl and become bitter enemies, that is. Overdramatization gives the story laughs it doesn't want, and the two racers seem a bit old to be battling like jealous high-school kids over a girl.

p, E. Stanley Williamson; d, Joe Kane; w, Maurice J. Hill; ph, Alan Stensvold (Techniscope, Technicolor); ed, Verna Fields.

Auto Racing   (PR:A   MPAA:NR)

TRADING HEARTS**

(1988) 88m Vista/Cineworld c (AKA: TWEENERS)

Raul Julia (Vinnie), Beverly D'Angelo (Donna), Jenny Lewis (Yvonne), Parris Buckner (Robert), Robert Gwaltney (Ducky), Ruben Rabasa (Pepe), Mark Harris (Ralph), Robin Caldwell, Earleen Carey, Tom Kouchalakos, Edward L. Koch.

Although written by Sports Illustrated's respected Frank Deford (who also penned the book upon which EVERYBODY'S ALL-AMERICAN was based) and starring Raul Julia and Beverly D'Angelo, TRADING HEARTS never saw a theatrical release and went directly to home video. A romantic comedy set in 1957, the film features Julia as Vinnie, a washed-up pitcher for the Boston Red Sox who has just been cut from the roster during spring training. Feeling sorry for himself, Vinnie hits the bar circuit, where he meets Donna (D'Angelo), a thirtysomething divorcee making a last-ditch attempt at a singing career in a local dive. Although Vinnie and Donna don't exactly hit it off, her precocious 11-year-old daughter, Yvonne (Jenny Lewis) —a baseball nut who recognizes Vinnie from her baseball cards—is determined to get her mom and the pitcher

hitched. This doesn't seem likely, however, until Donna's ex-husband succeeds in gaining custody of the child, uniting Donna and Vinnie in pursuit of a common dream. The film was directed by ace sports photographer Neil Leifer.

p, Herb Jaffe, Mort Engelberg; d, Neil Leifer; w, Frank Deford; ph, Karen Grossman (DeLuxe Color); ed, Rick Shaine; m, Stanley Myers.

Baseball   **Cas.**   (PR:A-C   MPAA:PG)

TRIPLE THREAT**

(1948) 71m COL bw

Richard Crane (Don Whitney), Gloria Henry (Ruth Nolan), Mary Stuart (Marian Rutherford), John Litel (Coach Snyder), Pat Phelan (Joe Nolan), Joseph Crehan (Coach Miller), Regina Wallace (Mrs. Nolan), Syd Saylor (Television Man), Dooley Wilson (Porter), Harry Wismer, Tom Harmon, Bob Kelley (Announcers), Sammy Baugh, Johnny Clement, "Boley" Dancewicz, Paul Christman, Bill Dudley, Paul Governall, "Indian" Jack Jacobs, Sid Luckman, Charles Trippi, Steve Van Buren, Bob Waterfield

Don Whitney (Richard Crane) is a conceited college football player who, when he graduates and goes into the professional arena, gets the stuffing knocked out of him. The dull plot plods along to a cliche ending in between lively shots of some gridiron greats in action, but those are newsreel clips and barely further the story. The football pros (Sid Luckman, Sammy Baugh, and others) and announcers (Tom Harmon, Harry Wismer, Bob Kelley) in the film are mostly just introduced and do little themselves to make the story sing.

p, Sam Katzman; d, Jean Yarbrough; w, Joseph Carole, Don Martin; ph, Vincent Farrar; ed, Jerome Thoms.

Football   (PR:A   MPAA:NR)

TROUBLE ALONG THE WAY***

(1953) 110m WB bw

John Wayne (Steve Aloysius Williams), Donna Reed (Alice Singleton), Charles Coburn (Father Burke), Tom Tully (Father Malone), Sherry Jackson (Carole Williams), Marie Windsor (Anne McCormick), Tom Helmore (Harold McCormick), Dabbs Greer (Father Mahoney), Leif Erickson (Father Provincial), Douglas Spencer (Procurator), Lester Matthews (Cardinal O'Shea), Chuck Connors (Stan Schwegler), Bill Radovich (Moose McCall), Richard Garrick (Judge), Murray Alper (Bus Driver), James Flavin (Buck Holman), Ned Glass (Pool Player).

St. Anthony's College is in big financial trouble, so its president, Fr. Burke (Charles Coburn), tries to persuade former big-time football coach Steve Williams (John Wayne) to take over the small Catholic school's football program in the hope that a winning team will mean big gate receipts. Steve, whose life is on the skids, refuses until his ex-wife (Marie Windsor) tries to gain custody of his beloved daughter, Carole (Sherry Jackson); then, to convince the authorities that he is a responsible parent, he takes the position.

By calling in favors, bending admission standards, and performing a little blackmail here and there, Steve transforms St. Anthony's pathetic squad into a winning team; however, when Fr. Burke learns the price of victory, Steve js out of a job. In the meantime, Steve and Alice Singleton (Donna Reed), who is Carole's case worker (and thinks Steve is "positively ziggidy"), have fallen for each other. She therefore comes to his rescue at the custody hearing, as does Fr. Burke, who rehires him. Gives you kind of a warm feeling, doesn't it? No, *really*. TROUBLE ALONG THE WAY is full of good old-fashioned emotions, plot twists, and performances, and as hokey as it may sound, there are a lot of worse ways to spend a couple of hours. Chuck Connors, TV's "Rifleman" who played baseball for the Dodgers and Cubs and basketball for the Boston Celtics, makes an early film appearance here as one of Steve's assistant coaches.

p, Melville Shavelson; d, Michael Curtiz; w, Melville Shavelson, Jack Rose (based on the story "It Figures" by Douglas Morrow, Robert H. Andrews); ph, Archie Stout; ed, Owen Marks; m, Max Steiner.

Football **(PR:O MPAA:R)**

TWO MINUTES TO PLAY**

(1937) 69m Victory bw

Herman Brix *(Martin Granville)*, Eddie Nugent *(Jack Gaines)*, Jeanne Martel *(Pat Meredith)*, Betty Compson *(Fluff Harding)*, Grady Sutton *(Hank Durkee)*, Duncan Renaldo *(Lew Ashley)*, David Sharpe *(Buzzy Vincent)*, Sammy Cohen *(Abie)*, Forrest Taylor *(Coach Rodney)*, Richard Tucker *(Gaines)*, Sam Flint *(Granville)*.

At Franklin University, another mythical movie college, Martin Granville (Herman Brix) and Jack Gaines (Eddie Nugent) are rivals in academics, on the football field, and for the affections of Pat Meredith (Jeanne Martel). This is in keeping with an old family tradition, for their fathers (Richard Tucker and Sam Flint) continue a similar rivalry that also began in their own days at good old Franklin U. All is settled on the football field, with only "two minutes to play," in this strictly by-the-book story.

p, Sam Katzman; d, Robert Hill; w, William Buchanan; ph, William Hyer; ed, Charles Henkel.

Football **(PR:A MPAA:NR)**

U V

UNDER MY SKIN***

(1950) 86m FOX bw

John Garfield *(Dan Butler)*, Micheline Presle *(Paule Manet)*, Luther Adler *(Louis Bork)*, Orley Lindgren *(Joe)*, Noel Drayton *(George Gardner)*, A.A. Merola *(Maurice)*, Ott George *(Rico)*, Paul Bryar *(Max)*, Ann Codee *(Henriette)*, Steve Geray *(Bartender)*, Joseph Warfield *(Rigoli)*,

Eugene Borden *(Doctor)*, Loulette Sablon *(Nurse)*, Alphonse Martell *(Detective)*, Ernesto Morelli *(Hotel Clerk)*, Jean Del Val *(Express Man)*, Hans Herbert *(Attendant)*, Esther Zeitlin *(Flower Woman)*, Maurice Brierre *(Doorman)*, Gordon Clark *(Barman)*.

Ernest Hemingway's spare, somewhat grim short story "My Old Man" was turned into something resembling THE CHAMP on horseback. Though Hemingway's story was considerably altered and expanded to fit a feature-length film, the resulting picture retains much of the basic flavor of the author's work. Dan Butler (John Garfield), a crooked jockey who has been barred from racing in the US and Italy, flees to France with his son Joe (Orley Lindgren), barely escaping death at the hands of some gangster. In Paris, Dan and his son run into Paule Manet (Micheline Presle, the star of the French classic DEVIL IN THE FLESH, in her first American role), a beautiful woman who owns her own nightclub on the Left Bank. In an effort to become the perfect dad that his son imagines him to be, Dan decides to run an honest race, and also become serious with Paule. However, pressure from gangster Louis Bork (Luther Adler), who demands that the rider throw a race in order to pay back a loan, puts Dan in a spot.

p, Casey Robinson; d, Jean Negulesco; w, Casey Robinson (based on the story "My Old Man" by Ernest Hemingway); ph, Joseph LaShelle; ed, Dorothy Spencer; m, Daniele Amfitheatrof.

Horse Racing **(PR:A MPAA:NR)**

UNHOLY ROLLERS**

(1972) 88m Roger Corman/AIP c (AKA: LEADER OF THE PACK)

Claudia Jennings *(Karen)*, Louis Quinn *(Stern)*, Betty Anne Rees *(Mickey)*, Roberta Collins *(Jennifer)*, Alan Vint *(Greg)*, Candice Roman *(Donna)*, Jay Varela *(Nick)*, Charlene Jones *(Beverly)*, Joe E. Tata *(Marshall)*, Maxine Gates *(Angie Striker)*, Kathleen Freeman *(Karen's Mother)*, John Harmon *(Doctor)*, John Mitchell *(Horace McKay)*, Dennis Redfield *(Duane)*, Carl Rizzo, Michael Miller *(Referees)*, John Steadman *(Guard)*, Roxanna Bonilla *(Consuelo)*, Louie and the Rockets *(Band in Bar)*.

This fast-paced look at the roller-derby circuit stars former *Playboy* Playmate of the Year Claudia Jennings as Karen, a factory worker who quits her job and takes up skating, then becomes tops in her field when she decides to ignore the staged brawls and violence and go in for the real thing. Her fellow players hate her, but she leaves the audience always wanting more. UNHOLY ROLLERS is heavy on violence and four-letter words, and short on character, but that makes the picture true to its source. Though filled with roller-derby action, it does manage to leave room for the usual exploitative elements of lesbianism and nudity. The producers had hoped to get it into the theaters before KANSAS CITY BOMBER (1972), another roller-derby picture with a larger budget, but the Raquel Welch starrer beat them to the punch.

p, John Prizer, Jack Bohrer; d, Vernon Zimmerman; w, Howard R. Cohen (based on a story by Zimmerman,

Cohen); ph, Mike Shea (DeLuxe Color); ed, George Trirogoff, Yeu-Bun Yee; m, Bobby Hart.

Roller Derby   Cas.   (PR:O   MPAA:R)

UNWELCOME STRANGER**½

(1935) 64m COL bw

Jack Holt *(Howard Chamberlain)*, Mona Barrie *(Madeline Chamberlain)*, Jackie Searl *(Gimpy)*, Ralph Morgan *(Mike)*, Bradley Page *(Lucky Palmer)*, Frankie Darro *(Charlie Anderson)*, Sam McDaniel *(Pot Roast)*, Frank Orth *(Jackson)*.

This harmless and rather sweet racetrack picture concerns a horse breeder, Howard Chamberlain (Jack Holt), who is suspicious of orphans—ponies and people alike—since he himself was raised in an orphanage. He is so serious about his superstition that he even gets rid of any foundling ponies he has, rather than let them jinx their stablemates. Little Gimpy (Jackie Searl) approaches Chamberlain with the hope of getting involved in racing, and the breeder takes him in and grows quite fond of him . . . then discovers that the child is an orphan. He's too attached to the boy, however, to turn him away and gives in to Gimpy's desire to jockey a horse. Gimpy takes first place and his mentor's superstition is broken.

d, Phil Rosen; w, Crane Wilbur (based on a story by William Jacobs); ph, John Stumar; ed, Arthur Hilton.

Horse Racing   (PR:A   MPAA:NR)

VICTORY**

(1981) 117m Victory-Lorimar/PAR c (GB: ESCAPE TO VICTORY)

Sylvester Stallone *(Robert Hatch)*, Michael Caine *(John Colby)*, Pele *(Luis Fernandez)*, Bobby Moore *(Terry Brady)*, Osvaldo Ardiles *(Carlos Rey)*, Paul Van Himst *(Michel Fileu)*, Kazimierz Deyna *(Paul Wolchek)*, Hallvar Thoren-sen *(Gunnar Hilsson)*, Mike Summerbee *(Sid Harmor)*, Co Prins *(Pieter Van Beck)*, Russell Osman *(Doug Clure)*, John Wark *(Arthur Hayes)*, Soren Linsted *(Erik Borge)*, Kevin O'Calloghan *(Tony Lewis)*, Max Von Sydow *(Maj. Karl Von Steiner)*, Gary Waldhorn *(Coach Mueller)*, George Mikell *(Kommandant)*, Laurie Sivell *(Goalie)*, Arthur Brauss *(Lutz)*, Robin Turner *(Player)*, Michael Wolf *(Lang)*, Jurgen Andersen *(Propaganda Civilian)*, David Shawyer *(Strauss)*, Werner Roth *(Team Captain Baumann)*, Amidou *(Andre)*, Benoit Ferreux *(Jean Paul)*, Jean Francois Stevenin *(Claude)*, Jack Lenoir *(Georges)*, Folton Gera *(Viktor)*, Carole Laure *(Renee)*, Tim Pigott-Smith *(Rose)*.

Part THE GREAT ESCAPE, part standard underdog-comes-from-behind sports movie, John Huston's VICTO-RY limps along unimaginatively for its first three-quarters, but hits full stride in the half-hour, brilliantly staged soccer sequence that provides the film's climax. The setting is a WW II POW camp, where Maj. Karl Von Steiner (Max von Sydow), a onetime member of the German national soccer team, spots John Colby (Michael Caine), a former English international player, among the Allied prisoners. The major persuades Colby to put together a team to play a "friendly" match against a German team, but with the intervention of the Nazi propaganda machine, the contest escalates into a confrontation between the German national team and an all-star squad of Allied prisoners to be played in Colombes Stadium in Paris. While the prisoners prepare for the match, Hatch (Sylvester Stallone), their American trainer, escapes, meets with the French Resistance to plan a half-time escape from the stadium, then reluctantly allows himself to be recaptured. Before 50,000 spectators and a worldwide radio audience, the Germans, aided by a biased referee, take a commanding 4-1 lead into the locker room at halftime, but instead of making good their escape, the Allies return to the field determined to win, despite the fact that the inexperienced Hatch is in goal. All of which leads to the well-shot, tightly edited, and, yes, exciting finale that features some extraordinary play by a number of real-life soccer stars, including Brazilian great Pele; Bobby Moore, captain of England's 1966 World Cup champions (who perhaps not coincidentally beat West Germany 4-2); and Argentine superstar Osvaldo Ardiles. Alternately hokey and inspiring, the climactic game, which features the crowd chanting *victoire* and bursting into "La Marseillaise," is unquestionably VICTORY's highlight, and good enough reason to sit through the rest of the film.

p, Freddie Fields; d, John Huston; w, Evan Jones, Yabo Yablonsky (based on a story by Yablonsky, Djordje Milicevic, Jeff Maguire); ph, Gerry Fisher (Panavision, Metrocolor); ed, Roberto Silvi; m, Bill Conti.

Soccer   Cas.   (PR:A-C   MPAA:PG)

VISION QUEST***

(1985) 107m Guber-Peters/WB c

Matthew Modine *(Louden Swain)*, Linda Fiorentino *(Carla)*, Michael Schoeffling *(Kuch)*, Ronny Cox *(Louden's Dad)*, Harold Sylvester *(Tanneran)*, Charles Hallahan *(Coach)*, J.C. Quinn *(Elmo)*, Daphne Zuniga *(Margie Epstein)*, R.H. Thomson *(Kevin)*, Gary Kasper *(Otto)*, Raphael Sbarge *(Schmoozler)*, Forest Whitaker *(Bulldozer)*, Frank Jasper *(Shute)*, Roberts Blossom *(Grandpa)*, James Gammon *(Kuch's Dad)*, Judith Hansen *(Elsie)*, Fred Miles *(Louden's Opponent)*, Sean Morgan *(Injured Salesman)*, Cash Stone *(Official)*, Ken Pelo *(Hoover Team Coach)*, Madonna

Earnest, warm, and often very funny, VISION QUEST features a finely etched performance by Matthew Modine as Louden Swain, an 18-year-old high-school wrestler who is equally determined to lose his virginity and some 20 pounds—the latter so that he can take on the state's finest grappler, 168-pound champion Shute (Frank Jasper). While Louden embarks upon his "vision quest"—a physical and spiritual quest to find his place in the world—the film introduces the intriguing cast of characters who most influence him, including his father (Ronny Cox), a failed farmer-cum-auto mechanic, and his friend and teammate Kuch (Michael Schoeffling). The two people who loom largest in Louden's life, however, are Shute and Carla (Linda Fiorentino), a 21-year-old art student from New Jersey who stays with the Swains while the car she just purchased is repaired, and who initiates Louden into the world of romance and sex. When she leaves abruptly, Louden contemplates abandoning his other obsession, but the cook at the hotel where he works (J.C. Quinn) persuades him not to give up. All of Louden's rigorous dieting and training pay off in his match against Shute, and guess who's come back to witness his triumph? Although this finale isn't going to surprise anyone, VISION QUEST is full of patiently developed characters that have more to do with real life than movie scripts, distinguishing it from many similarly plotted big-finish sports films. What's more, the performances (including Madonna's film debut, in a nightclub scene) are strong, the Spokane, Washington, setting is new and interesting, and the mat action is authentic (Modine spent four months preparing for the role—running, wrestling, and exercising). Based on a novel by Terry Davis, this rites-of-passage tale is far from perfect, but will leave few viewers disappointed.

p, Jon Peters, Peter Gruber; d, Harold Becker; w, Darryl Ponicsan (based on the novel by Terry Davis); ph, Owen Roizman (Panavision, Technicolor); ed, Maury Winetrobe; m, Tangerine Dream.

Wrestling   Cas.   (PR:O MPAA:R)

WALK, DON'T RUN***

(1966) 114m Granley/COL c

Cary Grant (Sir William Rutland), Samantha Eggar (Christine Easton), Jim Hutton (Steve Davis), John Standing (Julius P. Haversack), Miiko Taka (Aiko Kurawa), Ted Hartley (Yuri Andreyovitch), Ben Astar (Dimitri), George Takei (Police Captain), Teru Shimada (Mr. Kurawa), Lois Kiuchi (Mrs. Kurawa), Bob Okazaki (Plant Manager), James Yagi (Rutland's Driver), Craig Matsunaga (Boy), Patty Siu (Girl), Miyoshi Jingu (Woman), William Saito (Japanese Athlete), C.K. Yang (Chinese Athlete), Peggy Rea (Russian Shot Putter), Jane Tochihara (Japanese Mother), Randy Okazaki (Cab Driver), Rollin Moriyama (Manager), Sheri Yamasaki (Hostess), Vickey Cason (Contortionist).

A remake of THE MORE THE MERRIER (1943), this lighthearted comedy was Cary Grant's last film, and stars Grant as Sir William Rutland, an English industrialist who is unable to find hotel accommodations on the eve of the 1964 Tokyo Olympiad. Answering an ''apartment to share'' notice, he persuades Christine (Samantha Eggar) to allow him to stay with her, then talks her into letting Steve (Jim Hutton), a American race walker, bunk there as well. Christine's priggish fiance, Julius (John Standing), a

British embassy official, isn't very happy about the living arrangements, and matters become even more complicated when a Soviet agent begins to suspect that Steve and Christine are spies. Rutland, however, is set on bringing Steve and Christine together, and his maneuvering to do so—including stripping to his underclothes and accompanying Steve through the streets of Tokyo during the walk race—results in a happy, suitably romantic finale. Grant's final performance is delightful, and Eggar and Hutton offer strong support in this winning comedy.

p, Sol C. Siegel; d, Charles Walters; w, Sol Sak (based on a story by Robert Russell), Frank Ross; ph, Harry Stradling (Panavision, Technicolor); ed, Walter Thompson, James Wells; m, Quincy Jones.

Track and Field/
Comedy   Cas.   (PR:A MPAA:NR)

WALKOVER***

(1965, Pol.) 77m Syrena-Film Polski/New Yorker bw (WALKOWER)

Aleksandra Zawieruszanka (Teresa), Jerzy Skolimowski (Andrzej Leszczyc), Krzysztof Chamiec (Director), Franciszek Pieczka (Activist), Elizbieta Czyzewska (Girl at Train Station), Andrzej Herder (Pawlak), Tadeusz Kondrat (Old Man), Stanislaw Zaczyk (''Priest''), Henryk Kluba (Trainer Rogala), Krzysztof Litwin (Miecio).

Polish director Jerzy Skolimowski's third film stars Skolimowski himself as Andrzej, a 30-year-old amateur boxer who earns a meager living from the prize money of various bouts. A former college acquaintance, Teresa (Aleksandra Zawieruszanka), helps Andrzej get an engineering job, but he is drawn back to the ring when he learns the factory has a boxing team. At an upcoming fight, Andrzej is ruled the winner when his opponent doesn't show up. The opponent later arrives and reveals that he was bribed not to show, demanding his half of the prize money. Andrzej refuses to split his winnings, however, and the pair enter the ring for a rematch in which he is easily beaten. As a youth, Skolimowski had been a boxer, and his first directorial effort was a documentary starring himself called BOXER. What is most unique about WALKOVER is the filmmaking technique; while most boxing films are filled with heavily edited boxing montages, there are only a scant 29 shots in all of WALKOVER.

d, Jerzy Skolimowski; w, Jerzy Skolimowski; ph, Antoni Nurzynski; ed, Barbara Kryczmonik; m, Andrzej Trzaskowski.

Boxing   (PR:C MPAA:NR)

WALL OF NOISE**½

(1963) 112m WB bw

Suzanne Pleshette (Laura Rubio), Ty Hardin (Joel Tarrant), Dorothy Provine (Ann Conroy), Ralph Meeker (Matt Rubio), Simon Oakland (Johnny Papadakis), James Murphy (Bud Kelsey), Murray Matheson (Jack Matlock), Robert Simon (Dave McRaab), George Petrie (Mr. Harrington), Jean Byron (Mrs. Harrington), Fred Carson (Adam

Kasper), Bill Walker *(Money)*, Napoleon Whiting *(Preacher)*, Kitty White *(Singer)*, Jim Murray *(Sportswriter)*.

The lives and loves behind the scenes at the racetrack are detailed in this thoroughbred soap opera. An ambitious young trainer, Joel Tarrant (Ty Hardin), enters into an illicit affair with the stable owner's wealthy wife, hot-to-trot Laura Rubio (Suzanne Pleshette), in the hope that someday he'll have enough dough to buy his own horses and stable. Husband Matt (Ralph Meeker) suspects what is going on and fires Joel. Desperate, Joel borrows money from the boss of his former girl friend, Ann Conroy (Dorothy Provine), to buy a promising horse. When the horse wins big in a preliminary race, Joel gets his hopes up, but the horse loses in the final run and leaves Joel financially busted. Although his horse fails him, Ann promises to stick around. Onetime *Los Angeles Times* sportswriter Jim Murray is appropriately cast as a sportswriter. While the plot may be heavy on the melodrama, the horse-racing photography by Lucien Ballard, a veteran of numerous westerns, is excellent.

p, Joseph Landon; d, Richard Wilson; w, Joseph Landon (based on the novel by Daniel Michael Stein); ph, Lucien Ballard; ed, William Ziegler; m, William Lava.

Horse Racing (PR:A MPAA:NR)

WE WENT TO COLLEGE**

(1936) 64m MGM bw (GB: THE OLD SCHOOL TIE)

Charles Butterworth *(Glenn Harvey)*, Walter Abel *(Phil Talbot)*, Hugh Herbert *(Professor)*, Una Merkel *(Susan)*, Edith Atwater *(Nina)*, Walter Catlett *(Sen. Budger)*, Charles Trowbridge *(President Timlin)*, Tom Ricketts *(Grandpop)*.

College grad Glenn Harvey (Charles Butterworth) returns to his alma mater during homecoming week for three days of wild, youthful remembrances. Something of a wastrel, Glenn becomes the victim of too much alcohol, finds his way onto the field during the big game, and tries to prevent his team from being scored against by tackling a member of the opposing squad—a comic moment taken from a real life Princeton game in the 1935 football season.

p, Harry Rapf; d, Joseph Stanley; w, Richard Maibaum, Maurice Rapf (based on a story by George Oppenheimer, Finley Peter Dunne, Jr.); ph, Lester White; ed, James E. Newcom; m, Dr. William Axt.

Football/Comedy (PR:A MPAA:NR)

WEE GEORDIE***

(1956, Brit.) 93m Argonaut/Times (GB: GEORDIE)

Alistair Sim *(The Laird)*, Bill Travers *(Geordie MacTaggart)*, Norah Gorsen *(Jean Donaldson)*, Molly Urquhart *(Geordie's Mother)*, Francis de Wolff *(Henry Samson)*, Jack Radcliffe *(Rev. McNab)*, Brian Reece *(Dick Harley)*, Raymond Huntley *(Rawlins)*, Miles Malleson *(Lord Paunceton)*, Jameson Clarke *(Geordie's Father)*, Doris Godard *(Helga)*, Stanley Baxter *(Postman)*, Duncan Macrae *(Schoolmaster)*, Paul Young *(Young Geordie)*,

Anna Ferguson *(Young Jean)*, Margaret Boyd *(Laird's Housekeeper)*, Alex McCrindle *(Guard)*.

Set in the "past and present, with a wee glimpse into the future," this tender tale of a youngster's rise to fame is photographed against the picturesque Scottish highlands. Geordie (Paul Young) is a frail lad who takes a ribbing from his schoolmates because of his size, or lack of it. After seeing a muscleman ad in a magazine, he begins to get himself into shape, and, as he enters manhood (now played by Bill Travers), his pains begin to pay off when he is selected for Britain's Olympic squad in the hammer-throwing event in Australia. Leaving his local lassie (Norah Gorsen) behind, Geordie heads down under, where a muscular Danish damsel, Helga (Doris Godard), pounces on her reticent cocompetitor. The film includes a characteristically fine performance from Alastair Sim as the laird who employs Geordie's gamekeeper father.

p, Frank Launder, Sidney Gilliat; d, Frank Launder; w, Frank Launder, Sidney Gilliat (based on a novel by David Walker); ph, Wilkie Cooper (Technicolor); ed, Thelma Connell; m, William Alwyn.

Track and Field (PR:A MPAA:NR)

WHIPLASH**½

(1948) 91m WB bw

Dane Clark *(Michael Gordon)*, Alexis Smith *(Laurie Durant)*, Zachary Scott *(Rex Durant)*, Eve Arden *(Chris)*, Jeffrey Lynn *(Dr. Arnold Vincent)*, S.Z. Sakall *(Sam)*, Alan Hale, Sr. *(Terrance O'Leary)*, Douglas Kennedy *(Costello)*, Ransom Sherman *(Tex Sanders)*, Fred Steele *(Duke Carney)*, Robert Lowell *(Trask)*, Don McGuire *(Harkus)*, Clifton Young *(Gunman)*, Sam Hayes *(Announcer)*, Mike Lally *(Ring Announcer)*, Howard Mitchell *(Fight Announcer)*, Ralph Volkie *(Referee)*, Donald Kerr *(Vendor)*, Rudy Friml *(Orchestra Leader)*, Jimmy Dodd *(Bill)*, I. Stanford Jolley *(Artist)*, Maude Prickett *(Mrs. Gruman)*, Thomas Garland *(Rocky)*, John Daheim *(Kid Lucas)*, John Harmon *(Kid McGee)*, Wally Scott *(Drunk)*, Cliff Herd *(Waiter)*, Howard Negley *(Policeman)*, Larry McGrath *(Manager)*, Bob Perry *(Timekeeper)*.

It's amazing how many Hollywood boxing tales center on a fighter who, deep down inside, is sensitive and thoughtful and would rather be doing something else, but who has been forced into the ring out of necessity. WHIPLASH takes this premise to the hilt, sending Michael Gordon (Dane Clark) away from his painter's canvas in California to get his head knocked about in New York City after falling head over heels for Laurie Durant (Alexis Smith). Her husband, Rex (Zachary Scott), was a fighter, but because of an accident had to retire and now runs the nightclub where his wife sings. Rex uses Michael to fulfill vicariously his dream of becoming the world champ, while Michael benefits from Rex's pointers. Eventually, however, Rex gets wind of the affair between his wife and the artist-cum-fighter and does the best to see that Michael gets his brains knocked out. Of course, Michael proves victorious in the ring. The romantic triangle is formula all the way, but the fight sequences (the film opens in Madison Square

Garden) and a number of boxing montages lend excitement.

p, William Jacobs; d, Lewis Seiler; w, Maurice Geraghty, Harriet Frank, Jr., Gordon Kahn (based on a story by Kenneth Earl); ph, Peverell Marley; ed, Frank Magee; m, Franz Waxman.

Boxing (PR:A MPAA:NR)

WHITE LIGHTNING**

(1953) 61m AA/MON bw

Stanley Clements *(Mike)*, Steve Brodie *(Jack)*, Gloria Blondell *(Ann)*, Barbara Bestar *(Margaret)*, Lyle Talbot *(Rocky)*, Frank Jenks *(Benny)*, Paul Bryar *(Stew)*, Lee Van Cleef *(Brutus)*, Myron Healey *(Nelson)*, Riley Hill *(Norwin)*, Tom Hanlon *(Announcer)*, Jane Easton *(Girl)*, John Bleifer *(Tailor)*, Duncan Richardson *(Davey)*.

Hockey films have never been all that popular on the big screen, especially in the 1950s, when WHITE LIGHTNING gave fans their only chance to see slap shots in a moviehouse. When flashy egomaniac Mike (Stanley Clements) joins the Red Devils hockey team, the other players and the coaching staff are willing to indulge his brash personality because of his talent on the ice. The team goes on a successful winning streak thanks to his abilities, but this makes things difficult for his teammate Nelson (Myron Healey), who is secretly being paid by some mobsters to make the Red Devils lose. The coach (Steve Brodie) is also having problems with the fresh kid, and Mike seriously considers throwing games himself when confronted by the mob. But in the end honesty triumphs and the star leads the team on to victory in an important game. The formula material has good visual quality, of a type sometimes lacking in sports films.

p, Ben Schwalb; d, Edward Bernds; w, Charles R. Marion; ph, Lester White; ed, Bruce Schoengarth; m, Marlin Skiles.

Hockey (PR:A MPAA:NR)

WILD RACERS, THE*½

(1968) 79m Alta Vista-Filmakers/AIP c

Fabian *(Jo-Jo Quillico)*, Mimsy Farmer *(Katherine)*, Alan Haufrect *(Charlie)*, Judy Cornwell *(British Girl)*, Davis Landers *(Manager)*, Warwick Sims *(Jo-Jo's Partner)*, Talia Shire, Ursule Pauly, Dick Miller, Ron Gans, Fabienne Arel, Patricia Culbert, Mary Jo Kennedy, Kurt Boon.

This meager auto racing picture relies heavily on stock footage to tell its story, that of racer Jo-Jo Quillico (Fabian), who is hired by an auto tycoon to do some driving. His real talent is with the girls, however, and he chalks up conquests faster than laps. Katherine (Mimsy Farmer) is his favorite—until she mentions marriage, whereupon he drops her like a hot radiator cap and finds someone else with no desire for commitment. Francis Ford Coppola was the second-unit director on this film, which is quite similar to the 1962 AIP picture THE YOUNG RACERS. In a minor role is Francis' sister Talia, who later became Talia Shire and made her mark as Rocky Balboa's sweetheart in

ROCKY. Also notable is the photography by Nestor Almendros, who has since received numerous Oscar nominations for his work. This was the third year in a row in which Fabian played a championship racer: he also sat behind the wheel in 1966's FIREBALL 500 and in 1967's THUNDER ALLEY, playing a driver plagued with blackouts in the latter.

p, Joel Rapp; d, Daniel Haller; w, Max House; ph, Nestor Almendros, Daniel Lacambre (Pathe Color); ed, Verna Fields, Dennis Jacob; m, Mike Curb.

Auto Racing (PR:A-C MPAA:NR)

WILDCATS*½

(1986) 107m Hawn-Sylbert/WB c

Goldie Hawn *(Molly McGrath)*, Swoosie Kurtz *(Verna)*, Robyn Lively *(Alice McGrath)*, Brandy Gold *(Marian McGrath)*, James Keach *(Frank McGrath)*, Jan Hooks *(Stephanie)*, Bruce McGill *(Dan Darwell)*, Nipsey Russell *(Ben Edwards)*, Mykel T. Williamson *(Levander "Bird" Williams)*, Tab Thacker *(Finch)*, Wesley Snipes *(Trumaine)*, Nick Corri *(Cerulo)*, Woody Harrelson *(Krushinski)*, Willie J. Walton *(Marvel)*, Rodney Hill *(Peanut)*, Lindsey Orr *(Central Player)*, Albert Michel *(Alonzo)*, Eddie Frescas *(Translator)*, M. Emmet Walsh *(Coes)*, Ellia English *(Marva)*, Jenny Havens *(Jeannie)*, Tony Salome *(Mr. Remo)*, George Wyner *(Principal Walker)*, Noel De Souza *(Doctor)*, Ann Doran *(Mrs. Chatham)*, Gloria Stuart *(Mrs. Connoly)*.

This Goldie Hawn vehicle, Michael Ritchie's fourth sports film (DOWNHILL RACER; SEMI-TOUGH; and BAD NEWS BEARS preceded), offers few surprises, but does feature some nice moments from the ever-plucky comedienne. After being denied the head football coach's job at Prescott High—a nice school in a nice neighborhood where she is the girls track coach—Molly McGrath (Hawn) accepts a position as the grid coach at inner-city Central High. Predictably, the tough kids refuse to take Molly seriously and make life miserable for her, but in time she earns their respect; and, respecting themselves for the first time, the Wildcats begin winning. Problems arise on the home front, however, when Molly's ex-husband (James Keach) claims that her devotion to her coaching duties has made her an unfit mother. Rest assured that Molly comes out a winner both in the big game against good old Prescott and in her custody struggle. Silly but not always funny, WILDCATS relies too much on Hawn's familiar screen persona, getting little mileage from the actress' "serious" moments, yet it manages to provide more than a chuckle or two.

p, Anthea Sylbert; d, Michael Ritchie; w, Ezra Sacks; ph, Donald E. Thorin (Technicolor); ed, Richard A. Harris; m, Hawk Wolinski, James Newton Howard.

Football/Comedy Cas. (PR:C-O MPAA:R)

WINNER TAKE ALL***½

(1932) 68m WB bw

James Cagney *(Jim Kane)*, Marian Nixon *(Peggy Harmon)*, Virginia Bruce *(Joan Gibson)*, Guy Kibbee *(Pop Slavin)*,

Clarence Muse (Rosebud the Trainer), Dickie Moore (Dickie Harmon), Allan Lane (Monty), John Roche (Roger Elliott), Ralf Harolde (Legs Davis), Alan Mowbray (Forbes), Clarence Wilson (Ben Isaacs), Charles Coleman (Butler), Esther Howard (Ann), Renee Whitney (Lois), Harvey Perry (Al West), Julian Rivero (Pice), Selmer Jackson (Ring Announcer), Chris-Pin Martin (Manager).

For his first boxing picture, James Cagney plays Jim Kane, a fighter on the mend in a New Mexico health resort. He's been sent there courtesy of fans' donations, having spent most of his own money on alcohol and women. At the resort, he meets Peggy (Marian Nixon) and her small son, Dickie (Dickie Moore), who are about to be kicked out because she can't pay her bill. Jim agrees to help out by entering the ring once more, and wins the prize money, but gets his nose smashed for his efforts. Returning to New York City determined to take the town by storm, Jim meets socialite Joan (Virginia Bruce) and falls for her. He gets his nose fixed to impress her, and takes care to protect his new snooter in the ring, but his skills as a fighter suffer as a result, the fans turn on him, Joan begins to grow bored, and the pug begins to realize that his life has taken a wrong turn. Though the story is simplistic, this is a strong drama, delivered with gusto by the cast. Cagney is at his best, creating a realistic portrait of a fighter who lets his ego balloon out of proportion, and Roy Del Ruth's direction wisely concentrates on the characters, allowing the fine ensemble to give the drama its power. Cagney, who approached his role with the utmost seriousness and was determined to make his characterization realistic, trained with Harvey Perry, an ex-welterweight who also has a bit part in the film. The sparring sessions paid off, for Cagney's moves look like the real thing and it's obvious he's in the thick of the fray in both closeups and long shots. Cagney's skills in the film were so impressive that the rumor circulated for some time that the actor was a former prizefighter.

p, Roy Del Ruth; d, Roy Del Ruth; w, Wilson Mizner, Robert Lord (based on the story "133 at 3" by Gerald Beaumont); ph, Robert Kurrle; ed, Thomas Pratt; m, W. Franke Harling.

Boxing (PR:A MPAA:NR)

WINNER TAKE ALL**

(1939) 62m FOX bw

Tony Martin (Steve Bishop), Gloria Stuart (Julie Harrison), Henry Armetta (Papa Gambini), Slim Summerville (Muldoon), Kane Richmond (Paulie Mitchell), Robert Allen (Tom Walker), Inez Palange (Mama Gambini), Johnnie Pirrone, Jr. (Tony Gambini), Pedro De Cordoba (Pantrelli), Betty Greco (Maria Gambini), Eleanor Virzle (Rosa Gambini).

A prizefight picture with an interesting twist finds cowboy Steve Bishop (Tony Martin) working as a waiter in a spaghetti joint. He agrees to fight in a charity bout, scores a lucky knockout, and goes on to fame and fortune through a series of fights fixed, unbeknownst to Steve, by gamblers. Steve's success goes to his head, which does not sit well with sportswriter Julie Harrison (Gloria Stuart), who

likes him and believes he needs a comeuppance to set him straight.

p, Jerry Hoffman; d, Otto Brower; w, Frances Hyland, Albert Ray (based on a story by Jerry Cady); ph, Edward Cronjager; ed, Nick DeMaggio.

Boxing (PR:A MPAA:NR)

WINNER'S CIRCLE, THE**

(1948) 70m FOX bw

Johnny Longden, Morgan Farley, Robert S. Howard, William Gould, John Berardino, Russ Conway, Frank Dae, Jean Willes, Man O'War the Horse, Seabiscuit the Horse, Whirlaway the Horse, Alsab the Horse, Assault the Horse, Gallant Fox the Horse, Bold Venture the Horse, Stymie the Horse, Phar Lap the Horse, Bull Lea the Horse, Discovery the Horse, War Admiral the Horse, Sir Barton the Horse, Equipoise the Horse.

A neatly contrived horse race story, told from the viewpoint of the horse. The picture follows the thoroughbred from the time of its birth on a Kentucky farm, showing its training, its first setbacks, the loyalty and devotion of its owner (Jean Willes), and its first victory at Santa Anita—with famous jockey Johnny Longden, playing himself, in the saddle.

p, Richard K. Polimer; d, Felix Feist; w, Howard J. Green, Leonard Praskins; ph, Elmer Dyer; ed, Richard G. Wray; m, Lucien Caillet.

Horse Racing (PR:A MPAA:NR)

WINNERS TAKE ALL**

(1987) 105m Apollo-Embassy Home Entertainment/ Manson c

Don Michael Paul (Rick Melon), Kathleen York (Judy McCormick), Robert Krantz ("Bad" Billy Robinson), Deborah Richter (Cindy Wickes), Peter DeLuise (Wally Briskin), Courtney Gains (Goose Trammel), Paul Hampton (Frank Bushing), Gerardo Mejia (Johnny Rivera), Tony Longo ("Bear" Nolan), Isabel Grandin (Peggy Nolan), Broc Glover (Carl), Roger Hampton (Mongrel), Virgil Frye (Sam), Noon Orsatti (Brendt), Clarke Coleman (Kenny), Barbie Langmack (Amy), Bevie Langmack (Angie), Arthur Abelson (Art the Cameraman), Jeff MacGregor (Indian Head Announcer), David Stanfield, Rick Johnson, David Bailey, Larry Huffman (Themselves).

Finding personal salvation through sporting events is by now a well-worn theme in the post-ROCKY movie world. Though WINNERS TAKE ALL starts off as an interesting character study, it fails to deliver on its initial promise, eventually capitulating to formulaic development. "Bad" Billy Robinson (Robert Krantz) is a top motorcycle racer with a corporate-sponsored team. Frank (Paul Hampton), the team's devious manager, takes his boys on a tour of rural America that brings Billy back to the small town where he grew up. There he is reunited with Rick (Don Michael Paul), his best friend and constant rival ever since grammar school. Old jealousies emerge, and Rick decides to challenge Billy in motocross racing. Unlike other films of this nature, the characters here are well developed, and when director Fritz Kiersch sticks to depictions of small town life or friendship, WINNERS TAKE ALL is fairly engaging. The look and ambience are completely accurate, displaying an insider's understanding of this world. Unfortunately, these elements are largely subordinated to genre cliches or countless shots of motorcycles raising dirt. Once Kiersch gets past introducing us to his characters' milieu, he goes right for the obvious, reducing the film to another simple-minded sports drama.

p, Christopher W. Knight, Tom Tatum; d, Fritz Kiersch; w, Ed Turner (based on a story by Tom Tatum, Christopher W. Knight); ph, Fred V. Murphy II (Deluxe color); ed, Lorenzo DeStefano; m, Doug Timm.

Motorcycle Racing   Cas.   (PR:C MPAA:PG-13)

WINNING***

(1969) 123m Newman-Foreman/UNIV c

Paul Newman *(Frank)*, Joanne Woodward *(Elora)*, Robert Wagner *(Luther Erding)*, Richard Thomas *(Charley)*, David Sheiner *(Lee Crawford)*, Clu Gulager *(Larry Morechek)*, Barry Ford *(Les Bottineau)*, Toni Clayton *(The Girl)*, Maxine Stuart *(Miss Redburne's Mother)*, Eileen Wesson *(Miss Redburne)*, Robert Quarry *(Sam Jagin)*, Pauline Myers *(Cleaning Woman)*, Ray Ballard *(Trombone Player)*, Charles Seel *(Eshovo)*, Alma Platt *(Mrs. Eshovo)*, Harry Basch *(The Stranger)*, Allen Emerson *(Desk Clerk)*, Bobby Unser, Tony Hulman *(Themselves)*, Bruce Walkup, Timothy Galbraith *(Drivers)*, Dan Gurney, Roger Mc-Cluskey, Bobby Grim.

Frank Capua (Paul Newman) is a bit tipsy after celebrating his win at a 200-mile auto race. He meets Elora (Joanne Woodward), who works in a car rental store, talks her into going for a drive with him, and soon the two are in love. They marry, and he adopts her son, 13-year-old Charley (Richard Thomas), who idolizes Frank. The moment Frank weds, however, his sweet luck begins to turn sour as he loses race after race to his No. 1 competitor, Luther Erding (Robert Wagner). As the Indy 500 approaches, the situation begins to take its toll on the marriage. WINNING was originally planned as a TV movie, but was soon expanded for the big screen with the addition of Newman (who was also an uncredited producer) and others to the cast. Newman did his own race driving (the studio insured him for $3 million)—and still continues to do so with vigor, at age 64—and several other real-life racers appear, including Bobby Unser, Tony Hulman, Dan Gurney, Roger Mc-Cluskey, and Bobby Grim. The footage in the Indy race is of the awesome 17-car crackup that began the 1968 festivities. Its insertion lends the picture even greater authenticity, although the film stock used in the race scenes appears to differ slightly from that used in the rest of the movie.

p, John Foreman; d, James Goldstone; w, Howard Rodman; ph, Richard Moore (Panavision, Technicolor); ed, Edward A. Biery, Richard C. Meyer; m, Dave Grusin.

Auto Racing   Cas.   (PR:A-C MPAA:G/M)

WINNING TEAM, THE***

(1952) 98m WB bw

Doris Day *(Aimee Alexander)*, Ronald Reagan *(Grover Cleveland Alexander)*, Frank Lovejoy *(Rogers Hornsby)*, Eve Miller *(Margaret)*, James Millican *(Bill Killefer)*, Rusty Tamblyn *(Willie Alexander)*, Gordon Jones *(Glasheen)*, Hugh Sanders *(McCarthy)*, Frank Ferguson *(Sam Arrants)*, Walter Baldwin *(Pa Alexander)*, Dorothy Adams *(Ma Alexander)*, Bonnie Kay Eddie *(Sister)*, Jimmy Dodd *(Fred)*, Fred Millican *(Catcher)*, Pat Flaherty *(Bill Klem)*, Tom Greenway *(Foreman)*, Frank MacFarland *(Johnson)*, Arthur Page *(Preacher)*, Frank Marlowe *(Taxi Driver)*, Ken Patterson *(Dr. Conant)*, Bob Lemon, Jerry Priddy, George Metkovich, Hank Sauer, Peanuts Lowrey, Irving Noren, Al Zarilla, Gene Mauch *(Ball Players)*, Alex Sharp *(1st Baseman)*, William Kalvino *(Batter)*, Russ Clark *(Umpire)*.

After portraying the immortal George Gipp in KNUTE ROCKNE—ALL AMERICAN, Ronald Reagan took on the role of another sporting great in this well-made but sanitized screen biography of legendary pitcher Grover Cleveland Alexander. The film follows Alexander from his early days as a telephone lineman and barnstorming pro through his major-league pitching success with the Phillies and Cubs, and on to his strong-willed comeback after succumbing to the bottle. Plagued by double vision and dizzy spells—the result of a head injury that temporarily ended his career even before he reached the majors—Alexander turns to the bottle when his curse returns, driving away his loving wife, Aimee (Doris Day). Leaving the game again, Alexander hits bottom, supporting himself by working for a two-bit circus, but when Aimee persuades St. Louis Cardinal manager Roger Hornsby   (Frank Lovejoy) to give Alexander another shot, the pitcher leads   the Cards to a victory in the 1926 World Series. Reportedly, this was one of Reagan's favorite roles and he gives a credible performance, portraying Alexander as an incredible talent beset by all-too-human problems. To prepare for his role, Reagan trained with Arnold "Jigger" Statz, a contemporary of Alexander's, and Jerry Priddy, second baseman for the Detroit Tigers, spending two hours a day for three weeks working on his pitching.

p, Bryan Foy; d, Lewis Seiler; w, Ted Sherdeman, Seelag Lester, Merwin Gerard (based on the story by Lester, Gerard); ph, Sid Hickox; ed, Alan Crosland, Jr.; m, David Buttolph.

Baseball/Biography   (PR:A MPAA:NR)

WOMAN-WISE**

(1937) 71m FOX bw

Rochelle Hudson *(Alice Fuller)*, Michael Whalen *(Tracey Browne)*, Thomas Beck *(Clint De Witt)*, Alan Dinehart *(Richards)*, Douglas Fowley *(Stevens)*, George Hassell *(John De Witt)*, Astrid Allwyn *("Bubbles" Carson)*, Chick Chandler *(Bob Benton)*, Pat Flaherty *(Duke Fuller)*.

This lighthearted romp through the dusty halls of fixed prize fights is not beyond making a few moral comments as well. Tracey Browne (Michael Whalen) is a newspaper sports editor who wants to clean up the dirty racket. He sets his sights on shyster promoter Richards (Alan Dinehart) and takes on one of his ex-champs himself, knocking out the pug to show how easy it is. This annoys the champ's daughter, Alice (Rochelle Hudson), but eventually she and the editor come together, fall in love, and together clean up the game. Directed by Allan Dwan, the veteran journeyman filmmaker who helmed his first feature in 1911 and retired in 1961 with more than 400 films to his credit.

p, Sol M. Wurtzel; d, Allan Dwan; w, Ben Markson; ph, Robert Planck; ed, Al De Gaetano.

Boxing   (PR:A   MPAA:NR)

WORLD IN MY CORNER**½

(1956) 82m UNIV bw

Audie Murphy *(Tommy Shea)*, Barbara Rush *(Dorothy Mallinson)*, Jeff Morrow *(Robert Mallinson)*, John McIntire *(Dave Bernstein)*, Tommy Rall *(Ray Kacsmerek)*, Howard St. John *(Harry Cram)*, Chico Vejar *(Steve Carelli)*, Cisco Andrade *(Parker)*, Baby Ike *(Bailey)*, Sheila Bromley *(Mrs. Mallinson)*, Dani Crayne *(Doris)*, H. Tommy Hart *(Stretch Caplow)*, James Lennon *(Ring Announcer)*, Steve Ellis *(TV Announcer)*.

Tommy Shea (Audie Murphy) is a poor kid from the ghetto who quickly rises in the ranks of welterweight competition, but never gets a chance at a title fight. Anxious to wed his girl (Barbara Rush) and get her away from her overbearing father, Tommy agrees to throw a bout against the champ (played by real-life boxer Chico Vejar) in exchange for a hefty amount of cash, but the decision gnaws at his conscience. This standard Murphy vehicle is enlivened somewhat by the well-directed boxing scenes and relatively authentic milieu.

p, Aaron Rosenberg; d, Jesse Hibbs; w, Jack Sher (based on a story by Sher, Joseph Stone); ph, Maury Gertsman; ed, Milton Carruth.

Boxing   (PR:A   MPAA:NR)

WORLD'S GREATEST ATHLETE, THE***

(1973) 93m Disney/BV c

Tim Conway *(Milo Jackson)*, Jan-Michael Vincent *(Nanu)*, John Amos *(Coach Sam Archer)*, Roscoe Lee Browne *(Gazenga)*, Dayle Haddon *(Jane Douglas)*, Billy DeWolfe *(Maxwell)*, Nancy Walker *(Mrs. Petersen)*, Danny Goldman *(Leopold Maxwell)*, Vito Scotti *(Sports Fan)*, Don Pedro Colley *(Morumba)*, Clarence Muse *(Gazenga's Assistant)*, Liam Dunn *(Dr. Winslow)*, Leon Askin *(Dr. Gottlieb)*, Ivor Francis *(Dean Bellamy)*, Bill Toomey *(TV Spotter)*, Joe Kapp *(Buzzer Kozak)*, Howard Cosell, Frank Gifford, Jim McKay, Bud Palmer *(Announcers)*.

Coaches Sam Archer (John Amos) and Milo Jackson (Tim Conway) discover jungle boy Nanu (Jan-Michael Vincent)—showing off his amazing super-physical abilities in the wilds of Africa. They bring him back to their college and transform him into a track star, saving their team from once again becoming the laughingstock of the NCAA. A

snappy family entry that gently pokes fun at both the "Tarzan" myth and college athletics, THE WORLD'S GREATEST ATHLETE benefits from several cameos. Sportscaster Howard Cosell gets big laughs for his self-parody, while fellow broadcasters Bud Palmer, Frank Gifford, and Jim McKay are also on hand.

p, Bill Walsh; d, Richard Scheerer; w, Gerald Gardner, Dee Caruso; ph, Frank Phillips (Technicolor); ed, Cotton Warburton; m, Marvin Hamlisch.

Track and Field/
Comedy   **Cas.**   **(PR:AA   MPAA:G)**

WRESTLER, THE*

(1974) 95m Gagne-Frank/Entertainment Ventures c

Bill Robinson *(Billy Taylor)*, Edward Asner *(Frank Bass)*, Elaine Giftos *(Debbie)*, Verne Gagne *(Mike Bullard)*, Sarah Miller *(Betty Bullard)*, Harold Sakata *(Odd Job)*, Sam Menecker *(Mobster)*, Hardboiled Haggerty *(Bartender)*, Dusty Rhodes, Dick Murdoch, The Crusher, Dick The Bruiser, James Blears, Superstar Billy Graham *(Themselves)*.

This obscurity from the 1970s deserves to find a new audience now that pro wrestling has once again gripped the nation in a stranglehold. All the theatrical elements of the drop-kicking, full-nelsoning monsters of the mats are displayed in THE WRESTLER, the simple story of which pits the honest wrestlers managed by Frank Bass (Ed Asner) against a criminal faction who want a piece of the action—and the profits. Verne Gagne appropriately plays an aging champ (his real-life role) as well as acting as the film's executive producer. Also in the cast is announcer Sam Menecker, as one of the mobsters, and the granddaddies of wrestling—Dick the Bruiser and The Crusher.

p, W.R. Frank; d, Jim Westman; w, Eugene Gump; ph, Gil Hubbs; ed, Neal Chastain; m, William Loose, William Allen Castleman.

Wrestling   **Cas.**   **(PR:C   MPAA:PG)**

XYZ

YESTERDAY'S HERO*½

(1979, Brit.) 95m Cinema Seven/EMI c

Ian McShane *(Rod Turner)*, Suzanne Somers *(Cloudy Martin)*, Adam Faith *(Jake)*, Paul Nicholas *(Clint)*, Sam Kydd *(Sam Turner)*, Glynis Barber *(Susan)*, Trevor Thomas *(Speed)*, Sandy Ratcliffe *(Rita)*, Alan Lake *(Georgie Moore)*, Matthew Long *(Mack Gill)*.

Scripted by Jackie Collins—sister of Joan, author of such high-society potboilers as *Hollywood Wives*, and the source of numerous prime-time TV miniseries—YESTERDAY'S HERO tells the story of a has-been soccer player who again rises in the ranks. Suzanne Somers (TV's quintessential dippy blonde in "Three's Company") is second-billed as the woman who gets hooked up with the soccer player, Ian McShane. Paul Nicholas is cast as a pop star who owns the team, giving the filmmakers a feeble excuse to toss in some equally feeble music.

p, Oscar S. Lerman, Ken Regan; d, Neil Leifer; w, Jackie Collins; ph, Brian West; ed, Anthony Gibbs.

Soccer   **Cas.**   **(PR:C-O   MPAA:NR)**

YESTERDAY'S HEROES**

(1940) 65m FOX bw

Jean Rogers *(Lee)*, Robert Sterling *(Wyman)*, Ted North *(Hammond)*, Katharine Aldridge *(Janice)*, Russell Gleason *(Garrett)*, Richard Lane *(Slater)*, Edmund MacDonald *(Jones)*, George Irving *(Stovall)*, Emma Dunn *(Winnie)*, Harry Hayden *(Kellogg)*, Isabel Randolph *(Mrs. Kellogg)*, Pierre Watkin *(Mason)*, Frank Sully *(Walsh)*.

Robert Sterling plays Wyman, one of the title heroes, a doctor who recalls how his college gridiron heroics nearly sabotaged his studies and love life. Persuaded to join the football team, Wyman, in no time at all, abandoned his schoolwork for the sport and deserted his true love, Lee (Jean Rogers), for coed hussy Janice (Katharine Aldridge). Thanks to helpful chum Garrett (Russell Gleason), he got back on the right track.

p, Sol M. Wurtzel; d, Herbert I. Leeds; w, Irving Cummings, Jr., William Conselman, Jr. (based on the serialized novel by William Brent); ph, Charles Clarke; ed, Al De Gaetano.

Football   **(PR:A   MPAA:NR)**

YOUNG MAN OF MANHATTAN**½

(1930) 75m PAR bw

Claudette Colbert *(Ann Vaughn)*, Norman Foster *(Toby McLean)*, Ginger Rogers *(Puff Randolph)*, Charlie Ruggles *(Shorty Ross)*, Leslie Austin *(Dwight Knowles)*, H. Dudley Hawley *(Doctor)*, Lorraine Aalbu, Aileen Aalbu, Fern Aalbu, Harriet Aalbu *(Sherman Sisters)*.

Sportswriter Toby McLean (Norman Foster) meets fellow reporter Ann Vaughn (Claudette Colbert) during the Gene Tunney-Jack Dempsey fight. They fall in love and marry in short order, living in a small New York apartment. When he travels to St. Louis to cover the World Series, he is introduced to socialite Puff Randolph (Ginger Rogers), but he is still too much in love with Ann to pay attention to her. Soon, however, Ann becomes a well-known magazine writer and, jealous of her success, Toby throws himself into an affair. Ann tries to drown her sorrows with some bootleg Scotch and temporarily goes blind from the bad booze. Horror-stricken, Toby abandons Puff and devotes himself to his work, hoping for a reconciliation with Ann. This adequate romance has more historic than filmic interest: it was Rogers' first feature and one of Colbert's last dues-paying pictures before she became a major star. The writing is melodramatic and the direction is uninspired, as are the performances—likable though they are. The film has little else going for it, except for the glimpses of major sporting events like the above-mentioned fight, the Army-Navy football game, the World Series, a six-day bicycle race, and others. Perhaps the most significant thing about YOUNG MAN OF MANHATTAN is that it made Rogers' come-on line, "Cigarette me, big boy," one of the most popular catch-phrases of the 1930s.

d, Monta Bell; w, Robert Presnell, Daniel Reed (based on the novel by Katherine Brush); ph, Larry Williams; ed, Emma Hill; m, David Mendoza.

**Baseball/Boxing/
Football**   **(PR:A   MPAA:NR)**

YOUNG RACERS, THE**

(1963) 82m Alta Vista/AIP c

Mark Damon *(Stephen Children)*, William Campbell *(Joe Machin)*, Luana Anders *(Henny)*, Robert Campbell *(Robert Machin)*, Patrick Magee *(Sir William Dragonet)*, Bruce McLaren *(Lotus Team Manager)*, Milo Quesada *(Italian Driver)*, Anthony Marsh *(Announcer)*, Marie Versini *(Sesia Machin)*, Beatrice Altariba *(Monique)*, Margaret Robsahm *(Lea)*, Christina Gregg *(Daphne)*.

Joe Machin (William Campbell) is a womanizing Grand Prix racer on the European circuit who deceives his wife, Sesia (Marie Versini), at every pit stop; Stephen Children (Mark Damon) is a onetime driver, now a writer, who travels to Monte Carlo at race time to meet his fiancee, Monique (Beatrice Altariba). Piqued to discover her apparently embroiled in an affair with Joe, the disgruntled Stephen decides to write a book exposing the daredevil as a dirty driver. When Joe discovers this, he challenges Stephen to a racing duel, which Stephen accepts. Ever one to take advantage of ready sets and available locations, low-budget producer-director Roger Corman made this picture while on a European vacation, touring the racetracks in England, France, Belgium, and Monaco. Young Francis Ford Coppola, who served as sound man on the production, picked up some pointers from Corman; he used the major cast members and equipment to direct his horror film, DEMENTIA 13 (1963), in Ireland. Another fast learner on the set was prop man Menachem Golan, who was later to form Cannon Films with his partner, Yoram Globus.

p, Roger Corman; d, Roger Corman; w, R. Wright Campbell; ph, Floyd Crosby (Eastmancolor); ed, Ronald Sinclair; m, Les Baxter.

Auto Racing   **(PR:C   MPAA:NR)**

YOUNGBLOOD**½

(1986) 109m Guber-Peters/MGM—UA c

Rob Lowe *(Dean Youngblood)*, Cynthia Gibb *(Jessie Chadwick)*, Patrick Swayze *(Derek Sutton)*, Ed Lauter *(Coach Murray Chadwick)*, Jim Youngs *(Kelly Youngblood)*, Eric Nesterenko *(Blane Youngblood)*, George Finn *(Racki)*, Fionnula Flanagan *(Miss McGill)*, Ken James *(Frazier)*, Peter Faussett *(Huey)*, Walker Boone *(Assistant Coach)*, Keanu Reeves *(Hoover)*, Martin Donlevy *(Referee Hannah)*, Harry Spiegel *(Thunder Bay Coach)*, Rod Sapiensze *(Thunder Bay Assistant Coach)*, Bruce Edwards *(Thunder Bay Trainer)*, Lorraine Foreman *(Teacher)*, Barry Swatik *(Starting Guard)*, Michael Legros, Murray Evans

(Linesmen), Charlie Wasley *(Young Dean),* Ricky Davis *(Young Kelly),* Joe Bowen *(Radio Announcer).*

Brat Packer Rob Lowe takes to the ice as Dean Youngblood, a young hockey player who skates his way onto the Hamilton Mustangs, beating out the more physical Racki (George Finn) for the last remaining spot on the team. After an unsettling initiation period, including some good-natured hazing from his new teammates, Youngblood begins to fit in, growing particularly close to Derek (Patrick Swayze), one of the Mustangs' stars. Meantime, the new player becomes smitten with Jessie (Cynthia Gibb), the daughter of Mustang coach Murray Chadwick (Ed Lauter), who introduces him to the world of literature. Racki returns to haunt the Mustangs when they play his new team, the Thunder Bay Bombers, and he takes a vicious shot at Derek that results in a serious head injury. Unwilling to fight to defend his friend's honor, Youngblood quits the team and returns to his father's (onetime Chicago Blackhawk star Eric Nesterenko, who also served as the film's technical advisor) farm, where his brother (Jim Youngs), a failed hockey player himself, persuades Dean to give it another shot and helps him toughen up for his comeback. Dean returns for the big game with the Bombers, and of course Racki is waiting for him, but this time Dean is more than ready. Although YOUNGBLOOD stays the familiar never-say-die, snatch-victory-from-defeat course, the hockey action and acting are surprisingly good. Youngs and Swayze (DIRTY DANCING) are excellent in support of Lowe, who may not make the most of this star vehicle but does turn in a competent, believable performance. And as with so many other youth-oriented films, there's plenty of fancy backlighting, quickly cut montages, and a hard-pounding rock score.

p, Peter Bart, Patrick Wells; d, Peter Markle; w, Peter Markle (based on a story by Peter Markle, John Whitmore); ph, Mark Irwin (Metrocolor); ed, Stephen E. Rivkin, Jack Hofstra; m, William Orbit, Torchsong.

Hockey   Cas.   (PR:O MPAA:R)

ALTERNATE TITLE

Listed below are alternate, foreign, and Great Britain titles of films, followed by the title under which the film appears in this volume.

A

AFFAIR OF THE HEART, AN
(SEE: BODY AND SOUL)
ANGELS AND THE PIRATES
(SEE: ANGELS IN THE
OUTFIELD)

B

BATTLING BELLHOP, THE
(SEE: KID GALAHAD)
BIG MO (SEE: MAURIE)
BLAZE OF GLORY (SEE: BOY
FROM INDIANA)
BRAVE AND THE BEAUTIFUL, THE
(SEE: MAGNIFICENT MATADOR,
THE)

C

CALIFORNIA DOLLS, THE
(SEE: . . . ALL THE MARBLES)
CALIFORNIA HOLIDAY
(SEE: SPINOUT)

D

DERBY DAY (SEE: FOUR AGAINST
FATE)
DEVIL ON WHEELS
(SEE: INDIANAPOLIS
SPEEDWAY)

E

EDITH ET MARCEL (SEE: EDITH
AND MARCEL)
ESCAPE TO VICTORY
(SEE: VICTORY)
EVERY WOMAN'S MAN
(SEE: PRIZEFIGHTER AND THE
LADY, THE)
EVERYBODY'S CHEERING
(SEE: TAKE ME OUT TO THE
BALL GAME)

F

FIRST TIME, THE (SEE: FIGHTER,
THE)
FOOTBALL COACH
(SEE: COLLEGE COACH)

G

GENERALS OF TOMORROW
(SEE: TOUCHDOWN, ARMY)
GEORDIE (SEE: WEE GEORDIE)
GREAT SCHNOZZLE, THE
(SEE: PALOOKA)

H

HARD DRIVER (SEE: LAST
AMERICAN HERO, THE)
HARMONY PARADE
(SEE: PIGSKIN PARADE)
HOLD THAT GIRL (SEE: HOLD
THAT CO-ED)

I

IDOLS IN THE DUST
(SEE: SATURDAY'S HERO)
IMPOSSIBLE LOVER
(SEE: HUDDLE)

J

JOE PALOOKA (SEE: PALOOKA)
JOY PARADE, THE (SEE: LIFE
BEGINS IN COLLEGE)
JUNGLE TERROR (SEE: FIREBALL
JUNGLE)

K

KID COLOSSUS, THE
(SEE: ROOGIE'S BUMP)
KID'S LAST FIGHT, THE (SEE: LIFE
OF JIMMY DOLAN, THE)
KING OF THE ICE RINK
(SEE: KING OF HOCKEY)

L

LEADER OF THE PACK
(SEE: UNHOLY ROLLERS)
LUCK OF THE GAME, THE
(SEE: GRIDIRON FLASH)

M

MAN CALLED SULLIVAN, A
(SEE: GREAT JOHN L., THE)
MAN OF BRONZE (SEE: JIM
THORPE—ALL AMERICAN)
MANNY'S ORPHANS (SEE: HERE
COME THE TIGERS)
MASK OF DUST (SEE: RACE FOR
LIFE, A)
MEET WHIPLASH WILLIE
(SEE: FORTUNE COOKIE, THE)
MODERN HERO, A (SEE: KNUTE
ROCKNE—ALL AMERICAN)

N

NEIL SIMON'S THE SLUGGER'S
WIFE (SEE: SLUGGER'S WIFE,
THE)

O

OLD SCHOOL TIE, THE (SEE: WE
WENT TO COLLEGE)
ONCE A JOLLY SWAGMAN
(SEE: MANIACS ON WHEELS)
O'RILEY'S LUCK (SEE: ROSE
BOWL)
ORPHAN OF THE RING (SEE: KID
FROM KOKOMO, THE)

P

PHAR LAP—HEART OF A NATION
(SEE: PHAR LAP)
PLAYING THE GAME
(SEE: TOUCHDOWN)
PRIDE OF KENTUCKY
(SEE: STORY OF SEABISCUIT,
THE)
PRIDE OF THE BOWERY, THE
(SEE: MR. HEX)
PRINCE OF THE BLUE GRASS
(SEE: PRIDE OF THE BLUE
GRASS)
PRO, THE (SEE: NUMBER ONE)

R

RACING LUCK (SEE: RED HOT
TIRES)
REBEL WITH A CAUSE
(SEE: LONELINESS OF THE
LONG DISTANCE RUNNER,
THE)
RED HOT WHEELS (SEE: TO
PLEASE A LADY)
REMEMBER WHEN (SEE: RIDING
HIGH)
RHYTHM ON THE RIVER
(SEE: FRESHMAN LOVE)

S

STAND AND DELIVER
(SEE: BOWERY BLITZKRIEG)
STREETFIGHTER, THE
(SEE: HARD TIMES)
STRICTLY CONFIDENTIAL
(SEE: BROADWAY BILL)
SUCH MEN ARE DANGEROUS
(SEE: RACERS, THE)
SWINGING AFFAIR, A
(SEE: SWINGIN' AFFAIR, A)

T

THOROUGHBRED (SEE: RUN FOR
  THE ROSES)
TRANSATLANTIC TROUBLE
  (SEE: TAKE IT FROM ME)
TRETIY TAYM (SEE: LAST GAME,
  THE)
TWEENERS (SEE: TRADING
  HEARTS)

U

UN UOMO DALLA PELLE DURA
  (SEE: RIPPED-OFF)

V

VIGOUR OF YOUTH (SEE: SPIRIT
  OF NOTRE DAME, THE)
VIVIR DESVIVIENDOSE
  (SEE: MOMENT OF TRUTH,
  THE)

W

WALKOWER (SEE: WALKOVER)
WANTED (SEE: POLICE CALL)
WHAT LOLA WANTS (SEE: DAMN
  YANKEES)
WINNING WAY, THE
  (SEE: ALL-AMERICAN, THE)

INDEX

Individuals listed in the Index are grouped by function as follows:

Actors (major players only)
Cinematographers
Directors
Editors
Music Composers
Producers
Screenwriters
Source Authors (authors of the original material or creators of the characters upon which the film is based)

Individual names are followed by an alphabetical listing of the films in which they were involved.

Beaton, Norman
PLAYING AWAY

Beatty, Ned
LAST AMERICAN HERO, THE
STROKER ACE

Beatty, Warren
HEAVEN CAN WAIT

Bedelia, Bonnie
HEART LIKE A WHEEL

Beery, Jr., Noah
SOME BLONDES ARE DANGEROUS

Beery, Wallace
MIGHTY MC GURK, THE
FLESH
CHAMP, THE (1931)

Begley, Ed
GREEN HELMET, THE
IT HAPPENS EVERY SPRING
BOOTS MALONE

Bendix, William
KILL THE UMPIRE
BABE RUTH STORY, THE

Bennett, Joan
MAYBE IT'S LOVE
GUY WHO CAME BACK, THE

Benson, Robby
ONE ON ONE
RUNNING BRAVE
ICE CASTLES

Berardino, John
KID FROM LEFT FIELD, THE
KID FROM CLEVELAND, THE
WINNER'S CIRCLE, THE

Bergen, Polly
FAST COMPANY

Berry, Ken
EIGHT MEN OUT

Bickford, Charles
JIM THORPE—ALL AMERICAN
RIDING HIGH (1950)
BABE RUTH STORY, THE

Bishop, Julie
MAIN EVENT, THE (1938)

Bixby, Bill
SPEEDWAY

Black, Karen
SEPARATE WAYS
DRIVE, HE SAID

Blades, Ruben
LAST FIGHT, THE

Blake, Robert
RIPPED-OFF

Blakely, Susan
DREAMER

Blanchard, Felix "Doc"
SPIRIT OF WEST POINT, THE

Blondell, Joan
CROWD ROARS, THE (1932)

Blue, Monte
MILLION TO ONE, A

Bogarde, Dirk
MANIACS ON WHEELS

Bogart, Humphrey
KID GALAHAD (1937)
HARDER THEY FALL, THE
SWING YOUR LADY

Bologna, Joseph
MIXED COMPANY

Bond, Ward
HOME IN INDIANA
GENTLEMAN JIM
STRAIGHTAWAY
SALUTE
BOB MATHIAS STORY, THE
RIDING HIGH (1950)
RACKETY RAX
FLESH
CONFLICT

Boone, Ray
KID FROM CLEVELAND, THE

Borg, Bjorn
RACQUET

Borg, Veda Ann
GIRL FROM MONTEREY, THE

Borgnine, Ernest
SPIKE OF BENSONHURST
GREATEST, THE
SQUARE JUNGLE, THE
RIPPED-OFF

Boros, Julius
CADDY, THE

Bosley, Tom
MIXED COMPANY

Boudreau, Lou
KID FROM CLEVELAND, THE

Bouix, Evelyne
EDITH AND MARCEL

Boyd, Bill
RACING LUCK (1935)

Brabham, Jack
GRAND PRIX (1966)

Brady, Scott
IN THIS CORNER

Brandauer, Klaus Maria
STREETS OF GOLD

Brennan, Walter
HOME IN INDIANA
KENTUCKY
GLORY
RISE AND SHINE
DEATH ON THE DIAMOND
ALL-AMERICAN, THE (1932)
PRIDE OF THE YANKEES, THE

Brent, George
KID FROM CLEVELAND, THE

Breslin, Pat
GO, MAN, GO!

Brickhouse, Jack
GOLDEN GLOVES STORY, THE

Bridges, Beau
HEART LIKE A WHEEL

GREASED LIGHTNING
SILVER DREAM RACER

Bridges, Jeff
LAST AMERICAN HERO, THE
HALLS OF ANGER
STAY HUNGRY
FAT CITY

Bridges, Lloyd
KID FROM LEFT FIELD, THE
HARMON OF MICHIGAN
SPIRIT OF STANFORD, THE
PRIDE OF THE BLUE GRASS

Brimley, Wilford
NATURAL, THE

Brix, Herman
TWO MINUTES TO PLAY
FLYING FISTS, THE

Brolin, Josh
THRASHIN'

Bronson, Charles
HARD TIMES
TENNESSEE CHAMP

Brown, Blair
STEALING HOME

Brown, Joe E.
$1,000 A TOUCHDOWN
MAYBE IT'S LOVE
HOLD EVERYTHING
LOCAL BOY MAKES GOOD
FIREMAN, SAVE MY CHILD
RACKETY RAX
ELMER THE GREAT
ALIBI IKE
POLO JOE

Brown, Johnny Mack
70,000 WITNESSES
SATURDAY'S MILLIONS

Brown, Roger
PAPER LION

Brown, Tim
M*A*S*H

Brown, Tom
FAST COMPANIONS

Brown, Tommy
M*A*S*H

Buchanan, Buck
M*A*S*H

Budge, Don
PAT AND MIKE

Burlinson, Tom
PHAR LAP

Burstyn, Ellen
PIT STOP

Busey, Gary
BIG WEDNESDAY
LAST AMERICAN HERO, THE
BEAR, THE

Bushman, Francis X.
MR. CELEBRITY

Butkus, Dick
GUS

Caan, James
ROLLERBALL
RED LINE 7000

Cabot, Bruce
BIG GAME, THE

Cage, Nicolas
BOY IN BLUE, THE

Cagney, James
WINNER TAKE ALL (1932)
CROWD ROARS, THE (1932)
CITY FOR CONQUEST

Cagney, Jean
GOLDEN GLOVES

Caine, Michael
VICTORY

Calhoun, Rory
MAIN EVENT, THE (1979)
THUNDER IN CAROLINA

Campanella, Roy
ROOGIE'S BUMP

Campanis, Al
BIG LEAGUER

Cannon, Dyan
HEAVEN CAN WAIT

Cantor, Eddie
KID FROM SPAIN, THE

Cara, Irene
BUSTED UP

Carlson, Richard
MAN FROM DOWN UNDER, THE

Carnera, Primo
PRIZEFIGHTER AND THE LADY, THE

Caron, Leslie
GOLDENGIRL
GLORY ALLEY

Carrillo, Leo
RACETRACK
DECEPTION

Carson, Jack
MR. UNIVERSE
GENTLEMAN JIM

Casey, Bernie
MAURIE
CORNBREAD, EARL AND ME

Cerdan, Jr., Marcel
EDITH AND MARCEL

Chandler, Jeff
IRON MAN, THE (1951)

Chaney, Jr., Lon
ROAD DEMON
FIREBALL JUNGLE

Charleson, Ian
CHARIOTS OF FIRE

Chase, Chevy
CADDYSHACK

Chissell, Noble "Kid"
HOME IN INDIANA
KNOCKOUT
SET-UP, THE

Chitwood, Joie
FIREBALL JUNGLE

Chong, Rae Dawn
AMERICAN FLYERS

Christie, Julie
HEAVEN CAN WAIT

Christman, Paul
TRIPLE THREAT

Christopher, Dennis
BREAKING AWAY

Clark, Dane
GO, MAN, GO!
WHIPLASH

Clay, Cassius [Muhammad Ali]
REQUIEM FOR A HEAVYWEIGHT

Clayburgh, Jill
SEMI-TOUGH

Clements, Stanley
RACING LUCK (1948)
PRIDE OF MARYLAND

Close, Glenn
NATURAL, THE

Clyde, Andy
MILLION DOLLAR LEGS (1932)

Cobb, Lee J.
GOLDEN BOY
RACERS, THE
FIGHTER, THE

Coburn, Charles
TROUBLE ALONG THE WAY
PEGGY

Coburn, James
HARD TIMES
GOLDENGIRL

Coghlan, Junior
RACETRACK

Colbert, Claudette
YOUNG MAN OF MANHATTAN

Collier, Jr., Buster
SPORTING CHANCE

Collier, Jr., William
MARK IT PAID
FIGHTING GENTLEMAN, THE

Concannon, Jack
M*A*S*H

Conn, Billy
PITTSBURGH KID, THE

Conner, Bart
RAD

Conrad, William
BODY AND SOUL (1947)

Conte, Richard
RACE FOR LIFE, A
FIGHTER, THE

Converse, Frank
SPRING FEVER

Convy, Bert
RACQUET

Conway, Tim
GUS
WORLD'S GREATEST ATHLETE, THE
PRIZE FIGHTER, THE

Coogan, Jackie
MILLION DOLLAR LEGS (1939)
HOME ON THE RANGE

Cooper, Gary
PRIDE OF THE YANKEES, THE

Cooper, Jackie
CHAMP, THE (1931)

Cortez, Ricardo
FLESH

Cosby, Bill
LET'S DO IT AGAIN

Cosell, Howard
JOHNNY BE GOOD
WORLD'S GREATEST ATHLETE, THE

Costner, Kevin
BULL DURHAM
AMERICAN FLYERS

Courtenay, Tom
LONELINESS OF THE LONG DISTANCE
RUNNER, THE

Cowan, Charlie
HEAVEN CAN WAIT

Crabbe, Buster
CONTENDER, THE

Crabbe, Larry "Buster"
MILLION DOLLAR LEGS (1939)
HOLD 'EM YALE
ROSE BOWL

Crain, Jeanne
HOME IN INDIANA

Crane, Richard
TRIPLE THREAT

Crawford, Michael
GAMES, THE

Crenna, Richard
JOHN GOLDFARB, PLEASE COME
HOME

Crisp, Donald
NATIONAL VELVET
SERGEANT MURPHY

Crosby, Bing
RIDING HIGH (1950)
COLLEGE HUMOR

Crosby, Cathy Lee
COACH

Cross, Ben
CHARIOTS OF FIRE

Crouse, Lindsay
SLAP SHOT

Crowley, Jim
SPIRIT OF NOTRE DAME, THE

Cruise, Tom
ALL THE RIGHT MOVES
COLOR OF MONEY, THE

Culp, Robert
GOLDENGIRL

ACTORS

Curtis, Jamie Lee
AMAZING GRACE AND CHUCK

Curtis, Tony
JOHNNY DARK
BAD NEWS BEARS GO TO JAPAN, THE
SQUARE JUNGLE, THE
FLESH AND FURY
ALL-AMERICAN, THE (1953)

Cusack, Cyril
MANIACS ON WHEELS

D'Angelo, Beverly
TRADING HEARTS

Dailey, Dan
KID FROM LEFT FIELD, THE
PRIDE OF ST. LOUIS, THE

Dale, Virginia
QUARTERBACK, THE

Damon, Mark
YOUNG RACERS, THE

Dangerfield, Rodney
CADDYSHACK

Darby, Kim
ONE AND ONLY, THE

Darnell, Linda
GREAT JOHN L., THE
BLOOD AND SAND (1941)

Darren, James
LIVELY SET, THE

Darro, Frankie
BORN TO FIGHT

Davidson, Ben
M*A*S*H

Davies, Marion
CAIN AND MABEL

Davis, Bette
KID GALAHAD (1937)

Davis, Glenn
SPIRIT OF WEST POINT, THE

Davis, Mac
NORTH DALLAS FORTY
STING II, THE

Dawson, Len
PERSONAL BEST

Day, Doris
MR. CELEBRITY
WINNING TEAM, THE

de Havilland, Olivia
ALIBI IKE

de Marney, Derrick
FLYING FIFTY-FIVE

De Mornay, Rebecca
SLUGGER'S WIFE, THE

De Niro, Robert
BANG THE DRUM SLOWLY
RAGING BULL

Dee, Ruby
JACKIE ROBINSON STORY, THE

Demarest, William
SALTY O'ROURKE

RIDING HIGH (1950)

Demaret, James
FOLLOW THE SUN

Dempsey, Jack
REQUIEM FOR A HEAVYWEIGHT
PRIZEFIGHTER AND THE LADY, THE

Denning, Richard
GOLDEN GLOVES

Derek, John
LEATHER SAINT, THE
SATURDAY'S HERO

Dern, Bruce
ON THE EDGE
NUMBER ONE
THAT CHAMPIONSHIP SEASON
DRIVE, HE SAID

DeRogatis, Al
HEAVEN CAN WAIT

Dettweiler, Helen
PAT AND MIKE

Devane, William
BAD NEWS BEARS IN BREAKING
TRAINING, THE

Devine, Andy
BIG GAME, THE
HOLD 'EM YALE
LEATHER-PUSHERS, THE
SPIRIT OF NOTRE DAME, THE
SATURDAY'S MILLIONS
FIGHTING YOUTH
FAST COMPANIONS
DANGER ON WHEELS
ALL-AMERICAN, THE (1932)

Dewhurst, Colleen
ICE CASTLES

Dickey, Bill
STRATTON STORY, THE
PRIDE OF THE YANKEES, THE

Doby, Larry
KID FROM CLEVELAND, THE

Donlevy, Brian
KILLER McCOY
PIT STOP

Dorn, Philip
SKI PATROL

Dors, Diana
GREAT GAME, THE (1952)

Douglas, Kirk
RACERS, THE
CHAMPION

Douglas, Michael
RUNNING

Douglas, Paul
LEATHER SAINT, THE
GUY WHO CAME BACK, THE
IT HAPPENS EVERY SPRING
ANGELS IN THE OUTFIELD

Downey, Jr., Robert
JOHNNY BE GOOD

Dru, Joanne
PRIDE OF ST. LOUIS, THE

Duff, Howard
ROAR OF THE CROWD

Duke, Patty
BILLIE

Dullea, Keir
PAPERBACK HERO

Dunaway, Faye
CHAMP, THE (1979)

Dunn, James
SOCIETY GIRL

Dunphy, Don
MATILDA

Durante, Jimmy
PALOOKA

Durning, Charles
NORTH DALLAS FORTY

Duvall, Robert
NATURAL, THE
M*A*S*H
GREATEST, THE

Dvorak, Ann
RACING LADY
COLLEGE COACH

Dykes, Jimmy
STRATTON STORY, THE

Economaki, Chris
STROKER ACE
SIX PACK

Eden, Barbara
RIDE THE WILD SURF

Eggar, Samantha
WALK, DON'T RUN

Ellis, Patricia
FRESHMAN LOVE

Enberg, Dick
GUS

English, Alex
AMAZING GRACE AND CHUCK

Errol, Leon
JOE PALOOKA MEETS HUMPHREY
JOE PALOOKA IN THE
COUNTERPUNCH
JOE PALOOKA IN THE BIG FIGHT
JOE PALOOKA, CHAMP
FIGHTING MAD
HUMPHREY TAKES A CHANCE

Erskine, Carl
ROOGIE'S BUMP

Erving, Julius
FISH THAT SAVED PITTSBURGH, THE

Erwin, Stuart
PIGSKIN PARADE

Essex, David
SILVER DREAM RACER

Evashevski, Forest
HARMON OF MICHIGAN

Ewell, Tom
GREAT AMERICAN PASTIME, THE

Fabares, Shelley
SPINOUT

RIDE THE WILD SURF

Fabian
WILD RACERS, THE
THUNDER ALLEY
RIDE THE WILD SURF
FIREBALL 500

Fairbanks, Jr., Douglas
LIFE OF JIMMY DOLAN, THE

Falk, Peter
... ALL THE MARBLES

Farrell, Charles
FIGHTING YOUTH

Farrell, Glenda
PERSONALITY KID, THE

Fazenda, Louise
RACING YOUTH

Feller, Bob
KID FROM CLEVELAND, THE

Fellows, Edith
PRIDE OF THE BLUEGRASS

Fidrych, Mark
SLUGGER'S WIFE, THE

Field, Sally
STAY HUNGRY

Fields, W.C.
MILLION DOLLAR LEGS (1932)

Fiorentino, Linda
VISION QUEST

Fitzgerald, Barry
STORY OF SEABISCUIT, THE

Fitzgerald, Geraldine
LAST AMERICAN HERO, THE

Flynn, Erroll
GENTLEMAN JIM

Fonda, Jane
TALL STORY

Fontaine, Joan
MILLION TO ONE, A

Ford, Glenn
FOLLOW THE SUN
RETURN OF OCTOBER, THE

Ford, Whitey
SAFE AT HOME

Foreman, George
LET'S DO IT AGAIN

Foster, Jodie
STEALING HOME

Foster, Preston
ELMER THE GREAT
ALL-AMERICAN, THE (1932)

Francis, Anne
GREAT AMERICAN PASTIME, THE

Frawley, William
JOE PALOOKA IN WINNER TAKE ALL
IT HAPPENED IN FLATBUSH
SAFE AT HOME
ROSE BOWL

Frazier, Joe
ROCKY

Frederick, Vicki
... ALL THE MARBLES

Funicello, Annette
THUNDER ALLEY
FIREBALL 500

Furness, Betty
GRIDIRON FLASH

Gable, Clark
CAIN AND MABEL
TO PLEASE A LADY
SPORTING BLOOD (1931)
SARATOGA

Gagne, Verne
WRESTLER, THE

Gallagher, Richard "Skeets"
FAST COMPANY

Gallico, Paul
MADISON SQUARE GARDEN

Gardenia, Vincent
BANG THE DRUM SLOWLY

Gardner, Ava
SUNDAY PUNCH

Garfield, Allen
SKATEBOARD

Garfield, John
UNDER MY SKIN
THEY MADE ME A CRIMINAL
BODY AND SOUL (1947)

Garland, Judy
THOROUGHBREDS DON'T CRY

Garner, James
GRAND PRIX (1966)

Garr, Teri
STING II, THE
BLACK STALLION, THE

Garrett, Leif
SKATEBOARD

Gates, William "Pop"
HARLEM GLOBETROTTERS, THE

Gaylord, Mitch
AMERICAN ANTHEM

George, Lynda Day
RACQUET

Gibb, Cynthia
YOUNGBLOOD

Gielgud, John
CHARIOTS OF FIRE

Gifford, Frank
WORLD'S GREATEST ATHLETE, THE
ALL-AMERICAN, THE (1953)
PAPER LION

Giftos, Elaine
WRESTLER, THE

Gleason, Jackie
STING II, THE
REQUIEM FOR A HEAVYWEIGHT
HUSTLER, THE

Gleason, James
BIG GAME, THE
JOE PALOOKA IN TRIPLE CROSS

JOE PALOOKA IN THE SQUARED
CIRCLE
SWELLHEAD, THE
SWEEPSTAKES
RIDING HIGH (1950)
RETURN OF OCTOBER, THE
FAST COMPANIONS
ALL-AMERICAN, THE (1932)

Glenn, Scott
PERSONAL BEST

Gonzalez, Pancho
PLAYERS

Gorcey, Leo
MR. HEX
HOLD THAT LINE
THEY MADE ME A CRIMINAL
THAT GANG OF MINE
SUNDAY PUNCH
BOWERY BLITZKRIEG
FIGHTING FOOLS

Gordon, Joe
KID FROM CLEVELAND, THE

Gordy, John
PAPER LION

Gortner, Marjoe
SIDEWINDER ONE

Gould, Elliott
MATILDA
M*A*S*H

Gowdy, Curt
HEAVEN CAN WAIT

Grable, Betty
MILLION DOLLAR LEGS (1939)
PIGSKIN PARADE

Grant, Cary
WALK, DON'T RUN

Greco, Jose
MANOLETE

Greenberg, Hank
KID FROM CLEVELAND, THE

Greene, Richard
KENTUCKY

Greenwood, Charlotte
PEGGY

Greer, Jane
BILLIE

Grier, Pam
ON THE EDGE
GREASED LIGHTNING

Grodin, Charles
HEAVEN CAN WAIT

Guardino, Harry
MATILDA

Gumbel, Bryant
HEAVEN CAN WAIT

Gunn, Moses
CORNBREAD, EARL AND ME

Gurney, Dan
GRAND PRIX (1966)
WINNING

Hackman, Gene
SPLIT DECISIONS
HOOSIERS
DOWNHILL RACER

Haley, Jack
PIGSKIN PARADE

Haley, Jackie Earle
BAD NEWS BEARS IN BREAKING
TRAINING, THE
BAD NEWS BEARS GO TO JAPAN,
THE
BAD NEWS BEARS, THE
BREAKING AWAY

Hall, Anthony Michael
JOHNNY BE GOOD

Hall, Huntz
MR. HEX
HOLD THAT LINE
THEY MADE ME A CRIMINAL
BOWERY BLITZKRIEG
FIGHTING FOOLS

Hall, Lois
JOE PALOOKA IN THE SQUARED
CIRCLE

Hamilton, Murray
CASEY'S SHADOW

Hamlin, Harry
BLUE SKIES AGAIN

Harlow, Jean
IRON MAN, THE (1931)
SARATOGA

Harmon, Mark
STEALING HOME

Harmon, Tom
CADDY, THE
HARMON OF MICHIGAN
THAT'S MY BOY (1951)
SPIRIT OF WEST POINT, THE
ROSE BOWL STORY, THE
RETURN TO CAMPUS
ALL-AMERICAN, THE (1953)
PAT AND MIKE

Harris, Barbara
MIXED COMPANY

Harris, Julie
REQUIEM FOR A HEAVYWEIGHT

Harris, Michael
EIGHT MEN OUT

Harris, Richard
THIS SPORTING LIFE

Harrison, Gregory
NORTH SHORE

Haver, June
HOME IN INDIANA

Havoc, June
FOLLOW THE SUN

Hawkins, Alex
SLUGGER'S WIFE, THE

Hawn, Goldie
WILDCATS

Haynes, Marques
HARLEM GLOBETROTTERS, THE

Hayward, Susan
$1,000 A TOUCHDOWN
LUSTY MEN, THE

Hayworth, Rita
GAME THAT KILLS, THE
BLOOD AND SAND (1941)

Heflin, Van
SATURDAY'S HEROES

Hegan, Jim
KID FROM CLEVELAND, THE

Hemingway, Mariel
PERSONAL BEST

Henry, Gloria
RACING LUCK (1948)

Hepburn, Katharine
PAT AND MIKE

Herrmann, Edward
TAKE DOWN

Hershey, Barbara
NATURAL, THE
HOOSIERS

Heston, Charlton
NUMBER ONE

Hill, Graham
GRAND PRIX (1966)

Hill, Marianna
RED LINE 7000

Hill, Phil
GRAND PRIX (1966)

Hingle, Pat
RUNNING BRAVE

Hipple, Eric
BEAR, THE

Hirsch, Elroy "Crazylegs"
CRAZYLEGS, ALL AMERICAN

Hogan, Ben
CADDY, THE

Hogan, Hulk
ROCKY III

Holden, William
GOLDEN BOY
BOOTS MALONE

Holm, Ian
CHARIOTS OF FIRE

Hopper, Dennis
HOOSIERS

Hornung, Paul
SEMI-TOUGH

Horton, Edward Everett
HERE COMES MR. JORDAN

Houk, Ralph
SAFE AT HOME

Houseman, John
ROLLERBALL

Hrabosky, Al
SLUGGER'S WIFE, THE

Hubbell, Carl
BIG LEAGUER

Hughes, Wendy
SIDECAR RACERS

Hulman, Tony
WINNING

Hulme, Dennis
GRAND PRIX (1966)

Hundley, Rodney
MIXED COMPANY

Hunter, Tab
RIDE THE WILD SURF
DAMN YANKEES

Hurt, John
CHAMPIONS

Huston, Walter
PRIZEFIGHTER AND THE LADY, THE

Hutton, Jim
WALK, DON'T RUN

Hutton, Lauren
LITTLE FAUSS AND BIG HALSY
PAPER LION

Hutton, Timothy
EVERYBODY'S ALL-AMERICAN

Hyde-White, Wilfrid
RAINBOW JACKET, THE

Ireland, Jill
HARD TIMES

Ireland, John
BASKETBALL FIX, THE

Jackson, Anne
SAM'S SON

Jackson, Inman
HARLEM GLOBETROTTERS, THE

Jeffries, James J.
MR. CELEBRITY
PRIZEFIGHTER AND THE LADY, THE

Jennings, Claudia
UNHOLY ROLLERS

Johnson, Ben
JUNIOR BONNER
CHAMPIONS

Johnson, Jack
MADISON SQUARE GARDEN

Johnson, Lynn Holly
ICE CASTLES

Johnson, Rafer
GAMES, THE

Jones, Allan
MOONLIGHT IN HAVANA

Jones, Charlie
PERSONAL BEST

Jones, James Earl
BINGO LONG TRAVELING ALL-STARS
AND MOTOR KINGS, THE
GREAT WHITE HOPE, THE

Jones, Janet
AMERICAN ANTHEM

Jordan, Bobby
THAT GANG OF MINE

Josephson, Les
HEAVEN CAN WAIT

Julia, Raul
TRADING HEARTS

Jurgens, Curt
GOLDENGIRL

Kaplan, Gabriel
FAST BREAK

Kapp, Joe
LONGEST YARD, THE
WORLD'S GREATEST ATHLETE, THE
SEMI-TOUGH

Karns, Roscoe
RED HOT TIRES

Karras, Alex
PAPER LION

Katt, William
BIG WEDNESDAY

Kaye, Danny
KID FROM BROOKLYN, THE

Keach, Stacy
THAT CHAMPIONSHIP SEASON
FAT CITY

Keaton, Buster
COLLEGE
BATTLING BUTLER

Keaton, Michael
TOUCH AND GO

Keel, Howard
FAST COMPANY

Keller, Marthe
BOBBY DEERFIELD

Kellerman, Sally
M*A*S*H

Kelly, Gene
TAKE ME OUT TO THE BALL GAME

Kelly, Patsy
PIGSKIN PARADE

Keltner, Ken
KID FROM CLEVELAND, THE

Kennedy, Arthur
LUSTY MEN, THE
KNOCKOUT
CITY FOR CONQUEST
CHAMPION

Kennedy, Bob
KID FROM CLEVELAND, THE

Kennedy, Edgar
GIRL FROM MONTEREY, THE

Kennedy, Jayne
BODY AND SOUL (1981)

Kennedy, Leon Isaac
BODY AND SOUL (1981)

Kennedy, Merna
POLICE CALL

Keyes, Earl
RETURN TO CAMPUS

Kilcullen, Robert
FINNEY

King, Bernard
FAST BREAK

Kirk, Tom
TRACK OF THUNDER

Kirkwood, Jr., Joe
JOE PALOOKA MEETS HUMPHREY
JOE PALOOKA IN WINNER TAKE ALL
JOE PALOOKA IN TRIPLE CROSS
JOE PALOOKA IN THE SQUARED
CIRCLE
JOE PALOOKA IN THE
COUNTERPUNCH
JOE PALOOKA IN THE BIG FIGHT
JOE PALOOKA, CHAMP
FIGHTING MAD
HUMPHREY TAKES A CHANCE

Kline, Issy
GOLDEN GLOVES STORY, THE

Knight, Fuzzy
FLYING FISTS, THE

Knotts, Don
GUS
PRIZE FIGHTER, THE

Knox, Elyse
JOE PALOOKA IN WINNER TAKE ALL
JOE PALOOKA IN THE
COUNTERPUNCH
JOE PALOOKA, CHAMP

Koenig, Mark
PRIDE OF THE YANKEES, THE
BABE RUTH STORY, THE

Kristofferson, Kris
SEMI-TOUGH

Kurtz, Swoosie
WILDCATS

Kyser, Kay
SWING FEVER

Ladd, Alan
SALTY O'ROURKE

Lamas, Lorenzo
TAKE DOWN

Lancaster, Burt
JIM THORPE—ALL AMERICAN

Lane, Diane
SIX PACK

Lange, Jessica
EVERYBODY'S ALL-AMERICAN

Lansbury, Angela
NATIONAL VELVET

LaRue, Jack
GIRL FROM MONTEREY, THE

Laughton, Charles
MAN FROM DOWN UNDER, THE

Laurie, Piper
JOHNNY DARK
HUSTLER, THE

Lauter, Ed
LONGEST YARD, THE
YOUNGBLOOD

Lawford, Peter
GOOD NEWS (1947)
BODY AND SOUL (1981)

Layden, Elmer
SPIRIT OF NOTRE DAME, THE

Leibman, Ron
PHAR LAP

Leigh, Janet
ANGELS IN THE OUTFIELD

Lemmon, Jack
FORTUNE COOKIE, THE

Lemon, Bob
KID FROM CLEVELAND, THE
WINNING TEAM, THE

Lemon, Meadowlark
FISH THAT SAVED PITTSBURGH, THE

Lester, Vicki
MIRACLE KID

Lewis, Jerry
MONEY FROM HOME
CADDY, THE
THAT'S MY BOY (1951)

Lewis, Strangler
PRIZEFIGHTER AND THE LADY, THE

Lloyd, Harold
FRESHMAN, THE
MILKY WAY, THE

LoBianco, Tony
SEPARATE WAYS

Lockhart, Calvin
HALLS OF ANGER

Loes, Billy
ROOGIE'S BUMP

Loggia, Robert
OVER THE TOP

Lombard, Carole
FROM HELL TO HEAVEN

Lombardi, Vince
PAPER LION

Long, Richard
ALL-AMERICAN, THE (1953)

Longden, Johnny
WINNER'S CIRCLE, THE

Louis, Joe
SQUARE JUNGLE, THE
SPIRIT OF YOUTH

Lovejoy, Frank
WINNING TEAM, THE

Lowe, Edmund
SECRETS OF A NURSE

Lowe, Rob
YOUNGBLOOD

Lowrey, Peanuts
WINNING TEAM, THE

Loy, Myrna
BROADWAY BILL
PRIZEFIGHTER AND THE LADY, THE

Lucci, Mike
PAPER LION

ACTORS

Luckman, Sid
TRIPLE THREAT

Lupino, Ida
JUNIOR BONNER
DAREDEVILS OF EARTH

Lynch, Richard
EIGHT MEN OUT

Lynn, Diana
PEGGY

McCallion, James
PRIDE OF THE BLUEGRASS

McCallister, Lon
BOY FROM INDIANA

McCarthy, Kevin
KANSAS CITY BOMBER

McCluskey, Roger
WINNING

McCrea, Joel
SPORT PARADE, THE

McEnroe, John
PLAYERS

McGraw, Ali
PLAYERS

McHugh, Frank
FRESHMAN LOVE
COLLEGE LOVERS
PACE THAT THRILLS, THE

Mack, Helen
SECRETS OF A NURSE

McKay, Jim
WORLD'S GREATEST ATHLETE, THE

McLaglen, Victor
RACKETY RAX

MacLaine, Shirley
JOHN GOLDFARB, PLEASE COME
HOME

MacLane, Barton
KID COMES BACK, THE

McLaren, Bruce
GRAND PRIX (1966)

McMahon, Jim
JOHNNY BE GOOD

MacMurray, Fred
FATHER WAS A FULLBACK

McQueen, Steve
LE MANS
JUNIOR BONNER
SOMEBODY UP THERE LIKES ME

MacRae, Gordon
BIG PUNCH, THE

Madonna
VISION QUEST

Mahan, Larry
J.W. COOP

Main, Marjorie
FAST COMPANY

Malden, Karl
STING II, THE
FEAR STRIKES OUT

Mantle, Mickey
SAFE AT HOME

Maravich, Pete
SCORING

Maris, Roger
SAFE AT HOME

Marsh, Joan
MARK IT PAID

Martin, Dean
MONEY FROM HOME
CADDY, THE
THAT'S MY BOY (1951)

Martin, Dean Paul
PLAYERS

Martin, Strother
SLAP SHOT

Martin, Tony
WINNER TAKE ALL (1939)

Marx, Chico
HORSE FEATHERS

Marx, Groucho
HORSE FEATHERS

Marx, Harpo
HORSE FEATHERS

Marx, Zeppo
HORSE FEATHERS

Mason, James
HEAVEN CAN WAIT

Mastrantonio, Mary Elizabeth
COLOR OF MONEY, THE

Mateo, Miguel
MOMENT OF TRUTH, THE

Matheson, Tim
DREAMER

Mathias, Bob
BOB MATHIAS STORY, THE

Matthau, Walter
FORTUNE COOKIE, THE
BAD NEWS BEARS, THE
CASEY'S SHADOW

Mature, Victor
EASY LIVING

Matuszak, John
NORTH DALLAS FORTY

Mauch, Gene
WINNING TEAM, THE

Maxwell, Marilyn
CHAMPION

Mayo, Virginia
KID FROM BROOKLYN, THE

Meeker, Ralph
GLORY ALLEY
WALL OF NOISE

Menjou, Adolphe
MILKY WAY, THE
KING OF THE TURF
GOLDEN BOY
TO PLEASE A LADY

Meredith, Burgess
ROCKY III
ROCKY II
ROCKY
FAN'S NOTES, A

Metcalfe, Adrian
GAMES, THE

Metkovich, George
WINNING TEAM, THE

Middlecoff, Dr. Cary
FOLLOW THE SUN

Mifune, Toshiro
GRAND PRIX (1966)

Miles, Vera
RUN FOR THE ROSES
ROSE BOWL STORY, THE
PRIDE OF THE BLUE GRASS

Milland, Ray
IT HAPPENS EVERY SPRING
RHUBARB

Mitchell, Cameron
MONKEY ON MY BACK

Mitchell, Dale
KID FROM CLEVELAND, THE

Mitchell, Sasha
SPIKE OF BENSONHURST

Mitchell, Thomas
BIG WHEEL, THE

Mitchum, Robert
MATILDA
LUSTY MEN, THE
THAT CHAMPIONSHIP SEASON

Mizerak, Steve
COLOR OF MONEY, THE

Modine, Matthew
VISION QUEST

Monroe, Marilyn
FIREBALL, THE

Montalban, Ricardo
RIGHT CROSS

Montand, Yves
GRAND PRIX (1966)

Montgomery, Robert
HERE COMES MR. JORDAN

Moore, Archie
FORTUNE COOKIE, THE

Moore, Dickie
DECEPTION

Moore, Terry
RETURN OF OCTOBER, THE

Moorehead, Agnes
STRATTON STORY, THE

Moran, Gussie
PAT AND MIKE

Moreno, Rita
RING, THE

Moriarty, Cathy
RAGING BULL

Moriarty, Michael
BANG THE DRUM SLOWLY

Morley, Robert
RAINBOW JACKET, THE
FINAL TEST, THE

Morris, Chester
KING FOR A NIGHT

Morris, Wayne
BIG PUNCH, THE
KID COMES BACK, THE
QUARTERBACK, THE

Morrow, Vic
BAD NEWS BEARS, THE

Morse, David
INSIDE MOVES

Mosconi, Willie
HUSTLER, THE

Moss, Stirling
RACE FOR LIFE, A

Mr. T.
ROCKY III

Munshin, Jules
TAKE ME OUT TO THE BALL GAME

Murphy, Audie
WORLD IN MY CORNER

Murphy, Ben
SIDECAR RACERS

Murphy, George
HOLD THAT CO-ED
RISE AND SHINE
RINGSIDE MAISIE

Murray, Bill
CADDYSHACK

Murray, Jim
WALL OF NOISE

Nahan, Stu
ROCKY II

Naish, J. Carrol
GOLDEN GLOVES

Nastase, Ilie
PLAYERS

Naughton, James
SECOND WIND

Neagle, Anna
FOUR AGAINST FATE

Nelson, Byron
CADDY, THE

Nelson, Craig T.
ALL THE RIGHT MOVES

Nelson, Lindsay
SEMI-TOUGH

Nesterenko, Eric
YOUNGBLOOD

Nevers, Ernie
SPIRIT OF STANFORD, THE

Newman, Paul
WINNING
SOMEBODY UP THERE LIKES ME
SLAP SHOT

Nielsen, Brigitte
ROCKY IV

Nigh, Jane
RODEO

Nimoy, Leonard
KID MONK BARONI

Nitschke, Ray
LONGEST YARD, THE

Nolan, Lloyd
IT HAPPENED IN FLATBUSH
CRAZYLEGS, ALL AMERICAN

Nolte, Nick
NORTH DALLAS FORTY

Noren, Irving
WINNING TEAM, THE

Novarro, Ramon
HUDDLE

Novikoff, Lou
STRATTON STORY, THE

Nugent, Eddie
PRISON SHADOWS

O'Brien, George
SALUTE

O'Brien, Margaret
GLORY

O'Brien, Pat
KNUTE ROCKNE—ALL AMERICAN
KID FROM KOKOMO, THE
IRON MAJOR, THE
INDIANAPOLIS SPEEDWAY
FIREBALL, THE
COLLEGE COACH
PERSONALITY KID, THE

O'Connor, Donald
MILLION DOLLAR LEGS (1939)

O'Hara, Maureen
MAGNIFICENT MATADOR, THE
FATHER WAS A FULLBACK

O'Keefe, Dennis
GREAT DAN PATCH, THE
FOLLOW THE SUN
BURN 'EM UP O'CONNER

O'Keefe, Michael
SLUGGER'S WIFE, THE

O'Neal, Ryan
MAIN EVENT, THE (1979)
GAMES, THE

O'Neal, Tatum
BAD NEWS BEARS, THE

O'Sullivan, Maureen
SPORTING BLOOD (1940)
FAST COMPANIONS
CROWD ROARS, THE (1938)

O'Toole, Annette
ONE ON ONE

Oakie, Jack
MILLION DOLLAR LEGS (1932)
MAN I LOVE, THE
MADISON SQUARE GARDEN

FROM HELL TO HEAVEN
TOUCHDOWN
SOCIAL LION, THE
RISE AND SHINE
FAST COMPANY
COLLEGE RHYTHM
COLLEGE HUMOR

Ontkean, Michael
SLAP SHOT

Orbach, Jerry
FAN'S NOTES, A

Pacino, Al
BOBBY DEERFIELD

Page, Geraldine
J.W. COOP

Paige, Janis
MR. UNIVERSE

Paige, Satchel
KID FROM CLEVELAND, THE

Pallette, Eugene
RIDE, KELLY, RIDE

Palmer, Bud
WORLD'S GREATEST ATHLETE, THE

Palmer, Lilli
BODY AND SOUL (1947)

Parker, Frank
PAT AND MIKE

Parker, Jean
PITTSBURGH KID, THE

Parker, Willard
BODYHOLD

Parks, Michael
SPIKER
SIDEWINDER ONE

Payne, John
KID NIGHTINGALE
INDIANAPOLIS SPEEDWAY

Peck, Gregory
AMAZING GRACE AND CHUCK

Pegler, Westbrook
MADISON SQUARE GARDEN

Pele
HOT SHOT
VICTORY

Penner, Joe
COLLEGE RHYTHM

Pep, Willie
REQUIEM FOR A HEAVYWEIGHT

Perkins, Anthony
TALL STORY
FEAR STRIKES OUT

Perrine, Valerie
LAST AMERICAN HERO, THE

Peters, Bernadette
LONGEST YARD, THE

Peters, Jean
IT HAPPENS EVERY SPRING

Petersen, William L.
AMAZING GRACE AND CHUCK

ACTORS

Petty, Kyle
STROKER ACE

Petty, Richard
THUNDER IN DIXIE

Pevney, Joseph
BODY AND SOUL (1947)

Pidgeon, Walter
SARATOGA

Pleshette, Suzanne
WALL OF NOISE

Plummer, Christopher
BOY IN BLUE, THE

Poitier, Sidney
LET'S DO IT AGAIN
GO, MAN, GO!

Pollard, Michael J.
LITTLE FAUSS AND BIG HALSY

Powell, Dick
RIGHT CROSS
COLLEGE COACH

Powell, Sandy
CUP-TIE HONEYMOON

Power, Tyrone
BLOOD AND SAND (1941)

Presley, Elvis
KID GALAHAD (1962)
SPINOUT
SPEEDWAY

Pressley, Louis "Babe"
HARLEM GLOBETROTTERS, THE

Preston, Robert
JUNIOR BONNER
SEMI-TOUGH

Priddy, Jerry
WINNING TEAM, THE

Provine, Dorothy
WALL OF NOISE

Pryor, Richard
BINGO LONG TRAVELING ALL-STARS
AND MOTOR KINGS, THE
GREASED LIGHTNING

Quaid, Dennis
EVERYBODY'S ALL-AMERICAN
BREAKING AWAY

Quigley, Charles
GAME THAT KILLS, THE

Quillan, Eddie
SWEEPSTAKES

Quinn, Anthony
MAGNIFICENT MATADOR, THE
KNOCKOUT
REQUIEM FOR A HEAVYWEIGHT
BLOOD AND SAND (1941)

Raft, George
LADY'S FROM KENTUCKY, THE

Raines, Cristina
SILVER DREAM RACER

Rains, Claude
THEY MADE ME A CRIMINAL
HERE COMES MR. JORDAN

Ralston, Denis
PLAYERS

Ray, Aldo
SATURDAY'S HERO
PAT AND MIKE

Raye, Martha
$1,000 A TOUCHDOWN

Reagan, Ronald
KNUTE ROCKNE—ALL AMERICAN
WINNING TEAM, THE
SWING YOUR LADY
SERGEANT MURPHY

Reardon, John "Beans"
KID FROM LEFT FIELD, THE

Redford, Robert
NATURAL, THE
LITTLE FAUSS AND BIG HALSY
DOWNHILL RACER

Redgrave, Sir Michael
LONELINESS OF THE LONG DISTANCE
RUNNER, THE

Reed, Donna
MAN FROM DOWN UNDER, THE
CADDY, THE
TROUBLE ALONG THE WAY
SATURDAY'S HERO

Reed, Oliver
STING II, THE

Reed, Pamela
BEST OF TIMES, THE

Reid, Jr., Wally
RACING STRAIN, THE

Reiner, Rob
HALLS OF ANGER

Reno, Kelly
BLACK STALLION, THE

Revson, Peter
GRAND PRIX (1966)

Reynolds, Burt
LONGEST YARD, THE
STROKER ACE
SEMI-TOUGH

Rice, Grantland
MADISON SQUARE GARDEN
FOLLOW THE SUN

Riggs, Bobby
RACQUET

Robbins, Tim
BULL DURHAM

Robertson, Cliff
J.W. COOP

Robinson, Edward G.
BIG LEAGUER
KID GALAHAD (1937)

Robinson, Jackie
JACKIE ROBINSON STORY, THE

Robinson, Sugar Ray
PAPER LION

Rogers, Ginger
YOUNG MAN OF MANHATTAN

Rogers, Kenny
SIX PACK

Rogers, Mimi
BLUE SKIES AGAIN

Roland, Gilbert
BULLFIGHTER AND THE LADY, THE
RACERS, THE

Romero, Cesar
HOLD 'EM YALE
RACERS, THE

Rooney, Mickey
BIG WHEEL, THE
LIFE OF JIMMY DOLAN, THE
KILLER McCOY
LIGHTNING—THE WHITE STALLION
NATIONAL VELVET
THOROUGHBREDS DON'T CRY
REQUIEM FOR A HEAVYWEIGHT
FIREBALL, THE
BLACK STALLION, THE
FAST COMPANIONS
DEATH ON THE DIAMOND

Rosenbloom, Maxie
MR. UNIVERSE
KING FOR A NIGHT
KID FROM KOKOMO, THE
KID COMES BACK, THE
SWING FEVER
RINGSIDE MAISIE

Ross, Barney
REQUIEM FOR A HEAVYWEIGHT

Rossovich, Tim
JOHNNY BE GOOD
MAIN EVENT, THE (1979)
STING II, THE

Ruggles, Charlie
70,000 WITNESSES

Runyon, Damon
MADISON SQUARE GARDEN

Rush, Barbara
WORLD IN MY CORNER

Russell, Betsy
TOMBOY

Russell, Kurt
BEST OF TIMES, THE

Ruth, Babe
PRIDE OF THE YANKEES, THE

Ryan, Robert
SET-UP, THE
IRON MAJOR, THE

Saint, Eva Marie
GRAND PRIX (1966)

Sands, John
BORN TO SPEED

Sarandon, Susan
BULL DURHAM

Sauer, Hank
WINNING TEAM, THE

Savage, John
INSIDE MOVES

Schaap, Dick
SEMI-TOUGH

Schell, Maximilian
PLAYERS

Schenkel, Chris
MAURIE

Schmidt, Joe
PAPER LION

Schroder, Ricky
CHAMP, THE (1979)

Schwarzenegger, Arnold
STAY HUNGRY

Scott, George C.
HUSTLER, THE

Scott, Randolph
HOME ON THE RANGE

Shaw, Stan
BUSTED UP

Sheen, Martin
THAT CHAMPIONSHIP SEASON

Sheridan, Ann
HOME ON THE RANGE
THEY MADE ME A CRIMINAL
INDIANAPOLIS SPEEDWAY
FIGHTING YOUTH
CITY FOR CONQUEST

Shire, Talia
ROCKY IV
ROCKY III
ROCKY II
ROCKY
RAD

Shorter, Frank
PERSONAL BEST

Silvers, Phil
RACQUET

Sim, Alistair
WEE GEORDIE

Sinatra, Frank
TAKE ME OUT TO THE BALL GAME

Sinatra, Nancy
SPEEDWAY

Singleton, Penny
SWING YOUR LADY

Sixkiller, Sonny
LONGEST YARD, THE

Skerritt, Tom
M*A*S*H

Skolimowski, Jerzy
WALKOVER

Smith, Alexis
GENTLEMAN JIM
WHIPLASH
CASEY'S SHADOW

Smith, Bruce
SMITH OF MINNESOTA

Smith, Bubba
STROKER ACE

Smith, Nolan
M*A*S*H

Smith, William
BLOOD AND GUTS

Snead, Sam
CADDY, THE
FOLLOW THE SUN

Snow, Jack T.
HEAVEN CAN WAIT

Somers, Suzanne
YESTERDAY'S HERO

Sorvino, Paul
THAT CHAMPIONSHIP SEASON

Sothern, Ann
RINGSIDE MAISIE

Sparv, Camilla
DOWNHILL RACER

Speaker, Tris
KID FROM CLEVELAND, THE

Stack, Robert
BULLFIGHTER AND THE LADY, THE

Stagg, Alonzo
KNUTE ROCKNE—ALL AMERICAN

Stallone, Sylvester
OVER THE TOP
VICTORY
ROCKY IV
ROCKY III
ROCKY II
ROCKY
PARADISE ALLEY

Stanwyck, Barbara
GOLDEN BOY
TO PLEASE A LADY

Steel, Anthony
CHECKPOINT

Steele, Bob
FIGHTING CHAMP

Steiger, Rod
HARDER THEY FALL, THE

Sterling, Jan
HARDER THEY FALL, THE
RHUBARB
FLESH AND FURY

Sterling, Robert
RINGSIDE MAISIE
YESTERDAY'S HEROES

Stern, Bill
GO, MAN, GO!
SPIRIT OF WEST POINT, THE
PRIDE OF THE YANKEES, THE

Stern, Daniel
BREAKING AWAY

Stewart, James
NAVY BLUE AND GOLD
STRATTON STORY, THE
SPEED

Stewart, Paul
JOE LOUIS STORY, THE

Stockwell, Dean
MIGHTY MC GURK, THE

Stone, Lewis
SPORTING BLOOD (1940)

Streisand, Barbra
MAIN EVENT, THE (1979)

Stricklyn, Ray
TRACK OF THUNDER

Stuart, Nick
POLICE CALL

Studstill, Pat
PAPER LION

Stuhldreher, Harry
SPIRIT OF NOTRE DAME, THE

Sutherland, Donald
M*A*S*H

Svenson, Bo
NORTH DALLAS FORTY

Swayze, Patrick
YOUNGBLOOD

Swenson, Bo
MAURIE

Talbot, Lyle
RED HOT TIRES

Tamblyn, Rusty
KID FROM CLEVELAND, THE

Tarkenton, Fran
M*A*S*H

Tatum, Reese "Goose"
HARLEM GLOBETROTTERS, THE

Taylor, Elizabeth
NATIONAL VELVET

Taylor, Marjorie
RACING ROMANCE

Taylor, Robert
CROWD ROARS, THE (1938)

Temple, Shirley
STORY OF SEABISCUIT, THE

Thompson, Lea
ALL THE RIGHT MOVES

Thompson, Marshall
ROSE BOWL STORY, THE

Thorpe, Jim
TOUCHDOWN

Tiffin, Pamela
LIVELY SET, THE

Todd, Thelma
HORSE FEATHERS

Toomey, Bill
WORLD'S GREATEST ATHLETE, THE

Toomey, Regis
NAVY BOUND

Tracy, Spencer
SOCIETY GIRL
PAT AND MIKE

Trevor, Claire
BABE RUTH STORY, THE

Trippi, Charles
TRIPLE THREAT

Tucker, Forrest
SPIRIT OF STANFORD, THE

Tucker, Sophie
THOROUGHBREDS DON'T CRY

Turpin, Ben
MILLION DOLLAR LEGS (1932)

Unitas, Johnny
GUS

Unser, Bobby
WINNING

Ustinov, Peter
JOHN GOLDFARB, PLEASE COME HOME

Vale, Virginia
BLONDE COMET

Valentino, Rudolph
BLOOD AND SAND (1922)

Vallee, Rudy
FATHER WAS A FULLBACK

Van Buren, Steve
TRIPLE THREAT

Van Doren, Mamie
ALL-AMERICAN, THE (1953)

Veeck, Bill
KID FROM CLEVELAND, THE

Verdon, Gwen
DAMN YANKEES

Vernon, Mickey
KID FROM CLEVELAND, THE

Vilas, Guillermo
PLAYERS

Vincent, Jan-Michael
BIG WEDNESDAY
WORLD'S GREATEST ATHLETE, THE

Voight, Jon
ALL-AMERICAN BOY, THE
CHAMP, THE (1979)

Wagner, Lindsay
SECOND WIND

Wagner, Robert
WINNING

Walcott, Jersey Joe
HARDER THEY FALL, THE

Wallace, Coley
JOE LOUIS STORY, THE

Wallach, Eli
SAM'S SON

Walston, Ray
TALL STORY
DAMN YANKEES

Walter, Jessica
NUMBER ONE
SPRING FEVER

Warden, Jack
HEAVEN CAN WAIT
DREAMER
CHAMP, THE (1979)

Warner, Glenn "Pop"
KNUTE ROCKNE—ALL AMERICAN

Warner, Jack
SQUARE RING, THE

FINAL TEST, THE

Warren, Jennifer
SLAP SHOT

Warren, Michael
FAST BREAK
DRIVE, HE SAID

Warrick, Ruth
IRON MAJOR, THE
ROOGIE'S BUMP

Washington, Frank
HARLEM GLOBETROTTERS, THE

Waterfield, Bob
TRIPLE THREAT
CRAZYLEGS, ALL AMERICAN

Wayne, John
LIFE OF JIMMY DOLAN, THE
TROUBLE ALONG THE WAY
SALUTE
IDOL OF THE CROWDS
CONFLICT

Weathers, Carl
SEMI-TOUGH
ROCKY IV
ROCKY III
ROCKY II
ROCKY

Webber, Robert
CASEY'S SHADOW

Welch, Raquel
KANSAS CITY BOMBER

Wellman, Jr., William
SWINGIN' AFFAIR, A

Whalen, Michael
SPEED TO BURN

Wheeler, Bert
HOLD 'EM JAIL
COWBOY QUARTERBACK

Wheelwright, Ernie
LONGEST YARD, THE
GREATEST, THE

Whitman, Stuart
RUN FOR THE ROSES

Wilde, Cornel
DEVIL'S HAIRPIN, THE

Wilding, Michael
FOUR AGAINST FATE

Willard, Jess
PRIZEFIGHTER AND THE LADY, THE

Williams, Bill
BLUE GRASS OF KENTUCKY
PACE THAT THRILLS, THE

Williams, Billy Dee
BINGO LONG TRAVELING ALL-STARS AND MOTOR KINGS, THE

Williams, Esther
TAKE ME OUT TO THE BALL GAME

Williams, Garry
EIGHT MEN OUT

Williams, Robin
BEST OF TIMES, THE

Williamson, Fred
M*A*S*H
LAST FIGHT, THE

Willis, Norman
LIFE BEGINS IN COLLEGE

Wilson, Marie
COWBOY QUARTERBACK

Winkler, Henry
ONE AND ONLY, THE

Winters, Jonathan
FISH THAT SAVED PITTSBURGH, THE

Winters, Shelley
TENNESSEE CHAMP

Wismer, Harry
SPIRIT OF WEST POINT, THE
SOMEBODY UP THERE LIKES ME
BABE RUTH STORY, THE

Withers, Googie
FOUR AGAINST FATE

Withers, Grant
DUKE OF CHICAGO

Wolf, Warner
ROCKY IV

Wood, Natalie
ROSE BOWL STORY, THE
FATHER WAS A FULLBACK

Woodeschick, Tom
M*A*S*H

Woodward, Joanne
WINNING

Woolsey, Robert
HOLD 'EM JAIL

Wright, Teresa
PRIDE OF THE YANKEES, THE

Wyman, Jane
KID NIGHTINGALE
KID FROM KOKOMO, THE

Wynn, Keenan
TENNESSEE CHAMP
ANGELS IN THE OUTFIELD
COACH

Yang, C.K.
WALK, DON'T RUN

Yarborough, Cale
STROKER ACE

Young, Burt
ROCKY IV
ROCKY III
ROCKY II
ROCKY
... ALL THE MARBLES

Young, Gig
ARENA
KID GALAHAD (1962)

Young, Loretta
LIFE OF JIMMY DOLAN, THE
KENTUCKY

Young, Robert
NAVY BLUE AND GOLD
KID FROM SPAIN, THE
BAND PLAYS ON, THE

SPORTING BLOOD (1940)
SATURDAY'S MILLIONS
DEATH ON THE DIAMOND

Zaharias, Babe Didrikson
PAT AND MIKE

Zale, Tony
GOLDEN GLOVES STORY, THE

Zarilla, Al
WINNING TEAM, THE

CINEMATOGRAPHERS

Abrams, Barry
HERE COME THE TIGERS

Ahern, Lloyd
FATHER WAS A FULLBACK

Akers, I.W.
KENTUCKY BLUE STREAK

Albert, Arthur
STREETS OF GOLD

Almendros, Nestor
WILD RACERS, THE

Alonzo, John A.
BAD NEWS BEARS, THE
CASEY'S SHADOW

Andracke, Greg
HOT SHOT

Arling, Arthur E.
GREAT AMERICAN PASTIME, THE

Ash, Jerome
SHAKEDOWN, THE

Askins, Monroe
THUNDER ALLEY

August, Joseph
THAT'S MY BOY (1932)
SALUTE

Avil, Gordon
CHAMP, THE (1931)

Bailey, John
THAT CHAMPIONSHIP SEASON

Ballard, Lucien
MAGNIFICENT MATADOR, THE
JUNIOR BONNER
WALL OF NOISE

Ballhaus, Michael
COLOR OF MONEY, THE

Barnes, George
CAIN AND MABEL
SOCIETY GIRL
RIDING HIGH (1950)

Beascoechea, Frank
NADIA

Beeson, Paul
SILVER DREAM RACER

Biroc, Joseph
LONGEST YARD, THE
RIDE THE WILD SURF
... ALL THE MARBLES

Boffety, Jean
EDITH AND MARCEL

Boggs, Haskell
LEATHER SAINT, THE
RED LINE 7000
FEAR STRIKES OUT

Bogner, Ludvik
BUSTED UP
RENO AND THE DOC

Bouillet, George
GREASED LIGHTNING

Boyd, Russell
PHAR LAP

Boyle, Charles B.
FOLLOW THRU

Boyle, John W.
GRIDIRON FLASH

Bradford, William
THOROUGHBREDS

Bredell, Elwood
SWING THAT CHEER
SECRETS OF A NURSE
DANGER ON WHEELS

Brenner, Jules
CORNBREAD, EARL AND ME

Brodine, Norbert
RIGHT CROSS

Brown, James
MR. HEX

Brun, Joseph
JOE LOUIS STORY, THE
THUNDER IN CAROLINA

Butler, Bill
BINGO LONG TRAVELING ALL-STARS
AND MOTOR KINGS, THE
STING II, THE
ROCKY IV
ROCKY III
ROCKY II
DRIVE, HE SAID
ICE CASTLES

Byrne, Bobby
STEALING HOME
BULL DURHAM

Cave-Chinn, L.
MANIACS ON WHEELS

Chapman, Michael
RAGING BULL
PERSONAL BEST

Chavez, Julio C.
RACING FEVER

Clark, Dan
STRAIGHTAWAY

Clarke, Charles
IT HAPPENED IN FLATBUSH
YESTERDAY'S HEROES

Cline, Robert
THAT GANG OF MINE
CONTENDER, THE

Cline, Wilfrid M.
GLORY

STORY OF SEABISCUIT, THE

Colwell, Chuck
THRASHIN'

Contner, Durgi J.
ROOGIE'S BUMP

Coop, Denys
THIS SPORTING LIFE

Cooper, Wilkie
WEE GEORDIE

Correll, Charles
FAST BREAK

Cortez, Stanley
LEATHER-PUSHERS, THE
BASKETBALL FIX, THE

Crabe, James
ROCKY
PLAYERS

Cronjager, Edward
HOME IN INDIANA
WINNER TAKE ALL (1939)
RISE AND SHINE

Crosby, Floyd
FIREBALL 500
YOUNG RACERS, THE

Cross, Eric
SPORTING LOVE

Cundy, Dean
SEPARATE WAYS

Czapsky, Stefan
ON THE EDGE

Dalzell, Dennis
SIDEWINDER ONE

Daniels, William
GLORY ALLEY
PAT AND MIKE

de Grasse, Robert
IRON MAJOR, THE

De Santis, Pasquale
MOMENT OF TRUTH, THE

DeBont, Jan
ALL THE RIGHT MOVES

Decae, Henri
BOBBY DEERFIELD

Deschanel, Caleb
NATURAL, THE
SLUGGER'S WIFE, THE
BLACK STALLION, THE

Di Venanzo, Gianni
MOMENT OF TRUTH, THE

Diamond, James
MILLION TO ONE, A
THEY NEVER COME BACK

Dickinson, Desmond
ARSENAL STADIUM MYSTERY, THE

Dines, Gordon
SQUARE RING, THE

Dominguez, Raul
RUN FOR THE ROSES

CINEMATOGRAPHERS

Doran, Robert
RACING BLOOD (1938)

Draper, Jack
BULLFIGHTER AND THE LADY, THE

Drasner, Milton
HOLD 'EM YALE

Dupont, Max
HOT CURVES

Dyer, Elmer
WINNER'S CIRCLE, THE

Edeson, Arthur
PATENT LEATHER KID, THE
LIFE OF JIMMY DOLAN, THE
KID NIGHTINGALE
KID COMES BACK, THE
SWING YOUR LADY
FLESH
FAST COMPANIONS
PALOOKA

Elswit, Robert
AMAZING GRACE AND CHUCK

Emmott, Basil
GREAT GAME, THE (1930)
TAKE IT FROM ME

Faithfull, Geoffrey
GREEN HELMET, THE
STOCK CAR
RACING ROMANCE
FIFTY-SHILLING BOXER
CUP-TIE HONEYMOON

Fapp, Daniel L.
MONEY FROM HOME
CADDY, THE
SPINOUT
DEVIL'S HAIRPIN, THE

Farrar, Vincent
TRIPLE THREAT

Fierberg, Steven
SPIKE OF BENSONHURST

Fischbeck, Harry
MILLION DOLLAR LEGS (1939)

Fisher, Gerry
VICTORY

Folsey, George
TENNESSEE CHAMP
TAKE ME OUT TO THE BALL GAME

Forrest, James
BODY AND SOUL (1981)

Fowle, H.E.
MANIACS ON WHEELS

Fraker, William A.
HEAVEN CAN WAIT

Fredericks, Ellsworth
TALL STORY
BOB MATHIAS STORY, THE

Freeman, Mervyn
BLONDE COMET

Freulich, Henry
SPORT OF KINGS

Freund, Karl
GOLDEN BOY

Friedman, Eugene
PAPER LION

Fujimoto, Tak
HEART LIKE A WHEEL

Garbarini, Peter
PAPER LION

Garmes, Lee
LUSTY MEN, THE
THAT'S MY BOY (1951)
SATURDAY'S HERO

Gaudio, Tony
KNUTE ROCKNE—ALL AMERICAN
KID GALAHAD (1937)
THAT'S MY MAN

George, Laszlo
BEAR, THE
RUNNING

Gerard, Harry
MAN I LOVE, THE

Gerrard, Henry
FOLLOW THRU

Gertsman, Maury
MONKEY ON MY BACK
WORLD IN MY CORNER
ALL-AMERICAN, THE (1953)

Gilks, Alfred
MILKY WAY, THE

Glassberg, Irving
FLESH AND FURY

Glendinning, Hone
RIDING HIGH (1937)

Goldblatt, Stephen
EVERYBODY'S ALL-AMERICAN

Gornick, Jr., Allan
PERSONAL BEST

Gould, Harvey
THAT GANG OF MINE

Greene, Max
FOUR AGAINST FATE
THERE AIN'T NO JUSTICE

Greenhalgh, Jack
RACING BLOOD (1938)

Grindrod, Phil
GREAT GAME, THE (1952)

Grossman, Karen
TRADING HEARTS

Guerner, Enrique
MANOLETE

Guffey, Burnett
KID GALAHAD (1962)
HALLS OF ANGER
HARDER THEY FALL, THE
GREAT WHITE HOPE, THE

Guissart, Jr., Rene
LE MANS

Gurfinkel, David
OVER THE TOP

Guthrie, Carl
BIG PUNCH, THE
JOHNNY DARK

Haines, Bert
COLLEGE
BATTLING BUTLER

Haitkin, Jacques
PRIZE FIGHTER, THE

Hall, Conrad
FAT CITY

Haller, Ernest
JIM THORPE—ALL AMERICAN

Hamilton, Peter
SMALL TOWN STORY

Hammerus, Ralph
PATENT LEATHER KID, THE

Harlan, Russell
RING, THE

Hartzbrand, Morris
PAPER LION

Harvey, Jimmy
RACE FOR LIFE, A

Hauser, Robert B.
LE MANS

Heller, Otto
SQUARE RING, THE
RAINBOW JACKET, THE

Hickox, Sid
KID FROM KOKOMO, THE
GENTLEMAN JIM
FRESHMAN LOVE
WINNING TEAM, THE
INDIANAPOLIS SPEEDWAY
CROWD ROARS, THE (1932)

Hilburn, Percy
GOOD NEWS (1930)
IRON MAN, THE (1931)

Hines, William E.
SCORING

Hirschfield, Gerald
MR. UNIVERSE

Hoffman, Fred
PAPER LION

Hollander, Adam
J.W. COOP

Hora, John
MAURIE

Howe, James Wong
THEY MADE ME A CRIMINAL
BODY AND SOUL (1947)
FIGHTER, THE
CITY FOR CONQUEST

Hubbs, Gil
WRESTLER, THE

Hugo, Michel
NUMBER ONE

Hunt, J. Roy
SPORT PARADE, THE

Hyer, Bill
FLYING FISTS, THE

LIVELY SET, THE
IRON MAN, THE (1951)

Hyer, William
TWO MINUTES TO PLAY
RACING BLOOD (1938)
PRISON SHADOWS

Irwin, Mark
BLOOD AND GUTS
YOUNGBLOOD

Jackman, Jr., Fred
NAVY WAY, THE

Jackson, Harry
KID FROM LEFT FIELD, THE

Jago, Jo
SMALL TOWN STORY

Janet, Pierre
RETURN TO CAMPUS

Jennings, Dev
BATTLING BUTLER
HOLD EVERYTHING

Jennings, J. Devereux
COLLEGE

June, Ray
HORSE FEATHERS
SARATOGA

Kaufman, Lloyd
SQUEEZE PLAY

Kellman, Morris
PAPER LION

Kelsay, Ross
SKATEBOARD

Kemper, Victor J.
ONE AND ONLY, THE
STAY HUNGRY
SLAP SHOT

Kesson, Frank
COLLEGE LOVERS

Kline, Benjamin
GAME THAT KILLS, THE
JOE PALOOKA, CHAMP

Kline, Richard H.
TOUCH AND GO

Knechtel, Alvin
PATENT LEATHER KID, THE

Knowland, Nic
PLAYING AWAY

Koenekamp, Fred J.
KANSAS CITY BOMBER
BAD NEWS BEARS IN BREAKING
TRAINING, THE
CHAMP, THE (1979)

Kohler, Henry
FRESHMAN, THE

Kovacs, Laszlo
INSIDE MOVES
PARADISE ALLEY

Krasner, Milton
LAUGHING IRISH EYES
SKI PATROL
SET-UP, THE
RED LINE 7000
DEATH ON THE DIAMOND

Kull, Edward
HIGH GEAR
FIGHTING GENTLEMAN, THE

Kurrle, Robert
MAYBE IT'S LOVE
WINNER TAKE ALL (1932)

Lacambre, Daniel
WILD RACERS, THE

Lanning, Reggie
LAUGHING IRISH EYES
PITTSBURGH KID, THE

Larner, Stevan
CADDYSHACK
GOLDENGIRL

LaShelle, Joseph
GUY WHO CAME BACK, THE
FORTUNE COOKIE, THE
UNDER MY SKIN
IN THIS CORNER

Lassally, Walter
LONELINESS OF THE LONG DISTANCE
RUNNER, THE

Laszlo, Ernest
BIG WHEEL, THE
JACKIE ROBINSON STORY, THE
RIDING HIGH (1950)

Lathrop, Philip
HARD TIMES
ALL-AMERICAN BOY, THE

Lawton, Charles
RINGSIDE MAISIE

Lawton, Jr., Charles
KILL THE UMPIRE
BOOTS MALONE

Lazan, Stan
MIXED COMPANY

Le Picard, Marcel
HOLD THAT LINE
GIRL FROM MONTEREY, THE
JOE PALOOKA IN THE SQUARED
CIRCLE
BOWERY BLITZKRIEG

Leiterman, Richard
RAD

Lemmo, James
LAST FIGHT, THE

Leonetti, Matthew F.
BREAKING AWAY

Lindon, Lionel
GRAND PRIX (1966)
RHUBARB

Lippman, Irving
SAFE AT HOME

Lipstein, Harold
FAST COMPANY
DAMN YANKEES

Lohmann, Paul
NORTH DALLAS FORTY

Lowell, Ross
J.W. COOP

Lundin, Walter
FRESHMAN, THE
HARRIGAN'S KID

Lynch, Warren
OVER THE GOAL
RED HOT TIRES

Lyons, Chet
DECEPTION

Lyons, Edgar
RACING LUCK (1935)

McAlpine, Don
BLUE SKIES AGAIN
PUBERTY BLUES

MacBurnie, John
KING OF THE GAMBLERS
HEART OF VIRGINIA
DUKE OF CHICAGO
PRIDE OF MARYLAND

McCord, Ted
KNOCKOUT
SERGEANT MURPHY
COWBOY QUARTERBACK
PRIDE OF THE BLUEGRASS

MacDonald, Joe
IT HAPPENS EVERY SPRING
RACERS, THE

Mackenzie, Jack
BOY FROM INDIANA

McKinney, Austin
PIT STOP

McLean, Nick
STROKER ACE

McLeod, Bill
FINAL TEST, THE

McNaughton, Bruce
GREAT MACARTHY, THE

Makin, Harry
FAN'S NOTES, A

Marley, Peverell
WHIPLASH

Marta, Jack
KID FROM CLEVELAND, THE
FIGHTING THOROUGHBREDS
CROOKED CIRCLE, THE

Martin, John
RACING BLOOD (1954)

Martinelli, Arthur
MR. CELEBRITY
MIRACLE KID
TEN LAPS TO GO

Marx, David
PAPER LION

Mate, Rudolph
PRIDE OF THE YANKEES, THE

Maylam, Tony
BOBBY DEERFIELD

Meehan, George
HEART PUNCH

Mellor, William
$1,000 A TOUCHDOWN
BIG LEAGUER

CINEMATOGRAPHERS

HOME ON THE RANGE
Metty, Russell
PEGGY

Meyers, Paul
SUNNY SKIES

Mignot, Pierre
BOY IN BLUE, THE

Miller, Arthur
PIGSKIN PARADE

Miller, Virgil
BIG FIX, THE
RIGHT TO THE HEART
RIDE, KELLY, RIDE
CRAZYLEGS, ALL AMERICAN

Milner, Victor
TOUCHDOWN, ARMY

Moore, Richard
WINNING

Morgan, Donald M.
ONE ON ONE
LET'S DO IT AGAIN

Morgan, Ira
HIGH SCHOOL HERO
RACING LUCK (1948)

Morris, Reginald
SECOND WIND

Moura, Edgar
HOT SHOT

Murphy II, Fred V.
WINNERS TAKE ALL

Murphy, Fred
HOOSIERS

Murphy, Mike
COACH

Musuraca, Nicholas
GOLDEN BOY
SATURDAY'S HEROES

Neumann, Harry
NAVY BOUND
ROSE BOWL STORY, THE
RODEO
ROAR OF THE CROWD
IDOL OF THE CROWDS
PRIDE OF THE BLUE GRASS

Nobles, William
RACING STRAIN, THE

Nurzynski, Antoni
WALKOVER

O'Connell, L.W.
KING OF HOCKEY
RACKETY RAX
POLO JOE

Okazaki, Kozo
BAD NEWS BEARS GO TO JAPAN,
THE

Onorato, Paul
SIDECAR RACERS

Ornitz, Arthur J.
REQUIEM FOR A HEAVYWEIGHT

Palmer, Ernest
KENTUCKY
BLOOD AND SAND (1941)
FLYING FIFTY-FIVE

Parolin, Aiace
MOMENT OF TRUTH, THE

Paynter, Robert
GAMES, THE

Peterman, Don
AMERICAN FLYERS

Phillips, Frank
GUS
WORLD'S GREATEST ATHLETE, THE

Planck, Robert
HOLD THAT CO-ED
LIFE BEGINS IN COLLEGE
KING OF THE TURF
WOMAN-WISE

Planer, Franz
SPIRIT OF STANFORD, THE
CHAMPION

Poland, Clifford
FIREBALL JUNGLE

Polito, Jean
BAD NEWS BEARS GO TO JAPAN,
THE

Polito, Sol
LOCAL BOY MAKES GOOD
FIREMAN, SAVE MY CHILD
CITY FOR CONQUEST

Pollister, Richard
PAPER LION

Porrett, Fred
PAPER LION

Probyn, Brian
DOWNHILL RACER

Protat, Francois
RUNNING BRAVE

Redman, Frank
PACE THAT THRILLS, THE

Reed, Arthur
BORN TO FIGHT

Rees, William
PERSONALITY KID, THE

Reeves, Arthur
SWELLHEAD, THE
SUNNY SKIES

Rennahan, Ray
KENTUCKY
BLOOD AND SAND (1941)

Richards, Jack
FINNEY

Richardson, Robert
EIGHT MEN OUT

Robinson, George
SQUARE JUNGLE, THE
SPIRIT OF NOTRE DAME, THE
SOME BLONDES ARE DANGEROUS
RACING YOUTH
ALL-AMERICAN, THE (1932)
COLLEGE LOVE

Roe, Guy
IN THIS CORNER

Roizman, Owen
VISION QUEST

Rose, Jackson
SWELLHEAD, THE
BORN TO SPEED

Rosher, Charles
SWING FEVER

Rosher, Jr., Charles
SEMI-TOUGH

Rosson, Harold
TO PLEASE A LADY
STRATTON STORY, THE
SPORTING BLOOD (1931)

Russell, John
BILLIE

Russell, Jr., John L.
GOLDEN GLOVES STORY, THE

Ruttenberg, Joseph
KILLER McCOY
SPEEDWAY
SOMEBODY UP THERE LIKES ME

Sabol, Steve
PAPER LION

Sandor, Greg
JUMP

Schatz, Jack
PAPER LION

Schoenbaum, Charles
MIGHTY MC GURK, THE
GOOD NEWS (1947)
RACETRACK

Scholtz, Abe
POLICE CALL

Seitz, John
NAVY BLUE AND GOLD
CROWD ROARS, THE (1938)

Shamroy, Leon
JOHN GOLDFARB, PLEASE COME
HOME

Sharp, Henry
MADISON SQUARE GARDEN
HOLD 'EM NAVY!
GOLDEN GLOVES
FROM HELL TO HEAVEN
70,000 WITNESSES
ROSE BOWL

Shaw, Steven
LIGHTNING—THE WHITE STALLION

Shea, Mike
UNHOLY ROLLERS

Shelton, Joe
SPEED LOVERS

Sherry, Robert A.
SPIKER

Shore, Richard
BANG THE DRUM SLOWLY

Shufton, Gene
HUSTLER, THE

Shuttack, Steve
RETURN TO CAMPUS

Sickner, William
JOE PALOOKA MEETS HUMPHREY
JOE PALOOKA IN WINNER TAKE ALL
JOE PALOOKA IN TRIPLE CROSS
JOE PALOOKA IN THE
COUNTERPUNCH
FIGHTING MAD
FIGHTING FOOLS
HUMPHREY TAKES A CHANCE

Siegler, Allen
MOTOR MADNESS
MAIN EVENT, THE (1938)
BURNING UP
SOCIAL LION, THE

Silano, George
LAST AMERICAN HERO, THE

Slocombe, Douglas
ROLLERBALL

Smith, Leonard
HOLD 'EM JAIL
NATIONAL VELVET
BAND PLAYS ON, THE
THOROUGHBREDS DON'T CRY
THEY LEARNED ABOUT WOMEN
SO THIS IS COLLEGE

Smokler, Peter
NORTH SHORE

Smoot, Reed
TAKE DOWN

Snyder, Edward
SWEEPSTAKES
SPEED TO BURN
ROAD DEMON
FIGHTING YOUTH

Snyder, William
RETURN OF OCTOBER, THE

Spalding, Thomas E.
THUNDER IN DIXIE

Sparkuhl, Theodor
LADY'S FROM KENTUCKY, THE
SALTY O'ROURKE

Sprudin, Miklaj
BOXER

Stanley, Frank
FISH THAT SAVED PITTSBURGH, THE
J.W. COOP

Steiner, Phil
GO, MAN, GO!

Stengler, Mack
JOE PALOOKA IN THE BIG FIGHT

Stensvold, Alan
TRACK OF THUNDER

Stewart, Ernest
CHECKPOINT

Stine, Harold E.
M*A*S*H

Stout, Archie
TROUBLE ALONG THE WAY
FIGHTING CHAMP
COUNTY FAIR, THE

CONFLICT

Stradling, Harry
GREATEST, THE
WALK, DON'T RUN

Stumar, Charles
KING FOR A NIGHT
STEADY COMPANY
SPIRIT OF STANFORD, THE
SHAKEDOWN, THE
SATURDAY'S MILLIONS

Stumar, John
HARMON OF MICHIGAN
UNWELCOME STRANGER

Suhrstedt, Timothy
SPLIT DECISIONS

Surtees, Bruce
BIG WEDNESDAY
DREAMER

Taffet, Al
PAPER LION

Tannura, Phillip
SMITH OF MINNESOTA
HARLEM GLOBETROTTERS, THE
BABE RUTH STORY, THE

Taylor, Ronnie
CHAMPIONS

Tetzlaff, Teddy
HIGH SPEED
THIS SPORTING AGE
COLLEGE RHYTHM

Thorin, Donald E.
WILDCATS
AMERICAN ANTHEM

Todd, Arthur
MILLION DOLLAR LEGS (1932)
TOUCHDOWN
RED HOT TIRES
ELMER THE GREAT
ALIBI IKE
COLLEGE COACH

Toland, Gregg
KID FROM SPAIN, THE
KID FROM BROOKLYN, THE

Tosi, Mario
MAIN EVENT, THE (1979)
SIX PACK

Tover, Leo
FOLLOW THE SUN
QUARTERBACK, THE
COLLEGE RHYTHM
COLLEGE HUMOR
PRIDE OF ST. LOUIS, THE

Valentine, Joseph A.
SPEAKEASY

van der Enden, Eddie
GRUNT! THE WRESTLING MOVIE

Van Enger, Charles
MOONLIGHT IN HAVANA
KID MONK BARONI

Van Trees, James
GREAT JOHN L., THE

Vogel, Paul C.
ARENA
SUNDAY PUNCH
ANGELS IN THE OUTFIELD

Voigtlander, Ted
SAM'S SON

Wagner, Sidney
MAN FROM DOWN UNDER, THE
SPORTING BLOOD (1940)

Walker, Joseph
BROADWAY BILL
HERE COMES MR. JORDAN

Warrenton, Gilbert
GREAT DAN PATCH, THE
BLUE GRASS OF KENTUCKY
BLUE BLOOD
COWBOY AND THE PRIZEFIGHTER,
THE

Watkin, David
CHARIOTS OF FIRE

Waugh, Fred
J.W. COOP

Wenstrom, Harold
HUDDLE

West, Brian
YESTERDAY'S HERO

Wheeler, Charles F.
BEST OF TIMES, THE

Wheeler, Joseph
PAPER LION

White, Lester
WHITE LIGHTING
WE WENT TO COLLEGE
BURN 'EM UP O'CONNER
SPIRIT OF WEST POINT, THE
SPEED
PRIZEFIGHTER AND THE LADY, THE
FIREBALL, THE

Wild, Harry
BIG GAME, THE
RACING LADY
EASY LIVING

Wilder, Donald
SPRING FEVER
PAPERBACK HERO

Williams, Larry
YOUNG MAN OF MANHATTAN

Wilson, James
TAKE ME TO PARIS

Woolf, Jack
MATILDA

Woolsey, Ralph
LITTLE FAUSS AND BIG HALSY

Wooster, Kirk
NUMBER ONE

Wyckoff, Alvin
BLOOD AND SAND (1922)

Yarussi, Daniel
TOMBOY

Yeoman, Robert D.
JOHNNY BE GOOD

CINEMATOGRAPHERS

Zaytsev, Sergey
LAST GAME, THE

DIRECTORS

Abbott, George
DAMN YANKEES

Adolfi, John
COLLEGE LOVERS

Aldis, Will
STEALING HOME

Aldrich, Robert
BIG LEAGUER
LONGEST YARD, THE
. . . ALL THE MARBLES

Altman, Robert
M*A*S*H

Amy, George
KID NIGHTINGALE

Anderson, Lindsay
THIS SPORTING LIFE

Anspaugh, David
HOOSIERS

Arnold, Jack
LIVELY SET, THE

Ashby, Hal
SLUGGER'S WIFE, THE

Asher, William
FIREBALL 500

Asquith, Anthony
FINAL TEST, THE

Avedis, Howard
SEPARATE WAYS

Avildsen, John G.
ROCKY

Bacon, Lloyd
FIREMAN, SAVE MY CHILD
KNUTE ROCKNE—ALL AMERICAN
KILL THE UMPIRE
CAIN AND MABEL
IT HAPPENS EVERY SPRING
INDIANAPOLIS SPEEDWAY

Badham, John
BINGO LONG TRAVELING ALL-STARS
AND MOTOR KINGS, THE
AMERICAN FLYERS

Baker, David
GREAT MACARTHY, THE

Ballard, Carroll
BLACK STALLION, THE

Barry, Wesley
RACING BLOOD (1954)

Barsha, Leon
PACE THAT THRILLS, THE

Barton, Charles
HARMON OF MICHIGAN
SPIRIT OF STANFORD, THE
ROSE BOWL

Beatty, Warren
HEAVEN CAN WAIT

Beaudine, William
MR. HEX
MR. CELEBRITY
MIRACLE KID
HOLD THAT LINE
TAKE IT FROM ME
BLUE GRASS OF KENTUCKY
ROSE BOWL STORY, THE
RODEO
ROAR OF THE CROWD
BLONDE COMET
PRIDE OF THE BLUE GRASS

Becker, Harold
VISION QUEST

Bell, Monta
YOUNG MAN OF MANHATTAN

Bellamy, Earl
SIDEWINDER ONE
SIDECAR RACERS

Bennison, Andrew W.
THIS SPORTING AGE

Beresford, Bruce
PUBERTY BLUES

Berke, William
NAVY WAY, THE
RACING LUCK (1948)

Berkeley, Busby
THEY MADE ME A CRIMINAL
TAKE ME OUT TO THE BALL GAME

Bernds, Edward
WHITE LIGHTING

Berry, John
BAD NEWS BEARS GO TO JAPAN,
THE

Blair, George
KING OF THE GAMBLERS
THOROUGHBREDS
DUKE OF CHICAGO

Blakeley, John E.
CUP-TIE HONEYMOON

Boetticher, Budd
MAGNIFICENT MATADOR, THE
BULLFIGHTER AND THE LADY, THE

Bogart, Paul
HALLS OF ANGER

Borzage, Frank
THAT'S MY MAN

Bowers, George
BODY AND SOUL (1981)

Brabin, Charles
SPORTING BLOOD (1931)

Brower, Otto
WINNER TAKE ALL (1939)
STRAIGHTAWAY
SPEED TO BURN
ROAD DEMON

Brown, Clarence
NATIONAL VELVET
TO PLEASE A LADY
ANGELS IN THE OUTFIELD

Brown, Harry Joe
MADISON SQUARE GARDEN

Brown, Phil
HARLEM GLOBETROTTERS, THE

Browning, Tod
IRON MAN, THE (1931)

Butler, David
KENTUCKY
GLORY
STORY OF SEABISCUIT, THE
SALUTE
PIGSKIN PARADE

Cabanne, Christy
DANGER ON WHEELS

Cahn, Edward L.
BORN TO SPEED

Capra, Frank
BROADWAY BILL
RIDING HIGH (1950)

Carruth, Milton
SOME BLONDES ARE DANGEROUS

Chapman, Michael
ALL THE RIGHT MOVES

Clemens, William
KNOCKOUT

Clifton, Elmer
TEN LAPS TO GO

Cline, Edward
MILLION DOLLAR LEGS (1932)

Clowes, John L.
GRAND PRIX (1934)

Collins, Lewis D.
COWBOY AND THE PRIZEFIGHTER,
THE

Conway, Jack
THEY LEARNED ABOUT WOMEN
SARATOGA

Cooke, Alan
NADIA

Cooper, George A.
MANNEQUIN

Corman, Roger
YOUNG RACERS, THE

Cornsweet, Harold
RETURN TO CAMPUS

Corrigan, Lloyd
FOLLOW THRU

Creber, Lewis
IT HAPPENED IN FLATBUSH

Crosland, Alan
PERSONALITY KID, THE

Cruze, James
RACETRACK

Cukor, George
PAT AND MIKE

Cunningham, Sean S.
HERE COME THE TIGERS

Curtiz, Michael
KID GALAHAD (1937)

JIM THORPE—ALL AMERICAN
TROUBLE ALONG THE WAY

Dare, Danny
MAIN EVENT, THE (1938)

Day, Richard
IT HAPPENED IN FLATBUSH

de Cordova, Frederick
PEGGY

de Gaetano, Michael
SCORING

de Toth, Andre
MONKEY ON MY BACK

Dearden, Basil
SQUARE RING, THE
RAINBOW JACKET, THE

Del Ruth, Roy
HOLD EVERYTHING
WINNER TAKE ALL (1932)
BABE RUTH STORY, THE

Denham, Reginald
FLYING FIFTY-FIVE

Dennis, Charles
RENO AND THE DOC

Dickinson, Thorold
ARSENAL STADIUM MYSTERY, THE

Dieterle, William
BOOTS MALONE

Dmytryk, Edward
MILLION DOLLAR LEGS (1939)
GOLDEN GLOVES

Donen, Stanley
DAMN YANKEES

Doniger, Walter
SAFE AT HOME

Donner, Richard
INSIDE MOVES

Dreifuss, Arthur
HIGH SCHOOL HERO

Drury, David
SPLIT DECISIONS

Dwan, Allan
RISE AND SHINE
WOMAN-WISE

Dziedzina, Julian
BOXER

Eason, B. Reeves
KID COMES BACK, THE
SERGEANT MURPHY

Eason, Breezy
HEART PUNCH

Eastman, Charles
ALL-AMERICAN BOY, THE

Elvey, Maurice
GREAT GAME, THE (1952)

Endfield, Cyril
JOE PALOOKA IN THE BIG FIGHT

Enright, Ray
SWING YOUR LADY
IRON MAJOR, THE

ALIBI IKE

Erickson, A.F.
THIS SPORTING AGE

Everett, D.S.
RUNNING BRAVE

Feist, Felix
BASKETBALL FIX, THE
GOLDEN GLOVES STORY, THE
WINNER'S CIRCLE, THE

Fisher, Terence
RACE FOR LIFE, A

Fleischer, Richard
ARENA

Flood, James
BIG FIX, THE
SWELLHEAD, THE

Ford, John
SALUTE
FLESH

Ford, Philip
PRIDE OF MARYLAND

Forde, Eugene
RIGHT TO THE HEART

Forlong, Michael
GREEN HELMET, THE

Foster, Norman
RIDE, KELLY, RIDE

Fox, Wallace
GIRL FROM MONTEREY, THE
BOWERY BLITZKRIEG
RACING LADY

Frankenheimer, John
GRAND PRIX (1966)

Fraser, Harry
SPIRIT OF YOUTH

Freed, Herb
TOMBOY

Freedman, Jerrold
KANSAS CITY BOMBER

Friedman, Seymour
BODYHOLD

Furie, Sidney J.
LITTLE FAUSS AND BIG HALSY

Gage, George
SKATEBOARD

Ganzer, Alvin
LEATHER SAINT, THE

Garnett, Tay
FIREBALL, THE

Golan, Menahem
OVER THE TOP

Goldstone, James
WINNING

Gordon, Robert
JOE LOUIS STORY, THE
SPORT OF KINGS

Green, Alfred E.
KING OF THE TURF
THOROUGHBREDS DON'T CRY

JACKIE ROBINSON STORY, THE

Grefe, William
RACING FEVER

Gries, Tom
NUMBER ONE
GREATEST, THE

Grinde, Nick
MILLION DOLLAR LEGS (1939)
GOOD NEWS (1930)

Hackford, Taylor
EVERYBODY'S ALL-AMERICAN

Hale, Rex
RACING BLOOD (1938)

Hall, Alexander
LADY'S FROM KENTUCKY, THE
HERE COMES MR. JORDAN

Haller, Daniel
WILD RACERS, THE

Hancock, John
BANG THE DRUM SLOWLY

Hare, Bill
FINNEY

Harvey, Anthony
PLAYERS

Hathaway, Henry
HOME IN INDIANA
RACERS, THE

Hawks, Howard
RED LINE 7000
CROWD ROARS, THE (1932)

Helmick, Paul
THUNDER IN CAROLINA

Henry, Buck
HEAVEN CAN WAIT

Herman, Albert
SPORTING CHANCE

Hibbs, Jesse
WORLD IN MY CORNER
ALL-AMERICAN, THE (1953)

Hill, Bob
FLYING FISTS, THE

Hill, George Roy
SLAP SHOT

Hill, Jack
PIT STOP

Hill, Robert
TWO MINUTES TO PLAY
PRISON SHADOWS

Hill, Walter
HARD TIMES

Hoffman, Herman
GREAT AMERICAN PASTIME, THE

Hogan, James
$1,000 A TOUCHDOWN

Holzman, Allan
GRUNT! THE WRESTLING MOVIE

Hopper, Jerry
SQUARE JUNGLE, THE

Horne, James W.
COLLEGE

Howard, David
CONFLICT

Howe, James Wong
GO, MAN, GO!

Hudson, Hugh
CHARIOTS OF FIRE

Humberstone, H. Bruce
QUARTERBACK, THE

Huston, John
VICTORY
FAT CITY

Hutchinson, Charles
BORN TO FIGHT

Irvin, John
CHAMPIONS

Jacobson, Arthur
HOME ON THE RANGE

Jarrott, Charles
BOY IN BLUE, THE

Jason, Leigh
HIGH GEAR

Jewison, Norman
ROLLERBALL

Johnson, Lamont
ONE ON ONE
LAST AMERICAN HERO, THE

Johnson, Raymond K.
KENTUCKY BLUE STREAK

Jones, Harmon
KID FROM LEFT FIELD, THE
PRIDE OF ST. LOUIS, THE

Kagan, Jeremy Paul
STING II, THE

Kampmann, Steven
STEALING HOME

Kane, Joe
TRACK OF THUNDER
CROOKED CIRCLE, THE

Kaplan, Jonathan
HEART LIKE A WHEEL

Karelov, Y.
LAST GAME, THE

Karlson, Phil
KID GALAHAD (1962)

Katzin, Lee H.
LE MANS

Keaton, Buster
BATTLING BUTLER

Kenton, Erle
FROM HELL TO HEAVEN

Kiersch, Fritz
WINNERS TAKE ALL

Killy, Edward
SATURDAY'S HEROES

King, Louis
COUNTY FAIR, THE

King, Rick
HOT SHOT

Kline, Herbert
KID FROM CLEVELAND, THE
FIGHTER, THE

Kotcheff, Ted
NORTH DALLAS FORTY

Landers, Lew
SMITH OF MINNESOTA
SKI PATROL
BLUE BLOOD

Landon, Michael
SAM'S SON

Landres, Paul
NAVY BOUND

Lanfield, Sidney
HOLD 'EM YALE
FOLLOW THE SUN
SOCIETY GIRL

Launder, Frank
WEE GEORDIE

Lawrence, Jay O.
SWINGIN' AFFAIR, A

Le Borg, Reginald
JOE PALOOKA IN WINNER TAKE ALL
JOE PALOOKA IN TRIPLE CROSS
JOE PALOOKA IN THE SQUARED
CIRCLE
JOE PALOOKA IN THE
COUNTERPUNCH
JOE PALOOKA, CHAMP
FIGHTING MAD
FIGHTING FOOLS

Lederman, D. Ross
MOTOR MADNESS
MARK IT PAID
GAME THAT KILLS, THE
RED HOT TIRES

Lederman, Ross D.
HIGH SPEED

Lee, Jack
MANIACS ON WHEELS

Leeds, Herbert I.
YESTERDAY'S HEROES

Leifer, Neil
TRADING HEARTS
YESTERDAY'S HERO

Lelouch, Claude
EDITH AND MARCEL

Leonard, Robert Z.
MAN FROM DOWN UNDER, THE

Lerner, Joseph
MR. UNIVERSE

LeRoy, Mervyn
LOCAL BOY MAKES GOOD
ELMER THE GREAT

Levey, William A.
LIGHTNING—THE WHITE STALLION

Levin, Henry
RUN FOR THE ROSES

Levinson, Barry
NATURAL, THE

Lewis, Joseph H.
THAT GANG OF MINE
RETURN OF OCTOBER, THE

Litvak, Anatole
CITY FOR CONQUEST

Logan, Joshua
TALL STORY

Lubin, Arthur
SECRETS OF A NURSE
RHUBARB
IDOL OF THE CROWDS

Ludwig, Edward
BIG WHEEL, THE
STEADY COMPANY

Lynch, Paul
BLOOD AND GUTS

Lyon, Francis D.
BOB MATHIAS STORY, THE
CRAZYLEGS, ALL AMERICAN

McCarey, Leo
MILKY WAY, THE
KID FROM SPAIN, THE

McCarey, Ray
IT HAPPENED IN FLATBUSH

McCarthy, J.P.
FIGHTING CHAMP

Macdonald, David
RIDING HIGH (1937)

McEveety, Vincent
GUS

Macfadden, Hamilton
FIGHTING YOUTH

McGaha, William
SPEED LOVERS

McGann, William
FRESHMAN LOVE
PRIDE OF THE BLUEGRASS
POLO JOE

MacGregor, Edgar J.
GOOD NEWS (1930)

Mack, Russell
BAND PLAYS ON, THE
SPIRIT OF NOTRE DAME, THE
ALL-AMERICAN, THE (1932)

McLeod, Norman Z.
HORSE FEATHERS
KID FROM BROOKLYN, THE
TOUCHDOWN

McNaughton, R.Q.
MANIACS ON WHEELS

Magnoli, Albert
AMERICAN ANTHEM

Mamoulian, Rouben
GOLDEN BOY
BLOOD AND SAND (1941)

Mandel, Robert
TOUCH AND GO

Manduke, Joe
JUMP
CORNBREAD, EARL AND ME

Mann, Anthony
MOONLIGHT IN HAVANA

Mann, Daniel
MAURIE
MATILDA

March, Alex
PAPER LION

Marin, Edwin L.
SPEED
RINGSIDE MAISIE

Markle, Peter
YOUNGBLOOD

Marshall, George
MONEY FROM HOME
HOLD THAT CO-ED

Mayo, Archie
LIFE OF JIMMY DOLAN, THE

Merrill, Keith
TAKE DOWN

Michaels, Richard
BLUE SKIES AGAIN

Milius, John
BIG WEDNESDAY

Miller, David
SUNDAY PUNCH
SATURDAY'S HERO

Miller, Jason
THAT CHAMPIONSHIP SEASON

Milton, Dave
JOE PALOOKA MEETS HUMPHREY

Moore, Vin
RACING YOUTH

Morrissey, Paul
SPIKE OF BENSONHURST

Moses, Gilbert
FISH THAT SAVED PITTSBURGH, THE

Mulligan, Robert
FEAR STRIKES OUT

Murphy, Dudley
SPORT PARADE, THE

Murphy, Ralph
SPIRIT OF WEST POINT, THE
70,000 WITNESSES

Naud, William T.
THUNDER IN DIXIE

Needham, Hal
STROKER ACE
RAD

Negulesco, Jean
UNDER MY SKIN

Neill, Roy William
THAT'S MY BOY (1932)

Nelson, Ralph
REQUIEM FOR A HEAVYWEIGHT

Neumann, Kurt
HOLD 'EM NAVY!

KING FOR A NIGHT
TOUCHDOWN, ARMY
RING, THE
FAST COMPANIONS

Newell, Mike
AMAZING GRACE AND CHUCK

Newfield, Sam
RACING LUCK (1935)
CONTENDER, THE

Newman, Joseph
GUY WHO CAME BACK, THE
GREAT DAN PATCH, THE

Newmeyer, Fred
FRESHMAN, THE
THEY NEVER COME BACK
FIGHTING GENTLEMAN, THE

Niblo, Fred
BLOOD AND SAND (1922)

Nicholls, Jr., George
BIG GAME, THE

Nicholson, Jack
DRIVE, HE SAID

Nilsson, Rob
ON THE EDGE

Nosseck, Noel
DREAMER

Ove, Horace
PLAYING AWAY

Palmisano, Conrad E.
BUSTED UP

Pearson, Peter
PAPERBACK HERO

Peckinpah, Sam
JUNIOR BONNER

Petrie, Daniel
SIX PACK

Pevney, Joseph
IRON MAN, THE (1951)
FLESH AND FURY

Phelps, William
NORTH SHORE

Poitier, Sidney
LET'S DO IT AGAIN

Pollack, Sidney
BOBBY DEERFIELD

Preece, Michael
PRIZE FIGHTER, THE

Pressman, Michael
BAD NEWS BEARS IN BREAKING
TRAINING, THE

Prieto, Joseph
FIREBALL JUNGLE

Prosperi, Franco
RIPPED-OFF

Rafelson, Bob
STAY HUNGRY

Ramis, Harold
CADDYSHACK

Rawlins, John
LEATHER-PUSHERS, THE
BOY FROM INDIANA

Ray, Nicholas
LUSTY MEN, THE

Raymond, Jack
GREAT GAME, THE (1930)
TAKE ME TO PARIS

Reiner, Carl
ONE AND ONLY, THE

Reisner, Charles F.
HARRIGAN'S KID

Relph, Michael
SQUARE RING, THE

Rey, Florian
MANOLETE

Richardson, Tony
LONELINESS OF THE LONG DISTANCE
RUNNER, THE

Riesner, Charles F.
IN THIS CORNER

Rilla, Wolf
STOCK CAR

Ritchie, Michael
WILDCATS
BAD NEWS BEARS, THE
SEMI-TOUGH
DOWNHILL RACER

Ritt, Martin
GREAT WHITE HOPE, THE
CASEY'S SHADOW

Robertson, Cliff
J.W. COOP

Robson, Mark
HARDER THEY FALL, THE
CHAMPION

Rogell, Albert
SWEEPSTAKES

Rogers, Maclean
RACING ROMANCE
FIFTY-SHILLING BOXER

Rosen, Phil
UNWELCOME STRANGER

Rosi, Francesco
MOMENT OF TRUTH, THE

Ross, Nat
COLLEGE LOVE

Rossen, Robert
BODY AND SOUL (1947)
HUSTLER, THE

Roth, Joe
STREETS OF GOLD

Rowland, Roy
KILLER McCOY

Ruggles, Wesley
COLLEGE HUMOR

Rush, Richard
THUNDER ALLEY

Salkow, Sidney
FIGHTING THOROUGHBREDS

DIRECTORS

Santell, Alfred
PATENT LEATHER KID, THE

Santley, Joseph
LAUGHING IRISH EYES

Sarafian, Richard
BEAR, THE

Sargent, Joseph
GOLDENGIRL

Sayles, John
EIGHT MEN OUT

Scanlan, Joseph L.
SPRING FEVER

Scheerer, Richard
WORLD'S GREATEST ATHLETE, THE

Schultz, Michael
GREASED LIGHTNING

Schuster, Harold
KID MONK BARONI
SWING THAT CHEER

Schwab, Laurence
FOLLOW THRU

Scorsese, Martin
RAGING BULL
COLOR OF MONEY, THE

Sedgwick, Edward
BURN 'EM UP O'CONNER
SATURDAY'S MILLIONS
DEATH ON THE DIAMOND

Seiler, Lewis
KID FROM KOKOMO, THE
WINNING TEAM, THE
WHIPLASH
DECEPTION

Seiter, William A.
LIFE BEGINS IN COLLEGE

Shavelson, Melville
MIXED COMPANY

Shebib, Donald
SECOND WIND

Shelton, Ron
BULL DURHAM

Sherman, George
JOHNNY DARK

Shores, Lynn
MILLION TO ONE, A

Shourds, Sherry
BIG PUNCH, THE

Simon, S. Sylvan
SPORTING BLOOD (1940)

Skolimowski, Jerzy
WALKOVER

Smight, Jack
FAST BREAK

Smith, Bud
JOHNNY BE GOOD

Smith, Noel
OVER THE GOAL
KING OF HOCKEY
COWBOY QUARTERBACK

Spottiswoode, Roger
BEST OF TIMES, THE

Springsteen, R.G.
HEART OF VIRGINIA

Stahl, John M.
FATHER WAS A FULLBACK

Stallone, Sylvester
ROCKY IV
ROCKY III
ROCKY II
PARADISE ALLEY

Stanley, Joseph
WE WENT TO COLLEGE

Stark, Ray
CASEY'S SHADOW

Stern, Steven Hilliard
RUNNING

Stoloff, Benjamin
SPEAKEASY
PALOOKA

Storm, Jerome
RACING STRAIN, THE

Sturges, John
RIGHT CROSS
FAST COMPANY

Sutherland, A. Edward
SOCIAL LION, THE
FAST COMPANY

Sutherland, Edward A.
BURNING UP

Swerdloff, Arthur
ROADRACERS, THE

Taurog, Norman
HOT CURVES
HOLD 'EM JAIL
CADDY, THE
SUNNY SKIES
SPINOUT
SPEEDWAY
COLLEGE RHYTHM

Taylor, Don
RIDE THE WILD SURF

Taylor, Sam
FRESHMAN, THE

Tennyson, Penrose
THERE AIN'T NO JUSTICE

Thomas, Ralph
CHECKPOINT

Thompson, J. Lee
JOHN GOLDFARB, PLEASE COME
HOME

Thorpe, Richard
CROWD ROARS, THE (1938)

Till, Eric
FAN'S NOTES, A

Tilton, Roger
SPIKER

Tourneur, Jacques
EASY LIVING

Towne, Robert
PERSONAL BEST

Townley, Jack
PITTSBURGH KID, THE

Townsend, Bud
COACH

Tryon, Glenn
GRIDIRON FLASH

Tully, Montgomery
SMALL TOWN STORY

Tuttle, Frank
GREAT JOHN L., THE

Vadja, L.
LOVE ON SKIS

Van Dyke, W.S.
PRIZEFIGHTER AND THE LADY, THE

Vidor, King
CHAMP, THE (1931)

Vorhaus, Bernard
DAREDEVILS OF EARTH

Walker, Hal
THAT'S MY BOY (1951)

Walsh, Raoul
GLORY ALLEY
GENTLEMAN JIM
SALTY O'ROURKE

Walters, Charles
GOOD NEWS (1947)
WALK, DON'T RUN

Waters, John
MIGHTY MC GURK, THE

Weil, Samuel
SQUEEZE PLAY

Weis, Donald
BILLIE

Wellman, William A.
MAYBE IT'S LOVE
MAN I LOVE, THE
COLLEGE COACH

Werker, Alfred
RACKETY RAX

Westman, Jim
WRESTLER, THE

Whelan, Tim
SWING FEVER

Whitman, Philip H.
POLICE CALL

Wickes, David
SILVER DREAM RACER

Wilcox, Fred M.
TENNESSEE CHAMP

Wilcox, Herbert
FOUR AGAINST FATE

Wilde, Cornel
DEVIL'S HAIRPIN, THE

Wilder, Billy
FORTUNE COOKIE, THE

Williamson, Fred
LAST FIGHT, THE

Wills, J. Elder
SPORTING LOVE

Wilson, Richard
WALL OF NOISE

Wincer, Simon
PHAR LAP

Winner, Michael
GAMES, THE

Winters, David
THRASHIN'
RACQUET

Wise, Robert
SOMEBODY UP THERE LIKES ME
SET-UP, THE

Wood, Sam
HUDDLE
NAVY BLUE AND GOLD
THEY LEARNED ABOUT WOMEN
STRATTON STORY, THE
SO THIS IS COLLEGE
PRIDE OF THE YANKEES, THE

Wrye, Donald
ICE CASTLES

Wyler, William
SHAKEDOWN, THE

Yarbrough, Jean
JOE PALOOKA MEETS HUMPHREY
TRIPLE THREAT
HUMPHREY TAKES A CHANCE

Yates, Peter
BREAKING AWAY

Young, Harold
ROOGIE'S BUMP

Zeffirelli, Franco
CHAMP, THE (1979)

Zieff, Howard
MAIN EVENT, THE (1979)

Zimmerman, Vernon
UNHOLY ROLLERS

EDITORS

Adams, Warren
JOE PALOOKA IN THE
COUNTERPUNCH

Akst, Albert
GOOD NEWS (1947)
SUNDAY PUNCH
SOMEBODY UP THERE LIKES ME

Aleyeva, K.
LAST GAME, THE

Allen, Dede
SLAP SHOT
HUSTLER, THE

Allen, Fred
SPEED TO BURN

Allen, Stanford C.
ROCKY II

Amy, George
KID GALAHAD (1937)

Anderson, Philip W.
TALL STORY

Anderson, William
PUBERTY BLUES

Angus, Robert
SKATEBOARD

Archer, Nick
DOWNHILL RACER

Arzner, Dorothy
BLOOD AND SAND (1922)

Austin, William
HOLD THAT LINE
RODEO
ROAR OF THE CROWD
FIGHTING FOOLS
DECEPTION

Bain, Fred
FIGHTING GENTLEMAN, THE

Barber, Oscar
RACING FEVER

Batista, Henry
RACING LUCK (1948)

Beaton, Alex
J.W. COOP

Beetley, Samuel E.
PACE THAT THRILLS, THE

Bell, Cliff
DUKE OF CHICAGO

Bellinger, Theodore
GREAT JOHN L., THE

Bennett, Hugh
PATENT LEATHER KID, THE

Berg, Dave
SATURDAY'S MILLIONS

Berger, Fred W.
GREAT DAN PATCH, THE

Berlatsky, David
KANSAS CITY BOMBER

Bernie, Jason
KID MONK BARONI
KID FROM CLEVELAND, THE

Bezencenet, Peter
SQUARE RING, THE

Biery, Edward A.
WINNING

Bischoff, Robert
BLOOD AND SAND (1941)
RACKETY RAX

Blangsted, Folmar
JIM THORPE—ALL AMERICAN

Boemler, George
PAT AND MIKE

Booth, Marguerite
FAT CITY

Bornstein, Ken
LIGHTNING—THE WHITE STALLION

Bracht, Frank
SIDEWINDER ONE
DAMN YANKEES

Brame, Bill
RED LINE 7000

Brandt, Byron
GREATEST, THE

Bridgers, Raymond
NADIA

Brochu, Don
SLUGGER'S WIFE, THE

Brockway, Richard
NUMBER ONE

Brown, O. Nicholas
HEART LIKE A WHEEL

Brummer, Richard S.
SPIKER

Burton, Bernard W.
JOE PALOOKA, CHAMP

Cahn, Phil
KING FOR A NIGHT

Cahoon, Richard
MAGNIFICENT MATADOR, THE
SWELLHEAD, THE
SHAKEDOWN, THE

Cambas, Jacqueline
PERSONAL BEST

Cambern, Donn
DRIVE, HE SAID

Capacchione, Frank
LONGEST YARD, THE

Carlisle, Robert
SPIRIT OF NOTRE DAME, THE
SATURDAY'S MILLIONS

Carruth, Milton
WORLD IN MY CORNER
IRON MAN, THE (1931)

Carruth, William
CADDYSHACK

Carter, John
PAPER LION

Chastain, Neal
WRESTLER, THE

Chew, Richard
STREETS OF GOLD

Chialvo, Jeanine
PUBERTY BLUES

Chulack, Fred
DREAMER

Clancy, Margaret
SOCIETY GIRL

Clark, Al
MAIN EVENT, THE (1938)
BOOTS MALONE

Clark, James B.
RACERS, THE

Clarke, Frank
GREEN HELMET, THE

Claxton, William F.
GOLDEN GLOVES STORY, THE

Cohn, Martin G.
RACING BLOOD (1938)

Colbert, Norman
BIG FIX, THE
IN THIS CORNER

Connell, Thelma
WEE GEORDIE

Conrad, Scott
ROCKY

Craft, Charles
IDOL OF THE CROWDS

Crandall, Robert
MR. CELEBRITY
GIRL FROM MONTEREY, THE

Crane, Kenneth
THUNDER ALLEY

Cranston, Helga
FINAL TEST, THE

Craven, Garth
BEST OF TIMES, THE

Crone, George
GRIDIRON FLASH

Crosland, Jr., Alan
WINNING TEAM, THE

Currier, Richard
MR. HEX
HIGH SCHOOL HERO

Curtiss, Edward
JOHNNY DARK
SWING THAT CHEER
SKI PATROL
SECRETS OF A NURSE
ALL-AMERICAN, THE (1953)

Dalton, John
FIREBALL JUNGLE

Dalva, Robert
BLACK STALLION, THE

Darmois, Hugues
EDITH AND MARCEL

Davey, Ethel
RACING STRAIN, THE

Dawson, Ralph
LUSTY MEN, THE
KNUTE ROCKNE—ALL AMERICAN
PEGGY

De Gaetano, Al
BIG FIX, THE
WOMAN-WISE
IN THIS CORNER
YESTERDAY'S HEROES

DeMaggio, Nick
WINNER TAKE ALL (1939)

Dennis, Jack
HOME ON THE RANGE
HOLD 'EM YALE
THAT'S MY BOY (1932)

Dervim, Joseph
FAST COMPANY

Des Jonqueres, Ghislaine
LE MANS

DeStefano, Lorenzo
THRASHIN'
WINNERS TAKE ALL

Dewar, Frank
PRIDE OF THE BLUEGRASS

Digges, Jr., Richard H.
BURNING UP

Dixon, Ralph
THOROUGHBREDS

Dmytryk, Edward
HOLD 'EM NAVY!

Dodd, Everett
OVER THE GOAL

Elliott, Faith
GO, MAN, GO!

Ernst, Donald W.
LE MANS

Farrell, Richard
SPEEDWAY

Feitshans, Fred
FIREBALL 500

Fetterman, Richard
TAKE DOWN

Fields, Verna
WILD RACERS, THE
TRACK OF THUNDER

Fitzstephens, John
SPEED LOVERS

Florio, Robert
BEAR, THE

Frazan, Adrienne
BILLIE

Freda, William
SPEED LOVERS

Freeman, Jeff
SPLIT DECISIONS

Friedgen, Jr., Bud
FISH THAT SAVED PITTSBURGH, THE

Fuller, John
PRIDE OF THE BLUE GRASS

Garfield, David
STING II, THE
ALL THE RIGHT MOVES

Gerstad, Harry
CHAMPION

Gibbons, James
FRESHMAN LOVE
SERGEANT MURPHY

Gibbs, Anthony
STEALING HOME
LONELINESS OF THE LONG DISTANCE
RUNNER, THE
ROLLERBALL
YESTERDAY'S HERO

Gilmore, Stuart
MILLION DOLLAR LEGS (1939)
KID GALAHAD (1962)
RED LINE 7000

Golden, Robert
BOWERY BLITZKRIEG

Gordean, William
STROKER ACE

Gordon, Robert
NORTH SHORE
COACH

Gould, Doug
KNOCKOUT
COWBOY QUARTERBACK

Gray, William
SPORTING BLOOD (1931)
BLOOD AND GUTS
FLESH

Greene, Danford B.
M*A*S*H
BLUE SKIES AGAIN
ROCKY II

Gribble, Bernard
GAMES, THE

Gross, Frank
SOME BLONDES ARE DANGEROUS

Gross, Roland
SET-UP, THE

Hall, Ralph James
MIXED COMPANY

Halsey, Richard
THAT CHAMPIONSHIP SEASON
ROCKY

Hampton, Janice
ROCKY II

Hannemann, Walter
MAURIE
BOB MATHIAS STORY, THE
ROSE BOWL STORY, THE

Hare, Bill
FINNEY

Harkness, Richard
ON THE EDGE

Harris, Jack
MANIACS ON WHEELS
RAINBOW JACKET, THE

Harris, Richard A.
WILDCATS
BAD NEWS BEARS GO TO JAPAN,
THE
BAD NEWS BEARS, THE
SEMI-TOUGH

Harrison, Doanne
GOLDEN GLOVES

Havlick, Gene
BROADWAY BILL
RETURN OF OCTOBER, THE

Hayes, W. Donn
BORN TO SPEED

Heermance, Richard
BABE RUTH STORY, THE

Heisler, Stuart
KID FROM SPAIN, THE

Held, Tom
THEY LEARNED ABOUT WOMEN

Henkel, Charles
TWO MINUTES TO PLAY

Herdan, Earl
RUNNING BRAVE

Herman, Ace
HIGH SCHOOL HERO
RACING BLOOD (1954)

Herring, Pembroke J.
LET'S DO IT AGAIN

Hill, Emma
YOUNG MAN OF MANHATTAN

Hill, Jack
PIT STOP

Hilton, Arthur
LEATHER-PUSHERS, THE
UNWELCOME STRANGER

Hirschler, Kurt
RUNNING

Hively, George
LONGEST YARD, THE

Hofstra, Jack
YOUNGBLOOD

Hollywood, Peter
SILVER DREAM RACER
AMAZING GRACE AND CHUCK

Holmes, Christopher
GREASED LIGHTNING
DRIVE, HE SAID
ALL-AMERICAN BOY, THE

Holmes, William
HOLD EVERYTHING
CAIN AND MABEL
INDIANAPOLIS SPEEDWAY
CITY FOR CONQUEST

Holzman, Allan
GRUNT! THE WRESTLING MOVIE

Honess, Peter
CHAMPIONS

Hornbeck, William
RIDING HIGH (1950)

House, Chandler
$1,000 A TOUCHDOWN

Huggins, Jere
PERSONAL BEST

Humphreys, Ned
PERSONAL BEST

Hunt, Charles
RACING LUCK (1935)

Jacob, Dennis
WILD RACERS, THE

Jacobs, Allan
MATILDA
LONGEST YARD, THE

Johnson, Harvey
LADY'S FROM KENTUCKY, THE

Jones, Harmon
HOME IN INDIANA

Jones, Jeff
AMERICAN FLYERS

Jones, Kirk
SPRING FEVER
PAPERBACK HERO

Jones, Robert C.
HEAVEN CAN WAIT

Kahn, Michael
ICE CASTLES

Kamen, Jay
NORTH DALLAS FORTY

Kane, Joe
SWEEPSTAKES

Katz, Oliver B.
SCORING

Katz, Sidney
PAPER LION

Kell, J.S.
COLLEGE

Keller, Frank P.
SAFE AT HOME

Kern, Robert J.
NAVY BLUE AND GOLD
NATIONAL VELVET
TO PLEASE A LADY
PRIZEFIGHTER AND THE LADY, THE
ANGELS IN THE OUTFIELD

Killifer, Jack
LOCAL BOY MAKES GOOD
KID FROM KOKOMO, THE
GENTLEMAN JIM
THEY MADE ME A CRIMINAL
SWING YOUR LADY

Kimble, Robert L.
SIDECAR RACERS

Knudtson, Floyd
LEATHER SAINT, THE
DEVIL'S HAIRPIN, THE

Knudtson, Frederic
BIG GAME, THE
SATURDAY'S HEROES
EASY LIVING
CROOKED CIRCLE, THE

Kolster, Clarence
HOT CURVES
SUNNY SKIES
POLO JOE

Kress, Carl
STROKER ACE
RAD

Kryczmonik, Barbara
WALKOVER

Kummins, David
JOE LOUIS STORY, THE

Lahti, Jim
RENO AND THE DOC

Lane, Richard
. . . ALL THE MARBLES

Larson, Seth
MR. HEX

Lawrence, Viola
HERE COMES MR. JORDAN

Leeds, Robert
KING OF THE GAMBLERS

Leighton, Robert
BULL DURHAM

Lenny, Bill
RACE FOR LIFE, A

Lerner, Carl
REQUIEM FOR A HEAVYWEIGHT

Lerner, Geraldine
MR. UNIVERSE

Levanway, William
GOOD NEWS (1930)
BAND PLAYS ON, THE

Levin, Sidney
CASEY'S SHADOW

Levy, Bert
LIFE OF JIMMY DOLAN, THE

Lewis, Ben
BIG LEAGUER
MIGHTY MC GURK, THE
BURN 'EM UP O'CONNER
TENNESSEE CHAMP
STRATTON STORY, THE

Lewis, Joseph H.
LAUGHING IRISH EYES

Lewthwaite, Bill
FOUR AGAINST FATE

Linder, Stu
NATURAL, THE

Link II, John F.
STAY HUNGRY

Lipton, Rex
THUNDER IN CAROLINA

Livingston, Roy
BLUE GRASS OF KENTUCKY
BLUE BLOOD
FIGHTING MAD

Loeffler, John
SAM'S SON

Loeffler, Louis
HOLD THAT CO-ED
LIFE BEGINS IN COLLEGE
RIGHT TO THE HEART
RIDE, KELLY, RIDE

Loewenthal, Daniel
LAST FIGHT, THE

Loewinger, Rose E.
RACETRACK

Lovering, Otho
NAVY BOUND
JOE PALOOKA MEETS HUMPHREY
JOE PALOOKA IN WINNER TAKE ALL
SOCIAL LION, THE
BLUE GRASS OF KENTUCKY
HUMPHREY TAKES A CHANCE

Low, Warren
MONEY FROM HOME
CADDY, THE
KID COMES BACK, THE
THAT'S MY BOY (1951)

EDITORS

Lower, Tony
SPRING FEVER
RUNNING BRAVE

Luciano, Michael
LONGEST YARD, THE

Lyon, Francis D.
BASKETBALL FIX, THE

Lyon, William
SATURDAY'S HERO

McDermott, Edward
MAYBE IT'S LOVE

McGee, Frank
RED HOT TIRES

McKay, James
THEY LEARNED ABOUT WOMEN

McLean, Barbara
FOLLOW THE SUN

McLernon, Harold
KING OF HOCKEY

McNeil, Allen
FRESHMAN, THE
RISE AND SHINE

Macrorie, Alma
RHUBARB
QUARTERBACK, THE

Magee, Frank
BIG PUNCH, THE
WHIPLASH

Maguire, Fred
JOE PALOOKA IN THE BIG FIGHT

Mandell, Daniel
KID FROM BROOKLYN, THE
FORTUNE COOKIE, THE
PRIDE OF THE YANKEES, THE

Manger, Harvey
SPIRIT OF WEST POINT, THE

Mann, Edward
FIGHTER, THE

Marks, George
FIREMAN, SAVE MY CHILD

Marks, Owen
TROUBLE ALONG THE WAY

Marks, Richard
BANG THE DRUM SLOWLY

Marshek, Archie
LIVELY SET, THE

Martin, Jr., Philip
IRON MAJOR, THE

Mayer, Otto
STRAIGHTAWAY

Mazolla, Frank
FISH THAT SAVED PITTSBURGH, THE

Meyer, Otto
GOLDEN BOY

Meyer, Richard C.
WINNING

Milner, Daniel
PRISON SHADOWS

Miner, Stephen
HERE COME THE TIGERS

Minter, Harold
PRIDE OF MARYLAND

Molin, Bud
ONE AND ONLY, THE
HALLS OF ANGER

Morley, James
RACING LADY

Morra, Irene
KENTUCKY
GLORY
STORY OF SEABISCUIT, THE
PIGSKIN PARADE

Morriss, Frank
INSIDE MOVES
AMERICAN FLYERS

Morse, Terry
PERSONALITY KID, THE

Moscovitz, David
SPEED LOVERS

Mulconery, Walt
TOUCH AND GO
PERSONAL BEST

Murphy, William B.
GUY WHO CAME BACK, THE
JOHN GOLDFARB, PLEASE COME
HOME

Murray, Jack
ROAD DEMON

Nadel, Arthur H.
JACKIE ROBINSON STORY, THE

Nelson, Charles
KILL THE UMPIRE

Nelson, Jr., Argyle
LITTLE FAUSS AND BIG HALSY

Newcom, James E.
WE WENT TO COLLEGE
RIGHT CROSS

Newman, Eve
FIREBALL 500
PARADISE ALLEY

Nicholson, George
GOLDENGIRL

Nims, Ernest
FIGHTING THOROUGHBREDS
PITTSBURGH KID, THE

Norris, George T.
JUMP
SQUEEZE PLAY

Nosler, Lloyd
SHAKEDOWN, THE

O'Meara, C. Timothy
HOOSIERS

O'Meara, Tim
BIG WEDNESDAY

Ogilvie, Jack
CONFLICT

Oliver, James
AMERICAN ANTHEM

Parrish, Robert
BODY AND SOUL (1947)

Paterson, Tony
PHAR LAP

Pierce, Bruce
IT HAPPENS EVERY SPRING
RING, THE

Pierson, Carl
THAT GANG OF MINE

Pitt, Ray
THERE AIN'T NO JUSTICE

Pivar, Maurice
IRON MAN, THE (1931)

Pollard, Samm
BODY AND SOUL (1981)

Poppe, Harry
SPEED

Pratt, Thomas
WINNER TAKE ALL (1932)
ELMER THE GREAT
CROWD ROARS, THE (1932)
ALIBI IKE
COLLEGE COACH

Priego, Alfredo Rosas
RUN FOR THE ROSES

Puett, Dallas
AMERICAN FLYERS

Rawlings, Terry
CHARIOTS OF FIRE

Rawlins, David
BINGO LONG TRAVELING ALL-STARS
AND MOTOR KINGS, THE

Ray, Richard G.
BORN TO FIGHT

Reynolds, William
KID FROM LEFT FIELD, THE
GREAT WHITE HOPE, THE

Richards, Frederick
KID NIGHTINGALE

Rivkin, Stephen E.
YOUNGBLOOD

Robbins, J. Edwin
SPEAKEASY

Roberts, Artie
HOLD 'EM JAIL

Roberts, Randy
GREASED LIGHTNING
PLAYERS

Roberts, Robbe
ONE ON ONE
LAST AMERICAN HERO, THE

Robinson, Byrd
MOTOR MADNESS

Roland, Rita
SPINOUT
SIX PACK

Rolf, Tom
LAST AMERICAN HERO, THE

Romanis, L.
BOXER

Ropence
MANOLETE

Rosenblum, Irving C.
. . . ALL THE MARBLES

Ruggiero, Gene
GREAT AMERICAN PASTIME, THE
GLORY ALLEY

Salfas, Stan
SPIKE OF BENSONHURST
HOT SHOT

San Andres, Louis
PAPER LION

Schmidt, Arthur
FISH THAT SAVED PITTSBURGH, THE
TOUCHDOWN, ARMY

Schoenberg, Irving M.
HEART OF VIRGINIA

Schoengarth, Bruce
WHITE LIGHTING

Schoengarth, Russell
MOONLIGHT IN HAVANA
IRON MAN, THE (1951)

Schoolnick, Skip
BODY AND SOUL (1981)

Schoonmaker, Thelma
RAGING BULL
COLOR OF MONEY, THE

Schroeder, Edward
MILLION TO ONE, A
TEN LAPS TO GO

Scott, John
GREAT MACARTHY, THE

Seld, Arthur
HARMON OF MICHIGAN

Seldeen, Murray
LAUGHING IRISH EYES

Serandrei, Mario
MOMENT OF TRUTH, THE

Sewell, Blanche
TAKE ME OUT TO THE BALL GAME

Shaffer, Allyson
MAN I LOVE, THE

Shaine, Rick
TRADING HEARTS

Shapiro, Melvin
ICE CASTLES

Shasser, Alyson
FOLLOW THRU

Shea, William
SALTY O'ROURKE
ROSE BOWL

Shebib, Donald
SECOND WIND

Sheider, Cynthia
BREAKING AWAY

Sheridan, Michael J.
CHAMP, THE (1979)

Silvi, Roberto
VICTORY

Simpson, Robert
PRIDE OF ST. LOUIS, THE

Sinclair, Ronald
THUNDER ALLEY
YOUNG RACERS, THE

Smith, Bud
PERSONAL BEST

Smith, Fred
COLLEGE LOVERS

Smith, Frederick Y.
RINGSIDE MAISIE

Smith, Howard
NAVY WAY, THE
RIDE THE WILD SURF

Smith, Nicholas
THRASHIN'

Smith, Rose
POLICE CALL

Smith, Scott
JOHNNY BE GOOD

Somerset, Pat
DRIVE, HE SAID

Spencer, Dorothy
UNDER MY SKIN

Spencer, Jeanne
HEART PUNCH

Spottiswoode, Roger
HARD TIMES

Stafford, Robert
GUS

Stanford, Thomas
SPLIT DECISIONS

Steinkamp, Frederic
GRAND PRIX (1966)
BOBBY DEERFIELD

Stell, Aaron
SPORT OF KINGS
FEAR STRIKES OUT
CORNBREAD, EARL AND ME

Stone, LeRoy
MILKY WAY, THE

Suess, Maurie M.
JACKIE ROBINSON STORY, THE

Sullivan, Frank
SPORTING BLOOD (1940)
SO THIS IS COLLEGE
FIREBALL, THE
DEATH ON THE DIAMOND

Sweeney, James
HARLEM GLOBETROTTERS, THE
GAME THAT KILLS, THE
SPIRIT OF STANFORD, THE
BODYHOLD

Symons, James
OVER THE TOP
ROCKY II

Taylor, Peter
THIS SPORTING LIFE

Thayer, Jr., Guy V.
MIRACLE KID

Thompson, Walter
BIG WHEEL, THE
MIXED COMPANY
WALK, DON'T RUN

Thoms, Jerome
HARDER THEY FALL, THE
TRIPLE THREAT

Thorsen, Mel
SMITH OF MINNESOTA

Tintori, John
EIGHT MEN OUT

Todd, Holbrook N.
BLONDE COMET
CONTENDER, THE

Tordjmann, Fabien
PRIZE FIGHTER, THE

Trirogoff, George
UNHOLY ROLLERS

Troffey, Alex
SALUTE

Urioste, Frank J.
FAST BREAK

Van Enger, Richard L.
BULLFIGHTER AND THE LADY, THE
THAT'S MY MAN

Veron, Elmo
THOROUGHBREDS DON'T CRY
SARATOGA

Villasenor, George
SLUGGER'S WIFE, THE

Vogel, Virgil
FLESH AND FURY

Wallis, Rit
BOY IN BLUE, THE

Warburton, Cotton
ARENA
WORLD'S GREATEST ATHLETE, THE
CRAZYLEGS, ALL AMERICAN

Warner, Mark
ROCKY III

Warren, Eda
RIDE THE WILD SURF

Warschilka, Edward
MAIN EVENT, THE (1979)

Weatherwax, Paul
SQUARE JUNGLE, THE

Webb, J. Watson
IT HAPPENED IN FLATBUSH

Webb, Jr., J. Watson
FATHER WAS A FULLBACK

Webster, Ferris
HARRIGAN'S KID
SWING FEVER

Weiss, Adam
BULL DURHAM

Wells, James
WALK, DON'T RUN

Westover, Richard E.
TOMBOY

EDITORS

Wheeler, John W.
SPLIT DECISIONS
BAD NEWS BEARS IN BREAKING
TRAINING, THE
ROCKY IV

White, George
MAN FROM DOWN UNDER, THE

White, Merrill
BOY FROM INDIANA

Whitlock, Graham
PLAYING AWAY

Whytock, Grant
MONKEY ON MY BACK
KING OF THE TURF
PALOOKA

Wilder, Leslie F.
SO THIS IS COLLEGE

Wilkison, Mairin
RENO AND THE DOC

Wilson, Frederick
CHECKPOINT

Winetrobe, Maury
VISION QUEST
ICE CASTLES

Winters, Ralph E.
KILLER McCOY

Wise, Robert
IRON MAJOR, THE

Wolf, Robert
JUNIOR BONNER

Wolfe, Robert I.
DRIVE, HE SAID

Wolfe, Robert L.
BIG WEDNESDAY

Woodcock, John
LE MANS

Wray, Richard G.
WINNER'S CIRCLE, THE

Wright, John
SEPARATE WAYS

Wright, Maurice
THIS SPORTING AGE

Wyman, Bob
GREASED LIGHTNING

Wynn, Hugh
HUDDLE
CHAMP, THE (1931)

Yee, Yeu-Bun
UNHOLY ROLLERS

Zetlin, Barry
GRUNT! THE WRESTLING MOVIE

Ziegler, William
WALL OF NOISE

Zimmerman, Don
EVERYBODY'S ALL-AMERICAN
OVER THE TOP
HEAVEN CAN WAIT
ROCKY IV
ROCKY III

Zubeck, Gary
BUSTED UP

MUSIC COMPOSERS

Abeni, Maurizio
LIGHTNING—THE WHITE STALLION

Addison, John
LONELINESS OF THE LONG DISTANCE
RUNNER, THE

Albioni, Tomaso Giovanni
ROLLERBALL

Alexander, Jeff
KID GALAHAD (1962)
GREAT AMERICAN PASTIME, THE
SPEEDWAY

Alexander, Van
SAFE AT HOME

Alperson, Jr., Edward L.
MAGNIFICENT MATADOR, THE

Alwyn, William
WEE GEORDIE
RAINBOW JACKET, THE

Amfitheatrof, Daniele
HARRIGAN'S KID
UNDER MY SKIN
ANGELS IN THE OUTFIELD

Axt, Dr. William
WE WENT TO COLLEGE

Bach, Johann Sebastian
ROLLERBALL

Bakaleinkoff, Mischa
BODYHOLD

Barnes, Milton
BLOOD AND GUTS

Barnett, Charles
BUSTED UP

Barry, Jeff
SPIKER

Barry, John
INSIDE MOVES

Bassman, George
JOE LOUIS STORY, THE

Baxter, Les
FIREBALL 500
YOUNG RACERS, THE

Bell, Brian
RENO AND THE DOC

Bell, Thom
FISH THAT SAVED PITTSBURGH, THE

Berline, Byron
STAY HUNGRY

Bernstein, Elmer
SLAP SHOT
BOOTS MALONE
SATURDAY'S HERO
FEAR STRIKES OUT
AMAZING GRACE AND CHUCK

Broones, Martin
SO THIS IS COLLEGE

Brown, Lew
HOLD EVERYTHING

Brunner, Robert F.
GUS

Burke, Joe
HOLD EVERYTHING

Buttolph, David
WINNING TEAM, THE
STORY OF SEABISCUIT, THE

Byrd, Donald
CORNBREAD, EARL AND ME

Cacavas, John
SEPARATE WAYS

Cadkin, Emil
BIG FIX, THE

Caillet, Lucien
WINNER'S CIRCLE, THE

Calker, Darrell
JOE PALOOKA IN TRIPLE CROSS

Campbell, David
ALL THE RIGHT MOVES

Capps, Al
STROKER ACE

Castleman, William Allen
WRESTLER, THE

Caswell, Ozzie
BLUE BLOOD

Chattaway, Jay
LAST FIGHT, THE

Chihara, Paul
BAD NEWS BEARS GO TO JAPAN,
THE

Chudnow, David
JACKIE ROBINSON STORY, THE

Cleave, Van
RHUBARB

Coati Mundi
SPIKE OF BENSONHURST

Collier, Ron
FAN'S NOTES, A
PAPERBACK HERO

Colombo, Alberto
BIG LEAGUER

Conti, Bill
GOLDENGIRL
VICTORY
THAT CHAMPIONSHIP SEASON
BEAR, THE
ROCKY IV
ROCKY III
ROCKY II
ROCKY
DREAMER
PARADISE ALLEY

Convertino, Michael
BULL DURHAM

Coppola, Carmine
BLACK STALLION, THE

Curb, Mike
WILD RACERS, THE

Darin, Bobby
LIVELY SET, THE

Daring, Mason
EIGHT MEN OUT

Davis, Carl
CHAMPIONS

De Vol, Frank
LONGEST YARD, THE
. . . ALL THE MARBLES

Deutsch, Adolph
SWING YOUR LADY

DeVorzon, Barry
HARD TIMES

Di Pasquale, James
RAD
FAST BREAK

DiCola, Vince
ROCKY IV

Dolan, Robert Emmett
SALTY O'ROURKE

Dragon, Carmen
KID FROM BROOKLYN, THE

Dubin, Al
HOLD EVERYTHING

Duning, George
RETURN OF OCTOBER, THE

Edens, Robert
TAKE ME OUT TO THE BALL GAME

Ellis, Don
KANSAS CITY BOMBER

Engels, Lehman
ROOGIE'S BUMP

Essex, David
SILVER DREAM RACER

Feuer, Cy
FIGHTING THOROUGHBREDS

Fielding, Jerry
JUNIOR BONNER
BAD NEWS BEARS, THE
SEMI-TOUGH

Fields, Harry
RETURN TO CAMPUS

Finston, Nat
BIG WHEEL, THE

Foster, David
STEALING HOME

Fox, Charles
ONE ON ONE
LAST AMERICAN HERO, THE
SIX PACK

Frankel, Benjamin
FINAL TEST, THE

Fraser, Jill
PERSONAL BEST

Friedhofer, Hugo
HOME IN INDIANA
HARDER THEY FALL, THE

BODY AND SOUL (1947)

Frontiere, Dominic
NUMBER ONE
BILLIE

Gagnon, Andre
RUNNING

Gerhard, Roberto
THIS SPORTING LIFE

Gershenson, Joseph
JOHNNY DARK

Gilbert, Herschel Burke
KID MONK BARONI
RING, THE

Gock, Les
PUBERTY BLUES

Goldberg, Barry
THRASHIN'

Goldsmith, Jerry
HOOSIERS
PLAYERS

Goldstein, William
BINGO LONG TRAVELING ALL-STARS
AND MOTOR KINGS, THE

Gomez, Vicente
FIGHTER, THE

Green, Walter
THUNDER IN CAROLINA

Grusin, Dave
HEAVEN CAN WAIT
HALLS OF ANGER
WINNING
BOBBY DEERFIELD
CHAMP, THE (1979)

Hamlisch, Marvin
WORLD'S GREATEST ATHLETE, THE
FAT CITY
ICE CASTLES

Hardy, Hagood
SECOND WIND

Harline, Leigh
MONEY FROM HOME
GUY WHO CAME BACK, THE
THAT'S MY BOY (1951)
IT HAPPENS EVERY SPRING
PRIDE OF THE YANKEES, THE

Harling, W. Franke
WINNER TAKE ALL (1932)

Harris, Anthony
COACH

Hart, Bobby
UNHOLY ROLLERS

Heindorf, Ray
KNUTE ROCKNE—ALL AMERICAN

Henderson, Ray
HOLD EVERYTHING

Hooper, Les
FINNEY

Hopkins, Kenyon
DOWNHILL RACER
HUSTLER, THE

Howard, James Newton
EVERYBODY'S ALL-AMERICAN
WILDCATS

Irving, Ernest
THERE AIN'T NO JUSTICE

Jackson, Howard
COWBOY QUARTERBACK

Jarre, Maurice
GRAND PRIX (1966)

Jenson, Merrill B.
TAKE DOWN

Jerome, M.K.
FRESHMAN LOVE

Jones, Ken
GREEN HELMET, THE

Jones, Quincy
WALK, DON'T RUN

Justin, Susan
GRUNT! THE WRESTLING MOVIE

Kander, John
BLUE SKIES AGAIN

Kaper, Bronislau
TO PLEASE A LADY
SOMEBODY UP THERE LIKES ME

Karlin, Fred
MIXED COMPANY
GREASED LIGHTNING

Kay, Edward J.
HIGH SCHOOL HERO
JOE PALOOKA MEETS HUMPHREY
JOE PALOOKA IN WINNER TAKE ALL
JOE PALOOKA IN THE
COUNTERPUNCH
RACING BLOOD (1954)

Kellaway, Roger
PAPER LION

Klockar, Annakarin
LIGHTNING—THE WHITE STALLION

Kraushaar, Raoul
MAGNIFICENT MATADOR, THE
BASKETBALL FIX, THE
COWBOY AND THE PRIZEFIGHTER,
THE

Lai, Francis
GAMES, THE
EDITH AND MARCEL

Lange, Arthur
GOLDEN GLOVES STORY, THE
PRIDE OF ST. LOUIS, THE

Langehorne, Bruce
STAY HUNGRY

Lava, William
BIG PUNCH, THE
WALL OF NOISE

Lavista, Raul
RUN FOR THE ROSES

Lawrence, Elliot
THUNDER IN DIXIE

Lawrence, Jack
QUARTERBACK, THE

Lawrence, Stephen
BANG THE DRUM SLOWLY

Lazebnik, Betty
RENO AND THE DOC

Legrand, Michel
LE MANS

Levay, Sylvester
TOUCH AND GO

Levin, Albert
BORN TO SPEED

Lewis, Webster
BODY AND SOUL (1981)

Loesser, Frank
QUARTERBACK, THE

Loose, William
WRESTLER, THE

Lowe, Mundell
SIDEWINDER ONE

Malneck, Matty
QUARTERBACK, THE

Mandel, Johnny
CADDYSHACK
M*A*S*H

Manfredini, Harry
HERE COME THE TIGERS

Mann, Paul
QUARTERBACK, THE

Markowitz, Richard
ROADRACERS, THE

Masser, Michael
GREATEST, THE

Mathieson, Dock
SQUARE RING, THE

Mathieson, Greg
AMERICAN FLYERS

Matz, Peter
PRIZE FIGHTER, THE

Mayfield, Curtis
LET'S DO IT AGAIN

Mendoza, David
YOUNG MAN OF MANHATTAN

Moçkridge, Cyril J.
FOLLOW THE SUN
TALL STORY
FATHER WAS A FULLBACK

Mollin, Fred
SPRING FEVER

Montgomery, Bruce
CHECKPOINT

Moroder, Giorgio
OVER THE TOP

Morton, Arthur
HARLEM GLOBETROTTERS, THE

Myers, Stanley
TRADING HEARTS

Newman, Alfred
BLOOD AND SAND (1941)

Newman, Lionel
KID FROM LEFT FIELD, THE

GREAT WHITE HOPE, THE

Newman, Randy
NATURAL, THE

Nitzsche, Jack
STREETS OF GOLD
PERSONAL BEST

North, Alex
GO, MAN, GO!
RACERS, THE

Orbit, William
HOT SHOT
YOUNGBLOOD

Palmer, Carleton
SPEED LOVERS

Papathanassiou, Vangelis
CHARIOTS OF FIRE

Perkins, Frank
GLORY

Petrov, Andrey
LAST GAME, THE

Philhofer, Herb
ON THE EDGE

Phillips, Stu
RIDE THE WILD SURF

Piccioni, Piero
MOMENT OF TRUTH, THE

Poledouris, Basil
SPLIT DECISIONS
BIG WEDNESDAY

Post, Mike
RUNNING BRAVE

Previn, Andre
FORTUNE COOKIE, THE
ROLLERBALL

Raksin, David
RIGHT CROSS
PAT AND MIKE

Randi, Don
J.W. COOP

Reynolds, Dick
FINNEY

Riddle, Nelson
RED LINE 7000

Ritenour, Lee
AMERICAN FLYERS

Robertson, Robbie
COLOR OF MONEY, THE

Roemheld, Heinz
KNOCKOUT
KID GALAHAD (1937)
GENTLEMAN JIM
SQUARE JUNGLE, THE

Rose, David
SAM'S SON

Rosenthal, Laurence
HEART LIKE A WHEEL
REQUIEM FOR A HEAVYWEIGHT

Rowland, Bruce
PHAR LAP

Rubinstein, Arthur B.
BEST OF TIMES, THE

Rudolph, Dick
JOHNNY BE GOOD

Safan, Craig
BAD NEWS BEARS IN BREAKING
TRAINING, THE

Salinger, Conrad
TENNESSEE CHAMP

Salter, Hans J.
THAT'S MY MAN
FLESH AND FURY

Salzedo, Leonard
RACE FOR LIFE, A

Sawtell, Paul
MONKEY ON MY BACK

Schifrin, Lalo
STING II, THE

Scott, John
NORTH DALLAS FORTY

Scott, Nathan
KID FROM CLEVELAND, THE

Scott, Tom
SIDECAR RACERS

Shefter, Bert
MONKEY ON MY BACK

Shelton, Louie
J.W. COOP

Shire, David
FAST BREAK
DRIVE, HE SAID

Shostakovich, Dmitri
ROLLERBALL

Silvestri, Alan
AMERICAN ANTHEM

Skiles, Marlin
WHITE LIGHTING
ROSE BOWL STORY, THE
RODEO
ROAR OF THE CROWD
PRIDE OF THE BLUE GRASS

Smeaton, Bruce
GREAT MACARTHY, THE

Snell, David
MIGHTY MC GURK, THE
MAN FROM DOWN UNDER, THE
KILLER McCOY
RINGSIDE MAISIE

Snow, Mark
SKATEBOARD

Stahl, Willy
NAVY WAY, THE

Steiner, Max
HOLD 'EM JAIL
KID GALAHAD (1937)
GRIDIRON FLASH
JIM THORPE—ALL AMERICAN
TROUBLE ALONG THE WAY
THEY MADE ME A CRIMINAL
CITY FOR CONQUEST

Stevens, Bernard
MANIACS ON WHEELS

Stevens, Leith
CRAZYLEGS, ALL AMERICAN

Stoll, George
SPINOUT

Stoloff, Morris
GAME THAT KILLS, THE
HERE COMES MR. JORDAN

Stone, Christopher L.
NADIA

Stone, Richard
NORTH SHORE

Stothart, Herbert
NATIONAL VELVET

Talbot, Irvin
LEATHER SAINT, THE

Tangerine Dream
VISION QUEST

Tchaikovsky, Petr Ilich
ROLLERBALL

Timm, Doug
WINNERS TAKE ALL

Tiomkin, Dimitri
MR. UNIVERSE
CHAMPION

Torchsong
YOUNGBLOOD

Trzaskowski, Andrzej
WALKOVER

Ward, Edward
NAVY BLUE AND GOLD
SARATOGA
CROWD ROARS, THE (1938)
BABE RUTH STORY, THE

Waxman, Franz
WHIPLASH
SPORTING BLOOD (1940)

Webb, Roger
BOY IN BLUE, THE

Webb, Roy
LUSTY MEN, THE
IRON MAJOR, THE
EASY LIVING

Webb, Simon
PLAYING AWAY

Weiss, Stephen
QUARTERBACK, THE

Williams, Johnny
JOHN GOLDFARB, PLEASE COME
HOME

Williams, Patrick
ONE AND ONLY, THE
SLUGGER'S WIFE, THE
BREAKING AWAY
CASEY'S SHADOW

Wilson, Stanley
DUKE OF CHICAGO
PRIDE OF MARYLAND

Wolf, Eli
FINNEY

Wolinski, Hawk
WILDCATS

Young, Victor
GOLDEN BOY
BULLFIGHTER AND THE LADY, THE
FIREBALL, THE

Zahler, Gordon
RETURN TO CAMPUS

PRODUCERS

Abbott, George
DAMN YANKEES

Adler, Buddy
HARLEM GLOBETROTTERS, THE
SATURDAY'S HERO

Aldrich, William
... ALL THE MARBLES

Alland, William
JOHNNY DARK
LIVELY SET, THE

Alperson, Edward L.
MAGNIFICENT MATADOR, THE

Amarnani, Vijay
PLAYING AWAY

Arkoff, Samuel Z.
FIREBALL 500

Asher, E.M.
SOME BLONDES ARE DANGEROUS

Asher, Irving
TAKE IT FROM ME

Auer, Stephen
KING OF THE GAMBLERS
DUKE OF CHICAGO

Avedis, Howard
SEPARATE WAYS

Baker, David
GREAT MACARTHY, THE

Barry, Wesley
RACING BLOOD (1954)

Bart, Peter
YOUNGBLOOD

Bartlett, Hall
CRAZYLEGS, ALL AMERICAN

Bash, John
ROOGIE'S BUMP

Bassett, John F.
SPRING FEVER
PAPERBACK HERO

Batchellor, George R.
BLONDE COMET

Beatty, Warren
HEAVEN CAN WAIT

Beck, John
KILL THE UMPIRE

Bennett, Ken
SMALL TOWN STORY

Berman, Henry
GREAT AMERICAN PASTIME, THE
FAST COMPANY

Berman, Pandro S.
BIG GAME, THE
NATIONAL VELVET

Bernard, Sam
RAD

Bernerd, Jeffrey
BLUE GRASS OF KENTUCKY

Bischoff, Sam
CAIN AND MABEL
KID FROM KOKOMO, THE
RED HOT TIRES

Black, Todd
SPLIT DECISIONS

Blakeley, John E.
CUP-TIE HONEYMOON

Blauner, Steve
DRIVE, HE SAID

Blaustein, Julian
GUY WHO CAME BACK, THE
RACERS, THE

Bloom, William
SPORT OF KINGS

Blum, Harry N.
SKATEBOARD

Bohrer, Jack
UNHOLY ROLLERS

Borofsky, Michael
SPLIT DECISIONS

Borzage, Frank
THAT'S MY MAN

Botsford, A.M.
ROSE BOWL

Box, Betty E.
CHECKPOINT

Briskin, Mort
BIG WHEEL, THE
JACKIE ROBINSON STORY, THE

Broder, Jack
KID MONK BARONI

Broidy, William F.
NAVY BOUND

Brown, Clarence
TO PLEASE A LADY
ANGELS IN THE OUTFIELD

Brown, Harry Joe
SPIRIT OF WEST POINT, THE

Buckner, Robert
GENTLEMAN JIM

Burg, Mark
BULL DURHAM

Burr, C.C.
KENTUCKY BLUE STREAK

Burton, Bernard W.
MOONLIGHT IN HAVANA

PRODUCERS

Butler, David
GLORY

Capra, Frank
RIDING HIGH (1950)

Carr, Trem
FIGHTING CHAMP
IDOL OF THE CROWDS
CONFLICT

Carreras, Michael
RACE FOR LIFE, A

Carroll, Gordon
BEST OF TIMES, THE

Castle, Michael D.
TOMBOY

Cervi, Antonio
MOMENT OF TRUTH, THE

Chadwick, I.E.
COUNTY FAIR, THE

Chapin, Doug
AMERICAN ANTHEM

Chartoff, Robert
ROCKY IV
ROCKY III
ROCKY II
ROCKY
RAGING BULL

Chester, Hal E.
JOE PALOOKA MEETS HUMPHREY
JOE PALOOKA IN WINNER TAKE ALL
JOE PALOOKA IN TRIPLE CROSS
JOE PALOOKA IN THE SQUARED
CIRCLE
JOE PALOOKA IN THE
COUNTERPUNCH
JOE PALOOKA IN THE BIG FIGHT
JOE PALOOKA, CHAMP
FIGHTING MAD
HUMPHREY TAKES A CHANCE

Chodorov, Edward
ALIBI IKE

Clark, Colbert
LAUGHING IRISH EYES

Clowes, St. John L.
GRAND PRIX (1934)

Cohen, Rob
BINGO LONG TRAVELING ALL-STARS
AND MOTOR KINGS, THE

Cohen, Ronald
RUNNING

Cohn, Harry
BROADWAY BILL

Cohn, Ralph
MAIN EVENT, THE (1938)

Collins, Gunther
SWINGIN' AFFAIR, A

Colmes, Walter
KID FROM CLEVELAND, THE

Conn, Maurice A.
RACING BLOOD (1938)

Cooper, Robert
RUNNING

Corman, Roger
YOUNG RACERS, THE

Cornsweet, Harold
RETURN TO CAMPUS

Cowan, Maurice
FOUR AGAINST FATE

Coyle, John T.
MIRACLE KID

Crespo, Jr., Mario
RUN FOR THE ROSES

Cruze, James
RACETRACK

Cummings, Jack
STRATTON STORY, THE

Cunningham, Sean S.
HERE COME THE TIGERS

Cutts, John
LAST AMERICAN HERO, THE

Dalrymple, Ian
MANIACS ON WHEELS

Dashev, David
FISH THAT SAVED PITTSBURGH, THE

Daven, Andre
HOME IN INDIANA

De Fina, Barbara
COLOR OF MONEY, THE

de Gaetano, Michael
SCORING

Dearden, Basil
SQUARE RING, THE

DeHaven, Carter
HOOSIERS

Del Ruth, Roy
WINNER TAKE ALL (1932)
BABE RUTH STORY, THE

Delamar, Mickey
RACE FOR LIFE, A

Dell, Wanda
PRIZE FIGHTER, THE

Dent, David
GREAT GAME, THE (1952)

Deutsch, Armand
RIGHT CROSS

Deutsch, Stephen
ALL THE RIGHT MOVES

Dewey, Christopher C.
JUMP

Dickenson, Elizabeth
ROOGIE'S BUMP

Dietrich, Ralph
PEGGY

Donen, Stanley
DAMN YANKEES

Douglas, Warren
SKI PATROL

Dull, Orville O.
MAN FROM DOWN UNDER, THE

Dupont, Rene
SILVER DREAM RACER

Elfand, Marty
KANSAS CITY BOMBER

Elkins, Saul
BIG PUNCH, THE

Elliott, Lang
PRIZE FIGHTER, THE

Engel, Samuel G.
FOLLOW THE SUN

Engelberg, Mort
TRADING HEARTS

Englander, Ira
RUNNING BRAVE

Evans, Robert
PLAYERS

Fawcett, L'Estrange
GREAT GAME, THE (1930)

Feitshans, Buzz
BIG WEDNESDAY

Fellows, Robert
IRON MAJOR, THE

Field, David
AMAZING GRACE AND CHUCK

Fielding, Sol Baer
TENNESSEE CHAMP

Fields, Adam
JOHNNY BE GOOD

Fields, Freddie
VICTORY

Fier, Jack
SMITH OF MINNESOTA

Finnegan, William
NORTH SHORE

Flothow, Rudolph C.
BODYHOLD

Foote, John Taintor
GREAT DAN PATCH, THE

Foreman, John
WINNING

Foy, Bryan
OVER THE GOAL
KING OF HOCKEY
KID NIGHTINGALE
KID COMES BACK, THE
FRESHMAN LOVE
WINNING TEAM, THE
SERGEANT MURPHY
DECEPTION
PRIDE OF THE BLUEGRASS

Frank, W.R.
WRESTLER, THE

Freed, Arthur
GOOD NEWS (1947)
TAKE ME OUT TO THE BALL GAME

Freeman, Everett
JIM THORPE—ALL AMERICAN

Friedlob, Bert
FIREBALL, THE

Friedman, Stephen
TOUCH AND GO
SLAP SHOT
FAST BREAK

Gilliat, Sidney
WEE GEORDIE

Globus, Yoram
OVER THE TOP
THAT CHAMPIONSHIP SEASON
BODY AND SOUL (1981)

Goetz, Hayes
PRIDE OF THE BLUE GRASS

Golan, Menahem
OVER THE TOP
THAT CHAMPIONSHIP SEASON
BODY AND SOUL (1981)

Goldberg, Leonard
BAD NEWS BEARS IN BREAKING
TRAINING, THE

Golden, Max H.
SWING THAT CHEER

Golder, Lew
SPIRIT OF YOUTH

Goldstein, Leonard
KID FROM LEFT FIELD, THE
FLESH AND FURY

Goldstone, Richard
SET-UP, THE

Goldwyn, Samuel
KID FROM SPAIN, THE
KID FROM BROOKLYN, THE
PRIDE OF THE YANKEES, THE

Goodwin, R.W.
INSIDE MOVES

Gordon, Lawrence
HARD TIMES

Gordon, Steve
ONE AND ONLY, THE

Gottlieb, Alex
FIGHTER, THE

Grainger, Edmund
KNOCKOUT

Grant, James Edward
GREAT JOHN L., THE

Greene, Victor M.
FLYING FIFTY-FIVE

Grefe, William
RACING FEVER

Gregson, Richard
DOWNHILL RACER

Griffith, Ray
ELMER THE GREAT

Grippo, Jan
FIGHTING FOOLS

Gruber, Peter
VISION QUEST

Hackford, Taylor
EVERYBODY'S ALL-AMERICAN

Hagen, Julius
MANNEQUIN

Halstead, Henry
TAKE ME TO PARIS

Hare, Bill
FINNEY

Hawks, Howard
RED LINE 7000

Hayes, Jeffrey
ON THE EDGE

Heermance, Richard
ROSE BOWL STORY, THE
ROAR OF THE CROWD

Hellinger, Mark
RISE AND SHINE

Herliman, George
RACING LUCK (1935)

Herman, Albert
SPORTING CHANCE

Herz, Michael
SQUEEZE PLAY

Hirschman, Herbert
HALLS OF ANGER

Hoffman, Jerry
WINNER TAKE ALL (1939)
SPEED TO BURN
ROAD DEMON

Holmes, Milton
BOOTS MALONE

Hornstein, Martin
ONE ON ONE

Hubbard, Lucien
SPEED
DEATH ON THE DIAMOND

Hurley, Harold
HOME ON THE RANGE

Hyman, Bernard H.
SARATOGA

Irving, Richard
SIDECAR RACERS

Jacobs, William
WHIPLASH
STORY OF SEABISCUIT, THE

Jaffe, Herb
TRADING HEARTS

Jaffe, Stanley R.
BAD NEWS BEARS, THE

Jason, Leigh
HIGH GEAR

Jewison, Norman
ROLLERBALL

Johnson, Mark
NATURAL, THE

Jones, Paul
CADDY, THE

Kallis, Stanley
ROADRACERS, THE

Katzman, Sam
HIGH SCHOOL HERO
TWO MINUTES TO PLAY
TRIPLE THREAT

THAT GANG OF MINE
BOWERY BLITZKRIEG

Kaufman, Lloyd
SQUEEZE PLAY

Kelly, Burt
SECRETS OF A NURSE

Kelly, Margaret
PUBERTY BLUES

Kemeny, John
BOY IN BLUE, THE
ICE CASTLES

Kenney, Douglas
CADDYSHACK

Kent, Willis
RACING STRAIN, THE

King, Frank
RING, THE

King, George
RIDING HIGH (1937)

King, Herman
RING, THE

King, Maurice
RING, THE

Knight, Christopher W.
WINNERS TAKE ALL

Kohlmar, Fred
FATHER WAS A FULLBACK

Kramer, Stanley
CHAMPION

Krasna, Norman
LUSTY MEN, THE

Kreisler, Otto
SMALL TOWN STORY

Krueger, Carl
GOLDEN GLOVES STORY, THE

Krugman, Saul J.
ALL-AMERICAN BOY, THE

Lackey, William
PRIDE OF MARYLAND

Laemmle, Jr., Carl
IRON MAN, THE (1931)
SPIRIT OF NOTRE DAME, THE
SATURDAY'S MILLIONS
COLLEGE LOVE

Landon, Joseph
WALL OF NOISE

Lang, Jennings
STING II, THE

Launder, Frank
WEE GEORDIE

Laurence, Douglas
SPEEDWAY

Lazarus, Jeff
LADY'S FROM KENTUCKY, THE

Leader, Anton M.
GO, MAN, GO!

Lee, Damien
BUSTED UP

PRODUCERS

Lelouch, Claude
EDITH AND MARCEL

Leonard, Robert Z.
MAN FROM DOWN UNDER, THE

Lerman, Oscar S.
YESTERDAY'S HERO

Lerner, Joseph
MR. UNIVERSE

Leshin, E.D.
SALTY O'ROURKE

Leven, Edward
BASKETBALL FIX, THE

Levy, Robert L.
RAD

Lewis, Edward
GRAND PRIX (1966)

Linsk, Lester
GAMES, THE

Litvak, Anatole
CITY FOR CONQUEST

Lobell, Michael
DREAMER

Loew, Jr., Arthur M.
ARENA

Logan, Joshua
TALL STORY

Long, Joan
PUBERTY BLUES

Lord, Robert
LOCAL BOY MAKES GOOD
COLLEGE COACH

Lovell, Dyson
CHAMP, THE (1979)

Lowe, Edward T.
TOUCHDOWN, ARMY

Lyon, Nelson
SPIKE OF BENSONHURST

McCray, Kent
SAM'S SON

MacDonald, Wallace
HARMON OF MICHIGAN

McGaha, William
SPEED LOVERS

Malvern, Paul
IDOL OF THE CROWDS

Mandel, Frank
FOLLOW THRU

Manduke, Joe
CORNBREAD, EARL AND ME

Mankiewicz, Herman J.
MILLION DOLLAR LEGS (1932)

Margellos, James
SECOND WIND
PAPERBACK HERO

Markey, Gene
KENTUCKY

Marshall, John
GREATEST, THE

Mastroly, Frank R.
GREAT JOHN L., THE

Masucci, Jerry
LAST FIGHT, THE

Mate, Rudolph
RETURN OF OCTOBER, THE

Melford, Frank
BOY FROM INDIANA

Merrick, David
SEMI-TOUGH

Merrill, Keith
TAKE DOWN

Meyer, Fred S.
FIGHTING YOUTH

Millar, Stuart
PAPER LION

Miller, Ron
GUS

Miner, Stephen
HERE COME THE TIGERS

Minney, R.J.
FINAL TEST, THE

Mirisch, Walter
RODEO

Mitchell, David
BUSTED UP
RENO AND THE DOC

Mooney, Martin
MR. CELEBRITY

Moonjean, Hank
STEALING HOME
STROKER ACE

Morosco, Walter
IT HAPPENED IN FLATBUSH

Morrow, Douglas
MAURIE

Mount, Thom
STEALING HOME
BULL DURHAM

Naar, Joseph T.
ALL-AMERICAN BOY, THE

Napoleon, Art
RIDE THE WILD SURF

Napoleon, Jo
RIDE THE WILD SURF

Naud, Tom
SAFE AT HOME

Naud, William T.
THUNDER IN DIXIE

Nayfack, Nicholas
GLORY ALLEY

Nicholson, Jack
DRIVE, HE SAID

Nicholson, James H.
FIREBALL 500

Nilsson, Rob
ON THE EDGE

Nizich, Nicholas
SCORING

Normann, Don
GRUNT! THE WRESTLING MOVIE

Norton, Richard
ARSENAL STADIUM MYSTERY, THE

O'Brian, Peter
BLOOD AND GUTS

O'Donovan, Danny
GOLDENGIRL

Olenicoff, S. Rodger
ICE CASTLES

Pakula, Alan
FEAR STRIKES OUT

Pappas, Steve
HOT SHOT

Parker, Steve
JOHN GOLDFARB, PLEASE COME
HOME

Passmore, H. Fraser
SPORTING LOVE

Pasternak, Joe
SPINOUT

Perlberg, William
GOLDEN BOY
IT HAPPENS EVERY SPRING
RHUBARB

Perrin, Nat
MIGHTY MC GURK, THE

Peters, Jon
MAIN EVENT, THE (1979)
VISION QUEST

Picker, David V.
ONE AND ONLY, THE

Picker, Sidney
HEART OF VIRGINIA

Pillsbury, Sarah
EIGHT MEN OUT

Pine, William
NAVY WAY, THE

Pivar, Ben
LEATHER-PUSHERS, THE
DANGER ON WHEELS

Pizzo, Angelo
HOOSIERS

Polimer, Richard K.
WINNER'S CIRCLE, THE

Pollack, Sidney
BOBBY DEERFIELD

Popkin, Harry M.
BIG WHEEL, THE

Preminger, Ingo
M*A*S*H

Prizer, John
UNHOLY ROLLERS

Puttnam, David
CHARIOTS OF FIRE

Rachmil, Lewis J.
PACE THAT THRILLS, THE

Rafelson, Bob
STAY HUNGRY

Ralston, Rudy
CROOKED CIRCLE, THE

Randel, Anthony
GRUNT! THE WRESTLING MOVIE

Rapf, Harry
WE WENT TO COLLEGE
BURN 'EM UP O'CONNER
THOROUGHBREDS DON'T CRY
CHAMP, THE (1931)

Rapf, Matthew
BIG LEAGUER

Rapp, Joel
WILD RACERS, THE

Rawlinson, A.R.
STOCK CAR

Reddish, Jack N.
LE MANS

Regan, Ken
YESTERDAY'S HERO

Reisz, Karel
THIS SPORTING LIFE

Relph, Michael
SQUARE RING, THE
RAINBOW JACKET, THE

Retchin, Norman
LEATHER SAINT, THE

Richardson, Tony
LONELINESS OF THE LONG DISTANCE RUNNER, THE

Riskin, Everett
HERE COMES MR. JORDAN

Ritchie, Michael
BAD NEWS BEARS GO TO JAPAN, THE

Roach, John F.
PARADISE ALLEY

Roberts, Alan
RACQUET

Roberts, Bob
BODY AND SOUL (1947)

Roberts, G.B.
FIREBALL JUNGLE

Roberts, William
LAST AMERICAN HERO, THE

Robertson, Cliff
J.W. COOP

Robinson, Casey
UNDER MY SKIN

Rogers, Bogart
PIGSKIN PARADE

Rogers, Charles E.
SWEEPSTAKES

Rogers, Charles R.
MADISON SQUARE GARDEN
HOLD 'EM YALE
70,000 WITNESSES

Rogers, John W.
SPIRIT OF WEST POINT, THE

Roos, Fred
BLACK STALLION, THE

Rosenberg, Aaron
WORLD IN MY CORNER
IRON MAN, THE (1951)
ALL-AMERICAN, THE (1953)

Rosenfield, Lois
BANG THE DRUM SLOWLY

Rosenfield, Maurice
BANG THE DRUM SLOWLY

Rosi, Francesco
MOMENT OF TRUTH, THE

Ross, Frank
MAURIE

Rossen, Robert
HUSTLER, THE

Roth, Joe
STREETS OF GOLD

Roven, Charles
HEART LIKE A WHEEL

Royer, Fanchon
MILLION TO ONE, A
TEN LAPS TO GO

Ruben, J. Walter
RINGSIDE MAISIE

Ruddy, Albert S.
MATILDA
LONGEST YARD, THE
LITTLE FAUSS AND BIG HALSY

Ryerson, Sean
RENO AND THE DOC

Sacks, Alan
THRASHIN'

Sander, Ian
EVERYBODY'S ALL-AMERICAN

Sanford, Midge
EIGHT MEN OUT

Schaefer, Armand
FIGHTING THOROUGHBREDS
PITTSBURGH KID, THE

Schaffel, Robert
AMERICAN ANTHEM

Schermer, Jules
PRIDE OF ST. LOUIS, THE

Schmidt, Wolf
RUN FOR THE ROSES

Schnee, Charles
SOMEBODY UP THERE LIKES ME

Schneider, Harold
STAY HUNGRY

Schwab, Laurence
FOLLOW THRU

Schwalb, Ben
WHITE LIGHTING
BLUE BLOOD

Schwarz, Jack
GIRL FROM MONTEREY, THE

Seaton, George
RHUBARB

Sellers, Arlene
BLUE SKIES AGAIN

Seltzer, Walter
NUMBER ONE

Selwyn, William E.
BOB MATHIAS STORY, THE

Selznick, David O.
MAN I LOVE, THE

Sexton, John
PHAR LAP

Sharpe, Lester
THOROUGHBREDS

Shavelson, Melville
MIXED COMPANY
TROUBLE ALONG THE WAY

Shaw, Peter
CHAMPIONS

Siegel, Max
INDIANAPOLIS SPEEDWAY

Siegel, Sol C.
WALK, DON'T RUN

Silliphant, Stirling
JOE LOUIS STORY, THE

Silverman, Mark
SPIKE OF BENSONHURST

Sisk, Robert
SATURDAY'S HEROES

Sistrom, William
RACING LADY

Small, Edward
MONKEY ON MY BACK
KING OF THE TURF

Smith, A. George
RACING ROMANCE

Smith, George
FIFTY-SHILLING BOXER

Somio, Josef
ARSENAL STADIUM MYSTERY, THE

Spangler, Larry G.
BEAR, THE

Sparks, Robert
EASY LIVING

Stahl, Marvin D.
BIG FIX, THE

Stark, Ray
SLUGGER'S WIFE, THE
FAT CITY

Starr, Irving
HARRIGAN'S KID
SWING FEVER
SUNDAY PUNCH

Steifel, Samuel H.
BIG WHEEL, THE

Stephenson, David L.
IN THIS CORNER

Sternbach, Bert
CONTENDER, THE

Sternberg, Tom
BLACK STALLION, THE

PRODUCERS

Stock, L.S.
GRAND PRIX (1934)

Stoloff, Ben
BIG FIX, THE

Stonsnider, Lee
PIT STOP

Streisand, Barbra
MAIN EVENT, THE (1979)

Stromberg, Gary
FISH THAT SAVED PITTSBURGH, THE

Stromberg, Hunt
PRIZEFIGHTER AND THE LADY, THE

Suppa, Ronald A.
PARADISE ALLEY

Susskind, David
REQUIEM FOR A HEAVYWEIGHT

Sylbert, Anthea
WILDCATS

Tanz, Mark M.
INSIDE MOVES

Tatum, Tom
WINNERS TAKE ALL

Tenser, Marilyn J.
TOMBOY

Tenser, Mark
COACH

Thomas, Jerry
HOLD THAT LINE
COWBOY AND THE PRIZEFIGHTER, THE

Thomas, William
$1,000 A TOUCHDOWN
NAVY WAY, THE

Thompson, James E.
NADIA

Tilton, Roger
SPIKER

Topper, Burt
THUNDER ALLEY
FIREBALL 500

Towers, Harry Alan
LIGHTNING—THE WHITE STALLION

Towne, Robert
PERSONAL BEST

Trikilis, Michael
SIX PACK

Tucker, Melville
LET'S DO IT AGAIN

Turman, Lawrence
GREAT WHITE HOPE, THE

Ufland, Harry
STREETS OF GOLD

Veiller, Anthony
QUARTERBACK, THE

Wald, Jerry
LUSTY MEN, THE

Wallis, Hal B.
MONEY FROM HOME
KNUTE ROCKNE—ALL AMERICAN

KID GALAHAD (1937)
THEY MADE ME A CRIMINAL
THAT'S MY BOY (1951)
SWING YOUR LADY

Walsh, Bill
WORLD'S GREATEST ATHLETE, THE

Warner, Jack
KNUTE ROCKNE—ALL AMERICAN
THEY MADE ME A CRIMINAL

Wayne, John
BULLFIGHTER AND THE LADY, THE

Weingarten, Lawrence
PAT AND MIKE

Weinstein, Hannah
GREASED LIGHTNING

Weinstein, Paula
AMERICAN FLYERS

Weis, Donald
BILLIE

Weisbart, David
KID GALAHAD (1962)

Weisman, David
SPIKE OF BENSONHURST

Wells, Patrick
YOUNGBLOOD

White, J. Francis
THUNDER IN CAROLINA

White, Sam
SPIRIT OF STANFORD, THE

Wigan, Gareth
AMERICAN FLYERS

Wilcox, Herbert
FOUR AGAINST FATE

Wilde, Cornel
DEVIL'S HAIRPIN, THE

Wilder, Billy
FORTUNE COOKIE, THE

Williams, Elmo
SIDEWINDER ONE

Williamson, E. Stanley
TRACK OF THUNDER

Winitsky, Alex
BLUE SKIES AGAIN

Winkler, Irwin
ROCKY IV
ROCKY III
ROCKY II
ROCKY
RAGING BULL

Winters, David
RACQUET

Wizan, Joe
SPLIT DECISIONS
JUNIOR BONNER

Wolf, Richard A.
SKATEBOARD

Wunsch, Robert J.
SLAP SHOT

Wurtzel, Sol M.
RIGHT TO THE HEART
RIDE, KELLY, RIDE
WOMAN-WISE
YESTERDAY'S HEROES

Wyler, William
SHAKEDOWN, THE

Yablans, Frank
NORTH DALLAS FORTY

Yates, Peter
BREAKING AWAY

Yordan, Philip
HARDER THEY FALL, THE

Zanuck, Darryl F.
HOLD THAT CO-ED
KENTUCKY
BLOOD AND SAND (1941)

Zimbalist, Sam
NAVY BLUE AND GOLD
KILLER McCOY
CROWD ROARS, THE (1938)

Ziskin, Laura
EVERYBODY'S ALL-AMERICAN

Zugsmith, Albert
SQUARE JUNGLE, THE

SOURCE AUTHORS

Abbott, George
DAMN YANKEES

Abel, Robert
ROAR OF THE CROWD

Ade, George
FRESHMAN LOVE

Ahearn, Thomas
SWING THAT CHEER

Alexander, Ronald
BILLIE

Alland, William
LIVELY SET, THE
FLESH AND FURY

Andrews, Robert H.
TROUBLE ALONG THE WAY

Appet, Leah
SEPARATE WAYS

Archerd, Evan
AMERICAN ANTHEM

Arnold, Danny
CADDY, THE

Asinof, Eliot
EIGHT MEN OUT

Atkinson, Hugh
GAMES, THE

Austie, Arthur
FOUR AGAINST FATE

Avedis, Howard
SEPARATE WAYS

Bachman, Larry
SPEED

Bagnold, Enid
NATIONAL VELVET

Baim, Gary L.
ICE CASTLES

Baker, C. Graham
PERSONALITY KID, THE

Baldwin, Earl
COLLEGE LOVERS

Bancroft, Harold
JOE PALOOKA IN TRIPLE CROSS

Barber, Rowland
SOMEBODY UP THERE LIKES ME

Barrows, Nicholas
GRIDIRON FLASH

Barry, Wesley
RACING BLOOD (1954)

Bartlett, Sy
SERGEANT MURPHY

Beauchamp, D.D.
GOLDEN GLOVES STORY, THE

Beaumont, Gerald
WINNER TAKE ALL (1932)
FAST COMPANIONS

Benjamin, Jeff
AMERICAN ANTHEM

Benson, George
GREATEST, THE

Birdwell, Russell J.
JIM THORPE—ALL AMERICAN

Blasco-Ibanez, Vicente
BLOOD AND SAND (1922)

Bleecher, William F.
TEN LAPS TO GO

Boetticher, Budd
MAGNIFICENT MATADOR, THE
BULLFIGHTER AND THE LADY, THE

Borschchagovskiy, A.
LAST GAME, THE

Bren, J. Robert
BAND PLAYS ON, THE

Brennan, Frederick Hazlitt
FOLLOW THE SUN
SPORTING BLOOD (1931)

Brent, William
SPIRIT OF STANFORD, THE
YESTERDAY'S HEROES

Bricker, George
KING OF HOCKEY

Bright, John
KID FROM CLEVELAND, THE

Brightman, Stanley
BATTLING BUTLER

Brooks, Matt
SWING FEVER

Brown, George Carleton
BIG PUNCH, THE

Brown, Lew
GOOD NEWS (1947)
GOOD NEWS (1930)
FOLLOW THRU

Brown, Rowland
LADY'S FROM KENTUCKY, THE

Bruce, George
NAVY BLUE AND GOLD
KILLER McCOY
CROWD ROARS, THE (1938)

Brush, Katherine
YOUNG MAN OF MANHATTAN

Burnett, W.R.
IRON MAN, THE (1931)
SOME BLONDES ARE DANGEROUS
IRON MAN, THE (1951)

Burtis, Thomas
MADISON SQUARE GARDEN

Butler, Binyon
COLLEGE HUMOR

Cady, Jerry
WINNER TAKE ALL (1939)

Campbell, Sir Malcolm
BURN 'EM UP O'CONNER

Carey, Gabrielle
PUBERTY BLUES

Carrington, C.B.
KENTUCKY BLUE STREAK

Carter, Joseph
RAGING BULL

Cary, Lucian
SATURDAY'S MILLIONS
DUKE OF CHICAGO

Cavanaugh, Florence
IRON MAJOR, THE

Chamberlain, George Agnew
HOME IN INDIANA

Champion, Bob
CHAMPIONS

Chase, Borden
HARRIGAN'S KID

Cheney, J. Benton
GAME THAT KILLS, THE

Chernus, Sonja
BIG FIX, THE

Chester, Hal E.
JOE PALOOKA, CHAMP

Churchill, Robert B.
BORN TO SPEED

Clark, Frank Howard
HEART PUNCH

Clork, Harry
MILKY WAY, THE
KID FROM BROOKLYN, THE

Cockrell, Eustace
TENNESSEE CHAMP
FAST COMPANY

Cohan, George M.
FAST COMPANY
ELMER THE GREAT

COWBOY QUARTERBACK

Cohen, Howard R.
UNHOLY ROLLERS

Cohen, Octavus Roy
SOCIAL LION, THE
PITTSBURGH KID, THE

Conlin, Richard
ANGELS IN THE OUTFIELD

Considine, Bob
BABE RUTH STORY, THE

Conway, Gary
OVER THE TOP

Corbett, James J.
GENTLEMAN JIM

Crouse, Russel
TALL STORY

Curtis, James
THERE AIN'T NO JUSTICE

Cushing, Tom
BLOOD AND SAND (1922)

Daniels, Robin
BLONDE COMET

Dashev, David
FISH THAT SAVED PITTSBURGH, THE

Davies, Valentine
IT HAPPENS EVERY SPRING

Davis, Terry
VISION QUEST

Deford, Frank
EVERYBODY'S ALL-AMERICAN

DeSylva, B.G.
HOLD EVERYTHING
GOOD NEWS (1947)
GOOD NEWS (1930)
FOLLOW THRU

DeWolf, Karen
RETURN OF OCTOBER, THE

Dix, Beulah Marie
LIFE OF JIMMY DOLAN, THE
THEY MADE ME A CRIMINAL

Donen, Stanley
TAKE ME OUT TO THE BALL GAME

Dunne, Jr., Finley Peter
WE WENT TO COLLEGE

Earl, Kenneth
WHIPLASH

Edmiston, James
DEVIL'S HAIRPIN, THE

Engelbach, David C.
OVER THE TOP

Ettlinger, Don
HOLD THAT CO-ED

Exley, Frederick Earl
FAN'S NOTES, A

Fair, Ronald
CORNBREAD, EARL AND ME

Fales, Dean
COLLEGE HUMOR

Farley, Walter
BLACK STALLION, THE

Fay, William
GUY WHO CAME BACK, THE

Fessier, Michael
KNOCKOUT

Fisher, Ham
JOE PALOOKA MEETS HUMPHREY
JOE PALOOKA IN WINNER TAKE ALL
JOE PALOOKA IN TRIPLE CROSS
JOE PALOOKA IN THE SQUARED
CIRCLE
JOE PALOOKA IN THE
COUNTERPUNCH
JOE PALOOKA IN THE BIG FIGHT
JOE PALOOKA, CHAMP
PALOOKA

Fisher, Steve
THAT'S MY MAN

Fitzroy, Roy
COUNTY FAIR, THE

Fitzsimmons, Cortland
70,000 WITNESSES
DEATH ON THE DIAMOND

Flanagan, E.J.
KID COMES BACK, THE

Foote, John Taintor
KENTUCKY
STORY OF SEABISCUIT, THE

Foster, Lewis
MILLION DOLLAR LEGS (1939)

Frank, Frederic
HARMON OF MICHIGAN

Freeman, Leonard
ALL-AMERICAN, THE (1953)

Gaines, Charles
STAY HUNGRY

Gallico, Paul
MATILDA
PRIDE OF THE YANKEES, THE

Gardner, Leonard
FAT CITY

Gent, Peter
NORTH DALLAS FORTY

Gerard, Merwin
WINNING TEAM, THE

Gindorff, Bryan
HARD TIMES

Goldberg, Mel
LIVELY SET, THE

Goldsmith, Clifford
FATHER WAS A FULLBACK

Goldstone, Richard
HARMON OF MICHIGAN

Gordon, Robert
GIRL FROM MONTEREY, THE

Goulding, Edmund
FLESH

Grand, Gordon
SPORT OF KINGS

Graziano, Rocky
SOMEBODY UP THERE LIKES ME

Green, George
GIRL FROM MONTEREY, THE

Grey, Zane
HOME ON THE RANGE

Gribble, Leonard
ARSENAL STADIUM MYSTERY, THE

Griffin, Eleanore
THOROUGHBREDS DON'T CRY

Grippo, Jan
MR. HEX

Grossman, F. Maury
SWING THAT CHEER

Harman, Fred
COWBOY AND THE PRIZEFIGHTER,
THE

Harris, Mark
BANG THE DRUM SLOWLY

Harrison, William
ROLLERBALL

Hawkey, Rock
FLYING FISTS, THE

Hawks, Howard
RED LINE 7000
INDIANAPOLIS SPEEDWAY
CROWD ROARS, THE (1932)

Hawks, William
INDIANAPOLIS SPEEDWAY

Hazard, Lawrence
FROM HELL TO HEAVEN

Hellinger, Mark
BROADWAY BILL
RIDING HIGH (1950)

Hemingway, Ernest
UNDER MY SKIN

Hendershot, Eric
TAKE DOWN

Henderson, Ray
GOOD NEWS (1947)
GOOD NEWS (1930)
FOLLOW THRU

Henstell, Bruce
HARD TIMES

Hillyer, Lambert
STRAIGHTAWAY

Hirshberg, Albert S.
FEAR STRIKES OUT

Hoerl, Arthur
THEY NEVER COME BACK

Hoffman, Joseph
SWING FEVER

Holzman, Allan
GRUNT! THE WRESTLING MOVIE

Hooker, Richard
M*A*S*H

Horwin, Jerry
SPORT PARADE, THE

Howard, Cy
THAT'S MY BOY (1951)

Howard, Mary
SPIRIT OF WEST POINT, THE

Hughes, Rupert
PATENT LEATHER KID, THE

Hunter, William
GREAT GAME, THE (1930)

Ibanez, Vincente Blasco
BLOOD AND SAND (1941)

Jacobs, William
OVER THE GOAL
UNWELCOME STRANGER

Jenkins, Dan
SEMI-TOUGH

Johnson, Robert Lee
PACE THAT THRILLS, THE

Joslyn, Talbert
NAVY BOUND

Juergens, Philip
BLONDE COMET

Kallis, Stanley
ROADRACERS, THE

Kandel, Aben
CITY FOR CONQUEST

Kanin, Fay
SUNDAY PUNCH

Kanin, Michael
SUNDAY PUNCH

Kaplan, Marc
FAST BREAK

Katz, Lee
KID NIGHTINGALE

Keene, Norman
POLICE CALL

Kelly, Gene
TAKE ME OUT TO THE BALL GAME

Kelly, Mark
MAN FROM DOWN UNDER, THE
PIGSKIN PARADE

Key, Ted
GUS

King, Bradley
THAT'S MY MAN

Klein, Herbert
KID FROM CLEVELAND, THE

Kleiser, Randal
NORTH SHORE

Knight, Christopher W.
WINNERS TAKE ALL

Knoblock, Edward
SPEAKEASY

Krims, Milton
SPEED

Kyne, Peter B.
BORN TO FIGHT
BLUE BLOOD
RIDE, KELLY, RIDE
RACING BLOOD (1938)

LaMotta, Jake
RAGING BULL

Lampell, Millard
SATURDAY'S HERO

Lancaster, Bill
BAD NEWS BEARS IN BREAKING
TRAINING, THE

Lardner, Ring
FAST COMPANY
ELMER THE GREAT
COWBOY QUARTERBACK
ALIBI IKE
CHAMPION

Larkin, Jr., John
SOCIETY GIRL

Larner, Jeremy
DRIVE, HE SAID

Lear, Peter
GOLDENGIRL

Lee, Connie
RETURN OF OCTOBER, THE

Lee, Damien
RENO AND THE DOC

Lees, John
GREAT GAME, THE (1930)

Lennon, Thomas
KILLER McCOY

Lester, Seelag
WINNING TEAM, THE

Lette, Kathy
PUBERTY BLUES

LeVino, Albert Shelby
HOLD 'EM NAVY!

Lewis, Ralph S.
FIGHTING MAD

Lindsay, Howard
TALL STORY

Lipton, Lew
SWEEPSTAKES

Lipton, Lou
HOLD 'EM JAIL

Loew, Jr., Arthur M.
ARENA

Logue, Charles
SHAKEDOWN, THE
FAST COMPANIONS

London, Jack
FIGHTER, THE
CONFLICT

Lucats, Nick
SPIRIT OF STANFORD, THE

Luddy, Edward I.
STEADY COMPANY

Lupino, Stanley
SPORTING LOVE

McGinn, Jim
NADIA

McGowan, John
HOLD EVERYTHING

McGrath, Harold
RIGHT TO THE HEART

McGuinness, J.K.
THIS SPORTING AGE

McGuire, William Anthony
KING FOR A NIGHT

McNulty, John
BIG LEAGUER

McPhee, John
CASEY'S SHADOW

Maguire, Jeff
VICTORY

Magyar, Dezso
STREETS OF GOLD

Malamud, Bernard
NATURAL, THE

Malone, Joe
BIG FIX, THE

Mandel, Frank
GOOD NEWS (1947)
GOOD NEWS (1930)

Mankiewcz, Joseph L.
MILLION DOLLAR LEGS (1932)

March, Joseph Moncure
SET-UP, THE

March, Timothy
LET'S DO IT AGAIN

Marion, Charles R.
ROAR OF THE CROWD

Marion, Frances
PRIZEFIGHTER AND THE LADY, THE
CHAMP, THE (1979)
CHAMP, THE (1931)

Marion, Jr., George
COLLEGE RHYTHM

Marischka, Franz
SMALL TOWN STORY

Markey, Gene
GLORY

Markle, Peter
YOUNGBLOOD

Marks, Clarence E.
FIGHTING THOROUGHBREDS

Marsh, H.R.
SWING YOUR LADY

Martin, W. Thorton
BAND PLAYS ON, THE

Masucci, Jerry
LAST FIGHT, THE

Matthews, Marlene
SPIKER

Melford, Austin
BATTLING BUTLER

Melzer, B.F.
JOE PALOOKA IN THE SQUARED
CIRCLE

Meyer, Stanley
FIGHTING YOUTH

Milhauser, Bertram
LIFE OF JIMMY DOLAN, THE

Milicevic, Djordje
VICTORY

Miller, Jason
THAT CHAMPIONSHIP SEASON

Miller, Seaton I.
CROWD ROARS, THE (1932)

Millhauser, Bertram
THEY MADE ME A CRIMINAL

Mooney, Martin
MR. CELEBRITY

Morgan, Byron
BAND PLAYS ON, THE

Morheim, Louis
BIG LEAGUER

Morrow, Douglas
TROUBLE ALONG THE WAY
STRATTON STORY, THE

Mortimer, Frank
HOT CURVES

Naud, Tom
SAFE AT HOME

Nazarro, Ray
BULLFIGHTER AND THE LADY, THE

Neely, William
STROKER ACE

Nemerov, Howard
TALL STORY

Nicholson, Kenyon
SWING YOUR LADY

Norton, Grace
SPORTING BLOOD (1940)

Nugent, Elliott
LOCAL BOY MAKES GOOD

Nugent, J.C.
LOCAL BOY MAKES GOOD

Oakley, Barry
GREAT MACARTHY, THE

Odets, Clifford
GOLDEN BOY

Oppenheimer, George
KILLER McCOY
WE WENT TO COLLEGE

Ottum, Robert K.
STROKER ACE

Pendleton, Nat
DECEPTION

Perrin, Nat
PIGSKIN PARADE

Peterson, Ralph W.
SQUARE RING, THE

Phelps, William
NORTH SHORE

Piersall, James A.
FEAR STRIKES OUT

Pivar, Ben
DANGER ON WHEELS

SOURCE AUTHORS

Plimpton, George
PAPER LION

Pollock, Louis
JACKIE ROBINSON STORY, THE

Powell, Jonathan
CHAMPIONS

Praskins, Leonard
CHAMP, THE (1979)

Randel, Anthony
GRUNT! THE WRESTLING MOVIE

Rattigan, Terence
FINAL TEST, THE

Rauh, Stanley
HARMON OF MICHIGAN

Reid, Mrs. Wallace
RACING STRAIN, THE

Remarque, Erich Maria
BOBBY DEERFIELD

Reynolds, Quentin
SECRETS OF A NURSE

Ritch, Steve
SAFE AT HOME

Robinson, Charles
SWING YOUR LADY

Rockne, Mrs. Knute
KNUTE ROCKNE—ALL AMERICAN

Roeca, Sam
RACING BLOOD (1954)

Rogers, Bogart
MAN FROM DOWN UNDER, THE

Root, Lynn
MILKY WAY, THE
KID FROM BROOKLYN, THE

Root, Wells
RACETRACK

Rosener, George
SPEAKEASY

Rosi, Francesco
MOMENT OF TRUTH, THE

Ross, Frank
WALK, DON'T RUN

Ross, George
BIG FIX, THE

Ruben, J. Walter
THOROUGHBREDS DON'T CRY
RACETRACK

Ruddy, Albert S.
LONGEST YARD, THE

Ruesch, Hans
RACERS, THE

Runyon, Damon
MONEY FROM HOME
HOLD 'EM YALE
RACING LADY

Russell, Robert
WALK, DON'T RUN

Sackler, Howard
GREAT WHITE HOPE, THE

Samara, Spiro
DOWNHILL RACER

Samuels, Charles
MR. CELEBRITY

Sandler, Barry
KANSAS CITY BOMBER

Savage, Peter
RAGING BULL

Sayre, George
CONTENDER, THE

Sayre, Joel
RACKETY RAX

Schayer, Richard
SPIRIT OF NOTRE DAME, THE
ALL-AMERICAN, THE (1932)

Schmidt, Marlene
SEPARATE WAYS

Schulberg, Budd
HARDER THEY FALL, THE

Schwab, Lawrence
GOOD NEWS (1947)
GOOD NEWS (1930)
FOLLOW THRU

Scott, DeVallon
PACE THAT THRILLS, THE

Segall, Harry
HEAVEN CAN WAIT
HERE COMES MR. JORDAN

Sellers, William F.
GOLDEN GLOVES STORY, THE

Selznick, Joyce
ROOGIE'S BUMP

Serling, Rod
REQUIEM FOR A HEAVYWEIGHT

Shamberg, Bernard D.
FIGHTING MAD

Shane, Maxwell
GOLDEN GLOVES

Shaw, Irwin
EASY LIVING

Sheekman, Arthur
PIGSKIN PARADE

Sher, Jack
WORLD IN MY CORNER

Sherman, Vincent
PRIDE OF THE BLUEGRASS

Shulman, Irving
RING, THE

Shumate, Harold
MAIN EVENT, THE (1938)
HIGH SPEED
PRIDE OF THE BLUE GRASS
PRIDE OF ST. LOUIS, THE

Sillitoe, Alan
LONELINESS OF THE LONG DISTANCE
RUNNER, THE

Slater, Montagu
MANIACS ON WHEELS

Smith, H. Allen
RHUBARB

Smith, Shirley W.
IT HAPPENS EVERY SPRING

Snell, Earle
GRIDIRON FLASH

Stanush, Claude
LUSTY MEN, THE

Stein, Daniel Michael
WALL OF NOISE

Stone, Joseph
WORLD IN MY CORNER

Storey, David
THIS SPORTING LIFE

Stromberg, Gary
FISH THAT SAVED PITTSBURGH, THE

Stuhldreher, Harry
BAND PLAYS ON, THE

Sullivan, Wallace
LAUGHING IRISH EYES

Sutherland, Sidney
LAUGHING IRISH EYES

Tatum, Tom
WINNERS TAKE ALL

Templeton, George
SATURDAY'S HEROES

Tenser, Mark
TOMBOY
COACH

Tevis, Walter
COLOR OF MONEY, THE
HUSTLER, THE

Thomas, Basil
GREAT GAME, THE (1952)

Thorpe, Jim
JIM THORPE—ALL AMERICAN

Thurber, James
RISE AND SHINE

Tilton, Roger
SPIKER

Tomei, Lisa
GRUNT! THE WRESTLING MOVIE

Torgerson, Edwin Dial
SPEED TO BURN

Towne, Gene
PERSONALITY KID, THE

Trent, John
BOY IN BLUE, THE

Trumbo, Dalton
KID FROM KOKOMO, THE

Tunberg, Karl
HOLD THAT CO-ED

Tupper, Tristram
SALUTE
RED HOT TIRES

Van Every, Dale
SPIRIT OF NOTRE DAME, THE
ALL-AMERICAN, THE (1932)

Waggner, George
IDOL OF THE CROWDS

Walker, David
WEE GEORDIE

Wallace, Edgar
FLYING FIFTY-FIVE

Wallace, Francis
HUDDLE
BIG GAME, THE
KID GALAHAD (1962)
KID GALAHAD (1937)
TOUCHDOWN
THAT'S MY BOY (1932)
ROSE BOWL

Wallop, Douglas
DAMN YANKEES

Walton, Todd
INSIDE MOVES

Ware, Darrell
LIFE BEGINS IN COLLEGE

Ware, Leon
PEGGY

Warren, Frank
ROOGIE'S BUMP

Weissberger, Maurice
SMALL TOWN STORY

Wheelan, Tim
HOLD 'EM JAIL

White, Jon Manchip
RACE FOR LIFE, A

Whitman, Alan
THAT GANG OF MINE

Whitmore, John
YOUNGBLOOD

Wilkinson, Michael
PHAR LAP

Williams, Susan
AMERICAN ANTHEM

Witwer, H.C.
CAIN AND MABEL

Wolf, Richard A.
SKATEBOARD

Wolfe, Tom
LAST AMERICAN HERO, THE

Wyler, Robert
FIGHTING THOROUGHBREDS

Yablonsky, Yabo
VICTORY

Younger, A.P.
HOT CURVES
THEY LEARNED ABOUT WOMEN
SWELLHEAD, THE
SUNNY SKIES

Zanuck, Darryl F.
MAYBE IT'S LOVE

Zetlin, Barry
GRUNT! THE WRESTLING MOVIE

Zimmerman, Vernon
UNHOLY ROLLERS

Zuckerman, George
SQUARE JUNGLE, THE

SCREENWRITERS

Aaberg, Dennis
BIG WEDNESDAY

Abbott, George
DAMN YANKEES

Ackerman, Hal
SECOND WIND

Adams, Gerald Drayson
MIRACLE KID

Aldis, Will
STEALING HOME

Alexander, Ronald
BILLIE

Allardice, James
MONEY FROM HOME

Alsberg, Arthur
GUS

Andrews, Robert D.
SMITH OF MINNESOTA

Ansen, Joe
GOLDEN GLOVES STORY, THE

Appet, Leah
SEPARATE WAYS

Archerd, Evan
AMERICAN ANTHEM

Arnold, Danny
CADDY, THE

Asher, William
FIREBALL 500

Aurthur, Robert Alan
GRAND PRIX (1966)

Avins, Mimi
RUN FOR THE ROSES

Bacon, Lloyd
FIREMAN, SAVE MY CHILD

Baer, Arthur "Bugs"
THEY LEARNED ABOUT WOMEN

Baggott, King
SPORTING CHANCE

Baim, Gary L.
ICE CASTLES

Baines, John
FOUR AGAINST FATE

Baker, Herbert
BIG LEAGUER

Baranley, Sascha
BORN TO FIGHT

Barrows, Nick
MILLION DOLLAR LEGS (1932)

Bartlett, Hall
CRAZYLEGS, ALL AMERICAN

Barwood, Hal
BINGO LONG TRAVELING ALL-STARS
AND MOTOR KINGS, THE

Baxt, George
THUNDER IN DIXIE

Bean, Henry
RUNNING BRAVE

Beatty, Warren
HEAVEN CAN WAIT

Beauchamp, D.D.
ALL-AMERICAN, THE (1953)

Becker, Arnold
GO, MAN, GO!

Belden, Charles
KID NIGHTINGALE

Beltran, Pedro
MOMENT OF TRUTH, THE

Benchley, Nathaniel
GREAT AMERICAN PASTIME, THE

Benchley, Robert
SPORT PARADE, THE

Benjamin, Jeff
AMERICAN ANTHEM

Bennett, Charles
MANNEQUIN

Benson, Robby
ONE ON ONE

Berkeley, Martin
HARRIGAN'S KID

Berkman, Ted
FEAR STRIKES OUT

Berlin, Milton
BURN 'EM UP O'CONNER

Bernard, Sam
RAD

Bernstein, Walter
SEMI-TOUGH

Bettinson, Ralph Gilbert
GREAT GAME, THE (1930)

Binyon Butler, Claude
COLLEGE HUMOR

Bishoff, Larry
DREAMER

Blankfort, Henry
HARRIGAN'S KID
JOE PALOOKA MEETS HUMPHREY
JOE PALOOKA IN THE
COUNTERPUNCH
HUMPHREY TAKES A CHANCE

Blatty, William Peter
JOHN GOLDFARB, PLEASE COME
HOME

Blau, Raphael
FEAR STRIKES OUT

Bloom, Harold Jack
ARENA

Boasberg, Al
SO THIS IS COLLEGE

Boasberg, Albert
BATTLING BUTLER

Boehm, David
LIFE OF JIMMY DOLAN, THE
PERSONALITY KID, THE

Borshchagovskiy, A.
LAST GAME, THE

Bowie, Douglas
BOY IN BLUE, THE

Bowne, Alan
SPIKE OF BENSONHURST

Boylan, Malcolm Stuart
LADY'S FROM KENTUCKY, THE

Branch, Houston
PITTSBURGH KID, THE

Brennan, Frederick Hazlitt
KILLER McCOY
FOLLOW THE SUN
SPEAKEASY

Brent, William
SPIRIT OF STANFORD, THE

Breslow, Lou
RACKETY RAX

Bricker, George
BIG FIX, THE
KING OF HOCKEY
KID COMES BACK, THE
FRESHMAN LOVE
BODYHOLD

Brickman, Paul
BAD NEWS BEARS IN BREAKING
TRAINING, THE

Bright, John
KID FROM CLEVELAND, THE
FIGHTING MAD
CROWD ROARS, THE (1932)

Brodney, Oscar
MOONLIGHT IN HAVANA

Brooke, Peter R.
BASKETBALL FIX, THE

Brown, Paul
THRASHIN'

Bruce, George
NAVY BLUE AND GOLD
KING OF THE TURF
CROWD ROARS, THE (1938)

Bruckman, Clyde
FRESHMAN, THE

Buchanan, William
TWO MINUTES TO PLAY

Buchman, Harold
IT HAPPENED IN FLATBUSH

Buchman, Sidney
FROM HELL TO HEAVEN
SATURDAY'S HERO
HERE COMES MR. JORDAN

Buckley, Harold
IDOL OF THE CROWDS

Buckner, Robert
KNUTE ROCKNE—ALL AMERICAN

Buffington, Adele
HIGH SPEED
SWELLHEAD, THE

Buhai, Jeff
JOHNNY BE GOOD

Bull, Donald
ARSENAL STADIUM MYSTERY, THE

Bullock, Walter
RIGHT TO THE HEART

Burbridge, Betty
RACING STRAIN, THE

Burke, Edwin
SPEAKEASY

Busch, Niven
CROWD ROARS, THE (1932)
COLLEGE COACH

Butler, Frank
MILKY WAY, THE
COLLEGE HUMOR

Butler, John K.
HEART OF VIRGINIA
PRIDE OF MARYLAND

Butterfield, Walton
FAST COMPANY

Caesar, Arthur
FIREMAN, SAVE MY CHILD

Cahoon, Richard
SWELLHEAD, THE

Callahan, George
BABE RUTH STORY, THE

Campbell, R. Wright
YOUNG RACERS, THE

Capetanos, Leon
GREASED LIGHTNING

Carole, Joseph
TRIPLE THREAT
RACING LUCK (1948)

Carroll, Sidney
HUSTLER, THE

Cartwright, Gary
J.W. COOP

Caruso, Dee
WORLD'S GREATEST ATHLETE, THE

Carvalho, Claire
RACETRACK

Catto, Max
TAKE ME TO PARIS

Chapman, Ben
LEATHER-PUSHERS, THE

Chase, Borden
IRON MAN, THE (1951)

Churchill, Robert B.
BORN TO SPEED

Clancey, Vernon
FLYING FIFTY-FIVE

Clark, Harry
MIGHTY MC GURK, THE

Clarke, T.E.B.
RAINBOW JACKET, THE

Cleary, Jon
GREEN HELMET, THE
SIDECAR RACERS

Clements, Calvin
KANSAS CITY BOMBER

Cleveland, George
SUNNY SKIES

Clowes, John L.
GRAND PRIX (1934)

Clymer, John B.
COLLEGE LOVE

Cockrell, Francis
SPORT PARADE, THE
RHUBARB

Coen, Franklin
JOHNNY DARK
FIGHTING THOROUGHBREDS

Cohen, Howard R.
UNHOLY ROLLERS

Cohn, Art
GLORY ALLEY
TENNESSEE CHAMP
SET-UP, THE

Coldeway, Anthony
OVER THE GOAL

Cole, Lester
SOME BLONDES ARE DANGEROUS
SECRETS OF A NURSE

Cole, Tom
STREETS OF GOLD

Collins, Gunther
SWINGIN' AFFAIR, A

Collins, Hal
HIGH SCHOOL HERO

Collins, Jackie
YESTERDAY'S HERO

Collins, Monte
JOE PALOOKA IN WINNER TAKE ALL
FIGHTING MAD

Collins, Richard
BOB MATHIAS STORY, THE

Colomby, Harry
TOUCH AND GO

Comden, Betty
GOOD NEWS (1947)

Condon, Charles
MARK IT PAID
TEN LAPS TO GO

Connell, Richard
MILKY WAY, THE

Conselman, Jr., William
RIDE, KELLY, RIDE
YESTERDAY'S HEROES

Conselman, William
PIGSKIN PARADE

Considine, Bob
BABE RUTH STORY, THE

Conway, Tim
PRIZE FIGHTER, THE

Cooper, Olive
LAUGHING IRISH EYES

Cornsweet, Harold
RETURN TO CAMPUS

Corrigan, Lloyd
HOLD 'EM NAVY!
FOLLOW THRU
TOUCHDOWN, ARMY

Couderc, Pierre
COLLEGE LOVE

Coyle, John T.
MIRACLE KID

Crane, Harry
TAKE ME OUT TO THE BALL GAME

Crawford, Nancy Voyles
SIDEWINDER ONE

Cummings, Hugh
POLO JOE

Cummings, Jr., Irving
RIDE, KELLY, RIDE
YESTERDAY'S HEROES

Curtin, Valerie
INSIDE MOVES

Curtis, James
THERE AIN'T NO JUSTICE

D'Abbes, Ingram
SPORTING LOVE

Darling, W. Scott
BORN TO SPEED
BLUE GRASS OF KENTUCKY
BLUE BLOOD

Daves, Delmer
$1,000 A TOUCHDOWN
SO THIS IS COLLEGE

Davies, Valentine
IT HAPPENS EVERY SPRING

Davis, Frank
JIM THORPE—ALL AMERICAN

de Gaetano, Michael
SCORING

De Mond, Albert
SHAKEDOWN, THE
COLLEGE LOVE

Decker, Marge
TO PLEASE A LADY

Deford, Frank
TRADING HEARTS

DeLeon, Walter
HOLD 'EM JAIL
SPIRIT OF NOTRE DAME, THE
COLLEGE RHYTHM

DeMond, Albert
KING OF THE GAMBLERS
DUKE OF CHICAGO

Dennis, Charles
RENO AND THE DOC

DePina, Albert
JOE PALOOKA, CHAMP

Deutsch, Helen
NATIONAL VELVET

Diamond, I.A.L.
FORTUNE COOKIE, THE

Dickey, Basil
FLYING FISTS, THE

Dickinson, Thorold
ARSENAL STADIUM MYSTERY, THE

Dillon, Robert
SAFE AT HOME

Doherty, Ethel
HOME ON THE RANGE

Dolen, Jay
CONTENDER, THE

Dortort, David
LUSTY MEN, THE

Doty, Douglas
RACETRACK
COLLEGE LOVERS

Doud, Earle
RACQUET

Dowd, Nancy
SLAP SHOT

Doyle, Laird
CAIN AND MABEL

Doyle-Murray, Brian
CADDYSHACK

Dreifuss, Arthur
HIGH SCHOOL HERO

Dudley, Paul
MONKEY ON MY BACK

Duff, Warren
IRON MAJOR, THE

DuKore, Lawrence
GREASED LIGHTNING

Dunn, Winifred
PATENT LEATHER KID, THE

Durieux, Gilles
EDITH AND MARCEL

Dusenberry, Phil
NATURAL, THE

Eastman, Charles
LITTLE FAUSS AND BIG HALSY

Edmiston, James
DEVIL'S HAIRPIN, THE

Edwards, Geoffrey
RAD

Ellis, Robert
SPEED TO BURN
ROAD DEMON

Endfield, Cyril
MR. HEX
JOE PALOOKA IN THE
COUNTERPUNCH
JOE PALOOKA IN THE BIG FIGHT
JOE PALOOKA, CHAMP

Englander, Otto
BOY FROM INDIANA

English, Richard
MILLION DOLLAR LEGS (1939)

Englund, Ken
CADDY, THE

Enright, Ray
FIREMAN, SAVE MY CHILD

Epstein, Julius J.
TALL STORY

Estridge, Robin
CHECKPOINT

Ettlinger, Don
HOLD THAT CO-ED
LIFE BEGINS IN COLLEGE

Fallon, David
SPLIT DECISIONS

Faragoh, Francis Edward
IRON MAN, THE (1931)

Farnham, Joe
SO THIS IS COLLEGE

Fay, William
KID GALAHAD (1962)

Feist, Felix
GOLDEN GLOVES STORY, THE

Felton, Earl
FRESHMAN LOVE
PITTSBURGH KID, THE

Fessier, Michael
SPEED

Field, David
AMAZING GRACE AND CHUCK

Fields, Leonard
COLLEGE LOVE

Fisher, George
SMALL TOWN STORY

Fisher, Steve
THAT'S MY MAN

Fitzsimmons, Cortland
RACING LADY

Fletcher, Guy
FIFTY-SHILLING BOXER

Flicker, Theodore J.
SPINOUT

Foote, Bradbury
KING OF THE GAMBLERS

Foote, John Taintor
KENTUCKY
GREAT DAN PATCH, THE
STORY OF SEABISCUIT, THE

Ford, Corey
SPORT PARADE, THE

Foreman, Carl
CHAMPION

Fort, Garret
70,000 WITNESSES

Foster, Lewis
MILLION DOLLAR LEGS (1939)
GOLDEN GLOVES

Fox, Ray Errol
HOT SHOT

Foy, Bryan
COLLEGE

SCREENWRITERS

Franham, Joe
GOOD NEWS (1930)

Frank Ross
WALK, DON'T RUN

Frank, Jr., Harriet
WHIPLASH

Frank, Melvin
RETURN OF OCTOBER, THE

Freeman, Everett
JIM THORPE—ALL AMERICAN

Friedman, Alan
HARRIGAN'S KID

Friedman, Ken
HEART LIKE A WHEEL

Frohman, Mel
. . . ALL THE MARBLES

Gage, George
SKATEBOARD

Gaines, Charles
STAY HUNGRY

Galfas, Timothy
MATILDA

Ganzer, Alvin
LEATHER SAINT, THE

Gardner, Gerald
WORLD'S GREATEST ATHLETE, THE

Gardner, Leonard
FAT CITY

Garnett, Tay
FIREBALL, THE

Garrett, Grant
MIGHTY MC GURK, THE
HOME ON THE RANGE

Gates, Harvey
BAND PLAYS ON, THE
RACING LUCK (1948)
COUNTY FAIR, THE

Gelsey, Erwin
HOLD 'EM NAVY!
LIFE OF JIMMY DOLAN, THE
TOUCHDOWN, ARMY
PERSONALITY KID, THE

Gent, Peter
NORTH DALLAS FORTY

George, George W.
PEGGY

Geraghty, Maurice
WHIPLASH

Geraghty, Tom
ELMER THE GREAT

Gerard, Merwin
WINNING TEAM, THE

Gillard, Stuart
SPRING FEVER

Gilliat, Sidney
WEE GEORDIE

Gindorff, Bryan
HARD TIMES

Girard, Bernard
BIG PUNCH, THE

Glasmon, Kubec
CROWD ROARS, THE (1932)

Glass, Gaston
RACETRACK

Gleason, James
SWELLHEAD, THE

Goldberg, Mel
LIVELY SET, THE

Golden, Ray
LIFE BEGINS IN COLLEGE

Gordon, Bernard
FLESH AND FURY

Gordon, Cliff
MANIACS ON WHEELS

Gordon, Homer King
KENTUCKY BLUE STREAK

Gordon, Ruth
PAT AND MIKE

Gordon, Steve
ONE AND ONLY, THE

Gould, Heywood
STREETS OF GOLD

Grahame, Alec
SQUARE RING, THE

Grant, Edward
GREAT JOHN L., THE

Grant, James Edward
BULLFIGHTER AND THE LADY, THE

Gray, William
BLOOD AND GUTS

Grayson, Charles
SWING THAT CHEER

Green, Adolph
GOOD NEWS (1947)

Green, Howard J.
HARMON OF MICHIGAN
WINNER'S CIRCLE, THE
SPIRIT OF STANFORD, THE

Greene, Victor M.
FLYING FIFTY-FIVE

Grefe, William
RACING FEVER

Grey, John
FRESHMAN, THE

Gump, Eugene
WRESTLER, THE

Guttentag, Bill
HOT SHOT

Hanley, Bill
GRAND PRIX (1966)

Hanley, Jack
ROOGIE'S BUMP

Harbaugh, Carl
COLLEGE

Harding, Brooks B.
FRESHMAN, THE

Hare, Bill
FINNEY

Harris, Elmer
SOCIETY GIRL

Harris, Mark
BANG THE DRUM SLOWLY

Harrison, William
ROLLERBALL

Hart, Moss
FLESH

Hartley, Jean
POLICE CALL

Hartman, Don
KID FROM BROOKLYN, THE

Hartman, Edmund
CADDY, THE

Havez, Jean
FRESHMAN, THE

Hazard, Lawrence
THOROUGHBREDS DON'T CRY
SPORTING BLOOD (1940)

Heath, Percy
MAN I LOVE, THE
FROM HELL TO HEAVEN

Heerman, Victor
GOLDEN BOY

Hendershot, Eric
TAKE DOWN

Hendryx, Shirl
RUNNING BRAVE

Henstell, Bruce
HARD TIMES

Herbert, F. Hugh
PERSONALITY KID, THE

Herzig, Sig
THEY MADE ME A CRIMINAL
INDIANAPOLIS SPEEDWAY

Hill, Jack
PIT STOP

Hill, Maurice J.
TRACK OF THUNDER

Hill, Walter
HARD TIMES

Hillyer, Lambert
STRAIGHTAWAY

Hoerl, Arthur
GIRL FROM MONTEREY, THE
THEY NEVER COME BACK
SPIRIT OF YOUTH

Hoffe, Monckton
FOUR AGAINST FATE

Holmes, Milton
BOOTS MALONE
SALTY O'ROURKE

Hopkins, Robert
SARATOGA

Horne, Kenneth
FLYING FIFTY-FIVE

House, Max
WILD RACERS, THE

Howard, Cy
THAT'S MY BOY (1951)

Huebsch, Edward
SPORT OF KINGS

Hunter, John
BLOOD AND GUTS
RACING ROMANCE

Huston, Paul
SKI PATROL

Hyland, Frances
WINNER TAKE ALL (1939)

Hyman, Arthur S.
HUDDLE

Jackson, Harry
CUP-TIE HONEYMOON

Jackson, Joseph
MAYBE IT'S LOVE

Jacobs, William
OVER THE GOAL
SERGEANT MURPHY

Jason, Leigh
HIGH GEAR

Jeffrey, Jan
JOE PALOOKA IN TRIPLE CROSS
JOE PALOOKA IN THE SQUARED
CIRCLE

Jevne, Jack
PALOOKA

Johnson, Henry
FIGHTING YOUTH

Johnson, Robert Lee
HUDDLE
PACE THAT THRILLS, THE

Jones, Evan
VICTORY
CHAMPIONS

Jones, Grover
MILKY WAY, THE
BURNING UP
TOUCHDOWN

Kahn, Gordon
WHIPLASH

Kallis, Stanley
ROADRACERS, THE

Kalmar, Bert
HORSE FEATHERS
KID FROM SPAIN, THE

Kampmann, Steven
STEALING HOME

Kandel, Aben
KID MONK BARONI
IRON MAJOR, THE
FIGHTER, THE

Kane, Michael
BEAR, THE
ALL THE RIGHT MOVES

Kanin, Fay
SUNDAY PUNCH

Kanin, Garson
PAT AND MIKE

Kanin, Michael
SUNDAY PUNCH

Kanter, Hal
MONEY FROM HOME

Kaufman, Charles
SQUEEZE PLAY
SATURDAY'S HEROES
RACERS, THE

Kearney, Patrick
FAST COMPANY

Keene, Norman
POLICE CALL

Kelly, Margaret
PUBERTY BLUES

Kennedy, Leon Isaac
BODY AND SOUL (1981)

Kenney, Douglas
CADDYSHACK

Kent, Willis
RACING STRAIN, THE

King, Bradley
THAT'S MY MAN

King, Rick
HOT SHOT

Kingsley, Dorothy
ANGELS IN THE OUTFIELD

Kinsolving, William
FAN'S NOTES, A

Kirgo, George
SPINOUT
RED LINE 7000

Klein, Wally
INDIANAPOLIS SPEEDWAY

Kleiner, Harry
LE MANS

Kline, Herbert
FIGHTER, THE

Kober, Arthur
PALOOKA

Kohn, John
GOLDENGIRL

Kotcheff, Ted
NORTH DALLAS FORTY

Kramer, Searle
MR. UNIVERSE

Krasna, Norman
THAT'S MY BOY (1932)

Kuller, Sidney
LIFE BEGINS IN COLLEGE

La Capria, Raffaele
MOMENT OF TRUTH, THE

Lachman, Mort
MIXED COMPANY

Lamensdorf, Leonard
CORNBREAD, EARL AND ME

Lampell, Millard
SATURDAY'S HERO

Lancaster, Bill
BAD NEWS BEARS GO TO JAPAN,
THE
BAD NEWS BEARS, THE

Landau, Richard
RACE FOR LIFE, A

Landon, Joseph
WALL OF NOISE

Landon, Michael
SAM'S SON

Lang, Charles
MAGNIFICENT MATADOR, THE

Lang, Walter
RACETRACK

Lardner, Jr., Ring
M*A*S*H
GREATEST, THE

Larner, Jeremy
DRIVE, HE SAID

Larson, Nancy
COACH

Lasko, Ed
ROADRACERS, THE

Launder, Frank
WEE GEORDIE

Lawrence, Bert
HOLD THAT LINE
FIGHTING FOOLS

Lawrence, Vincent
GENTLEMAN JIM

Leahy, Agnes Brand
SOCIAL LION, THE

Lee, Damien
BUSTED UP

Lee, Jack
MANIACS ON WHEELS

Lee, Robert N.
70,000 WITNESSES

Lehman, Ernest
SOMEBODY UP THERE LIKES ME

Lelouch, Claude
EDITH AND MARCEL

Lennon, Thomas
SECRETS OF A NURSE
RACING LADY
CROWD ROARS, THE (1938)

Leo, Maurice
SWING YOUR LADY

Leslie, Aleen
FATHER WAS A FULLBACK

Lester, Seelag
WINNING TEAM, THE

Levinson, Barry
INSIDE MOVES

Libett, Robert Yale
ALL-AMERICAN, THE (1953)

Lipman, William R.
MIGHTY MC GURK, THE

Lipscomb, W.P.
GREAT GAME, THE (1930)

Lipton, Lew
SWEEPSTAKES

Lively, William
THAT GANG OF MINE

Loeb, Lee
MAIN EVENT, THE (1938)
SWING THAT CHEER
IT HAPPENED IN FLATBUSH

Logan, Helen
SPEED TO BURN
ROAD DEMON

Logue, Charles A.
HOME ON THE RANGE
SHAKEDOWN, THE
CONFLICT

Loos, Anita
SARATOGA

Loos, Mary
FATHER WAS A FULLBACK

Lord, Robert
HOLD EVERYTHING
LOCAL BOY MAKES GOOD
FIREMAN, SAVE MY CHILD
WINNER TAKE ALL (1932)

Lowe, Sherman
THEY NEVER COME BACK

Lucats, Nick
SPIRIT OF STANFORD, THE

Lyndon, Barre
TO PLEASE A LADY

Lyndon, Victor
STOCK CAR

Macauley, Richard
KID FROM KOKOMO, THE

McBride, Joseph
BLOOD AND GUTS

McCall, Jr., Mary C.
RINGSIDE MAISIE

McCanlies, Tim
NORTH SHORE

McCoy, Arch
HERE COME THE TIGERS

McCoy, Horace
LUSTY MEN, THE
GENTLEMAN JIM
FIREBALL, THE

McDermott, John
COLLEGE RHYTHM

Macfadden, Hamilton
FIGHTING YOUTH

McGaha, William
SPEED LOVERS

McGinn, Jim
NADIA

McGuinness, James Kevin
SALUTE

McGuire, William Anthony
KING FOR A NIGHT

KID FROM SPAIN, THE

Mack, Willard
SPORTING BLOOD (1931)

McMahon, Thomas A.
SIDEWINDER ONE

McNutt, William Slavens
BURNING UP
TOUCHDOWN

Mahin, Jr., John Lee
PRIZEFIGHTER AND THE LADY, THE

Maibaum, Richard
WE WENT TO COLLEGE

Mankiewicz, Don
FAST COMPANY

Mankiewicz, Herman J.
MAN I LOVE, THE
RISE AND SHINE
PRIDE OF THE YANKEES, THE
PRIDE OF ST. LOUIS, THE

Mankiewicz, Joseph L.
SOCIAL LION, THE
FAST COMPANY

Mann, Arthur
JACKIE ROBINSON STORY, THE

Mannheimer, Albert
SPORTING BLOOD (1940)

Manning, Roger D.
GRUNT! THE WRESTLING MOVIE

Manzano, Llovety
MANOLETE

Marion, Charles R.
HOLD THAT LINE
WHITE LIGHTING
ROSE BOWL STORY, THE
RODEO
ROAR OF THE CROWD

Marion, Frances
GOOD NEWS (1930)

Markle, Peter
YOUNGBLOOD

Marks, C.J.
FAST COMPANIONS

Marks, Clarence
SHAKEDOWN, THE

Markson, Ben
WOMAN-WISE
RACKETY RAX

Martin, Al
RACING LUCK (1948)
PRISON SHADOWS

Martin, Don
TRIPLE THREAT

Martin, Frances
COLLEGE RHYTHM

Martin, Mardik
RAGING BULL

Marvin, Mike
SIX PACK

Mason, Sarah Y.
GOLDEN BOY

THEY LEARNED ABOUT WOMEN

Mathison, Melissa
BLACK STALLION, THE

Matter, Alex
SIX PACK

Matthews, Marlene
SPIKER

Matthis, June
BLOOD AND SAND (1922)

May, Elaine
HEAVEN CAN WAIT

Mear, H. Fowler
RIDING HIGH (1937)

Meehan, John
PRIZEFIGHTER AND THE LADY, THE

Meehan, Jr., John
TAKE IT FROM ME

Meltzer, Lewis
GOLDEN BOY

Melville, Alan
FOUR AGAINST FATE

Merrill, Keith
TAKE DOWN

Michaels, Steve
RACQUET

Milius, John
BIG WEDNESDAY

Miller, Jason
THAT CHAMPIONSHIP SEASON

Miller, Seton I.
KID GALAHAD (1937)
HERE COMES MR. JORDAN

Miller, Winston
HOME IN INDIANA

Milne, Peter
GLORY
POLO JOE

Mizner, Wilson
WINNER TAKE ALL (1932)

Moessinger, David
NUMBER ONE

Mooney, Martin
MR. CELEBRITY
BLONDE COMET

Morgan, Byron
BURN 'EM UP O'CONNER

Morrissey, Paul
SPIKE OF BENSONHURST

Morrow, Douglas
MAURIE
JIM THORPE—ALL AMERICAN
STRATTON STORY, THE

Mortimer, Frank
HOT CURVES

Muir, Florabel
FIGHTING YOUTH

Murray, Ralph F.
SWEEPSTAKES

Myers, Henry
MILLION DOLLAR LEGS (1932)

Myers, Peter
SQUARE RING, THE

Myhers, John
PRIZE FIGHTER, THE

Napoleon, Jo
RIDE THE WILD SURF

Napoleons, Art
RIDE THE WILD SURF

Neal, Lex
FRESHMAN, THE
BATTLING BUTLER

Needham, Hal
STROKER ACE

Nelson, Don
GUS

Neville, Grace
MOTOR MADNESS
GAME THAT KILLS, THE

Neville, John T.
MILLION TO ONE, A
HEART PUNCH

Newman, Walter
CHAMP, THE (1979)

Niblo, Jr., Fred
MOTOR MADNESS
GAME THAT KILLS, THE
IN THIS CORNER
COWBOY QUARTERBACK

Nichols, Dudley
THIS SPORTING AGE

Nicholson, Jack
DRIVE, HE SAID

Nilsson, Rob
ON THE EDGE

Nolbandov, Sergei
THERE AIN'T NO JUSTICE

Norris, Stephen
RACING BLOOD (1938)

O'Donnell, Jack
KING FOR A NIGHT
RACING LUCK (1935)

Obst, David
JOHNNY BE GOOD

Oppenheimer, George
CROWD ROARS, THE (1938)

Ormsby, Alan
TOUCH AND GO

Orton, J.O.C.
TAKE IT FROM ME

Pagano, Ernest
RACETRACK

Palca, Alfred
HARLEM GLOBETROTTERS, THE

Panama, Norman
RETURN OF OCTOBER, THE

Parent, Gail
MAIN EVENT, THE (1979)

Pearson, Barry
PAPERBACK HERO

Peck, Jr., Charles K.
BASKETBALL FIX, THE

Pekelis, Haim
SQUEEZE PLAY

Pembroke, Scott
KING FOR A NIGHT

Perelman, S.J.
HORSE FEATHERS
HOLD 'EM JAIL

Perrin, Nat
SWING FEVER

Phelps, William
NORTH SHORE

Phillips, Caryl
PLAYING AWAY

Pirosh, Robert
QUARTERBACK, THE

Pizzo, Angelo
HOOSIERS

Pokrass, Samuel
LIFE BEGINS IN COLLEGE

Polonsky, Abraham
BODY AND SOUL (1947)

Ponicsan, Darryl
VISION QUEST

Portabella, Pedro
MOMENT OF TRUTH, THE

Prager, Stanley
JOE PALOOKA IN THE BIG FIGHT

Praskins, Leonard
WINNER'S CIRCLE, THE
FLESH
CHAMP, THE (1931)

Presnell, Robert
YOUNG MAN OF MANHATTAN

Price, Richard
STREETS OF GOLD
COLOR OF MONEY, THE

Prieto, Joseph G.
RUN FOR THE ROSES

Proctor, James
DREAMER

Purcell, Gertrude
PALOOKA

Rafelson, Bob
STAY HUNGRY

Ramis, Harold
CADDYSHACK

Ramrus, Al
HALLS OF ANGER

Rapf, Maurice
WE WENT TO COLLEGE

Rattigan, Terence
FINAL TEST, THE

Rauh, Stanley
LAUGHING IRISH EYES

Rawlinson, A.R.
STOCK CAR

Ray, Albert
HOLD 'EM JAIL
WINNER TAKE ALL (1939)

Reed, Daniel
YOUNG MAN OF MANHATTAN

Reed, Tom
SPIRIT OF WEST POINT, THE

Reeves, Theodore
NATIONAL VELVET

Reid, Dorothy
RHUBARB

Retchin, Norman
LEATHER SAINT, THE

Reyney, Ferdinand
ALL-AMERICAN, THE (1932)

Rhine, Larry
LEATHER-PUSHERS, THE

Richards, Alexander
THUNDER IN CAROLINA

Rickman, Thomas
EVERYBODY'S ALL-AMERICAN
KANSAS CITY BOMBER

Riskin, Robert
BROADWAY BILL
RIDING HIGH (1950)

Rivkin, Allen
MADISON SQUARE GARDEN
SUNDAY PUNCH
70,000 WITNESSES

Robbins, Matthew
BINGO LONG TRAVELING ALL-STARS
AND MOTOR KINGS, THE

Roberts, Marguerite
ROSE BOWL

Roberts, William
LAST AMERICAN HERO, THE
FAST COMPANY

Robertson, Cliff
J.W. COOP

Robins, Sam
BOWERY BLITZKRIEG

Robinson, Casey
UNDER MY SKIN
FATHER WAS A FULLBACK

Rodman, Howard
WINNING

Roeca, Sam
NAVY BOUND
RACING BLOOD (1954)

Roman, Lawrence
PAPER LION

Romeril, John
GREAT MACARTHY, THE

Root, Wells
MAN FROM DOWN UNDER, THE

Rose, Jack
TROUBLE ALONG THE WAY
RIDING HIGH (1950)

SCREENWRITERS

Rose, Les
PAPERBACK HERO

Rose, Stephen Bruce
COACH

Rose, William
MANIACS ON WHEELS

Rosebrook, Jeb
JUNIOR BONNER

Rosenberg, Jeanne
BLACK STALLION, THE

Rosi, Francesco
MOMENT OF TRUTH, THE

Rossen, Robert
HUSTLER, THE

Roth, Murray
PALOOKA

Rubin, Benny
HOT CURVES

Rubin, Stanley
JOE PALOOKA IN WINNER TAKE ALL

Ruby, Harry
HORSE FEATHERS
KID FROM SPAIN, THE

Ruddy, Albert S.
MATILDA

Ryan, Ben
LAUGHING IRISH EYES
PALOOKA

Ryan, Tim
HOLD THAT LINE

Ryerson, Florence
FAST COMPANY

Sackheim, Jerry
HEART OF VIRGINIA

Sackler, Howard
GREAT WHITE HOPE, THE

Sacks, Alan
THRASHIN'

Sacks, Ezra
WILDCATS

St. John, Adela Rogers
PATENT LEATHER KID, THE

Sak, Sol
WALK, DON'T RUN

Sale, Richard
FATHER WAS A FULLBACK

Salkowitz, Sy
THUNDER ALLEY

Salter, James
DOWNHILL RACER

Sand, Bob
TOUCH AND GO

Sandrich, Mark
HOLD 'EM JAIL

Sargent, Alvin
BOBBY DEERFIELD

Sauter, Joe
HOT SHOT

Saxton, Charles
HIGH GEAR

Sayles, John
EIGHT MEN OUT

Sayre, George
RACING LUCK (1935)
CONTENDER, THE

Schary, Dore
RED HOT TIRES

Schnee, Charles
RIGHT CROSS
EASY LIVING

Schnitzer, Gerald
FIGHTING FOOLS

Schrader, Paul
RAGING BULL

Schrank, Joseph
SWING YOUR LADY

Schrock, Raymond
KID NIGHTINGALE
CONTENDER, THE

Schubert, Bernard
BAND PLAYS ON, THE

Schulman, Arnold
PLAYERS

Schwab, Laurence
FOLLOW THRU

Scott, Allan
GUY WHO CAME BACK, THE

Scott, DeVallon
PACE THAT THRILLS, THE

Seff, Manuel
COLLEGE COACH

Segal, Eric
GAMES, THE

Segal, Jerry
ONE ON ONE

Seller, Thomas
MAN FROM DOWN UNDER, THE

Sellers, Kevin
BLUE SKIES AGAIN

Serling, Rod
REQUIEM FOR A HEAVYWEIGHT

Seward, Edmond
FIGHTING FOOLS

Shane, Maxwell
NAVY WAY, THE
LEATHER-PUSHERS, THE
GOLDEN GLOVES

Shaner, John
HALLS OF ANGER

Shavelson, Melville
MIXED COMPANY
KID FROM BROOKLYN, THE
TROUBLE ALONG THE WAY
RIDING HIGH (1950)

Shaw, Irwin
BIG GAME, THE

Shelton, Ron
BULL DURHAM
BEST OF TIMES, THE

Sher, Jack
KID FROM LEFT FIELD, THE
WORLD IN MY CORNER

Sherdeman, Ted
WINNING TEAM, THE

Sherie, Fenn
SPORTING LOVE

Sherman, Joseph
DEATH ON THE DIAMOND

Sherman, Vincent
PRIDE OF THE BLUEGRASS

Shrake, Bud
J.W. COOP

Shuken, Phillip
SPEEDWAY

Shulman, Irving
RING, THE

Shumate, Harold
HOME ON THE RANGE
PRIDE OF THE BLUE GRASS

Silliphant, Stirling
OVER THE TOP

Sillitoe, Alan
LONELINESS OF THE LONG DISTANCE
RUNNER, THE

Silverstein, David
SATURDAY'S HEROES

Simon, Neil
SLUGGER'S WIFE, THE

Sinclair, Edward
FIGHTING GENTLEMAN, THE

Skolimowski, Jerzy
WALKOVER

Slavin, George F.
PEGGY

Smith, Andrew
MAIN EVENT, THE (1979)

Smith, Charles
BATTLING BUTLER

Smith, Paul Gerard
BATTLING BUTLER
HOLD 'EM YALE

Smith, Robert
BIG WHEEL, THE

Smith, Walton Hall
HUDDLE

Snell, Earle
HOT CURVES
SUNNY SKIES
STEADY COMPANY
RACING YOUTH
FAST COMPANIONS

Sobieski, Carol
CASEY'S SHADOW

Spence, Ralph
BAND PLAYS ON, THE
DEATH ON THE DIAMOND

Stallone, Sylvester
OVER THE TOP
ROCKY IV
ROCKY III
ROCKY II
ROCKY
PARADISE ALLEY

Starkes, Jaison
FISH THAT SAVED PITTSBURGH, THE

Stefan, Fred
SPRING FEVER

Stern, David
RHUBARB

Stern, Sandor
FAST BREAK

Stern, Steven Hilliard
RUNNING

Stevens, Edmond
FISH THAT SAVED PITTSBURGH, THE

Stone, John
SALUTE

Storey, David
THIS SPORTING LIFE

Suay, Ricardo Munoz
MOMENT OF TRUTH, THE

Sucher, Henry
MIRACLE KID

Sullivan, C. Gardner
HUDDLE

Suszko, Jerzy
BOXER

Swerling, Jo
BLOOD AND SAND (1941)
PRIDE OF THE YANKEES, THE

Sylvester, Robert
JOE LOUIS STORY, THE

Symon, Burk
IN THIS CORNER

Tabori, Paul
RACE FOR LIFE, A

Taradash, Daniel
GOLDEN BOY

Tarshis, Harold
DECEPTION

Tashlin, Frank
KILL THE UMPIRE

Taylor, Lawrence
JACKIE ROBINSON STORY, THE

Taylor, Rex
HIGH GEAR

Taylor, Sam
FRESHMAN, THE

Tennyson, Penrose
THERE AIN'T NO JUSTICE

Tesich, Steve
BREAKING AWAY
AMERICAN FLYERS

Thew, Harvey
DEATH ON THE DIAMOND

Thomas, Jerry
COWBOY AND THE PRIZEFIGHTER,
THE

Tomaszewski, Bohdan
BOXER

Tombragel, Maurice
DANGER ON WHEELS

Toner, Anthony
CUP-TIE HONEYMOON

Totheroh, Dan
ROOGIE'S BUMP

Totman, Wellyn
THOROUGHBREDS
FIGHTING THOROUGHBREDS
FIGHTING CHAMP

Towne, Robert
PERSONAL BEST

Towne, Roger
NATURAL, THE

Townley, Jack
CROOKED CIRCLE, THE

Townsend, Leo
FIREBALL 500

Trosper, Guy
STRATTON STORY, THE

Trotti, Lamar
KENTUCKY

Tryon, Glenn
GRIDIRON FLASH

Tuch, Fred
SPEED LOVERS

Tuchock, Wanda
SPORTING BLOOD (1931)

Tugend, Harry
TAKE ME OUT TO THE BALL GAME
PIGSKIN PARADE

Tunberg, Karl
HOLD THAT CO-ED
LIFE BEGINS IN COLLEGE

Tupper, Tristram
RED HOT TIRES

Turner, Ed
WINNERS TAKE ALL

Uytterhoeven, Pierre
EDITH AND MARCEL

Van Every, Dale
SATURDAY'S MILLIONS

Van Peebles, Melvin
GREASED LIGHTNING

Veiller, Anthony
MONKEY ON MY BACK

Vose, Kenneth
GREASED LIGHTNING

Waggner, George
IDOL OF THE CROWDS

Wald, Jerry
KID FROM KOKOMO, THE

Walsh, Christy
SPIRIT OF NOTRE DAME, THE

Ward, David S.
STING II, THE

Webster, M. Coates
KNOCKOUT

Weed, Frank
ALL-AMERICAN, THE (1932)

Weems, Walter
CONFLICT

Welbeck, Peter
LIGHTNING—THE WHITE STALLION

Welch, Eddie
HOLD 'EM YALE

Welland, Colin
CHARIOTS OF FIRE

Wells, George
TAKE ME OUT TO THE BALL GAME
ANGELS IN THE OUTFIELD

Wenning, Tom
SPORT PARADE, THE

Wesley, Richard
LET'S DO IT AGAIN

Westerby, Robert
SQUARE RING, THE

Wexley, John
CITY FOR CONQUEST

Wheelan, Tim
FRESHMAN, THE

Wheelwright, Richard
JUMP

Whittington, Harry
FIREBALL JUNGLE

Wickes, David
SILVER DREAM RACER

Wilbur, Crane
MONKEY ON MY BACK
UNWELCOME STRANGER
BORN TO SPEED

Wilde, Cornel
DEVIL'S HAIRPIN, THE

Wilde, Ted
FRESHMAN, THE

Wilder, Billy
FORTUNE COOKIE, THE

Wilhelm, Wolfgang
GREAT GAME, THE (1952)

Wilkerson, Elaine
SPEED LOVERS

Williamson, David
PHAR LAP

Williamson, Fred
LAST FIGHT, THE

Willis, F. McGrew
FIGHTING GENTLEMAN, THE

Wilson, Hugh
STROKER ACE

Wilson, Warren
SWING FEVER

Wisberg, Aubrey
BIG FIX, THE

SCREENWRITERS

Wister, William
ALIBI IKE

Witliff, William
BLACK STALLION, THE

Wolf, Richard A.
SKATEBOARD

Wolfson, P.J.
MADISON SQUARE GARDEN
70,000 WITNESSES

Wood, William
LIVELY SET, THE

Woolf, Edgar Allen
FLESH

Wrye, Donald
ICE CASTLES

Wynn, Tracy Keenan
LONGEST YARD, THE

Yablans, Frank
NORTH DALLAS FORTY

Yablonsky, Yabo
VICTORY

Yawitz, Paul
SATURDAY'S HEROES

Yellen, Jack
HOLD THAT CO-ED
PIGSKIN PARADE

Yordan, Philip
HARDER THEY FALL, THE

Yost, Dorothy
SPORTING BLOOD (1940)
RACING LADY

Zacharias, Steve
JOHNNY BE GOOD

Zelig, Ben
TOMBOY

Zuckerman, George
SQUARE JUNGLE, THE
IRON MAN, THE (1951)